W9-CMP-845

Indian Ocean Studies

Routledge Indian Ocean Series

SERIES EDITORS: RUTH BARNES AND ZULFIKAR HIRJI

'Borderline: Sulu Stories' by Yee I-Lann (2005, 61 x 61 cm, Digital Print on Kodak Endura Paper) with acknowledgement to Valentine Willie Fine Art: www.vwfa.net

Indian Ocean Studies

Cultural, Social, and Political Perspectives

**Edited by Shanti Moorthy
and Ashraf Jamal**

Routledge
Taylor & Francis Group
New York   London

First published 2010
by Routledge
270 Madison Ave, New York, NY 10016

Simultaneously published in the UK
by Routledge
2 Park Square, Milton Park, Abingdon, Oxon OX14 4RN

Routledge is an imprint of the Taylor & Francis Group, an informa business

Typeset in Sabon by IBT Global.
Printed and bound in the United States of America on acid-free paper by IBT Global.

Library of Congress Cataloging in Publication Data

Indian Ocean studies : cultural, social, and political perspectives / edited by Shanti Moorthy and Ashraf Jamal.
    p. cm.—(Routledge Indian Ocean series ; 6)
Includes bibliographical references and index.
1. Indian Ocean—Study and teaching (Higher) 2. Indian Ocean Region—Study and teaching (Higher) 3. Islands of the Indian Ocean—Study and teaching (Higher)
4. Indian Ocean Region—Intellectual life. 5. Indian Ocean Region—Social conditions. 6. Indian Ocean Region—Politics and government. I. Moorthy, Shanti. II. Jamal, Ashraf.
    DS339.8.I53 2009
    909'.09824—dc22
    2009021563

ISBN10: 0-415-80390-X (hbk)
ISBN10: 0-203-86743-2 (ebk)

ISBN13: 978-0-415-80390-8 (hbk)
ISBN13: 978-0-203-86743-3 (ebk)

Contents

Figures

Preface

Michael Pearson

Oceanic studies have expanded greatly in the last few years. Historians, and the editors of this volume, still find inspiration in Braudel's classic study of the Mediterranean, though we need also to keep in mind his cautionary note: "A historical study centred on a stretch of water has all the charms but undoubtedly all the dangers of a new departure."[1] Within the discipline of history there has been something of a resurgence of interest in the seas. The small maritime area of the Mediterranean still attracts eminent scholars, as seen in Horden and Purcell's important recent work.[2] The major publisher Routledge has under way a series called *Seas in History*, in which studies of the Atlantic Ocean, the Baltic and North Seas, and the Indian Ocean have appeared thus far.[3] It is gratifying that this volume also comes from Routledge, in the now well-established series *Indian Ocean Studies*.

A recent discussion in the very prestigious and widely read *American Historical Review* was guilty of a major sin of omission.[4] A long introduction by Karen Wigen was followed by analyses of the Mediterranean, the Atlantic, and the Pacific. Curious indeed that the Indian Ocean was ignored. Could the reason for this be that for most of its history the Indian Ocean was crossed and used by people from its littorals, not by Europeans, while the three examples chosen by Wigen were all dominated by Europeans for most or all of their histories? This complaint about a Eurocentric approach applies to an extent to a very recent book, *Seascapes*,[5] where again the Indian Ocean is largely absent and European- and American-controlled oceans and subjects are privileged. Indeed this Eurocentric bias goes back a long way. Braudel's study of the Mediterranean was notoriously weak on the southern, Islamic, shore of the sea. Even before this, early in the twentieth century, many European authorities considered the Indian Ocean to be only a "half ocean" as it did not extend far into the Northern Hemisphere!

Despite this neglect from the American academic mainstream, historical studies of the Indian Ocean are in fact flourishing. Very recently Markus P.M. Vink rectified the parochialism of the *American Historical Review* with an excellent overview of the state of Indian Ocean studies today.[6] Some years ago I attempted a general overview of its history, and more recently Sugata Bose wrote a stunning analysis of the last two centuries.[7]

So much for histories of the Indian Ocean. Other social scientists have also contributed, for example in strategic studies and in political science. However, an essential question for any study focusing on a body of water is to consider whether seas are legitimate objects of academic inquiry. Karen Wigen has written several provocative introductions to collections about maritime studies recently. In one of them she sets out the alternatives: either maritime studies secedes from the land and proceeds alone, or more modestly it at least, when given its due, modifies and enriches traditional social sciences. "Most current categories of social analysis were initially developed to understand land-based societies. How those categories need to be transformed by perspectives from the sea—and how far they can be stretched, bent, and reworked to accommodate ocean-centered realities—is perhaps the most important unresolved agenda hanging over this collection . . . Whether this means that maritime scholarship can and should give rise to an alternative set of social categories is another question . . . will ocean histories yield new constructs and new metanarratives to frame our social imaginations? Or will their value lie rather in replacing such fixed categories in favor of discrepant temporalities and amphibious identities . . . ?"[8]

The question then is whether studies of oceans can generate new and distinctive paradigms, or if they will merely add a little to existing land-based models. It could be that a cultural studies approach to the sea will contribute to the first, very ambitious, possibility. Several recent and forthcoming publications lend some weight to this bold claim. The team led by Stephen Muecke, based at the University of Technology in Sydney, has been pioneers here. They produced "The Indian Ocean," *The UTS Review*, VI, 2, 2000, and a revised, more accessible version in *Cultures of Trade: Indian Ocean Exchanges*, edited by Devleena Ghosh and Stephen Muecke (Cambridge Scholars Press, 2007). The same team, of which I am a member, has run two conferences, one in Leiden in 2006 called "Culture and Commerce in the Indian Ocean" and another in Perth in 2008 called "Ocean of Stories: Intercoloniality, Networks and Cultural Exchange Around the Indian Ocean." It is encouraging that others are on the same path. Colleagues at the University of the Witwatersrand in Johannesburg have initiated a research thrust called "South Africa–India: Connections and Comparisons," of which the first product was a conference: "Eyes Across the Water: Navigating the Indian Ocean," held in August 2007. A book based on this conference is being prepared. A Centre for Indian Studies in Africa has just been set up at Wits, and this will inevitably involve a focus on the Indian Ocean. Another very recent book takes a much more anthropological view of the Indian Ocean.[9] Finally, there is an excellent cultural studies-oriented collection, edited by Meg Samuelson and Shaun Viljoen, called *Oceanic Worlds/Bordered Worlds*, which has contributions from several disciplines.[10]

The present collection more explicitly advances the case for a Cultural Studies approach to the Indian Ocean. It originated at a conference organized by Ashraf Jamal and Shanti Moorthy at University Malaya in Kuala

Lumpur, Malaysia, in August 2007. Several contributors subsequently revised their presentations for publication and, along with other invited contributions, here is the result. The editors will locate the various chapters in their Introduction; for my part, and with my own background as an historian, I have found them all to be stimulating and provocative. The contributors are an agreeable mix of younger scholars and more established people. I must risk being invidious by singling out two of them. Lakshmi Subramanian, famous for her historical studies of Gujarat in the eighteenth century, here deftly takes a more cultural studies approach. The result is a very successful chapter from a quite new theoretical perspective. It is indicative of how fruitful a marriage of the Indian Ocean and cultural studies can be that the lead chapter is by Stephen Muecke, an internationally known cultural studies practitioner who now, we are pleased to see, has turned his attention to the Indian Ocean. The stunning results are on display at the start of this volume. Even if new paradigms are not yet evident, at the least, all the chapters in this important volume demonstrate unequivocally that cultural studies can move forward, even reorient, studies of the Indian Ocean, and indeed maritime studies in general.

NOTES

1. Fernand Braudel, *The Mediterranean and the Mediterranean World in the Age of Philip II, Volume II* (London: Harper & Row, 1972) 19.
2. Peregrine Horden and Nicholas Purcell, *The Corrupting Sea: A Study of Mediterranean History, Volume I* (Oxford, UK: Blackwell, 2000).
3. Paul Butel, *The Atlantic* (London: Routledge, 1999); David Kirby and Merja-Liisa Hinkkanen, *The Baltic and North Seas* (London: Routledge, 2000); Michael Pearson, *The Indian Ocean* (London: Routledge, 2003, and paperback edition 2007).
4. Various authors, section entitled "AHR Forum: Oceans of History," *American Historical Review* 111(3; June 2006): 717–780.
5. Jerry H. Bentley, Renate Bridenthal, and Karen Wigen, eds., *Seascapes: Maritime History, Littoral Cultures and Transoceanic Exchanges* (Honolulu, HI: University of Hawai'i Press, 2007).
6. Markus P.M. Vink, "Indian Ocean Studies and the 'New Thalassology,'" *Journal of Global History* 2(1; 2007): 41–62.
7. Pearson, *The Indian Ocean*; Sugata Bose, *A Hundred Horizons: The Indian Ocean in the Age of Global Empire* (Cambridge, MA: Harvard University Press, 2006).
8. Karen Wigen, "Introduction," *Seascapes: Maritime History, Littoral Cultures and Transoceanic Exchanges*, 17.
9. Edward Simpson and Kai Kresse, eds., *Struggling with History: Islam and Cosmopolitanism in the Western Indian Ocean* (New York: Columbia University Press, 2007).
10. Special issue of *Social Dynamics* 33(2; December 2007).

1 Introduction
New Conjunctures in Maritime Imaginaries

Shanti Moorthy and Ashraf Jamal

The ocean must be anthropomorphized, as though it could not exist or possess a meaning were it not a mirror of humankind. The "wheel of human fortune" has "determined the destiny of the sea," Braudel observes, inextricably binding the fates of human beings and that of the waters which encircle their received earthly domain.[1] To write a story of an ocean, then, is to write the story of those who have traversed it, who have inhabited its shores, and who, through the power of the imagination, have conjured its many meanings.

Evelyn Waugh observed that the Mediterranean has been on the "beaten track" for centuries; it is "fully labelled"[2] and holds no secrets. As the so-called cradle of European civilization, its rim holds a position of familiarity within the Western imaginary as, after Homer and Virgil, its history conjures various images: Cato in the Roman Senate, ending his every speech with *"Ceterum censeo Carthaginem esse delendam"* ("Moreover, I advise that Carthage must be destroyed"); the once fertile Sahara feeding an empire; Charlemagne contra the Saracens; later, the ships of the Umayyad Caliphate turning the Mediterranean into a "Muslim lake," when the Golden Age of Islam coincided with Europe's own "Dark Ages"; right down to more modern colonial and military conquests and current stories of desperate North Africans in overcrowded boats, drowning at sea in an attempt to reach an increasingly fortresslike European Union.

In its turn, the Atlantic has long been the site of Euro-American exchange since the Columbine "discovery," as evinced by the plaque on the Statue of Liberty (which, significantly, stands facing Europe) stating:

> "Keep, ancient lands, your storied pomp!" cries she
> With silent lips. "Give me your tired, your poor,
> Your huddled masses yearning to breathe free,
> The wretched refuse of your teeming shore.
> Send these, the homeless, tempest-tossed to me,
> I lift my lamp beside the golden door!"[3]

La liberté éclairant le monde (liberty enlightening the world), the statue strategically faces Europe at America's most porous border, her beckoning welcome commemorating the millions from Europe who made the hazardous crossing in their search for liberty, prosperity, the American dream. That triumphalist narrative has been undermined by scholarship, notably by Paul Gilroy in *The Black Atlantic*, which exposes the horror of other, more enforced, Atlantic crossings, which did not have liberty as their goal. The exposure raises the possibility of belated redress, while providing a major corrective to Enlightenment faith in collective human reason, in revealing, along with the Holocaust of the twentieth century, what Hannah Arendt describes as the "fearsome, word-and-thought defying banality of evil."[4]

Pacific Ocean scholarship similarly reflects Anglo-American preoccupations, the convoluted mutual dependency of East Asian trade and government bond transactions with the United States, China being central in "the mythic construction of the Pacific Rim as telos"[5]; the Pacific Rim becoming, in capitalist "Rimspeak," "that imaginary space of growth beyond regions of stagnation and market decline."[6] A space, furthermore, of hegemonic militarization, Hollywood-style acculturation, and the recent resurgence of indigenous Oceanic, Filipino, and Westernised Japanese rejoinders.[7]

As interest in maritime cultural studies has evolved, Indian Ocean studies represents a relatively recent and exciting development, emerging from the invaluable historical revisionism of Michael Pearson, Sugata Bose, K.N. Chaudhuri, Gwynn Campbell, Randall Pouwells, Kenneth McPherson, Ed Simpson, Erik Gilbert, John Hawley, and many others. Where Gilroy recovers the most wretched of subaltern histories, Indian Ocean studies reveals what John Hawley describes as "subaltern cosmopolitanism."[8] Its merchants and labourers circulated on its rim, and across its waters, from time immemorial, as recorded for instance in the Greek *Periplus of the Erythraen Sea* (circa first century AD), and continue to do so today. Its more wretched travellers assimilated, to leave trace communities such as the Sidis in India and the Bombay Africans of Mombasa.[9]

The history of the Indian Ocean, as the oldest human ocean, is relatively seamless. With few of the traumas or pathologies and without the newness of the Atlantic, the Indian Ocean holds no comparable sway on contemporary Western or local political imaginary, either as a route to liberty or the site of redress. The history of the Indian Ocean does not bear the stripes of the Atlantic, as witnessed by the modern day persistence of disadvantaged diasporas who suffered during Hurricane Katrina in New Orleans, for instance, while the nation's then president reportedly hovered overhead in a helicopter, clutching his pet dog.

In the age of European empire, however, the Indian Ocean was imagined in the West as a route to fantastical riches and possible Shangri-La, eternal youth, the supine alluring East surrendering her honeyed secrets to the intrepid bourgeois European adventurer. To control the Indian Ocean was to control its trade and riches, and was a guarantee, historically, to global ascendancy. The Portuguese Tomé Pires states that "whoever is lord of Malacca has his hands on the throat of Venice."[10] Or, in the words of that famous pirate in service of his Queen, Sir Walter Raleigh:

> He who commands the sea commands the trade routes of the world.
> He who commands the trade routes, commands the trade.
> He who commands the trade, commands the riches of the world.[11]

Enduring colonial hegemony failed, however, whether it be Portuguese, Dutch, or British, from the expulsion of the Portuguese from East Africa, to the unprecedented Japanese victories against the Europeans during the Second World War. The lesson almost seems to be "to have but not to hold." Then again, it may be argued that the "will to power" does not surrender easily, replaced as it were by "indirect rule" in new avatars, with multinational companies, the IMF and the WTO replacing the residents of old.

The point being that as an ocean, and an "ocean of notions"[12] at that, the Indian Ocean is no poor cousin. As the most embayed ocean, it yields a rich harvest for the imagination, both in its poetics and politics. Where Eric Hobsbawm warns against the turn to micronarratives as fragmenting collective human agency,[13] against so many social apartheids one could argue that the viscera of the particular embodies a universality in itself, or a "diversality" (diversity as a universal project) after Walter Mignolo.[14] Hence the turn to indigenous histories and narratives does not invent them; it merely, as Walter Ong would say, "technologizes" them.[15] These narratives exist, in the manner of Berkeley's tree,[16] whether or not there is anyone listening; and academic scholarship serves to disseminate these narratives.[17]

The purpose of this book is manifold. We aim to introduce to the reader an Indian Ocean poetics, as the chapters describe the movement of people, beliefs and ideas, plants, holy body parts, and so forth, reiterating Sugata Bose's notion of circulation: the Indian Ocean being a region constantly in circulation and recirculation, in flux, suppliant and yet enormously resilient. Its watery currents and airy *musim* (monsoons) making impossible the parochialism such as was seen in Northern Europe following the fall of the Roman Empire, and, some would argue, making a resurgence today in Europe's drift to the Right.

As we inscribe the movements or fluxes of the Indian Ocean, we counter Philip Steinberg's notion of the Indian Ocean as a void,[18] as anonymous high seas to merely be charted, plotted and mapped onto an impersonal grid,[19] in an Enlightenment inspired exercise of anxious classifications[20] and proprietorial enclosures.[21] The high seas of the Indian Ocean have never been *mare liberum* in the opportunistic Grotian sense, or *mare clausum*,[22] but a shared communal space with intensely local capital and social intercourse.[23] Hence, any study of the Indian Ocean will reveal the collision of the global and the local, not as a site for vulgar power and conquest, but genuine and by and large peaceable exchange, prior to the development of European expansionism.

While history casts a long shadow in any consideration of human activity in and around the Indian Ocean, the dangers of historicism lie in writing off the relevance of the Indian Ocean region today as merely another site of exotic minoritarian contest, a region in decline, a historical has-been. As fortunes wax and wane in time, as contemporary Chinese capital penetrates the African hinterland in a modern day "Scramble for Africa,"[24] the apparent decline of Wall Street and the seeming resurgence of China and India today must all remind us, at the dawn of what Kevin Rudd, like Ronald Reagan before him, terms "the Asia Pacific century,"[25] that, just as people and ideas have circulated, so can history itself recirculate and, vitally, reinvigorate the imagination, as we move beyond the Eurocentric, beyond yet again self-congratulatory indigenism, to an alternative mode of being in the world that has always been.

CONFIGURING GEOGRAPHY: A RETURN TO AREA STUDIES?

So what exactly does Indian Ocean studies entail? Our focus is the Indian Ocean region, by which we mean the ocean itself, its littoral and hinterland, fully embedded in the global, and viewed from the perspective of contemporary human interests, human histories, human movements. This region encompasses Africa's southern and eastern coasts, Michael Pearson's "Afrasian Sea,"[26] the coasts of the Arabian peninsula and South Asia, the Malay archipelago (encroaching on the South China Sea), and the northern and western coasts of Australia. We propose that the Indian Ocean region possesses an internal commonality which enables us to view it as an area in itself: commonalities of history, geography, merchant capital and trade, ethnicity, culture, and religion. This we contrast to Sugata Bose's notion of an "interregional arena." While usefully raising the possibility of viewing the Indian Ocean region as a human theatre which occupies interstices and straddles several regions,[27] "interregionalism" runs the risk of diminishing the Indian Ocean region as a unique space,[28] locking it into being a region between more significant regions, overshadowed by the concerns of nations with fixed borders and orchestrated histories, and continents that dominate by virtue of sheer mass. We prefer to treat the Indian Ocean region as one, among many, liminal spaces of hybrid evolution, an area whose boundaries are both moveable and porous, which brings us close to Devleena Ghosh and Stephen Muecke's notion of transnational imaginative geography.[29] As Erik Gilbert notes, "Where there are boats and trade, the sea connects more than it divides."[30]

Area studies, popularized in the aftermath of the partition of the world between Cold War ideologues following the end of World War II,[31] was the subject of much castigation by centre-Left intellectuals such as Edward Said.[32] Viewed as a thinly disguised North American sponsored modernization of the old Orientalist marriage between knowledge and power, or rather knowledge in service of power,[33] it reified artificial geopolitico-cultural boundaries, for the convenience of discourse, up until the collapse of the Soviet Union and the dismantling of the Berlin Wall in 1989.[34]

Not to cast the baby out with the proverbial bath water, area studies being the study of non-Western societies, while guilty of gross oversimplifications and undue subservience to patriotic ideology, also served to democratize or internationalise the social sciences. Area studies treated as authentic the objects of their study, despite the fevered paranoia of liberalism seeking to identify potential friends or foes, or capitalist quest for possible sources of raw materials and markets. Furthermore, area studies interrogated the separation between disciplines in the social sciences, an interrogation we foster in this volume.

In constituting the Indian Ocean region as a contemporary object of study, it is not our purpose to serve the interests of hegemonic power, be they political or economic. Where the invaluable scholarship of Arif Dirlik, for instance, constitutes the Pacific Rim as a site of indigenous contestation to the distant hegemony of either the United States or Japan,[35] we are placed now at the interregnum of several world orders. By this we mean that, rather than subscribing to Francis Fukuyama's imaginary of global neoliberalism or the end-of-history as desirable and already attained, Immanuel Wallerstein's apocalyptic prophecies of the impending collapse of the current world-system[36] seems more immediate, the hysteria of the world press notwithstanding. In the chaotic years of 2007 and 2008, we see the culmination of the fiscal unravelling set in motion with the end of the Bretton Woods Accord, the Thatcher/Reaganite market deregulation and abandonment of the welfare state of the 1970s and 1980s, the end of new markets, and increasing competition for fuel, natural resources, and water. Like Nikolai Kondratieff[37] before him, Wallerstein believes that crises[38] are inscribed into the very nature of capitalism.

In such uncertain times, the notion of resistance, in the Dirlik sense[39] (admittedly he was writing in 1994),[40] becomes not only futile,[41] but irrelevant.[42] Leaving aside consideration of the mobility and fixity[43] of heartless capitalism, it is our belief that the indigenes of the Indian Ocean littoral today experience no anxiety at the penetration of exogenous cultural capital, unlike Western anthropologists who bemoan the vanishing of authentic indigenous cultures. If Pacific Islanders now embrace hip hop, who are we to force the hula on them? And if, as Gordon Hughes says, "one of the lessons of history is that cultures progress by bastardization,"[44] history reveals that exogenous cultures have been and are, by and large, successfully indigenised or resisted.[45]

As a mode of discourse, our recourse to area studies is neither a newer Orientalism nor a means of "minoritarian" cultural reclamation or rehabilitation, which perhaps leaves us open to accusations, not unfamiliar to practitioners of cultural studies, of celebratory elitism or political vacillation. Our defence is this: there is no question of the Indian Ocean rim being either numerically, historically, or culturally minoritarian.[46] To admit to a centre-periphery discourse is to reify its binaries, which is where we part company from our esteemed colleagues Ghosh and Muecke, who in that context propose the contemporary Indian Ocean world as "a set of transnational relations alternative to hegemonic northern globalisation."[47] Much blood has been shed—from the Birmingham School, Edward Said, the Subaltern Studies Group onwards—to bring us to the crest of this battle for a place in the public arena; as we reap the benefits of the work of our predecessors, the "battle" concerning affirmation and redress is now in the public space; to continue to go over old ground locks us in the self-defeating logic of always being at the margins, a position we renounce in the name of Indian Ocean studies. Where Michel Foucault and Jacques Derrida, both French poststructuralists, have unmasked systems of knowledge mediated by the centre, emergent discourse occurring in the current era need no longer subscribe to a plaintive and outmoded hermeneutics of suspicion. It is impossible for us to return to the naïveté that had our forefathers swallowing Macaulay's infamous Minute[48] over a century ago.

Alert, conversely, to the dangers of Occidentalism and the inversion of binaries,[49] we celebrate the many cross-pollinations that have and are occurring across the Indian Ocean, resulting in successful hybridity both at the macro- and microscopic level. We have no investment in the fixity of ethnocultural essentialisms, the ghetto of recriminations, reactionary exceptionalisms, regardless of their geopolitical origin. Hermeneutic aggression matures into a conditional quietism, a confidence that critiques the celebratory "subalternism" of the Indian Ocean as arbitrarily assigned and demeaning; we would ask, "subaltern to whom?"[50] as we keep the language of revolution at the ready in our armamentarium: our apparent aestheticism should not be mistaken for asthenia.

A rehabilitated area studies enables the study of human activity and preoccupations in a specific region, in the engagements of cultural studies with the vernacular practices of everyday life. While we are wary of the dangers of cultural groupings and universalisms that fail to recognise heterogeneity, we reject the nihilism of what Clifford Geertz warns is postmodern scepticism that "leaves us with little to say, save that difference is difference."[51] He urges an explicit recognition of diversity "not as a negation of similarity [but] as comprising it: locating it, concretizing it, giving it form"[52] and delicately balances that position, precariously for a structuralist, against reducing heterogeneity to "so many lumps of sameness marked out by the limits of consensus."[53] Nonetheless, in modernity's dissimulation between the public and private performative aspects of identity or difference,[54] we are still left with its palpability, or, in Charles Taylor's sense, a "deep diversity."[55]

Postmodern conceptualizations of diversity and the Anglo-American identity revolutions of the 1970s have facilitated critique of the failure of modernity, in its political manifestation as liberal secularism, to provide "minoritarian" recourse to the public sphere: the promise of "difference blindness" ultimately becoming culturally and ideologically coercive. The current heated debate in Europe—and particularly in France, where the rise of antitraditional humanism, which contests cultural heterogeneity as leading to many exclusionary microfascisms[56] with a necessary renegotiation of the social contract between state, public culture, citizen, and various monist-materialist or identitarian communities—cannot be translated to the contemporary Indian Ocean world. Postmodern radical subjectivities, fragmentary identities, depersonalization or evacuation of selfhood and antihumanism, while valuable interrogations of the Western bourgeois subject, are not so useful in the context of Indian Ocean studies. Here, against a background of failed and corrupt postcolonial states, inequitable global trade practices, evolving industrialization, disease and hunger, the concerns of identity politics appear narcissistic,[57] even while the postmodern embrace of the "irrational" may usefully converge with a non-Western world view.

Any discussion of diversity then becomes politically loaded, in the sense that an awareness of heterogeneity imposed or constructed from outside the Indian Ocean region, by Western-trained academia, may prove to be condescending, misleading, culturally alien, and divisive. It was indeed the aim of modern colonialism to divide and rule, to sequester "types," to annihilate hybridity;[58] this is an intellectual position we would prefer not to reiterate. Conversely, if hybridity as contingency has become the somewhat hackneyed cliché of a late-twentieth-century neo-Bloomsbury intellectual posturing that posits itself as being both fashionable and marginal, a marginality of privilege, this notion of hybridity has no place in Indian Ocean studies.

Hence it would emerge that Geertz's view of diversity, despite its worthy connotations of recognition and respect, may, on closer examination, turn out to be subject to a culturally specific liberalism, posing as universalism or cultural neutrality, privileging certain modes of being or seeing.[59] Thus, while affirming the dual themes of integration and fragmentation,[60] it is important, in our opinion, to see heterogeneity in the Indian Ocean context as radically different, more deeply nuanced, more widely accepted a priori within the region and certainly more traditional in its connectedness to the past. Where historical secularism in the West ultimately failed to accommodate diversity, despite its foundational premise, heterogeneity has been an immutable fact of life in the Indian Ocean world, assailed now by the advent of Western-style modernity (with its concomitant intolerances) and nation-states. All of which, as Amitav Ghosh puts it, compels everyone to "travel in the West."[61] As Indian Ocean populations transit, negotiate, and indigenise modernity and its discontents, it is necessary that we who inhabit and are formed by historically "Western" discourse and production of meanings, acknowledge with humility that there is much that we can neither comprehend nor define; we must remember that being, ultimately, transcends identity or essence.[62]

In the heterogeneous Indian Ocean world, Michael Pearson rhetorically sums up the dilemma facing analysts, "The central question is whether indeed there is such a thing as an Indian Ocean which can be studied, analysed and used as heuristic tool just like say a state or a village."[63] Here, area studies as methodology, emerges as an instance of contingent "strategic essentialism,"[64] mooted by Gayatri Spivak, along with her more recent "critical regionalism."[65] Area studies becomes a springboard, allowing cultural studies to negotiate a convergence between extremes, between the abstractions of political theory and international relations and the thick descriptions of ethnography, anthropology, and archival history, to produce new conjunctures.

Without diminishing the importance of regional history or transregional commerce in the Indian Ocean, self-admitted preoccupations for Ghosh and Muecke, movement as a trope is our central referent, as a means of interrogating older forms of area studies. We now take hybridity as the new and always universal, remaining alert to our responsibilities to both being and difference, as comprising a series of moving vectors, after James Clifford:

> For the region called 'Europe' has been constantly remade, and traversed, by influences from its borders (Blaut, 1993; Menocal, 1987). And is not this interactive process relevant, in varying degrees, to any local, national, or regional domain? Virtually everywhere one looks, the processes of human movement and encounter are long-established and complex. Cultural centres, discrete regions and territories, do not exist prior to contacts, but are sustained through them, appropriating and disciplining the restless movements of people and things.[66]

Our study of the Indian Ocean region yields no hermetically sealed arenas, stable populations, magisterial formulations, or unchanging cultures, in a marked departure from the confident assumptions of mid-twentieth-century area studies. We find instead so many concentric and overlapping Venn diagrams that elude reduction, in "deep calling unto deep"[67] heterogeneity. Our view from the ocean completely inverts the land- and continent-based approach of the older area studies, which leaned heavily on modern and postcolonial nation-states as units of homogenous continents; this shift is now central to maritime studies. The Indian Ocean region shares and overlaps with adjacent regions: the Pacific Rim, the Malay Archipelago, the South China Sea, the Indian Subcontinent, the Arabian Peninsula, the Persian Gulf, Eastern and Southern Africa, and the African continent beyond. The uniquely littoral nature of Indian Ocean societies makes engagements between regions inevitable, so there is no fear of a return to the constraints of an area studies discipline that subscribes to patrolled geographic, historical, or cultural boundaries.

Thus, while we may speak of the Indian Ocean region as sharing some internal consistencies and variegated similarities, its boundaries are porous rather than arbitrary, it is both rooted and portable as an imaginary that transcends geopolitical regionalism. It can be dispersed into distant and diasporic spaces, as Bose describes with regard to transregional nationalism at the demise of the British Raj, whose Empress Victoria never set foot in the heartland of her empire, despite it occasioning and constituting her power as spectacle. To extend that line of reasoning further, if, after Andre Gunder Frank, American gold and silver were sought in order to acquire colonial hegemony in the Indian Ocean,[68] then the European Industrial Revolution and the flowering of nineteenth- and twentieth-century Western capitalism may be studied under the rubric of Indian Ocean studies![69] Which brings us to a consideration of global interconnectedness and world system analysis.

WORLD SYSTEM ANALYSIS: THE USES AND ABUSES OF HISTORY

While area studies appears to inhere in the notion of Indian Ocean studies, this in no way diminishes the region's global interconnectedness, either now or throughout history.[70] In fact, as a paradigm, the Indian Ocean region mediates between the expansive homogeneity of the global and the minutiae of the local in its rooted particularity. Furthermore, the Indian Ocean as the "cradle of human globalization"[71] served as testing ground for the integration into the international economy of a provincial Western Europe, newly emergent from the throes of eight hundred years of Carolingian feudalism. The Indian Ocean still today, along with the Pacific Rim, serves as the telos of global capital, production, and consumption.

So while area studies provides the close-ups, world system analysis pans out to the long view, the panoptic, the *"longue durèe,"* borrowed from Fernand Braudel.[72] In this it avoids arbitrary "periodization," and rehabilitates the once discredited telling of world histories, previously consigned to the dump heap of glibness. The camera pans out and we see the weave of the patterns of historical cycles, the particular and the general intertwined. In this three-dimensional polyphonic and perspectival sequence of world history, British rule in India, lasting a mere ninety years (1857–1947), appears almost inconsequential beside centuries of, for example, the Mongol-Moghul-Ottoman[73] dominance of China, India, Central Asia, and Byzantium.[74]

Reorienting significance and temporality features large in Andre Gunder Frank's application of world system analysis, advocating one, rather than many, world systems.[75] This not only restores the Indian Ocean world to its place in the panoply of human history, but allows this region to be treated as a unit for analysis in a contemporary world which Frank proposes has always been international, economically integrated and globally interconnected. In this context, the answer to Edward Lorenz's question—"Does the flap of a butterfly's wings in Brazil set off a tornado in Texas?"—would be "Yes."[76]

In a view reminiscent to us of Confucius' notion of the household as the lowest common denominator in a cascade of socially networked hierarchies, Chase-Dunn and Hall explain, and we quote at length:

> The modern world-system is understood as a set of nested and overlapping interaction networks that link all units of social analysis—individuals, households, neighbourhoods, firms, towns and cities, classes and regions, national states and societies, transnational actors, international regions, and global structures. The world-system is all of the economic, political, social, and cultural relations among the people of the earth. Thus, the world system is not just "international relations" or the "world market." It is the whole interactive system, where the whole is greater than the sum of the parts. All boundaries are socially structured and socially reproduced, as are the identities of individuals, ethnic groups, and nations.[77]

Thus world-system analysis reveals how social processes dynamically construct space and time, and, by extension, how the ocean and oceanic trade occupy a space within, rather than between, societies, leading some to propose that "the modern world system is, characteristically and importantly, an oceanic system."[78]

"World system" or "world-systems analysis?"[79] Though Immanuel Wallerstein and Samir Amin are lead players, after Braudel, in the field of world-systems analysis, we are inclined to the nonhyphenated[80] version promulgated by Frank, who admits to only one world system, globally interconnected for five millennia, the whole being more than the sum of its parts.[81] This contrasts with Wallerstein, Amin, and even Braudel's notion of multiple autonomous competing world-systems, that as Franz Fanon would propose, compartmentalize the world.[82] Wallerstein's world-systems approach privileges recent (and, according to Frank, temporary) Euro-American successes, while failing to move beyond European exceptionalism, born of an Enlightenment secularization of a Judaeo-Christian sense of superiority, mission, destiny, and the improvability of a particular subgroup of humanity, taken to an extreme in Northern European predestinarianism.

Wallerstein's approach has been denounced as the "inverted Orientalism of ahistorical American liberalism."[83] His position provides no explanation, for instance, of the Bullion Panic of the late seventeenth century.[84] In contrast, Frank's world system analysis is far more democratic, as he integrates[85] what he terms "Afro-Eurasia,"[86] both past and present, in a unified analysis that reveals long and short cycles of economic ascendancy and decline, in a manner that confounds linear Eurocentric causal history. Frank envisages so many parallel arenas and histories, which, without privileging Europe, allows the Indian Ocean region to emerge, though not unscathed, from its temporary decline in the colonial era. He decentres the notion of the "centre," by making the centre appear mobile, contingent, and simulacral, with an always highly contested, slippery grip on power. Furthermore, his analysis unmasks the ideological investment bolstering contemporary theories of globalization, in their need to appear both global or universal, and also new. The preoccupation with novelty, the need for newness and the break with the past is another consequence of early modern Enlightenment, which Friedrich Nietzsche deftly exposes as fallacious.

The catchphrase "now we are globalized," along with a consideration of the supposed novelty of Western cosmopolitanism, provincialises the "emergent" world, erases its history, brings no recourse to lessons learned since time immemorial, such as Bose's stunning revelation of the extent to which the British Empire was bankrolled by South Asian financiers, for instance.[87] Modern historians, in throwing the voyages of Vespucci, Columbus, Vasco da Gama, and Ferdinand Magellan into sharp relief, serve to make the year 1500 a watershed in human history.[88] To our minds, Europe's "discoveries" represent a bildungsroman, where Europe comes of age and is ready to move beyond the familiar of the local, but ultimately becomes the bully who, as the saying goes, does not play well with others.

Rather than European explorations, the only thing remarkable about this period was John Calvin's revolt against the long-standing Judaeo-Christian prohibition on usury,[89] which led to an unprecedented mobility of capital, newly injected in the form of gold and silver from the Americas, leading to the birth of capitalism, the success of predestinarian Dutch and Scots at the helm of their national East India Companies.[90] So rather than images of heroic muscular travellers with windswept locks, sailing over the edge of the world, to find continents that were alternately described as fabulously wealthy, civilized, barbaric, teeming with people or strangely empty of people and ripe for the picking, the "subaltern" history of Europe bears more resemblance to the backroom wheelings and dealings of Charles Dickens' Uriah Heep, pudgy, pasty-faced, insincere, treacherous, greedy. Viewed from the Indian Ocean, triumphalist Eurocentric histories, as the founding myths of modernity, start to look like fascist reinventions of the past.[91]

Wallerstein's own attachment to the mythic Eurocentric heroism of the year 1500 makes this his blind spot, and leads him to make much of miniscule shifts of "modern" European hegemonic cores from Amsterdam to London and New York in the space of two hundred years, whilst he dismissively homogenises far longer lasting and internally diverse pre-1500 empires. He discredits Janet Abu-Lughod's claims for the existence of premodern globalism and capitalism on the grounds that what is new today is new modes of production (synonymous with accumulation). We counter that what is really new today is not mobile capital, but surplus on an

unprecedented scale, waste beyond belief, inhuman global disparity, futur-
ism that is unable to see beyond the next ballot box, where we get, once
again, to surrender our "rights" to a proxy financed to the hilt by unscru-
pulous, globally acquired capital.[92]

Premodern globalism anticipates "modern" industrial capitalism, but
not as inevitable or necessarily sequential, to avoid the dangers of "presentism."[93] The lessons of history are that there is no guarantee that contemporary "progress" will persist, just as Europe misplaced the technology
to make saunas, flushing toilets, and domed roofs, at the fall of the Roman
Empire. Hence, while neither globalism nor cosmopolitanism are new in
the Indian Ocean world, what is new of course, is speed, space–time com-
pression, the magnitude and scope of globalization, occurring in the context where human life is stripped of value to an unprecedented level, as a
measure of the triumph of sciencism.[94] We can take some comfort, however, through world system analysis, in the fact that all this has occurred in
what amounts to a blip on the scale of human temporality, soon to be over;
nonetheless, one person's blip may be another's eternity.

THE HUMAN OCEAN

What is missing from world system analysis, whether hyphenated or not,
is the individual, the particular. Frank has been criticised for deliberately
not taking into consideration, variously, women, cultures, tribes, and
nations, in short, the intricacies of human existence, as he brushes broad
swathes on the canvas of human history. In the mode of meta-analysis,
Frank provides a vital corrective to Eurocentric fixations with the "modern" world/s as being unprecedented, as he warns against excessive attachment to the particular:

> All attempts to write any particular, let alone national[ist], history in
> disregard and isolation of its world historical context is subject to dan-
> gerous particularist [nationalist] bias. Euro-, Western-centric history,
> but also its Sino-, Islamo-, Afro-centric alternatives, should be replaced
> by a more humano-centric history, and indeed also an (sic) world-wide
> eco-centric one. World system history is an attempt to offer such a sys-
> temic analysis of otherwise apparently disparate and unrelated events,
> which are really part of the single historical stream of wo/mankind
> [humanity?]. As Mikhail Gorbachev said addressing the United Na-
> tions, there is unity in diversity.[95]

Frank's position is unexceptionable. However, the predictive extrapola-
tions of world(-)system/s analysis are in danger of sounding determinist,
remarkably like Hari Seldon's[96] mechanistic computations, devoid of play,
that Mallarmean and Deleuzean hazard which the chance throw of the

dice can never abolish and has the dazzling potential, therefore, to change everything. In short, the pulsatile flesh and blood of the human factor, in our hopes, yearnings and fears, so vividly encapsulated in this confessional by 'Umar ibn al Khattab, a seventh-century caliph:

> The sea is a boundless expanse, whereon great ships look tiny specks; nought but the heavens above and waters beneath; when calm, the sailor's heart is broken; when tempestuous, his senses reel. Trust it little, fear it much. Man at sea is an insect on a splinter, now engulfed, now scared to death . . . How should I trust my people on its accursed bosom? Remember al-'Ala'. Nay my friend, the safety of my people is dearer to me than all the treasures of Greece.[97]

Does a world defined by a system that is so interconnected, with destinies so interlocked, preclude the Brownian motion of molecules that randomly collide and create new tangents, new genetic permutations, new thought? We think not. So we turn now to the pointillism of the particular, under the aegis of Frank's broad swathes, as we humanize the Indian Ocean world. Fernand Braudel helps us here in linking:

> "those two great human oceans, China and India" linked in turn by so many "small and shallow epicontinental seas . . . The seas in fact are so many 'Mediterraneans', surrounded by land and dotted with islands: they are already on a human scale . . . each such entity keeps its own permanent characteristics; but the sea performed miracles of culture-contact, encouraging interchange and leading to mutual resemblances."[98]

It is the humanizing of the ocean which is our book's key objective and theme. Whether as historian, geographer, literary analyst, or ethnographer, each of our contributors addresses a specific human factor. This may be an empirical analysis of creolization as a globalized phenomenon, with specific reference to the Indian Ocean. Or, the lives of seafarers then and now; the lives of those who inhabit the ocean's littoral. Or, the visceral reflection on home and homelessness, migrancy and diaspora, through the works of specific writers of fiction. Or, the seaborne nature of belief systems or plant growths. What binds these various approaches is, as Spivak recognises, the vital role of the humanities as a disciplinary entry point that can prepare us for "an 'other' principle of study. [. . .] The ethico-political task of the humanities has always been the rearrangement of desires,"[99] the possibility for new imaginative conjunctures.

These conjunctures, or "miracles of culture-contact," could never have been possible without the seas and oceans, hence the critical shift from terrestrial to maritime cultural logics, or rather, the emergent coalescence of these perceptual modalities. If maritime cultural studies is still in its infancy, this does not of course mean that its cultural *practice* is similarly so. Our amphibian natures have long ago been recognized by Strabo[100] while Alphonso Lingus adumbrates: "The form and the substance of our bodies are not clay shaped by Jehovah and then driven by his breath; they are coral reefs full of polyps, sponges, gorgonians, and free-swimming macrophages continually stirred by monsoon climates of moist air, blood, and biles."[101] To speak of a "human ocean," then, is not merely to speak adjectivally, or metaphorically, but to harness human cultural practice to the element which has made it possible. Moreover, to think the oceanic human is also to affirm "the rearrangement of desires" within the ethico-political sphere of the humanities.

While the logic of each chapter is its own, rather than one enforced from outside, each chapter is answerable to the book's central concern: the human factor in the Indian Ocean. In Chapter 2, Stephen Muecke sets the reflexive tone designed to motivate and celebrate cultural engagements from within the region. Muecke's preferred focus is Australasia, a contact zone he shares with the chapter that follows by Haripriya Rangan and Christian Kull. If Muecke's "fictocritical" chapter allows for a speculative drift, Rangan and Kull's empirical geographical orientation recounts quite another drift, that of plant and animal life. Both chapters, in distinct ways, produce a groundswell of emergent takes on Indian Ocean studies. This groundswell, with its tactile sense of what Michael Pearson calls the fungibility and permeability of land and water, serves to evoke the pliability and looseness of the connection which this book seeks to make. Rather than working through rigorous and often misleading subsections, the sequence of chapters presented here evoke what Gaston Bachelard in *Water and Dreams* calls *la pate*.[102]

Estate agents never cease to remind one of that cherished abstract asset: location. The next chapters, by Shanti Moorthy and Fernando Rosa Ribeiro, demystify the fetish of place, reminding us that being in situ always incorporates drift, that one is never in one place. If *kala pani*—black waters— names a watery world outside the circuitry of the known and familiar, it also casts out those who choose to inhabit that world. This exilic state, which need not be negatively received, is reprised, and developed otherwise, in chapters by Lakshmi Subramanian and Heather Goodall. These chapters address the lives of those seamen who, cast out, nevertheless sustain a dream of returning to their native land. This dream of origins, however, cannot quite be realised, given the a priori drift which makes the return to origins, while compelling, nevertheless partial and illusory. Salman Rushdie broaches this matter perceptively in his essay "Imaginary Homelands" and also in the following reflection:

> The effect of mass migrations has been the creation of radically new types of human being: people who root themselves in ideas rather than places, in memories as much as in material things; people who have

been obliged to define themselves—because they are so defined by others—by their otherness; people in whose deepest selves strange fusions occur, unprecedented unions between what they were and having experienced several ways of being, he understands their illusory nature. To see things plainly, you have to cross a frontier.[103]

The next three chapters sustain the matter of selfhood and its discontents. The chapters focus upon three luminaries, Francis Xavier, Zheng He, and Rabindranath Tagore, each of whom has assumed a mytho-poetic provenance within the Indian Ocean imaginary. While the approaches of the contributors are distinct, what connects them is the power of storytelling or mythmaking, and the connections of these myths to oceanic migration. While Pamila Gupta's chapter examines the weaving of the fantastical and the everyday in the determination of the fate of a sacred body, Susan Philip addresses a contemporary theatrical reconfiguration of the myth of Zheng He. Mark Frost, in turn, addresses the fate of a mystical idea of a pan-Asian consciousness.

Charles Baudelaire's appeal to a world elsewhere, outside the known, finds its riposte in the reflections of those who live their lives on the obscure littoral of an obscure ocean. For if it is all well and good to long to escape from Paris,[104] it is quite another matter to address the matter of making a home in zones of relative obscurity along the Indian Ocean rim, a thematic developed by Miki Flockemann and Meg Samuelson.

The toxic matter of racism continues to plague the most encompassing of liberal social systems. It is as if the world were always strange and the assertion of colour, as an extension of selfhood and identity, ceaselessly imperative; as though the masks constructed before, and naturalized today, will continue to haunt us. It is this racial haunting which forms the theme of chapters by Rochelle Pinto and Arun Saldanha. Linking racial practice in the distant and recent past, Pinto's and Saldanha's chapters reveal the continuance of disturbing, once mainstream and now resurgent, racial assemblages.

The next chapters, by Christian Ghasarian and David Picard, address La Reunion; the method and focus is ethnographic, exploring the island's history, its beliefs, and its place in global tourism. A "forgotten island," La Reunion also emerges in a short fiction as a final place of exile. The penultimate critical chapter by Ashraf Jamal—"Telling and Selling on the Indian Ocean Rim"—returns us to the Indian Ocean as a dreaming tool or dream time of cultural studies, as does the concluding poem by Stephen Muecke, "Post-Orientalism."

While the ocean itself is gaining ascendancy as a factor in contemporary thought, postcolonial studies, to which it is directly connected, will find new life in connecting its concerns thereto. If the trade winds of Atlantic economy—West Africa, America, Europe—have dominated cultural discourse, it is clear that the monsoon winds are gaining increased currency, not least for the reason that the Indian Ocean is by far the most poetic of the watery regions on earth.[105] It becomes apparent that the scale of the Indian Ocean is vast, the continental players diverse, and the unity of the field impossible to fix. However, if there is one important aspect of our book which sets it apart, then it is the African component. Countering K.N. Chaudhuri's scandalous disregard for the role of Southern and Eastern Africa in Indian Ocean cultural and economic exchanges,[106] we have deliberately sought to engage with reflections on this region. That said, the overall intention was not to address a lack but to engage in the complex linkages which make up the Indian Ocean littoral, and to do so by connecting with academics working within these regions. This of course has not meant the exclusion of practitioners from Europe. Location—conceived under erasure—neverthe-less matters, as with any critique of Western exceptionalism.

THE INTERDISCIPLINARY APPROACH

While there has been a proliferation of many texts on maritime stud-ies, this book draws on the interdisciplinary expertise of its contributors, partly influenced by Thomas Kuhn and Bruno Latour's postmodern take on the sociocultural and contextual construction of disciplines.[107] Aca-demics as recently as the 1980s, in studying the same region (or even the human body, for that matter) were often unable to communicate with one another across the yawning abyss created by jargon and disciplinary purities hallowed by tradition. Each discipline brings, without a doubt, invaluable and highly evolved skills, but, considered in isolation, raises the danger of creating as many objects of study as there are disciplines. While stopping short of outright deconstruction, despite the spirit of the times, which would leave us with a mere aestheticization of the Indian Ocean region, our praxis, beyond the fascination with theory, allows for much interdisciplinary dialogue and borrowings, or as Gallagher and Greenblatt quip "intellectual hand-me-downs" that look good in the pur-view of other disciplines.[108]

The object of study must transcend any methodological fidelity. To this end we draw on innovations pioneered by Braudel, whose combination of the intellectual practices of history, economics, anthropology, philosophy, and literature contributed to the emergence of that disciplinary hybrid, cul-tural studies. We are fully conscious of Spivak's admonition:

> Over against such restrictive specialism, there is a generalism that tries to make connections, assembling ad hoc scholarship as an aid to think-ing. This problem-solving model is more like the strategy of paramedi-cal primary health care—where the fieldworkers learn about a disease from volunteer doctors when they encounter it—than like the assured competence of qualified medical practitioners. The problem with mere

generalism is ignorant speculation. What one wants is supplementation from "volunteer doctors." The root sense of "doctor" is teacher, after all.[109]

Spivak inadvertently raises the spectre not only of the amateur bypassing the scene of an accident for fear of incurring liability, but the prospect of medical practitioners still practising bloodletting as a cure-all, if they hadn't finally taken William Harvey, that maverick of his time, seriously. Hence we propose interdisciplinarity as risk taking, while rejuvenating the imagination, for which the humanities are responsible, beyond the endless litany of the faithful reproduction of received wisdom, the alliterations of mechanical, and mass-produced opinion.

In studying the Indian Ocean world, in itself the most hybrid of cultural interpenetrations, our methodology must likewise be hybrid, as we forge an alliance between structuralist methodology and interdisciplinary coalitions; this in the context of a postmodern consciousness that comes of age in its accountability. Where methodology derives from the "West," this is a West more portable and flexible than ever; we believe we are able to indigenise and particularize the methodology while subverting the prejudices. Abandoning cherished notions of marginality, we see more danger today from conceited academic fixity and unassailable consensus, which is something that interdisciplinarity goes some way towards undermining. In providing the common ground, interdisciplinarity not only vitalizes discourse, providing unitary and deliberately transient holism, but allows the kaleidoscopic flow of knowledges as epiphenomena, to variously converge and diverge, like a flickering slide show. As Geertz proposes, contra Wittgenstein's notion of a single thread, "It is the overlappings of differing threads, intersecting, entwined, one taking up where another breaks off, all of them posed in effective tensions with one another to form a composite body, a body locally disparate, global integral."[110]

Our book deliberately breaks away from hermetic orientations, immanence becomes the key. This is where cultural studies breaks with historiography, which of a necessity constructs psychic distance between the subject and the object of its study, in a process of defamiliarization that facilitates historical research.[111] This is something we would critique, after Michel de Certeau, as leading to an epistemic haunting, by which we mean a return of knowledges that such epistemes violently repress.[112] Cultural studies demands no such epistemological rupture, as Bachelard described;[113] we remain very much up close and personal, as neither we nor our reader is expected to assume a detached relation to an authoritative text; we must become implicated in a set of searching questions relevant to the contemporary moment, fully conscious of context. In other words, while never prescriptive, the chapters are designed as zones of reflection and application: one *does* cultural analysis in the reading, with the possibility, as Gallagher and Greenblatt propose, "of treating all of the written and visual traces of a particular culture as a mutually intelligible network of signs."[114] While accepting the notion of the coherent subject of history,[115] we treat history and cultures as texts, as revealing a series of palimpsests, each impinging in turn in a cascade of effects reaching the contemporary world.[116] Our intellectual base necessarily maintains fluidity, self-reflexivity; all systematised knowledges produced (and they are undoubtedly produced) are, to borrow from deconstruction, cultural artefacts: contextual, contemporary, contingent, subject to change and value judgements, and hence, fair game for cultural studies.

We advocate retaining the freshness and spirit of enquiry of amateurs;[117] open to thinking beyond the limits, we expect to arrive at no eternal, unchanging truths, but always "see in a mirror, darkly."[118] We ask sober questions of ourselves and our students, questions that don't always have neatly packaged, palatable answers. Some of the overarching issues that our book addresses are (1) why the Indian Ocean region lends itself to an imaginative/poetic and new/radical critical discursive discourse, (2) why area studies and world-systems analysis collude with Euro-American exceptionalism, and why they must be revised, (3) why a humano-centric/interdisciplinary approach allows a key shift from the intertia and arrogance of a panoptic or overly empowered contingent approach, (4) and why cultural studies, in the broadest sense, while the darling of current tertiary education culture, also harbours the seeds of a countercritique without disavowing a functional poetics.

CULTURAL STUDIES: BETWEEN POETICS AND POLITICS

Where the postmodern turn in cultural studies leaves us open to accusations of irresponsible and toxic elisions of fact, fiction, and indeterminate methodology, in a swirling cauldron that emits fumes that seem, to our detractors, to have us lurching about intoxicated, spouting more style than substance, we counter that cultural studies is the ideal workhorse for Indian Ocean studies. It enables us to confront the burdens of history that potentially repackage colonial histories as new takes on how the contemporary world is fashioned, reiterating latent prejudices; it provides a forum for the interstitia occupied by narrative gaps and silences, for micronarratives, endangered cultures and ecologies; it spotlights the hitherto marginal while celebrating the popular, and deftly subverts the hegemony of the elite.

Admittedly, the 1970s saw cultural studies retreat from the public sphere of the Marxist/ Frankfurt school and cultural materialist sociopolitical critique of pragmatism and consumerism, into the cloistered austerities of identity politics, under the sway of the anticapitalist masters of *la pensees* '68.[119] This drift, defensible at the time, saw cultural studies turn into an elite, scholastic, conservative,[120] university-based discourse on itself, along with a spectatorship of the bourgeois popular, fatally hijacked by opportunistic consumerist collusion. Nonetheless, if global regulation is to follow the 2008 world financial crisis, which free-marketeers worry will take us "down the slippery slope to socialism," as a backlash against a market and its financiers and politicians who appear unable to regulate themselves, cultural studies can prove its continuing relevance by emerging from the autoerotic opium den of pensive disenchanted navel-gazing, and confront what is more than "a crisis of verse,"[121] to meet a life-or-death struggle for the right to not just read or write, but to think boldly and independently.[122] By reclaiming its intellectual heritage, cultural studies can provide not only a powerful social critique of the historical present, but a politically engaged thrust for global social justice, grace, and reconciliation. The time is ripe for action and enunciation, to move beyond mere symbolic or semantic critique and armchair critical reading practices, to a revolutionary remaking of the present; to addressing inequitable practices everywhere, be they economic, political, cultural, or ecological; to providing pathways for the resuscitation of now extinct Anglophone public intellectuals. To make the space in which they may risk dissident transcommunitarian speech and, importantly, be heard, free from vested economic interests and world-weary cynical aporias, in concert with a symphonic groundswell of voices from elsewhere, as our work on the Indian Ocean will go some way towards providing.

In a sense our aim in this book is archaeological, but not to make a fetish of the past, though there is no doubt that the relevance of the Indian Ocean region rests on an appeal to history. We aim to excavate the Indian Ocean world, both past and present, and bring to the surface a fruitful area of interdisciplinary scholarship, valuable in itself, made available through the modalities of area studies and world system analysis. As inhabitants of that geographical world, as descendants of Gujarati traders and Ceylon Tamil civil servants that circulated on its rim and across its waters, this is a project dear to our hearts. Because what matters in the end is the lived human experience, and how our narratives connect in a large but small world, how to counter the gross indifference of a mediatised world with a short memory span and an amnesia for the past. A civilization, and we use that term advisedly in a "post-9/11" world, that has forgotten how to tell and hear stories, inevitably involutes, much like the newborn in the incubator that dies, despite the best of care, if it is not cuddled: love and stories being immutable facts of human existence. Poised as we are at the end of Wallerstein's epoch, we do believe that our stories about the Indian Ocean world, in its peaceable exchanges and sense of mutual worth, form a repository, a cargo of ideas, which can be used to heal the future of a world that has commodified even the future.

NOTES

1. See Bose, 4.

2. *Labels: A Mediterranean Journal*, Waugh's first travel book, provides an extremely humorous account of an Englishman abroad in 1929; imbued with an urbane ennui, he visits places on the beaten track ("there's a reason why the track is beaten"), places which he felt were "fully labeled" and left no scope for the imagination.

3. A line from a poem, "The New Colossus," by the nineteenth-century American poet Emma Lazarus. "The New Colossus," describing the Statue of Liberty, appears on a plaque at the base of the statue. It ends with the statue itself speaking (*New Dictionary of Cultural Literacy*, 3rd ed, 2002)

4. The banality of evil is the subtitle and final phrase of Arendt's most controversial book, describing the trial of Adolf Eichmann in Jerusalem in 1961. In this book she "de-demonises" evil, presents it as pedestrian, thoughtless, a terrifying picture of evil perpetrated by average people.

5. Connery, 1994, 31–32: He argues that "Pacific Rim discourse is an imagining of U.S. multinational capitalism in an era when the socialist 'bloc' still existed, and it is the socialist bloc that is the principle and discursive Other . . . Pacific Rim discourse [itself] presumes a kind of metonymic equivalence." See also Rob Wilson and Arif Dirlik, *Asia/Pacific as Space of Cultural Production*, 1994. Margaret Jolly contrasts the American vision of the "Pacific Rim" with the Australian discourse of the "Pacific region" (Jolly, 526).

6. Greg Dening as quoted in Klein and Mackenthun, 18.

7. See Wilson and Dirlik.

8. Hawley, 1.

9. Hawley, 4, 5. See also Edward A. Alpers, *Sailing Into the Past:The African Experience in India* at http://www.samarmagazine.org/archive/article. php?id=20. Accessed 26 December 2008.

10. Tome Pirès, the late-fifteenth-century CE Portuguese apothecary, wrote *Suma Oriental* (a "Summa of the East") circa 1515, an account of his travels in the East. Cited in Frank, 58.

11. Philip Steinberg, 18.

12. Adapted from Salman Rushdie's *Haroun and the Sea of Stories* (15), where the protagonist's father is a famous storyteller, also known as "Rashid the Ocean of Notions" or "the Shah of Blah." While Rushdie's storyteller is likened to an ocean, we anthropomorphize the Indian Ocean—it becomes its own storyteller.

13. "Today, both the Right and to the Left are saddled with identity politics. Unfortunately, the danger of disintegrating into a pure alliance of minorities is unusually great on the Left, because [. . .] the decline of the great universalist slogans of the Enlightenment [. . .] leaves it without any obvious way of formulating a common interest across sectional boundaries. The only one of the so-called 'new social movements' which crosses all such boundaries is that of the ecologists. But, alas, its political appeal is limited and is likely to remain so." (Hobsbawm, 45).

14. "Epistemic diversality shall be the ground for political and ethical cosmopolitan projects. In other words, diversity as a as a universal project (that is, diversality) shall be the aim instead of longing for a new abstract universal and rehearsing a new universality grounded in the 'true' Greek or Enlightenment legacy. Diversality as the horizon of critical and dialogic cosmopolitanism presupposes border thinking or border epistemology grounded on the critique of all possible fundamentalism (Western and non-Western, national and religious, neoliberal and neosocialist) and on the faith in accumulation at any cost that sustains capitalist organizations of the economy" (Mignolo, 743).

15. "Writing or script differs as such from speech in that is does not inevitably well up out of the unconscious . . . To say writing is artificial is not to

condemn it but to praise it. Like other artificial creations [. . .] it is utterly
invaluable and indeed essential for the realization of fuller, interior human
potentials. Technologies are not mere exterior aids, but also interior transformations of consciousness, and never more when they affect the word.[. . .]
Writing heightens consciousness [. . .] as deeply interiorized technology. But
[. . .] the fact that it is technology must be honestly faced" (Ong, 81–82).

16. George Berkeley's famous meditation on the metaphysics of existence, "I was
thinking of a tree in a solitary place, where no one was present to see it."

17. See Hawley (4) for his notion of "hidden transcripts" of South-South cultural
exchanges through history.

18. To our minds, Steinberg makes an overly artificial distinction between the
social constructions of the Indian Ocean and Micronesian seas, "The Indian
Ocean societies viewed the ocean as a special trading space outside society
and therefore immune to societal, land-like territorial control. The Microne-
sians govern the sea much as they govern land: as a set of discrete places to
be demarcated and controlled according to the general organizing principles
of territoriality in Micronesian society" (Steinberg, 60). Thus he ignores the
fact that not all trade across and around the Indian Ocean was long distance
or for luxury goods alone; there was much petty trade between local and distant entrepots along sea routes that were familiar, as Erik Gilbert (Gilbert,
17–20) describes.

19. Steinberg provides excellent examples of early modern cartographic representations of the sea as initially "wild, unruly, and untameable" populated
by fearsome mythic creatures and an anthropomorphized Nature in 1548,
representations which were replaced by the early seventeenth century by
"maps portraying a grid over an essentially featureless ocean [. . .] to be
crossed by atomistic ships" (Steinberg, 99–105).

20. We refer to Diderot and the Encyclopedists, circa 1751, Linnaeus' plants classification of 1778. The Enlightenment generated a wellspring of arbitrary
classifications, categorizations, dictionaries, the division of time by the fob
watch rather than the medieval European calls to prayer by church bells.
The anxiety lay in the obssessional nature of the classifications, down to the
almost spurious minutiae of abundant detail.

21. Roy Porter describes the enclosures of spaces previously held in common
during Enlightenment era Britain, "With over 2000 enclosure Acts and more
than six million acres of land affected, enclosure and progressive agriculture
in general presented a model to enlightened minds of proper environmental
superintendence, wedding profit to paternalism . . . [F]inally the Protestant
ethic would serve as fertilizer: labor consecrated private gain into a public
and ecological good" (Porter, 310). The flip side of manicured gardens and
land reserved for large-scale profitable projects like mills and factories was
loss of market garden space, loss of grazing space for small holders, massive
rural poverty and, ultimately, with the banning of relief of the poor in their
own homes, the displacement of poor peasantry to work houses and urban
areas (proletarianization of the peasantry, as Frantz Fanon would say).

22. See Steinberg's Chapter 3 ("Ocean-Space and Merchant Capitalism") for an
immensely readable account of the early development of European international relations with regard to the oceans. He outlines the Dutch Hugo Grotius' *Mare Liberum (The freedom of the seas;* written in 1608, forty years
prior to the treaty of Westphalia), a seminal text in modern ocean law and
modern international law (Steinberg, 31). Grotius' aim was to undermine
the Iberian claim to stewardship (not possession) of ocean routes; he does
not dispute stewardship (modeled on ancient Rome in the Mediterranean)
as such, but proposed universal access to ocean routes. Steinberg continues

with the Portuguese Seraphim de Freitas notion of the sea as *res communis*, with rights to patrol but not control the seas parceled between competent rulers; and the Englishman John Seldon's notion of *mare clausum* (pertaining to territorial claims to regional waters).

23. As Erik Gilbert, in a survey of how trade that persisted through the colonial era, states "The low cost of dhows, their ability to use virtually any beach as a port and the informal economic linkages they created between the various colonies of the western Indian Ocean made the dhow economy deeply subversive of the colonial project in Zanzibar . . . Even as [colonial] officials predicted the decline of the dhow, their steamers ran virtually empty and dhows carried the bulk of the cargo between points served by the government steamer service. Like our historians, colonial officials were so wedded to their faith in modernization that they were blind to economic reality . . . [in] a Whiggish notion of progress" (Gilbert 3, 5). Indigenous global and trade, sometimes labeled as piracy (Subramanian, 29), persisted even through the era of the colonial steamship. See also Isabel Hofmeyr's observation on regionalism: "But what of transnationalism within the south itself? What of non-western sources of globalisation, or processes of transnationalism that happen without reference to the west?" (Hofmeyr, 3); "non-Europeans entered into relations with locals that were more intimate, sticky, and prolonged than the Europeans could countenance" (Hofmeyr, 7).

24. Refers to the partitioning of Africa among European colonial powers between 1880 and 1914. See excellent account in Thomas Pakenham's book by that name.

25. "The 21st century will be the Asia-Pacific century, so we need to make sure that in decades ahead we are fully engaged with the region," said Mr Rudd. "It will be the global powerhouse and there are great opportunities if we engage properly and engage now," he told an OzAsia symposium in the southern city of Adelaide. http://www.straitstimes.com/Breaking%2BNews/World/Story/STIStory_280661.html

26. Pearson, *The Indian Ocean*, 13.

27. Bose, 6.

28. As Erik Gilbert queries, "Should we see contiguous bits of land as culturally and historically related? Or should we see areas connected by easy-to-cross water as more related and interconnected than areas with contiguous but difficult- to-cross land?" Michael Pearson succinctly states: " . . . the seas and shores of the Indian Ocean [. . .] being a discrete unit that can be investigated like a state, or a city, or a ruler" (Pearson, 1998, 8). See also Michael Pearson's "Littoral Society: The Concept and The Problems" for a development of the idea of the littoral.

29. Ghosh and Muecke, 2.

30. Gilbert, 12. He elaborates that critics of area studies believe "that [. . .] continentally defined units make little sense from a cultural perspective and [. . .] rely on essentialized visions of cultural and civilizational uniformity. They argue for new, less continental units of analysis, but they fail to consider the possibility that bodies of water may at times make good units of analysis" (Gilbert, 13).

31. " . . . the way area studies have defined the units of analysis that constrain most research. The area studies divide the world into components mostly based on continents, and assume that those continents define historical and cultural realities. Further they assume that these units of analysis—originally defined during the cold war as a means of apportioning research money—make sense now and made sense deeper in the past" (Gilbert, 12).

32. "Compared with *Oriental studies* or *area studies*, it is true that the term *Orientalism* is less preferred by specialists today, both because it is too vague and too general and because it connotes the high-handed executive attitude of nineteenth-century and early twentieth century European colonialism. [...] The point is that even if it does not survive as it once did, Orientalism lives on academically through its doctrine and theses about the Orient and the Oriental" (Said, 2). "[H.A.R. Gibb] could use the ugly neologism 'area study' for Orientalism as a way of showing that [the two] were interchangeable geographical titles" (Said, 53).
33. Said refers to H.A.R Gibbs' "Area Studies Reconsidered" in stating, "Oriental studies were to be thought of not so much as scholarly activities but as instruments of national policy towards the newly independent, and possibly intractable, nations of the postcolonial world. Armed with a refocused awareness of his importance to the Atlantic commonwealth, the Orientalist was to be the guide of policymakers, of businessmen, of a fresh generation of scholars" (Said, 276). Said seems to suggest that these activities were unscholarly!
34. In a strange dichotomy between theory and practice, while regions were constituted for academic research, the West was always uneasy with, and treated as subversive, the political realities of new regionalism, such as the Bandung initiative that spawned the Non-Aligned Movement and South-South dialogue. Referring to the South African-sponsored Bandung initiative of 1955, Zygmunt Bauman observes "[T]he two super-blocks [of the Cold War] . . . stayed unanimous on at least one point: they both treated the rest of the world as the twentieth century equivalent of the 'blank spots' of the nineteenth-century state-building and state-enclosure race. [...] Non-alignment, refusal to join either one or the other of the two super-blocks [...] was seen as the blocks era equivalent of that 'no-man's land' ambivalence which was fought off tooth and nail, competitively yet in unison, by modern states at their formative stage" (Bauman, 63).
35. "[T]he invention, circulation and maintenance of this [ie the Pacific Rim] geographically vast and culturally heteroglossic region [. . .] was dominantly [...] to serve Euro-American interests in the name of God, imperial glory, catapulting profit, and national (/transnational) management" (Wilson and Dirlik, 2).
36. See Immanuel Wallerstein's *Alternatives: The United States Confronts the World*.
37. See Nikolai Kondratiev's *The Major Economic Cyles* (1925) which posits the existence in capitalist economies of fifty- to sixty-year-long cyles of boom followed by financial collapse or depression.
38. See Immanuel Wallerstein's *World-Systems Analysis: An Introduction*.
39. "[T]he Pacific Rim powers very promotion and circulation of such an Asia-Pacific community as an integrated economic region [...] has meant that the so-called Pacific Basin countries contained in the region are habitually excluded from mapping and contesting these megatrend visions of 'economic cooperation' and 'cultural exchange' that bear down upon their heteroglossic well-being and threaten their local survival as distinct cultures and alternative histories" (Wilson and Dirlik, 4).
40. Further reading: Arif Dirlik, *The Postcolonial Aura: Third World Criticism in the Age of Global Capitalism*. The key essays being "The Global and the Local (84–104) and "There is More in the Rim than Meets the Eye: Thoughts on the 'Pacific Idea'" (129–145).
41. By "futile" we don't mean to diminish attempts to preserve local, indigenous, traditional culture or to say that resistance is impossible. We do feel,

however, that there should be no collusion between the sympathetic observer/ ethnographer and the spokespeople for traditional societies who fear cultural admixtures as socially subversive in terms of creating disaffected youth or new subcultures; the root of that fear, in our opinion, is an immense distrust of the cultures that flow in the wake of modernity.

42. The irrelevancy of resistance is apparent, at the time of this writing (September 2008), in the meltdown of "core" (in the Wallerstein sense) Western economies, which has and will profoundly destabilize centre-periphery discourse for decades to come, as we ask, where is the centre that we must resist?

43. Freewheeling capital "fixes" in docile emergent states and flees "unstable" or recalcitrant states, rewarding totalitarian states that have deregulated markets and porous borders and punishing resistance by folding up and making a quick exit without accountability; the ultimate capitalist employers' dream, of being able to sack the striking proletariat without fear of industrial action.

44. Hughes, 948.

45. To quote Wilson and Dirlik again, "Uncanny knowledges of culture, politics, and economics are kept segregated and isolated across the Asia/Pacific region even as a complex new micropolitics of location and memory begins to flourish and interact. 'Let resistance write its own geography,' Chris Connery trenchantly warns in his analysis of Pacific Rim Discourse as a transnational American construct emanating from the boom-cycle geopolitics of the 1980s as well as from a residual Cold War imaginary" (Wilson and Dirlik, 6). We propose that indigenous cultures are more self-aware today than ever before: vaccinated now against measles, no Western plague is going to wipe them out.

46. Notwithstanding Deleuze's affirmative use of the minoritarian—after all it was he who introduced the term as something radical. See *Kafka: Towards a Minor Literature* for Deleuze's discussion on the minor.

47. Ghosh and Muecke, 2. Rather than providing alternatives, there is a greater likelihood, speaking in 2008, of "hegemonic globalization" being hijacked by emergent economic giants such as India and China. Furthermore, we would propose that transnationalism precedes and gives rise to globalization, rather than the reverse.

48. Cited by Spivak in Ashcroft et al., 31.

49. See Ian Buruma et al., *Occidentalism*, for a timely warning on the dangers of reverse Orientalism and the politics of resentment/ressentiment.

50. Spivak's seminal essay, "Can the Subaltern Speak?" provides an excellent critique of the appropriation of Antonio Gramsci's Marxist/materialist notion of the subaltern (as economically dispossessed) by admittedly invaluable subaltern studies (where the subaltern is seen as culturally and historically dispossessed) and assumes a solidarity among subalterns while attempting to speak on their behalf, which Spivak warns is totalizing and essentialist. Our point is that to accept a subaltern position from a materialist/historicist/ culturalist position, in 2008, is to perpetuate our own subordination.

51. Geertz, 222.

52. Ibid., 226, 227.

53. Ibid., 254.

54. In the way public displays of sexual preference are encouraged, for instance, while religious affiliations must be kept private.

55. Geertz, 224.

56. Seyla Benhabib cited in Cusset, 308.

57. See Sigmund Freud's "Civilization and Its Discontents" for a discussion of the "narcissism of minor differences."

58. Discourse that centres on hybridity, sameness, and difference starts to look reactionary, contra a nineteenth-century Victorian epistemological fixity, with its concomitant aversion to cultural and racial miscegenation. Bearing in mind recent scholarship revealing links between English and Islamic jurisprudence resulting from cultural cross-fertilizations dating back to the Knights Templars and the Crusades. BBC New online, 24 Sept, 2008. http://news.bbc.co.uk/2/hi/uk_news/magazine/7631388.stm. This article ignores the crucial link of Greece and Byzantium in Islamic history. If the West is derivative of an Islamic heyday of a thousand years ago, Islamic empires developed from earlier Greek and Eastern Roman civilizations. The causal chain in cultural psyches stretches back into the distant mists of time.
59. See *Multiculturalism* by Charles Taylor (Amy Gutmann, ed.).
60. Vink, 53.
61. See Amitav Ghosh's "In an Antique Land" (236).
62. See Thomas Aquinas' "On Being and Essence," a foundational text drawing on Aristotle as refracted by Avicenna aka Ibnu Sina.
63. Simpson and Kresse, 364.
64. Strategic essentialism, as developed by Spivak, refers to adopting a position temporarily, or role-playing, for a purpose: "a strategic use of positive essentialism in a scrupulously visible political interest" (*The Spivak Reader*, 214) . Spivak, in her *boundary* 2 interview, laments the misuse that the term has incurred, in attributing unchanging fixed characteristics to the subject, which, rather than emancipating, perpetuate subordination.
65. Spivak, 1.
66. Clifford, 3.
67. Colloquialism derived from Psalm 42: 7, KJV.
68. "[A] major consequence of the Columbian exchange was the New World's contribution of gold and silver to the world's stocks and flows of money, which certainly also gave a new boost to economic activity and trade in the Old World economy from the sixteenth century onward" (Frank, 60)."[A]lmost the only world economic business of the Europeans, who were not able to sell anything else—especially of their own non-competitive production—in the thriving markets of Asia. Asians would buy nothing else from Europe other than the silver it got out of its colonies in the Americas" (Frank, 134).
69. As Franz Fanon says, "In concrete terms Europe has been bloated out of all proportions by the gold and raw materials from such colonial countries as Latin America, China and Africa. Today Europe's tower of opulence faces these continents, for centuries the point of departure of their shipments of diamonds, oil, silk and cotton, timber, and exotic products to this very same Europe. Europe is literally the creation of the Third World. The riches which are choking it are those plundered from the underdeveloped peoples" (Fanon, 58).
70. See Marcus Vink's article for an excellent though inherently Wallersteinian overview of methodology.
71. The phrase "cradle of globalization" is attributed to Lee Cassanelli et al., *Indian Ocean: Cradle of Globalization* http://ccat.sas.upenn.edu/indian-ocean/ Accessed 26 December 2008.
72. Braudel, 122.
73. Considered here as a unitary politic-cultural unit.
74. The Baudrillardian erasure of memory and the emphasis on the contemporary has effectively cancelled out this longer view. It is precisely the artificiality of the postmodern, as a Western strategy of dominance, which it seems has won/is winning?

75. l) The existence and development of the world system stretches back not just five hundred but some five thousand years; 2) The world economy and its long-distance trade relations form a centerpiece of this world system; 3) The process of capital accumulation is the motor force of world system history; 4) The center-periphery structure is one of the characteristics of the world system; 5) Alternation between hegemony and rivalry is depictive of the world system, although system wide hegemony has been rare or non-existent; and 6) Long economic cycles of ascending and descending phases underlie economic growth in the world system. (Frank and Gills).

76. Edward Lorenz, meteorologist at MIT, pioneered chaos theory and the so-called "butterfly effect" in a 1972 paper entitled "Predictability: Does the Flap of a Butterfly's Wings in Brazil Set Off a Tornado in Texas?" Our "Yes" is qualified because Lorenz, in developing chaos theory, concluded that while very small changes in a system can have large and unexpected consequences, precise long-range forecasts are impossible. World systems analysis looks both to the past and the future, considering the latter being the calculable and inevitable outcome of the former.

77. Chase-Dunn and Hall, cited in Chase-Dunn and Grimes, 388.

78. Steinberg, 23.

79. Frank appears to use the terms world system 'history' and 'approach' interchangeably with 'analysis.'

80. The hyphen denotes a certain loyalty to Wallerstein's approach.

81. We can list the following among the criteria of participation in the same world system:
    1. extensive and persistent trade connections.
    2. persistent or recurrent political relations with particular regions or peoples, including especially center-periphery-hinterland relations and hegemony/rivalry relations and processes.
    3. sharing economic, political, and perhaps also cultural cycles. The identification of these cycles and their bearing on the extent of the world system play a crucial role in our inquiry.
    Indeed, the identification of the geographical extent of near- simultaneity of these cycles may serve as an important operational definition of the extent of the world system. If distant parts of Afro-Eurasia experiences economic expansions and contractions nearly simultaneously, that would be evidence that they participate in the same world system. (Frank and Gills).

82. Fanon, 15.

83. Vink, 51.

84. Marcus Vink cites Chaudhuri, contra Wallerstein, "Some even wonder as to which was the actual 'core' and the 'periphery' in view of contemporary mercantilist concerns in England and the Dutch Republic, and elsewhere over the 'fundamental structural imbalance in Indo-European trade' and resulting outflow or 'drain' of bullion and the 'near panic' among European textile producers and the perceived threats of de-industrializing Europe in response to the invasion by textiles from India ('the world's greatest producer of cotton textiles') in the late seventeenth century" (Vink, 50).

85. "Integrates" here refers in the political economist sense.

86. Frank, 2.

87. See Bose, *A Hundred Horizons*, Chapter 3. David Washbrook echoes, "British capitalism [and colonialism] rode on the back of South Asian dynamics . . . [T]he Company was bankrolled by Indian capital, serviced by local scribe elites and sustained by indigenous military forces," (cited by Vink, 51).

88. This brings to mind Adam Smith's claim that the discovery of America and the rounding of the Cape were the two most significant moments in history!

89. Max Weber develops this thesis at length, in exposing the dichotomy between Protestant rejection of Catholic exteriority (of the salvific through sacraments), but promulgation of their own famous work ethic as the path to and evidence of salvation, made explicit in the Calvinist attitudes towards entitlement and material possessions.
90. Which goes some way to explain the collapse of the Iberian colonial enterprise: the failure to embrace "usury."
91. We are reminded here of Mauricio Obregon's chastening throwaway remark in *Beyond the Edge of the Sea* (New York: The Modern Library, 2002): "When the Polynesians sailed across the Indian Ocean to Madagascar, their legends also went with them, but, unfortunately, they lacked a bard" (3–4). It's all about who gets to do the telling.
92. This cynicism is wonderfully interrupted by the election of Barack Obama to the U.S. Presidency, financed not by powerful lobbyists, but average people donating twenty, fifty, or one hundred U.S. dollars in a vote for change.
93. Presentism is a mode of historical analysis in which present-day ideas and perspectives are anachronistically introduced into depictions or interpretations of the past. Most modern historians seek to avoid presentism in their work because they believe it creates a distorted understanding of their subject matter.The Oxford English Dictionary gives the first citation for *presentism* in its historiographic sense from 1916, and the word may have been in use in this meaning as early as the 1870s. Historian David Hackett Fischer identifies presentism as a logical fallacy also known as the "fallacy of *nunc pro tunc*". He has written that the "classic example" of presentism was the so-called "Whig history", in which certain eighteenth- and nineteenth-century British historians wrote history in a way that used the past to validate their own political beliefs. This interpretation was presentist because it did not depict the past in objective historical context, but instead viewed history only through the lens of contemporary Whig beliefs. In this kind of approach, which emphasizes the relevance of history to the present, things which do not seem relevant receive little attention, resulting in a misleading portrayal of the past. "Whig history" or "whiggishness" are often used as synonyms for presentism, particularly when the historical depiction in question is teleological or *triumphalist*. (Wikipedia).
94. See Paul Virilio's *Speed and Politics* for further discussion.
95. Lecture by Frank entitled "World System History" Prepared for presentation at the annual meeting of The New England Historical Association, Bentley College, Waltham, MA, April 23, 1994. *http://www.hartford-hwp.com/archives/10/034.html* Accessed September 21, 2008.
96. Hari Seldon, fictional character in Isaac Asimov's Foundation series, was a professor of mathematics and developed "psychohistory" to predict the future as a series of long cycles lasting thousands of years. He establishes a secret, mirror society to replace the dying galactic empire that he serves.
97. Cited in Steinberg, 45.
98. Braudel 1995, 256–257.
99. Spivak, *Other Asias*, 2, 3.
100. "We are in a certain sense amphibious, not exclusively connected with the land, but with the sea as well . . . The sea and the land in which we dwell furnish theatres for action, limited for limited actions and vast for grander deeds" (Strabo cited in Stenberg, 9).
101. Dangerous Emotions, 28, University of California Press, Berkeley, Los Angeles, London, 2000.
102. Bachelard, 13.
103. Rushdie, 1991, 124.

104. Baudelaire took his spleen to the Indian Ocean, travelling in the region and spending three weeks in Mauritius in 1841, commemorated in *Exotic Perfume*. His *Black Venus* cycle refers to his long association with Jeanne Duvall, a mulatto actress and prostitute, immortalized by Edouard Manet in his 1862 painting *Baudelaire's Mistress, Reclining*.
105. Bailyn states "Nobody I know is or has been poetically enraptured by the Atlantic world" (cited in Bose, 5).
106. See K.N. Chaudhuri's *Asia Before Europe*, 36.
107. "Our intellectual life is out of kilter. Epistemology, the social sciences, the science of texts—all have their privileged vantage point, provided they remain separate. If the creatures we are pursuing cross all three spaces, we are no longer understood" (Latour, 5). Latour was influenced by Michael Polanyi's notion of "tacit knowledge."
108. Gallagher and Greenblatt, 3.
109. Spivak, 9.
110. Geertz, 227.
111. "[T]he notion of a distinct culture, particulary a culture distant in time or space, as a text—a notion we got more from Geertz and the structuralists than the historicists—is powerfully attractive for several reasons. It carries the core hermeneutical presumption that one can occupy a position from which one can discover meanings that those who left traces of themselves could not have articulated. Explication and paraphrase are not enough; we seek something more, something that the authors we study would not have had sufficient distance upon themselves and their own era to grasp" (Gallagher and Greenblatt, 8).
112. "Thus founded on the rupture between a past that is its object, and a present that is the place of its practice, history endlessly finds the present in its object and the past in its practice. Inhabited by the uncanniness that it seeks, history imposes its law upon the faraway places that it conquers when it fosters the illusion that it is bringing them back to life" (De Certeau, 36).
113. Epistemological rupture, or *coupure epistemologique*, is a term coined by Gaston Bachelard in *La Formation De L'Esprit Scientifique*, in a fascinating application of psychoanalysis to the development of scientific knowledges.
114. Gallagher and Greenblatt, 7.
115. Coherence and the Subject/Self have undergone much deconstruction by Western academia, useful in countering triumphalist modernist narratives. Obviously, from the point of agency and historical revisionism in the Indian Ocean region, extreme narrative skepticism is counter-productive and can be reserved for emergent fundamentalist postcolonial histories. This is purely utilitarian, and not a theoretical regression! Treason to postmodern ahistorical autonomy frees us from the prison of slavish conservative adherence to cherished theory! For further reading see Slavoj Zizek's "The Ticklish Subject."
116. See Michael Pearson's notion of "ressac," or mutual dependence, with the mixture varying from time to time, in *Littoral Society: The Concept and the Problems*.
117. See Edward Said on the amateur in *Representations of the Intellectual*.
118. From St. Paul's first letter to the Corinthians 13.12, refers to partial sightings, imperfect visions.
119. See Francois Cusset, *French Theory: How Foucault, Derrida, Deleuze, & Co. Transformed the Intellectual Life of the United States*. 316.
120. Conservative in the conformity of nonconformity.
121. Cusset, 324.
122. "The secular republic found the last idol to smash in thought itself" (Cusset, 311).

BIBLIOGRAPHY

Bachelard, Gaston. *Water and Dreams: An Essay On the Imagination of Water.* Dallas, TX: The Pegasus Foundation—Dallas Institute of Humanities and Culture Publications, 1983.
Bauman, Zygmunt. *Globalization: The Human Consequences.* New York: Columbia University Press, 1998.
Bose, Sugata. *A Hundred Horizons: The Indian Ocean in the Age of Global Empire.* Cambridge, MA: Harvard University Press, 2006.
Braudel, Fernand. *On History.* Translated by Sarah Matthews. Chicago, IL: University of Chicago Press, 1980.
———. *A History of Civilizations.* New York: Penguin, 1995.
Chase-Dunn, Christopher, and Peter Grimes. "World-Systems Analysis." *Annual Review of Sociology* 21(1995): 387–417.
Clifford, James. *Routes: Travel and Translation in the Late Twentieth Century.* Cambridge, MA: Harvard University Press, 1997.
Connery, Christopher L. "Pacific Rim Discourse: The US Global Imaginary in the Late Cold War Years." *boundary 2* 21(1; 1994): 30–56.
Cusset, Francois. *French Theory: How Foucault, Derrida, Deleuze & Co. Transformed the Intellectual Life of the United States.* Translated by Jeff Fort. Minneapolis, MN: University of Minnesota Press, 2008.
De Certeau, Michel. *The Writing of History.* New York: Columbia University Press, 1988.
Fanon, Frantz. *The Wretched of the Earth.* New York: Grove, 2004.
Frank, Andre Gunder. *ReOrient: Global Economy in the Asian Age.* Los Angeles, CA: University of California Press, 1998.
Frank, Andre Gunder, and Barry K. Gills. *The Five Thousand Year World System in Theory and Praxis.* http://www.rrojasdatabank.info/agfrank/theory_praxis.html (accessed September 21, 2008).
Gallagher, Catherine, and Stephen Greenblatt. *Practicing New Historicism.* Chicago, IL: University of Chicago Press, 2000.
Geertz, Clifford. *Available Light: Anthropological Reflections on Philosophical Topics.* Princeton, NJ: Princeton University Press, 2000.
Ghosh, Amitav. *In An Antique Land.* New York: Vintage, 1994.
Ghosh, Devleena, and Stephen Muecke, eds. *Cultures of Trade: Indian Ocean Exchanges.* Newcastle, UK: Cambridge Scholars Publishing, 2007.
Gilbert, Erik. *Dhows and the Colonial Economy of Zanzibar.* Oxford, UK: James Curry, 2004.
Hawley, John C., ed. *India in Africa, Africa in India: Indian Ocean Cosmopolitanisms.* Bloomington, IN: Indiana University Press, 2008.
Hobsbawm, Eric. "Identity Politics and the Left." *New Left Review* 217 (May/June; 1996).
Hofmeyr, Isabel. "The Black Atlantic Meets the Indian Ocean: Forging New Paradigms of Transnationalism for the Global South—Literary and Cultural Perspectives." Special Issue of *Social Dynamics* 33(2; December 2007), Oceanic Worlds/Bordered Worlds, Meg Samuelson and Shaun Viljoen, eds.
Hughes, Gordon. "Community Cohesion, Asylum Seeking and the Question of the 'Stranger.'" *Cultural Studies* 21(6): 931–951.
Klein, Bernard, and Gesa Mackenthun. *Sea Changes.* New York and London: Routledge, 2004.
Latour, Bruno. *We Have Never Been Modern.* Translated by Catherine Porter. Cambridge, MA: Harvard University Press, 1993.
Mignolo, Walter. "The Many Faces of Cosmo-polis: Border Thinking and Critical Cosmopolitanism." *Public Culture* 12(3): 721–748.

Obregon, Mauricio. *Beyond the Edge of the Sea.* New York: The Modern Library, 2002.

Ong, Walter J. *Orality and Literacy.* London: Routledge, 2002.

Pearson, Michael N. *Port Cities and Intruders: The Swahili Coast, India and Portugal in the Early Modern Era.* Baltimore, MD: Johns Hopkins University Press, 1998.

———. *The Indian Ocean.* New York: Routledge, 2003.

Porter, Roy. *Enlightenment: Britain and the Creation of the Modern World.* London: Penguin, 2000.

Rushdie, Salman. *Imaginary Homelands: Essays and Criticism 1981–1991.* London: Granta, 1991.

———. *Haroun and the Sea of Stories.* London: Granta, 1990

Said, Edward W. *Orientalism.* London: Penguin, 1978.

Spivak, Gayatri Chakravorty. *Other Asias.* Oxford, UK: Blackwell Publishing, 2008.

———. *The Spivak Reader.* London: Routledge, 1996.

———. "Can The Subaltern Speak?" In *The Post-Colonial Studies Reader,* edited by Ed Ashcroft, Gareth Griffiths, Helen Tiffin, 28–37. Oxford, UK: Routledge, 1995.

Steinberg, Philip E. *The Social Construction of the Ocean.* Cambridge, UK: Cambridge University Press, 2001.

Subramanian, Lakshmi. "Of Pirates and Potentates: Maritime Jurisdiction and the Construction of Piracy in the Indian Ocean." In *Cultures of Trade: Indian Ocean Exchanges,* edited by Devleena Ghosh and Stephen Muecke, 19–30. Newcastle, UK: Cambridge Scholars Publishing, 2007.

Wilson, Rob, and Arif Dirlik. "Asia/Pacific as Space of Cultural Production." *boundary 2* 21(1; 1994): 1–14.

FURTHER READING

Arendt, Hannah. *Eichmann in Jerusalem: A Report on the Banality of Evil.* New York: Penguin, 1994.

Buruma, Ian, and Avishai Margalit. *Occidentalism.* London: Atlantic, 2005.

Chaudhuri, K.N. *Asia Before Europe: Economy and Civilization of the Indian Ocean from the Rise of Islam to 1750.* Cambridge, UK: Cambridge University Press, 1991.

Deleuze, Gilles, and Felix Guattari. *Kafka: Towards a Minor Literature.* Minneapolis, MN: University of Minnesota Press, 1986.

Dirlik, Arif. *The Postcolonial Aura: Third World Criticism in the Age of Global Capitalism.* Boulder, CO: Westview Press, 1997.

Fukuyama, Francis. *The End of History and The Last Man.* New York: Free Press, 1992.

Gilroy, Paul. *The Black Atlantic: Modernity and Double Consciousness.* Cambridge, MA: Harvard University Press, 1993.

Jolly, Margaret. "Imagining Oceania: Indigenous and Foreign Representations of a Sea of Islands." *The Contemporary Pacific* 19(2; 2007): 508–545.

Pakenham, Thomas. *The Scramble for Africa: White Man's Conquest of the Dark Continent from 1876–1912.* London: Abacus, 1991.

Pearson, Michael N. "Littoral Society: The Concept and the Problems." *Journal of World History* 17(4; 2006): 353–373.

Rushdie, Salman. *Haroun and the Sea of Stories.* New York: Penguin, 1991.

Said, Edward W. *Representations of the Intellectual.* New York: Vintage, 1994.

Taylor, Charles. *Multiculturalism*. Edited by Amy Gutmann. NJ: Princeton University Press, 1994.

Vink, Marcus. "Indian Ocean Studies and the 'New Thalassology.'" *Journal of Global History* 2(2007): 41–62.

Virilio, Paul. *Speed and Politics*. New York: Semiotext(e), 2007.

Wallerstein, Immanuel. *Alternatives: The United States Confronts the World*. Boulder, CO: Paradigm Publishers, 2004.

———. *World-Systems Analysis*. London: Duke University Press, 2004.

Waugh, Evelyn. *Labels: A Mediterranean Journal*. London: Penguin, 1995.

Zizek, Slavoj. *The Ticklish Subject: The Absent Centre of Political Ontology*. London: Verso, 2000.

2 Fabulation

Flying Carpets and Artful Politics in the Indian Ocean

Stephen Muecke

In the 1990s I started to take an interest in the networking capacity for cultural studies when I saw how Kuan-Hsing Chen set up the Inter-Asia Cultural Studies Group, an alternative intellectual knowledge exchange which now has an eponymous (Taylor and Francis) journal and a vital and well-funded network of scholars working in Taiwan, China, Japan, Hong Kong, Singapore, India, Korea, etc. For younger scholars in the humanities this network has effectively displaced any need for them to work within the older area studies frameworks controlled by Anglo-American universities, nor do they necessarily feel the need to go to one of those universities for their graduate training. The local training in Taiwan or Hong Kong still uses English a lot, as a lingua franca, and still uses many canonical cultural studies texts, but the decolonisation process is well-advanced. It is an extraordinarily successful network, using interdisciplinary theory as another kind of lingua franca, breaking the hegemonic hold of the older disciplines and their area studies foci, and opening up new specific areas of study not visible to those older networks: new media, gender studies, alternative globalisation studies.

This creates, in the process, a new set of intellectual voices, ones that don't sound like the older "tone" in the language of the social sciences, some of which makes me want to characterise it as "cargo knowledge."[1] The speaking subject enunciates with assurance: "*This* is what I have found out, this is the true. Here's a 'transparent' language with a 'load' of content." But this "true" is a fictional truth of the coloniser, by virtue of what it does not reveal and by the way it is distributed. The cargo knowledge the coloniser unloads goes only one way. It does not appear on the jetties of the South, it is packed up and shipped to the port cities of the North. It is "packed" in the kinds of stories it tells, and in the kinds of stories it responds to; a fiction created by the encounter with different kinds of discourses which are selectively heard and translated. Stories are thus crafted with selected omissions and/or excesses, things which can't always be contained by the available concepts. Ethnography, for instance, is often a fiction to the extent that it masks its conditions of possibility: the funding from the Ford Foundation or some research council. Or, historically, a story about the "fabulous" wealth of the East blinds the European merchant-adventurer to the likelihood of the more meagre realities he will find on arrival.

This is why neither the language of fact nor the language of fiction is sufficient for describing how our new networking might work; neither the ostensibly transparent language of the social sciences that "delivers" knowledge in its authoritative tone, nor the beautiful truth of nationalised and standardised literatures that also return ideas and images to the centre to be judged as more cargo of a different sort: "commonwealth literatures" is the name for that particular kind of package.

A language which travels and inspires is not a uniform one, but it might have the kind of "magic" implied by *fabulation*, a Bergsonian concept reused by Gilles Deleuze. Fabulation involves *inventing* in relation to a problem or a situation that must be remedied, particularly with regard to the situation of "the people who are missing."[2] If a contemporary Indian Ocean body of literature is "missing" in that sense, it remains to be invented, something I attempted recently in a creolised retelling of Paul and Virginia.[3] So fabulation involves the writer and the people *moving towards one another*. Fiction in this model is freed from the imperative to create a true world, just as the "cargo" social scientific voice is freed from the model of transparency to the true fact. Fabulation works best hovering between the oral and written, the real or the imaginary, being neither a document nor a fiction, but a fictocritical form of enunciation that oscillates between these poles. This is not the romance of the indeterminate; it is a listening method which "hears" not only the words but the discursive frameworks which are the practice for putting words together as knowledge. The new southern networks, I argue, are ones that are developing in conjunction with new digitally vehicled audiovisual literacies. They will be the future.

This is something I learned from the storytelling of Nyigina elder Paddy Roe,[4] when I started my association with the Indian Ocean in the northwest of Western Australia, sitting on the beach and gazing out "to the islands" (to borrow the title of the famous Randolph Stow novel), the islands to which the spirits of the Aboriginal coastal people return, out in the Indian Ocean where the great storm clouds of the wet season gather and come rolling in like monstrous heads and give the northwest peoples the iconography of the Wandjina figures that they call their gods today.

There I began to take an interest in the links between oral histories and stories and the literary mainstream, with me as link and scribe. Were the Broome stories I recorded destined to be just a marginal note in the story that the Australian nation was constructing for itself, based on the traditions of England? Less than one hundred years ago *that* small island, still rich from its imperial trade, invested its surplus in a cultural superstructure, a nationalism that involved the locals turning their attention from the illusion of the purity of the classical languages to make their own Creole (English as a combination of Romance, Germanic, Anglo-Saxon, and

Nordic languages) into a Great Tradition, a great literary tradition through the institutionalisation of a canon of great writers. Once these cultural heroes had their reputations secured, they were also exported to the colonies: quite a network, quite a turnaround in the fortunes of a once despised vernacular. So that is what I was working against with "Paul and Virginia," projecting Paddy Roe's vernacular across the Indian Ocean towards Mauritius and its canonical Rousseauian text of 1788 by Bernardin de St Pierre, *Paul et Virginie*. The Indian Ocean might have a new network, but it would have to be invented.

Gilles Deleuze, in his *Time Image*[5] book about cinema conjures a moment of fabulation in which cultural forces regroup and start to generate their own stories. The places and the materials, in the form they take and the way they can be transformed, talk to the writing or to the way stories are told. This reassemblage of forces is a way of re-creating the Indian Ocean world, an ancient world reconstituted as a contemporary world through the practice of what I call "artful politics."

This is a politics of seeing and hearing such that a strange kind of language will have to come into being, a language which will challenge any firm distinction between description and fictionalisation and which will introduce a queer defamiliarisation into the heart of the most familiar experiences in order to project reality and not normalise it. The language of fabulation is one which "deterritorialises" the cargo language, which in effect creolises it. "What has to be filmed", says Deleuze, "is the frontier, on condition that this is equally crossed by the filmmaker in one direction and by the real character in the opposite direction: time is necessary here: a certain time is necessary which constitutes an integral part of the film."[6]

Whether it is a matter of making films, telling stories, or writing academic papers, we who are in the business of inventing cultures as we describe them have a stake in our own performances, like getting immersed in Indian Ocean studies, in which the time of the performance is an integral part of its quality. For some, time does not matter, and so the effect is delayed or displaced (anachronic or anatopic). Here, you could say, *here* is my piece of cargo writing, my academic report, delivered on time to the funding body, to act on in *their* good time, or not act on at all, in which case one might have to question the value of the cargo. So delivery matters, and delivery involves thinking about: the mode of enunciation, the decolonisation of the subject–object (master–slave) relation, and do I hear also a trumpet call for the retreat of the forward march of European modernity around the world?

But wait, you may say, wait a minute, these theoretical and rhetorical adjustments are all very well, but what if the delivery of cargo knowledge is not only on time but valued, and does a good job with International Monetary Fund money reforming government and industry in third world countries? Social indicators are improving, there is some economic growth and environmental sustainability as well. Maybe so, but that analysis belongs in someone else's paper. My thesis would be that the World Bank needs its spin doctors too; the red carpet is not always rolled out and waiting for the agents of capitalist reform; it too has to "fabulate," to tie its threads of institutional thinking in with local desires and aspirations, to also make things become, to make virtual realities before they exist concretely.

What I am seeking to do is to trace, as Bruno Latour says, "the unique signature drawn by associations and substitutions through the conceptual space."[7] The fascinating "conceptual space" that is constituted by Indian Ocean studies today is a historically formed image where we see European enlightenment thought (reflected back in waves to the seventeenth century) meeting the transcontinental mercantile-religious complex that was the pre-colonial Indian Ocean. That particular conjunction gives us the potential to see postcolonial thought, which, after all, developed out of the meshing of European theory and empirical analysis of the colonial situation, further localised in the Indian Ocean, instead of developed only elsewhere, in the northern diaspora for instance.

So let us consider different chains of associations drawn through that heterogeneous space that is the Indian Ocean, creating the "unique signatures" that will be our renovated languages of analysis. Yes, the new area studies—let's call it the Indian Ocean network—is both a critical intellectual project *and* a radically empirical one. One chain is the annual monsoon rhythm (OED: Arabic *mawsim*, lit. "season," *wasama* to mark) and the way it brings rains to the Subcontinent, enriching the agriculture there. The rains link to vitality, to ritual, to the interlocking lives of plants, animals, and humans. The monsoon becomes a sacred thing, not in itself, but precisely in the manner that, in its network of relations, it crafts a "unique signature." Between October and April it turns around, and blows from the northeast, encouraging departures, sailing, and eventually trade; another network of associations is established here, one based on working the relations of the scarcity and abundance of goods. Techniques for the transcription of value have to be developed (coinage or letters of credit), the character of the merchant has to be forged as trustworthy by the way he dresses and speaks and can trace his social relations. Does all this culture trace back to the monsoon? Yes, at that time it was a natural–cultural continuum of connections which couldn't be broken.

And when the Portuguese, with da Gama, finally succeed in rounding the Cape in ships designed for "remote control," as it were, since they are going such a distance, a different conceptual structure appears on the Indian Ocean scene.[8] The notion of imperial force appears, as the sovereign drives these expeditions from a distance for the profit of the national capital; and there is a singular god overseeing a global world which remained to be envisioned by Copernicus, but which Camoens was later to "give" to da Gama in the great Portuguese national epic, the *Lusiad*, written some seventy years after the voyage. In India, a goddess speaks to da Gama, in Canto X,[9] of the extraordinary *máquina do mundo*:

'To you, my hero, God in his divine wisdom has granted to see with your bodily eyes what is denied to other mortals, whose vain strivings after knowledge but lead them into error and misery. Follow me, you and your men, with firm and courageous, yet prudent, step up this densely-wooded slope.' And so saying, she led him into a thicket where a mortal might only with extreme difficulty make his way.

Soon they found themselves on a lofty mountain-top, in a meadow studded with emeralds and rubies that proclaimed to the eye it was no earthly ground they trod. And there they beheld, suspended in the air, a globe of such transparency that the light shone right through it and the centre was as visible as the outer surface. What it was made of could not be divined, but it clearly consisted of a series of spheres contrived by the wand of God to rotate about a simple fixed centre in such a way that, however they revolved or rose or fell, the whole neither rose nor fell but showed the same from every angle. Its supernatural artifice in short had neither beginning nor ending, but was in all things uniform, perfect, and self-sustained like God its maker.

As da Gama gazed at it he was deeply moved, and stood lost in curiosity and amazement. Then the goddess spoke: 'This thing you see before you is a representation in miniature of the universe, that you may see where your path lies, whither it leads, and what the end of your desires. This is the mighty fabric of creation, ethereal and elemental . . .

I think it is significant that this fiction, this spectacle of the Machine of the World (*Máquina do Mundo*), and of the power of science, is located in India as a blessing bestowed on an imperial explorer. Its vision of the world as a universal system, obeying mechanical laws whose evolution, as J-F Lyotard says, will "trace a foreseeable trajectory and give[s] rise to continual 'normal' functions."[10] Thus Da Gama's goddess, rather than simply prophesying in the classical manner of the Odyssey, provides a machine so that "you may see where your path lies". This will become the predictive capacity of the scientific laws of the mastery of nature that will reach their height with Newton and Descartes. By 1800, says Michel Serres:

Science alone is universal, in its practice of a verifiable reality, since it provides the very laws of the universe, whatever the latitudes. This is how our fathers saw it, and how we ourselves believed it to be. And this is why eighteenth-century Europe celebrated the Enlightenment. And this is why the nineteenth century wrote of Absolute Knowledge.[11]

Nature and culture will be driven into separate realms by this line of thought, as A.N. Whitehead and William James, and more recently Bruno Latour and other scholars have shown.[12] It is the physicist who has privileged access to the facts of the natural world in a relentless drive for immutable laws, but the multifarious and contingent experiences of the real world are lost in this: smells, aberrations, stray facts, beautiful sunsets—all this has to be bracketed out. It is the dream of the navigator rather than the pathfinder. It creates a different chain of associations to the one I described of the mariner linking to the monsoon.

But the rationalist Enlightenment had its rivals, in a different geneal-ogy traceable from Montaigne to Rousseau and Diderot, who celebrated contingency and experimentalism, adapting themselves to the landscape as they proceeded, rejoicing at chance and the unexpected. "Everything has its outcome in nature, the most extravagant as well as the most reasoned experiment. Experimental philosophy is always happy with what comes its way," Diderot said in *De l'intérpretation de la nature*.[13]

My version of a contemporary cultural studies finds itself descended from this rival enlightenment because we proceed from the contingencies of encounter rather than from founding principles. Strangers meet, like ships in the Conradian night, and ask each other what the game is, what the stakes are, what the matter is. They begin to fabulate. They don't seek to confirm available fictions, or fictionalise a truth. They meet with maturity and respect, and share wry humour, because they know that "things must go both ways," as my old mentor Paddy Roe in Broome used to say. But their fabulations are not just for fun; they can be a valid and sturdy mode of existence, well-crafted yarns and memories reinforcing each other, lasting longer, perhaps, than mere paper knowledge.

Is it by chance that I thought of Alan Villiers and his experience of pearl-ing, and picked up *Monsoon Seas* once again to prepare this chapter? Is it by chance that Villiers found himself in the Persian Gulf waters before World War II and then wrote (and I quote at length for you to experi-ence the fabulation or con-fabulation that goes on here as strangers meet respectfully and knowledge is disseminated through a story):

The waters of the Persian Gulf are rich with pearl oysters, particularly on the chain of reefs and banks near Bahrein, farther up the Gulf not far from the Bay of Kuwait, and off the coast of Trucial Oman. The best banks are on the Arab side of the Gulf. The season lasts for four months and ten days in summer, when the water is hot, for all diving is without gear except for a sort of clothespin nipped on the nose and a stone to go down with. In 1905 there were 4, 500 boats and 75, 000 men employed in Gulf pearling, according to statistics kept at Bahrein.[14]

[In 1939] I spent some time with them on the banks, pearling, and also made a buyer's run among the fleets of Kuwait and Bahrein, with the expert buyer Sheik Mohammed Abdul-Razzaq, who had with him interesting paraphernalia, consisting of pieces of red flannel, a minute pair of scales which he held by hand, a large box of silver rupees, his brother, a clerk, a servant and a handyman, five sheep, several goats, and a large supply of sherbet, rice, ghee, and other necessities. We trav-elled in a small motorboat, and it was our custom to spend the day among the pearling vessels and the nights at anchor close off some pleasant beach, where we drew up our carpets out of the reach of the tide and slept on the sand, beneath the stars. It was a good life.[15]

(...)

The sheik practiced a most curious method in his bargaining. When we approached a little pearler, or a big one, we would go aboard with quiet and unhurried dignity, be received with coffee and sweet confections, and discuss all manner of things for an hour or so before the subject of pearls was mentioned. Then in due course, out would come a piece of red flannel or an old black sock, and the nakhoda would carefully untie the bundle to display his take. They were always a lovely sight, and the sheik's eyes used to gleam, though he would invariably begin by decrying the gems and lamenting that the waters of the Gulf no longer produced pearls worth a buyer's attention. Then, in another hour or so, he would condescend to examine the take properly, sieving it and weighing the various grades, and examining some through a small magnifying glass. Only after several hours would the subject of a price be mentioned. Then would follow the usual sparring, always cheerful and conducted according to rule.

If he really intended to buy the pearls, the sheik would at last grab a spare piece of his red flannel, throw it over his right hand, grasp the right hand of the nakhoda beneath this flannel, and conduct the final negotiations by manipulation of fingers, according to some ancient code, in solemn and complete silence. Sometimes he varied the procedure by grabbing his brother's hand in the same manner, and working on his fingers, but this was when he wanted to get his brother's idea of the value of the parcel he was considering.[16]

This to me is a kind of quintessential scene of Indian Ocean trade, where a chain of relations links natural value to cultural value in a describable continuum. Nature is not hidden, as in the Western imaginary where the savant removes Nature's veil to uncover her secrets.[17] Here the art of concealment is openly cultural: the piece of red flannel clearly signals, in something of a ritualised performance, what it is we should *not* know.

In any case, truth was never literal or transparent, that is only one of its fictions, as if anyone could be constantly exposed to its burning light. Truth was always a process of masking and unmasking, or a dancing movement between the general and the specific—proofs cast as syllogisms, for instance. It exists, I'm afraid, only in the movements of discourse, which is saying that it is never singular and never quite present either. Attached to the strings of artifice, it burst onto the scene like a *deus ex machina*, or like a flying carpet bearing Douglas Fairbanks in *The Thief of Baghdad*.

Ah yes, popular culture, it too, is part of our Indian Ocean scene, as I want to work to conclude by taking everything in this Indian Ocean world back to a fundamental idea: *everything in it is in a natural–cultural continuum.* Everything has some value; everything is worthy of respect. "Everything has its outcome in nature" said Diderot. The Indian Ocean is full of popular culture, let's not exclude it because it might seem trivial. Each story, artifact, or flying carpet carries a bit of cultural value which, if you follow a zigzag path of associations is linked to natural things and beings. In "*A Thousand and One Nights* at the Movies," Robert Irwin says that the thousand and one productions of *that* story in film:

> . . . are an important part of Orientalism, and they need to be considered as part of a broader cultural phenomenon that includes such diverse things as Turkish cigarettes, Flying Carpet Travel Agents, Flying Carpet Dry Cleaning outlets, cinemas called the Alhambra, Egyptian music halls, Orientalist sheet music, camel jokes, the Genie in advertisements for brass polish, three wishes jokes, Wilson, Keppel and Betty's Egyptian sand dance, Kettleby's 'In a Persian Market', the Bonzo Dog Doo Dah Band's 'Ali Baba and his camel', Fry's Turkish Delight, the posters for conjuring and circus shows, Tommy Cooper's fez, night club versions of the Dance of the Seven Veils . . . '[18]

Strange stuff, this popular orientalism, fabulations out of control, asking the analytic writing what it has learned. Said didn't deal much with the popular, coming as he did out of a literary tradition. And he had an epistemological framework that doesn't help the schema I am trying to construct. His problem was one of representation, or rather misrepresentation. The reality of Asian worlds has nothing to do with the false representations made of them in Western discourses. But the way he has set up the problem (not just him, but any critique of ideology) based on two characters, subject and object, self and world, facing each other across the abyss of the mystery of representation, will never be able to grasp anything new, because the only winner in that game is language, and metalanguage, and the constant exhortation to close the gap:

> If by 'epistemology' we name the discipline that tries to understand how we manage to bridge the gap between representations and reality, the only conclusion to be drawn about it is that this discipline has no subject matter whatever, because we never bridge such a gap—not, mind you because we don't know anything objectively, but because *there is never such a gap*. The gap is an artefact due to the wrong positioning of the knowledge acquisition pathway.[19]

Why should we acquire knowledge about Indian Ocean popular culture? Because it will tell us how people are connected via what they share, and today this extends with new media beyond the geography of the ocean. The flows are different now. Michael Pearson sets up a problem to do with the Indian Ocean, a familiar and important one about littoral cultures: "Surat and Mombasa have more in common with each other than they do with inland cities such as Nairobi or Ahmadabad."[20] The question is set up as an area studies one, in which the similarity matters to us as scholars, but how do we go from there—where we scholars now have a set of terms to debate in common—to making it matter to the poor fisherfolk who supposedly have the actual littoral culture in common? Perhaps now they continue to have cultures in common with a contemporary popular culture overlay; they are watching the same Bollywood movies for instance, so they are a part of an evolving network.

An artful politics expresses what matters for networks and helps improve the network, which involves time and construction work. People will build associations to deal with matters of concern that arise for their fishing, commercial, and cultural communities: NGO and trade union linkages, research institutes that monitor ecosystems that provide livelihoods and export income.

At the same time there are networks working towards completely different ends, for instance in the Australian Indian Ocean Territories, including Christmas Island. At the time of the 2001 *Tampa* Crisis, Christmas Island could have been a possible destination for asylum seekers because it was still Australian sovereign territory at that stage. Then a new law was passed excising it from Australia for that purpose, so any asylum seekers ("boat people") landing there could not expect to be processed. A new detention facility was built at huge expense (up to half a billion Australian dollars). But it is not a singular thing, it is part of a network that makes it possible. This installation is only partly functional, designed for up to eight hundred detainees, but now with a change of government it may never house any. With what did it link? What is it or was it good for? It was clearly going to be good for the private security corporation that would have run it on a lucrative government contract, it was good for the builder Baulderstone and the labourers flown in from Australia at great expense, it underscored the previous Australian government's vote-winning exercise about being tough on refugees with brown complexions, it networked with a broader global coalition of creating security fears as part of a capitalist-militarist complex (the so-called War on Terror), it even linked to those individual shareholders who have no qualms about investing in one of the world's most lucrative investment lines: correctional management companies.

Networks thus coexist, and are sometimes in competition. The right-wing Australian government voted out in 2007 wanted to build up associations of the things they believed would "work," and they took the trouble to destroy networks that exist as alternatives, like trade unions and student associations. It is no exaggeration to say that they spent propaganda money to destroy the idea of such associations as well.

To return to Latour's idea, the point for critical theory and its place in Indian Ocean studies is to stop doing critical theory! That is to say, it is pointless continuing with a mode of discourse whose main platform, repeated endlessly, is one of scepticism about representations. "There is a gap between what the government is telling us and what is real, they are not being truthful," as if, if they finally told the truth, we could trust them and all would be well. That is not the point, if what they are really doing is building up associations, and that includes stories, texts, objects, ideologies, military forces, cash, etc. That kind of "constructive" effort creates a powerful network, tending to leave all opposition drowning in its wake. The facility at Christmas Island, looking like one of its failures, is a kind of eloquent expression of that network's capacity to mobilise itself rapidly and then move on.

I am not a political scientist, but my discussion of politics is designed to make us reconsider our modes of knowledge acquisition as we recraft Indian Ocean studies. The framework suggests that knowledge is a living, transforming set of relations, not a cargo traded on the cheap and deposited back in the rich North in single-discipline warehouses. Interdisciplinarity makes new things visible (like popular culture and security centres). Nor is knowledge a set of representations lagging behind the real, always trying to catch up, reporting on it. It is part of the real; it is in itself a mode of existence as well as but much more than language and representation.

Within that interdisciplinary discourse, or set of discourses, the abandonment of ideology critique will pave the way for the introduction of a radical empiricism that again will make new objects visible in their working relationships with other things.

I have worked with two concepts in this chapter: fabulation and the network (artful politics). Fabulations are the kind of storytelling that takes off on a flight of becoming rather than repeating the available discourses and genres. It is fabulations that enable a subject to begin to feel engaged or disengaged, to either belong or depart, but in any case to continue a process of becoming. Traditionally, literature is a set of textual mechanisms, commercialised into an industry, that create and distribute forms of subjectivity. To the extent that it becomes fixed to a set of social values it doesn't work so well. But when it is articulated with feelings like "hope for the future" then it engages a community and a set of subjects in a process of becoming— that is the task of fabulation. So it is not airy-fairy, it provides valid modes of existence. And one can see how it links to the politics of the network.

The type of network I have been sketching owes a lot to the science studies of Bruno Latour and other scholars. But not being purely in the domain of science, my framework integrates human subjects via the mechanism of the fable, oscillating between description and fictionalisation, between speech and writing. There is no compulsion of the fact or of the fully present truth. The network is not the domain of objective facts or things of the world (the world "out there" that humans come to, trotting over the bridge of representations). It is a natural–cultural continuum of real empirical linkages which our analysis will have to trace in their complexity. Concepts, fish, sails, monsoon winds, songs, ceremonies, slave beads: all these are possible actors in the network.

As a concluding example, let us consider the position of my Réunion colleagues Françoise Vergès and Carapin Marimoutou in *Amarres: Créolisations india-océanes*:

> When Europe used to think of itself as the centre of the world, and organised the world around this centre, we were somewhere over there at the end of the world. Then, we were moored to France, but it was an imposed mooring which strangled us on occasions. Today, now that Europe has become one of the provinces of the world, we are rethinking our moorings. Our project is now one of decentering the gaze and redrawing the cartography of the world from the Indian ocean viewpoint, here where France, Africa, Europe, Asia and the Muslim worlds cross paths.[21]

There is something politically at stake for this island culture; it does not see itself as "just one culture among many," it must perforce see itself in somewhat more absolutist terms as it throws these mooring ropes overboard. This is a process of cultural negotiation: the more we jettison, the closer we get to what matters to us absolutely, that which we will *never* give away in a negotiation about how we share a culture with France. We can do without philosopher J-P Sartre in the Indian Ocean they might say; splash. Here are all of the popular songs of Trenet and Piaf, and Halliday may as well go too. Splash, we have our own music. *Nouvelle cuisine?* Splash, we have our fish curry and rice. What about Sarkozy? Wait, that might be illegal—after all, here in Réunion we are a *Department d'Outre Mer*. And having thrown off one set of moorings in a critical gesture, what new links do we make, whom do we pull on board? Drowning souls who have yet to discover the joys of Indian Ocean scholarship and its networks?

Culture by its very nature is excessive, and like nature it is an organic set of strange and wonderful things that we can never quite pin down. If in Réunion someone finds a rusted iron shackle that once held a slave's ankle, then this rare artifact might appear in Francoise Vergès' museum to focus a regional identity centred on the history and identity of the slave or the *marron*. With scraps of historical evidence, with useful concepts like *créolisation*, a culture is assembled which has room to move even within the constraints of the French State. The president of the republic can't be thrown overboard, not yet, nor the French language, nor, ultimately, the power of the State which finds its absolute in its right to impose military force if necessary. These are the new questions for networking research in the Indian Ocean that I would modestly propose. Not so much the question of "have we got the representations right," but, as we construct the network of associations of facts, values, institutions, scholars, activists, and fish: what can we afford to jettison? And then, what further allies can we acquire? Unlike the Inter-Asia Cultural Studies Group, which is well established, the Indian Ocean cultural studies network of scholars and activists is just beginning.

Crossing languages, old imperial affiliations, vastly different continents (Africa, South Asia, Australia), the network faces difficulties that have yet to be analysed, let alone resolved.

NOTES

1. This has also been termed the "authoritative plain style" of the English-speaking Protestant scientific community; see Karen Bennett, "Galileo's Revenge: Ways of Construing Knowledge and Translation Strategies in the Era of Globalization." *Social Semiotics* 17(2; June 2007): 171–193.
2. Deleuze, 1991, 4.
3. Muecke, 2006.
4. Roe, 1983.
5. Deleuze, 1989.
6. Deleuze, 1989, 153–154.
7. Latour, 1999, 161.
8. John Law, "On the Methods of Long Distance Control: Vessels, Navigation and the Portuguese Route to India." In *Power, Action and Belief: A New Sociology of Knowledge?* Edited by John Law, 234–263. London: Routledge, 1986.
9. Camoens, 1952, 233–234.
10. Lyotard, 1984, 90.
11. Serres, 1980, 128.
12. Latour, 2004.
13. Saint-Amand, 1997, 102.
14. Villiers, 1952, 236.
15. Ibid., 237.
16. Ibid., 238–239.
17. Hadot, 2006.
18. Irwin, 230.
19. Latour, 2007, 90.
20. Pearson, 2006, 345.
21. Vergès, 2005, 8.

BIBLIOGRAPHY

Camoens, Luis Vaz de. *The Lusiads*. Translated by W.C. Atkinson. Harmondsworth, UK: Penguin, 1952.

Deleuze, Gilles. *Cinema 2: The Time Image*. Translated by Hugh Tomlinson and Robert Galeta. Minneapolis, MN: University of Minneapolis Press, 1989.

Deleuze, Gilles. *Coldness and Cruelty*. New York: Zone Books, 1991.

Hackett, Edward J., Olga Amsterdamska, Michael Lynch, and Judy Wajcman, eds. *The Handbook of Science and Technology Studies, Third Edition*. Cambridge, MA: MIT Press, 2007, 83–112.

Hadot, Pierre. *The Veil of Isis: An Essay on the History of the Idea of Nature*. Translated by Michael Chase. Cambridge, MA: Harvard, 2006.

Irwin, Robert. "A Thousand and One Nights at the Movies." *Middle Eastern Literatures* 7(2; 2004): 223–233.

Latour, Bruno. *Pandora's Hope*. Cambridge, MA: Harvard University Press, 1999.

———. *Politics of Nature*. Cambridge, MA, Harvard University Pres, 2004.

————. "A Textbook Case Revisited. Knowledge as Mode of Existence." In *The Handbook of Science and Technology Studies, Third Edition*, edited by Edward J. Hackett, Olga Amsterdamska, Michael Lynch, and Judy Wajcman, 83–112. Cambridge, MA: MIT Press, 2007.

Lyotard, Jean François. *The Postmodern Condition: A Report on Knowledge.* Minneapolis, MN: University of Minnesota Press, 1979.

Muecke, Stephen. "Paul and Virginia." *Journal of Mauritian Studies, New Series* 3(1; 2006): 109–117. Also: http://stephenmuecke.blogspot.com/2006/11/paul-and-virginia.html

Pearson, Michael N. "Littoral Society: The Concept and the Problems." *Journal of World History* 17(4; 2006): 353–373.

Roe, Paddy. *Gularabulu: Stories from the West Kimberley.* Fremantle, Western Australia: Fremantle Arts Centre Press, 1983.

Saint-Amand, Pierre. "Contingency and the Enlightenment." *SubStance 83* 26(2; 1997): 96–109.

Serres, Michel. *Hermès V Le Passage du Nord-Ouest.* Paris: Minuit, 1980.

Taussig, Michael. *Walter Benjamin's Grave.* Chicago, IL: Chicago University Press, 2006.

Vergès, Françoise, and Carapin Marimoutou. *Amarres: Créolisations india-océanes.* Paris: L'Harmattan, 2005.

Villiers, Alan. *Monsoon Seas.* New York, McGraw Hill, 1952.

3 The Indian Ocean and the Making of Outback Australia

An Ecocultural Odyssey

Haripriya Rangan and Christian Kull

National histories, by their very definition, tend to be parochial and territorial in scope. The fluidity of change wrought by diverse interactions and movements of plants, animals, and people across lands and oceans are restricted and solidified in narratives that seek to assert a territorial integrity based on a few biophysical factors and human actions within tightly defined national political boundaries. We would expect environmental and ecological histories to be different, to adopt more expansive perspectives to convey the fluidity and dynamism of interactions between social and biophysical nature in the making of landscapes without being constrained by national boundaries. Oddly enough, few do. It seems as though most environmental and ecological histories submit to the disciplining practices of nation-making narratives, tending to reproduce and reinforce the parochial visions and insular territorial imaginations of their nationalist counterparts.[1]

This chapter travels across the Indian Ocean and beyond the bounded territorial imagination of nation-making narratives to tell a different kind of ecocultural history about the making of Outback Australia. It centres on the enigma behind the widespread presence of *Acacia farnesiana* in the Outback landscape of Australia. About 1,000 of the 1,350 or so known species of acacia are considered native to Australia, but *A. farnesiana* is not one of them. According to biologists, this many-branched and shrubby thorn tree has its origins in Central America and the Caribbean, and is now widespread across various parts of southern Europe, southern and eastern Africa, Afghanistan, Pakistan, India, Southeast Asia, and the Pacific. It has more than forty vernacular names in different countries: cassie, huisache, sweet acacia, needle bush, and Ellington's Curse are some examples.[2] Its botanical name derives from the fact that it was first brought to Europe in 1611 from the West Indies and cultivated in the gardens of Cardinal Odoardo Farnese.[3]

Figure 3.1   Acacia farnesiana in its home range in Texas. Courtesy of Campbell and Lynn Loughmiller, Lady Bird Johnson Wildflower Center.

Acacia farnesiana is found across much of the Australian Outback, and is commonly known as the mimosa bush. Its presence in Australia is regarded as an enigma because the plant arrived here well before Captain James Cook did in 1770. Australian botanists generally use 1788 as the decisive date for classifying plants as "native" or "introduced" to the island continent.[4] The idea that this plant arrived in Australia without the agency of British settlers is seen as remarkable in itself; that it made its way into the interior of the continent before British explorers appears even more mystifying when seen through the lens of popular Australian history. As far as mainstream national narratives are concerned, the island continent had no "real" history to speak of before 1788, the year that the First Fleet landed on the eastern coast near Sydney carrying its cargo of convicts to establish the first British settlement in the colony of New South Wales. As the historian, Paul Carter observes:

> Almost the greatest barrier to Australia's spatial history is the date 1788. On the one side, anterior to and beyond the limits of Australian 'history', lies a hazy geo-historical tradition of surmise, a blank sea scored at intervals down the centuries by the prows of dug-outs, outriggers, and latterly, three-masters; it is a 'thick horizon', a rewarding site of myth and speculation. But it lacks substance; cause and effect do not converge in its events, but spread out behind like the wake. After 1788, all is solid. Even the weather seems arrested. In alighting at Botany Bay, Phillip steps out of Myth into History. His first concern is not like Cook, to water his ships but to protect them permanently

from offshore gales. He removes almost immediately to Sydney Cove: his means of passage become marks of place. Cook is cast off. A substantial history is inaugurated, an imperial tradition of names, years, floggings, heads of cattle, salaries. The sea, formerly an asylum, itself becomes a prison, a turbulent, unavoidable barrier to progress.[5]

The great historical barrier of 1788 plays a central role in the way the Outback is configured in Australian consciousness and formation of national identity. If, as Carter says, from this moment onwards the ocean was transformed from asylum to a barrier representing "the tyranny of distance"[6] from the metropolitan centres of imperial Britain, it was also the moment when the inland of the island continent emerged as an unknown void and foil to the ambitions of progress in this outpost of Empire. Girt by sea[7] and held back by a vast inland wilderness, Australian consciousness and history has clung to the southern and eastern coastlines, the liminal spaces of refuge that, since 1788, have embodied the "restive fringe"[8] of British settlement. For most Australians, the imagined geography of the continent centres on coastal cities and their agricultural hinterlands followed by the Bush, which not only marks the edge of civilisation but also stands as a repository of settler yearnings for European pastoral idylls and environmental sensibilities.[9] Beyond the Bush lies the Outback, appearing in the Australian imagination as a harsh and unyielding expanse of wilderness that resists the reach of historical progress.

Figure 3.2 Acacia farnesiana in northwest Queensland. Rangan 2006.

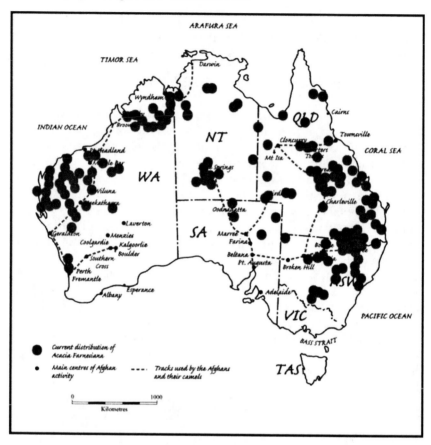

Figure 3.3   Distribution of *Acacia farnesiana*. Based on *Flora of Australia online*, 2007.

The widespread presence of *Acacia farnesiana* in the Outback is an enigma because it problematises both the historical barrier of 1788 and associated geographic imaginings of Australia. Having arrived from else-where before 1788, it escapes botanical classification as either native or introduced. Its presence in the interior of the continent challenges main-stream geographical imaginings of Outback Australia as a remote and inhospitable terrain isolated from the rest of the world. The real enigma of *Acacia farnesiana* is that it offers the opportunity to rethink the geographi-cal history of the Australian Outback in other ways—not as the desolate heart of an island continent at the antipodean edge of European civilisation, but as a landscape connected and changed by its interaction and engage-ment with surrounding oceans and worlds. The plant compels us to look beyond prevailing insular and parochial barriers and cartographic visuali-sations and seek new ways of understanding the history of the making of Outback Australia.

CARTOGRAPHIC OPENINGS

Most people, while looking at maps, see them as authoritative representations of territories, political boundaries, and locations of places, resources, and physical features. Some may look closer to examine the details of measurement, the artwork, the aesthetics, or the power brought into representation. But very few people, other than geographers,[10] are likely to look at maps and see them as processes by which worlds are drawn into being.

The process of drawing Australia into a world of interaction antecedes the arrival of Captain Cook at Botany Bay in 1770 and subsequent British settlement of the southeastern coast. It is said that Indian Ocean traders may have landed on the northern shores of the continent during the fifteenth century. Arab traders carrying rice and spices across the Indian Ocean from Banda and neighbouring islands during the fifteenth and sixteenth centuries may have encountered the northern and northwestern coast of Australia; some of them are said to have described a large uninhabited country to the south of Borneo where they saw large, flightless birds. It is known that Makassan proas or fishing boats regularly visited the northern shores to collect and trade *trepang* or sea cucumbers with the indigenous groups of these regions. The narratives of these sightings, encounters, and exchanges may not have been recorded or charted on paper, but were drawn on rocks[11] and into symbols, techniques, and cultural practices.[12]

Australia's geography was brought into cartographic existence through a series of maps drawn by Portuguese navigators crossing the Indian Ocean. Following Vasco da Gama's arrival in the southwest coast of India in 1497 and capture of the spice trade between India and western Indian Ocean cities, the Portuguese established their base in Goa and pressed on to gain control of the trade in the eastern Indian Ocean. By 1511, Alfonso de Albuquerque, the Governor of Goa, had captured Malacca (Melaka), the port where Malay, Chinese, Arab, and Indian traders operated; in 1512, his deputies António de Abreu and Francisco Serrão arrived in the Moluccas (Maluku); in 1516, the Portuguese established a colony in Timor, the island closest to mainland Australia.

Between 1516 and 1606, the year when the Dutch navigator Willem Jansz sighted the north coast of the continent, Australia began appearing in cartographic form in Portuguese maps. It first shows its tentative presence in broken lines in the southeast corner of the *Carta Anonima Portuguesa* drawn in 1533; the southern coast of Java is open and uncharted and the eastern coastlines of Borneo and Celebes (Sulawesi) are also drawn in broken lines. The Dauphin chart, which is dated 1536 and part of a collection called the Dieppe maps, draws Australia in an unfamiliar but prominent form, identifying it as Iave La Grande or Greater Java. The drawing visualises the western coast of the continent as adjacent to Java and separated by a Rio Grande. What is currently represented as the southern coast of Australia is truncated, with the southwestern parts appearing as the western edge, and the southeastern parts appearing on the right hand side of the map.[13] By the 1620s, the maps of the eastern parts of the Indian Ocean began drawing the northwest coast of Australia in greater detail. One map, probably drawn in the 1620s, is based on the evidence of Manoel Godinho de Erédia's travels to the northwest of the continent in 1601 and records the arrival of Dutch seafarers on a ship named Eendracht in 1616. In this map, the gap between Java and the northwest coastline is no longer separated by a river, but by sea. Timor is more clearly oriented in relation to Arnhem Land, which is referred to as Nuca Antara,[14] and shows the island of New Guinea as connected to the mainland of the continent.

The cartographic production of Australia was continually shaped and altered during the seventeenth and eighteenth centuries by the expansion of Dutch mercantile interest across the Indian Ocean, and with increased movement of Spanish and French explorers across the Pacific. Each sighting, skirting, wreck, and landfall added a new inscription on navigation charts and each new mark created openings through which plants from new and old worlds made their way into the northern coastline.

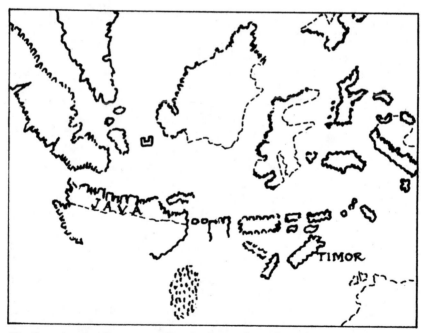

The Carta Anonima Portuguesa. The Carta Anonima utilises the older cartographic conventions, with bays shown as semi-circles, capes shown as arrows, and islands as rectangles. These coasts are shown in black on the above map and existing land-shapes (including Australia) are indicated by broken lines. Note particularly the shape of Java, and the open south coasts of Java and Sumbawa.

Figure 3.4   Carta Anonima, circa 1533. McIntyre 1977.

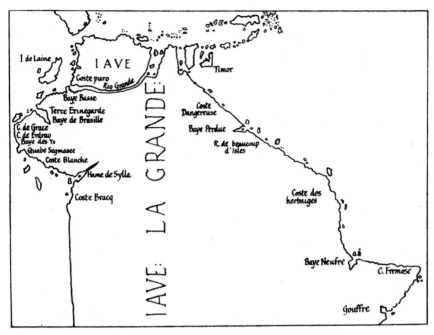

Figure 3.5   Dauphin chart, circa 1536. McIntyre 1977.

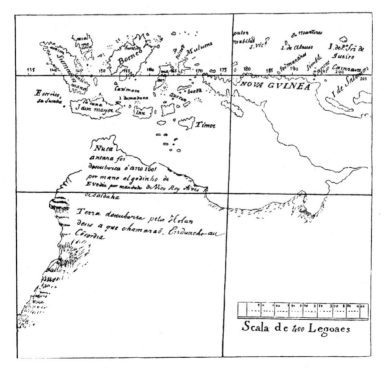

Figure 3.6   Nuca Antara map after Erédia, circa 1620s. Yarrow 1980.

A. farnesiana may have arrived on the Australian continent by a number of ways: it could have travelled across the Indian Ocean on Portuguese or Dutch merchant ships to Timor and Java, or across the Pacific on the ships of Spanish explorers travelling from the Americas to the Philippines. George Birdwood, an Anglo-Indian official and botanical enthusiast, made the following observations about the plant:

> It is described as a native Chilian plant by Molina, in the 16th century, from which date it is gradually traced through a succession of writers eastward, in Italy, the Morea and Greek Islands, in the gardens of Egypt and Arabia, and in Western India. From Buenos Ayres, it was carried by Europeans into Louisiana, and as far north as Charleston, and again by Europeans it was carried from America westward to Tahiti and the Philippines, to Timor and Java, and apparently to Burmah and the Coromandel coast of India. It has now overspread all India. Everwhere its name seems to be derived from its exquisite "aroma," and as the Greek writers do not refer to this, its overwhelming characteristic, I accepted it as a plant of exclusively American origin, and one of the most delightful gifts of the old world to the new [sic]. It is first botanically described in Hyancinthus Ambrosium in AD1605–72.[15]

The seedpods of *A. farnesiana* may have floated across from Timor or Flores and taken root along the northern coast of Australia,[16] or the seeds may have been exchanged by Malay and Makassan fishermen with the indigenous groups of the region.[17] Whatever its mode of travel across the oceans, *A. farnesiana* had not only arrived well before Captain Cook, but also established its presence in the interior of the continent. In 1845, when Sir Thomas Livingstone Mitchell, then Surveyor General of New South Wales, journeyed northwards on one of the early exploratory expeditions to find an inland route from Sydney to the Gulf of Carpentaria, he recorded the presence of *A. farnesiana* near the Belyando River (roughly 300 km inland from the coastal town of Mackay in present day Queensland), and added a sample to his plant collection.[18] It is possible that coastal indigenous groups in the north may have played a role in its inland diffusion; they may have valued *A. farnesiana* seeds for their protein and exchanged them with inland indigenous groups that, in turn, may have planted the seeds along river courses and sites of settlement in their territories.

The current distribution of *A. farnesiana* in Australia is not limited to northern coastal areas or particular sites near northern rivers, but is spread wide across the interior of the continent. How did this come about? To answer this question, we first need to describe the plant's characteristics and its modes of propagation. *A. farnesiana* is a woody, deciduous, and thorny shrub that can grow between 1.5 to 4 metres in height. It ranges across warm temperate dry through tropical desert to moist forest zones between sea level and 1,000 metres elevation. It thrives in dry localities and on loamy and sandy soils, often acting as a soil binder and a shade tree; in Australia, the plant grows in rangelands and farmlands in semiarid and arid areas and in the unoccupied inland deserts. It often grows as scattered plants, but may form spiny thickets near watercourses. It is also one of few plant species that can persist near highly saline artesian watering drains.[19] Its flowers are small, round, orangeish yellow in colour, and very fragrant;

Figure 3.7 *Acacia farnesiana*: foliage, flowers, and pods. Courtesy of Forest & Kim Starr 2008.

it produces seedpods roughly 4 to 8 cm. long, and each pod can contain between twelve and fourteen seeds.

Once established, *A. farnesiana* seedlings can grow readily and resprout quickly after damage by fire or browsing; and although the aerial portions of the plant may be killed by fire, it can regenerate through basal shoots. The seeds have a protein content of around 18 percent, and are used as food in some parts of the world. The plant is used in traditional medicinal treatments for a range of illnesses; the bark and pods have high tannin content and are used in leather tanning and other ways. Most important, though, is that its foliage is an excellent source of forage for ungulates or hoofed animals such as cattle, sheep, and goats. The seedpods are nutritious and readily eaten by them, and the seeds are transported in their droppings; these animals are the main agents for assisting its dispersal across land.[20]

Given these hoofed transporters of *A. farnesiana* seeds were not part of the continent's native fauna, how did they arrive in the remote reaches of inland Australia? The answer may seem fairly simple if we accept the arguments of the environmental historian, Alfred Crosby. He argues that the wheat- and livestock-based settler colonialism in the temperate zones of the Americas, southern Africa, and Australasia was, in effect, a "biological expansion of Europe" aided by the "portmanteau of biota" that accompanied European settlers to these regions. The animals, plants, insects, and organisms that settlers brought with them were the biological means by which these regions were transformed into "neo-Europes."[21] Based on this perspective, the logical answer would be that as British settlers extended their livestock farming into inland areas, their cattle and sheep would have aided the dispersal of *A. farnesiana*. But this reasoning does not make much sense when placed within the historical context of settlement expansion in inland Australia. By the 1830s, squatters and colonists had grabbed or occupied much of the land near the southern coastal belts, and there was growing pressure to expand settlement further inland. Settlers clung to visions of "yeoman farms in little Englands,"[22] but were faced with an inland terrain and environment that provided little succour for such aspirations. Much of the continent's inland was unexplored, and the few forays into the semiarid and desert areas beyond the bushland fringe offered no prospect of "making a nation of sheep-walks."[23] Exploring the interior and getting European settlers and their livestock to move into inland Australia required the agency of another kind of hoofed animal that was brought across the Indian Ocean from the northwestern regions of the Indian subcontinent rather than Europe. This was the camel.

MAKING THE OUTBACK

Many of the colonists arriving in Australia during the early decades of the nineteenth century had served the East India Company in various military capacities and campaigns in the Indian subcontinent.[24] Several of them were familiar with the use of camels and knew their advantages over horses and bullock teams in traversing desert and arid terrains. Some presented proposals to their colonial governments for inland exploration using camels. The urgency for inland exploration was spurred by the commencement of a trade in horses between the colony of New South Wales and the East India Company for the purpose of remounting its cavalry and other administrative units in the subcontinent. The Torres Straits proved dangerous for navigation, and hence travel from Sydney to India involved lengthier journeys around the southern and western coasts of Australia. Sir Thomas Livingstone Mitchell's exploratory expedition to the interior was chiefly motivated by the desire to find an overland route from Sydney to the head of the Gulf of Carpentaria. In outlining the objectives of his expedition, Sir Mitchell wrote:

> But other considerations, not less important to the colonists of New South Wales, made it very desirable that a way should be opened to the shores of the Indian Ocean. That sea was already connected with England by steam navigation, and to render it accessible to Sydney by land, was an object in itself worthy of an exploratory expedition. In short, the commencement of such a journey seemed the first step in the direct road home to England, for it was not to be doubted that on the discovery of a good overland route between Sydney and the head of the Gulf of Carpentaria, a line of steam communication would thereupon be introduced from that point to meet the English line at Singapore.[25]

The proposal to import camels from India seemed feasible in principle; steamers carrying horses to Calcutta, Madras, and Bombay could return with cargoes of camels. In 1836, a government official of the colony of New South Wales presented the Governor a memo exploring the practicality of introducing camels from the upper reaches of the Ganges. He observed that while it was possible to obtain camels from northwest India for purposes of inland exploration, the foremost difficulty would be in procuring drivers and handlers to accompany the animals.[26]

Overall, there were various pressures on colonial governments during the 1840s and 1850s to mount expeditions to the interior and claim new inland territories. The newer colonies of South Australia and Victoria were keen to compete against New South Wales for territory and overland trade routes to the Gulf of Carpentaria. The discovery of copper and lead deposits in areas north of Adelaide and the rising demand from English manufacturers for wool added to the urgency of exploration for minerals, pastoral expansion, and more direct inland routes that linked up to established steamship routes in the Indian Ocean archipelago.[27]

In 1840, six camels were shipped from the Canary Islands to Port Adelaide in South Australia, but only one survived the journey. Two more camels arrived the same year in Melbourne, and were displayed as curiosities at the fairgrounds before being sent to Sydney, where they remained on display in the Government House.[28] In 1846, the sole surviving camel shipped from the Canary Island to Adelaide was used in a minor exploratory expedition led by John Horrocks, a South Australian pastoralist. Horrocks was unaccustomed to handling the animal and was severely injured while riding it. He died from the injury and "Horrocks' beast" was put to death.[29]

The first successful importation of camels was achieved under the aegis of George Landells, an ex-British army officer from India. Landells travelled to Peshawar and into the tribal areas of Afghanistan in 1858 to buy camels and recruit drivers. He returned to Melbourne with twenty-four camels and three cameleers, well in time for the Victorian expedition to traverse the interior to the Gulf of Carpentaria. In 1860, the famously ill-fated Burke and Wills expedition set off from Melbourne with much fanfare to race against other colonial expeditions across the interior, but neither of the leaders had much understanding or experience of negotiating desert terrain. Burke quarrelled with Landells, the only European with some understanding of using camels in arid terrains; Landells abandoned the expedition and returned to Melbourne. Burke then left the Afghan cameleers behind at camps in Coopers Creek and Menindie, and departed with Wills and two assistants to win the race to the northern coast. Only one of the assistants, John King, survived the expedition.[30]

Figure 3.8   View of Government House, Sydney, NSW, as it appeared when vacated by Sir George Gipps in 1845, circa 1845. Painting by G.E. Peacock. Courtesy of the Mitchell Library, State Library of New South Wales.

Figure 3.9   Departure of Burke and Wills from Melbourne; lithograph, circa 1860–circa 1880, Massina & Co. Courtesy of the State Library of Victoria.

From the 1860s onwards, camels were imported in larger numbers. Thomas Elder, a colonist with pastoral and mining interests, established a camel stud in Beltana, a small settlement north of Port Augusta, and recruited Afghan camel drivers to rear and train the animals. He financed five expeditions into the interior from South Australia and supplied them with camels and Afghan cameleers. The 1870s were the decade of great inland expeditions and desert crossings, and almost every major expedition relied on the camels and their Afghan handlers for transport. The 1880s were the years of consolidation, with graziers extending into the newly explored areas and obtaining leases for setting up vast sheep stations in the semiarid areas and desert fringes. Prospecting and mining expanded in the interior, and railways began to be built to service and connect these interior towns to the coastal cities. Afghan cameleers became commercial operators, camel breeders, and small-scale merchants, hauling wool from Outback sheep stations and bringing back supplies of flour and other necessities during the dry season. The 1890s brought another spurt in explorations using camels and Afghans to prospect for new mines and grazing land. They transported ore from mines, supplied water to mining settlements, and were used in surveying and constructing the Rabbit-Proof Fence, the Overland Telegraph Line, and the trans-Australian railway.[31]

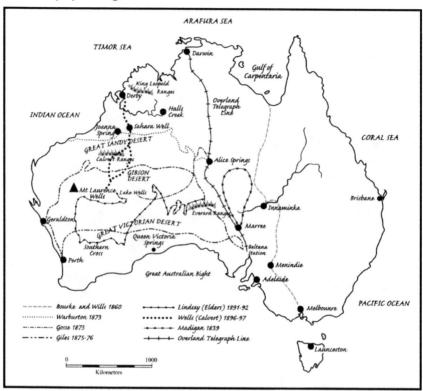

Figure 3.10   Desert explorations using camels and Afghan cameleers. Based on Stevens 1989, p. 43.

Figure 3.11   Camels carrying flour in a dry season, circa 1895. Courtesy of the Mitchell Library, State Library of New South Wales.

Figure 3.12 The "Happy Thought" prospecting party, circa 1900. Courtesy of the Battye Library, State Library of Western Australia.

By the 1900s, the Australian Outback was conceived as the place where adventurous men of hardy Anglo-Celtic stock sought their fortunes and forged the prosperity of their colonies and empire. Yet, regardless of the bravado and rhetoric, the Outback could not have been produced or imagined in such terms without the work of camels and their handlers. In his memoirs of working as a camel haulage operator in the West Australian

Figure 3.13 Surveyor canning and party on the survey trip to mark out the line of the Rabbit-Proof Fence, Western Australia, circa 1901. E.J. Brady Collection, Courtesy of the National Library of Australia.

Outback, Herbert Baker describes the importance and extent of the Afghan pack camel transport:

> Camels were seen in all the parched outback towns from Coolgardie and Marble Bar to Cloncurry and Broken Hill. Where they did the most work would be difficult to say, but packing copper from the dry ranges to Cloncurry railway station or Burketown wharf kept a few thousand camels busy for years. Camels were indispensable in the vast region bordered by Broken Hill, Marree, Oodnadatta, Alice Springs and Birdsville, a region embracing part of New South Wales, South Australia, the Northern Territory and Queensland. In this area, they were used for packing bore casing, six-, eight-, and ten-inch steel tubing in 12-ft. lengths . . . The camels' main work in the dry pastoral areas was carrying stores and fencing material to sheep stations and returning with their wool . . . camels were used extensively in sinking dams, being harnessed to pull ploughs and scoops. Perhaps the largest colony of camels was on the West Australian goldfields, where the dry plains were tailored for no other animal.[32]

By the first two decades of the twentieth century, camels had become a ubiquitous feature in the everyday life and landscape of the Outback in

Figure 3.14 Camel with bags of ore from Mt. Isa copper mines, ready to go to Cloncurry, 1932. Courtesy of the John Oxley Library, State Library of Queensland.

Western Australia, Northern Territory, northwest Queensland, and the interior of New South Wales. Cameleers continued to import them from the northwest regions of the Indian subcontinent such as Baluchistan, Sind, and Rajasthan for maintaining and supplementing the breeding stock. The governments of South Australia and Western Australia set up camel stud stations for breeding and recruited Afghan cameleers to train young camels. It is estimated that there were over 20,000 camels used in trains or harnessed for transporting goods and construction works. Camels tracked across the Outback to deliver mail and supplies to stations, the inland police used them to patrol the Rabbit-Proof Fence, and many men and women belonging to indigenous communities took up camel droving.[33]

REMAKING THE OUTBACK

For nearly sixty years following their arrival in Australia, camels and their Afghan handlers provided the most economic and reliable forms of transport for goods and services in the Outback. Pack camel trains operated across every mainland state except Victoria, covering nearly three-quarters of the continent. Between the late 1800s and the first decade of the twentieth century, they helped inland sheep farmers survive and keep

Figure 3.15 Unloading camels at Port Augusta, circa 1920. Mortlock Pictorial Collection, Courtesy of the State Library of South Australia.

Figure 3.16   Native woman camel driving, postcard 1913. Courtesy of the National Library of Australia.

their businesses going through periods of severe drought, several crashes in wool prices, and economic recession.[34]

What did camels eat? Camels, as we know, are hardy creatures that can survive on the vegetation in arid zones. They are fairly flexible in their foraging habits, and can browse on both shrubs and grasses. Nearly 80 percent of the vegetation types in the arid parts of inland Australia are edible for camels. But camels, being browsers, are also selective: they like fresh forage and show distinct preferences for particular plant species. The foraging preferences of camels and cattle are quite different. Cattle prefer grasses, and only forage on shrubs and trees when fresh grass is not available; in contrast, camels prefer eating leaves and pods from trees and shrubs, and feed on grasses when tree forage is not available. Camels in Australia feed up to 95 percent on dicotyledons or leguminous plants, and only feed on grass during the wet season when forbs are not yet available.[35]

Research on the foraging habits of camels in central Australia shows that there are between 340 to 350 plant species that are palatable to them. Of these palatable species, camels have a very strong preference for forty-four varieties of trees and shrubs. Among the twenty-two Acacia varieties palatable to them, camels are extremely fond of six species, of which two are immigrants: one is *Acacia farnesiana*, and the second is *Acacia nilotica*, another traveller across the Indian Ocean.[36] *A. nilotica* has a wide home range stretching from eastern and southern Africa all the way into northern India. It was introduced during the turn of the twentieth century into cattle and sheep stations in central and western Queensland. While official records state that *A. nilotica* was sourced from the Saharanpur Botanical Gardens in northwestern India around 1897, some station owners claim that those who served in the Anglo–Boer wars and in the Afghan wars may have brought back the plant from these regions.[37] *A. nilotica*'s current distribution is limited to the western and northern Outback of Queensland and extends to parts of the Northern Territory. The plant was considered useful for the sheep industry in Queensland because its wide and relatively low canopy provided good shade and forage for sheep during the lambing and hot dry seasons.

Figure 3.17   Camels browsing prickly acacia, northwest Queensland. Courtesy of Anna Egan 2007.

Given that *A. farnesiana* is one of the varieties of acacia highly favoured by camels for browsing, it is likely that the plant's dispersal was aided to some extent by the droppings of the animals in grazing paddocks near the makeshift Afghan camps or "Ghan towns," and along transport routes across the Outback.[38] Since *A. farnesiana* is resilient and can regenerate quickly and vigorously after heavy browsing, it is likely to have thrived in the areas traversed by camels. Baker mentions the enthusiasm with which camels browsed on trees with thorns, and notes their special fondness for a particular prickly tree (most likely *A. farnesiana*)—which he does not name, but describes as similar to the "Mexican mesquite tree" (*Prosopsis spp.*)—as the "number one camel feed."[39]

Camel transport in the Outback declined in the 1920s due to a combination of climatic, technological, and economic factors. The long drought between 1925 and 1929, the arrival and gradual spread of motorised vehicles, and the Great Depression placed extraordinary pressures on camel

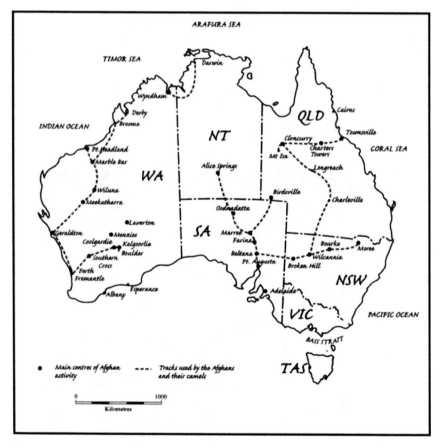

Figure 3.18   Centres of Afghan activity and pack camel routes. Based on Stevens 1989 and Baker 1964.

haulage businesses. In addition, increased agistment rates imposed by governments made it more expensive to feed and maintain the animals, and forced most camel operators into debt and penury. Afghan cameleers were denied citizenship by the new immigration laws instituted after Federation in 1901,[40] so most had little option but to release their camels into the unoccupied Outback and return to their country. Herbert Baker recounted meeting in 1927 one of the last remaining group of Afghan cameleers in the Marble Bar district of Western Australia, whose pack transport business had been bankrupt with the coming of motor lorries. They travelled some thirty miles inland from Marble Bar, and drove their pack of hundred or more camels across a low range of hills and watched them disappear over the ridge into unoccupied country. As Baker rode up to one of the Afghan cameleers, the old man said: "I say good-bye, my cameel"; he writes:

> I did not speak; he seemed so deep in thought I felt it best to wait till he got things straightened out. I had appeared at an extremely critical moment, perhaps the saddest, of a hard life. Finally he turned and said: "Fifty years I stop this country, work all the time, now I finish."[41]

By the 1940s and 1950s, camels became a rare sight in Outback towns and transport routes, and almost none of their Afghan handlers or their makeshift "Ghan towns" remained. As Baker observed, both "Afghans and camels were unwanted in the automobile age."[42]

The projected distribution of *A. farnesiana* differs across the unoccupied and occupied Outback.[43] The release of camels into the unoccupied Outback may have contributed to the further spread of *A. farnesiana*, but the plant is likely to have been kept in check by their browsing preference

Figure 3.19   Last camel train used in central Australia to deliver mail, December 1925. Courtesy of the National Archives of Australia.

and ability to digest the seed to a substantial extent through rumination.[44] The spread of *A. farnesiana* in the occupied Outback is likely to have occurred through a different combination of factors. Recurrent collapse of wool prices through the 1930s to the 1960s led many inland pastoralists to reduce sheep numbers and restock their stations with cattle. Cattle, like sheep, browse on trees and shrubs such as *A. farnesiana* and *A. nilotica* during the dry season when fresh grasses are not available; but unlike sheep (and camels), cattle do not sufficiently break down acacia seeds through their rumination, with the result that the seeds may be relatively undamaged as they pass through the animal's digestive system. They remain dormant until the wet season when the cattle dung provides congenial conditions for the embedded seeds to germinate and enables the seedlings to establish fairly quickly. *A. farnesiana*'s distribution in the occupied Outback has thus been aided by the conversion from a sheep- to cattle-based economy.

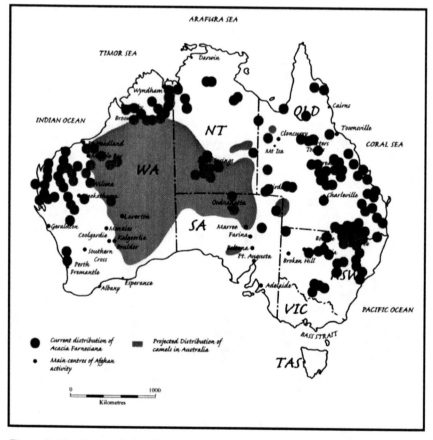

Figure 3.20 Projected distribution of *A. Farnesiana* and camels in the Outback. Based on Flora of Australia Online 2007, Stevens 1988, Baker 1964, Siebert and Newman 1989.

RE-VISIONING THE OUTBACK

Today, A. *farnesiana* and its fellow oceanic traveller, A. *nilotica*, are considered weeds in various parts of the occupied Outback because their thorny presence make cattle mustering more difficult, and because they reduce grazing areas when they occur in dense stands.[45] But unlike A. *nilotica*, A. *farnesiana* has escaped classification as a "Weed of National Significance" because it arrived in the continent before 1788. Although A. *nilotica* is not as widespread as A. *farnesiana* and is limited to parts of central and northern Queensland and small parts of the Northern Territory, both its identity and fate have been determined on the basis of its post-1788 arrival. Natural resource management agencies in Queensland identify A. *nilotica* as an "introduced" and "invasive" species and have targeted it for extermination from the landscape.[46]

A. *farnesiana* offers a way of looking beyond the historical barrier of 1788, of seeing the Outback as connected by old and new movements across lands and oceans, and as an inland landscape that records these travels and migrations. While A. *farnesiana*'s enigma of arrival may have won it current reprieve from being condemned as an invasive immigrant and targeted for extermination, its presence also problematises the logic underlying botanical and ecological classifications of "native" and "introduced" species based on the date of British occupation of Australia. Being neither native nor introduced, A. *farnesiana*'s presence in the Australian Outback calls for a more open and dynamic way of thinking about "nativeness" and "natural" landscapes.

Herbert Baker was of the view that "[o]n saltbush-mulga country there was no other animal that thrived as well as the camel and none, with the exception of kangaroos and emus, that suited the landscape so perfectly."[47] The same could be said for the camel's favourite acacia species; together these pre- and post-1788 travellers across the Indian Ocean were fundamental to the making of the Outback, in making its nature and landscape visible and comprehensible to a population that clung to its parochial Anglo-Celtic visions of Empire and to the coastal edge of the continent.

The cartographic visualisation of Australia in early Portuguese maps shows a coastline of openings, possibilities, and connections to the world of the Indian Ocean. Sir Thomas Livingstone Mitchell saw his expedition across the interior of the continent as a way of drawing Australia into what he called "the Indian Archipelago," of linking old and new movements, connections, memories, and histories. That he recorded in passing, without any expression of surprise, the presence of A. *farnesiana*—a plant he would have recognised from his past travels in Portugal and India—near the Belyando River in interior Queensland might indicate his openness to seeing the inland as connected, rather than isolated, from the Indian Ocean world.

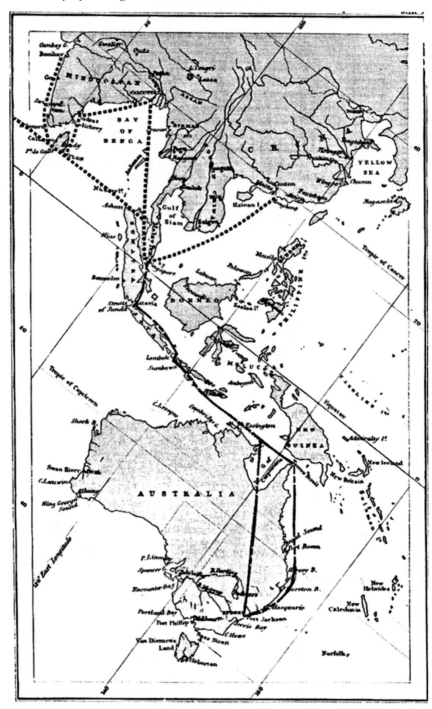

Figure 3.21   "The Indian Archipelago." T.L. Mitchell, 1848.

If the Outback is to figure in the articulation of an authentic nativeness or Australianness, then these Indian Ocean travellers and migrants to inland Australia must be seen as an integral part of that imagining. *A. farnesiana*, the camel, and *A. nilotica* may be judged useless by today's economic calculus or considered non-native, feral, and invasive by botanists and conservation agencies, but their very presence in the Outback landscape signals the possibility of a richer, more generous, eclectic consciousness of the continent's geographical history and imagining of Australian identity.

ACKNOWLEDGEMENTS

The research for this chapter is part of a larger research project on the exchange of acacia species across the Indian Ocean, funded by the Australian Research Council (DP0666131). The authors are grateful to Elissa Sutherland and Craig Thorburn for their comments on previous drafts; to Anna Egan and Alyse Weyman for research assistance; and to Kara Rasmanis for cartographic and imaging assistance.

NOTES

1. R. White, "The Nationalization of Nature," *The Journal of American History* 86(3; 1999): 976–986; I. Tyrrell, *True Garden of the Gods: Californian-Australian Environmental Reform, 1860–1930* (Berkeley, CA: University of California Press, 1999).
2. ILDIS. World Database of Legumes. www.ildis.org/ Legume Web, accessed 20 July 2006, published 2005.
3. W.-A. Roland, Australian acacias in Europe, www.acacia-world.net/html/lecture_melbourne.html, accessed 30 July 2007, published 2006; also see F.A. Fluckiger, "The Essential Oil Industry in Grasse, Botanical Medicine Monographs and Sundry," *American Journal of Pharmacy* 57(3; March 1885).
4. A. Bean, "A New System for Determining Which Plant Species Are Indigenous in Australia," *Australian Systematic Botany* 20(2007): 1–43.
5. P. Carter, *The Road to Botany Bay: An Exploration of Landscape and History* (Chicago, IL: University of Chicago Press, 1987), 34.
6. G. Blainey, *The Tyranny of Distance.* (Melbourne: Sun Books, 1958).
7. "Girt by sea" is a phrase that appears in the Australian national anthem.
8. J.M. Powell, *A Historical Geography of Modern Australia: The Restive Fringe* (Cambridge, UK: Cambridge University Press, 1988).
9. P. Kane, "'Woeful Shepherds': Anti-pastoral in Australian poetry," in *Imagining Australia: Literature and Culture in the New New World*, eds. J. Wright and C. Wallace-Crabbe, 269–284 (Cambridge, MA: Harvard University Press, 2004).
10. M. Monmonier, *Mapping It Out: Expository Cartography for the Humanities and Social Sciences* (Chicago, IL: University of Chicago Press, 1993); D. Wood, *The Power of Maps* (New York: Guildford Press, 1992); D. Turnbull, *Maps Are Territories, Science Is An Atlas: A Portfolio of Exhibits* (Chicago, IL: University of Chicago Press, 1993); J.B. Harley, "Deconstructing

the Map," in *Writing Worlds: Discourse, Text and Metaphor in the Representation of Landscape*, eds. T.J. Barnes and J.S. Duncan, XX–XX (London: Routledge, 1992 pp. 231–253).

11. K. McIntyre, *The Secret Discovery of Australia: Portuguese Ventures 250 Years Before Captain Cook* (first published in 1977; Sydney: Picador, 1982). McIntyre refers to the Wandjina paintings discovered by George Grey near Collier Bay.

12. S. Yarrow, *We Discovered an Island* (Booragoon, WA: Regency Publications, 1980).

13. McIntyre provides an extensive analysis of the Dauphin map and explains how Portuguese navigators used the cartographic conventions and methods of projection to draw this map. He superimposes the drawing on present methods of projection to show how this outline resembles the current representations of Australia. Some anomalies in McIntyre's interpretation of the maps have been resolved by Peter Trickett in his excellent attempt to establish Portuguese discoveries of Australia. See P. Trickett, *Beyond Capricorn: How Portuguese Adventurers Secretly Discovered and Mapped Australia and New Zealand 250 Years Before Captain Cook* (Adelaide: East Street Publications, 2007).

14. "Nuca Antara" is probably a Portuguese rendering of the Javanese-Malay term "Nusantara," in which "nusa" stands for nation, and "antara" means beyond (i.e., transnational territories that make up "the whole" world of interaction). Vlekke notes that the original meaning is "the other islands" as seen from Java or Bali, and hence it took the more general meaning of "the outside world" or "abroad." Javanese texts of the fifteenth century use the term in this original sense. See B.H.M. Vlekke, *Nusantara: A History of Indonesia* (The Hague: W. van Hoeve Ltd., 1965), p. 6 n. 5.

15. G. Birdwood, "The Migrations of the Tobacco Plant, the Farnesian Cassia, and the Lombardy Poplar," *Journal of the Society of Arts* 44(1896): 467.

16. H. Ridley, *The Dispersal of Plants Throughout the World* (Ashford: L. Reeve, 1930); *cf.* C. Duvall, "On the Origin of the Tree *Spondias mombin* in Africa," *Journal of Historical Geography* 32(2006): 249–266.

17. J. Isaacs, *Bush Food* (McMahons Point, NSW: Weldons, 1987).

18. T.L. Mitchell, *Journal of an Expedition into the Interior of Tropical Australia: In Search of a Route from Sydney to the Gulf of Carpentaria* (London: Longman, Brown, Green and Longmans, 1848), 256.

19. Le Houérou, *Acacia farnesiana (L.) Willd.*, www.fao.org/ag/AGP/AGPC/doc/Gbase/DATA/Pf000113.HTM, accessed 2 August 2007.

20. Global Invasive Species Database, *A. Farnesiana*, www.issg.org/database/species/ecology.asp?si=49&fr=1&sts=, accessed 2 August 2007; D. O'Dowd, and A. Gill, "Seed Dispersal Syndromes in Australian Acacias," in *Seed Dispersal*, ed. D. Murray, 87–121 (Sydney: Academic Press, 1986).

21. A. Crosby, *Ecological Imperialism* (Cambridge, UK: Cambridge University Press, 1986).

22. J.M. Powell, 56.

23. Ibid.

24. Until 1858, the Australian colonies came under the administrative oversight of the East India Company Government in Calcutta; see T.L. Mitchell (1848) and also W.J. Lines, *Taming the Great South Land: A History of the Conquest of Nature in Australia*, 2ⁿᵈ edition (Athens, GA: University of Georgia Press, 1999), 34.

25. Mitchell, 3.

26. C. Stevens, *Tin Mosques and Ghan Towns: A History of Afghan Cameldrivers in Australia* (Melbourne: Oxford University Press, 1989), 13.

27. Ibid., 28.
28. Ibid., 13–14.
29. Ibid., 28.
30. Ibid., 31–33. The full names of the expedition leaders are Robert O'Hara Burke and William John Wills.
31. Ibid., 34–56.
32. H., Baker, *Camels and the Outback* (Melbourne: Sir Isaac Pitman, 1964), 90.
33. Stevens, 261; A.K. Fazal, *Trade History of Afghan Cameleers in Australia, 1860–1935* (Kabul: UNO/Education Press, 2004).
34. Well-known pack camel routes linked inland settlements such as Marree, Farina, and Oodnadatta in South Australia across the Lake Eyre Basin and Simpson Desert to Alice Springs and Birdsville. In Western Australia and the Northern Territory, camels worked the track between Wiluna and Hall's Creek through the Great Sandy Desert and Gibson Desert, which later became the Canning Stock Route. They linked the inland mining settlements of Meekatharra, Marble Bar, and Wiluna with the coastal towns of Geraldton, Port Hedland, Derby, Broome, Wyndham, and Darwin, and the major mining towns of Kalgoorlie and Coolgardie to Fremantle. Camel trains operated between the mining settlements at Mount Isa, Dutchess, Cloncurry, and Charters Towers in northern Queensland, and carried ore and wool from Broken Hill, Wilcannia, Bourke, and Moree to railhead and ports in eastern New South Wales. See Stevens (1989) and Baker (1964, op. cit.), and P. Jones, and A. Kenny, *Australia's Muslim Cameleers: Pioneers of the Inland, 1860s–1930s* (South Australian Museum, Adelaide: Wakefield Press, 2007).
35. B. Siebert, and D. Newman, "Camelidae," in *Fauna of Australia, Volume 1B, Mammalia*, eds. D. Walton, and B. Richardson, no. 60: 1–9 (Canberra: Australian Government Publishing Service, 1989); A. Phillips, J. Heucke, B. Dörges, and G. O'Reilly, *Co-grazing Cattle and Camels: A Report for the Rural Industries Research and Development Corporation* (Canberra: RIRDC, 2001).
36. B. Dörges, J. Heucke, and R. Dance, *The Palatability of Central Australian Plant Species to Camels* (Alice Springs: Central Australian Camel Industry Association [CACIA]).
37. Field interviews carried out by the authors in April 2006, and by their research assistants, Anna Egan and Alyse Weyman in April–June 2007.
38. The distribution of *A. farnesiana* based on specimen collections in Australian herbaria shows a remarkable overlap with the centres of Afghan activity and transport routes.
39. Baker, op.cit., p.129. *A. farnesiana*, *A. nilotica*, *Prosopsis spp.*, and *Parkinsonia spp.* are generally referred to as "prickle bushes" and often confused with each other. They are officially classified as "introduced" (excluding *A. farnesiana*, because it arrived before 1788) and "invasive" and targeted for control. See Spies, P. and March N., 2004. *Prickly Acacia National Case Studies Manual* (Cloncurry: Queensland Department of Natural Resources, Mines and Energy).
40. Australia's emergence as a nation and sense of identity at the time of Federation in 1901 was embodied in the establishment of the "White Australia" policy. The Immigration Restriction Act of 1901 passed by the government of Australia's first Prime Minister, Edmund Barton, excluded "coloured people" from migrating to the country or awarding citizenship to those already in Australia. See Stevens, op. cit., 148; M. M. de Lepervanche, *Indians in a White Australia: An Account of Race, Class and Indian Immigration to Eastern Australia* (Sydney: George Allen & Unwin, 1984) 56–61.

41. Baker, H. op.cit., 2.
42. Baker, H. ibid.
43. This may in part reflect the methods used for specimen collections maintained in Australian herbaria. Since *A. farnesiana* is not officially classified as a weed of national significance, there are no map projections of the plant's spread and density.
44. Based on estimates of camel numbers during the 1920s and 1930s, some researchers have projected the current camel population to be over 600,000. Studies of camel distribution show their major concentration in the Great Sandy Desert, the Gibson and Simpson Deserts, and the Lake Eyre Basin, with minor and scattered concentrations in the areas near Marble Bar, between Hall's Creek and Tanami, Oodnadatta and Alice Springs, and near Birdsville, Mount Isa, and Cloncurry. See Siebert and Newman (1989). Also see B. Dörges, and J. Heucke, *Demonstration of Ecologically Sustainable Management of Camels on Aboriginal and Pastoral Land.* Final report on project number 200046 for the Natural Heritage Trust (Alice Springs: CACIA, 2003).
45. N. March, 2000. *Prickly Acacia Best Practice Manual* (Brisbane: Queensland Department of Natural Resources).
46. http://www.weeds.org.au/WoNS/pricklyacacia/, http://www.nrw.qld.gov.au/ factsheets/pdf/pest/pp9.pdf, http://www.environment.gov.au/biodiversity/ invasive/publications/a-nilotica.html, accessed 2 August 2007.
47. Baker, op. cit., 129.

4   Abdulrazak Gurnah and Littoral Cosmopolitanism

Shanti Moorthy

> The others that obsess me in the Other do not affect me as examples
> of the same genus united with my neighbor by resemblance or com-
> mon nature, individuations of the human race, or chips off the old
> block . . . The others concern me from the first. Here fraternity pre-
> cedes the commonness of a genus. My relationship with the Other as
> neighbor gives meaning to my relations with all the others.
>
> Emanuel Levinas in *Otherwise than Being or Beyond Essence*

On reading Abdulrazak Gurnah's writings one is struck by the thriving
and "cosmopolitan" nature of East African coastal towns, at least up until
the 1960s. Cosmopolitanism in general, and on the Indian Ocean rim in
particular, is a hot topic in current academic discourse. It is my purpose
here to not only survey current thinking in regard to cosmopolitanism in
Indian Ocean studies but to examine how Gurnah illustrates and contests
depictions by Indian Ocean scholars of apparently idyllic premodern East
African societies. His writings lend themselves to more nuanced and problematic readings of these societies as cosmopolitan.

In its simplest incarnation, cosmopolitanism refers to a subjective consciousness of ethnic heterogeneity occurring within a specific geographical
locale. It refers to a society that is at once urban and urbane, sophisticated, racially diverse. A society that concedes diversity as inherent in its
members, and acceptable in the public arena; where notions of difference
or legitimacy do not provide the basis for conflict, armed or otherwise. A
society, furthermore, that is able to live with difference, and the inevitable
sociocultural miscegenations, without fear, or the imposition of repressive
homogeneity. A society not of enforced ghettoes and exclusionary apartheids, but with hierarchies, admittedly, that derive from timeless and universal preoccupations such as economic solvency, the rich lording it over the
poor; and by extension, in the premodern context, other quasi-mediaeval
conceptions of the haves and have-nots: citizen and slave, man and woman,
civilized and savage. A society, nonetheless, where all are equally at home,
citizen, subject, diasporas; a situation that has become problematic in
today's world of territorial sovereignty, passports, visas, and border checks,

of unwelcome asylum seekers and refugees; of the "nativism"[1] of the Europe of the Schengen accord, that struggles with the notion of hospitality as an ethic in itself. As Jacques Derrida reflects, "At a time when we claim to be lifting internal borders, we proceed to bolt the external borders of the European Union tightly."[2]

Against the rootedness of cosmopolitan "places," a significant proportion of the members of cosmopolitan societies are, or may have been, personally or ancestrally, physically mobile, and possessing an apprehension of the world that is anything but parochial. In the modern context, mobility is complicated by the speed and rapidity of travel, media, and communication technologies; however, in the premodern scenario, mobility and rootlessness were real and arduous, rather than predominantly virtual.

The crucial hallmarks of a cosmopolitan society are worldliness, and the ethical treatment of the stranger, the Other. It is my thesis that Abdulrazak Gurnah does indeed present us with word pictures of a premodern East Africa that not only possesses a cosmopolitan diversity, a diversity furthermore that needs to be read differently to contemporary Western notions of cosmopolitanism, but also with depictions of a failure of cosmopolitanism in ethical terms. This brings to the fore considerations which are both "secular" in their worldliness and "metaphysical" in the values one may attach to social behaviour.

Cosmopolitan worldliness connotes, in the first instance, a society that posseses a marked degree of human diversity or heterogeneity as a mode of being in the world. Where the term "secular," in its original Roman Catholic or Latinate sense, referred to living an immortal salvific life whose initial "mortal" span was subject to a worldly existence that was often unconscious of eternity, secularism in that context being regarded as a spiritual failing. Its usage shifted with the rise of European political secularism, to denote a society, living in the world, comprising individuals or groups who were different from each other; difference in the early modern European sense meaning Christians of different denominations, Deists, Freemasons, and atheists living peaceably together in a civil monarchical or republican society. In its contemporary Western incarnation, and in the context of unprecedented human mobility in a globalised world, cosmopolitanism now refers to a society that is multiracial and "multicultural,"[3] that actively fosters the ethnic, cultural, and economic survival of its minoritity groups. As is evident here, secularism has moved far beyond spiritual admonition, to the celebratory.

An initial reading of Gurnah's texts seem to confirm that the East African littoral was indeed cosmopolitan prior to and during the era of European colonialism; peacable coexistence being the mark of this civilized heterotopia,[4] as one of Gurnah's protagonists, describes:

> We liked to think of ourselves as a moderate and mild people. Arab African Indian Comorian: we lived alongside each other, quarrelled and sometimes intermarried. Civilized, that's what we were.[5]

Legitimacy, or the myths comprising ethnic authenticity in relation to claims for territoriality, does not figure large in local public discourse prior to postcolonial independence. Gurnah's East African coastal towns appear to have no self-admitted indigenes, everyone seems to have come from elsewhere in the recent or distant past, all in competing, and as it turns out, ultimately incompatible postcolonial claims for legitimacy. "Origins" may have been the African interior, the Arabian peninsula, South Asia, or the Swahili with their fabled Shirazi connections: " . . . the founding myth of the original inhabitants of the coast from Lamu to Kilwa, has in it somewhere the arrival of a ship from Persia."[6] The image of people arriving on ships reinforces the notion of the littoral as a Foucauldian heterotopia or "other" space,[7] the thematic of my essay on the littoral.[8] This, along with accounts, sightings, and encounters with the English in *Desertion*,[9] the Germans in *Paradise*,[10] and the Portuguese in *By The Sea*,[11] gels with depictions of coastal towns around the Indian Ocean rim in history, as Manuel Godinho found in Surat in 1663:

> [. . .] white Mughals, Indian Muslims, all types of pagans, Christians of various nationalities and, in fact, people from all over the world who have either settled in Surat or have come to port on business. In Surat we find Spaniards, Frenchmen, Germans, English, Dutch, Flemish, Dunkirkians, Italians, Hungarians, Poles, Swedes, Turks, Arabs, Persians, Tartars, Georgians, Scythians, Chinese, Malabaris, Bengalis, Sinhalese, Armenians and an endless variety of other strange barbarian people.[12]

More so than the creolised "Arab-Omanis," who intermarried extensively with inhabitants of the littoral, Indians remained a visible minority,[13] their movies, culture, food absorbed into the texture of life in the urban littoral, as Gurnah recollects from his own childhood:

> The Sultana cinema was Indian-owned, as were the two other cinemas in the town, the Empire and the Majestic. The Sultana was built by the Parsi S. H. Talati who also owned the Empire Cinema, under a separate management. The Majestic Cinema was owned by the Ismaili Amir 'Ngozi'. There were many Indians in Zanzibar then: Hindu, Ismaili, Ithnaasheri, Bohra, Parsi. In my first-year class in secondary school, which was the year before the revolution in 1964, there were 15 Indian students out of 30. The grocer's shop where our family had an account, just a short walk from our house and on the other side of the mosque, was Indian-owned. The carpenter on this side of the mosque and the barber down towards the main road were also Indian. In fact most of the barbers, tailors, haberdashers, doctors, motor dealers and, of course, lawyers were Indian.[14]

Both Arab-Omanis and Indians had stable communities on the East African littoral from well before the arrival of European colonialists.[15] If the adoption of the rupee,[16] a South Asian currency, in colonial East Africa reveals the role of Indians as intermediaries of European colonial interests, it also shows the extent of early modern "globalised" fiscal networks. Even food becomes a cross-cultural common denominator on the East African coast, as evident in Gurnah's description of the Indian food served at Saleh Omar's non-Indian wedding banquet:

> . . . they put on a full three-day extravaganza, with music and song and dance, and a biriani banquet after the ceremony and a special halwa ordered for the occasion and a procession with music and song to convey her to my house. For the rest of the three days it was non-stop food, samosas and mahamri, curries and sesame bread, almond ice-cream and jelabis.[17]

Both Michael Pearson and Gurnah agree that what makes the East African littoral unique is its historical position within the trade network that linked it with other coasts and port cities around the Indian Ocean rim, as Pearson reflects:

> . . . littoral society is much more cosmopolitan than parochial inland people for, at the great ports which constitute the nodes of the littoral, traders and travellers from all over the ocean, and far beyond, were to be found.[18]

Pearson further cites Robert Anthony who writes, " . . . of a water world of 'shared social, economic and cultural activities, and patterns that are not easily defined and delimited by ethnic and linguistic differences or by national boundaries.'"[19] In the same vein, Michael Lambek proposes, " . . . their littoral locations have allowed the inhabitants of the ports to escape some of the predations of land-based states, while also enabling them to expand in trade in both directions (that is, both maritime and terrestrial)."[20] Littoral societies were transformed by humans who crossed the ocean to reach them, as Gurnah's Saleh Omar describes in *By The Sea*:

> For centuries, intrepid traders and sailors, most of them barbarous and poor no doubt, made the annual journey to that stretch of the coast on the eastern side of the [African] continent, which had cusped so long ago to receive the musim winds. They brought with them their goods and their God and their way of looking at the world, their stories and their songs and prayers, and just a glimpse of the learning which was the jewel of their endeavours.[21]

This amphibious symbiosis or mutual dependence linking it to both land and sea is a salient feature of the littoral. Pearson illustrates by developing the idea of *ressac*, which translates from the French as undertow, backwash, or surf:

A complementary way to conceptualize land-sea relations and connections is Jean-Claude Penrad's notion of *ressac*, the threefold violent movement of the waves, turning back on themselves as they crash against the shore. He uses this image to elucidate the way in which the to-and-fro movements of the Indian Ocean mirror coastal and inland influences that keep coming back at each other just as do waves.[22]

What emerges in this conceptualization of littoral society is an interpersonal hybridity that is both biological and psychological. Littoral society is autonomous in its Foucauldian heterotopia, rootless though located, multiracial and multilingual, and differs from its adjoining inland regions, in a feathering of networks that forge links across the Indian Ocean, rather than into the hinterland, as Pearson proposes:

> . . . look[ing] at people around the coasts . . . Here it is a question of whether there is something which we can call a littoral society which shows certain commonalities around the shores of the ocean. These coastal communities will have more in common with each other than with their hinterlands. Their most important connections are with their maritime forelands. So Kilwa and the surrounding coast has, in terms of culture, religion, food, livelihood and so on more in common with Aden or Calicut than with the Mutapa 'state' to its west[23]

Gurnah's depicts life on the littoral as severed from the fetishes of both language and land. The itinerant trader was held in high esteem, as Mohammad Abdalla, the leader of Aziz's expedition to the African interior in Gurnah's *Paradise,* explains:

> "This is what we are on earth to do," Mohammad Abdalla said. "To trade. We go to the driest deserts and the darkest forests, and care nothing whether we trade with a king or a savage, or whether we live or die. It's all the same to us. You'll see some of the places we pass, where people have not yet been brought to life by trade, and they live like paralysed insects. There are no people more clever than traders, no calling more noble. It is what gives us life."[24]

If trade is a marker of being either civilized or sophisticated, then the East African littoral was both. Trade comprised both short- and long-haul essential and luxury goods, the traders and sailors, or *nahodha,* travelling seasonally with the *musim,* or monsoons. As Gurnah has Saleh Omar saying:

> The man I obtained the ud-al-qamari [costly Cambodian incense] from was a Persian trader from Bahrain who had come to our part of the world with the musim, the winds of the monsoons, he and thousands of other traders from Arabia, the Gulf, India and Sind, and the Horn

of Africa. They had been doing this every year for at least a thousand years. In the last months of the year, the winds blow steadily across the Indian Ocean towards the coast of Africa, where the currents obligingly provide a channel to harbour. Then in the early months of the new year, the winds turn around and blow in the opposite direction, ready to speed the traders home.[25]

Nature and her monsoons, Pearson's "deep structures,"[26] had favoured the development of East African littoral port cities, as Saleh Omar elaborates:

> It was all as if intended to be exactly thus, that the winds and currents would only reach the stretch of coast from southern Somalia to Sofala, at the northern end of what has become known as the Mozambique Channel. South of this stretch, the currents turned evil and cold, and ships that strayed beyond there were never heard of again. South of Sofala was an impenetrable sea of strange mists, and whirlpools a mile wide, and giant luminescent stingrays rising to the surface in the dead of the night and monstrous squids obscuring the horizon.[27]

Trade was the lynchpin in the social edifice of Zanzibar, the social structure maintained by familial and faith networks that reinforced trade links, in an endless circulation of ambition, desire, and utility, as Anne Bang describes:

> . . . from 1932 when [the Omani] Sultan made Zanzibar Town his capital . . . the new trade entrepot of East Africa was marked by a high degree of human influx, lasting trade and family networks with overseas locations, as well as a high degree of awareness of foreign places that shaped its everyday life. In total, the nineteenth century experience had enabled Zanzibar Town dwellers to think and act beyond the local.[28]

Port cities represent the meeting point of the global with the local, as Pearson reveals, citing Rhoads Murphey:

> Port functions, more than anything else, make a city cosmopolitan . . . A port city is open to the world, or at least to a varied section of it. In it races, cultures, and ideas as well as goods from a variety of places jostle, mix, and enrich each other and the life of the city. The smell of the sea and the harbour, still to be found . . . in all of them, like the sound of boat whistles or the moving tides, is a symbol of their multiple links with a wider world, samples of which are present in microcosm within their own urban areas.[29]

Here is a region whose inhabitants occupy a coast that for centuries has seen the busy to-ing and fro-ing of people and goods. People provided the vectors not only for economic exchanges, but a cross-pollination of genes, culture, food, faith, and ideas. Their main preoccupation seems to have been almost universally commerce, in either direct or indirect involvement. In this Gurnah contests the fictional narratives of Chinua Achebe, Ngugi wa Thiongo, and Ayi Kwei Armah, as Jacqueline Bardolph postulates:

> As opposed to the insistence on land or language, we have a community of traders always on the move, ready to explore far-away countries. They are not attached to a particular soil, neither are they hungry for land. And we have seen how Gurnah insists on the translations and modes of coexistence of many languages, how he brings to light the many intermarriages through generations that render notions of purity and authenticity ludicrous.[30]

The itinerant trader, the sailor, the missionary, the portfolio financier, many of whom operate in the realm of exchange, desire, and advertising, would need to be multilingual in a polyglot society, as Gurnah's Saleh Omar portrays it, "Sometimes people called to sit with them and listen and chat, [. . .] and they all spoke in loud voices mixing English and Arabic and Kiswahili in polyglot good humour, and the laughter and noise from the room filled the whole house."[31]

Languages occupied a shared communal space, and most inhabitants of the urban East African littoral moved easily in the inbetween realm of translation; for instance, in *Desertion*, Zakariya, who moves from India to the then Omani-administered Mombasa on the East African coast and marries a local woman, soon becomes multilingual:

> He had a gift for languages, their father, and spoke Kiswahili, Arabic and Gujarati fluently. His Kiswahili was quite perfect. It was not only that he could make himself understood in this language, but that he felt it, and made his way in it with an intimacy and assurance that was like an instinct, like walking, a skill so profoundly learned that it seemed natural.[32]

Despite longstanding trade and caravan routes to the hinterland from the littoral, translation, rather than a shared language, was the hallmark of social and commercial exchange, as Gurnah depicts in *Paradise*:

> Nyundo had been sent into the town as the messenger, because he could speak the language of the people here. Uncle Aziz said he remembered the sultan could speak Kiswahili, but he agreed it would be more courteous to address him in his own language first.[33]

Translation, in its original sense referring to physical mobility, becomes, in Salman Rushdie's view, cause for celebration:

The word 'translation' comes, etymologically, from the Latin for 'bearing across'. Having been born across the world, we are translated men. It is normally supposed that something always gets lost in translation; I cling obstinately, to the notion that something can also be gained.[34]

In the intricacies of plural multilingual societies, diversity was regarded as a strength rather than a liability. Diversity produced creolisation, as Pearson elucidates the development of creole lingua franca:

> . . . cosmopolitanism produced another element of unity [in creole lingua franca]. Certain languages achieved wide currency, such as Arabic in the earlier centuries. There are some 5000 words of Arabic influence in Malay, and many more than that in Swahili, and about 80% of these are the same, that is in Malay and Swahili, so we have a 'corpus of travelling Arabic words.'[35]

Later, nautical Portuguese, and more recently English, attained similar lingua franca status,[36] in usage beside, not in place of, other more community-specific languages.

Where race and language embody difference, necessitating the forging of bridges across barriers, today's historians see Islam as the great universal link, Gwynn Campbell's *Pax Islamica*,[37] on most of the Indian Ocean littoral; Islam as a religion of urban spaces, the connection substantiated by merchants, traders and sailors, scholars, saints, intermarriages, and the universal obligation of the hajj and lesser Sufi pilgrimages. Gurnah appears to present Islam as the great universal ideal across the Indian Ocean:

> Their father Zakariya [from India] had always said that he was a Muslim living among Muslims, and that was enough for him. Where he was born or came from was neither here nor there, they all lived in the house of God, dar-al-Islam, which stretched across mountains and forests and deserts and oceans, and where all were the same in submission to God.[38]

Gurnah concurs here again with Pearson, who reflects on the hybrid indigenisation of belief practices on the littoral:

> There is I think, an Islamic bond all around the shores of the ocean, with important commonalities and similarities . . . David Parkin has written that 'the idea of prayer in the mosque connotes unambiguous Islamic piety, while that outside points towards the possibility of other kinds of worship'[. . .] My claim is that while the 'other kinds of worship' clearly show some regional variations, all are still 'coastal' variants of Islam, while obviously 'prayer in the mosque' has strong commonalities all over the Islamic Indian Ocean world, indeed the Islamic world *tout court*.[39]

Pearson foreshadows the contested nature of Islamic legitimacy and authority that plays itself out in the contemporary Indian Ocean world and beyond, with the current rise of Wahhabi Islam and the suppression of heterogeneous local cults and Sufism in the public arena. Linked as it is to urban nodes in networks of trade, Islam becomes a marker for cosmopolitanism, as Pearson elucidates:

> Littoral people, living in a more cosmopolitan environment than those inland, are more likely to convert. In the case of the Indian Ocean, the cosmopolitan, international aspect of Islam has often been cited as a prime motivation for conversion, and while this applied most strongly in the port cities, it is also evident on the coasts between them.[40]

Under the influence of Islam, the Swahili were literate, unlike the inhabitants of the inland regions, as Gurnah reveals:

> My first language is Kiswahili, and unlike many African languages, it was a written language before European colonisation. The earliest examples of discursive writing date back to the late seventeenth century, and when I was an adolescent, this writing still had meaning and use as both writing as well as part of the oral currency of the language.[41]

Literacy was considered a distinguishing feature of the littoral, as Hamid reveals to Yusuf:

> 'Do you know that we who are from the coast all call ourselves waungwana?' Hamid asked. 'Do you know what this means? It means people of honour. [. . .] If you cannot read His word or follow His law, you are no better than these worshippers of rocks and trees. Little better than a beast'[42]

The East African littoral, worldly and cosmopolitan as it was, predates European colonial conquests, survives the partitioning of the world by Europe, and suddenly, unthinkably, inexplicably, goes into decline at independence in the 1960s. This is not to say that there have never been thriving ports on the Indian Ocean rim that have gone into irreversible decline— witness Rangoon, Malacca and Aceh in the Far East, Cambay, Surat and Calicut in South Asia, Basra and Aden in the Middle East, to name but a few more recent examples.[43] But with East Africa, the situation is different. A whole swathe of its coast has been erased from the map of the world's imaginary of places of cultural and economic significance. Emboldened by this erasure, or in ignorance masquerading as informed opinion, K.N. Chaudhuri has the audacity to state the following:

> The exclusion of East Africa from our civilizational identities needs a special word of explanation. In spite of its close connection with the

Islamic world, the indigenous African communities appear to have been structured by a historical logic separate and independent from the rest of the Indian Ocean.[44]

At a stroke, Chaudhuri commits the unforgivable error of erasing the whole Swahili coast and its culture, in his consideration of the history of the Indian Ocean, not only leaving himself unable to account for centuries of economic and cultural thriving,[45] but unconsciously echoing Georg Hegel's infamous comments on Africa that anticipate social darwinism:

> At this point we leave Africa, not to mention it again. For it is no historical part of the World; it has no movement or development to exhibit. Historical movements in it—that is in its northern part—belong to the Asiatic or European World. Carthage displayed there an important transitionary phase of civilization; but, as a Phoenician colony, it belongs to Asia. Egypt will be considered in reference to the passage of the human mind from its Eastern to its Western phase, but it does not belong to the African Spirit. What we properly understand by Africa, is the Unhistorical, Undeveloped Spirit, still involved in the conditions of mere nature, and which had to be presented here only as on the threshold of the World's History.[46]

Both Chaudhuri and Hegel ignore centuries of recorded premodern history which attest to links forged between the Swahili coast, the Arabian peninsula, South Asia and the Far East, to say nothing of colonial ventures in the region. On the other hand, there is no doubt that the East African littoral is today no longer a hub in the Indian Ocean world: it now appears to be predominantly monoethnic, after a long period of violence against minorities and dissenters. Its towns are derelict, its national economies struggling and dependent on foreign aid; this in the context of nascent economies elsewhere on the Indian Ocean rim. Which leads me to reexamine the notion of cosmopolitanism in general, and as it applies to the premodern and modern East African littoral as depicted by Gurnah.

It would be easy at this juncture to point a finger, along with a thousand other accusatory postcolonial fingers, at European colonialism as providing the start of the end for the East African littoral, the turning point in the subsequent decline of cosmopolitanism and the rise of interethnic conflicts. Such a position serves to displace blame and responsibility for contemporary problems, by scapegoating the now long-departed colonialists, in a cunning exercise in determinism. The simple reductionism of this position is not shared either by Gurnah or modern historians.

Contrary to expectations, European colonialism actually heightened cosmopolitan sensibilities around the Indian Ocean rim; and this for several reasons, such as the role of "indigenous"[47] Indian Ocean capital in bankrolling European colonial enterprise, the increased circulation of indigenous merchants, traders, sailors, soldiers, and indentured workers in the colonial era,[48] and the influx of colonial administrators, entrepreneurs, and military personnel.[49] This, along with the accelerated development of urban townships,[50] industrialization, and the spread of secular philosophies, was an era of rich international cultural exchange on many levels.

There is no doubt however that the colonial era resulted in a qualitative change in the cosmopolitanism of the East African littoral. Where premodern cosmopolitanism is considered to be largely voluntary, fuelled by trade with resultant cultural exchanges, the burgeoning of cosmopolitanism during the colonial era was not necessarily cause for celebration: certainly not on the part of indentured workers or impoverished soldiers,[51] often forced into these professions by the poverty resulting from colonial demands for cash crops; nor the often unwelcome imposition of European administrators or residents on traditional native rulers. Ackbar Abbas develops the idea of "enforced" cosmopolitanism:

> The ideal of cosmopolitanism, to quote a much discussed essay of Ulf Hannerz's, as "an orientation, a willingness to engage with the Other . . . an intellectual and aesthetic stance of openness toward divergent cultural experiences" may be an admirable one, but it is sustainable only in metropolitan centres where movement and travel are undertaken with ease and where the encounter with other cultures is a matter of free choice, negotiated on favourable terms. But what about a situation where these conditions are not available—a situation where "divergent cultural experiences" are not freely chosen but forced on us, as they are under colonialism? What form of "openness" should we cultivate then, and would this constitute a cosmopolitan stance or a compradorist one? Could cosmopolitanism be one version of "cultural imperialism"?[52]

Furthermore, some features of colonial administration had more lasting sequelae on the ways in which difference, or the Other, was viewed; such as the colonial fetish for defining differences and attempting to eradicate the inbetweenness of hybridity, which had until then been the bedrock of littoral port cities, as Anne Bang describes:

> Zanzibari society [comprised] a 'mixedness', 'heterogeneity' or 'cosmopolitanism' [which posited] the contradiction or outright incompatibility between the colonial urge to create fixed categories and a social structure which essentially eluded classification.[53]

Gurnah himself describes a premodern society of hybrid immigrants, indifferent to their places of "origin":

> After all that time, the people who lived on that coast hardly knew who they were, but knew enough to cling to what made them different from

those they despised, among themselves as well as among the outlying progeny of the human race in the interior of the continent.[54]

Enumeration and classification, as Enlightenment-inspired preoccupations with rationalizing or comprehending a world that, though demystified, was strangely uncanny, became powerful tools for containment in the colonial era. Edward Said was the first to highlight the Orientalist preoccupation with types, in proposing:

> . . . rhetorically speaking, orientalism is absolutely anatomical and enu-
> merative, to use its vocabulary is to engage in the particularizing and
> dividing of things Oriental into manageable parts.[55]

Colonial mapmaking was a case in point, as Gurnah's Saleh Omar reflects on the shift from living with the world on the horizon, to an imperial parochialism, which should have been, but wasn't, an oxymoron:

> Before maps the world was limitless. It was maps that gave it shape and
> made it seem like territory, like something that could be possessed, not
> just laid waste and plundered. Maps made places on the edges of the
> imagination seem graspable and placeable. And later when it became
> necessary, geography became biology in order to construct a hierar-
> chy in which to place the people who lived in their inaccessibility and
> primitiveness in other places on the map.[56]

In the case of India, Arjun Appadurai suggests that the British colonial body count based on caste served to turn differences, which had been inconsequential during Moghul rule, into the pretext for modern postcolonial India's turn to communal politics:

> . . . the idea of political representation . . . tied not to essentially similar
> citizens and individuals but to communities conceived as inherently
> special . . . provides the crucial link between [colonial] census clas-
> sifications and caste and community politics . . . and contemporary
> democratic politics. The enumeration of the social body, conceived as
> aggregations of individuals whose bodies were inherently both collec-
> tive and exotic, sets the stage for group difference to be the central
> principle of politics. Linking the idea of representation to the idea of
> communities characterized by bioracial commonalities (internally) and
> bioracial differences (externally) seems to be the critical marker of the
> colonial twist in the politics of the modern nation-state.[57]

Similarly, in a society dominated by immigrants, Anne Bang's account of the introduction of passports by the British administration in Zanzibar flags the entry of places of origin into the public discourse of the time:

Identification of person and origin was something new in East Africa at this time [1915]. The issue of passports touches directly on issues of identity. While the [Omani] Sultanate [of Zanzibar] had few classification categories beyond the free/slave, Muslim/non-Muslim and Ibadi-Omani/other Muslim dichotomies, the British administrators were more prone to closely categorise the governed peoples . . . [and] placed much emphasis on where people came from (literally, where people arrived from) . . . and more prone to translate these categories into access to political representation, housing, food rations, education and employment.[. . .] The persistent emphasis on origin, expressed in a language of ethnography, caused new organizations to emerge which were based precisely on origin.[58]

Thus, for the sake of administrative convenience in the colonial era, categories of different types of "natives" were not only reified, but sometimes invented, or plucked out of obscure antiquity. These categories intervened in the supposed "difference blindness"[59] of precolonial subjecthood, and as Appadurai describes, went on to become the basis for communal politics in newly formed postcolonial states. Furthermore, the new rulers of postcolonial states were inclined to dispatch their troublesome or overly successful minority groups back to where they, or as is more often the case, their ancestors of many generations earlier, had "come from": as with the young independent state of Zanzibar's forced eviction of Omani and other Arabs in 1964, and the gradual repression of its Indian communities.

While in no way nullifying the impact of colonial prejudices, Gurnah contests the notion of premodern East African cosmopolitanism, in the first instance with his description of the layering of society by the legacies of slavery and premodern primitivism. If we return to the excerpt that we examined at the start of this chapter, and read what follows, Gurnah looks beneath the surface of premodern heterogeneity and encounters seething, festering resentments:

We liked to think of ourselves as a moderate and mild people. Arab African Indian Comorian: we lived alongside each other, quarrelled and sometimes intermarried. Civilized, that's what we were. In reality, we were nowhere near *we*, but us in our separate yards, locked in our historical ghettoes, self-forgiving and seething with intolerances, with racisms, and with resentments. And politics brought all that into the open. It was not that we did not know these things about ourselves, about slavery, about inequalities about the contempt with which everyone spoke about the barbarity of the savage in the interior who had been captured and brought to work on our island. We read about these things in our colonized history books, but there these events seem lurid and far away from the way we lived, and sometimes they seemed like self-magnifying lies.[60]

In the light of this excerpt it becomes apparent that all was not well with premodern East African society. European-inspired colonial identities were superimposed on preexisting prejudices, as Anne Bang describes: "The Sultanate [. . .] distinguished sharply between the coastal, 'civilized' culture and the 'barbarian' interior."[61] These identities exacerbated difference consciousness and developed new social hierarchies. Kwame Appiah raises the issue of condescension as a potential pitfall: " . . . 'cosmopolitanism', [its] meaning is . . . disputed, and celebrations of the 'cosmopolitan' can suggest an unpleasant posture of superiority toward the putative provincial."[62] As Hamid tells Yusuf in Gurnah's *Paradise*:

> 'Do you know that we who are from the coast call ourselves waung-wana?' Hamid asked. 'Do you know what that means? It means people of honour. That's what we call ourselves, especially up here among fiends and savages. Why do we call ourselves that? It is God who gives us the right. We are honourable because we submit ourselves to the Creator, and understand and adhere to our obligations to Him. If you cannot read His word or follow His law, you are no better than these worshippers of rocks and trees. Little better than a beast.'[63]

Prejudices sanctioned by religious beliefs are powerful indeed, as Mohammad Abdalla sneers:

> Their trade goods were mostly cloth and iron, he explained. [. . .] Any of it was better than the stinking goatskin the savages wore when left to themselves. That is if they wore anything at all, for God made heathens shameless so that the faithful can recognize them and resolve how to deal with them . . . [In] the very depths of the dark and green mountain country [. . .] cloth was still the most common item of exchange. The savage did not trade for money.[64]

When it comes to the slave trade, the premodern history of Zanzibar is even more grim, as Aziz explains to Yusuf in *Paradise*:

> You'll be thinking: how did so many of these Arabs come to be here in such a short time? When they started to come here, buying slaves from these parts was like picking fruit off a tree. They didn't even have to capture their victims themselves, although some of them did so for the pleasure of it. There were enough people eager to sell their cousins and neighbours for trinkets. And the markets were open everywhere [. . .]. There were good profits to be made. Indian merchants gave credit to these Arabs to trade in ivory and slaves.[65]

It becomes apparent that celebratory accounts of the civilised and cosmopolitan nature of Indian Ocean trade risk eclipsing that most inhuman of exchanges: the slave trade. Indeed the traffic in people, considered luxury goods, formed the bedrock of trade in and out of Africa for centuries; the East African littoral was no exception, as Pearson reveals:

> The trade in slaves represents another extensive and high-value item of exchange. This trade, using 'product' from East Africa, began in earnest in the eighth and ninth centuries, though Zanj, that is African, slaves are first mentioned in Sassanian Persia, shortly before Islam in the early seventh century.[66]

It emerges that Arabs and South Asians colluded in the slave trade; Indian moneylenders acquired prominence in both premodern and colonial East Africa, as Gurnah's Frederick Turner muses in *Desertion*:

> . . . wherever Indians went, there prosperity followed, although of course it depended on the class of Indians. In Zanzibar he had seen the street sweeping variety that clogged Indian cities, living in degrading penury and begging in the streets, whining and screeching their grating racket, and most of the vendors of the hole-in-the wall shops were Indians. But the general idea was true: get the right kind of banyan in your district and prosperity will surely follow.[67]

Where the involvement of Indian financiers with the slave trade was covert, Arabs and Omanis were at the forefront, and they were badly affected when the slave trade finally ended. While the previous excerpt contests the homogeneity of East African Indians, the following exchange between Aziz and Mohammad Abdalla reflecting on the failure of slave-dependent East African Arab financial enterprise in *Paradise*, reveals more sinister prejudices:

> Uncle Aziz said '[At emancipation the] slaves just hid or ran away. The Arabs were left without food or comforts and had no choice but to leave. [. . .] Now the Indians have taken over with the Germans as their lords and the savages at their mercy.' 'Never trust the Indian,' Mohammad Abdalla said angrily. 'He will sell you his own mother if there's profit in it. His desire for money knows no limits. When you see him he looks craven and feeble, but he will go anywhere and do anything for money.' Uncle Aziz shook his head [. . .], 'The Indian knows how to deal with the European. We have no choice but to work with him.'[68]

Indians were object of resentment, functioning as the middlemen and financiers for Omani and European colonial interests, as Gurnah's protagonist reflects:

> The real money was in the hands of the Indian merchants and creditors, of course. God has given them a gift for business but has denied

them charity. They were the only ones who could afford to bring in the goods that were needed, which traders bought from them on credit, and repaid with interest. From the beginning, when the Omanis made themselves lords in these parts two hundred years ago, they brought Indian bankers to look after their affairs. [. . .] Sooner or later, the creditors owned the land and the princes and lords lived in a pretence of prosperity which the Indian merchants prudently and wisely financed. While the sultans and their nobles arrogantly strutted in their tarnished finery, and intrigued and plotted endlessly, the merchants were in control of affairs.[69]

The history of South Asia is intertwined with the African hinterland and the East African littoral, as Frederick Turner reveals in *Desertion*:

The Indians have been here a long time, or at least they were already here when the Portuguese came to plant their cross. It's even said that the pilot Da Gama picked up from here for the final run to Calicut was an Indian sailor. I can believe it, or more likely he was an Indian slave. Everything was done by slaves, and even the slaves owned slaves.[70]

Rehana, in *Desertion*, presents the ending of slavery as almost accidental, "Baluchi troops . . . had been brought here to guard the slaves on plantations. That was until the mad Sultan Khalifa of Zanzibar sent an Englishman to run his plantations for him and he freed all the slaves."[71] There was no political intervention on behalf of the oppressed, no indigenous outrage at the injustice of slavery, as Hussein reveals, " . . . Zanzibar? There even slaves defend slavery."[72] No truth and reconciliation commissions, there was only an overwhelming fatalism, that left it to a foreigner, an Englishman, to attempt to restore humanity to the debased.

The premodern economies of the littoral went into decline with the ending of the slave trade, until the turn to plantation-based cash crops, cloves in the case of Zanzibar. This necessitated the importing of cheap indentured labour, more often than not from South Asia, because attempts to draw former slaves into the workforce failed, as Frederick Turner describes:

. . . you can't get people to work as they should. You can't get them to make any effort. It's slavery that did it, you see. Slavery and diseases that sap their strength, but slavery most of all. In slavery they learned idleness and evasion, and now cannot conceive of the idea of working with any kind of endeavour or responsibility, even for payment. What passes for work in this town is men sitting under a tree waiting for the mangoes to ripen.[73]

Involvement with the trafficking of slaves, and prejudice against the Africans of the interior, cast long shadows on the attempts to form modern democratic postcolonial societies on the East African littoral, as Gurnah reveals in *Admiring Silence*:

> So when the time came to begin thinking of ourselves in the future, we persuaded ourselves that the objects of this abuse had not noticed what had happened to them, or had forgiven and would now like to embrace a new rhetoric of unity and nationalism. To enter into a mature compromise in everyone's interest. But they didn't. They wanted to glory in grievance, in promises of vengeance, in their past oppression, in their present poverty and in the nobility of their darker skins.[74]

This is something I explore further elsewhere. For now, it suffices to say that Gurnah presents a picture of premodern society on the East African littoral that is riven by fissures, with factions that divide society along the lines of ethnic loyalties and communal grievances, even before the advent of European colonialism. Africans and slaves from the interior, urban Swahili, Indian entrepreneurs and indentured workers, and Arab-Omani rulers and traders, each subgroup deals with its Others in terms of the recognition of familiar stereotypes, even whilst tolerating hybridity.

The words "recognition" and "familiar" undermine the notion of cosmopolitanism as living in a world of *strangers* who merely recognise a shared humanity. It is conceivable, and highly likely, that in the premodern non-Western world view there was no possibility of anyone being a "stranger." I say this for several reasons: many of these urban communities were "face-to-face," in the ancient Greek sense; small enough for direct connections to be established between its members, in contrast to the anonymity of today's "megalopolises," as Gurnah reveals:

> It was a small place, and no neighbour was that distant nor were any acquaintances that vague, and everyone knew who everyone was. In any case, none of them were willing to give up their right to talk about and interfere in other people's lives, to be aghast at that one's infraction and the other one's dereliction, and to expect yet another one to bring calamity down on his family, you mark my words. Some of them were merely familiar faces in the streets [. . .] without names or connection . . . [75]

Furthermore, much social interaction in "traditional" non-Western societies was dictated by communal practices and expectations, whether it be elaborate courtesies, the practice of hospitality, the conduct of disputes, and so forth. By and large most people were members of specific communities; the recognition of the familiar, in this setting, would refer to individuals conforming to "types," whether gendered, familial, ethnic, or religious. The type, or more cynically, the stereotype, was socially formed, as is the modern Western conception of identity. This is a theme that Ed Simpson and Kai Kresse develop, from K.N. Chaudhuri's notion of equivalence as being the basis of "recognition" of new landscapes and people:

> Beyond the stereotype however each figure [. . .] is suggestive of a broader community [. . .] whose practices and customs [. . .] have migrated with them, albeit changing as they do so. [. . .] The traveller, sailor or migrant recognises these people as the equivalents of people and communities from home [and even] imagine an appropriate social position in relation to the new but superficially familiar stranger.[. . .] a form of equivalence which [. . .] makes travel possible, eases discomfort, and essentially allows people to be blind (to not see) to the differences between home and the place they have travelled to.[76]

The mobile cosmopolitans of the Indian Ocean world who reached the East African littoral tended to circulate within communal, faith, ethnic, or familial networks, as does Hassanali's erstwhile brother-in-law from India:

> His name was Azad. He had come to Mombasa in the last musim from Calicut . . . [T]he captain asked Azad to stay behind and act as his agent until his return the following year, to arrange for goods and merchandise to be ready for him when he came back. They were related in a way . . . It was important, that relative part, because it meant he was obliged to be trustworthy in his dealings and his word was as good as his brother's, the captain.[77]

There is a sense here of many parallel communal networks, that intersect only in the most superficial and public spaces, rather than a fully assimilated cosmopolitan society with difference evenly distributed throughout. Carol A. Keller suggests a need to:

> . . . rethink the notion of "cosmopolitanism" as applied to Indian Ocean port cities in the past and present. We have tended to emphasize the multi-ethnic, multi-linguistic, and multi-religious character of these cities, and there is historical evidence to demonstrate that Indian Ocean merchants commonly cooperated and even partnered across ethnic and religious lines. But it is also the case that these townspeople of the Indian Ocean littoral typically maintained communal boundaries in the residential, marriage, and inheritance patterns. It may be useful, then, to revive an old concept and think about these port cities as "plural societies" (i.e., societies where distinct cultural, racial, or religious communities live side by side and cooperate in certain restricted spheres of activity while maintaining clear communal boundaries between and among themselves).[78]

This notion of community among communities is in stark contrast to the fourth century BC Cynic ideal of the cosmopolitan as "citizen of the cosmos," a form of elite individualism, as Appiah elucidates:

The formulation was meant to be paradoxical and reflected the general Cynic scepticism toward custom and tradition. A citizen—a *polites*—belonged to a particular polis, a city to which he or she owed loyalty. The cosmos referred to the world, not in the sense of the earth, but in the sense of the universe. Talk of cosmopolitanism originally signalled, then, a rejection of the conventional view that every civilized person belonged to a community among communities.[79]

This is different again from modern liberal societies, which are massively sceptical towards the notion of community, leading to a severance of the individual from "traditional" communities, as Slavoj Zizek describes in his critique of liberal multiculturalism as being a mode of expressing identity within society:

> In liberalism, culture survives, but as privatised: as a way of life, a set of beliefs and practices, not the public network of norms and rules. Culture is then literally transubstantiated: the same set of beliefs and practices change from the binding power of a collective into an expression of personal and private idiosyncrasies.[80]

Thus cosmopolitanism, as an ideal way of ethical living among strangers, becomes an issue in modern liberal societies, where socially constructed identities are contingent and unpredictable. As Jean Baudrillard reflects:

> Urban societies are populated with what we could call artificial strangers. There is an artificial production of strangeness. In this case, strangeness is not produced by the ellipsis of the Other but by the eclipse of the Other or, to use a more linguistic word, the elision of the Other.[81]

Which brings us to the crux of our discussion: it is impossible and dangerous to equate premodern notions of heterogeneity with current debates in Europe and America. To do so would be to indulge in Whiggish notions of the past, or presentism, and what's worse, from the perspective of Western discourse, someone else's past. This is an issue raised by David Morley, as he cites Jean-Luc Nancy:

> . . . Heimat fever has its roots in the West's long obsession with the "loss of community." As Nancy puts it, "at every moment in its history, the Occident has given itself over to the nostalgia for a more archaic community that has disappeared, and to deploring a loss of familiarity, fraternity and conviviality."[82]

My point is that imputing an idyllic cosmopolitanism to premodern societies runs the risk of a displaced nostalgia by proxy. Furthermore, it represents a subtle form of condescension towards non-Western societies, which, if they are "traditional," also become anthropological showpieces, "their" recent present coincides with the past of a now more advanced West, reinforcing the superiority of the West, even as it laments the loss of its own prelapsarian simplicity. Ackbar Abbas turns the argument on its head by revealing that any reading of cosmopolitanism is influenced by hegemonic norms:

> In Borges's case, cosmopolitanism was, first, a modernist argument against the tyranny of "tradition" as narrow parochialisms and ethnocentricism: this was the critical aspect of his cultural universalism ("our patrimony is the universe")—in much the same way that the universalism of "structure" was to Claude Levi-Strauss a critical safeguard against ethnocentric bias. The problem begins when this universalism is identified with Western culture ("I believe our tradition is all of Western culture . . ."). This identification did not happen by chance. In the modern era, which corresponded to the economic and political dominance of Western nations, cosmopolitanism by and large meant being versed in Western ways, and the vision of "one world" culture was only a sometimes unconscious, sometimes unconscionable, euphemism for "First World" culture. This relationship of cosmopolitanism to power suggests that it cannot be thought of simply as an honorific or a universalist term, connoting an ability to transcend narrow loyalties and ethnocentric prejudices or a sympathetic disposition to "the other."[83]

Abbas usefully reveals the Eurocentric universalism of discourse about cosmopolitanism, in regard to what may be valued as sophisticated, and what constitutes the ethical treatment of strangers. The point being that much of the premodern interethnic behaviour occurs outside of Western paradigmatic frameworks. And such behaviour occurred in the *a priori* context of there being no strangers. Furthermore, seemingly unethical behaviour was often condoned by religious faiths, which problematises and necessarily relativises any discussion of what constitutes ethics or good or value. Islam has no prohibitions against slavery, and teaches that salvation is available only to the believer; furthermore Islam is no monolith, if one considers, for instance, the ethnic quotas for university entry in Pakistan as pointing to a subjective consciousness of difference within the *ummah*, as I elaborate later. Similarly, the religious, rather than utilitarian, basis for the Hindu caste system sanctions behaviour and prejudices that would, in another cultural context, be considered unethical.

Gurnah's fictions deliberately complicate representations of pre-independence littoral societies, as he admits to trying to suggest:

> . . . a complicated balancing act between different societies—the very reason that the coastal regions are so vulnerable when European imperialism comes—is because society is already at full stretch. All sorts of

cruelties existed within it which it couldn't account for even to itself. Cruelties against women, cruelties against children, cruelties against those people you see as weak, as every society does.[84]

Problematising the notion of universal ethics, Gurnah's fictional writings abound with critiques of Swahili patriarchal hierarchies, of bondage and submission and impotence, of foolish bankrupt fathers forced to sell their children to redeem their debts,[85] of the practice of forced marriages;[86] of uncles who represent authority but whose wafting perfume fails to hide their cloying paedophilia and sexual abuse;[87] of powerful senior henchmen, emancipated former slaves, who sodomize young boys, as Latif Mahmud reproaches Saleh Omar:

> You must have known that he was a notorious predator on young boys, tormenting them week after week with offers of coins and packets of halwa until they succumbed, or until his interest forced someone else to make them succumb, after which in their shame they submitted to others. Him and others like him, who thought themselves strong and manly because they could stalk and torment and intimidate young boys until they forced them to submit in shame. [. . .] I saw a cannibal who swaggered in his cruelty, a tormentor of the flesh of the young and poor.[88]

Themes of sexual abuse of the young and helpless recur in Gurnah's fiction. Of young men who run away from home never to be heard of again, saying "I never wrote to them [my family], and I guessed they would not know where I was so they would never be able to write to me. I wanted nothing to do with them, and their hatreds and demands."[89] Conflict and corrosion, the themes of bitterness and psychic violence, repeat themselves in each of Gurnah's fictions, as the slave Yusuf flees the amorous overtures of his master's wife in *Paradise*:

> But he had done nothing shameful, it was the way they had forced him to live, forced all of them to live, which was shameful. Their intrigues and hatreds and vengeful acquisitiveness had forced even simple virtues into tokens of exchange and barter. He would go away, there was nothing simpler. Somewhere where he could escape the oppressive claims everything made on him. But he knew that a hard lump of loneliness had long ago formed in his displaced heart, that wherever he went it would be with him, to diminish and disperse any plot he could hatch for small fulfilment.[90]

Gurnah depicts social castigation, real and surrogate family ties that are transgressive, powerlessness and abuse of power leading to bitterness and wrecked lives, and the betrayals that occur within the intimate spaces of family, disillusionment that occurs well before the advent of Western-inspired abandonment of the idea of the extended family. Of family feuds that continue for generations, sometimes as allegories for the contests between the various sacred families and future sects of Islam:

> Have you noticed how the history of Islam is so tied up with family squabbles? Let me put that another way lest I offend you. I know what a sensitive lot we Muslims are. Have you noticed the incredible consequences of family squabbles in the history of Islamic societies? [. . .] I hate families.[91]

This contradicts depictions of Islam as providing a timeless and transnational sense of belonging, as provided for instance by Ross Dunn:

> In the Middle East an individual's sense of being part of an international social order varied considerably with his education and position in life. But in the Indian Ocean lands where Islam was a minority faith, all Muslims shared acutely this feeling of participation. Simply to be a Muslim in East Africa, southern India, or Malaysia in the fourteenth century was to have a cosmopolitan frame of mind.[92]

However, Gwynn Campbell's *Pax Islamica* did not eradicate communal differences within the Muslim *ummah* through the ages, as Pearson notes:

> Ibn Battuta is merely one self-proclaimed expert from the heartland, or near enough, who had a pronounced air of superiority as he mingled with the indigenous Muslims around the ocean. His praise is reserved for those who like himself were Arabs from the heartland, and indeed he always commented on their presence, and praised them, while ignoring or belittling the locals.[93]

Variations in Islamic practices provided another layering of difference. Some may concede perhaps minor local variations of beliefs as instances of indigenous acculturation, as Pearson elaborates:

> Conversion, even if 'partial', served to further distinguish the shore dwellers, the Swahili, from their inland neighbours. This coastal society, because of its location, was much more open to wider influences from across the Indian Ocean than were people in the interior; their acceptance of Islam is part of this greater exposure. Yet their new religion was heavily impregnated with pre-Islamic indigenous beliefs . . . [94]

However, this spectrum of religious practices, as gaps between public and private piety, were source for anxiety among itinerant Islamic scholars, as Pearson describes, "Yet this division has often worried exemplars of the faith, who ever since coastal communities accepted Islam have been concerned to 'purify' practice and rectify deviations."[95]

Gurnah has his protagonist in *Admiring Silence* display an immense scepticism towards the unity of Islam, and reveals how the rise of the Wahhabi sect, viewed uncritically by Felicitas Becker as "Islamic globalisation,"[96] from the premodern and colonial eras onwards, has led to internecine conflict. The psychically and semantically violent suppression of heterogeneous local cults and Sufism in the public arena undermines unified notions of Islam as a monolith free of conflict:

> . . . [the] Wahhabi, those lovers of the unadorned word of God, zealots of the Sunna, muwahiddun. The original Wahhabis were the fundamentalists of fundamentalists, and could probably take their place among the fanatical crazies of any religion. They banned music, dancing, poetry, silk, gold and jewellery, and probably a few other little pleasures which it would not become their holinesses to mention aloud. They abhorred begging and the veneration of holy men. If their greatest historical act of vandalism was to destroy the tomb of Imam Hussein, the Prophet's grandson, at Kerbala, their most persistent persecution has been reserved for sceptics and philosophers, for the Sufi orders. Some of their modern ikhwan have doubts about whether God would have sanctioned the telephone or television, let alone rockets to the moon.[97]

Gurnah alludes to the contested nature of Islamic legitimacy and authority that plays itself out in the contemporary Indian Ocean world and beyond; and the cultural genocide waged on more heterogeneous forms of Islam by Wahhabi Islam, which is where I part company with Simpson and Kresse who suggest:

> . . . competing interpretations of orthodoxy and legitimacy can be seen as rival forms of cosmopolitanism: all share the goal of uniting Muslims by insisting on universal standards and practices; yet, propagating a sectarian agenda also inevitably gives rise to the disunity of factionalism.[98]

It is my opinion that the dissemination of sectarian loyalties which subscribe to idiosyncratic "universalisms" is incompatible with the notion of cosmopolitanism, but may possibly be reconciled with ideas about globalisation. The term cosmopolitanism is imbued with notions of ethics, whereas globalisation is indiscriminate, and operates in an ethical vacuum.

There is no doubt that the inhabitants of premodern and colonial port cities on the Indian Ocean rim had a cosmopolitan consciousness of the world beyond the local. However, this consciousness did not translate into necessarily recognisable ethical behaviour towards either their Others or their own. Furthermore, while there is no doubt that these societies were multiethnic and multicultural, this does not mean that they were blind to difference, as the current sense of cosmopolitanism requires. Admittedly, though, differences were not fetishized as they are in contemporary Western liberal notions of celebrating difference.

Hence, within the existing parameters of discourse about cosmopolitanism, especially in the light of Western standards of ethics, it impossible to give unqualified support to the idea of either premodern or colonial societies on the East African littoral as being, in the broadest sense, cosmopolitan. However, these societies were cosmopolitan to the extent that the imposition of the postcolonial nation-state was to prove a profound rupture, with an almost complete evacuation of cosmopolitanism on the littoral, for instance following the Zanzibari Revolution of 1964, with the brutal killing and expulsion of "nonindigenous" Omani and Indian Zanzibaris.

Anthony Reid pronounces Asian (and, by extension, Indian Ocean) maritime cities models of cosmopolitanism until the mid-twentieth century, due to their "vast maritime reach and diverse hinterlands," their religious pluralism, and the diversity encouraged by their rulers. However this changed with the "arrival of homogenising nationalism, [t]he kind of modern nationalism (with racial undertones never far from the surface) which sought cultural and ethnic homogeneity within state borders," after the modern European and American model.[99]

This gels with Gurnah's own admission of attempting to portray the fragmented nature of the littoral prior to independence, as:

> . . . a society that was actually fragmented. Fragmented doesn't mean that it doesn't work. It just means that it worked in a different way. So I wanted to write about a world that had always been fragmented but still manages to have something approaching civic and social life. [. . .] I didn't simply want to say, 'Look it worked before the European colonial encounter' but instead, 'Look how hard it had to try to work and look at the things it had to do to make itself work.'[100]

Gurnah's narrator in *Desertion*, in referring to failed pre-independence elections and riots, seems to suggest that the arrival of modern political ideologies heralded a loss of innocence:

> There had been a failed election six months earlier, ruined by riots and a stalemate result. Political differences between the parties had become irreconcilable, as perhaps they do in small places with intimate histories and grievances that never fade, or at least that rarely need to be re-examined in the light of pressing events. There were few events pressing enough to make people think twice about their loyalties. Not yet. The riots were a shock to young people [. . . and] would be put in perspective by later events, but in the innocence of the times, they seemed like an appalling lapse in manners, like family members abusing each other in public. There was still a great deal for us to learn

about what harm we were capable of doing to each other, and how easy it would become once we had begun.[101]

The cosmopolitanism of the East African littoral in no way prepared it for the imposition of the modern nation-state; indeed, its postcolonial rulers went to great lengths to expel its minority communities, ostensibly in revenge for the abuses of the slave trade and the desire to erase centuries of Arab influence, as Gurnah's Saleh Omar recounts the expulsion of mixed race "Omanis":

> The government had been using the island as a detention centre [built by British colonialists] since independence. They rounded up whole families of people of Omani descent, especially those who lived in the country or wore beards and turbans or were related to the ousted sultan, and transported them to the small island some distance off shore . . . [Photographs] showed a scene which was not unfamiliar from press photographs of other disasters—a crowd of people squatting on the ground, some of them with heads bent, some looking towards the camera with tired melting eyes, some with cautious interest, bearded men capless and worn out, women with heads shawled and eyes cast down, children staring.[102]

Saleh Omar sees parallels between the postcolonial ethnic cleansing in Zanzibar and the Jewish Holocaust in Nazi Germany. Recalling his years of incarceration by the dictatorship in postcolonial Zanzibar, he says:

> I have taught myself not to speak of the years which followed, although I have forgotten little of them. The years were written in the language of the body, and it is not a language I can speak with words. Sometimes I see photographs of people in distress, and the image of their misery and pain echoes in my body and makes me ache with them.[103]

Saleh Omar echoes Hannah Arendt's notion of the sheer banality of evil, committed by ordinary people, as he describes how photographs he has seen of the humiliation of Jews forced to scrub pavements on their hands and knees strikes a chord in his own memory:

> All around them, close up to them, on the pavement behind them and in the front of them, stood crowds of Viennese, grinning and looking on. People of all ages, mothers and fathers and grandfathers and children, some leaning on bicycles, others carrying shopping bags, standing smiling in their ordinary respectability while those three men were degraded in front of them. Not a swastika in sight, just ordinary people laughing at the humiliation of three Jews.[104]

Ordinary people, dehumanized by psychic and literal violence, reveal how closely the narrative of civilization is intertwined with that of unspeakable human atrocities, and how individuals are to be held responsible for the actions of their leaders and their nations.

The new postcolonial Zanzibari government severed all trade and cultural links with the Indian Ocean world, through the banning of musim trade and the undermining of entrepots, in an ultimately failed bid for fiscal self-sufficiency through the pursuit of disastrous agrarian policies. The motives ostensibly are ideological, as they attempted to force conventional postcolonial notions of nationalism, of unitary language and culture, and native claims for land, on a mobile polyglot littoral society. The impact of hegemonic political ideology on littoral heterotopia is something I explore at greater length in another essay.[105]

On another level, the State's instinctive antipathy to cosmopolitanism brings us full circle to the several millennia-old debate about whether it is possible to be both cosmopolitan and patriotic: as with the Stoics dealing with the demands of their city-states, the early Christians in the Roman Empire, rootless Jews in mediaeval Europe, Catholics in post-Reformation England, transnational Muslims in the post-9/11 United States. Any discussion of the desirability of cosmopolitanism must thus struggle to accommodate two extreme positions: subscription to the ideologies of patriotic nationalism versus the universal value of responsibility to fellow human beings irrespective of race, creed, or nationality, all against the backdrop of unprecedented twentieth-century worldwide immigration and the Holocaust.

The tragedy remains, nonetheless, that a cosmopolitan littoral society such as Zanzibar, that has over centuries been assailed by different ideas, open to a variety of cultures, languages, and ways of being, has, with regard to the collapse of its modern nation-state, experienced a failure of "discursive translation—that is, the transfer of thought patterns between one historical arena and another";[106] the ideologies of the modern nation-state have not been successfully assimilated. The failure of the modern Zanzibari state is more than abstraction. It has resulted in unspeakable suffering to its citizens, as Saleh Omar reveals:

> So many people had left or been expelled or died. So many evils and hardships had befallen and were still befalling those who remained, and no one had a monopoly of suffering and loss. So I [. . .] devoted myself to a quiet life, speaking without rancour about what it was necessary to say, listening with fortitude to the anguished stories of the life that had become our lot. [. . .] And later, when I was on my own in the darkness of my crumbling store, I lamented the loss of my loved ones and grieved for them, and when that grief palled I was saddened by the wasted life I had lived.[107]

Saleh Omar's experience parallels that of the East African littoral, his only recourse is silence, a failure of speech, the abandonment of translation. Most of Gurnah's protagonists occupy silent gaps in his narratives, as polyglot tongues fall silent, stricken in the wake of the violence that has dogged their experience of modernity.

If cosmopolitanism is an impossibly utopian ideal, it nonetheless remains an extremely seductive one, as Saint Paul proclaims "So then you Gentiles are not foreigners or strangers any longer; you are now citizens together with God's people and members of the family of God."[108] This is not an ideal that I would subject to the depredations of utility: I believe it is important for human societies to maintain and work towards ethical goals that make for a better world, both within and between societies. And, more importantly, to develop immanent ways of seeing and thinking about Others, at the intimate level of human and humanising encounters.

NOTES

1. Even Europe can be "nativist"! In actuality, nativity refers to birth. Can the German Turk or the British Pakistani ever be at "home"?
2. Derrida, 13.
3. Kwame Appiah describes multiculturalism as "another shape shifter, which so often designates the disease it purports to cure" (xiii).
4. Drawing on Foucault's notion of heterotopia.
5. Gurnah, *Admiring Silence*, 66.
6. Gurnah, *An Idea of the Past*, 290.
7. Foucault, 27.
8. See my *Littoral as Heterotopia and the Idea of Ressac* (forthcoming).
9. Gurnah, *Desertion*, 3.
10. Gurnah, *Paradise*, 169, 244.
11. Gurnah, *By The Sea*, 15.
12. Cited by Pearson in Simpson and Kresse, 366.
13. McPherson, 78.
14. Gurnah, *The Dancers*.
15. McPherson, 78.
16. In Zanzibar in 1908, see Anne Bang in Simpson and Kresse, 169.
17. *By The Sea*, 148.
18. Pearson, *Indian Ocean*, 39.
19. Pearson in Simpson and Kresse, 368.
20. Lambek, xv.
21. *By The Sea*, 13.
22. Pearson, *Littoral*, 359.
23. Pearson in Simpson and Kresse, 366.
24. *Paradise*, 119.
25. *By The Sea*, 14.
26. Pearson, *Indian Ocean*, 12.
27. Ibid., 15.
28. Bang, 168.
29. Pearson, *Indian Ocean*, 32.
30. Bardolph, 84.
31. *By The Sea*, 87.
32. *Desertion*, 62.
33. *Paradise*, 137.
34. Rushdie, 17.
35. Pearson, *Indian Ocean*, 39.
36. Ibid.
37. Campbell, 43.
38. *Desertion*, 62.
39. Pearson in Simpson and Kresse, 367.

40. Pearson, *Littoral*, 365.
41. Gurnah, *Writing and Place*.
42. *Paradise*, 100.
43. McPherson, 85.
44. Chaudhuri, 36.
45. In K.N. Chaudhuri's hands we return to a nineteenth-century European discourse that saw Africa as a dark continent without history.
46. Hegel, 99.
47. Indigenous being a slippery term in Indian Ocean studies discourse: Which inhabitant of the Indian Ocean rim is not indigenous?
48. Bose, 27; Vink, 50.
49. Bang, 171.
50. Ibid., 176, for her description of the explosive urbanization of Zanzibar in the nineteenth century.
51. Indentured workers were little better than slaves, soldiers were shuttled around the colonies and often placed at the front lines of battles that were not "theirs." See Bose, 124–126.
52. Abbas, 771.
53. Bang, 170.
54. *By The Sea*, 13.
55. Said, 72.
56. *By The Sea*, 35.
57. Appadurai, 130.
58. Bang, 172, 173.
59. Taylor, 40.
60. *Admiring Silence*, 66–67, emphasis in the original.
61. Bang, 174.
62. Appiah, xiii.
63. *Paradise*, 100.
64. Ibid., 119.
65. Ibid., 131–132.
66. Pearson, *Indian Ocean*, 85.
67. *Desertion*, 39–40.
68. *Paradise*, 133.
69. *Admiring Silence*, 140.
70. *Desertion*, 46.
71. Ibid., 66.
72. Ibid., 88.
73. Ibid., 45.
74. *Admiring Silence*, 67.
75. *Desertion*, 125.
76. Simpson and Kresse, 21, 23.
77. *Desertion*, 61.
78. Carol A. Keller on Lee Cassanelli, http://www.accd.edu/sac/history/keller/IndianO/Cassan.html. Accessed 26 December 2008.
79. Appiah, xiv.
80. Zizek, 142.
81. Baudrillard, 27.
82. Morley, 254.
83. Abbas, 770–771.
84. Nasta, 361.
85. *Paradise*, 24.
86. Ibid., 207.
87. *By The Sea*, 95.
88. *By The Sea*, 156. See also *Paradise*, 47, *By The Sea*, 100.

89. *By The Sea*, 239. See also *Admiring Silence*, 128.
90. *Desertion*, 236.
91. *By The Sea*, 195.
92. Cited by Pearson, *Indian Ocean*, 77.
93. Pearson, *Indian Ocean*, 81.
94. Ibid., 78.
95. Ibid., 80.
96. Becker, 288.
97. *Admiring Silence*, 136.
98. Simpson and Kresse, 26.
99. Anthony Reid keynote lecture.
100. Nasta, 360.
101. *Desertion*, 176.
102. *By The Sea*, 222, 223.
103. Ibid., 231.
104. Ibid., 231.
105. See my *The Debacle of Nationhood* (forthcoming).
106. Klein and McKenthun, 9.
107. *By The Sea*, 235.
108. St. Paul's *Letter to the Ephesians 2.19*.

BIBLIOGRAPHY

Abbas, Ackbar. "Cosmopolitan De-scriptions: Shanghai and Hong Kong." *Public Culture* 12(3; 2000): 769–786.

Appadurai, Arjun. *Modernity at Large: Cultural Dimensions of Globalization.* Minneapolis, MN: University of Minnesota Press, 1996.

Appiah, Kwame Anthony. *Cosmopolitanism: Ethics in a World of Strangers.* New York: Norton, 2007.

Bang, Anne. "Cosmopolitanism Colonised? Three Cases from Zanzibar 1890–1920." In *Struggling with History: Islam and Cosmopolitanism in the Western Indian Ocean*, edited by Edward Simpson and Kai Kresse, 167–188. New York: Columbia University Press, 2008.

Bardolph, Jacqueline. "Abdulrazak Gurnah's *Paradise* and *Admiring Silence*: History, Stories and the Figure of the Uncle." In *Contemporary African Fiction*, edited by Derek Wright, 77–89. Bayreuth, Germany: Bayreuth University Press, 1997.

Baudrillard, Jean. *Radical Alterity.* Translated by Marc Guillaume. Los Angeles: Semiotext, 2008.

Becker, Felicita. "Cosmoplitanism Beyond the Towns: Rural-Urban relations in the History of the Southern Swahili Coast in the Twentieth Century." Eds. Simpson and Kresse, 261–290.

Bose, Sugata. *A Hundred Horizons: The Indian Ocean in the Age of Global Empire.* Cambridge, MA: Harvard University Press, 2006.

Breckenridge, Carol A., et al., eds. "Cosmopolitanism: Millenial Quartet." *Public Culture* 12(3; 2000): 577–804.

Campbell, Gwynn. "Islam in Indian Ocean Africa Prior to the Scramble." In *Struggling with History: Islam and Cosmopolitanism in the Western Indian Ocean*, edited by Edward Simpson and Kai Kresse, 43–92. New York: Columbia University Press, 2008.

Chaudhuri, K.N. *Asia Before Europe: Economy and Civilization of the Indian Ocean from the Rise of Islam to 1750.* Cambridge, UK: Cambridge University Press, 1990.

Derrida, Jacques. *On Cosmopolitanism and Forgiveness*. Translated by Mark Dooley and Michael Hughes. New York: Routledge, 2001.

Foucault, Michel. "Of Other Spaces." Translated by J. Miskowiec. *Diacritics* 16(1; 1986): 22–27.

Gurnah, Abdulrazak. *Admiring Silence*. New York: New Press, 1996.

———. *By The Sea*. London: Bloomsbury, 2002.

———. *Desertion*. London: Bloomsbury, 2006.

———. *Paradise*. London: Bloomsbury, 1994.

———. "An Idea of the Past." In *A Twentieth Century Literature Reader*, edited by Suman Gupta and David Johnson, 289–292. London: Routledge, 2005.

———. "The Dancers." South Asian Diaspora Literature and Arts Archive. http://www.salidaa.org.uk/salidaa/docrep/docs/projects/backchat/The%20Dancers/docm_render.html. Accessed 6 January 2009.

———. "Writing and Place." World Literature Today Essays. http://www.ou.edu/worldlit/essays/Gurnah-Writing-and-Place.html. Accessed 6 January 2009.

Gutmann, Amy, ed. *Multiculturalism: Examining the Politics of Recognition*. Princeton, NJ: Princeton University Press, 1994.

Hegel, G.W.F. *The Philosophy of History*. New York: Cosimo Classics, 2007.

Klein, Bernard, and Gresa Mackunthen, eds. *Sea Champs and Historicizing the Ocean*. London and New York: Routledge, 2004.

Lambek, Michael. Foreword to *Struggling with History: Islam and Cosmopolitanism in the Western Indian Ocean*, edited by Edward Simpson and Kai Kresse, xiv–xix. New York: Columbia University Press, 2008.

McPherson, Kenneth. "Port Cities as Nodal Points of Change: The Indian Ocean 1890s–1920s." In *Modernity and Culture: From the Mediterranean to the Indian Ocean*, edited by Leila Tarazi Fawaz and C.A. Bayly, 75–95. New York: Columbia University Press, 2002.

Morley, David. *Home Territories: Media, Mobility and Identity*. London: Routledge, 2000.

Nasta, Susheila, ed. *Writing Across World: Contemporary Writers Talk*. New York: Routledge, 2004.

Pearson, Michael. *The Indian Ocean*. London: Routledge, 2003.

———. Afterword to *Struggling with History: Islam and Cosmopolitanism in the Western Indian Ocean*, edited by Edward Simpson and Kai Kresse, 357–372. New York: Columbia University Press, 2008.

———. "Littoral Society: The Concept and the Problems." *Journal of World History* 17.4 (2006): 353–373.

Reid, Anthony. "The Cosmopolitan City as an Asian Maritime Tradition." Keynote lecture at Conference on Towards the Construction of Urban Cultural Theories. Urban-Culture Research Centre, Osaka City University. 18 March 2006.

Rushdie, Salman. *Imaginary Homelands: Essays and Criticism 1981–1991*. London: Granta, 1991.

Said, Edward W. *Orientalism*. New York: Vintage, 1979.

Simpson, Edward, and Kai Kresse, eds. *Struggling with History: Islam and Cosmopolitanism in the Western Indian Ocean*. New York: Columbia University Press, 2008.

Taylor, Charles. "The Politics of Recognition." In *Multiculturalism: Examining the Politics of Recognition*, edited by Amy Gutmann, 25–74. Princeton, NJ: Princeton University Press, 1994.

Wright, Derek, ed. *Contemporary African Fiction*. Bayreuth, Germany: Bayreuth University Press, 1997.

Vink, Marcus. "Indian Ocean Studies and the 'new thalassology'." *Journal of Gloval History* 2 (2007): 41–62.

Zizek, Slavoj. *On Violence*. New York: Picador, 2008.

5 Destined to Disappear Without a Trace

Gender and the Languages of Creolisation in the Indian Ocean, Africa, Brazil, and the Caribbean

Fernando Rosa Ribeiro

This chapter proposes to tackle a theoretically complex subject, namely, the representation of intimate relationships in contexts intensely marked both by rather ancient processes of creolisation as well as colonial and post-colonial imaginings of local identities and nationhood. The aim of these imaginings may be to construct an internally homogeneous nation or ethnic group, or at least to construct an image of the nation where differences can be accounted for and negotiated within a common imaginative framework. As I have previously argued, intimate relationships in creolised contexts seem to have historically originated in precolonial times in the Indian Ocean area (and perhaps also the Mediterranean, with which the Indian Ocean has very ancient links) and spread from there to other areas. At any rate, there seems to be an interconnected set of both imaginings and social practices related to those relationships that is quite widespread.[1]

Several genres have been powerful vehicles for discussing intimate relationships in creolised contexts, from various kinds of colonial reports and documents, travelogues, and ethnographic and other studies, to novels and poetry, not to mention media such as photography, film, or music. I have previously worked on scholarly and literary representations in what concerns the work of some Brazilian, Netherlands Indies (i.e. colonial Indonesian) and South African authors.[2] What follows will concentrate on literary representations, especially those found in novels, with occasional forays into representations in other domains such as poetry. With one or two exceptions, the period covered is the late nineteenth to the mid- to late twentieth centuries. The domain covered ranges from works from the literature of the Dutch Caribbean (especially that of Curaçao) in both Dutch and Papiamentu, to that of Brazil (in Portuguese), former French West Africa (in French), South Africa (in both English and Afrikaans), and Indonesia (in

Dutch and Malay-Indonesian). Vast areas of the world (for instance, Latin America outside of Brazil) as well as huge swathes of literary history (for instance, black American writing) have been left out of this chapter.

My aim here therefore is not to produce an inventory of diverse local literatures, not even one circumscribed to the central concern of this chapter.[3] Rather, I will attempt, through a highly selective reading of some works that will be taken as representative from several areas, to show that the subject of intimate relationships in creolised contexts has often been quite central to at least part of the writing of several authors. This certainly has to do, in part, with the fact that in their novels those writers could think creatively about nation, colonialism, and identity, as well as the intimate sphere, in ways that were exploratory and tentative, but also potentially novel and even subversive. Needless to say that more than a modicum of official censure was also exercised in more than one case, several works having been banned when they were first published (as in the case of works by both Nelson Rodrigues and Peter Abrahams, both of which will be discussed later). Even when there was not any official ban, however, a measure of opprobrium and public censure were the lot of many authors (as in the case of William Plomer and his *Turbott Wolfe* as well as Edgar du Perron and his *Het land van herkomst*, both analysed later). Self-censorship could also be exercised (as in the case of C.P. Leipoldt).

Furthermore, the subject, though heavily laden with local inflections in each case, also has a transregional and transcontinental reach that is quite at odds with current notions of national literary historiographies in discrete, distinct languages. The often tragic ending of the relationships described seems to point to connections to a translocal imaginative framework not entirely encompassed within any single language or geographical domain, let alone colonial or postcolonial sphere. It may be that, being highly transgressive in relation to colonial and other boundary markers of identity, those novels inevitably share a good deal of common ground, regardless of their local context of production, their readership, and the process of literary canonisation to which they were eventually submitted. Furthermore, there were more than passing similarities in various colonial areas related to the creolisation of colonial subjects.[4] In this way, it is also possible to look at those writings as literary products that belong together within a social history that is much larger than, though never disconnected from, the local ones in which they were first engendered. The main theoretical inspiration here comes from the work of Sanjay Subrahmanyam as it articulates local and transregional imaginings within the framework of a connected history.[5] A tentative and at this point necessarily fragmentary connected history of those literary representations is therefore a good way to approach them. At any rate, it may be a novel way that will hopefully allow for a renewed emphasis on the apparent inherent connectedness of those imaginings wherever they seem to have come up.

II

> Somiela was stopped by his words. "I don't know of any white man who has married a slave. I'm a slave, and a Mohametan."
> "And I'm a baster.[6]"
> She didn't understand.
> . . . .
> "The woman you served coffee to is not my mother."
> "What?"
> "My mother was Sonqua. I found out when I was sixteen years old. My father told me."
> "You are—you're a—"
> "Yes. I'm like you. Not one, not the other. In the middle somewhere."[7]

Rayda Jacobs' novel is most probably the first novel about slavery written by a descendant of slaves in the Cape. It certainly is the first novel about slavery written by a Muslim woman in South Africa.[8] Fifty years before, another writer whom the South African government (before and during apartheid) would classify as "Coloured," just as in the case of Rayda Jacobs, wrote a novel about a love affair between a Coloured teacher, Lanny, from Cape Town, and Sarie, an Afrikaner woman in a Karoo *dorp* (small town or village) in the interior of the Cape. Harman, in Jacobs' novel, was considered white, but actually was not. He revealed himself to Somiela because he wanted to marry her. He would also convert to Islam in order to do that. Lanny is Christian, just as Sarie. But that made no difference in Peter Abrahams' ominously titled *The Path of Thunder*:

> Forgotten was the cardinal sin of their land, the sin condemned by everyone, from the church downward to the Labour party: the free and equal mixture of colours. Forgotten was the ugly word "miscegenation" that would be used to label their love. Forgotten were the stupid fears and prejudices that hemmed in and enchained the minds of men.
> They were alone and free and happy and in love. A boy and a girl in love.[9]

In another passage, Celia—a close friend of Lanny's from Cape Town—and Sarie have a conversation about him.

> "I want you to leave him alone."
> "For you?" Sarie asked softly.
> [. . . .]
> "No. Not for me but because nothing could ever come of it. You are white, he's Coloured. Nothing can ever come of it. There are lots

of white men from whom you could have chosen. Why did you have to choose him? Leave him alone for his own sake". [10]

Unsurprisingly, the apartheid government banned the novel. Previously, Peter Abrahams had immigrated to England (and later he would immigrate to Jamaica, where he still lives). He is one of South Africa's very first black writers (and its first Coloured novelist). Like many others after him, he felt that he could not be a normal person in the country of his birth, and hence his self-exile. At one point in this poignant novel, Sarie and Lanny think about leaving for Portuguese East Africa (namely, Moçambique) where they would be able to pursue their love freely (see, however, the description of Mendes' novel below, written in Moçambique in the years after the publication of *The Path of Thunder*—though a far cry from South Africa, colonial Moçambique was no "racial paradise").

Rayda Jacobs' postapartheid novel seems even more revolutionary when contrasted with one of South Africa's first novels about "miscegenation," namely Sarah Gertrude Millin's *God's Stepchildren* (that is, Coloureds, the people that Harman describes in the first excerpt as "in the middle somewhere"). It was first published in 1924 and, perhaps unsurprisingly, was first a success in the United States.[11] It is a historical novel that follows the progeny of an English missionary and a Koranna woman for a period close to one hundred years, until their descendant, the hapless white-looking Barry, returns to his relatives in the Cape interior, unable to live up to his whiteness (this last is presented as fake in the novel). Harman's father says, when his son tells him that he is marrying Somiela: "Black blood's a funny thing. You never know when it'll surface."[12] Millin would have agreed. Her novel is about the inevitability of failure due to racial taint even after generations of intermarriage and "whitening." As a *roman à thèse*, the novel makes for difficult reading nowadays, and seems hopelessly dated. Barry Lindsell could never be happy with the knowledge that he was not really white:

> Cape Town is as brown as it is white. Barry shuddered before the brown, and shivered before the white. One day, he was afraid, some Cape boy [i.e., "brown"] would come along and sense the hidden association between Barry and himself, claiming kinship. One day, he dreaded, some white person would feel that Barry was not what he was, and searching, would discover why. [13]

Interestingly, Barry will have a child from an Englishwoman whom he met while living in England, but the child will stay in England with her mother, not in the Cape. The narrator in Millin's novel briefly considers the possibility that people could successfully pass for white in the Cape's very ancient, creolised colonial society.[14] However, that possibility—sociologically speaking a fairly common one until well into the twentieth century[15]—is quickly brushed aside by the narrator so that Barry's relentless fall from grace can go on. Not the least irony in this whole saga is the fact that Millin was Jewish, and came from an immigrant family from Lithuania who were newcomers to South Africa. Jews were discriminated against in South Africa, and perhaps would only come to be officially once and for all classified as white as from 1948 with the onset of apartheid.[16] Then the National Party closed (white) ranks against what it saw as the rising threat of the masses of "Natives." It is very hard not to see her work retrospectively as a precursor of that view.[17]

Even without those biographical details, however, it is not too hard for the reader to suspect that Millin might be keeping a good deal of race-related ambiguity and doubt at bay by obsessively sketching a story of inevitable racial downfall for those "in the middle." The man who should actually be given the title of first Coloured writer, even though he never wrote a novel or a poem, Abdullah Abdurahman, was a good deal more sophisticated and ironic than Millin. He wrote in the years just before the publication of *God's Stepchildren*, namely, the first two decades of the twentieth century (though he would in fact be active as both journalist and politician until his death in 1940). He was also a keen social observer who loathed people who passed for white, but for somewhat different reasons. In a way, rather than racial traitors, as in Millin's novel, to him they were political traitors. However, race was actually also part of his discourse, and perhaps in this way he was not so far apart from Millin. He wanted Coloureds to be considered "civilised people" just as whites and be given the same rights. He was however often far less enthusiastic about the rights of "Natives." Abdurahman was the first Muslim to become a doctor in the Cape (he studied in Scotland). He was the grandson of slaves, and the son of a Muslim theologian trained at Al-Azhar in Cairo. He wrote a satirical column in the newspaper of his African Political Organization (APO) named "Straatpraatjes" ("Street Chat"), under the pseudonym of Piet Uithaalder, between 1909 and 1922.[18] In it he delivered some scathing political and social commentary. In 1911, for instance, he wrote:

> . . . da is bruine mense wat skaam is om op die straat met hulle vader of moeder te loop of met hulle te praat. En die mense wil graag hulle kinners in e wit school krij. [. . .] Dit is die soort van mense wat altoes die portret van hulle groot vader in die voor-kamer op hang, so laat alga kan sien dat hulle van Scotse of Hollandse afkomsel is. Ma as jij hulle vraa vir hulle ou ma sij portret dan al wat hulle kan se is "mij ou ma was e Kaapse vrou." Hulle kan jou nooit hulle ou ma s' portret weis nie.[19]

> . . . there are brown people who are ashamed of walking on the street with their father or mother or talk to them. And those people will prefer to put their children in a white school. [. . .] That is the kind of

people who always hang the portrait of their grandfather in the living
room, so as to let all see that they are of Scottish or Dutch origin. But
if you ask them for their mother's portrait then all they can say is that
"my mother was a Cape woman."[20] They can never show you a portrait
of their mother.[21]

In fact, Abdurahman was pointing out a good deal of ambiguity that prevailed in the Coloured community, as well as pointing out the varied origins
of that community. His irony and humour however would turn in later writers such as Millin and even Abrahams into sombre tragedy: in *The Path
of Thunder*, Lanny is killed because he is seeing a white woman. Another
novel, published just one year after Millin's, also has a tragic ending, as the
title character, Turbott Wolfe, dies. Natal in the 1920s was however a very
different place to the Cape. Namely, it was a province inhabited by English settlers and their descendants, a very small Afrikaans community, the
descendants of Indian indentured labourers, and Zulus. The community that
was the butt of Abdurahman's satire in the Cape was therefore not substantial enough. As a consequence William Plomer's *Turbott Wolfe* is not about
Coloureds, but about an Englishman who falls in love with a Zulu woman.
His love for her is however strictly platonic (perhaps unsurprisingly, as the
writer was gay).[22] Plomer was also a speaker of isiZulu, what was extremely
uncommon for a South African white writer of his generation.[23]
    Nonetheless, Turbott Wolfe gathers around himself a small group of
people to set up an organization—Young Africa—in favour of "miscegenation" (sic). Among them, there is an Afrikaans woman, Mabel van der
Horst, and Zachary, a Zulu man.[24]

> I allowed myself to reflect that these Colonial girls of very mixed an-
> cestry—not innocent of German blood—perhaps with a touch of the
> tar-brush, as they say—that girls who could marry blacks—. Yes, but
> as she walked away in her springing stride . . . she was no less than a
> goddess. [. . .]
>   What was her name? Her name was Eurafrica.[25]

Turbott Wolfe shocked many people in Natal.[26] As Plomer perhaps did
not have an axe to grind, unlike Millin, he felt freer to describe an actual
"interracial" relationship in fairly nonjudgmental terms. Though nowadays
a political grouping devoted to miscegenation seems a ludicrous thing (with
members of the group actually practicing it), differently to Millin's, Plomer's
novel is not a *roman à thèse*, not even in a sense opposite to that intended
by Millin. It has therefore retained a certain freshness that Millin's novel
does not have.
    There is no contemporary Afrikaans equivalent of Millin's or Plomer's
novels. It is not difficult to figure out why. Elsa Joubert has pointed out the
problem in her travelogue on Indonesia that is also an account of Leipoldt's

life and work. C. Louis Leipoldt was a famous Afrikaans poet who had served as a ship's doctor on a trip to the Indonesian archipelago—then the Dutch East Indies or Netherlands Indies—in 1912.[27] As a result of that trip, he had become interested in an Indo-European historical figure, that is, in a person of "mixed race." He started a poem on Pieter Elberfeld, and even published some of it, without, however, letting his South African readers know that his character was in fact of mixed ancestry. The Elberfeld poem was related to the project of writing a longer play that was actually never carried out.[28] As Joubert shows, Leipoldt in fact had praise to bestow on the Netherlands Indies government because it allowed mixed marriages and the children issuing from those marriages would often become legally European. That opinion would certainly not have gone down well in South Africa at the time (the late 1920s and early 1930s), let alone in the mouth of a cultural figure of renown such as Leipoldt, a "geliefde volksdigter," namely, a "beloved poet of the (Afrikaans) people."[29] That was about the time when the Afrikaans official cultural milieu was to become even more intolerant towards "miscegenation" than the English colonial milieu had been. Of course, Afrikaners also had a chip on their shoulder, as they had been despised by the English and their families were at times of mixed origins (therefore, not unlike Dutch families in the Netherlands Indies—as discussed later). Naturally, they had more than a few links to the Coloured population (who usually spoke the same language as they did and some-times professed the same religion as well—namely, a variety of Calvinism). Abdullah Abdurahman, particularly, often satirised Coloureds who passed as white Afrikaners.[30] It is therefore perhaps not a coincidence that both William Plomer and Peter Abrahams would choose an Afrikaans woman as the white partner in their respective stories of "miscegenation," and that Rayda Jacobs' more recent novel also centres on an Afrikaner (though this time it is a man). That those who were the product of "miscegenation" should have a horror of it is however commonplace in literary representations, where the mestizo or mulatto is often the most racist character in the narratives (as in Sadji's novel, discussed later in this chapter).

In fact, Herbert Dhlomo, a pioneering Zulu playwright and poet, would write a short story in 1935—called "An Experiment in Colour"—about an African man who had discovered a scientific secret, namely, how to turn himself into a white man through an injection, and then back into his old self through another injection.[31] This gripping short story shows an anguished man who decided to enjoy the privileges of whitedom to the point that he would get involved with a white woman, even though he was married (to an African one, of course). The story ends tragically, as South African stories related to "miscegenation" usually did: the man exposes his scientific feat in a public session, where both his wife and his white girlfriend are sitting side by side, and is shot dead—by an Afrikaans man. Afrikaans men are also Lanny's killers in *The Path of Thunder* (and Harman's killers as well in *The Slave Book*). This is the only story with a theme akin to "miscegenation" by an African author in South Africa that I have been able to trace. It is however a very poignant one as it depicts the inner workings of the segregation system (i.e., the system that preceded apartheid before 1948) and the toll it exacted.

Tragic novels would in fact continue to be published in South Africa, the most famous being perhaps the autobiographical *A Question of Power*, by Bessie Head, a South African writer from Natal (Plomer's birth province) who went into exile in Botswana during the heyday of apartheid.[32] In André Brink's *Gerugte van Reën* (*Rumours of Rain* in the English version), a slave man and a white woman born in the Cape rove around the far interior of the Cape colony after a disaster befell their party in the eighteenth century.[33] Skilfully written on the basis of a scrap of documented history, it weaves a tale of love that could only have happened in the wilderness. As the couple returns to the Cape, the man is, of course, killed. Colonial society cannot tolerate "miscegenation." Abdullah Abdurahman however indicated that it was not so in the early twentieth century.[34] One of the puzzling aspects of trying to understand South African narratives against their historical backgrounds is that for centuries South African society remained in practice fairly tolerant towards creolisation of various kinds. In this sense, it is hard to think of *Gerugte van Reën* as a typical eighteenth-century story, even though it is based on documentary evidence: in fact, it is rather easier to read it as an apartheid story. Namely, as a story engendered within the same society that caused Bessie Head, a Coloured writer, to exile herself in Botswana.[35]

Naturally, this incredibly negative picture has a counterpart not only in social practices but also in the law: in 1927 the new South African state (created in 1910) issued its first law about the matter, a precursor of the famous "Immorality Act" (sic) or Prohibition of Mixed Marriages Act of 1949.[36] This last would only be abolished in the 1980s. Throughout a good deal of the twentieth century, therefore, South Africa was a country where "miscegenation" was punishable by law. Nonetheless, the excerpt from Abdurahman's "Straatpraatjes" shows that at least the Cape (and in particular Cape Town) had an ancient history of creolisation, that in fact predated by well over two centuries the advent of the South African state in 1910. The Cape colony had been an outpost of the Dutch East Indies Company since 1652, and as such it belonged in the logic of the Company's Indian Ocean trade network (where it was initially just a refreshment station for ships bound to Asia or on the return trip from there to Europe). Of course, it is hard to think of another colonial space in the Indian Ocean where a highly creolised society eventually came to be so heavily penalized by an upcoming national state and its racial policies.[37] Nonetheless, in spite of its peculiarities, South Africa belongs in fact to a much vaster network centred on the Indian Ocean.

As I have argued elsewhere, there is an ancient Indian Ocean "technology" of creolisation of social practices, including marriages across ethnic and religious lines as well as what used to be called in colonial societies *"concubinage."*[38] This "technology" was perhaps exported to West Africa, the Caribbean, and the rest of the Americas with European colonization. However, it predates European presence in Asia by at least several centuries, as shown by the work of Amitav Ghosh, which highlights the relationship between a Tunisian Jewish trader and an Indian slave woman in Malabar in the twelfth century.[39] If anything, the South African case—if we may call it so—is one where the creolised society was seen, for various reasons, as a major threat to the rising national state. It would not be too exaggerated to say that apartheid eventually would arise as a system to control and discipline the creolised society as much as the "Natives," especially considering that the creolised society was seen as keeping an open door towards the Natives, at one end, and white society, at the other end. If there was something that worried the apartheid system, that was surely a certain fluidity of ethnic and other boundaries that was the hallmark of Cape just as of many other Indian Ocean societies.[40]

However, the highly creolised Cape world that we glimpsed in the quote from "Straatpraatjes" is actually a far cry even from a colonial society as near to South Africa as Southern Rhodesia (today's Zimbabwe). In Doris Lessing's story "The Antheap," part of the first volume of her *Collected African Stories*, Tommy, a white boy growing up in an isolated place where practically everybody else is African, wonders why his playmate, Dirk, is not the same colour as other "Kaffirs." His mother then tells him that Dirk is a "half-caste." She does not however explain to him what that is. There is a "rule of silence" about the subject that the boy has tried to break.[41] Tommy will brood for a long time until he finds out that Dirk is in fact the child of his father's boss, the mine owner, and an African woman. Then, as both boys grow up together, there will be a good deal to struggle for before both of them manage to obtain that Dirk's father pays for his education as well as Tommy's (of whom he is very fond even though he is only his employee's son). It is an oppressive story, set in a socially very harsh environment (an open-air mine), in what is, compared to a good deal of South Africa, a very new settler society where hardly any creolisation of the colonial kind had taken place. Dirk therefore does not belong to any proper social group, as would have been the case in the Cape. The story ends with both boys eventually going to South Africa for their further education, on scholarships provided by the mine owner himself.

III

Neighbouring colonial Moçambique, however, seems quite different from either country, and not only because it did not have South Africa's elaborate racial legislation nor Rhodesia/Zimbabwe's historically more recent (and much smaller) settler society. It is perhaps not a coincidence that Lanny and Sarie, in Abrahams' *The Path of Thunder*, at one point dream of leaving the Karoo and moving to Portuguese East Africa (i.e., Moçambique).

In the poem beginning with "Eu tenho uma lírica poesia" ("I have a lyrical poem"), originally written in 1959, Craveirinha sketches an encounter between a man and a *mulata*.[42] José Craveirinha is a *mulato* himself, and one of the leading figures in Moçambican letters. In one of his poems— "Mulata Margarida"—he intimates a world of sensuality and transnational contacts that has existed on the Moçambican coast for many centuries, linking it to other parts of the Indian Ocean as well as, after European presence began, other parts of the world (Brazil, for instance, has received a modicum of slaves and other immigrants from Mozambique, and so has the Cape[43]). In another poem, also about a woman, "Felismina," he describes her as she slowly strips herself on stage: "vais evoluindo alvejada a focos na barriga" ("you evolve as the spotlights aim at your belly").[44]

Orlando Mendes is a writer, one of Moçambique's first novelists. In his *Portagem*,[45] a novel written in the 1950s but only published in 1960, he tells the story of João Xilim, a *mulato*. He grows up in a small place, and becomes the *moleque* (i.e., the houseboy) of Maria Helena, a locally born Portuguese woman of the same age as him.[46] Just as in Doris Lessing's story, this one is also initially set in a mine in an isolated location (quite possibly just across the border from the place in colonial Rhodesia where Lessing sets her story). As they grow up, they eventually sleep together. However, as this was highly improper, João Xilim leaves for the wide world and becomes a sailor and stevedore, besides a foreman and a fisherman. In fact, it turns out that João Xilim was the son of an African woman and Maria Helena's father. He eventually comes across Patrão Campos ("Boss Campos"), his father, and Negra Kati ("Black Kati"), his mother, having sex in the bush.[47] He then runs away, though he will one day come back, only to leave again because Maria Helena and he are still attracted to each other. Prostitution is very common in João Xilim's surroundings.[48] One of the novel's characters, Marcelino, blurts out at one point:

> Os brancos pagam, levam as raparigas e depois cansam depressa e querem outras novas. Depois elas não voltam mais ao bairro onde nasceram. Andam de mão em mão, por todo o lado, até ficarem trinta anos mais velhas do que são. Às vezes, nasce um filho. Filho de ninguém, esta porcaria com pele nem preta nem branca que toda a gente cospe em cima. Para quê tudo isso?[49]

> The white men pay, take the young women away and then quickly become tired and want new ones. Next the women will not come back to their neighbourhoods. They go from hand to hand, all over the place, until they look thirty years older than their age. Some times a child is born. Nobody's child, just filth with a skin that is neither black nor white. Everybody spits on it. What is the point of all this?

João Xilim is a tortured soul who plans revenge. He will eventually set fire to the warehouse that hides the contraband business of Maria Helena's husband. He will however find a companion in Luísa, whom he (barely) saves from a sexual assault perpetrated by a white man as the novel comes to a close.

Mulatos are in fact even more important figures in Brazilian literature than in Moçambican letters. At any rate, they seem to be more abundant. A classic of naturalism, a literary current of the late nineteenth century, is for instance Aluísio Azevedo's O *Mulato*, first published in 1881. The *mulato* in question is a young white-looking, attractive, and wealthy man who, however, had a slave mother (of whose existence he was not aware as he was sent to Portugal at an early age[50]). Azevedo also published O *Cortiço* (1890), where there are couples where one partner is a Portuguese man, the other a black woman. The nonwhite partners in the couples in both novels meet a tragic end. The main character in O *Mulato* is killed by a Portuguese man (who happens to be racially superior to, but at the same time socially inferior to the *mulato*) who then marries his white fiancée after this last loses the *mulato*'s child which she had been carrying in her womb. Then would come another naturalist work, this time a short novel, *Bom-Crioulo* (literally, "Good Creole," in fact, a black man's name), by Adolfo Caminha, published in 1895. In it, a black sailor has an affair with a younger white sailor, and eventually kills the latter out of jealousy, as the boy had become the lover of a Portuguese woman in Rio. All these nineteenth-century novels are therefore very colonial in a way, even though Brazil was formally independent as from 1822. In all of them, colour hierarchies, as well as slave origin, are well marked (slavery would in fact only be abolished as late as 1888).

However, perhaps the most accomplished writer of the creolised society, at least in what concerns Rio de Janeiro, is Lima Barreto, a *mulato* himself. His writing is both tragic and satirical, and quite often is also very descriptive of working-class life in Rio in the first two decades of the twentieth century. His *Clara dos Anjos* (literally, Claire of the Angels), written in 1921–1922, is the story of the seduction and fall of a young *mulata* in the hands of a white con man, Cassi. She becomes pregnant from him. He then flees to São Paulo, also to escape the police who are after him for murder. Lima Barreto wrote a didactic novel: his point was to show how the main character had been misled because of overprotection on the part of her parents, as well as a certain lack of character and willpower (interestingly, it is a German woman who provides an example of both character and willpower in the novel). [51] The novel ends with Clara exclaiming in despair to her mother: 'Nós não somos nada nesta vida" ("We are nothing in this life" or, perhaps, "We are worth nothing at all"). [52]

In a story belonging to a collection first published in 1915, "Um Especialista," a Portuguese *comendador*[53] who is very fond of *mulheres de cor* or "women of colour" meets another Portuguese friend in Rio.[54] Alice, a *mulata*, is with them. As they talk, slowly it dawns on the *comendador* that Alice is actually his daughter. He had abandoned both Alice and her mother many years before, in Recife. The theme of male white seduction of women of colour is therefore a recurrent one in Lima Barreto's work. It also reminds the reader of Mendes' novel, *Portagem*, where there is also a blood tie between João Xilim and Maria Helena, though they are brother and sister (just as in Cola Debrot's novel, which will be discussed later) instead of father and daughter. Moreover, just as Clara dos Anjos, Alice too is a very sensual young woman (see also Nini in Sadji's novel, which will be discussed later, and Somiela in Jacobs' previously discussed novel). The trope of the beautiful, sensual, mulatto woman is an age-old trope in literature that seems to be truly transnational. In Pramoedya Ananta Toer's novel below, Anneliese is also a beautiful, doll-like Indo-European woman, and so is An, a mixed race prostitute, in Du Perron's *Het land van herkomst*. Lima Barreto is not nearly the accomplished poetic sensualist that Craveirinha is. However, it is very interesting that in his writings too there is a close link between sensuality and the body of a woman who is not white (and is not African either, as in Craveirinha's "Mulata Margarida"). That trope would become, in Brazil, practically an established one in many cultural spheres other than the literary one (for instance, in television, cinema, and vaudeville theatre, not to mention Carnival). Even if we restrict ourselves only to fiction and poetry, its ramifications are so multifarious as to make it hard to make a proper inventory. Though much less common, the image of the sensuous *mulato* is in fact also part of this imaginary.[55] In Menotti del Picchia's famous modernist poem, *Juca Mulato*, for instance, first published in 1917, the narrator describes an earthy man in a poetic language for which it is difficult to provide a proper translation (therefore what follows is only a very rough translation of this beautiful poem):

> E um prazer bestial lhe encrespa a carne e os nervos,
> afla a narina; o peito arqueja; uma lasciva
> onda de sangue lhe incha as veias do pescoço . . .
> . . . . . .
> e um pubescente ansiar de abraços e de beijos
> incendeia-lhe a pele e estua-lhe no sangue.

> And bestial pleasure tenses his flesh and nerves,
> dilates his nostrils; his chest heaves; a lascivious
> flush of blood thickens the veins of his neck . . .
> . . . . . .
> and a pubescent desire for embracing and kissing
> sets fire to his skin and curdles his blood. [56]

Juca Mulato is attracted to the daughter of his boss, not unlike João Xilim to Maria Helena in Mendes' *Portagem*. However, differently to what happens in *Portagem*, he does not sleep with her (nor is he said to be her brother). He is actually hurt by this love that cannot be, and this pain is the base of a good deal of the poem.[57]

Nelson Rodrigues is perhaps one of Brazil's most famous playwrights. One of his first plays is about an interracial couple. *Anjo Negro* ("Black Angel") was first staged in 1948 (it was written in 1946), after having been briefly censored by the Brazilian government. Ironically the play was both censored and then staged in the same year that the apartheid government was elected in South Africa. It is also the year when Peter Abrahams published his *The Path of Thunder* in London, also censored in South Africa. Obviously, on both sides of the South Atlantic the mention of white and black couples caused unease in official circles.[58] The play is a complex one. It is one of Rodrigues' "mythic" plays, namely, it is not to be taken as a realist piece of work. A black doctor marries a white woman, who has a child by his brother, Elias (who is however white, as he is an adopted child; Elias is also blind). The plot is thick with all kinds of intrigue and ambiguity, as well as infanticide, and in this it is a fairly typical Rodrigues play. Virgínia, even though she married a black man, is shown to be racist. Ismael in fact is also said to hate blacks and consequently to be steeped in self-hatred. The characters in the play give vent to a good deal of fairly typical colour stereotypes in Brazil, especially the white characters. As he learns that his wife has betrayed him with his white brother and had a child by him, Ismael thinks aloud:

> É castigo . . . Sempre tive ódio de ser negro. Desprezei, e não devia, o meu suor de preto . . . Só desejei o ventre das mulheres brancas . . . Odiei minha mãe, porque nasci de cor . . . Invejei Elias porque tinha o peito claro . . . Agora estou pagando . . . Um Cristo preto marcou minha carne . . . Tudo porque desprezei meu suor.[59]

> It is a punishment . . . I have always felt hatred for being black. I have despised my black man's sweat, even though I should not have . . . I have also desired only the womb of white women . . . I have hated my mother, because I was born of colour . . . I have envied Elias because he had a white chest . . . Now I am paying for it . . . A black Christ has branded my flesh . . . All because I have despised my own sweat . . .

Ismael blinds his white daughter Ana Maria (that is, the daughter of Virgínia and Elias), and therefore she grows up believing that he is a white man. In the end, both Ismael and Virgínia will enclose Ana Maria alive in a glass grave in the backyard. Virgínia had previously killed all her other children as infants because they were not white. After burying their daughter alive, Ismael and Virgínia go into the house to make love and the play ends.

Rodrigues would also mention black and white relationships in his other plays. In *Os Sete Gatinhos* ("The Seven Kittens"), a white teenage girl covertly pays a group of black men to carry out a gang rape—of herself. In *Toda Nudez Será Castigada* ("All Nakedness Shall Be Punished"), the young scion of a wealthy family ends up in jail and is raped by a Bolivian

Indian. He will eventually leave for La Paz with the Indian man, leaving behind a tearful stepmother who was a former prostitute (whom his widowed father had taken out of the brothel and made into his lawfully wedded wife). She has fallen in love with him and will kill herself after he leaves. Rodrigues spares the viewer nothing in terms of family conflict, sexuality, guilt, and betrayal (Rodrigues, 2003). Whereas Lima Barreto is a lower middle-class man of colour whose characters fight to keep a precarious foothold in the world of respectability (and usually fail, especially if they are women), Rodrigues pitilessly dissects the world that Lima Barreto's characters aspire to, exposing its many ambiguities and dark corners.

Brazil therefore presents a cornucopia of many different images and representations of black and white relationships (with the occasional Amerindian thrown in).[60] That sensuousness and sensuality should be part of a good deal of them is, to my mind, a far less researched aspect (perhaps because it is a much more complex one too: it is fairly easy to condemn such representations as merely racist or sexist, thereby throwing the baby out with the water).[61] However, this is not in the least a Brazilian characteristic only: it shows up in the work of authors such as Craveirinha, and, unsurprisingly, also in the work of authors writing in the Caribbean outside the Lusophone area proper. Recently, a friend who is a Curaçaoan scholar pointed out to me, for instance, that the work of one of Papiamentu's greatest poets, Pierre Lauffer, is often considered sexist. Curaçaoan literature in fact finds itself at the very intersection between South America and the larger Caribbean region (it somehow replicates therefore the geographical location of Curaçao, an island close to the Venezuelan coast). Papiamentu too is a Creole language that is inbetween South America and the Caribbean, as it has a lexical heritage derived from Portuguese (and, to a lesser extent, Spanish) as well as a West African past.[62] In "Karta na mi negra," Lauffer describes a black woman's body and the desire it inspires in him.[63] In a poem of 1961, "Shi Kanin'e Rosaminta," Lauffer writes about Shi Kanina's walking through an alley in Punda (Curaçao) and her earrings swinging to the rhythm of her hips.[64] Habibe rightly compares Lauffer's poetry to that of another Caribbean poet, namely, Luis Palés Matos from Puerto Rico. Palés Matos also writes about a queen that swings her hips.[65] The poem begins with the line "Culipaleando la Reina avanza" or "The Queen progresses swinging" her hips. Then her hips become a bed for "rivers of sugar and molasses." In another of Lauffer's poems, "Nigra Dea," the poet mentions a "tongue of flame" licking a "beast of tar." In yet another poem, he mentions a "black love" that has a flame of "ferocious passion."[66]

Interestingly, if we change both language and skin colour, the Creole love is still there, but the poetics of it becomes far less appealing to the reader. Cola Debrot was a Creole white writer, also from Curaçao (Lauffer was not white, but someone who might have been called a *mulato* in Brazil). He wrote in Dutch, however. His *Mijn zuster de negerin* (literally,

"My Sister the Black Woman") caused some impact when it first came out in the Netherlands in 1935.[67] It is a far cry both from the rich sensuality of Lauffer's poems and the tragedy oozing out of South Africa's novels on "miscegenation." Compared to the latter, Debrot's short novel is in fact a balm to read. There is not a chance that anybody will be killed or even disgraced. Frits Ruprecht is a kind of Dutch-Antillean version of Lima Barreto's Portuguese *comendador*, namely, a wealthy white man who openly wants to indulge in his taste for black women.[68] He comes home to Curaçao from the Netherlands to live in the family *plantage*, a kind of middle sized farming operation bringing only moderate profit at best (being small and fairly dry, Curaçao is historically a trading island rather than a source of plantation products—the *plantages* and their *landhuizen* were therefore rather symbols of prestige and status). There he meets Maria, whom he remembers from his childhood. She is Theodoor's (a black labourer on the *plantage*) daughter. She became a teacher, but, somewhat mysteriously, came back to live and work on the *plantage*. The fact that she had managed to study to become a teacher—an unusual career for a labourer's daughter, the novel intimates—is already a sign that Maria is no common woman.

> Frits herinnerde zich levendig dit jonge zwarte meisje. Zij was zo zwart als men onder de vrij gemengde negers van het eiland bijna niet aantrof. Maar er was iets zeer bijzonders aan haar: haar schedelvorm, haar neus, haar lippen waren die van een blanke, hadden niets negers.

> Frits had a lively memory of that young black woman. You almost never came across someone so black among the very mixed *negers* of the island. But there was something peculiar about her: her skull shape, her nose, her lips were those of a white person, they had nothing *negers* in them.[69]

As the story proceeds, Frits begins to suspect that Maria is in fact not Theodoor's daughter, but his own father's. It was common for white Creoles to foist their offspring on a subaltern black man. It was equally common for them to take an interest in the fate of their children (hence Maria's teacher's diploma).[70] Frits finds himself spending the night alone with Maria, who is the housemaid, inside the *landhuis*, the family big house. Frits is about to sleep with Maria when Wantsjo, the old caretaker, knocks at his door. Frits sends him away, but as he is going back to the bedroom (that had been his mother's) and to Maria, Wantsjo screams through the door: "Maria is de dochter van uw vader!!" ("Maria is your father's daughter!!"). Frits then resigns himself to the fact that he had found a sister and lost a lover: the novel ends with both of them in a close embrace as tears roll down Maria's cheeks.

IV

Colonial novels from Indonesia are full of references to "concubines" (*huishoudsters* in Dutch ("householders") or *njai* in Javanese and Malay[71]), "Indos" (i.e., Indo-Europeans or people of mixed descent, usually with legal European status) and *Indische mensen* ("Indies people," that is, commonly local people with European legal status but often with non-European ancestors in the archipelago). What in Brazil and the rest of Latin America and the Caribbean is a fairly common literary product, in what concerns Indonesia is, as far as I know, more often than not branded with the name "colonial" or, in the Netherlands, with the epithet *Nederlands-Indisch* or literature pertaining to the Netherlands Indies.[72] Therefore, in an exercise such as this one that takes into account various kinds of writing in different languages and colonial and postcolonial spheres, the inclusion of Indonesia is problematic from the beginning, as there is a language split (between Dutch and Malay/Bahasa Indonesia) that is also largely a split between a colonial and a postcolonial literature. As my access to Indonesian-language books in Brazil has been nil, I am at a loss to cover literature that strides the momentous divide of independence and language change (namely, from the Netherlands Indies to Indonesia, and from Dutch into Indonesian). It is therefore much more difficult to see someone as Edgar du Perron, for instance, a famous Java-born Indies writer, as an Indonesian writer than it is to see Cola Debrot as a Curaçao one.[73] However it may be, as we will see later, the Creole society comes up powerfully in the works of many colonial writers, as well as in that of at least one postcolonial author.

Before proceeding, however, I would like to call the reader's attention to one detail: the label "colonial" hides in fact an incredibly nuanced and complex literary environment. For instance, modern Indonesian fiction has strong roots in Chinese Malay fiction written in Indonesia (especially in Java) as it developed between 1880 and 1940. That fiction however has traditionally been largely deleted from official histories of Indonesian literature, and hardly anybody except for a few scholars will read Chinese Malay works nowadays. However, at least some of those works revealed themes and concerns that were clearly similar to that of Dutch Indies literature in Dutch, and postcolonial Indonesian literature as well. Nevertheless, as literary historiographies are segregated by language, as well as nationality, not to mention ethnicity, that fact has become historically largely invisible. Just for the record, there are a few Chinese Malay novels that deal with relationships across the legally enforced racial lines of the Netherlands Indies. For instance, Liem Khing Hoo published *Manoesia Machloek Gila* ("Mankind as Crazy Spirits") in 1939. It is the story of the marriage between a Chinese man and an *Inlander* or "Native" woman that ends in tragedy. Before that, Soe Lie Piet had published *Oeler jang Tjantik* ("The Pretty Leech" [sic]) in 1929.[74] The novel is about a Peranakan man (that is, a Javanese Chinese) who had a "Native" concubine (*nyai*) and therefore neglected his wife. Njoo Cheong Seng (pen name, Monsieur d'Amour) wrote *Nona Olanda sebagai Istri Tionghoa* ("A Dutchwoman as Chinese Wife"), published in 1925. The wife dies and the husband suffers. Nor was the subject restricted to Peranakan writers. Abdul Muis published in 1928 *Salah Asuhan* ("Poor Upbringing") about the marriage between a "Native" man and an Indo-European woman that also ends in tragedy.[75] Madelon Székely-Lulofs, a well-known Indies writer whose works used to be widely read and were translated into several languages from the 1930s to the 1950s, wrote *De andere wereld* ("The Other World"). The novel tells the story of a Dutch-man in Sumatra (a kind of Van Oudijck as in Couperus' novel, a discussion of which will follow) whose Dutch wife discovers that her husband had a *njai* (householder or "concubine") and children before marrying her.[76] In "Isah," a short story from the collection *Emigranten* by the same author, a Javanese labourer on a very isolated plantation in Sumatra goes to live with a young Dutch *assistant* (a kind of overseer) as his *njai*. The story is not devoid of eroticism (the couple is very young). However, the Dutchman is eventually murdered by Iman, Isah's former Muslim companion.[77]

From the postcolonial end, Pramoedya Ananta Toer is a writer whose themes and writing often straddle the temporal, linguistic, and concep-tual borders between colony and postcolonial state (incidentally, he was once the most vocal postcolonial writer in the country when it came to denouncing state persecution against Chinese Indonesians). *Bumi Manusia* is the first book in the Buru Quartet, a tetralogy first thought out on Buru Island, where the author was sent into exile by the Indonesian government. Though first published in 1980 (and banned soon afterwards), it first saw life on Buru as an oral tale committed to memory by his creator that was only written down much later.[78]

> Bukan hanya Mevrow Télinga atau aku, rasanya siapa pun tahu, begitulah tingkat susila keluarga nyai-nyai: rendah, jorok, tanpa ke-budayaan, perhatiannya hanya pada soal-soal berahi-mata. Mereka hanya keluarga pelacur, manusia tanpa pribadi, dikodratkan akan tenggelam dalam ketiadaan tanpa bekas. (. . .) Semuah lapisan ke-hidupan menghukum keluarga nyai-nyai; juga semua bangsa: Pribumi, Eropa, Tionghoa, Arab.

> It is not only Mrs. Télinga or I, but, I believe, everybody else as well, who thinks that the moral level in the families of *nyai* [i.e., "concu-bines"] is low, filthy, uncultured, and that all they are concerned about is sexual matters. Those families are immoral, their members without individual personality, destined to disappear without a trace. (. . .) Ev-ery class of society [existence] passes judgment on the families of *nyai*; also, every people: Native, European, Chinese, Arab.[79]

A good deal of the novel is concerned with the relationship between a young man from the traditional Javanese aristocracy, Minke, and Anneliese, the daughter of Nyai Ontosoroh and a demented Dutchman. The relationship (depicted as a very chaste one as if to give the lie to colonial and postcolonial imaginings of "immorality" related to families of *njai*) ends as Anneliese is eventually claimed by her Dutch half-brother in the Netherlands and is therefore forcefully sent to Europe by the authorities. Nyai Ontosoroh and Minke are totally powerless to do anything about it, and so is Anneliese herself. Interestingly, by this device the Indo-European character leaves the nation-to-be and moves to its proper place, namely, Europe, the place where most Indo-Europeans would in fact eventually end up after decolonization: "destined to disappear without a trace" (and, indeed, there are hardly any traces of Indo-Europeans in postcolonial Indonesia).[80] Interestingly, that is also somehow the fate of Ducroo, Edgar du Perron's persona in his literary autobiography, *Het land van herkomst*.[81] This is probably the most ironically titled novel of all Netherlands Indies literature, as the "The Country of Origin" is by definition somebody else's country (namely, the country of the Javanese). Ducroo is officially European (the author however had an Asian slave ancestress as many Indies families did, and just as some Afrikaans families in the Cape). He has had affairs with local women, like An, a Sundanese mestizo woman, but, differently to his elder brother, refuses to give in to colonial practice and take in a *nyai*.[82] He eventually goes to Europe where he finds a European woman, as many a colonial before him. Pramoedya Ananta Toer's subversive postcolonial reading of Indies society, where Nyai Ontosoroh is a figure of great strength and is clearly the main character in the novel after Minke, though not absent, for Du Perron is very critical of Indies society, is however not so marked in *Het land van herkomst*. Perhaps not the least difference in perspective is that in Du Perron's narrative colonial males (including some very unsavoury figures) are clearly the main characters. Perhaps this difference of both perspective and emphasis, more than anything else, is what marks Du Perron's classic as a colonial work (or perhaps, more properly, as a hybrid product, standing as it does at the tail end of the colonial era).

Set at about the same time as Pramoedya Ananta Toer's much later novel, an early classic of Netherlands Indies literature is Louis Couperus' *De stille kracht* ("The Silent Force"), first published in 1900. It is clearly a colonial work. It is a strange book by a famous Dutch author that lay half-forgotten for many decades after his death, until it was resuscitated a couple of decades ago (the 1990s in particular saw a spat of renewed interest in Netherlands Indies literature in the Netherlands). It reminds the reader of a contemporary work by a more accomplished writer, namely, Joseph Conrad's *Almayer's Folly*, first published in 1895. Just as in the case of Couperus, Conrad is also a European man with life experience in the Indies who later goes on to write about the region (however, his narrative is set in the Outer Islands rather than in Java as in Couperus' case).

The perspective of the narrator in both novels is not too different: namely, he is critical and even scornful of local society, but his characters actually have to give in to it in the narrative. Also, a good deal of local detail comes out in both novels. Almayer—a Dutchman born in Java—is destroyed by the milieu where he finds himself in one of the Outer Islands. Though a much stronger and more august personage, Van Oudijck, a high colonial official, this time of Netherlands origin, ultimately suffers a not too dissimilar fate in Java (Almayer, however, ends up dead). Namely, he gives in to local society and ends up cohabiting with a "Native" woman (in his case, for the second time in his life). One of the main characters in *De stille kracht* is Léontine, an Indies born woman full of sensuousness, Van Oudijck's wife. She eventually finds herself in love with Addy, a Sundanese mestizo of a local aristocratic family of the area where her husband is *Resident* (a kind of glorified "Native" commissioner, to use a term from British Africa). There is even an intimation of homosexuality as Addy apparently also seduces Theo, Van Oudijck's mixed race but officially European son. In both novels, the European man is at a loss to impose himself in a highly creolised society: rather, he is imposed upon. Almayer ends up becoming an opium addict in a Muslim-controlled society as his house (a would-be trading station) is taken over by a Chinese man. His local wife has since long left him. The silent force ominously wins over Europe.

The irony is that what in Indies society was somewhat shameful in European circles, though quite common, namely, a complex creolised past (and, it is important to add, present), became quite useful during the Japanese occupation between 1942 and 1945. Then some people of official European status would desperately try to stay out of the internment camps by invoking their non-European ancestry, as Adriaan van Dis, a Dutch writer of Indies origin, mentions in his poignant postcolonial portrait of Indies life reminisced in exile (namely, in the Netherlands). Van Dis in fact describes a process that is the exact opposite of that described by Abdullah Abdurahman in his "Straatpraatjes," presented earlier in the chapter, when people in the Cape were never able to produce a portrait of their non-European ancestress: "Voor de oorlog stopte iedereen zijn inlandse oma's in de doofpot, maar onder de jap wisten de mensen niet hoe gauw ze ze te voorschijn moesten toveren."[83] In translation: "Before the war people hid their Native grandmothers in the closet,[84] but under the Jap [sic] they could not charm them into appearing fast enough." The postcolonial era had been ushered in.

V

The family album that deletes "Native" (in this case, African) ancestry also has a prominent place in Abdoulaye Sadji's intricately woven narrative, *Nini mulâtresse du Sénégal* ("Nini the mulatto woman of Senegal").[85] The novel is still read in Senegal, where its author—an early intellectual of *négritude*—still enjoys considerable fame almost half a century after his death in 1961. This novel is by far the most interesting one I have come across in all my readings. It is not so because of its aesthetic quality (some of the other authors that I have read are more accomplished writers than Abdoulaye Sadji), though it is a well-written novel. Intriguingly, perhaps because it was written by someone who is neither someone "in the middle" nor a European himself (the case of the vast majority of writers whose work has been considered here bar Pramoedya Ananta Toer), but a Senegalese Muslim man, or perhaps because he was suffused with the ideals of *négritude* (and was therefore very sensitive about racial hierarchies), Abdoulaye Sadji has written the most detailed, intimate and descriptive novel I know about a Creole life "in the middle." The work reminds the reader of, for instance, *Clara dos Anjos* (perhaps the novel in Brazil that offers the clearest counterpart to *Nini*). The narrator's perspective is clearly male, and his language usually ironic and even condemnatory as he describes Nini's lifestyle and that of her milieu in the old colonial town of Saint-Louis nestled at the mouth of the Senegal river. He however is never didactic, differently to Lima Barreto's narrator.[86] In fact, his language and perspective reminds the reader of that of his contemporary, Frantz Fanon, as he wrote at about the same time, in another French colony, namely, Martinique, his famous *Peau noire, masques blancs*. In it, Fanon condemns vehemently the works of another Martinican writer, Mayotte Capécia, who is a local *mulâtresse*. Through a critique of Capécia's works, Fanon inveighs against the same kind of prejudices and Eurocentric perspective that Sadji's narrator deprecates in *Nini*.[87] In fact, Sadji's narrator often portrays Nini as a racist, narrow-minded, petit-bourgeois, provincial, and even utterly silly, self-complacent and superficial young woman. In spite of all this—or even more intriguingly, perhaps because of all this—Sadji's novel counts, to my mind, as a major accomplishment, both in the literary field and in the domain of deep descriptions of the intricacies of a Creole life.[88]

Nini is white-looking, just as several other Creole characters—for instance, Harman in Rayda Jacobs' novel, Theo van Oudijck and use Couperus," or Raimundo in Azevedo's classic *O mulato*.[89] Differently to those characters, however, she does not quite pass as white (though she likes to think of herself as such). Her dream, we are told, is that of every young *mulâtresse* in Saint-Louis, namely, to marry a European man (from Europe—differently to Java and, to a lesser degree, Martinique, locally born European men apparently do not exist in Saint-Louis). In fact, Nini comes from a long lineage of *signares* (from Portuguese *senhoras*)[90] who for centuries would amass riches and children from passing European traders in the Senegambian coast, in a process quite similar to what happened on the coasts of the Indian Ocean since well before colonial times.[91] It is only on page 185, however, that the reader learns that Nini's real name is Virginie (Virginie Maerle, in fact), as the *mulâtresses* are always called, so the narrator assures the reader, by short names such as Nini, Nana, Dedée,

Madou, and so on. The racial hierarchy, even in a comparatively privileged location such as Saint-Louis in late colonial Senegal, is like an iron fist in your face: the main employer, the government, has three types of contracts, according to whether you are European (in which case you would benefit from the most advantageous contract), *mulâtre* or *noir* (that is, African. Africans get of course the worst contracts).[92] In Nini's family album, there are no portraits of the family's African relatives who, however, live in a neighbourhood just across the bridge from her home. Nini has also another album, with photographs of her French boyfriends (who mostly leave her when they go back to France), where there are some nude pictures of herself too. She will show these only to selected viewers. A highly placed African man proposes to her, and she refuses, in horror. She will also demission as she discovers that she got a European-type contract (which is very unusual for a young *mulâtresse*) because of her Tante Hortense's (and therefore her own) African relations across the river (Senegal—and the whole of French West Africa—is just a few years away from its independence, and France is handing over power and influence to locals).

Her *beau*, Martineau, is a Frenchman who eventually loses his job in the private enterprise where Nini also used to work as a typist (the quintessential job for young *mulâtresses* in the novel). He promises to marry Nini, but leaves the country and later she learns that he will return, but to distant French Equatorial Africa, and accompanied by his European wife (in this, Martineau is like Ducroo in Du Perron's narrative, who would not marry An—and, differently to Martineau, not even promise to do so—but instead would also go to Europe to marry a European woman). Though she is an attractive young woman, very adroit in the arts of seduction like many a Creole woman (as the narrator stresses again and again in rich detail), like the vast majority of her peers in fact she cannot hook a European man. As Martineau leaves after having promised to marry her on his return, Nini in fact falls prey to an uneasy feeling.

> Son cœur s'alourdit; elle se reproche son attitude de quémandeuse vis-à-vis de Martineau et de tous les Blancs. [. . .] Pourquoi faut-il qu'elle soit éternellement celle qui convoite, quémande, supplie ? Est-elle donc une mendiante d'amour ? Elle songe à disparaître de la terre, à s'en aller quelquer part . . . Le mensonge de son existence et de celle de toutes les mulâtresses, ses consœurs, lui apparaît clairement, grossi par la déception que vient de lui infliger le départ brusque de l'amant. [. . .] Le destin les a toutes condamnées à cette vie sentimentale de bohème qui tantôt s'illumine d'une certitude ou d'un espoir, tantôt se trouve empoisonnée par leur condition d'hybrides n'appartenant à aucune société normale.[93]

Her heart is heavy; she reproaches herself for her pleading stance towards Martineau and all the white men. [. . .] Why does she have to be eternally the woman who desires, pleads, supplicates? Is she by any chance a beggar of love? She dreams of disappearing from the face of the earth, of going away somewhere. . . . The deception of her existence and that of all *mulâtresses*, her sisters, appears clearly to her, made worse by the disappointment that she has just suffered on account of her lover's sudden departure. [. . .] Fate has condemned all of them to this sentimental life of a *bohème*. This life at times is illuminated by either certainty or hope, and at other times is poisoned by their condition of hybrid women that do not belong to any normal society.

Like many before her, she has been duped and is now the object of ridicule in her provincial town (she is also scorned because people suspect that she ingratiated herself with a man from the rising African elite in order to get her government job with a European contract. Tante Hortense only much later tells her about her asking her relatives across the river to use their influence on her behalf. She will heftily condemn Nini for quitting her hard-won job and will ostracize her niece inside the family home). Differently to Anneliese's fate in Pramoedya Ananta Toer's *Bumi Manusia*, who is mostly a passive character, Nini sells a house that she has inherited and ends up leaving for France in self-imposed exile. She is actually portrayed as a very courageous young woman as she gives up her prestigious job and sells part of the family property without telling her Tante Hortense, as well as leaves without telling anyone outside her family (as all her *mulâtresse* friends had failed her). She has therefore virtually severed ties with her milieu and her country (in this, she is not unlike Anneliese). She will probably never come back. Considering her life, her desires, and prospects in Saint-Louis, it is very hard for the reader not to sympathize with her decision. The novel finishes as she boards the daily Air France flight plying the route from South America to Paris and stopping over in Dakar (by the way, that was the flight that for many decades would fly the route between Argentina, Brazil, Senegal, and France). Now she will soon belong to the metropolis as she has left for good the colonial space: Saint-Louis, a fluvial island at the mouth of the Senegal river, a suffocating enclave where she inhabited a provincial milieu far away from Europe and yet forever keeping Africa at arm's length. A milieu that just like herself could not survive far into the postcolonial era (or so the novel seems to intimate).

Just as in Pramoedya Ananta Toer's novel, here too the Creole woman— as in the case of the Indo-European beauty, Anneliese—belongs properly to the metropolis rather than to the postcolonial nation in waiting. In Azevedo's *O Mulato*, Raimundo's returning to São Luís from Portugal eventually causes his death; in Millin's *God's Stepchildren*, Barry's child will have to be born in England, where the colonial stigma of race will not reach it. The colonial space is deadly for the white-looking Creole. Accordingly, even in Rayda Jacobs' postapartheid historical novel Harman is killed towards the end, after having converted to Islam, marrying a slave (having first secured her freedom) and having a child by her.

Therefore, not even the postcolonial, postapartheid nation seems to be able to bear the ambiguity posed by the existence of the white-looking Creole! Unwittingly or not, Millin therefore does seem to have touched in her novel a deep chord in what concerns powerful and deeply rooted racial imaginings. Cronjé, an Afrikaans sociologist who wrote on the desirability of apartheid in the 1940s, had as his nemesis the figure of the white-looking Coloured man who would "infiltrate" his black blood into the white community by seducing a white woman. To Cronjé, he is the most dangerous figure in the South African social landscape, for he opens the door to the *mengelmoes-samelewing*, namely, a society where there is no distinction between the races and consequently every identity boundary has collapsed.[95] In Brazil, however, the white-looking Creole is not necessarily doomed.[96]

VI

Perusing the various kinds of writing explored in this chapter has actually given rise to even more questions. The first, and perhaps most impressive, is that which is related to national literary historiographies, and even national histories. All these novels and other writings are clearly related in theme and perspective, even though they were written in places very far away from each other, and in languages and literary traditions that are not necessarily directly conversant with each other. This commonality is somewhat hard to account for, and even harder to ignore. The overwhelming importance of gender relations in their connectedness to "race" and colour is equally hard to ignore. Also, it is clear that the theme straddles not only oceans and continents, but also the impressive divide between precolonial, colonial, and postcolonial times. Though the materials examined here are mostly of the twentieth century, it is important to indicate that the time span in which the Creole societies that have been their subject matter have developed can be incredibly long. Also, those Creole societies seem to have been both enormously resilient and fluid.

Another aspect that comes out powerfully can sometimes be condemned as a mixture of racism and sexism: Nini's subjectivity, for instance, so skilfully described by Abdoulaye Sadji, is not necessarily easy to understand nor accept. Nor are Lauffer's poems in Curaçao and Craveirinha's in Moçambique, not to mention Palés Matos' in Puerto Rico. Jorge Amado's famous novel, *Gabriela, Cravo e Canela* also comes to mind here. They all sing about the beauty and sensuality of the Creole woman, a subject to which Indian Ocean writers and poets such as Craveirinha and Mendes were also not indifferent. In comparison to them, writing coming out of Indonesia, for instance, seems almost reticent about eroticism and sensuality (this is perhaps one major difference between Asian, on the one hand, and Caribbean, African, and much Lusophone writing, on the other hand).

This aspect—that comes out powerfully even in Abdoulaye Sadji's otherwise somewhat sober writing—needs further research. It is clearly not a marginal phenomenon, nor one that is merely ancillary to the writing in question. In fact, it is perhaps a fundamental aspect to the Creole societies that inspired the imaginary behind the writing. These have been societies where, at least in their literary renderings, sensuality and eroticism are virtually interwoven not only in the fabric of gender relations, but also in the very subjectivity of the people concerned (Nini is a case in point). It is perhaps also the most subversive aspect of Creole societies as it threatens all kinds of hierarchies and boundaries: not unsurprisingly, one of the first acts of the postcolonial Moçambican government was to destroy the bohemian quarter in Maputo from which Craveirinha and many other Moçambicans had received their creative inspiration. Also, significantly, next door to Moçambique, in an earlier time the very first law of the apartheid government had been the Mixed Marriages Act of 1949, also ominously called the "Immorality Act."[96]

The whiff of "prostitution" and "immorality" that comes off the novels and poems is therefore almost impossible to separate from the eroticism and sensuality that are also part and parcel of many of them, as well as from their more properly sociological contexts and historical backgrounds. Nini's milieu, for instance, is almost strangely bourgeois as well as skillfully geared towards seduction of the white man. In *Clara dos Anjos*, the tension between petit-bourgeois respectability and narrow-mindedness, on the one hand, and free-wheeling bohemian life and crime, on the other hand, is at times so strong that the narrative almost bursts at the seams (in this sense, Sadji's novel is perhaps a more contained or accomplished narrative). Pramoedya's Nyai Ontosoroh, written from the perspective of the postcolonial nation, is presented to the reader as a strong moral pillar, as well as an excellent mother to Anneliese, her Indo-European, fairly passive, doll-like daughter. She is also a highly competent manager of her hopelessly deranged Dutch husband's dairy business. She is moreover a politically very combatant person who is deeply aware of colonial inequalities. It is hard to believe that the author is not, say, overcompensating for the colonial stereotype of the *nyai* by presenting us with a staunchly anticolonial subaltern that stands up for her rights at all times, even when she has no chance to win, as in the court case that eventually leads to Anneliese's forceful withdrawal from the colonial space. What could be more subaltern than a *nyai* sold as a teenager by her peasant parents to a white man, as happened with Nyai Ontosoroh as well as many of her real life counterparts in colonial times? In fact, Pramoedya's portrait of Nyai Ontosoroh—probably the most famous *nyai* in Indonesian literature—is so forceful as to be almost un-lifelike.

Lima Barreto's Clara dos Anjos is by far the weakest of the three characters, as she gives in to Cassi, becomes pregnant and is abandoned like many before her (and like her Senegalese counterpart, Nini, though this last does not become pregnant). One of the women that Cassi had previously seduced, also black, appears to him again in a very derelict part of the centre of Rio in a harrowing scene: after his dumping her, she had become a low-life prostitute. In fact, the threat and whiff of prostitution envelops all the young female characters here (again, Nini comes to mind, as does Anneliese, even though this last is from a very rich milieu. In fact, Anneliese's association with Minke, a Javanese man, casts a shadow of immorality over her that will eventually lead to her official abduction from the colonial space into the protected space of the metropolis). However, as Lima Barreto's novel closes, the narrator shows Clara the way ahead in this didactic novel: she has to become as strong as Margarida, the German woman, who is not wholly unlike Nyai Ontosoroh in this last's also Germanic-like determination and strength. Nini in fact turns out to be strong: she has been abandoned, and family and friends have utterly failed her, not to mention her would-be fiancé, but she shows that she has a mind of her own as she sells her property and leaves the country in search of a better life in the metropolis (a space to which Clara has no access as she lives in a postcolonial state). The narrators in the three novels, therefore, only turn their characters into figures of respect as they clearly outgrow their allotted destinies. The poems, however—Craveirinha's, Lauffer's, and Palés Matos'—do not seem to be in the least didactic. The women are sung and admired as they are, whether queens or prostitutes (or both). In a way, the poems are much more complex than the novels, as they point to a quotidian world of sensuousness and eroticism that the moral and national frameworks within which the novels inevitably move perhaps can barely contain except in irony and condemnation.[97]

In this light, even Rayda Jacobs' *The Slave Book* is not really an exception. True, Somiela's officially white man, Harman, makes her pregnant in a seduction scene that is overtly erotic (it is however the only erotic moment in the whole novel). He does not later abandon her, though she is a slave, a Muslim and a beautiful, sensual woman of colour. However, they go into exile to a remote part of the colony and as they get there Harman is killed by the Boers (like the African character in Dhlomo's short story and Lanny in Abraham's novel). A far cry from the likes of Cassi in *Clara dos Anjos*, Harman cannot survive. Somiela is not exactly abandoned, but she is left without a husband, in the care of ageing and fairly powerless in-laws, in a desolate part of the colony where locals have just killed the father of her child. As the novel closes, it is impossible to believe that she and her infant daughter will not face great hardship. In a way, both have also been cast out of colonial society. In fact, even Nelson Rodrigues' plays, which seem at first subversive of the established order, are not above moral frameworks (albeit very complex ones that are continually exposed by the narrator). The poems provide therefore a window onto Creole society that even as accomplished a novel as *Nini*—or a sociological and psychological work such as Fanon's—can only very fleetingly offer.

That varied body of writing, therefore, invites us to revisit again the sites of hybridity from which both the colony and the postcolonial nation have sprung. Those sites, at least in what concerns the Indian Ocean, are moreover often far older than colonialism itself. Traditional historiography (literary or otherwise), not to mention anthropology and the social sciences, has unfortunately ill-prepared us for this task. It is perhaps only by breaking out of the boundaries of national and area studies that we will be able to reconnect what has apparently always been more or less connected under the guise of several forms of Creolisation, all of which sit more or less uncomfortably with our current ways of looking at cherished categories such as colonialism, nation, gender, or "race."

ACKNOWLEDGEMENTS

I am grateful to Sephis in the Netherlands for having financed my stay in the Caribbean between 1996–1998; to Fapesp in São Paulo for giving me a postdoctoral scholarship between 1999 and 2001; and to CNPq in Brasília for giving me another scholarship in 2003 and 2004. Back in 1993, the Ford Foundation and Centro de Estudos Afro-Asiáticos in Rio de Janeiro also gave me a generous grant that allowed me to go to South Africa for my doctoral research. More recently, support from Stellenbosch University in South Africa has been fundamental. There are, however, far too many institutions and people to whom I owe a debt of gratitude in Brazil, the Caribbean, the Netherlands, and South Africa, for me to be able to mention all of them here.

NOTES

1. See Rosa Ribeiro (1995, 2002, 2005, 2007).
2. See Rosa Ribeiro (2007).
3. In fact, I doubt very much that any such comprehensive inventory exists, even for relatively circumscribed areas such as, for instance, the Atlantic world. First, there are language barriers. Most books have probably never been translated into English or another major European language (often a precondition for being noticed in a good deal of academia). Also, there is the predominance of area studies in academia. In particular, this has meant that there is a virtual gulf that divides Latin American, Caribbean, African, and Asian studies. All this has rendered difficult any attempt to construct a connected history of even limited aspects of processes of creolisation.
4. See, for instance, Stoler (1992) for French Indochina and the Netherlands Indies, and Clancy-Smith and Gouda for Dutch and French colonialism in general.
5. See, in particular, Subrahmanyam (1997).
6. Dutch-Afrikaans for "bastard," "mongrel," "mixed." The sense of "illegitimate," though not absent, is not necessarily the principal meaning in Dutch colonial times (see Ross, 1999, 30, footnote 60).
7. Jacobs (1998, 142).

8. Usually novels on slavery are written by white authors, especially Afrikaans ones. I have never come across a single literary work about slavery written by an African South African author.
9. Abrahams (1984, 171).
10. Ibid., 213.
11. See Tony Voss' introduction to Millin's *God's Stepchildren* (1986, 7). .
12. Jacobs (1998, 137).
13. Millin, 246.
14. Millin, 250.
15. In fact, it was not unheard of even far into the apartheid era. See Fredrickson (1981), Adhikari (1996).
16. See Voss' introduction to Millin's *God's Stepchildren*.
17. Unsurprisingly, according to Tony Voss, her work went through a revival in the 1950s.
18. See Adhikari (1996, 1).
19. Ibid., 97.
20. The denomination "van die Kaap" (of the Cape, i.e., the Cape of Good Hope) was quite common as a slave surname. As Millin's novel also shows (1986, 250), saying that someone was a Cape woman or man was often in fact a thinly coded way of saying that they were not white.
21. This passage is in a language that is neither Dutch nor Afrikaans as it would become standardized soon afterwards.
22. See for instance http://en.wikipedia.org/wiki/William_Plomer (accessed on September 16, 2008).
23. Interestingly, however, there is a "coloured" (sic, not capitalized) man mentioned very briefly in the novel, Alfred (Plomer, 1985, 147–48). He is, however, not of South African origin. On Plomer, see the introduction by Laurens van der Post (Plomer, 44). Speaking isiZulu fluently remains as uncommon for white writers now as it was back in Plomer's time.
24. Plomer, 172, 175–176.
25. Plomer, 193.
26. See the lengthy introduction by writer and Plomer's friend Laurens van der Post (Plomer, 1985, page 44 in particular).
27. See his poems under the heading "Uit my Oosterse Dagboek," or "Out of My Eastern Diary" (Leipoldt, 1934, 75–104).
28. Joubert (1997, 36–43).
29. Ibid., 43. As far as I know, the Afrikaans literary establishment would have to wait until Brink's *Gerugte van Reën* in the 1970s to have a full-fledged novel on the subject (Brink, 1978).
30. Adhikari (1996).
31. The story is eerily reminiscent of a now largely forgotten novel by Monteiro Lobato, a Brazilian writer of the first half of the twentieth century, *O Presidente Negro*, first published in 1926 (Lobato, 1948). In Lobato's novel, race and scientific experimentation are also welded together in a strange literary experiment in transnational (as it is set both in Brazil and in the United States) science fiction. The novel also ends tragically.
32. Head (1974).
33. Brink (1978).
34. Adhikari (1996).
35. Unsurprisingly, she also published her book in the 1970s (Head, 1974).
36. See, for instance, Furlong (1983).
37. Even postcolonial Indonesia and its racial state policies against *nonpribumi* (i.e., Chinese) are a far cry from apartheid South Africa (see Heryanto [1997] and Rosa Ribeiro [2006]).

38. Rosa Ribeiro (2007).
39. Ghosh (1992). Ghosh's novel is an incredible book, part travelogue, part ethnography, part historical research. It is also a major contemporary Indian work dealing with creolisation in the distant precolonial past. See also Ghosh's article in the prestigious *Subaltern Studies* (Ghosh, 1993). Furthermore, see Salman Rushdie's *The Moor's Last Sigh* for another contemporary work that is also concerned with creolisation and in part with the same area as Ghosh's work (namely, the Malabar coast or today's Kerala), but in colonial and postcolonial times (Rushdie, 1995).
40. For obsession with racial boundaries, see, for instance, the work of an Afrikaans sociologist of the 1940s, Cronjé (1945); see also Coetzee (1991) and Rosa Ribeiro (1995 and 2007).
41. Lessing (1986, 353)—it was first published in 1953.
42. Craveirinha (1999, 38). I am grateful to Patricia Hayes from the University of the Western Cape in Cape Town for having called my attention to Craveirinha's work as well as for showing me reproductions of Ricardo Rangel's photographs of night life in late colonial Maputo that are closely related to Craveirinha's poetry.
43. In fact, just as Goans went to Moçambique, Moçambicans also went as far as Timor Leste.
44. Craveirinha (1999, 85).
45. "Portagem" means either "tollhouse" or a "tollgate" or simply "toll": figuratively it means a barrier that has to be crossed in order to get somewhere. In Brazil, *pedágio* would have been used instead.
46. Incidentally, *moleque* is a word also used in Brazil (where it means either a brat or a black boy), and is, in fact, of Angolan origin, from Kimbundo *muleke*. Incidentally, this reveals how complex intercolonial contacts have been.
47. Mendes (1981, 21).
48. Mendes, 44, 55.
49. Mendes, 67–68.
50. Sending elite children with non-European backgrounds to Europe at an early age was in fact also a colonial practice well-entrenched in the Netherlands Indies (Taylor, 1983).
51. Barreto (2006, 152).
52. *Clara dos Anjos* was actually first published as a short story in 1920 (see Barreto, 2006, 199–207). The plot is quite similar in both short story and novel.
53. That is an honorary title.
54. Lima Barreto (2005, 17).
55. It also comes up in Louis Couperus' *De stille kracht* in the figure of Addy, who is a sensual mixed race Sundanese man (Couperus, 1993). There is also a suggestion of homosexuality when Addy and Theo van Oudijck meet in the former's bedroom. Addy is also the seducer of Léontine van Oudijck, Theo's stepmother, who is depicted as given to sensuousness as she is a white woman (a Creole) born and raised in the Javanese tropics.
56. Del Picchia (2001, 22).
57. Del Picchia, 28.
58. Ismael's role in the play was cut out for Abdias do Nascimento, a famous black actor, intellectual, and militant for black rights. Rodrigues' close friendship with Nascimento was also at the root of his writing the play. Therefore, the play is, strictly speaking, not only the brainchild of a white playwright. See Moutinho, (2004, 149). Moutinho's work is also a good source for Brazilian novels on Creole relationships.

59. Rodrigues (2005, 55).
60. Amerindians were main characters in many romantic nineteenth-century novels, such as José de Alencar's *Iracema* (first published in 1865 and still read to this day). Iracema is perhaps the most famous Indian woman character in Brazilian literature. Of course, she falls in love with a Portuguese—on top of that, a blue-eyed one, which makes him even whiter and therefore more attractive in the prevailing colour hierarchies of the country—and suffers a sad fate.
61. *Gabriela, Cravo e Canela*, by Jorge Amado (first published in 1958), is perhaps the most widely circulated Brazilian novel about a sensual woman "in the middle." Also made into a well-known film, the story is about Gabriela and her Arab companion, Nasib. Before the current New Age craze around Paulo Coelho's work, Jorge Amado was the most widely translated Brazilian author, also behind the former Iron Curtain.
62. See the dissertation by Curaçaoan writer Frank Martinus (1996).
63. This poem is called "Karta na mi negra" ("A letter to my *negra*"), from Lauffer's collection of poems, *Kumbu*, published in 1955. I have quoted the poem from Habibie (1994, 30). I am very grateful to Henry Habibe in Curaçao for having given me a copy of his book. Habibe's translations are into Dutch and I have taken the liberty of both taking inspiration as well as departing from them, as Papiamentu is much closer to my mother tongue than it is to Dutch.
64. Habibe (1994, 30).
65. Habibe, 34–35
66. Habibe, 36–37.
67. Curaçao is historically the seat of the Netherlands Antilles, a former Dutch colony that became officially an integral, noncolonial part of the Kingdom of the Netherlands in 1954.
68. However, as Cassi, the seducer in *Clara dos Anjos*, as well as at least two working-class Portuguese characters in Aluísio Azevedo's *O Cortiço*, show, there was no need for the white man to be wealthy. His whiteness was often enough for him to conquer a black woman. An interesting aspect of all these novels, however, is that the white man, as in the case of both the *comendador* and Frits Ruprecht, is often right from the beginning presented to the reader as someone who is after black or mulatto women.
69. Debrot (1995, 42–43).
70. Incidentally, white parentage, even illegitimate, as an avenue towards social mobility, is an indication of the incredible poverty prevailing in Curaçao even after the oil industry had arrived in the 1920s (the novel is from the 1930s). See Hoetink (1987) and Allen (2007).
71. The plural in Malay (Indonesian) is *njai-njai*.
72. In fact, the same might be said of similar literature in what concerns former French Indochina. I doubt that Marguerite Duras' autobiographical *L'amant*, for instance, which describers the relationship between a young French girl and an older Chinese lover, is considered part of Vietnamese literature, especially as it was published in the postcolonial era (Duras, 1984). However, in the Philippines, at least some nineteenth-century literature in Spanish is part and parcel of Filipino literature, as in the case of the work of José Rizal (however, he is almost only read in translation nowadays), a man of creolised origins himself and who described the Creole society of the Philippines in Spanish late colonial times in his novels (Rizal, 1996, 1997, and 2000).
73. The situation on the ground, however, is not too different: in Curaçao, publishing in Dutch and (invariably) in the Netherlands, as many writers still do, means that they will not be widely read in Curaçao, where most people

only read in Papiamentu outside their schooling and formal jobs. Therefore, though different, the fate of a novel in Dutch such as Debrot's in Curaçao and Du Perron's in Indonesia is not altogether too disparate: namely, they are mostly not locally read.

74. *Uler* (in today's spelling) can also be a worm (and the word is both Javanese and Malay); and *ular* is a snake.

75. Suryadinata (1996, 18–19). I have never held a copy of any of those novels in my hands, and only know about them because of Suryadinata's work. They are seldom or never read in Indonesia nowadays.

76. Székely-Lulofs (1934).

77. Székely-Lulofs (1933, 161–205). I am grateful to Siegfried Huigen from the Stellenbosch University for having given me a copy of the story.

78. Toer (2001, 50–51). This novel has been widely translated into many languages, as Pram (as he is affectionately known) is still Indonesia's most famous writer. Unfortunately, I do not have access to the English translation of the novel. Also, needless to say, there is no Brazilian translation (it is quite possible that no Indonesian writer has ever been translated in Brazil). The translation below the original text is therefore my own, as is the case with all other translations as well.

79. Of course, the narrator is here referring to the famous colonial *landaarden* or juridical nationality groups, that is, groups of ethno-legal status into which the Netherlands Indies society was divided roughly between the mid-nineteenth century to the time of the Japanese invasion in 1942. Those groups determined the right of access (or lack thereof) to land, schools, certain residential areas, medical care, finance, public office, inheritance, and so on. They therefore impinged on practically every sphere of life in the colony. See Fasseur (1992).

80. Willem (2001).

81. Perron (1997); Bosma and Ribeiro (2007). The book was first published in 1935.

82. Perron (1997, 279).

83. Van Dis (1996, 132).

84. The phrase "stopte . . . in de doofpot" is in fact much more graphic and intense than "hiding in the closet": the *doofpot* is a recipient where you keep coal and other fuel that has been used until it can be used again. For lack of oxygen, the fuel stops burning inside in.

85. Not even a visit to the website of the Bibliothèque Nationale de France has helped to ascertain beyond a doubt the date of first publication of this novel. It was, however, probably first published in 1954, and therefore six years before Senegal's independence in 1960. I am very grateful to Alain Pascal Kaly with University of Campinas, for providing me both with a copy of the novel and valuable insight about its importance as well as about Sadji's importance as a writer in Senegal.

86. It is difficult to avoid the impression that perhaps his subject matter touched Lima Barreto almost too closely, whereas in Abdoulaye Sadji's case he was very familiar with it, but, as a Muslim African man, also kept his distance from it (see note 89).

87. Fanon (1952).

88. Just like his character Nini, Sadji was also born in one of the famous *quatre communes* (instead of Saint-Louis, he came however from Rufisque), where the inhabitants, regardless of race or religion, often enjoyed some of the same legal and political rights as metropolitan French citizens as from the mid-nineteenth century (the other two *communes* were the island of Gorée and Dakar), differently to the vast majority of more properly colonial subjects

living in the so-called *protectorat* territory. Therefore, Sadji, also being a kind of Creole, was in all likelihood well-acquainted with the colonial society he describes in his novel.

89. Or the famous nineteenth century character Isaura, a white slave, in Bernardo Guimarães' classic *A Escrava Isaura*, first published in 1875. As a soap opera, at one point it also became the most widely watched Brazilian visual product, aired as faraway as China. It has been revived in recent years in Brazil as yet another soap. In fact, the powerful image of the beautiful white slave is an enduring visual sign that is far more gripping than the written text that has originated it. Also, Isaura's story does *not* end tragically. See, for instance, http://pt.wikipedia.org/wiki/Imagem:EscravaIsaura.jpg (accessed on April 25, 2008).

90. Boilat (1994, 5).

91. For a description from the first half of the nineteenth century, which also includes unique visual material, see Boilat (1994). Boilat was also a person "in the middle," born in Saint-Louis to a local woman who was most likely a *signare* and a Frenchman. Sadji also mentions the fact that Nini comes from a long lineage of *signaras* (Sadji, 1988, 198). The more usual spelling is *signares*. The locally born, male counterpart of the *signares* was called *habitant* (Boilat, 1994, 5), which, in Martinique, was the name given to Creole whites.

92. Sadji (1988, 207–209).

93. Ibid., 177–78.

94. See Cronjé (1945), Coetzee (1991) and Rosa Ribeiro (2007).

95. See Isaura as mentioned in note 90 above.

96. Furlong (1983).

BIBLIOGRAPHY

Abrahams, Peter. *The Path of Thunder.* Introduction by Richard Rive. Cape Town and Johannesburg: David Philip, 1984.

Adhikari, Mohamed, ed. *Straatpraatjes. Language, Politics and Popular Culture in Cape Town, 1909–1922.* Cape Town: Van Schaik, 1996.

Alencar, José de. *Iracema.* Rio de Janeiro: Casa Garnier, 1865.

Allen, Rose Mary. *Di ki manera? A Social History of Afro-Curaçaoans, 1863–1917.* Amsterdam: SWP, 2007.

Amado, Jorge. *Gabriela, Cravo e Canela.* São Paulo: Martins, 1958.

Azevedo, Aluísio de. *O Mulato.* São Luís: Tipografia de País, 1881.

———. *O Cortiço.* Rio de Janeiro: Casa Garnier, 1890.

Barreto, Lima. *Contos Reunidos.* Belo Horizonte: Crisálida, 2005.

———.*Clara dos Anjos.* São Paulo: Martin Claret, 2006.

Boilat, Abbé David. *Esquisses sénégalaises.* Paris: Karthala, 1994.

Bosma, Ulbe, and Fenando Rosa Ribeiro. "Late Colonial Estrangement and Miscegenation. Identity and Authenticity in the Colonial Imagination in the Dutch and Lusophone (Post) Colonial Worlds." *Cultural and Social History* 4 (1; 2007): 29–50.

Brink, André. *Gerugte van Reën.* Cape Town: Human & Rousseau, 1978.

Caminha, Adolfo. *Bom-Crioulo.* São Paulo: Martin Claret, 2007.

Clancy-Smith, J., and Frances Gouda, eds. *Domesticating the Empire.* Charlottesville, VA: University Press of Virginia, 1998.

Coetzee, J.M. "The Mind of Apartheid: Geoffrey Cronjé—1902." *Social Dynamics* 1 (1991): 1–35.

134 *Fernando Rosa Ribeiro*

Conrad, Joseph. *Almayer's Folly*. New York: Dover, 2003.
Couperus, Louis. *De stille kracht*. Amsterdam: Querido, 1993.
Craveirinha, José. *Obra Poética I*. Lisbon: Editorial Caminho, 1999.
Cronjé, Geoffrey. *'n Tuiste vir die Nageslag*. Johannesburg: Publicité, 1945.
Debrot, Cola. *Mijn zuster de negerin*. Amsterdam: De Bijzige Bij, 1995.
Dhlomo, H.I.E. "An Experiment in Colour." In *Collected Works*, edited by Nick Visser and Tim Couzens, 489–499. Johannesburg: Ravan Press, 1985.
Duras, Marguerite. *L'amant*. Paris: Ed. de Minuit, 1984.
Fanon, Frantz. *Peau noire, masques blancs*. Paris: Seuil, 1952.
Fasseur, Cees. Fasseur. "Hoeksteen en struikelblok. Rasonderscheid en overheidsbeleid in Nederlands-Indië." *Tijdschrift voor Geschiedenis* 105 (1992): 218–242.
Fredrickson, George. *White Supremacy: A Comparative Study in American and South African History*. New York: Oxford University Press, 1981.
Furlong, Patrick J. *The Mixed Marriages Act. An Historical and Theological Study*. Cape Town: Centre for African Studies, University of Cape Town, Communications No. 8, 1983.
Ghosh, Amitav. *In An Antique Land*. New York: Vintage, 1992.
———. "The Slave of MS. H.6." In *Subaltern Studies 7 (Writings on South Asian History and Society)*, edited by Partha Chatterjee and Gyanendra Pandey, 159–220. Delhi: Oxford University Press, 1993.
Habibe, Henry. *Un Herida Bida Ta. Een verkenning van het poëtisch oeuvre van Pierre Lauffer*. Curaçao: Intergrafia, 1994.
Head, Bessie. *A Question of Power*. London: Heineman, 1974.
Heryanto, Ariel. "Silence in Indonesian Literary Discourse: The Case of the Indonesian Chinese." *Sojourn* 12(1; 1997): 6–45.
Hoetink, Harry. *Het patroon van de oude Curaçaose samenleving*. Amsterdam: Emmering, 1987.
Jacobs, Rayda. *The Slave Book. A Novel*. Cape Town: Kwela, 1998.
Joubert, Elsa. *Gordel van smarag. 'n Reis met Leipoldt*. Cape Town: Tafelberg, 1997.
Leipoldt, C. Louis. *Uit Drie Wêrelddele*. Cape Town: Nasionale Pers, 1934.
Lessing, Doris. "The Antheap." In *Collected African Stories. Volume One. This was the Old Chief's Country*, 342–397. London: Grafton, 1986.
Lobato, Monteiro. *"O Presidente Negro ou o Choque das Raças" ("Romance Americano do ano 2228")*. In *A Onda Verde e o Presidente Negro*, 125–330. São Paulo: Brasiliense, 1948. .
Martinus, Efraim Frank. *The Kiss of a Slave: Papiamentu's West African Connections*. Doctoral dissertation, University of Amsterdam, 1996.
Mendes, Orlando. *Portagem*. São Paulo: Ática, 1981.
Millin, Sarah Gertrude. *God's Stepchildren*. Introduction by Tony Voss. Craighall: Ad. Donker, 1986.
Moutinho, Laura. *Razão, 'Cor'e Desejo*. São Paulo: Editora Unesp, 2004.
Perron, Edgar du. *Het land van herkomst*. Amsterdam: G.A. van Oorschot, 1997.
Picchia, Menotti Del. *Juca Mulato*. Belo Horizonte: Editora Itatiaia, 2001.
Plomer, William. *Turbott Wolfe*. Introduction by Laurens van der Post. Oxford: Oxford University Press, 1985.
Rizal, José. *El Filibusterismo: subversion*. Translated by Maria Soledad Lacson-Lacsin. Makati City: Bookmark, 1996.
———. *Noli me tangere*. Translated by Maria Soledad Lacson-Lacsin. Edited by Raul L. Locsin. Honolulu: University of Hawai'i Press, 1997.
———. *Noli me tangere*. Translated into Tagalog by Benjamin C. de la Fuente. Manila: De La Salle University Press, 2000.
Rodrigues, Nelson. *Teatro Completo*. Rio de Janeiro: Aguilar, 2003.

————. *Anjo Negro*. Rio de Janeiro: Nova Fronteira, 2005.

Rosa Ribeiro, Fernando. "A Construção da Nação Na África do Sul: A Ideologia Individualista e o Apartheid." *Anuário Antropológico* 94(1995): 161–188.

————. "A Construção da Nação Pós-Colonial: África do Sul e Suriname, 1933–1948." *Estudos Afro-Asiáticos* 24(3; 2002): 483–512.

————. "*Bahasa Persatuan*: Idioma e Nação na Indonésia Colonial (1915–1950)." *Afro-Ásia* 32(2005): 29–81.

————. "Pribumi e Não-Pribumi: colonialismo e a contrução do Estado-nação indonésio." *Estudos Afro-Asiáticos* 28(2006): 275–318.

————. "*Fornicatie* and *Hoerendom* or the Long Shadow of the Portuguese: Connected Histories, Languages and Gender in the Indian Ocean and Beyond." *Social Dynamics* 33(2; 2007): 33–60.

Ross, Robert. *Status and Respectability in the Cape Colony, 1750–1870. A Tragedy of Manners*. Cambridge, UK: Cambridge University Press, 1999.

Rushdie, Salman. *The Moor's Last Sigh*. London: Cape, 1995.

Sadji, Abdoulaye. *Nini mulâtresse du Sénégal*. Paris: Présence Africaine, 1988.

Stoler, Ann. "Sexual Affronts and Racial Frontiers: European Identities and the Cultural Politics of Exclusion in Colonial Southeast Asia." *Comparative Studies in Society and History* (1992): 514–551.

Subrahmanyam, Sanjay. "Connected Histories: Notes towards a Reconfiguration of Early Modern Eurasia." *Modern Asian Studies* 31(3; 1997): 735–762.

Suryadinata, Leo. "Dari Sastra Peranakan ke Sastra Indonesia." In *Sastra Peranakan Tionghoa Indonesia*. Jakarta: Grasindo, 1996.

Székely-Lulofs, Madelon. *Emigranten en andere verhalen*. Amsterdam: Elsevier, 1933.

————. *De andere wereld*. Amsterdam: Elsevier, 1934.

Swart, Sandra. "'Bushveld Magic' and 'Miracle Doctors'—a discussion of Eugène Marais and C. Louis Leipoldt's experiences in the Waterberg, c. 1906–1917." *Journal of African History* 45(2004): 237–255.

Taylor, Jean Gelman. *The Social World of Batavia: European and Eurasian in Dutch Asia*. Madison, WI: Wisconsin University Press, 1983.

Toer, Pramoedya Ananta. *Bumi Manusia. Sebuah Novel Sejarah*. Jakarta: Hasta Mitra, 2001.

Willems, Willem Hendrik. *De uittocht uit Indië, 1945–1995. De geschiedenis van Indische Nederlanders*. Amsterdam: Bakker, 2001.

Van Dis, Adriaan. *Indische Duinen*. Amsterdam: Meulenhoff, 1996.

6 Commerce, Circulation, and Consumption

Indian Ocean Communities in Historical Perspective

Lakshmi Subramanian

This chapter is an attempt to look at the dynamics and processes of identity formation among trading communities whose social profile was predicated upon cultural and commercial practices within the Indian Ocean. The Indian Ocean functioned as a transnational zone of interaction with connections extending far across discrete civilisational units from which migrant merchant communities were drawn and thrown together to negotiate cross-cultural and commercial interflows and overlaps. The temporal dimensions of these interactions were important; the world of Islam generated one set of conditions for dialogue while the intervention of Western political domination served to introduce a very different set of demands and variables in the region. Equally influential was the assertion of nationalist aspirations and its accompanying cultural dynamics that at a later date inflected very distinctly, the processes of community definition and aspirations. Documenting these processes as an empirical exercise, especially in the context of the more recent debates on diaspora models and regimes of circulation in the Indian Ocean, and how the latter served as sites of nationalist and transnationalist imaginings, forms some of the concerns of this chapter.

While some of my empirical research is drawn from communities based in and operating from Southern India, I hope to make some general formulations that attempt a broader conversation with certain thematic issues pertaining to the notion of an Indian Ocean subject and its negotiations with competing ideologies and practices. Among the communities that I have chosen for my investigation are the Muslim trading communities from the Coromandel—known as the Marakkayars, of whom the Chulias formed one subsection and who dominated the external or overseas trade of Southern India in the eighteenth and early quarter of the nineteenth century. The second case study looks at the Chettiars, or more specifically the Nagarathars or Nattukottai Chettiars, a Hindu mercantile group whose presence in Southeast Asia was integrally connected with the

colonial trading structure and whose ties with Southern India were mediated through cultural practices, community networks of marriage and kin,
and also through consumption markers. Just how these became constitutive
of complex and cross-cultural identities will form the focus of this chapter.
The profiles of these two communities, their rise and evolution, encom-
pass two significant if not defining moments, in the history of the Indian
Ocean; one that saw the working of cross-cultural transactions across the
Indian Ocean at a time when the world of premodern global trade fostered
a particular form of cosmopolitanism predicated upon religious and social
networks that trade generated and the other which was a direct offshoot
of colonialism that introduced new elements coming in the wake of capitalism, bourgeois modernity, and nation-state aspirations. If one contributed directly to the blurring of boundaries and to the making of a genuine
Indian Ocean subject the other produced a deep and growing angst about
recovery from homes, languages, and cultures left behind.

DIASPORA AND TRADING NETWORKS: PROBLEMS OF DEFINITION

Studies on merchant groups and networks in the Indian Ocean have indicated how these evolved over time and occupied a certain location in the
ocean's trading grid. These networks fulfilled a complex set of social and
mercantile functions, and acquired in the process a complex identity that
could be composite as well as hybrid. For a long time, Philip Curtin's important work on the diaspora dominated our understanding of its cultural role
in transacting between diverse groups in a common trading environment.[1]
More recent scholarship on Indian trading networks has begun to focus
on how culture, family life, and religious and business practices of dispersed merchant communities in the Indian Ocean were affected by long
range travels. Claude Markovits, for instance, focuses on the existence of
a wide spread circulation of merchants and commercial employees operating between India and the Indian Ocean, a phenomenon that spanned the
transition between indigenous and colonial regimes.[2] In doing this, he not
only questions the assumptions of looking at a unitary notion of a diaspora,
arguing that in many cases especially in the precolonial period, the majority of Indians were temporary residents and also that the community of
migrants was differentiated in terms of class and occupation. There was in
fact, no long-term separation from a real or originary homeland and that
the invocation of the nation was only one and often provisional strategy in
the formation of identities. For Markovits, therefore, it appears more rea-
sonable to look at the movement of merchants as networks that were rooted
in a local reality in South Asia and combine local history with that of global
history rather than engage with national history, which "is largely meaningless in this case."[3] Here he would appear to be in agreement with the

new kinds of concerns that have come to bear on the field of Indian Ocean studies, especially from the perspective of cultural studies that attempts to "rethink an imaginative geography, that of the space of the Indian Ocean, by articulating a form of trans-national analysis."[4]

Cultural studies and new writing on the Indian Ocean have in recent years offered innovative approaches to the retrieval of cultures of the Indian Ocean—from the ethnography of fishing and boatbuilding to maritime lore and to performance traditions: these have become the staple of new ways of looking at the Indian Ocean as a terrain of mnemonic traces and cultural transactions. My own approach in this chapter will be somewhere inbetween and will look at two atypical modes of merchant interaction and the devices they adopted and deployed to constitute themselves as a community whose self-definition was predicated upon a set of distinct cultural practices that were both endogenous in terms of religion and status as well as exogenous in terms of consumption and commerce. Here I shall draw substantially from Enseng Ho's outstanding work on the Hadrami diaspora that he has characterised as a composite paralleling what he calls the British model.[5]

CHULIAS: BEFORE AND AFTER EMPIRE

The expanding presence of the Chulias in the trading world of the Indian Ocean, especially in the Bay of Bengal segment, was particularly marked in the seventeenth century, which constituted the golden period for Indian overseas trade. South Asia, by virtue of its location and commercial and manufacturing potential enjoyed a particular preeminence in the Indian Ocean trading system—Indian merchants of different denominations enjoyed an unprecedented visibility as peripatetic carriers of staple as well as short-term residents in the ports of the Indian Ocean.[6] Gujaratis, by and large tended to concentrate in the ports of the western Indian Ocean while Tamils from the Cormandel region were oriented to the Southeast Asian archipelago. Tamil merchants included Chettis and Chulias who in different capacities were active agents in overseas trade and made up the category of Kling mentioned in Portuguese as well as subsequent European documentation.[7] As late as the first quarter of the nineteenth century, Indians in Southeast Asia were referred to as the Klings and Chulias, who T.J. Newbold described as "traders and settlers, both Musalmans and Hindus from the Cormandel Coast." He observed that these names had been given to them by the Malays since times of early commercial intercourse, that Kling was a corruption from Teling or Telinga.[8] John Crawfurd writing two decades earlier also commented on the frequency of communication between the Coromandel and Southeast Asia, dominated largely by the Chulias whose trading enterprise persuaded them "to seek their fortunes in a country richer by nature than their own, less occupied and the natives of which are easily circumvented."[9]

The coherence of the Chulia presence in the trading segment of the Bay of Bengal is generally dated to the expansion of Arab maritime contacts with the peninsula from the eighth century. The centrality of the Coromandel in the international trade linking South Asia with Southeast and West Asia brought increasing numbers of Arab merchants to Indian Ocean ports where they intermarried with local women, built networks of commercial, religious, and personal contacts, and maintained relationships with local rulers supplying their requirements, from warhorses to spices. A testimony to the success of these networks was their importance in local courts all through South and Southeast Asia, the vitality of their religious life largely serviced by Sufi lineages and the vibrancy of the chain of coastal towns that they developed.[10] Most of these towns at least in the Coromandel were dominated by the Marakkayars, an endogamous body of Tamil-speaking merchants and shipowners who maintained contacts with the Arab centres of pilgrimage on the one hand and developed new ties in Southeast Asia on the other. The Marakkayars belonged to the Sh'afi order and maintained a distance from other Tamil-speaking Muslims called the Labbais who were Hanafis. Marakkayars maintained the division by marrying with fellow Sha'fis from the Malabar Coast and Southeast Asia in preference to Tamil-speaking Hanafis. They prized their Arab connection, claimed that knowledge of Arabic was nonexistent among Labbais and that these converts had deviated from proper Islamic domestic custom by adopting murai or cross-cousin marriages of the kind prevalent in South India. The Marakkayars adhered to a particular lifestyle that emphasized acts of public piety, of promoting religious knowledge and scholarship, and building centres like madrasas, dargahs, and mosques.

Historians working on maritime India have commented on the extensive dealings of the Marakkayars, their networks in Southeast Asia and their resistance to the attempts of the European trading companies in the seventeenth century to engross the major proceeds of the country trade in the Indian Ocean. Merchants from the Coromandel—Pulicat, Nagore, Nagapatnam—had since very early times maintained regular connections with Southeast Asia. Malacca, the great sixteenth-century emporium, as we know from Tome Pires' account, housed an extensive Kling settlement—the Portuguese writer Duarte Barbosa referred to them as "men of great taste and owning many great ships" and to the corpulent Chettis with great big bellies.[11] Both these groups were identified as different from peripatetic itinerant traders and seen to have substantial stakes in local society. Of the two groups, Chulias seem to have responded vigorously to the rise of new Malay ports in the late fourteenth and early fifteenth century, notably the rise of Malacca as an important emporium. The arrival of the Portuguese and their attempts at monopolising the traffic of the Indian Ocean did not seriously deflect or undermine Chulia enterprise, which opted for new ports that did not fall under formal Portuguese dispensation.

Subsequent developments, related to the internal reorganisation of states in Southeast Asia in the seventeenth century, benefited and enabled merchant networks to regroup effectively; Chulias in fact fared well during these years of political transformation and expanded their operations, consolidated their presence in regional courts, and even assumed administrative functions. We hear of substantial Marakkayar investments in shipping; of their close connections with local Malay rulers and of their preponderance in the textile trade of the Coromandel that continued to retain its vitality until the early eighteenth century. The succeeding decades introduced new pressures and strains in the situation; conditions of political insecurity in South Asia, combined with the expansion of English private trade, eroded the foundations of Chulia enterprise and caused a major jolt to the existing networks. However, this was not entirely irreversible—in fact the Nagore Acheh trade route remained the most important route in the Bay of Bengal in the eighteenth century largely as a consequence of the Chulia Southeast Asia connection. Recent research suggests that the Chulia connection remained more enduring than was previously thought and that their activities remained robust well into the closing decades of the eighteenth century. According to Bhaswati Bhattacharya, for instance, a considerable part of the trade between Coromandel ports and Kedah, Acheh, and Malacca was in the hands of the Chulias or their counterparts on the other side of the bay. The trade peaked in the 1770s and was principally in textiles and enjoyed the encouragement and patronage of local Southeast Asian rulers.

The main centres of Chulia activity on the Coromandel Coast were Porto Novo and Nagore, which directed the traffic with Southeast Asia. Chulia merchants settled in the archipelago focused on Nagore and emphasized its importance. Local Southeast Asian rulers, as a result, endeavoured to keep this channel of communication as open as possible and even mounted a partial offensive when English private trade threatened to alter the existing arrangements.[12] Chulias were also important court officials; contemporary Europeans had occasion to comment on the close linkages between rulers of Acheh, Johore, and Perak with Chulia merchant networks, some of the Chulias becoming important court officials. The rulers along with their clients resisted the strong-arm tactics of English private traders, partly in response to their own increasing involvement with trade and partly in deference to the demands of the local networks of trading interests, notably the Chulias.

The Chulias were to be found in virtually all the major courts in the archipelago in the capacity of prime ministers and senior officers. In 1783, the Kedah ruler's minister was a keen Chulia called Jemmal. Chulia enterprise dominated the trade of Acheh. Thomas Forrest in 1792 had occasion to remark, "in India, vessels fitted out and sailed by natives alone sail at much less expense even less than one half of what they do when fitted out by Europeans although sailed by an Indian crew. Such is the frugal management and among these islands, the lascars could merely maintain themselves with fishing from inexhaustible stores and find many articles to fill up their vessels that Europeans would never think of."[13] He noted the regularity with which Chulia vessels arrived every year at Acheh from Porto Novo. These were medium sized vessels and brought piece goods of all kinds, chiefly long cloth white and blue, chintz with dark grounds, and a great deal of long cloth unbleached. The merchants sold at leisure and, according to Forrest, were not above deception, as they showed their "goods to the natives in as dark a part of their shop" as they could. It was their frugality and the cheapness of their prices that made it impossible for Europeans to compete with them.[14] The ramifications of Chulia enterprise were in full display in the states of Kedah, Perak, and Johore. Even in the nascent English settlement of Bencoolen, English private enterprise failed to deflect Chulia enterprise for the greater part of the eighteenth century, at least until the very closing decades of the eighteenth century, when the political geography was entirely redrawn.

Thomas Forrest's observations on Chulia duplicity and its role in enabling the community to withstand the pressures of European competition were not singular or even exceptional in terms of representing the dominant European voice. This was in a sense the heyday of the Nabobs when European private traders engaged in every act of deception, rapacity, and duplicity, even if they chose to cloak it in the language of rationality and fair trade. The observations become more transparent when read in the context of the larger narrative of European expansion that saw local commercial practices as inimical to the pursuit of free trade, or local strategies as irrational. A closer reading in fact yields a very different picture of mobility and diaspora formation that was able to take on universalist aspirations. The modalities of Marakkayar interaction between South India and Southeast Asia and their linkages, symbolic as well as real with Arabia, enabled them to operate very much on the lines that the Hadramis pursued and function as a composite diaspora that Ho likens to what he calls the British model as against the Jewish one. He suggests that just as the British diaspora never became ethnic minorities in the lands they colonised but took on universalising aspirations, forged loyalties around institutions such as private property, free trade, and protest according to law, and organised the diaspora in the form of an empire, the Hadrami Arabs too expressed their universalist ambitions in the form of a religious mission.[15] It brought together not just people from the homeland but from throughout the Indian Ocean as well. They married into the local population and became locals while at the same time, the men and their offspring continued to move throughout the oceanic space for trade, study, pilgrimage, and politics throughout the space. In the arc of ports around the Indian Ocean, a skein of networks arose in which people socialised with foreigners and locals as kinsmen and as Muslim. Like the British model, the movement in the

Hadrami diaspora brought together separated peoples not in an empire but in a religion.

Religion in this case was not only a spiritual space but a civil and political one as well. As bearers of Islamic knowledge and prestige, Hadramis were creators of Islamic knowledge; Hadramis were everywhere potential creators of public spaces and institutions. Not surprisingly Hadramis were welcomed in the new port cities and states where they made local alliances and functioned in important capacities. What is fairly remarkable about the Hadrami experience is that they were able to retain a distinct identity at one level, and at the same time create a completely new one.

From this perspective it is tempting to see the Chulias experiencing the transregional Indian Ocean network of peaceful trade and social exchange as an extensive domestic realm that was simultaneously local, global, and Muslim. The Arab connection as mentioned before was central to the Chulias as indeed was their commitment to scholarship and the public urban expression of Islamic lifestyle. Their facility with language was an important cultural asset that they deployed to advantage. Trade, local marriage alliances, and linguistic adeptness became important strategies in configuring the Chulias, who were part of the hadrami circle, and yet were local Tamils at one end and Malays at the other. The intersection of multiple identities, of practices and networks, proved to be extremely important in stabilising Chulia presence in Southeast Asia and in enabling some sections of the community to negotiate European political and commercial influence.

The importance of social strategies and cultural practices adopted by the Chulias is especially important to recall in the eighteenth-century context when they had to renegotiate their operations and transactions. As traders, they were not unused to sudden contingencies or having to respond to changing circumstances and stimuli; they had for a long time demonstrated a level of cosmopolitanism that characterised certain other trading networks in the Indian Ocean like, for example, the Armenians. However, what made the eighteenth-century experience especially striking was the intensity and rapidity of change that the trading structure underwent in the aftermath of formal European colonial control and the resilience displayed by Chulia networks in the changing circumstances. Their communication skills, penmanship, and local contacts were substantial assets that they put to use in developing political contacts and in expanding their operations amidst conditions of competition and aggression. This combination of cultural integration and linguistic and communication skills would appear to have featured as a central organising principle of the Chulia conglomerate.

CHULIAS AND THE NEW COLONIAL DISPENSATION

Chulia networks had to readjust to the radical transformation of the trading world in the aftermath of formal European colonisation. The making of the Anglo-Dutch maritime empires introduced new elements in the existing equation, compelling indigenous groups to come up with new strategies. The thrust of British private trade meant new, even if limited, opportunities for informal partnerships. At the same time, the shift towards new commodities, especially the movement of exotic southeast wares for the growing China market downsized Indian textile trade, which faced constraints even at the level of production in Southeastern India. The traffic did not die out entirely; going by trade estimates of Penang, it would appear that Indian piece goods continued to be a major item in the trade and that Chetties and Chulias continued to be principal exporters of cloth along with English private traders. Even though British piece goods had made an appreciable dent by the 1820s, the quantity of Indian piece goods imported into Penang was still larger than that of the Europe article. John Anderson, in 1846, estimated that exports of cotton and cloth from the Coromandel continued to be high even though he argued that the figure given by an earlier writer of its value at Rs. 25,000,000 annually was somewhat inflated. Betel nuts were another important item of trade. He estimated the export of betel nuts at not less than 150,000 to 160,000 tons. Anderson specifically referred to ten to twelve ships coming every year from the Coromandel bringing in piece goods of all kinds, white and blue, longish cloth, chintz, and salt. During the season in June, July, and August, there were seldom less than twelve or fifteen ships and brigs, which proceeded to Pedir for cargoes, and these along with Achenese Prahus provided the country with a variety of imports from Europe, India, and China.[16] Anderson was in many ways confirming the observations of Crawford, when he wrote about the numerous vessels of the Chulias. "The numerous vessels of their nation bring annually with the setting in of the western monsoon, shoals of these people literally to seek their fortunes in a country richer than their own, less occupied and the natives of which are strictly circumvented."[17] The Chulias were shrewd, supple, unwarlike, and mendacious according to Crawford and carried cargoes of cloth in their vessels that were around two hundred tons dead weight.

The continuity of commercial exchanges facilitated the operations of older Tamil networks that persisted at middle and lower levels. At the same time, some of them would appear to have moved with the expanding presence of the English and taken up permanent residence in the new settlement of Singapore while continuing with their operations at Penang, Perak, and Malacca. In the new centre at Singapore, they opted for newer functions that were largely ancillary to English and Chinese enterprise. The dominance of European and Chinese carriage in the transportation of European cloth and a variety of Chinese and Southeast Asian ware inevitably meant that the Chulias concentrated increasingly on lower levels of retail trade in Indian cloth and of port functions related to the handling of cargo and boatbuilding. The terms of trade had changed; the political dispensation was no longer the same, staple Indian calico had made way for the cloths of

Lancashire. The Chinese emerged as the new distributors of British goods, displacing the older Asian groups. Thus in the new centres of Penang and Singapore, Chulias became small-time shop owners handling a minor proportion of retail trade. They had perforce to dovetail their operations to suit the imperatives of the new economy and in the process opted for lower levels of retail trade or for collaboration with the English authorities as dependents and not partners. The perceptible decline in the trade of Indian textiles, whose marketing and sourcing had been the basis of their economic success in the earlier centuries, undermined their operations and resulted in a downgrading of their reputation. It is likely that their commercial practices that came in for sharp criticism by locals and Europeans alike manifested their basic weakness in adjusting to a new situation and was in the nature of a desperate strategy in keeping afloat their small ventures. They catered to the local population whose consumption of Indian textiles would appear to have continued. In 1855, a report in the *Singapore Free Press* underscored the unsavoury reputation that the Chulias had earned and also the nature of their functions and location in the commercial society of Malaya. "Many of my nation," the report by a Malay resident read, "the Orang Malaya, who come from sequestered localities and the interiors of rivers, people who are very simple and men of the different tribe of the Bugis who are not accustomed to resort to Singapore for trade are cheated and deceived in the cloth shops of the Klings because their shops being shut by screens of cloth next the public street are nearly quite dark and the verandas are also rendered impossible by benches and stools on which many persons sit in the darkness and confusion thus produced, goods which are coarse become fine, good silver money is transmitted into copper, doits which were sufficient in tael lose part of their number and measures become deficient. Sellers are rude and overbearing to the simple buyers and insist on their purchasing. If they don't admit to the exactions of the Klings, then a row is kicked up and buyers are hustled about by the Klings. Hence disturbances take place but the police cannot really find out the scene of disturbance on account of the screens of cloth which enclose verandas."[18]

MULTICULTURAL NEGOTIATIONS: THE CHULIAS AS A DIASPORA

These details help us reconstruct the residual nature of Chulia trade dealings at a time when European maritime aggression had dismantled the existing political and commercial regimes in Southeast Asia and British textiles displaced Indian textiles from Asian markets and transformed existing channels and conduits of distribution. Under the colonial dispensation, new groups came into prominence—the Chinese being a notable one—while old networks had to reinvent themselves outside the formal apparatus of empire and thereby remained obscure in the colonial archive.

There were some exceptions, like, for example, the narrative of Munshi Abdulla, the secretary to Sir Stamford Raffles, whose account offers us a fascinating insight into the emergence and functioning of Creole Muslim communities in Southeast Asia of which Chulias were a notable case study. Abdullah's account captures the complexities and nuances of what it meant to be part of a trading network in the eighteenth century. What is even more fascinating about the narrative is how in the process of operating as a cosmopolitan, transnational community, Hadramis and Chulias became in fact entrenched local Malays. The process was marked during the pre-colonial period; cross-cultural negotiations do not seem to have been viable or possible after the formalisation of colonialism and the new labour and commercial flows it supported. In fact we hear of Chulias and Klings coming in from India under the category of indentured labour, working within an assigned and somewhat lower rung of commercial society, and whose existence and profile was no longer predicated on the older transnational cultural space the ocean represented. Likewise, the Arabs coming into Southeast Asia in the nineteenth century were described as pirates and slave drivers who had to be repressed ruthlessly by the British if their aspirations of free trade and order had to be worked out. "It is seldom that the east is visited by Arabian merchants of large capital but there are numerous adventurers who carry on a coasting trade from port to port and by asserting the religious titles of sheikhs and Sayyids claim and generally obtain an exemption from all port duties in the Malay states; they are very frequently concerned in acts of piracy and great promoters of the slave trade. This class of adventurers it will be our object to repress but a regulated trade with any of the commercial state of Arabia as Muscat, Mocha and Judda may prove extremely advantageously to the Malay countries."[19]

It is in the context of the early modern period of transition in the Indian Ocean, that we shall analyse the narrative of Munshi Abdulla (born 1797) to reconstruct the older world of multicultural negotiations that made the Chulia a transnational subject in the most comprehensive sense of the term. I cannot resist quoting J.T. Thomson here, who, writing of the 1940s, when Abdullah had already reached middle age, says, "In physiognomy, he was a Tamilian of southern Hindustan: slightly bent forward, spare, energetic, bronze in complexion, oval faced, high nosed, one eye squinting outwards a little. He dressed in the usual style of Malacca Tamils. Acheen seluar, check sarong, printed baju, square skullcap and sandals. He had the vigour and pride of the Arab, the perseverance and subtlety of the Hindoo—in language and national sympathy only was he a Malay."[20] The biographical details of Munshi's family bring to life the ramifications of Hadrami diaspora and of the Chulia component within it. In reading his Hikayat[21] closely it is evident that not only was he born in a period of great change, but also that the linguistic resources of his community combined with their commercial contacts were especially valued assets. Munshi Abdullah came from a family of Arab traders and scribes who had married into local Tamil and Malay society in the Coromandel and Malacca respectively. His great-grandfather Abdul Kadir was a Yemeni Arab who had migrated to Nagore in Southeastern India, where he married a local Tamil. He had four sons, three of whom settled in Java, Sumatra, and Amboina. His fourth son took up residence in Malacca, where he married Peria Achi, the daughter of a Tamil Labbi merchant. Their son Abdul Kadir took up trade and combined it with religious instruction to supplement his income and forge deeper connections with local society. He went on to marry an up-country Malay woman, whom he later divorced after the birth of two children. Subsequently, he married a Malacca born half Indian called Selama, whose fifth surviving child was Abdullah. Abdul Kadir was a man of enterprise and worked with the European traders in several capacities—as scribe preparing contracts and petitions, as harbour master, and even as a local contact for accessing manuscripts that Europeans were interested in. The family was held in respect as they performed vital religious functions of familiarising the locals with the scriptures—Abdullah mentions his grandmother organising classes for young children in the study of the Koran. Their skills as scribes held them in good stead as merchants flocked to their chambers to arrange for documentation. Abdullah in fact mentions that good scribes were not easy to come by. "In Malacca of those days, it was very hard to find people who could do letter writing. There were four or five who altogether practiced it as a profession. There was first Khoja Muhammed, the son of a Malacca Tamil who became the Company's tolk, second Jamal Muhammed bin Nur Muhammed of Surat, third my father Abdul Kadir bin Muhammed Ibrahim, fourth Mahidin Ahmed Labbai."[22]

While it is clear that Abdulla's family belonged to the larger Hadrami diaspora which forged a local Tamil-Malay identity, it is also clear from his account how central the Tamil-Muslim network was in Southeast Asia and how knowledge of Tamil as an important commercial language was prized by his family as well as local merchants. Abdulla mentions time and again the attention he paid to learning Tamil. His own father spoke Tamil fluently, read and wrote accounts in it, and insisted on his son acquiring fluency in Tamil and a whole range of other languages. As he observed, "soon after having learnt Arabic and my Koran lessons well, my father sent me to a teacher to learn Tamil, an Indian language because it had been the custom from the time of our forefathers in Malacca for all children of good and well to do families to learn it. It was useful for doing compilations and accounts and for conversation because at the time Malacca was crowded with Indian merchants. Many were the men who had become rich by trading in Malacca so much so that names of Tamil traders had become famous."[23]

Commercial skills, literacy and linguistic proficiency, and networks of sociability and religious sentiment combined to give Tamil Muslims a special niche in the trading world of the Indian Ocean right until the middle decades of the nineteenth century. Thereafter, it would seem that some among them were completely integrated into local society, becoming the kind of Malays that Munshi Abdulla's family represented: functioning as part-time scribes, part-time traders, and part-time teachers, writing contracts, moving residence, and collecting local manuscripts for their European associates. Abdullah's father seems to have been a middle level trader who was scrupulous in transmitting his skills to his son. Abdullah describes him as a hard taskmaster who made it a point never to praise or smile. His efforts yielded fruit, for Abdullah learnt to speak, read, and write a number of languages—Tamil, Hindustani, and Malay—and deployed this to good effect. He built up extensive and excellent connections with the English authorities, who found his skills and knowledge of local conditions extremely useful. He left Malacca permanently for Singapore in 1840 and stayed there until his death in 1854.

The Munshi's experience was undoubtedly an exceptional one in that he made the transition from a premodern world into the modern with great facility and thereby positioned himself in the new trading order of Southeast Asia with an easy elegance. He demonstrated his openness by working in close collaboration with traders and missionaries and even tried his hand at printing technology that the missionaries sponsored. While his experiences were unique and not shared by many, his account is revealing in that it illustrates the web of interconnectedness between local traders, immigrants, and religious leaders who combined the business of God and Mammon, and lent a unique dimension to the peripatetic world of Islam in Southeast Asia. His account also testifies to the dynamism of the trading milieu, which the European presence had not entirely undermined and which continued to support and sustain movements of men, goods, and ideas. Arab traders and Tamil Muslims who had merged with Malay society, who had invested in kin and marriage networks, and had deployed to good effect their literacy and linguistic skills, struck enduring roots in the trading world of the Indian Ocean even if they were small players in the global economy of the nineteenth century. There were others who did not make the transition so swiftly or successfully, who retained their immediate connections with their base in the Coromandel and who oversaw the traffic in labour for the nineteenth-century colonial trading economy and who reconciled to a new status in the commercial hierarchy of the colonial trading world of maritime Asia. Their identities would appear to have lost some of the older diasporic mobility and moral exchanges.

At the heart of the cosmopolitanism that Abdullah's enterprise reflected, lay language and literacy networks, marriage connections, and a readiness to respond to new changes. Penmanship was especially valued in Malay society and in its commercial environment; it was extremely useful for earning a living by writing letters and bills of contracts. Religion and communication were equally important qualifications and it was in the simultaneous deployment of these practices that the family demonstrated its receptivity to change. Admittedly, Abdullah veered towards the European dispensation and earned the disapproval of his critics for being "unpatriotic," but the fact remains that his response was part of an older and embedded social strategy that the community had embraced in its pursuit of a universal cultural space charted at a personal and intimate level through wives and relatives, and at a larger one through religion and representations. Religion and pilgrimage were significant in cementing the world of trade and traffic and in creating a genuinely cosmopolitan space at least before the mid-nineteenth century; later representations decrying the religious zeal of the Arabs testify not so much to religious militancy among Arabs as to the anxiety of the British in clearing the maritime channels of competition and rivalry. Not surprisingly, British observers, including Raffles, wrote of Arabs as intolerant sycophants who managed to hoodwink natives and secure high offices, which they held "as robbers" and "cover all with the sanctimonious veil of religious hypocrisy."[24]

THE CHETTIS: HOME AND THE WORLD

On the other end of the spectrum were the Chetties, whose location, response, and aspirations remained more local even as they operated in an expanding global trading system. In 1879, J.D. Vaughan, describing the Chetties in the Straits Settlements, observed that they "may be regarded as mere visitors who have the command of fabulous sums of money it is true, but are not as a rule rich individually. They are agents of wealthy men at Madras, they take very little interest in the colony and hasten back again to their country as quickly as they can."[25]

Vaughan's observations at one level demonstrate the fundamental difference between the profiles of the late-nineteenth-century Chetty immigrants and the earlier Chulia-Hadrami diaspora in Southeast Asia. In part this was to do with the nature of the business undertaken by the Nagarathars and their commercial and religious practices that tied them very strongly and integrally to the hinterland in Tamilnadu. The connection also meant that their political and social identity in the twentieth century was determined very closely by developments in South India. Yet this was not a mere expression of an extended overseas nationalism; a close examination of the practices of the Tamil-Hindu diaspora and within it the Chettiar component in Singapore and Malaysia is enough to reveal the complexities accompanying the formation of new circulating groups within the Indian Ocean under a formal regime of colonialism. The identities of new migrant merchant groups configured differently around the issues of language, religion and reform, and cultural performance. Additionally, there was a sense of material advancement that was potentially possible in the diaspora outside the home and one which invested the community with a different sense of empowerment that distinguished them from their kinsmen at home. The case of the Chettiars in fact would appear to reinforce

Markovits' suggestions about locating merchant networks in a local–global continuum, wherein the sense of common religious mission with its secular and philanthropic dimensions gave the diaspora a very distinct identity.

The Nattukottai Chettiars or Nagarathars of the nineteenth century were not part of the old mercantile groups of Beri and Balija Chetties mentioned in European factory records. This community would appear to have emerged in the late seventeenth century as small-scale itinerant traders in salt. By the eighteenth century, some of them had extended business operations as far south as Ceylon even as they became prominent as moneylenders to the zamindari estates of Ramnad and Sivaganaga.[26] This connection gave the community not only its clear and identifiable territorial basis but also its initial capital stock which they employed in their subsequent business ventures in Ceylon and Southeast Asia. Propelled by the British connection, they moved into these areas where they deployed their distinct accounting and partnership system in undertaking the marketing, financing of agricultural produce, and thereby determining the bazaar rates of interest and exchange.[27] What enabled the Nattukottai Chettiars to expand was their system of agency, whereby trusted caste members were sent out as triennial agents to conduct loan operations in overseas British colonies. By the late nineteenth century, they were an established community and identified as an influential class of merchants engaged in money lending. They assiduously maintained their connections with their ancestral base and closely participated in politics, articulating their views through several newspapers that they ran—the *Vysian, Oolian,* and *Vysyamitran.* A close study of these newspapers is in fact an excellent means of accessing the changing self-perception of the community as they consolidated their position in the Straits, formed associations on the lines that had emerged in Tamilnadu, and kept in close touch with its political and social developments. Social reform of the community featured as a major subject of discussion—the need to regulate consumption practices like dowry and the need to reform religious and ritual practices was continuously articulated.

IDENTITIES IN FLUX: BEYOND THE NATION?

How were these connections maintained over time? Did the community transform itself in course of the twentieth century when the experience of being nationalist, Indian, and Malay figured significantly in the making of the community's identity? How far did the new symbols of nationalism alter the traditional sources of community formation? We know from David Rudner's work on the Nagarathars, that investment in rituals and traditional forms of religious offering was a critical determinant in the expansion and consolidation of their networks in Tamilnadu. From the late nineteenth century, investment in temple endowments was followed by large-scale involvement in secular philanthropy that provided an illustration of the dynamic quality of investment in the symbolic quality of elite-hood, the social relationships it created, and the social changes it affected.

Looked at from the vantage point of the colony, it would seem that these processes were replicated. Chetty newspapers and the Nagarathar associations referred to the community's extensive investment in large-scale acts of temple building and social and educational reform in Malaysia and which were seen as major sites for self-assertion. What complicated the process was that the community of Chettiars constituted only one strand in the larger Tamil diaspora in the region and who did not necessarily see eye to eye on a wide range of issues with the rest of the Tamil population fragmented by caste, occupation, and ethnic identity. In fact, a close reading of Indian-run newspapers in Singapore and Malaysia would suggest a complex process of identity reordering at work—one that makes for any unitary understanding of the Tamil diaspora impossible. While at one level, the Hindu Tamil community representing capital (Chettiars and Mudaliars) echoed the sentiments of their kinsmen back home, were moved by similar aspirations, and echoed the same concerns of caste politics and language devotion, their politics and identity-related aspirations were fractured by competing claims that developed from within their own immediate location in the Straits. The community had to accommodate a double set of pressures developing from within their own community and from within the larger situation of modernization they found themselves in.

The Tamil community in Malaysia and Singapore was for the most part drawn from two different segments of Tamil society—workers recruited from the most destitute, landless labourers in Tamilnadu, while the overseers were recruited from educated, English-speaking graduates of Jaffna College. These groups were so different both sociolinguistically and socio-economically that there was never a question of developing common interests. The Chetties did not figure in this equation although their cohesiveness as a distinct community with very close natal connections did enable them to assume the initiative when it came to regulation of their community affairs. To that extent, one may well locate the Chetties and the Jaffna Tamils within the larger context of a changing public sphere within the Indian Ocean where the Western-educated elite—drawn from lawyers, teachers, and merchants—began to evolve into an intelligentsia that demanded social and cultural reform. Chettiars would seem to have formed part of this complex conglomerate and undertook, for instance, a vigorous programme for cultural and social reform. Initially, the emphasis was on the development of language and literary activity—in 1938, the Tamil Kody was organised in Malacca by Arunachalam Chettiar who came to Malacca in 1920 and in 1936 made the first move towards Tamil literary advancement by setting up the Thiruvalluvar Library. The library served as a centre for encouraging Tamil language and culture and enlisted the support of other groups interested in the issue. Language in fact brought Tamil Muslims to the fold as well—corresponding to developments in Tamilnadu, we have the instance of Tamil Muslims, led by Abdul Kadir in 1937, speaking on behalf of language reform and social empowerment.[28]

However, what distinguished the Chettiar's cultural profile in Southeast Asia was the engagement with religious practices and performance, which was in fact a traditional means of accumulating and demonstrating symbolic capital. Following the footsteps of their counterparts in Madras, the community assumed the lead in forming urban associations to sponsor cultural performances and to take the lead in the reform of religious and social practices that no longer conformed to their appreciation of tradition. The reform interventions were also seen as absolutely vital in providing a solid base for reconstituting Indian identity in Malaysia, for retaining their links with the homeland and yet consolidating their special identity as Malay Tamils. This was not a continuation of the older heritage of being an Indian Ocean subject where the various identities were melded to form a third one. The case of the Malacca Chetties was frequently cited to make the point that they had lost their language, dress, and customs and now spoke and dressed like Malays and followed only a few select customs in relation to death ceremonies. This was not seen as ideal and associations continued to insist on retaining links with India, promoting cultural activities and building up a sustainable base for the community.

It was in this connection that the circulation of cultural practices, of music, dance, and drama, within the diaspora became an object of overriding importance from the 1930s. As staunch advocates of Tamil, the community felt compelled to keep in step with developments in India; this could be ensured only by investing substantially in the promotion of theatre in the diaspora. Drama troupes and musicians from Madras were regularly invited. This had important consequences. On the one hand, it fed into important networks of sociability, mediated through a number of cultural associations that sprang up in the 1930s. This in turn reinforced the sense of belonging to a larger community of speakers but with a difference that arose out of being located outside the nation and within the diaspora. Like theatre, music too was considered as an important cultural resource. The pleasures of listening to music and learning it constituted part of a process of self-definition on the part of Indian elites and which tended to be replicated by certain groups, Chetties being an important case in point. A number of musical associations or sabhas sprang up in Singapore and Malaysia—the chief among them being the Indian Musical Arts Society, Singai Sangeetha Abhivriddhi Sabha, and the Malacca Sangeetha Abhivriddhi Sabha, which on almost every occasion announced their decision to spread music to all musically inclined people.[29] Accepting almost verbatim the Indian nationalist discourse on musical reform, these associations emphasized the necessity of culture in national life and regeneration and replayed the discourse on music and its reclamation as the most significant element in India's cultural heritage.

For the emergent middle-class Tamils in Malaysia, music became a critical tool in maintaining their identity as well as social status. For the Chettiar community, classical music had always been a marker of status and taste—in fact the community often extolled patrons of the art form. Recalling Alagappa Chettiar's contributions for instance, it was mentioned that his service to the cause of classical music had been impressive. As leading members of Malaysia's Indian community, Chetttiars took the lead in sponsoring classical music, which was both a marker of taste and cultured sociability as well as an important resource to which the community wanted to have access. From the late 1920s, there was a strident demand for instruction in classical music. The concern was to ensure scientific training very much on the lines musical reform was being engineered in Madras. A correspondent from Kuala Lumpur to the Indian Pioneer advocated in 1929 that direct instruction was critical when it came to musical training . To quote from his observation, "every Indian parent in Malaya is anxious to give a real good scientific training in music to his children but the difficulty is to secure the services of the right type of man and that in sufficient numbers to be spread over the whole peninsula. It is a matter of great importance for the Indian community in the country to take immediate steps to remedy the defects, as otherwise the chances are that Indian music as an art will be entirely lost to future generations of Indians in this country." He suggested that an all Malaya Sangeetha Sabha should be established in which every parent or guardian as well as lover of music should contribute an initial donation to enable the sabha to bring from India at least half a dozen qualified music teachers to be located in different towns. In every town, there should be a working committee to make arrangements to start a music school to give lessons to children of the locality. Weekly music parties should be held under the sabha or other existing organisation, which will provide children with a taste for music. As musicians now stand, musicians possessing various degrees of knowledge come to the country off and on, stay in a particular place for a few months or so, during which time they easily secure more students than they can cope with and, whether the students entrusted to them have received sufficient training or not, they move to other places or leave the country altogether and parents or guardians console themselves by repeating the dictum, "Be content with what you have."[30]

While advocating regular renewal of cultural ties with India to maintain standards of excellence in the arts which was seen as critical in consolidating identity, the Malay Tamils were keen on developing their cultural scene that could not be entirely dependent on musical talent from India. Consequently, the concerns were about developing an indigenous pool of talent for public performance and radio broadcasting. A letter to the editor of the *Indian Daily Mail* dated 21 May 1949 observed, "It is no exaggeration to say that every Indian is heartily sick of these programmes. First look at the Tamil news broadcasts. It is neither Tamil nor news. Compare these to the

Delhi Tamil broadcast. What an ocean of difference. Then musical programmes. There are some able singers in Malaya. There are some who can play on the violin excellently. Why not get these? Why always relay rotten low type Indian records."[31]

It is not clear whether these sentiments were representative of the entire Tamil community or whether these were the views of a small elite group, in which the Chettiars dominated. For it is important to keep in mind that many of these associations had a substantial Chettiar presence along with relatively new high-caste migrants who went for blue-collar jobs after independence. Likewise, the Chettiars were in the forefront of reform activity that centered around the issue of temple reform and reordering of certain rituals like the practice of taking out kavadis and body piercings which were identified as premodern unenlightened practices. In fact what stands out as far as the Chettiar community was concerned, is the proximity they maintained with their ancestral base and how the large and growing network of Nagarathar associations was tied together by speaking in one voice on issues of cultural consumption and religious practice and secular philanthropy. This set the community very distinctly apart from other Malay Tamils. The self-definition of the community was organised around the biographies of great men like Annamalai Chettiar, whose services, wealth, and involvement with Tamil scholarship and culture were frequently invoked by both Chetty associations in Kuala Lumpur and Singapore as well as by the Malay Indian Association, which had a strong Chettiar presence. At the same time, the associations, in keeping with the reformist temper that characterised their politics in Southern India, pressed for reform of temple management and eradication of caste privileges. Here the Malay experiment was interesting in that the orthodox opinion did not have the same weight or even presence as in India. The Malay Indian Association in fact stated that the reforms relating to temple management did not meet with opposition and that resistance to change in Malaya was not especially marked as the Malayan Tamils felt it was doubly necessary to carry them out in consideration of their self-image in the country. In fact it would seem that even in those temples where the responsibility for management lay with labouring castes, the resistance to reform was not marked—in fact one may well see the making of a new identity that was contingent on improved economic status, and on a more considered appreciation of public space where religious practices had to be reworked. The image that we have of the proud agent showing off his household effects to new arrivals indicates just how perceptions of better lifestyles were factored into the new self-perceptions of the diasporic community. And yet in the advocacy of religious practices, cultural tastes, and even dress, it is clear that the community clung to notions of what constituted the appropriate subject. To this was added an appreciation of their commitment to business ventures that integrated them into local commercial society as well. As Leong Yew pointed out in his address to the farewell ceremony of Alagappa Chettiar in 1946, "Speaking as an old resident (in Singapore) if I were asked which two classes of people who have contributed most to the material wealth of this land, I would unhesitatingly say the Chettiars and Chinese sundry shopkeepers. These two classes of people are bankers and financiers of the poor."[32]

There was obviously more than an element of exaggeration in the statement. However, what is noticeable is the distinct subjectivity that coalesced around the new diaspora subject, wherein the continuity of an older inheritance was transformed by a growing sense of what the new situation demanded in terms of politics, social and cultural practices that included language in a big way. If the Chulias and Hadramis worked within the contours of a polylingual domain of cross-cultural and commercial transactions, the Chettiars would appear to have operated within a narrower domain of linguistic and cultural politics that collapsed the nation, the community, and the diaspora into a less inclusive continuum.

RESISTING CONCLUSIONS

This chapter has hopefully raised more questions than it has answered. I began with the premise that the story of Asian networks in the Indian Ocean in the nineteenth and twentieth centuries requires to be retold with an emphasis on the transformation of the Indian Ocean merchant subjects, some of whom, like the Chulias, maintained a curiously dual profile of the peripatetic with the sedentary. For the nineteenth-century merchant, the world had changed but with some space left for him to articulate his sense of profit and affinity. Arabs interacted with Malays and Tamils to form a dynamic interface between premodern commerce and that of colonial power regimes. The cumulative aspects of premodern commercial experience grounded in a variety of religious practice, commercial techniques, and marriage networks were deployed with full effect enabling the formation of complex conglomerates that could also make a partial transition to the European dispensation. As Munshi Abdullah observed so engagingly, "Since Singapore has become a settlement, chintzes from Europe have been used as bathing clouts, broad cloth as trousers, Bugis satin and the Batek silk of Java as hats. People carry silk umbrellas in their hands and wear leather sandals and talk fluently in English, Bengali and Tamil. If an Englishman addresses them in Malay, they reply in English. As for the things I have mentioned above, I am astonished to see how markedly our world is changing. A new world is being created, the old world destroyed. The very jungle becomes a settled district, while elsewhere, a settlement reverts to jungle."[33]

For the Nagarathar Chetties, on the other hand, colonialism with all its attendant implications and structural adjustments forced upon the world of commerce in Southeast Asia, gave them a canvas to work out their enterprise. British linkages enabled them to assume a crucial position in the trading world of Southeast Asia and to consolidate it by adopting cultural and commercial strategies. As a nineteenth-century formation, Chettiars were closely connected with their natal base which meant that their stakes as a diaspora remained closely tied up with narratives of nationalism and subnationalism based on language. Colonialism produced new narratives of the self and subjectivity in Tamilnadu and the Nagarthars responded to these pressures, which made them essentially an extension of the original community quite unlike that of the earlier Malacca Chetties and the Hadrami-Chulia conglomerate. The dynamics of the Nagarathar presence in Southeast Asia, the political and social formations that they sponsored and initiated, and the nature of subject-hood they visualised for themselves in an independent Malaysia, while retaining their religious and marriage linkages with their natal base, needs to be examined more closely if we are to reevaluate the impact and interface of colonial domination on the Indian Ocean trading world.

NOTES

1. Philip D.Curtin, *Cross Cultural Trade in World History*. Cambridge, UK: Cambridge University Press, 1984.
2. Claude Markovits, The Global World of Indian Merchants, 1750–1947: Traders of Sind from Bukhara to Panama (Cambridge Studies in Indian History and Society). Cambridge, UK: Cambridge University Press, 2000, 1–9.
3. Ibid., 8.
4. "Introduction." *The UTS Review: The Indian Ocean Cultural Studies and New Writing*, Vol.6 Number 2, 2000, pp. 1–5.
5. Enseng Ho, "Empire Through Diasporic Eyes: A View from the Other Boat." *Comparative Studies in Society and History* 46(2004): 210–246.
6. Ashin Dasgupta, "Indian Merchants and the trade of the Indian Ocean, c. 1500–1750." In *The Cambridge Economic History of India Vol. I c.1200–1750*, ed. T.Raychaudhuri and I. Habib, pp. 407–433. Cambridge, UK: Orient Longman edition in association with Cambridge University Press, 1982.
7. John Crawford observed in 1820 that trade between India and Southeast Asia had always been conducted from the ports of the Coromandel and by the nation called the Kalinga or Telinga and that the shipping in which the trade was carried on by the people of the peninsula was on small vessels of 100 to 200 tons and manned by Indians, generally Muslims. See John Crawfurd, *History of the Indian Archipelago: Containing an Account of the Manners, Arts, Languages, Religions, Institutions and Commerce of Its Inhabitants in Three Volumes*. London: Hurst, Robinson & Co., Vol. I, 1820, 133ff.
8. T.J. Newbold, *Political and Statistical Account of the British Settlements in the Straits of Malacca in Two Volumes*. Singapore: Oxford University Press (2 Vols) 1971 (Reprint of 1839 edition) (Original publisher John Marray, London, 1839. I)
9. John Crawfurd, *History of the Indian Archipelago: Containing an Account of the Manners, Arts, Languages, Religions, Institutions and Commerce of Its Inhabitants in Three Volumes*. London: Hurst, Robinson & Co., Vol. I, 1820, 133ff.
10. Susan Bayly, *Saints, Goddesses and Kings: Muslims and Christians in South Indian Society*. Cambridge, UK: Cambridge University Press, 1989, 78–79ff.

11. The Book of Duarte Barbosa. An account of the Countries bordering on the Indian Ocean and their Inhabitants. Trans Longworth Dames, 2 volumes, London 1918 and 1921.

12. Bhaswati Bhattacharya, "The Dutch East India Company and the Trade of the Chulias in the Bay of Bengal in the Late Eighteenth Century," in *Mariners, merchants and Oceans Studies in Maritime History*, ed. K.S.Mathew, 348–350. India: Manohar, 1995. For a brief historical overview of Chulias see Kenneth McPherson, "Chulias and Kings: Indigenous Trade Diasporas and European Penetration of the Indian Ocean Littoral," in *Trade and Politics in the Indian Ocean: Historical and Contemporary Perspectives*, ed., G.Borsa, 33–46. India: Manohar, 1990.

13. Thomas Forrest, *A Voyage from Calcutta to the Mergui Archipelago Lying on the East Side of the Bay of Bengal.* London: J.Robson, 1792, 24, 37–40, 41–42.

14. *Ibid.* 41–42.

15. Enseng Ho, "Empire Through Diasporic Eyes: A View from the Other Boat." *Comparative Studies in Society and History* 46(2004): 210–246.

16. John Anderson, *Acheen and the Ports on the North and East Coasts of Sumatra with Incidental Notices of the Trade in the Eastern Seas and the Aggressions of the Dutch.* London: W.H. Allen & Co., 1840, 160–161.

17. John Crawfurd, *History of the Indian Archipelago: Containing an Account of the Manners, Arts, Languages, Religions, Institutions and Commerce of Its Inhabitants in Three Volumes.* London: Hurst, Robinson & Co., Vol. I, 1820.

18. Quoted in *An Anecdotal History of Old Times in Singapore by Charles Burton Buckley in Two Volumes.* Singapore, 1902 O.U.P. Reprint, 1984. Vol.II, 626–627.

19. Journal of the Malayan branch of the Royal Asiatic Society. Vol. XXII Part I 1949. Pp. 162–65.

20. Introduction to Abdullah Bin Abdul Kadir, *The Hikayat Abdullah*, An annotated translation by A.H. Hill, XPublisher CityX: XPublisherX, 1954. See 5.

21. A.H. Hill, "*The Hikayat Abdullah*, an Annotated Translation." *Journal of the Malayan Branch of the Royal Asiatic Society* (Singapore: Malayan Publishing House, Ltd.) Vol. 28 Part III, 1955, No. 171.

22. A.H. Hill, "*The Hikayat Abdullah*, an Annotated Translation." *Journal of the Malayan Branch of the Royal Asiatic Society* (Singapore: Malayan Publishing House, Ltd.) Vol. 28 Part III, 1955, No. 171, 41. "It happened that at that time in Malacca," Abdullah writes, "my grandmother on my mother's side became a great teacher at Kampong Pali. Some two hundred children learnt the Koran."

23. *Ibid.*, 48–50.

24. "Under the pretext of instructing the Malays in the principles of the Mohemedan religion they inculcate the most intolerant bigotry and render them incapable of receiving any species of useful knowledge," see J.A.E. Morley, "The Arabs and the Eastern Trade," in *Journal of the Malayan Branch of the Royal Asiatic Society* Vol. XXII (1949): 143–44.

25. J.D. Vaughan, *The Manners and Customs of the Chinese of the Straits Settlements.* Singapore: Oxford University Press, 1970 Reprint. First printed at the Mission Press, 1879, 1–2.

26. For an account of the Chettiars in Colonial India see David Rudner, *Caste and Capitalism in Colonial India: The Nattukottai Chettiars.* Berkeley, CA: University of California Berkeley, 1994.

27. Rajat Kanta Ray, "Asian Capital in the Age of European Domination: The Rise of the Bazaar, 1800–1914," *Modern Asian Studies* 29(3; 1995): 449–454.

28. *The Indian* (published every Sunday from Kuala Lumpur) 6 March, 1937. This carried a report on the Tamil Reforms Conference where Abdul Cadiri spoke in favour of the Tamil language, which to him embodied a spirit of egalitarianism: "I feel that the intention of the promoters of these conferences in using the word Tamil is to work towards reform and socialism among the members of the Tamil speaking population without any prejudice whatever. I am sure that Tamil would embrace all Tamil speaking people in the Malay Peninsula without any kind of religious or caste prejudice."
29. *The Indian*, Kuala Lumpur. 19 January, 1938.
30. *The Indian Pioneer*, 17 May 1929.
31. *The Indian Daily Mail*, 21 May, 1949.
32. Leong Yew's address. *The Indian Daily Mail*, 29 November, 1946.
33. A.H. Hill, "*The Hikayat Abdullah*, an Annotated Translation." *Journal of the Malayan Branch of the Royal Asiatic Society* (Singapore: Malayan Publishing House, Ltd.) Vol. 28 Part III, 1955, No. 171, 144–145.

7 Shared Hopes, New Worlds
Indians, Australians, and Indonesians in the Boycott of Dutch Shipping, 1945–1949

Heather Goodall

The drama which began to unfold in Australia in August 1945 brought together people from countries now known as India, Pakistan, Bangladesh, Indonesia, Malaysia, and Australia. Central to the story were the South Asian seamen in Sydney and Brisbane who, with Australian maritime workers, responded to a call from Indonesian nationalists to support their unilateral declaration of independence by boycotting all Dutch shipping in Australian waters. This was a powerful strategy: 559 ships were immobilised between October 1945 and the eventual achievement of Indonesian nationhood in 1949.[1] Such events often leave only the public statements of leaders. This struggle, however, has given us a rare glimpse of deeper relationships: the links made between the everyday working people involved, the ordinary seamen and their supporters.[2] We find people who, despite wide differences in background and outlook, still shared the powerful hopes with which they were trying to shape their vision of new worlds.

This story is about crossings of the Indian Ocean, already a rich source of fables to enliven cultures around its shores. It is ironic because this story is so recent, but the extraordinary hopes and optimism of these 1945 events seem just as much a fable to us today as any tale from the distant and imaginary past. This was a time when not only the possibility of creating formal alliances and vivid human relationships around the Indian Ocean was alive but it seemed to be unfolding in reality. Many of the peoples of the region felt they were poised on the edge of a very new future. Such optimism was fragile: by 1950 it had shriveled in the icy blasts of the Cold War into national isolationism and distrust. The stories have been ignored or lost, the people themselves seem to have been made to disappear. But finally, we can make the people visible again. In doing so, we can ask if this brief time of fable might show new pathways into the future.

The years from 1945 to 1949 have been studied in each of these places as national histories, revealing dynamic change as decolonization formed new nations, new alliances, and new directions. The perspective from the Indian Ocean, however, demands that we think outside the national boundaries that are such a defining part of today's analysis and indeed of its daily news. It asks how interactions and flows of people, trade, nature, and ideas might have been occurring around the Indian Ocean, regardless of national borders. This chapter considers this question in three sections. In the first, the uneasy tensions between national and international politics are outlined to suggest why the story of the Indian seamen has been ignored not only in Australia but also in India. In the second, the chapter draws on new documents and oral evidence to sketch the biographies of the people, particularly the Australians and Indians, involved in the boycott of Dutch shipping in Australia.[3] The final, concluding section compares the transnational goals of these actors with their nationalist aspirations and asks whether their hopes of cross-border communication were achieved.

In August 1945, the Indonesians had unilaterally declared independence from their Dutch colonizers when the Japanese surrendered. They hoped to block any effort by the Dutch to reenter what they still called the Netherlands East Indies (NEI). The Dutch expectation, however, was directly supported by the British government, in its twin roles as military leader of the South East Asian Command taking orderly possession of the surrendered Japanese-held areas and as the government of India and therefore the regulator of the labour of Indian seamen. Australia was still politically and militarily tied to Britain. Although from 1907 Australia was called a Dominion rather than a colony, it followed Britain unquestioningly into both world wars,[4] only to face abandonment in Singapore, losing its entire 8th Division in the fighting and to the grim Malayan Prisoner of War camps, then experiencing nerve-wracking isolation in its own ensuing war against the Japanese. The Indonesian declaration of independence forced the Australian Labor Party (ALP) government into a dilemma which touched on its own deepest conflicts. Some of its members wanted to support the British in their enforcement of Dutch reentry into the NEI while others, embittered by what they saw as the betrayal in Singapore, wanted to act in decisive support for the Indonesian nationalists, carving out a new independent future in what was expected to be an alliance of equality with the United States.

The hopes of 1945 were expressed for many Indian Ocean peoples by the Atlantic Charter, signed in 1941 by Roosevelt and Churchill and later endorsed by Stalin. Although it was drawn up in a different ocean, by leaders tainted by colonial rule and big power dominance, this charter nevertheless spoke of principles for a new world. The Indians, the Indonesians, and the Australians in our story repeatedly referred to its guarantees that "the peoples had a right to self-determination," that there was to be "freedom from want and fear" which was to be enforced by global partnerships, that there was to be freedom of the seas and that there was to be common, global postwar disarmament. To them, this charter promised the end of empires. There were many others who read the charter in this way: it was as much of a beacon for Vietnamese nationalists as for Philippinos and Africans. In the early months of 1945 it seemed like this Atlantic Charter was a pathway to find the new worlds they wanted so badly to rise from the ashes of war.

The possibility of finding common threads in the histories of this period in Australia as well as in India and Indonesia is not usually recognized because the differences between them seem to be too great. The positions of India and Indonesia seem much easier to compare: each had large populations colonized and exploited by small numbers of Europeans who enacted the political and military power of distant Europe. Both had increasingly powerful nationalist movements which were taking their challenge to the world stage and demanding decolonization. Australia has seemed very different: it was a settled colony, composed by 1945 predominantly of settlers from the British Isles with a sprinkling of other Europeans. It had militarily and demographically suppressed its indigenous colonized minority and isolated itself racially with the White Australia policy, apparently aligning itself firmly with Britain on all issues up to that time.

Yet this apparent homogeneity was unstable. Since first settlement there had been a large and powerful Irish working-class component in the Australian population, which had long resented British control and its demands for loyalty, often against nationalists in Ireland. The anger generated by the British retreat after Singapore built on this underlying resistance to British colonialism and it was combined as well with the rising sense of the power of left-wing movements which had been generated by the united front between the Western powers and the Soviet Union during the war years. This led many in Australia to look towards a new direction for the future. The United States was seen as an important new ally but in this period before the heaviest impact of the Cold War, there were many Australians for whom this was not the only choice. They were looking to a future with a greater degree of national independence than ever before and a new recognition of the surrounding Indian and Pacific Ocean regions in which Australian troops had built alliances over the war.

Into this situation came the call from nationalists inside Java for the independence of Indonesia from Dutch colonial control. There had been many Indonesians residing in Australia since the fall of the NEI in 1942. Some had come with the retreating Dutch into exile in Australia and others were the crews on ships caught outside NEI waters when the Japanese invaded. Among the ships' crews were ordinary seamen, mostly Javanese, Muslim, and lower class, but there were also substantial numbers of Indonesian petty officers recruited from other regions, principally Manadonese men from eastern Sulawesi, who tended to be from more elite groups in Indonesian traditional society, had more colonial education, were more affluent and Christian.[5] Finally there were many Indonesians, again principally Javanese but from a wider range of elite and nonelite traditional groups, who had been long-time Dutch political prisoners in Tanah Merah camp, at Boven Digul in West Irian, because of their nationalist agitation and, for many, their affiliation to the Communist Party.[6] Set free in Australia through the intervention of the Federal ALP government, these activists had unprecedented communication with the Australian Left, including not only Communists and left-wing trade union members but far more widely into the Australian public. Never before had white Australians had such extensive and sympathetic exposure to non-Europeans. Molly Warner, who later married the activist Mohamad Bondan and returned with him to Indonesia, has recorded the process many average Australians went through in the early years of the war, of first feeling the need to build relationships with some of the neighbouring peoples who were all facing similar threats from Japanese expansion, then looking around to find some people with whom to build those relationships. The Indonesians were on hand, almost coincidentally, which allowed an unprecedented network of personal friendships to develop, alongside a sympathy for the nationalist goals of independence which were evident even in 1943.[7]

So when Sukarno issued his plea on 8 October 1945 for support specifically from the four nationalist statesmen he thought would be most sympathetic—Ho Chi Minh of Vietnam, Herbert Evatt of Australia (and Minister for Foreign Affairs in the ALP Government), Jawaharlal Nehru of India, and Carlos Romulo of the Philippines[8]—the Australian Left and its unions were ready to respond. The usual accounts of these events have stressed the rapid, enthusiastic role of the Australian unions who had never before expressed such sustained solidarity with non-Europeans nor with calls to act against a European power.[9] They carried out a tactic well known among seamen and dockworkers: the boycott of shipping in port. This meant that no ships could be loaded, repaired, refueled, or crewed to leave if they were under the ban. This strategy had been used by Indian seamen in London in the early days of the war to bargain for higher wages.[10] The Black Bans on coal freighters in Port Kembla had been the strategy of Australian maritime workers in 1938 to prevent the sale of Australian pig iron for processing to Japan in 1938 arguing it would be turned into bullets to repress the occupied Chinese or later used against Australia in the feared, coming war.[11]

Indian seamen played a key role in the 1945 boycott of Dutch shipping. Yet their presence is barely registered in the Australian histories, which focus only on the roles of Australian unions, and in particular the wharfies working on the docks. Australian seamen were not the crews of these Dutch vessels nor did they crew any of the other international shipping in any numbers. The Australian Seamen's Union (ASU) only controlled the crews on local shipping routes around the Australian coast or between Australia and New Zealand. It had no control over crews recruited in other places by foreign-owned shipping, which of course accounted for the majority of shipping in Australian ports. Ships travelling between Australia and the NEI included those owned by Dutch lines like KPM and by the smaller British-owned fleets of Burns Philp and others, as well as the giant British P&O. Some Indonesian ordinary seamen had initiated the boycott by walking off Dutch ships in Brisbane on 21 September 1945.[12] Most Indonesians, with the exception of key activists, were, however, repatriated on the *Esperance Bay* and other ships to independent areas of Indonesia, leaving Sydney on 13 October 1945. Those Indonesian seamen who remained were predominantly the petty officers, most of whom were Manadonese, who were strongly sympathetic towards the strike and fraternized with the Indonesian, Indian, and Australian activists, but did not walk off the ships nor stop them sailing.[13]

The majority of working seamen, the people who *could* actually stop the ships from sailing, were in fact Indians. It was Indian seafarers who did the political spade work, talking with Indian crews and persuading them to leave their ships despite the very real risks they all faced at the time and for the future. As they all knew only too well, their "continuous discharge" papers which had to be shown when they applied for all their later international jobs would bear the record of their defiance if the shipping companies decided to stamp the "Report of Character" column with the words "unsatisfactory" or "deserter."[14] Yet the Indians took this risk, with over two hundred men actually walking off their ships and another one thousand remaining on ships in Melbourne, Sydney, and Brisbane but refusing to sail them. They held up over 180,000 tons of arms and supplies being sent to the Dutch.[15]

The role of the Indian seamen was not just largely ignored at the time by the Australian union leadership but was denigrated by some senior Labor Party politicians. Herbert Evatt himself dismissed them as strikebreakers, using that most bitter of all Australian abuse by saying "All Indians are scabs."[16] Why has the Indian role been largely written out of the histories of the boycott produced later both from within the Australian unions[17] and from academics?[18] There are a number of reasons, as I have discussed in greater length elsewhere,[19] which include gross ignorance on the part of much of the media and of the public which confused "Indonesians" with "Indians." Most of the cause, however, as G. Balachandran, Frank Broeze, and Janet Ewald[20] have demonstrated, lay in the long history of colonialism and the power of colonial shipping companies, since the late eighteenth century, to construct and then embed racial differences. Indian seafarers, usually designated "lascars," became increasingly important as the major unskilled labour force of the colonial sea trade. Despite their essential role in the industry, and precisely because they were present in British ports in high numbers, Britain viewed Indians as a threat in that they might move from their ships into the port city populations of the metropole or its settler colonies, establishing racially and culturally distinct minority populations. A series of increasingly proscriptive laws, including the tightly defined contracts designed for Indians and the regulations imposed on the shipping companies and known collectively as "Asian Articles," forced shipping owners who recruited Indian and other "coloured" seafarers to record and monitor their movements during their contracts and commit to returning them to their home nation.

The "Asian Articles" proliferated on the basis of the alleged characteristics of different racial groups, such as Arabs, Indians, and Sri Lankans. Colonial conditions meant that the contracts they were forced to work under acted in very concrete ways to constrain Indian seafarers' wages and undermine their conditions of labour. Indian seamen made increasingly powerful challenges to these acts in the early twentieth century, mobilizing through the seafarers' unions which formed in Calcutta as early as 1918 and were active in both Bombay and Calcutta through the 1920s.[21] By 1936, they had achieved the highest rate of union coverage in any industry in India.[22] Yet, as both Balachandran and Broeze have documented, the Indian unions were defeated in each conflict because British shipping companies had direct influence on the British government, which consistently supported the companies in each case. Australian unions tended to seek their own advantage by endorsing shipping company strategies of dividing and ruling on racial lines, and blamed Indian "lascars" for their own oppression. In this they drew heavily on the confused stereotyping which had developed under colonialism involving religion, physical differences, and supposedly inherent character traits. "Lascars" were defined by the cluster developed to refer to "Hindoos," such as timidity, caution, and a lack of combativeness, as if this reflected some fixed biological category.[23] This is an irony given that the majority of seafarers in Australia were Muslims from the northwestern provinces of India, who might be considered also under another confused set of stereotypes, depicting the "mussalman" as aggressive, fanatical, and certainly combative, a characterization which although quite different was similarly derogatory.[24]

The ASU had a weaker but continuing counter force arising from the influence on its membership of the International Workers of the World (IWW) or "Wobblies", whose tenacious defence of antiracist internationalism, with the vision of the One Big Union, motivated the Darwin branch of the ASU to work on recruiting Indians in 1915.[25] In this spirit, the ASU offered substantial support to any "coloured" seamen who wanted to set up their own union, and it argued strongly in the International Labour Organisation after its formation in 1926, for the rights of Indian and other non-European seamen[26]. Its support however was paternalistically framed as assistance to "ignorant, illiterate" and "poverty stricken" foreign seamen to learn about unions, as if they were unfamiliar with industrial action and in need of tuition and guidance.[27] The ASU was still refusing during World War II to enroll Indian seamen directly into its membership.

Yet if ignorance, racism, and paternalism had rendered Indian seamen and their militancy invisible to Australians, it could not be said that Australia was invisible to Indians. The research documenting the history of Indians and Afghanis in Australia has been exemplary in its depth of analysis of Australian documents, oral histories, and material evidence. Yet it has been limited by Australian national borders and does not look for international Indian opinion on the rising tide of racism which overtook Australian federation at the end of the nineteenth century.[28] Once we start considering the oceanic crossings of the seafarers, however, it becomes more pressing to search for the ways in which Indians outside Australia might have learnt about and understood Australian politics before they arrived.

Since the 1880s, Indians around the world had been aware of increasing Australian hostility towards Asians in general and Indians in particular.[29] Their concerns had begun appearing in popular media with an Indian readership in England, South Africa, and within India itself from at least the turn of the twentieth century. It was an issue which was particularly widely canvassed in the Islamic newspapers which circulated actively across the British Empire.[30] This was because so much Australian racial denigration of the time was focused on those Indians who formed a majority of immigrants from the subcontinent, the Muslim Afghans, Pathans, and Punjabis who had come from the 1860s to work with camels in what continued to be the essential transport system for Australia's arid Outback. While few of these camelmen had come from Bengal and the eastern areas like the seafarers, the widespread Islamic affiliation among these eastern seamen and the interpenetration of ideas between elite, reformist Islam and "folk" Islam[31] ensured that news about Australian attitudes circulated widely. It was a particular matter of debate and caustic attack in the 1910s, not only among educated and upper-class Indians but among working people frustrated in their attempts to work in Australia.[32] This must have formed a substantial part of the knowledge which Indian seafarers carried with them when they docked in any Australian ports.

* * *

The key to opening up the story of Indian seamen and their relationships with Australians and Indonesians in 1945 comes from the emergence in 2006 of a previously unexamined archive until then languishing in a library for union and business records. The archive was created because in October 1945, five hundred Indians did form a union called the Indian Seamen's Union in Australia (ISUiA) to cover their interests while they were in Australian waters and active from 1945 to 1949. Their key Australian supporter, Clarrie Campbell, was a man who kept impeccable records so the Union's archive holds the names, addresses, ships, and job titles of more than nine hundred Indian seafarers who joined up in those years, as well as their letters to the Union and the letters and notes of speeches made by the Indian ISUiA spokespeople. We suddenly have a body not only of the words of these Indian seamen themselves but pointers to newspaper coverage which includes photographs. So now there are faces as well as words to help us see who these people were. Finally, the certainty that this movement and these people, although ignored, really did exist has made it possible to search out the surviving Australians who knew them and to learn more from their memories about what these days were like.

The ISUiA was most active in Sydney, although it had links to the other major ports involved in the boycott, Fremantle in Western Australia, Melbourne, and Brisbane. The Australians we can trace who were connected with it were each born outside Sydney but had gravitated to it by the war years. At the centre of the Australian connection was Clarrie Campbell, born in 1890 in South Australia and a plumber by trade. His long relationships with Indians began as he was travelling in England and then in India in 1913.[33] He had returned to Australia by the beginning of the First

World War and enlisted there, finding himself at Gallipoli fighting alongside Indians, under British orders and on behalf of the British Empire.[34] The Indian soldiers he met seemed to have been Punjabis and Pathans from the northwestern areas of India, most of whom were Muslim. These were people, along with Sikhs and some Hindus from the same northwestern areas, whom the British deliberately targeted for recruitment to the army as they believed them to be "the martial races."[35] Clarrie was clearly disturbed by the experiences he himself had in Gallipoli and after he returned wounded to Australia he immersed himself in the anti-conscription campaign of 1916. But the Indians in Gallipoli were in a far more difficult position. Not only were they being asked to fight for the British, in a time when the Indian nationalist movement was emerging more strongly, but they were being ordered to turn their guns against fellow Muslims, the Turks whose country they were invading from the west. The stresses on Indian soldiers in the imperial army were intense. Just two months after the final evacuation of Gallipoli, the whole 15th Indian Lancers were transferred from France to Basra to fight the Turks from the east. They rebelled, signing an oath

Figure 7.1 Clarrie Campbell in a formal business card photograph taken in the late 1940s. Courtesy Noel Butlin Archives of Business and Labour, Australian National University.

they would not fight against fellow Muslims. Tried by the British Army, the officers were pardoned but all 492 members of the subaltern ranks were severely punished.[36] Similar stresses must have been resonating among the Indians serving in Gallipoli and can only have convinced Australians like Clarrie, as they built friendships with Indian soldiers, that for all their differences they shared a common antagonism to British rule.

Sustaining his contacts with Indians during long periods of overseas travel in the 1920s, he trained as an industrial chemist and returned to Australia, opening a small garage in Glebe in inner city Sydney, along with a business making bitumen for road surfacing. One of his small companies, United Lubricants, conducted substantial trade with India in the 1930s.[37] He was active politically, supporting working people's campaigns against eviction in the Depression and sustaining close personal friendships with Federal Labor Party politicians, standing for the Federal Labor seat of West Sydney in 1934 and opposing the right-wing Labor icon J.T. Lang in 1941.

Campbell managed Ben Chifley's first election campaign for the seat of Macquarie in 1929 and remained in contact with him while Chifley was ALP Prime Minister during the 1940s, although Campbell was closer to the Federal member for East Sydney and Minister for External Territories, Eddie Ward.[38] At the same time, however, Campbell was involved with the Communist Party, never becoming a member as far as the Australian Security Intelligence Organisation (ASIO) could find, but working closely enough with the party to ensure regular security reports.

Although his links with the Communist Party of Australia (CPA) were regarded as sinister by ASIO and it spent years trying to prove that he was channeling money into Australia from the USSR, the documentation of Campbell's Indian connections suggests something rather different. He spent most of his time when he was involved with Indian seamen doing social welfare and individual support work as he and the seamen tried to sort out the complexities of retrieving unpaid wages, prosecuting violent ship captains and covering onshore medical and sometimes funeral expenses. During the mid 1930s he initiated and nurtured an Australia-India Association, among whose patrons were a wide range of Sydney's establishment as well as its politically Left advocates for civil rights like Jessie Street. This organization sent funds to India to aid in the Famines in 1944 and 1946. Of greater significance in the longer term was its backing of the Indian Club which grew out of Campbell's meetings with Indians in Sydney. Most of these were seafarers, in port between ships, and they faced many social and industrial problems, including overcrowded and poorly serviced "labour pool" accommodation while in Australian ports.[39]

Campbell's strategy was to find a place to establish a social club, which he had managed to do by 1943, located within the Anglican Seamen's Mission in the dockland area in Sydney, where Indian seamen could meet each other and mix with Australian visitors and volunteers, as well as interested seamen from other places, like the Indonesians. This was directly parallel to the organization and running of a range of "Servicemen's clubs" which were operating for visiting Allied servicemen through the war years.[40] The situation in Australia, of US-enforced and Australian-endorsed racial segregation in social clubs, was echoed in the provision the Anglican Seamen's Mission offered to the Indians. While Campbell's letters stressed the generosity of the mission in allowing the Indian Club to take up a whole floor, the space given them was on the remote upper floor of the old building, strictly segregated from the "white" seamen's recreation areas on the first floor and ground levels. The Indian Social Club was, in fact, located in what its volunteer workers routinely called "the black part" of the Seamen's Mission.

Campbell and his partner, Ada Boyce were regulars three nights a week at this club, making tea, talking, dancing, organizing picnics and trips to the South Coast for the day, running Hindustani films, organizing a prayer space, or filling up the room with chairs for the annual celebration of Id-Uz-Zuha, which allowed the Indians to meet and interact with a wide range of Sydney Muslims to share this enriching time of renewal which marks the end of the month of Ramadan.[41]

The Indians had the space at the club to talk over not only social affairs but the conflicts they might be embroiled in with ship's captains and shipping companies, the unfair withholding of wages or the brutality of a first mate, the inadequate medical provision on some ships and the abuse they suffered on others. These exploited industrial conditions were familiar to other regular visitors to the Social Club, like Mick Ryan and Barney Smith from the Seamen's Union, and in 1943 or 1944 they assisted at a meeting with some hundreds of Indians to talk with representatives of that union about gaining temporary memberships so they would have some support when they were in Australian waters. The ASU told them to organize an independent union, like the Chinese or the Indonesians had just done, and the Australians would support them. But the Indians had no resident population and the possibility of maintaining an advocacy structure was unworkable when most of them were only in port for a matter of weeks. Rebuffed, the Indians continued to draw on the individual assistance which people like Campbell and Smith could offer as they battled through the next few years.[42]

Clarrie's main focus was always on relationships with Indians, as Molly Bondan pointed out in her writings about those days, but in mid 1946, the small group of Indonesians remaining in Australia, largely in the Brisbane-based Committee for Indonesian Independence (KIM), asked for Clarrie's help.[43] Bondan, Molly's husband, wrote personally to Clarrie explaining that the tightening Dutch blockade around the Republican areas had choked off supplies of essential goods, particularly medical supplies. As a counter measure, the Republic was desperately trying to establish a shipping route to take in firstly these vital relief supplies but then to open an ongoing trade connection. The Indonesians based in Singapore had already negotiated with an Indian businessman, Dr. Rasanayagam, and three members of the Overseas Chinese Association to hire the ship with a British Captain, but the Indian insisted on an Indonesian crew. Bondan asked Clarrie for his political support and for his assistance to recruit the crew and to organize the loading of the ship from Sydney, in collaboration with the Waterside Workers Federation, but then to expand it to an ongoing import/export operation.

Another of the regulars to the Indian Club from 1944 onwards was Phyllis Johnson, born in 1907 in Perth, making her a woman of the Indian Ocean. She was married to Johnno Johnson, a violin maker, and both were members of the CPA in Sydney and had become friends with Clarrie through his connections there. I spoke with Phyllis in 2007, just before she turned ninety years of age. After her move to Sydney and marriage to

Figure 7.2   Phyllis Johnson, photograph taken during 1940s.

Johnno, Phyllis was an outspoken young activist in the CPA, and was jailed in the early years of the war (presumably before the Nazis turned on the Soviet Union) for publicly speaking as an advocate of an end to the fighting. She remembers however that jail wasn't so bad over those three months, because the chief wardress had herself been a spokesperson for the anti-conscription campaign like Phyllis's father, and she would open the cell door and bring Phyllis over for tea and cakes after lights out.

Phyllis and Johnno came to the Indian Club a few nights each week, serving tea and chatting and they went with Clarrie, Ada and groups of Indians to the picnics and trips to the South Coast. She had been drawn in through knowing Clarrie in the CPA campaigns and became interested in his friendships with Indians at the time of the Bengal Famine.

Most of the club's volunteers, who were mainly young women, had been drawn in through their connections with the party, rather than through links with the maritime unions. Phyllis jokes as she recalls these highly politicized young people, including herself, in intense conversations with the seamen which were often at cross-purposes: the Indians were trying to practice their skills in spoken English with polite questions about the girls' jobs and families, while the enthusiastic young Communists wanted to quiz them about conditions in India and how long it would be before the British were driven out. "We were do-gooders!" Phyllis laughed.

Sylvia Mullins, younger than Phyllis, was from an impoverished family west of Sydney. She had always known she wanted to make political changes and she had joined the Communist Party as soon as she was able to move to Sydney and take a job. She was also one of the regulars at the Indian Social Club, introduced by other young members of the party and excited by the chance to meet so many young men, as much as by the glimpses she was gaining of a whole world of activists and politics beyond Australian shores. Right in the thick of the Australian campaign to support the Indonesian declaration of independence, she was in a Sydney dockside demonstration with many other Communist Party members, including Phyllis and Johnno, against a British troopship carrying Dutch servicemen to conduct the military recolonisation of the NEI. The Dutch troops threw refuse at them and then hosed them down, and Sylvia, caught in the water and the light, became the subject of one of the most memorable photographs taken during the strike.

She became close friends with the Indonesians who visited the Indian Club as well as with the Indians themselves, and describes being invited to dinner on a Dutch ship by one of the Indonesian petty officers. She gained an insight then into the complex racialised politics at sea. The Indian engine room crew had already walked off on strike, but the Indian catering staff remained on duty, serving these middle-class Indonesians who were sympathetic to the strike but who chose to remain onboard ship.

The Indian seafarers in Australia were overwhelmingly working men, many of whom moved between agriculture and seafaring to support their

Figure 7.3 Sylvia Mullins and other protesters being hosed by Dutch troops aboard a British ship, during a Sydney demonstration against the transport of Dutch military support to the Netherlands East Indies. *The Sun*, 9 November 1945.

families.[44] There were only a very few members of any Indian elite groups, arising from either traditional status or from colonial education, among the seamen in Australia. One was the middle-class Goan Joseph Noronha, fluent in English, who had met Clarrie at the Social Club early in 1945 and who continued to write to him. He had not joined the ISUiA when it began, however, because, as he pointed out to Clarrie, "my people are class conscious and did not trust me."[45] There appear to have been virtually no members of elite groups in the Indian seafarers' union itself, where the men signed themselves on invariably as working in the engine room, as ordinary deckhands, or as cooks and assistants in the catering departments of the English and Dutch ships on which they had come.[46] Some Indians had affiliations to the Communist Party of India[47] but far more common among the seafarers' was union membership in India and this too was consistent with the relatively high level of unionization within the industry compared to other industries in India, despite high unemployment.[48]

There were some regional differences, with Goans, Pathans, Punjabis, and Bengalis forming the major groupings, with diversity in religion as well between Catholic Goans and the majority of the others who were Muslims. While their regional variation made the Indians similar to the Indonesians, in class terms they were very different. Whereas the Indonesians had a higher number of educated or elite members among the petty officers and the freed political internees, the Indians were almost entirely working people.[49] High numbers of Indians had been passing through Australian ports for at least a century and yet Australians were almost entirely ignorant about them. Indians had remained invisible to all except those few people who had begun to make contacts through channels like the Indian Social Club. We now have some images and fragmentary records of their words, both public and private, and, for just a few, we have film. The Dutch filmmaker Joris Ivens was commissioned by his government to record the anticipated triumphal reentry of the Dutch into the NEI, but he became sympathetic to the Indonesian republicans and began filming their boycott in secret. Unable to film the actual events in Sydney, however, because he was still officially employed by the Dutch, he orchestrated reenactments, usually within days or weeks of each of the individual events taking place. The key roles were filled by the union activists themselves, although they were not always taking the roles they had carried out in real life.[50]

The person who made the most dramatic impact on the Australians was Dasrath Singh, known universally to his Australian friends as "Danny."[51] A seamen employed in the catering department of various ships but in Sydney "between voyages," Singh's name suggests a northwestern Indian origin and a Sikh affiliation, but neither are certain. A cook or a cook's assistant, he had been in Australia for some time before the boycott of Dutch shipping began and had been a regular visitor to the Indian Social Club, where Phyllis remembers him for his fluency in English and Indian languages and for his mercurial, engaging character.

When the call came to support the Indonesians, Singh turned all his energies to organizing the Indians who were the crews of British and Dutch vessels.[52]

Singh's role, journalist Lockwood pointed out in his eyewitness account of the boycott, *Black Armada*, was crucial to more than the Indian campaign. As Clarrie Campbell put it in the character reference to trade union officials and Indian nationalist leaders which he wrote for Singh at the end of January, 1946, when Singh was finally being deported because of his political challenge of the Dutch:

> The bearer, D. Singh, is leaving Australia tomorrow for repatriation to India, under Dutch orders . . . It was the bearer who took the first active steps to warn the Australian Trades Unions of the impending Dutch plans of running their boats from Australia to Java with munitions of war to be used against the Indonesian people in their fight for Independence. From the moment this warning was given, the whole of the Trades Union movement in this country was geared up for action. With Mr Singh goes the deep appreciation of the whole of the Australian Trades Unions, as expressed at the ACTU conference yesterday, together with the gratitude and appreciation of the Indian Seamens Union in Australia.[53]

Lockwood agreed that Singh had had a major initiating role in the dispute, and argues that the original Black Ban had been against all Dutch shipping,

Figure 7.4 Dasrath Singh, known as Danny Singh by Australians, in a newspaper report on his harassment by Dutch plain clothes security officers in Sydney during the Boycott. *Tribune,* 9 November 1945.

whatever its cargo, without specific expectations that arms would be discovered. Dasrath Singh's news had caught the Australians off guard, bringing information from Indian crews that the Dutch were loading commercial cargo ships with guns and bullets. [54] The Indians reported that there had been Australian unionists as well as Dutch troops hauling the crates. It had been this evidence which swung the Prime Minister, Ben Chifley, into support of the Black Ban at a time when others, like the then Foreign Minister, H.V. Evatt, were only increasingly anxious to end the boycott in order to crush the rising power of the unions, particularly those with Communist leadership, which he argued were intervening in foreign policy.[55] This was the first time Australian activists became aware of loading guns and bullets onto commercial cargo vessels in Sydney ports.[56]

Phyllis Johnson has described the night when Danny Singh brought the news. He burst into "the black section of the Seamen's Mission" around 10 p.m. one evening early in October, just days after the Indonesians had called for a general boycott. Singh had three seamen from the *Japara* with him and he came with a message the Australians hadn't heard before, urging Clarrie Campbell, Barney Smith from the Seamen's Union, and the Johnsons to help him to take urgent action. Phyllis remembers him to have said:

> There's a ship at Ball's Head (one of the North Sydney docks). There are Indian seamen on it and the Dutch are loading munitions! The Indian seamen are very concerned about it but they don't know what to do. We've got to get those men off!

Phyllis and Johnno went across the harbour with Danny, but because it was a Dutch ship, Phyllis didn't go down below decks to where the seamen were meeting. Instead she stayed on the dock, but it was dark, cold and raining. She remembers waiting for hours, hunched on the pier:

> Johnno went onto the ship with Danny and it took a long time . . . because the Indians had to be sure. They had to be sure that Johnno was fair dinkum. And John said, "My wife is sitting on the wharf in the rain waiting for you to come off!" And it WAS raining I can tell you! Well, we got them all off . . . they came up with their prayer mats and they had very very little, but they were the first seamen to walk off [in Sydney] and they were all Indian, all of them![57]

This was a grave step for the Indian sailors—where they had taken direct action such as this previously in Britain, there had been a substantial resident South Asian population to support them.[58] This was not the case in Australia, so the seamen were risking everything and needed clear assurances that they would be supported not just financially but also politically.

Once the campaign got underway, the Indians decided that they should set up the ISUiA to provide a base. They tried to counter the problem of not having a resident population by electing one non-Indian member onto the Executive. Campbell became the Honorary Treasurer and began keeping those impeccable books. The Indians needed to build the membership up rapidly to give the organization weight, and they used the Social Club to recruit, asking seamen who came to it to list all the seamen and ships they knew. The Union's organizers then went round to the labour pools and boarding houses to find the men, gaining contact addresses and signatures to sign them up formally. Campbell funded a small commission for each of the men who eventually agreed to sign on.[59]

Dasrath Singh was one of the key people carrying out recruiting searches and Campbell's reference went on to describe Singh's energetic role—as well as its consequences:

> Through the whole of this campaign, D. Singh has constantly worked in a voluntary capacity and because of his stand to implement the spirit of the Atlantic Charter, the Dutch are returning him to India . . . D. Singh has been one of the most active members in building this Union, giving almost the whole of his time, day and night, to it.

The extent to which the membership built up was impressive: within the first few months there were over 600 members and in the next year there were 300 more added. Campbell ensured that every one of them filled in a membership form which included their name and contact address, their ship and occupation on it, and their preferred language (English, Goanese, Urdu, or Bengali). This gives a rare glimpse of the origin and community affiliation of these Indian workers, about whom many general records had been gathered by British and Indian governments and by shipping companies over decades, but with few such personal details.

Campbell went on to point out that Dasrath Singh had been targeted as he became more effective, indicating the collaboration of some members of the Indian High Commission staff, still loyal to the British, who had worked against the strikers. The active role played by the Dutch military and secret service in Australia, with the reluctant support of the Australian police, was deeply resented by the general Australian public, who were already disenchanted with the British and who saw the heavy-handed Dutch attempts to intimidate both Indonesians and Indians as evidence of a colonialism they wanted to put behind them. Jack, Sylvia Mullins' younger brother, on leave for four days from the Australian Air Force, helped to protect Danny Singh as he went from meeting to meeting, calling on Indians to boycott the Dutch ships and on Australians to contribute to the strike funds to support the Indians. Jack has described the scene as he and his Air Force mate Harry moved Dasrath Singh from place to place, with the Dutch following them threateningly in a car crawling along the curb beside them.[60]

> We were shadowed by a couple of big heavy Dutch blokes in a car. I got on the outside, then there was Danny and then there was Harry on the inside because he was the short bloke—although he's a good wrestler. And at one stage they pulled up along side us, and one started to get out and said, "Singh come here." And I turned around and I said, "Piss off. He's not going anywhere with you." So they decided they'd better not tackle us. We were in Air Force uniforms. So away they went . . . but there was a certain amount of apprehension all the time there. The

Indians were very game because there were stand over tactics, and of course the Dutch were putting all sorts of pressure on our government I suppose to see that these people were deported.

Once the boycott was well underway, the Dutch moved even more aggressively against Singh. In one incident, Dutch guards and intelligence officers, with the help of the New South Wales (NSW) Police, grappled with Singh and a group of Pathan unionists at the busy Central Railway station, in full view of shocked Australian peak hour commuters. The Dutch guards had been trying to stop Singh from talking to newly arrived Indian seamen, brought into the country with British cooperation to break the strike, as they were being transferred by train to Brisbane where a strike-bound ship waited.[61] Finally, the Dutch demands led to the forced "repatriation" of an unwilling Singh, on 1 February 1946.

Despite the many vivid memories which Australians hold of Dasrath Singh, there are no examples anywhere in the Indian Seamen's Union records of his writing. In fact, Campbell's notes suggest that Singh hated paperwork, never filled in forms and discarded letters unread.[62] Before he left, he took part in Joris Ivens' film *Indonesia Calling*, playing the part of one of the Indian seamen who had been brought to Australia to break the strike. The film reenacted the Indians' pursuit of the huge Dutch steamer *Patras* making its way out of Sydney Harbour with its newly arrived Indian crew forced to work by Dutch soldiers.

This was not the only ship which sailed with Indian crews, but all those which did sail were doing so at gunpoint. Another such incident occurred, with better documentation, showing that a reluctant Indian crew had been forced to leave Sydney after having tried to walk off. Indian unionists got word to friends in Brisbane, including Molly and Bondan at KIM. Molly wrote back in cautious, cryptic terms to convey their bad news:

> Not possible . . . to do much with Indians on these ships . . . [we know] that the 90 men are *strikers* . . . if they hadn't been stopped, they too would have swam ashore and become strikers . . . it was evident that the men came up under Dutch guard . . . [But] we have been down to the ships (two of them) this morning, and we all believe that it is not possible to get the chaps off. We believe that maybe a dozen could be got off safely, but that the rest would be stopped, and that, being a Dutch wharf there is little we could do about it under all the other circumstances. . . . And therefore, as our reason for wishing to remove the men was to provide them with protection against reprisals for their Sydney attempts, to fetch only a few off is worse that to fetch off none. So I believe it will remain as it is at the moment—we will warn the Republic to expect them, and state all the circumstances, and they must make a concerted attempt in Batavia.[63]

Molly's description means there can be no underestimating the real danger to crews or activists in attempts to encourage the men to leave the ships. In the actual *Patras* event in November 1945, Singh had been onboard the small motorboat which was driven at speed alongside the steamer, using a megaphone to sustain an impassioned speech to the crewmen in their own languages to abandon ship. Although the *Patras* left the harbour, the crew mutinied in open waters just to the north and forced the ship to limp humiliatingly back into port where the Indians walked off to join the strike. In the filmed reenactment, it is Abdul Rehman, the President of the Union, who is shown with others, including Campbell, on the speeding motorboat, with an unknown voice-over calling in Urdu to the crew to stop the ship. Singh appeared in the next scenes, playing the part of one of the mutineers speaking at an impromptu meeting to celebrate, as if he had only just arrived in Australia.

Introduced by Indonesian seamen and activist, Tukliwan, Dasrath Singh can be seen and heard on the footage, his identity confirmed by Phyllis Johnson and Jack Mullins, as he reads from the script for the first lines and then, looking up, breaks into his own animated style to deliver the climax:

Figure 7.5   Dasrath Singh during reenactment of the rally after the Patras crew had mutinied and returned to port to join the strike. Still taken from film *Indonesia Calling*, 1946, courtesy Heritage Films and the National Film and Sound Archive of Australia.

Friends we were informed that we were to take a light ship to take
wood to Banyu . . .

But we found ourselves put on a Dutch ship carrying arms and munitions to Indonesia.

But we refused to sail with them.

The Dutch threatened us with their guns but still we refused.

And now we will not sail with the ship!

Their Struggle is Our Struggle,

Their Victory is Our Victory!

It is not only Dasrath Singh who has become visible to us through the
archive and memory, although perhaps it is only "Danny" we see, the man
Australians knew. We can as well see the faces of other Indian Seamen's
Union members. One of the earliest photographs of the Indian activists
meeting with the Indonesians shows Ligorio de Costa, who with another
important Goan activist, Joe Gonsalves, reflected the sizable 10 percent
minority within the Union.[64]

Unlike the elite Joseph Noronha, who would have been more comfortable writing in Portuguese, these Goan unionists were literate in

Figure 7.6 Abdul Rehman (later chairman of ISUiA, seated centre), Ligurio de
Costa (standing left) and Clarrie Campbell (standing right) with Indonesian activists
in Sydney 12 October 1945 as they signed statement of support for Indonesian Independence and for the Boycott against Dutch shipping. *Tribune*, 12 October 1945.

Konkani, which they used in correspondence with the ISUiA, and they ensured that one of the four languages on the Union's badge and membership book was, as they called it then, "Goanese." Their ISUiA membership recorded their addresses as the chummeries where they stayed together in Bombay. These were the clubs or collective lodgings named after the villages from which they came, where they shared household costs and gathered useful recipes from each other which they could use in ships' catering departments.[65]

We have none of the words of these two photographed men, although Clarrie wrote warmly to Joe Gonsalves after he was repatriated,[66] but we do have the words of Joseph Noronha, who wrote a long, fluent letter to Clarrie Campbell from Melbourne, excited about the Union and all the work he felt it had to do. He was at the same time scathingly critical of the Seamen's Mission in Melbourne because, apart from having amalgamated with what he called "the Protestant Parasites," the social club operating for seamen out of the Mission was discriminatory, offering supper but refusing to allow Indian seafarers and other "coloured" seamen to dance with the young white women who were volunteers at the club because "they came from high and respectable families." Noronha's response to the Seamen's Mission staff member who told him had been " . . . to keep his Ladies in glass cases and our seamen were not hungry for their supper!" The Mission's picnic parties were completely racially segregated: Noronha was invited as an upper-class exception to the rule, but refused to attend "when I heard no coloured people were allowed to participate." He and his friends described the Melbourne Club to Campbell as "not even a shadow compared to the Club in Sydney."[67]

The person for whom we have both photographs and a few more fragments of his writing is Abdul Rehman. Like Dasrath Singh and many of the Punjabis and Pathans who together formed around 25 percent of the union membership, Rehman had shipped through Bombay.[68] He was not from the northwestern provinces, like many of the groups whom Clarrie had met in Gallipoli who formed a large proportion of the British land army from India. Instead, coming from Poona, southeast of Bombay, he was from the communities of coastal Muslim seafarers who had long been involved in trade along India's west coast and the western Indian Ocean. It was members of these communities who had been most actively involved in the formation of the National Seamen's Union of India, based in Bombay.[69]

We first see Abdul Rehman seated at the centre of the discussion in photographs showing the Indians pledging continued support to the Indonesians. Then he appears in photos of the Union's inauguration and in others he is shown on the desk recording memberships and collecting the donations new members made to the strike fund. We see him, along with Dasrath Singh, as they welcome Mohammad Hasan to be the Imam for the religious ceremonies at Eid, held in November 1945, to mark the end of the lunar fasting month of Ramadan.[70] Rehman's quiet presence was a major factor in the Union's rapid capacity to gather members and manage their political strategies as well as house and feed some hundreds of men on strike. The NSW Trades and Labour Council offered support and Phyllis Johnson and others helped Dasrath Singh as he tramped from one Australian job site to another, calling on Australian workers to respond with donations. But it was Abdul Rehman who pulled it all together, gathered more members and kept an eye on their interests beyond those of the political action, to continue the industrial work to improve wages, safety, and conditions. It was Abdul Rehman on whom Clarrie Campbell relied for advice and guidance. It is also Abdul Rehman whom we see, again unacknowledged, in footage in *Indonesia Calling* in the speeding small boat pursuing the *Patras*, standing alongside Clarrie as they called and waved to get the message to the seafarers onboard.

Figure 7.7   Reenactment of the small speed boat pursuit of the Dutch ship *Patras* as it tried to leave Sydney Harbour with its Indian crew working at gunpoint. Still taken from film *Indonesia Calling*, 1946, courtesy Heritage Films and the National Film and Sound Archive of Australia.

Figure 7.8 Abdul Rehman, with Clarrie Campbell, calling on *Patras* seamen to mutiny during reenactment of small boat chase. Still taken from film *Indonesia Calling*, 1946, courtesy Heritage Films and the National Film and Sound Archive of Australia.

A voice, perhaps Rehman's, can be heard in voice-over, calling out in Hindi or Urdu: "Brothers, leave the ship! Don't work for them!"

When Rehman was deported in December 1945, the Union used the occasion to write a letter to unions in India to allow him to talk about the work the Union was doing in Australia. The letter opened:

> The Bearer, Abdul Rehman, has been the Chairman of the Indian Seamen's Union in Australia since its formation recently. He has proved himself worthy of the confidence placed in him by all the Members of the Union, and we look forward to his return to Australia when he can take up the work he has had to leave off because of his forced return to India.[71]

Abdul Rehman made the journey home expecting to return soon to Australia. He wrote a number of letters, including a Christmas card, to Clarrie and Ada on the trip and encouraged Clarrie to send him the Union membership book as quickly as possible. It had still been at the printers when he left and, as he told Clarrie, "you know I have to do great work with it."[72] After seeing his family, he tried to find more work but faced extreme difficulty getting a place on any international shipping. Many ISUiA members found, when they returned to India after walking off their ships in protest, that, just as they had feared, their continuous discharge certificate had been stamped "Deserter," a warning for future shipping masters of a troublesome or unreliable sailor. This stigma meant that many of these seamen never worked on international ships again. Rehman, probably in this position and unable to gain work on the overseas lines, fell back on local cargo vessels working round the coast of India. Clarrie wrote back, catching Rehman up on the union news, and pleading with him to hurry back:

> Most of the Indonesian trouble is over as far as it affects Indian seamen, so have been able to give more time to the Union work. The membership has grown to 800, but it would have been much higher with somebody like yourself on the job. We have been hoping that you were coming back to be with us permanently, and put some punch into the work.
> I am very anxious to hear how the men got on who were on strike . . .
> I will be very glad to hear from you, Abdul, better still, we would be pleased to know you were coming back.[73]

When Rehman wrote again in May, he had a sombre tone: his life had been overwhelmed with family tragedy. His young son and daughter had both fallen gravely ill in Poona when he was away working. He'd left his ship at Calcutta and rushed home. His daughter had recovered but his fourteen-year-old son died. Still grieving, with his savings exhausted during his family's difficulties and unable to get a job to work his passage to Australia, he wrote sadly to Clarrie, assuring him that he would come back to Australia to assist the union if it was really needed but making it clear that his family's needs came first.[74]

The final but largest group among the seamen who joined the union were those like Mohamed T. Hussain, a butler (i.e., foreman) in a ship's catering department. Hussain was a Muslim, like Rehman and those from the west, but he came from Bengal in the east, in which a long tradition of seafaring reinforced a sense of regional solidarity. The seafarers who, like Hussain, shipped through Calcutta formed at least 60 percent of the union's membership.[75] Some gave Calcutta boarding houses as their address, while a few gave rural western Bengal or even Bihar contacts. Around half of them, that is 30 percent of all the union's members, identified themselves with the closely connected eastern areas of the port of Chittagong, the coastal Nowakhali and its hinterland, and the rural Sylhet, all areas which were later to become part of East Pakistan and then Bangladesh. The ISUiA archive offers documentary proof of the ways these men moved between agriculture and seafaring as economic conditions dictated, but in the hope of eventually acquiring land.[76] In May 1946, Shamsul Haq, a signed-up member of the union in both Australia and India, organized for both the Union in Sydney and the Australia-India Association, along with the commander of his ship, the *Empire Singapore*, to write to the "Collector of Nowa Khali":

> Some considerable time ago, I made an application for a grant of Kacha Char land to support myself and family.
>
> Unfortunately for us, I have received no word of your consideration of my application. This has meant that I have had to go to sea to maintain my family.
>
> In view of the very serious food situation in India which calls for the utmost food production, and my capability to properly farm the land, I would be forever grateful for receiving your favourable consideration.[77]

Some of the men who lived in Calcutta, that is around 30 percent of the total ISUiA membership, may have been there only in the short periods while they were waiting for ships, but many seemed to have become well established in the city. Their boarding house lodgings in Calcutta were transitory and insecure, wedged into impoverished and cramped slum areas. They moved from room to room, from building to building. Yet they were surrounded in the neighbourhood, as has become obvious in our field work in Kolkata recently,[78] by networks of family, fellow villagers and fellow Muslims, which allowed them a web of familiarity which at least echoed the Clubs of the Goans in Bombay in the mutual support these working people gave to each other.

There are no confirmed photographs of Mohamed T. Hussain among the Union's photographs. Yet his words are some of the most moving of those recorded in the Union's archive. He made a speech at a dinner hosted by the Indians to thank the Australian, Chinese, and Indonesian unionists and activists who had supported them while they were on strike. Abdul Rehman had already been deported, but Dasrath Singh was still in Sydney and signed the card given to Clarrie that night. Phyllis and Johnno Johnson were there, and Phyllis has warm memories of sharing the night with the Indians and more good friends like Mick Ryan, Barney Smith, and other ASU members who had been particularly stalwart. Hussain welcomed them all and said:

> *On behalf of my brother Indians and myself I extend to you all a warm welcome . . . We are Indian seamen without a ship and we have not been able to do all we would of liked for you . . . But what is missing we hope we will make up for with the warmth of our welcome . . .*
>
> *Those who have controlled our country for so many years, think that because we are Indians we must be slaves . . . There can be no new world while there are any people who are slaves of others . . . The*

winning of freedom in Indonesia will surely be followed by the free-
dom of India. For that reason we must do everything possible to see
that the Dutch are driven out of Indonesia.[79]

* * *

The hopes of 1945 lay in ashes by 1950. In India, independence had indeed
come after further struggles, but it had been undermined by the intense
bitterness of Partition. Many of the Indians who had participated in the
boycott in Australia and who had joined the Union were from areas which
became East or West Pakistan, so at best the communication between them
and those who remained in India was disrupted and their organizations
disbanded. At worst, Muslims on both sides of these new borders faced
violence and displacement. Some of the most active of the Calcutta-based
unionists known to those who had been in Australia moved to East Pakistan (later Bangladesh), like Aftab Ali, and played a major role in building
the union movement there in the maritime and other industries, contributing to the international labour movement. For most whom we cannot yet
trace, it meant years of disruption.[80]

In Indonesia, the Dutch military push to retake the NEI accelerated after
the Renville negotiations late in 1947 and then the agreement signed with
support from the United States and United Kingdom in January 1948. The
new Republic was subjected to escalating military aggression, relentless
naval blockade, and international isolation. The rising impact of the Cold
War was being felt in intensifying pressures to align new and emerging
nations with either the United States and the West or with the Soviet Bloc.
India resisted this pressure and became a key force in building the Non-
Aligned Nations movement. The Indonesian republicans, however, were
losing the military battle against the Dutch. Facing interminable political siege, the Indonesians finally succumbed. The widening differences
between factions within the nationalist movement became a bloody conflict at Madiun in July 1948 when many of the Left, including the newly
reestablished Communist Party, were executed in an internal conflict which
delivered a Republican movement which the United States was happy to
support against the Dutch, allowing final independence in 1949. Many of
the Indonesian activists who had lived in Australia died at Madiun, breaking the links which had developed in the war years and beginning a long
period of uneasy isolation between the two countries.[81]

In Australia, the Cold War pressures split the ALP government wide
open. The Chifley government had already been divided on how to handle
the boycott of Dutch shipping in 1945. Evatt and the mainstream trades
union movement, along with an emerging and deeply conservative Catholic network among working class organizations, opposed the militancy of
the Communist-led maritime unions. Rising pressures to align closely with
the United States led to a sequence of public conflicts between the Labor

Government and trade unionists, culminating in aggressive government intervention with troops when coal miners struck over a series of moderate demands on safety and wages issues. The resulting immense social contestation saw the Labor vote split and the conservative Liberal-National coalition under Menzies come to power in the Federal election, launching rapidly into a series of legal and legislative attempts to ban the Communist Party and dismantle its influence in union and public affairs. While the Communist Party survived, the emergence of the anti-Communist Democratic Labor Party enshrined the divided Labor vote and ensured that the Left was kept out of power for over twenty years.

We can ask what was really shared in those brief years at the end of the war when we look at the interactions between Indians, Australians, and Indonesians over the boycott of Dutch shipping. It is clear there was short-term political collaboration and each group had both a strong commitment to the national independence of their own country and supported the campaigns for national independence in the others. Yet there were certainly also misunderstandings and failures to communicate. What can we trace of new conversations opening up or of real shared visions?

The ideals of international socialism can be seen readily in the rhetoric of the times but it is also evident that there were many common commitments among the seafarers and activists on all sides to equity across national borders in industrial relations and in democratic organization. There were certainly some members of Communist parties who shared visions of an internationalist socialism despite the Soviet retreat into "socialism in one country." The Australians Phyllis Johnson and Sylvia and Jack Mullins were all members of the CPA and Clarrie Campbell was certainly committed to the Communist movement in spirit. Among the Indonesians who had lived in Australia, a number confirmed their continued membership of the Indonesian Communist Party (PKI) in 1948. Many of the Indians in the widely reported Sydney demonstrations against the KPM shipping company wore a "red star" as well as the badge of the new union. The Communist Party of India continued to be an important player in the Seafarers' unions.[82]

But there were others on all sides who were working seafarers and activists who might not have identified as Communists, but who held a strong commitment to the idea of international equality in access to justice and fair working conditions. The Indonesian Bondan had a long background as a nationalist, but did not actively identify as Communist or even socialist, while the younger Tukliwan was another who was at the time an active Left organizer rather than a cadre of any party, although he was later to disappear in the Indonesian purges of 1965. This more general commitment to strengthening working people's equity and alliances across national borders was seen in the Indian action in joining the boycott, even at such a high risk to themselves.

Hostility was expressed by some of the elite Indonesians over the need to organize politically with Indians whom they regarded as "coolies."[83]

The Indians, however, argued that such racial and class differences were constructions of colonialism, as one Indian organizer put it when he spoke formally to the Indonesians at a shared function:

> We Indians are indeed grateful that you accepted our invitation to join us in this picnic today. We feel that in doing so, we have welded a chain of fraternal friendship which no force can break . . . In the past there have been small conflicts between Indian and Indonesian seamen . . . We know now that in spite of the urgency of winning the war, certain shipping companies in their greed for profits, and even at the risk of losing the war, were prepared to use the people of one country against another . . . The unity of our people, the people of two important countries . . . ensures our ultimate emancipation.

Many Indonesians agreed with this, as they showed on another occasion when thanking the ISUiA for its support. They expressed the national goals they felt the two peoples shared as well as the sense of potential international alliances across borders among working people:

> "We hope for an everlasting friendship and cooperation between the Indonesian and Indian people in general, and the Indonesian and Indian workers in particular, both struggling for national independence, freedom and humanity." [84]

These hopes were framed in terms of recognizing and dismantling barriers which the "divide and rule" strategies of colonizers and shipping companies had set up, to build stronger, international solidarity. It was an analysis which was new to Australians and this political collaboration around the boycott offers a rare opportunity to see it unfolding.

Yet if there were some common hopes around international industrial equity, there was no such shared understanding on the question of the internationalism of Islam, which was a dimension of these events which was largely unrecognized by Australians, other than Clarrie Campbell. He had become very familiar over many years with Indian Muslims and was interested in meeting the needs of the union members and friends in the Indian Social Club, which was regularly turned over for prayers and religious meetings. More generally, Australians failed to recognize the roles played in India by activists with a religious affiliation alongside their politics. Those from the range of Left ideologies in Australia, from the CPA to the Labor Party, were committed to a rationalist and secular social vision which precluded religion. All the Australians involved with Indians in the boycott campaign, from Lockwood and the other *Tribune* journalists through to Phyllis and Sylvia in their memories of the events, stressed with approval the ecumenical and tolerant interactions of all the Indian seamen towards each other in cramped strike accommodation and the Social Club.

They read this as a disinterest in religion rather than what it was more likely to have been, that is as expectations that everyone would have a religious affiliation, that there would be diversity among them, that protocols existed and ways could be negotiated to find accommodations between them. This form of secularity which included diverse religious affiliations rather than denying religion altogether was largely foreign to the Western Left at the time.

But for many of the Indians and the Indonesians, the role of Islam in fostering an international unity among Muslims was a high priority:

> The Indians point out . . ."The Indonesians are 98% Mohammedan and the Indian seamen in Sydney are 98% Mohammedans," said one Indian spokesman. "Thus the shipping companies are trying to force us to take part in a war on our brother Mohammedans. This is against our conscience, as well as being against the law."[85]

This sentiment was consistent with the internationalism inherent in Islamic beliefs in general. It also reflected many decades of reporting and debate from within the South Asian Muslim diaspora in the United Kingdom, South Africa, Australia, Southeast Asia, and elsewhere. While there were a range of affiliations among Muslims who lived in those various diasporic communities and some of the publications which circulated among them reflected the missionary zeal of particular sects, nevertheless, the general reporting in the Indian press and international Islamic newspapers had fostered a consciousness of the extended network of Muslims across the colonies.[86] Just as important had been the rising numbers of Indonesian Hajjis who had been, since the 1860s, able to make the Indian Ocean crossing to carry out their pilgrimage to Mecca. Their passages had invariably been on ships crewed by Indians, most of whom were Muslims.[87] These journeys consolidated a growing awareness of shared religious faith. It was this counter to the divide-and-rule strategies of shipping companies to which the Indian picnic hosts alluded when they spoke to their Indonesian guests.

Ideas of national independence expressed by the Indians are relevant in considering how the internationalism of Islam was understood. Evidence of Muslim participation in broad nationalist politics has been well recorded, as has the role of Muslim seafarers in the emergence of militant unionism in maritime industries.[88] Key union activists in both Bombay and Calcutta were all Muslims. Broeze's work, tracing union formation and membership inside India, points out that it was the Bengali Muslim "lascar" community—led by a lawyer, Mahomed Daud—who were responsible for the "remarkable rise of the ISU at Calcutta as a solid organisation" in the 1920s.[89] During the 1930s, both the Communist-led and the moderate-led unions, in Calcutta and Bombay respectively, drew much of their support from Muslim seamen.[90] Indians in Australia in 1945 and 1946 had made public commitments to the new nation not in terms of a separatist Islam, but of broad national unity for independence from British rule and with the goal of social and industrial equity into the future. They had spoken not in support of a religiously defined independent nation nor of the All-India Muslim League in India. In March 1947, when the extent of the severe reprisals faced by the returned Indian strikers was clear, the ISUiA wrote to both Jawarhalal Nehru and Muhammad Ali Jinnah to seek assistance in defending the seamen whom Campbell called "courageous freedom fighters." By this time, however, Partition had been reluctantly accepted by Congress and it was clear there were going to be two independent nations in the near future. The ISUiA recognized it would require intervention by leaders of these two nations to protect the seamen. While there was interest in the All-India Muslim League among Indian seamen in Australia in 1945, all their statements and actions were framed within the longer history of Indian Muslim political activism in the broadest sense—syndicalist, nationalist, socialist, and even Communist as well as religiously informed.

In this intense period of shared political work, perhaps the most lasting legacy lay in the interactions which had occurred on a personal level, opening up expectations that future communication could take place and that common ground might emerge. The letters which were exchanged between repatriated Indians and Australians during 1946 and 1947 have glimpses of warmth and camaraderie which underpin the formal language of greeting and remembrance in which they are couched.[91]

Many of these relationships proved impossible to sustain across distance and in times of increasing pressure. Clarrie Campbell's early time in Singapore gave him ready access to Indonesia where he consolidated his close friendship with Haryono, an Indonesian who had lived in Brisbane during the war and had returned to help establish the Republic's trade unions.[92] Campbell worked closely with a number of Chinese and Indonesian activists trying to set up a fleet of cargo airplanes which would ferry trade goods between Australia, Malaya/Singapore, and Indonesia.[93] Given the bitter military struggle going on early in 1948, with a tightening Dutch blockade of the Indonesian Republic, an airline would have allowed the Republic to trade with its allies untouched by the Dutch shipping around the coastline. The Australian Security Intelligence Organisation (ASIO) file on Campbell suggests his continued contact with the Australian CPA and his growing communication with the Chinese Communists brought the full attention of the American and British security services onto the airline, dooming it with a flurry of unsubstantiated rumours of drug running and corruption.[94] Campbell's Chinese business partner died early in 1948 in a plane crash in mysterious circumstances and Campbell faced increasing frustration in his attempts to get back into Indonesia. Yet his friendship with Haryono continued and led Clarrie to approach an Englishman working for the Republican government, John Coast, who had better access to Java. Clarrie had an important package he felt he had waited too long to deliver to Haryono and so he entrusted it to Coast, who wrote later:

> I felt very sorry for Campbell. Such a line [an airline] to Jogja would have been admirable for us, and its failure was undoubtedly personally serious for him. He struck me as both genuine and tough. . . . He confided to my care . . . two glass eyes, which he asked me to take to Jogja on my next blockade-run for his friend Hariono [sic], the chairman of the Central Trades Union which had just merged with the new Communist Party. He handed me the eyes in a small tin box, telling me that Hariono's glass eye was loose and that he had long promised to send these spares to him. . . . . But by the time I next reached Jogja, the Communist revolt in Madiun had already broken out and I was forced to leave the eyes with one of the staff . . asking him to pass them onto Hariono if a peaceful settlement with the Communists were reached. Hariono, who had impressed me earlier as a sincere, suspicious trade union leader, was later killed.[95]

The loss of Haryono and other good friends at Madiun in July 1948 not only further isolated Clarrie, but it contributed to the severing of those powerful, unprecedented relationships which had allowed the Australian blockade to occur in the first place. Some activists, like Bondan, survived to maintain the links with Australia, but others, like Tukliwan, lived through Madiun only to face increasing marginalization themselves until they too disappeared in the 1965–1966 massacres of left-wing activists and Chinese Indonesians.[96]

Although opportunities to continue such close personal relationships had been lost, the experiences of those years shaped the way the surviving activists challenged the isolationism of the Cold War and the militarization it generated. We have not yet been able to trace the impact of Partition on the Indian seamen who had been in Australia, but we do know about some Australians. Phyllis Johnson was one who believed the friendships of the time with Indians and Indonesians strengthened the beliefs she had learnt from her father, a staunch unionist and an opponent of war, about the paramount importance of peace and the potential to make it between peoples of very different cultures. She learnt this lesson from the time she spent with the Indian seamen and other workers during this strike; she explains:

> I told everyone, I oppose war because it solves nothing. There are differences amongst people, but these differences can be talked over, even if it's going to take a much longer time. . . . . I mean 660,000 people in Iraq have already been killed. No more war! I'll speak against war for as long as I can.[97]

Phyllis's words resonate with those recorded from the Indian Seaman's Union officials like Mohammed Hossain and Dasrath Singh in their appeals for a world where the struggle for freedom was shared among people of different nations and where no one was the slave of any others. Their moving expressions of hope, far more than any old world leaders' agreement, like the Atlantic Charter, offered a genuinely new charter for freedom. It was an Indian Ocean charter which promised that the shared hopes and new worlds would be those linking everyday, working people, challenging all the borders around the ocean's shores.

ACKNOWLEDGEMENTS

This chapter is based on a paper delivered to the *Indian Ocean World* Conference, University of Malaya, Kuala Lumpur, August 2007.

I am indebted to G. Balachandran, Jan Lingard, Devleena Ghosh, Drew Cottle, Suchetana Chattopadhyay, and Duncan Waterson for their generosity, advice, and fine scholarship. Invaluable research assistance has been provided by Titas Chakaraborty and Prakriti Mitra in Kolkata to trace families of or stories about the seamen who gave this city as a home address in their union membership forms. Lola Sharon Davidson from the Indian Ocean *Intercoloniality* project at the University of Technology Sydney has once again assisted with fine editing. Shanti Moorthy has offered valuable editorial advice. Heritage Films (who hold copyright of the film *Indonesia Calling*) and the Maritime Union of Australia have been enthusiastic supporters of the project. The staff of the Noel Butlin Archives of Business and Labour, where the papers of the ISUiA are held, have offered unfailing assistance and support. This chapter is dedicated to the people who made these events happen: to the memory of the Indians, Indonesians, and Australians who worked together for justice and peace and to Sylvia and Jack Mullins and Phyllis Johnson, whose memories and continued commitment have kept the story alive.

NOTES

1. Rupert Lockwood, *Black Armada: Australia and the Struggle for Indonesian Independence, 1942–1949*. Sydney: Hale and Iremonger, 1982.
2. This chapter will use a definition of "working people" which includes those who might have identified themselves as "working class" in the socialist categories of the day, but also those people from nonelite groups who, although not directly associated with an industrial proletariat, were nevertheless "working" in the labour structures of colonialism.
3. We have even less information at this stage into the Indonesian activists and their story must wait till later. Recent work by Jan Lingard in her *Refugees and Rebels: Indonesian Exiles in Wartime Australia*. Melbourne: Australian Scholorly Publishing, 2008, explains events in Australia from 1943 to 1945. Otherwise there are only fragments of the life stories of the Indonesian activists scattered across journalistic records like Rupert Lockwood's account of the Boycott. Molly Bondan wrote movingly (recorded in Hardjono and Warner, 1995, 34) about her work in Indonesia, but was largely silent on the personal and even biographical details of her own life and that of her husband, Mohamad Bondan, although she offers us the closest glimpse we have so far. There are, finally, some warm memories from the Australians

who worked most closely with the Indians but who remember something of the Indonesians they met, like Tukliwan, who worked in Sydney and is warmly remembered by Australian activists interviewed for this research. Also known as Tuk or S. Toekliwon, we can find glimpses of his story in Sydney from 1944, and later in Indonesia in 1956–1958 in Brian Fitzpatrick and Rowan J. Cahill's *The Seamen's Union of Australia, 1872–1972: A History* (1981, 170–171).

4. Australia, in fact, only ratified the 1931 U.K. Statue of Westminster in 1942.

5. Hardjono and Warner, 31–33.

6. The Indonesian Communist Party (PKI) had been banned and disbanded by the Dutch some years before the war. Although formally no longer in existence, the internees and other nationalists in Australia and within the Netherlands East Indies continued to sustain interest in and contact with the International Communist Network. Although factionalised, this continued affiliation became apparent both in Australia and when the Communist Party of Indonesia reformed in 1948. See Benedict Anderson, *Java in a Time of Revolution: Occupation and Resistance, 1944–1946* (Djakarta and Singapore: Equinox, 1976 and 2006).

7. Ibid., 33–34.

8. Anderson, 179, citing Osman Raliby Documenta Historica, p. 52, Djakarta, Bulan-Bintang, 1953.

9. Fitzpatrick and Cahill; Beasley; Lockwood.

10. G. Gopalan Balachandran, "Cultures of Protest in Transnational Contexts: Indian Seamen Abroad, 1885–1945"; Broeze, *Island Nation*; Fitzpatrick and Cahill.

11. Ibid.

12. Hardjono and Warner, 38–39. Also, please again refer to Note 3.

13. Ibid., 34; interview conducted by Heather Goodall with Phyllis Johnson, 10 May 2007; interview conducted by Heather Goodall with Sylvia Mullins, 13 Mar 2007.

14. Lockwood, *Black Armada*; Archive of the Indian Seamen's Union in Australia [ISUiA], E 177/4 and E 177/5, throughout 1946, eg D. Furtado to CHC, Treasurer for ISUiA, 28 Mar 1946, and Md Sultan, Village Oambar, MWFP to CHC, Treasurer, for ISUiA, undated. Both in ISUiA Archive E 177/5.

15. C.H. Campbell [CHC] on behalf of ISUiA to Indian Unions, 1 Mar 1946, repeated 3 Oct 1946, ISUiA archive E 177/4. Based on figures per ship, Disbursement of Strike Pay, ISUiA E 177/17.

16. CHC to Phyllis and Johnno Johnson, 6 Mar 1946, ISUiA Archive E 177/4.

17. Fitzpatrick and Cahill; Beasley.

18. Cottle and Keys, "From Colonial Film Commissioner to Political Pariah."

19. I have discussed this elsewhere at greater length, see Heather Goodall, "Port Politics: Indian Seamen, Australian unionists and Indonesian Independence, 1945–1947."

20. The following details are derived from their work, particularly in G. Balachandran, "Circulation through Seafaring," 89–130; G. Balachandran, "Searching for the Sardar," 206–236; Janet Ewald.

21. Chattopadhyay, 229.

22. Broeze, "The Muscles of Empire."

23. Robert Miles, *Racism* (London: Routledge, 1989), p 35.

24. It was widely used in the British Raj as one of the approaches towards recruiting "martial races," who were understood to be drawn from both Sikh and Muslim northwestern province areas, into army positions (Deshpande) but was also reflected in the racial attacks by Australians on Afghanis as the

restricted immigration laws were formulated (Germain, 132). For examples in Australia, see *The Coolgardie Miner*, almost any issue, but 15 April 1897 is representative in its inclusion of phrases like: "rising fanatics," and "awful horrors that follow even the temporary triumphs of the black man over the white, or the Moslem over the Christian." Cited in Cigler, 82–83.

25. Burgmann, 1995, 90, on the 1915 attempt to assist Cinghalese seamen in Darwin for a branch of the OBU, For union members' recollections of relations with Indians and others, see Robert Haworth, personal communication with author.
26. Fitzpatrick and Cahill, 182–183.
27. Ibid., 169.
28. Christine Stevens, *Tin Mosques and Ghantowns: A History of Afghan Cameldrivers in Australia* (Melbourne: Oxford University Press, 1989); Pamela Rajdowski, *In the Tracks of the Camelmen* (Sydney: Angus and Robertson, 1987); Cigler.
29. Australian attitudes towards violent attacks on and parliamentary debates about Afghans and Indians (both "Mussalman" and "Hindoo") in Western Australia, South Australia, and New South Wales from the 1890s extensively documented in Rajdowski, *In the Tracks of the Camelmen*, 149–165.
30. Djinguiz.
31. Reetz, 23.
32. *The Argus*, 17 July 1917; cited in Bilal Cleland, "The Great War", Islamic Council of Victoria, www.icv.org.au/history6.shtml. Article in Calcutta paper *Habl oul-Matin*, 19 Jly 1915, translated into *Revue du monde musulman*, 1917–1918, pp 253–4; Calcutta based *Mulk and Millut*, 9 Apr 1907, both cited in Eric Germain: "Southern Hemispheric Diasporic Communities in the Building of an International Muslim Public Opinion at the Turn of the Twentieth Century", in *Comparative Studies of South Asia, Africa and the Middle East*, 27 (1) pp 126–138.
33. W.H. Barnwell, Inquiry Officer, ASIO biographical report on Campbell, 8 Jly 1947, Commonwealth of Australia. Volume 1, Series A6119/79. Important research on Clarrie's early life has been undertaken by Professor Duncan Waterson.
34. CHC to Ben Chifley, PM, 6 June 1946, C.H. Campbell Papers, P81/31
35. Deshpande.
36. David Omissi, *Indian Voices of the Great War* (London: Palgrave Macmillan, 1999).
37. CHC to Sir Raghunath Paranjpye, Indian High Commissioner to Australia, Canberra, 26 Feb 1946, ISUiA Archive, E177/4
38. Federal Labour Member for East Sydney and Minister for External Territories during this period.
39. Finally noticed by the Australian Left as a result of the Indian's action in 1945, the conditions of the labour pools were described in *Tribune*, 30 October 1945. An account of one Indian's protest, the seaman F.B. Lobo, over the conditions in the pools in 1946, his employing shipping company's resulting decision to terminate his contract without compensation, and Lobo's subsequent industrial challenge to them with the support of the ISUiA, is in Campbell's reference for him, CHC to Whom It May Concern, 4 July 1946. E 177/4.
40. Damousi and Lake. It was also parallel to some extent to the International Seamen's Social Club run by the ASU Seamen's Women's Auxilliary from 1939 to 1945. Photographs of it appear in Fitzpatrick and Cahill, 253–254. All officials and participants appear to be of Anglo or European background and this project has not yet investigated the question of how this organization might or might not have been linked to groups like the Australia-India

Foundation and the Australian-Indian Social Club. For comparable U.S. conflicts over interracial servicemen's clubs, see Margaret Halsey's *Some of My Best Friends Are Soldiers.*

41. Annual Report Indian Club, 1945, undated, ISUiA archives E 177/4; Careful attention was paid to inviting respected men to act as Imams for the Id ceremonies. In 1945 it was Mumammad Hasan, a barrister, later working in Fiji and in 1946 it was a local man, Mr Alam. *Tribune* 23 Nov 1945; CHC to over 20 Sydney families of Indian origin and to others including 'Syrian Muslim Families." 30 Oct 1946, ISUiA E177/4

42. CHC to Aftab Ali and Calcutta Unions and later to unnamed Bombay Seafarers' Union officer, detailing history of ISUiA. 3 Oct 1946. Found in ISUiA Archive, E 177/4

43. *Komite Indonesia Merdeko* (KIM) or Commitee on Indonesian Independence; Clarrie Campbell on Indians and on trade relationships, Hardjono and Warner, 19–20; 53–54.

44. G. Balachandran, "Searching for the Sardar" and "Circulation through seafaring."

45. Joseph Noronha to C.H.C, 28 Oct 1945, ISUiA Archives, E177/4. Noronha's statement reflects the tension between Goan working people and the middle classes discussed by Rochelle Pinto in *Between Empires: Print and Politics in Goa* (Delhi: Oxford University Press, 2007).

46. Database developed from ISUiA membership records, ISUiA Archive E 177/10

47. Frank Broeze, "The Muscles of Empire," 39.

48. Ibid., 66.

49. Lockwood, like Sylvia Mullins and Phyllis Johnson, commented on the wide class differences between the Indonesians in Australia, including some of aristocratic Javanese background who looked down on the Indians as "coolies" (*Black Armada*, 165).

50. Cottle and Keys, "From Colonial Film Commissioner to Political Pariah."

51. Singh's name suggests he had a northwestern origin, and was either from a Sikh or Hindu background.

52. Singh made a major impression too on Rupert Lockwood, the activist and journalist-author of the major account of the strike to date, *Black Armada*. Lockwood wrote that he had talked with Danny Singh most days and gathered the latest dockside news from Singh's colourful accounts (Lockwood, 149–164).

53. CHC, to Indian Seamen's Unions [in India] on behalf of Dasrath Singh, 31 Jan 1946, E177/5

54. Lockwood:p 152; Campbell for ISUiA to Hon. R.A. King, MLC and Sec., NSW Trades and Labor Council., 29 Jan 1946 ISUiA E177/4

55. CHC for ISUiA to Hon. R.A. King, MLC and secretary NSW Trades and Labor Council. 29 Jan 1946 E177/4; CHC for ISUiA to Waterside Workers, NSW and Federal, Ironworkers Federal, Seamen's Federal, ALP [Sharkey], Indonesian Seamen's Union 8 Apr 1946 ISUiA Archive E 177/4

56. Hardjono and Warner, 39; Lockwood, 101. Both works discuss sounding of alert on 25 September that the Dutch would be attempting to load munitions.

57. Interview conducted by Heather Goodall with Phyllis Johnson, 10 May 2007. Phyllis recorded the key elements of this story with Jan Lingard in the mid 1990s, but expanded it in this recent interview. Rupert Lockward's account, in *Black Armada* (151–152), supports Phyllis's memory, as do the archives of the ISUiA.

58. Tabili, 161–177.

59. Undated flyer in ISUiA Archive, E 177/4, advertising commission to Indian seamen at Indian Club, written three weeks after ISUiA formed.

60. Both quotes from transcript of interview with Jack Mullins recorded by the author, 2 March 2007. Another incident of harassment of Singh by Dutch security personnel is reported in *Tribune* 9 November 1945.
61. *Tribune*, 27 November 1945.
62. CHC to Phyllis and Johnno Johnson, 6 Mar 1946, ISUiA Archive E 177/4.
63. Molly Bondan to CHC 15 Dec 1946, p3, in C.H.Campbell papers, P81/2.
64. Photograph, *Tribune*, 12 Oct 1945; ISUiA membership database, compiled from full set of membership records, ISUiA Archive, E 177/10.
65. The complex questions around class, migrancy, and the Goan use of Konkani in writing is explored by Rochelle Pinto in her book, *Between Empires: Print and Politics in Goa*.
66. CHC to Joe Gonsalves, 9 Apr 1946, ISUiA Archives E 177/4.
67. Joseph Noronha to C.H.C, 28 Oct 1945, ISUiA Archives, E177/4.
68. ISUiA membership database, compiled from full set of membership records, ISUiA Archive, E 177/10.
69. *Constitution and Rules*, National Seamen's Union of India, Bombay, ISUiA Archive, E 177/2.
70. *Tribune*, 12 Oct; 9 November; 23 November 1945.
71. CHC to Whom it May Concern, 11 December 1945, ISUiA archive, E177/5.
72. Abdul Rehman to CHC, 14 January 1956, Colombo, ISUiA archive E177/4.
73. CHC to Abdul Rehman, 9 April 1946, ISUiA Archive, E177/4.
74. Abdul Rehman to CHC, 26 May 1946, ISUiA Archive E 177/4.
75. ISUiA membership database, compiled from full set of membership records, ISUiA Archive, E 177/10.
76. See discussions in Balachandran ("Searching for the Sardar," "Circulation through Seafaring") about the assumptions made by both shipping companies and governments that this movement between seafaring and agriculture was taking place. There had been no systematic attempt however to trace the movements of seafarers themselves.
77. Shamsul Haq to Collector of Nowa Khali, 22 May 1946, ISUiA Archive E 177/4.
78. Research undertaken by Titas Chakraborty and Prakriti Mithra, Jadavpur University, with Heather Goodall.
79. Draft speech, Mohamed T. Hussain, Butler, 13.1.46; 'thank you' letter from Clarrie to Mohamed on 16.1.46, ISUiA Archives, E177/5.
80. Broeze, "The Muscles of Empire." 66.
81. Anderson, 370–403; Vickers, 109–112.
82. Broeze, "The Muscles of Empire," 61.
83. Lockwood, 165.
84. Arif Fadilla, President and Achmad Soemadi, Secretary, Indonesian Political Exiles Association, Mackay, Qld, 4 Dec 1945, ISUiA Archive, E177/5.
85. FN 'Indians Reply to Indonesians' typescript, nd [possibly September 1945 but also may have been pre-August as it refers to the war as if it had not yet ended], ISUiA Archive E177/5.
86. Germain, "Southern Hemisphere Diasporic Communities"; Reetz, 11–51.
87. Michael B. Miller, "Pilgrims' Progress: The Business of the Haj," *Past and Present* 191(May; 2006): 189–228.
88. Chattopadhyay, 229; Deitrich Reetz.
89. Broeze, "The Muscles of Empire," 43–67, 54.
90. Ibid., 61, 66; Suchetana Chattopadhyay, Jadavpur University, Kolkata, in as yet unpublished doctoral research, has traced the active role of Muslims in Calcutta in the socialist and Communist movements.

91. Those between Abdul Rehman and Clarrie Campbell have this tone, as do many others, including those from D. Furtado to CHC, Treasurer for ISUiA, 28 Mar 1946, and Md Sultan, Village Oambar, MWFP to CHC, Treasurer, for ISUiA, undated. Both in ISUiA Archive E 177/5.
92. Haryono was by then chairing the Indonesian Trades Union peak body, SOBSI. He announced his sustained affiliation with the Communist Party when the Indonesian Communist Party (PKI) reestablished itself in 1948. See Lockwood, *Black Armada*, 141.
93. Cottle and Keys, "Asian Airlines: An Early Australian Cold War Mystery," unpublished paper.
94. Australian Security Intelligence Organisation [ASIO] CAMPBELL, Clarence Hart 'Steve'. 1933–1947 Vol 1–5 [*Barcode*: 12155800; Series A6119/79. Opened with exception: 6 Jun 1997] National Archives of Australia [NAA], online: http://www.naa.gov.au/
95. Coast, 185–186.
96. Fitzpatrick and Cahill, 170.
97. Interview with Heather Goodall, 10 May 2007.

BIBLIOGRAPHY

Interviews

Interview conducted by Heather Goodall with Jack Mullins, 2 March 2007, Glebe.
Interview conducted by Heather Goodall with Sylvia Mullins, 13 March 2007, Normanhurst.
Interview conducted by Heather Goodall with Phyllis Johnson, 10 May 2007, Padstow.

Archives and Primary Sources

C.H. Campbell papers. Archive Deposit number: P81, 1944–1947 (Noel Butlin Archive of Business & Labour, [NBBL]within the Archives Library of the Australian National University).
Indian Seamen's Union in Australia Archive Deposit number: E177, 1945–1949 (Noel Butlin Archive of Business & Labour [NBBL] in Archives Library of the Australian National University).
Australian Security Intelligence Organisation [ASIO] CAMPBELL, Clarence Hart 'Steve'. 1933—1947 Vol 1-5 [*Barcode*: 12155800; Series A6119/79. Opened with exception: 6 Jun 1997] National Archives of Australia [NAA], online: http://www.naa.gov.au/

Newspapers and Journals

Argus
Daily Mirror
Daily Telegraph
Habl oul-Matin (Calcutta)
Mulk and Millut (Calcutta)
Revue du monde musulman
Seamen's Journal

Sun
Sydney Morning Herald
Tribune

Books and Journal Articles

Anderson, Benedict: *Java in a Time of Revolution: Occupation and Resistance, 1944–1946*. Djakarta and Singapore: Equinox, 1976 and 2006.

Balachandran, Gopalan. "Searching for the sardar: the state, pre-capitalist institutions and human agency in the maritime labour market, Calcutta, 1880–1935." In *Institutions and Economic Change in South Asia*, edited by Burton Stein and Sanjay Subrahmanyam, 206–236. Bombay: Oxford University Press, 1996.

———. "Circulation through Seafaring: Indian Seamen 1890–1945." In *Society and Circulation: Mobile Peoples and Itinerant Cultures in South Asia, 1750–1950*, edited by Claude Markovits, Jacques Pouchepadass and Sanjay Subrahmanyam, 89–130. New Delhi: Permanent Black, 2003.

———. "Cultures of Protest in Transnational Contexts: Indian Seamen Abroad, 1885–1945." In *Culture and Commerce in the Indian Ocean*, edited by Devleena Ghosh and Stephen Muecke, *Trans/forming Cultures eJournal* 3(2) 2008: 45–75.

Beasley, Margo. *Wharfies: A History of the Waterside Workers' Federation of Australia*. Sydney: Halstead Press, 1996

Broeze, Frank. *Island Nation: A History of Australians and the Sea*. Sydney: Allen and Unwin, 1998

———. "The Muscles of Empire—Indian Seamen and the Raj 1919–1939." *Indian Economic and Social History Review* 1(1981): 43–67.

Burgmann, Verity. *Revolutionary Industrial Unionism: the Industrial Workers of the World in Australia*. Melbourne: Cambridge University Press, 1995.

Cigler, Michael. *The Afghans in Australia*. Melbourne: Australian Ethnic Heritage Series, 1986.

Coast, John. *Recruit to Revolution*. London: Christophers, 1952.

Cleland, Bilal. "The Great War," Islamic Council of Victoria, www.icv.org.au/history6.shtml, accessed 27 Aug 2007.

Chattopadhyay, Suchetana. "War, Migration and Alienation in Colonial Calcutta: The Remaking of Muzaffar Ahmad." *History Workshop Journal* 64(2007): 212–239.

Cottle, Drew, and Angela Keys. "From Colonial Film Commissioner to Political Pariah: Joris Ivens and the Making of Indonesia Calling." Paper presented at the Film and History, Melbourne 2006.

———. "Asian Airlines: An Early Australian Cold War Mystery," unpublished paper

Damousi, Joy, and Marilyn Lake, eds. *Gender and War: Australians at War in the Twentieth Century*. New York: Cambridge University Press, 1995.

Deshpande, Anirudh. "Sailors and the Crowd: Popular Protest in Karachi, 1946." *Indian Economic and Social History Review* 26(1; 1989): 1–28.

Djinguizm Mohammed. "'L'Islam en Australie et en Polynésie" ("Islam in Australia and Polynesia") in *Revue du Monde Musulman*, January 1908, 78–79.

Ewald, Janet. "Crossers of the Sea: Slaves, Freedmen, and Other Migrants in the Northwestern Indian Ocean, c. 1750–1914." *American Historical Review* 105(2000): 1–42.

Fitzpatrick, Brian, and Rowan J. Cahill. *The Seamen's Union of Australia, 1872–1972: A History*. Sydney, 1981.

Germain, Eric. "Southern Hemisphere Diasporic Communities in the Building of an International Muslim Public Opinion at the Turn of the Twentieth Century."

Comparative Studies of South Asia, Africa and the Middle East 27(1; 2007): 126–138.

Goodall, Heather. "Port Politics: Indian Seamen, Australian Unionists and Indonesian Independence, 1945–1947." In *Labour History*, 94 (2008): 43–68.

Halsey, Margaret. *Some of My Best Friends Are Soldiers.* New York: Simon & Schuster, 1944.

Hardjono, Joan, and Charles Warner, eds. *In Love with a Nation: Molly Bondan and Indonesia, Her Own Story in Her Own Words.* Sydney: Southwood Press, 1995.

Lingard, Jan. *Refugees and Rebels: Indonesian Exlies in Wartime Australia.* Melbourne: Australian Scholarly Publishing, 2008.

Reetz, Deitrich. *Islam in the Public Sphere: Religious Groups in India, 1900–1947.* New Delhi: Oxford University Press, 2006.

Tabili, Laura. *"We Ask for British Justice": Workers and Racial Difference in Late Imperial Britain.* New York: Cornell, 1994.

Vickers, Adrian. *A History of Modern Indonesia.* Cambridge, UK: Cambridge University Press, 2005.

Works Cited

Balachandran, Gopalan. "Cultures of Protest in Transnational Contexts: Indian Seamen Abroad, 1885–1945." In *Culture and Commerce in the Indian Ocean,* edited by Devleena Ghosh and Stephen Muecke, *Trans/forming Cultures eJournal* 3(2007): XX–XX.

Broeze, Frank. *Island Nation: A History of Australians and the Sea.* Sydney: Allen and Unwin, 1998.

———. "The Muscles of Empire—Indian Seamen and the Raj, 1919–1939." *Indian Economic and Social History Review* 1(1981): 43–67.

Chattopadhyay, Suchetana. "War, Migration and Alienation in Colonial Calcutta: The Remaking of Muzaffar Ahmad." *History Workshop Journal* 64(2007): 212–239.

Fitzpatrick, Brian, and Rowan J. Cahill. *The Seamen's Union of Australia, 1872–1972: A History.* Sydney: The Seamen's Union of Australia, 1981.

Hardjono, Joan, and Charles Warner, eds. *In Love with a Nation: Molly Bondan and Indonesia, Her Own Story in Her Own Words.* Sydney: Southwood Press, 1995.

Lockwood, Rupert. *Black Armada: Australia and the Struggle for Indonesian Independence, 1942–1949.* Sydney: Hale and Iremonger, 1982.

Reetz, Deitrich. *Islam in the Public Sphere: Religious Groups in India, 1900–1947.* New Delhi: Oxford University Press, 2006.

Tabili, Laura. *"We Ask for British Justice": Workers and Racial Difference in Late Imperial Britain.* New York: Cornell University Press, 1994.

8 "Signs of Wonder"

The Postmortem Travels of Francis Xavier in the Indian Ocean World

Pamila Gupta

INTRODUCTION

This chapter is premised on the idea that Jesuits circulating in the Indian Ocean world during the sixteenth century interspersed this space with "signs of wonder"[1] to sanctify both the land and sea as well as their larger civilizing mission; they also circulated these stories of (re)enchantment to a wider public. To this end, I examine the multiple "translations" in death of the corpse of Francis Xavier (1506–1552), a Spanish (Basque) Jesuit who died after ten years of missionizing with the sanction of the Portuguese crown in the East Indies. That his body increasingly exhibited multiple "signs of wonder" throughout its postmortem travels suggests their value for understanding early modern networks of religion, colonialism, and trade in the Indian Ocean. A set of Jesuit hagiographic biographies of this saint-in-the-making are my point of entry to access the details of Xavier's biography in both life and death.

I first examine the death and initial burial of Xavier's body on the desolate island of Sancian (or San João, as the Portuguese called it) off the coast of China in 1552, and its attendant "signs of wonder" such that this place is deemed unsuitable for housing Xavier's increasingly valued corpse. Next I turn to the second "translation" of his corpse from Sancian to Malacca (Malaysia) in 1553, once a burgeoning Portuguese colonial outpost. Here I trace the "signs of wonder" that get assigned to both (potential) saint and state, and which, although deemed a more suitable site than Sancian for Xavier's corpse, fails in the end for his permanent residency in death. Eventually, his corpse travels, via Ceylon and Cochin destined for Goa (India), the centre of the Portuguese empire in Asia, now the only place deemed worthy as a home for Xavier's invaluable corpse. In tracing the travels of this missionary's biography in death, I also trace his biography in life, only in reverse. This chapter both reveals the remarkable (hi)story of a saint-in-the-making and develops a discourse of sanctity ("signs of wonder") around Xavier's corpse such that it maintains a power of contagion, its ability to rub off (or not) onto land and sea both determining the suitability of future travels (of people, ideologies, and objects), and creating a larger circuit for

Portuguese publics, Catholic faith, pilgrimage, and conversion networks, and finally, storytelling in the Indian Ocean world.

SECTION I: (TELLING) INDIAN OCEAN STORIES

This chapter takes the idea of locating and telling "stories" from Ghosh and Muecke to develop further a cultural analytics for studying the Indian Ocean world.[2] These stories have the potential to act as a window onto wider political, economic, social, and cultural processes by way of their "seaborne connectivity"[3]; joining seemingly disparate nodal points located within the Indian Ocean through the motivations, passions, experiences, and narrations of travel undertaken by individuals, provides a human and historical specificity to these stories and conceptualizes the region's cultural landscape as one of dynamism and interconnectedness.[4] At the same time, these oceanic stories are necessarily "multivocal, discontinuous, imbricated, and recursive in [their] art of narration"[5]; hence their analytical value. Lastly, Ghosh and Muecke remind us that the (act of) telling the story is as important as the story itself for the texts themselves literally attribute value to those very objects of storytelling.[6] This is a point not lost on the Jesuit biographers whose stories of Xavier's postmortem travels in the Indian Ocean I take up in following sections of this chapter.

A second interrelated aspect of telling Indian Ocean stories is that of defining the subject under analysis or rather, the object of storytelling. An anthropological approach of following the path of an object through space and time is utilized here[7] to trace a specific cultural formation across and within multiple sites of activity.[8] Moreover, I adopt a cultural economy approach, one that "negotiates [an] object of study rather than taking [the] economic object as a given."[9] Specifically, by approaching Xavier's corpse as becoming (and not already as) a valued object of storytelling I am able to tentatively define the human motivations underwriting his postmortem travels.[10] Nor am I only tracing commoditization *as process*[11]—here the corpse of a would-be saint in the Indian Ocean—as well as its attendant metaphoric qualities ("signs of wonder"); rather, I am writing the cultural biography of an unusual object that is simultaneously a person and a thing.[12]

A third aspect of telling Indian Ocean stories involves rethinking histories of colonialism in relation to horizontal movements *between* colonial outposts located within this same ocean. Thomas Metcalf makes a compelling argument for studying "webs of empire" in the Indian Ocean arena[13] and which involves studying the circulation of goods, people, and ideologies that often bypassed imperial centers. This approach has the potential to unearth lesser known colonial narratives, experiences, and practices, such as the transportation of a potential saint's corpse over a period of eighteen months and one guided by the monsoon patterns of the Indian Ocean.

One of my attempts here is to excavate older and less familiar terrains of Indian Ocean storytelling, but from the vantage point of these newer theoretical understandings,[14] and that imports both a cultural studies approach and a nuanced historical sensibility to the study of an object that is simultaneously a commodity, a gift, a relic, a person, and a thing; its analysis in turn reveals circuits of religion, commerce, and colonialism operating in the early modern Indian Ocean world.

SECTION II: BIOGRAPHIES OF A CORPSE

Exploring a missionary's postmortem travels in the Indian Ocean first requires that the figure of Xavier be situated within a larger Portuguese Catholic and colonial context, one that both adopts a "biographical approach"[15] to viewing social history and provides the contours of the mutually constituting practices of the *Society of Jesus* and the *Estado da Índia* during the mid-sixteenth century. I do so, however briefly, before turning to a discussion of my extant source materials, a set of Jesuit biographies dedicated to Xavier.

More generally, this time frame can be characterized as one of both advances and setbacks after a period of unremitting success in building a high profile empire in Asia, centered at Goa(India), and initiated under Affonso de Albuquerque in 1510.[16] At the same time that Portuguese colonial officials were invested in expanding their "seaborne empire" to include various Asian colonial outposts beyond Goa, they were carving out niches and negotiating colonial spaces in the midst of a larger Indian Ocean world to create longstanding networks of culture, faith, and commerce. Meanwhile, the *Society of Jesus*, its members in a constant search for new converts to the fold of Roman Catholicism,[17] was invested in expanding its overseas mission to coincide with Portugal's acquisition of new territories, a mission that Xavier himself had initiated from Goa in 1542.[18] The Jesuits were also busy expanding on the example set by Xavier in the ten years he spent in Asia[19] through the development of institutions and codifications supporting the ideology and practice of (Roman) Catholicism.[20] Travelling Jesuits in the Indian Ocean world acted on Xavier's potential in *death* because he was explicitly linked to the successes of the *Society of Jesus* and the *Estado da Índia* in *life*.[21]

A rich set of source materials provides a window onto the remarkable (hi)story of Xavier's corpse. I rely on Jesuit biographies of Xavier written in the one hundred year period following his death in 1552, particularly those written during his canonization drive (1554–1622),[22] to trace the development of a discourse of sanctity surrounding his corpse. That these Jesuit chroniclers[23]—the majority writing from Goa, one from Lisbon, some who knew Xavier in life, others only in death—chose to include his journey to sainthood within their biographies of Xavier is revealing, suggesting both his defining role (in both life and death) in the expansion of their religious order overseas and their investment in incorporating his story into their larger histories of the *Society of Jesus*.[24] That these same Jesuit biographers also address aspects of Portuguese colonial state building in Asia[25] suggests that colonial and missionary officials were jointly involved in their efforts to Lusitanize and Christianize the far-flung territories of their East Indies Empire in the mid-sixteenth century.

As a set of source materials, these biographies are situated between "history and hagiography"[26] an aspect that does not detract but rather adds to their historical value insofar as they provide a perspective on a topic that would not be included in more narrowly defined historical sources of this same period.[27] Thus, on the one hand, these texts are hagiographical to the extent that they are wholly concerned with Xavier, the Jesuits and a larger Catholic "spiritual" conquest in Portuguese Asia.[28] According to historian Inés Županov, this genre of texts characteristically report only the most positive outcomes of Jesuit missionary travels, tend to neglect time and chronology, and remain anchored to particular sites—a ship, an island, or a church—on land or at sea.[29] On the other hand, these Jesuit biographies are historical to the extent that they are connected to real persons, places, and events that took place during the sixteenth century.[30] There is a "territorial dimension" to these Jesuit biographies that is invaluable for both historical and historiographical reasons.[31] Thus, it is precisely because of their dual hagiographical and historical perspectives that they are able to envision a particular mid-sixteenth-century Indian Ocean world—one that involves the structure and structuring of church and state,[32] their mutual constitution in specific sites under Portuguese dominion, changing (Portuguese Catholic) ideas of sanctity and sainthood, and a diversity of native and Catholic publics located in various colonial outposts. Moreover, these Jesuit biographies function by way of their accretion of information and infinite circulation; in the continual retelling of Xavier's remarkable "story" in death, they not only add value to the object of storytelling (Xavier himself, including his corpse[33]), but also by extension, to those places (both land and sea) wherein he exhibits multiple "signs of wonder."

SECTION III: "SIGNS OF WONDER"

The most potent moment in the Jesuit "discovery" of Asia was the realization that it could function as a practical utopia, a dreamland of possibilities and projects . . . It was with unprecedented enthusiasm, or as the Jesuits termed it themselves, with "fervours" that the missionaries embarked on geographical, political, linguistic and cultural journeys without return. Or, that is how it seemed—as no return—and what happened to most of the Jesuits. The passage to India was often a one way ticket to the worlds of Asia where an individual Jesuit continued to travel extensively.[34]

Xavier's holy presence in Asia . . . was particularly propitious to the Portuguese. His "apostolic" journeys sanctified not only the newly acquired territories through the foundation of religious institutions, improvement of social mores and Christianization, but also the vessels on which he traveled and the sea passages he plowed through. Whatever he *touched* became a mark on the map of Portuguese possession, even if it proved to be a temporary one.[35]

In tracing the development of a discourse of sanctity ("signs of wonder"[36]) as it was produced and circulated in conjunction with the three sites where Xavier's corpse was located either temporarily (Sancian and Malacca) or permanently (Goa) at subsequent points in time (1552–1554),[37] I explore the many "saintly" qualities that were attributed to this Jesuit missionary and exhibited by his corpse at each of these Portuguese colonial outposts that, not coincidentally, Xavier had also visited in life. Specifically, I pay special attention to those moments in which bodily signs, as "proof" of the miraculous capabilities of a potential saint-in-the-making, are invoked at each of the above locations by his multiple Jesuit biographers.[38] Moreover, it will be suggested that these "signs of wonder" while initially centered on Xavier's physical corpse,[39] steadily and metaphorically spread by contagion onto other bodies, those of land and sea, man and woman, ship and cross, a process which increasingly determines the (future) path not only of this would-be saint's travels in death, but also that of additional future travellers in the Indian Ocean world, Jesuit and Portuguese alike.

The story of Xavier's "miraculous" corpse as it was moved to multiple sites within Portuguese Asia thus make him a viable candidate for sainthood by initiating and circulating a discourse of sanctity that is directly tied to the machinations of the *Society of Jesus* as it operated under the imperial umbrella of the *Estado da Índia*.[40] My analysis then, of the many "signs of wonder" associated with Xavier's postmortem travels will suggest that these same corporeal displays—very often ritualized[41]—also evidence the ideologies and practices of the Jesuits at these various Portuguese colonial outposts in the East Indies.[42] By investing themselves in the sanctity of Xavier's corpse and its ability to rub off (or not) onto other objects through a process of "translation,"[43] Jesuits reveal much about themselves and their relations not only to one another, but also certain places (Sancian, Malacca, and Goa) and peoples, including Portuguese colonial officials, (European) traders and merchants, and various "Portuguese Catholic" and "native" publics located at these same sites during the mid-sixteenth century.[44] Jesuit investments in Xavier's sanctity also reveal the history of their own seaborne and territorial claims in the Indian Ocean.[45] Thus, in spite of attempts on their behalf to transform Sancian and Malacca[46]—not only through Xavier's biographical ties, but also through physical contact with his corpse—[47]into thriving spiritual, commercial, and colonial bases with a sense of community all connected via ships and monsoon patterns operating in the Indian Ocean world, this potential saint's many "signs of wonder" expose instead the attendant weaknesses of church, state, and public, thus compelling his final emplacement in Goa,[48] not insignificantly the site where this Jesuit had started his journey to sainthood ten years earlier. Here I follow historian Inés Županov to suggest that Xavier's apostolic journeys, not only in life but also in death, were directly connected to the mapping of a Portuguese empire in Asia,[49] a saintly fashioning that, as will become evident here, was "not without problems."[50] Lastly, it is in the act of (re)telling this remarkable Indian Ocean story (by Jesuit biographers, their followers, and now myself) that Xavier's value endures.[51]

A. Sancian (1552)

> Portuguese trade reached far beyond the country's Indian possessions. Thus, for instance, for nearly three decades[1518–1548] . . . they maintained an illicit trade along the Checkiang and Fukien coasts, using temporary bases in Kwantung. That is how St. Francis Xavier found his last resting place in Shanchuan taon [Sancian], one of the Portuguese smugglers' base[s].[52]

According to his many Jesuit biographers, Francis Xavier died during the night between 2 and 3 December in the year 1552[53] on the island of Sancian,[54] after awaiting news to enter China to start up a Jesuit mission.[55] In the following section, I trace how a discourse of sanctity was first developed in relation to Xavier's death at this site by the few available eyewitnesses— including several Jesuits, Portuguese traders and settlers, and one member of Sancian's "native" Chinese public. My approach is thematic, summarizing the central defining characteristics of his first "translation" as recorded by Jesuit biographers of this saint-in-the making. Xavier's corpse exhibits numerous "signs of wonder" upon his first disinterment, three months after his initial burial here. Interestingly, however, his incorrupt corporeal state does not spread by way of contagion onto this burgeoning Portuguese colonial outpost, excepting the waters surrounding it, and despite his biographical attachments to this place. My analysis will reveal Xavier's ill treatment in death, expose the weaknesses of church and state activity in Sancian, and finally, suggest why his (Jesuit) companions were propelled to translate his sacred remains to a more suitable site, the discursive power of his sanctity conveniently expanded in the process of travel in the Indian Ocean world.

Xavier is first accorded the status of a martyr and given a proper Christian burial by those present in Sancian at the time of his death.[56] Not only did he have his eyes fixed on the crucifix in his hands at the moment that he "surrendered his soul completely to God,"[57] but his death was "deeply regretted and mourned by everyone there," writes biographer Pinto.[58] Jesuit Valignano informs us that it was Antonio, Xavier's Chinese interpreter and servant, a converted native who "loved him so much," who first reported his death to the men onboard an unnamed Portuguese ship anchored in the harbor of Sancian.[59] Several of these "devoted ones" then left the ship to assist in Xavier's burial.[60] Lucena reports that despite the "grace and vivacity of his[Xavier's] features," this same group of men, including several Portuguese settlers of Sancian, "cried as he was deceased."[61] Next his corpse—dressed with his priestly vestments—is placed inside a "fitted box," a Chinese "custom" that Valignano reflects on as paralleling death practices "in Italy and other parts of Europe."[62] He also reports that inside this coffin was placed fresh lime "so that his flesh would be consumed more quickly."[63] De Souza tells us that his coffin was then carried and placed inside a hollow grave by the same devoted Antonio who was assisted only by two "mulattos" since many Portuguese settlers chose to remain inside their huts due to the "great cold that prevailed that day."[64]

Gonçalves informs us that "they buried him in a hillock, at the feet of a cross, placing many stones at the head so that if someone passed there later, [he] would know the place of the grave."[65] He also reports that on the day of Xavier's death, a religious image of a crucified Christ located in the castle in Navarra[Spain] where he was born stopped sweating, a practice that had regularly occurred during the ten years of Xavier's overseas missionary activities. Instead, on this auspicious day and on every Friday thereafter, the image began to issue drops of blood to "signify the greatest works he suffered," yet another marker of Xavier's martyrdom, sanctity, and biographical ties in life and death.[66]

Second, Xavier's corpse exhibits certain qualities of sanctity at the time of his disinterment three months after his initial burial. Despite the use of lime as an agent of decomposition that acts to "clean" his bones of their flesh, his corpse defies deterioration in death, signifying once again his potential saintliness. Teixeira informs us that it was on 17 February of the following year (1553) that the ship of Diogo Pereira—a friend of Xavier's in life and a wealthy Portuguese merchant—stopped off in Sancian as part of its continuing journey to Malacca, the *Santa Cruz* not coincidentally the same ship that Xavier himself had earlier travelled in to reach Sancian.[67] It is the same Antonio of earlier accounts who informs Pereira of Xavier's death and the location of his grave; Pereira, in turn, appoints a "trusted" Portuguese sailor from his ship to examine the condition of Xavier's corpse.[68] Upon opening his coffin, he found it "whole and healthy, like when they buried him, being near three months that he was buried, without any bad smell."[69] Biographer Pinto tells us that Xavier's corpse was without any signs of deterioration, nor "even the shroud and the cassock he wore were found to have any spots or blemishes, for both were as clean and white as if they had just been washed."[70] Just as his sanctity had now spread to his priestly vestments, so too did they emit "a very pleasant smell that all found comforting," according to Valignano.[71] This latter detail is echoed in the account of de Souza who describes the smell as "surpassing in sweetness the combined aroma of the most fragrant flowers,"[72] proof once again of Xavier's saintliness.

Third, Xavier's sanctity is reinforced through the practice of producing and distributing relics. While Gonçalves informs us that upon further examination of his corpse, his insides were determined to be "full of juice and blood,"[73] de Souza describes how the same Diogo Pereira requested that "a slice of flesh about one finger's length [be] cut off of Xavier's left knee so as to determine if he exhibited additional signs of incorruptibility, a jet of fresh blood gushing at once from the wound, as though the flesh had been that of a living man."[74] This confirmed Pereira's suspicions which he proceeded to label as yet another "mark of the incorruption of [his] sacred body."[75] Moreover, the production and circulation of relics was not restricted to his corpse; this same biographer informs us that a large piece of his cassock was also divided into relics and distributed amongst the Portuguese settlers present on the island,[76] a practice not uncommon to a potential saint's relics.

Fourth, his (Jesuit) companions are compelled to initiate his translation from this site by the fact that Xavier is not fully appreciated in Sancian.[77] Specifically, it is because of the limits of Portuguese statehood—Sancian was less a colonial outpost than a temporary safe haven for commercial traffic at this time—that enforces the need for his translation to a more suitable site.[78] While Mendes attests to the limited "local conditions" for Xavier's proper burial there,[79] Valignano characterizes Sancian as "deserted and uncultivated," as a "place of heathens" that he briefly passed by during his own travels in Portuguese Asia.[80] Meanwhile, Lucena describes the "poor huts" that the scant numbers of Portuguese "settlers" inhabit,[81] and de Souza informs us of the constant cold and fierce winds that regularly enveloped Sancian, and that Xavier also experienced personally during his last days, thus contributing to his untimely death.[82]

Specific factors then are emphasized by Xavier's Jesuit biographers in order to reinforce Sancian's unsuitability as a Portuguese colonial and missionary outpost.[83] Pinto describes how many of these same Portuguese settlers, upon their first viewing of Xavier's incorrupt corpse three months after his death, "smote themselves repeatedly for their past error" in not attending to Xavier's initial burial due to the extreme cold of that now momentous day.[84] Similarly, de Souza informs us that "the sight of such a marvel . . . moved some to a transport of spiritual fervour, others to repentance for having forsaken the saint in his last illness."[85] Lastly, Gonçalves points out that the burial of Xavier took place at the foot of the one (and only) cross planted by the Portuguese on this island, and was overseen by a "native" as opposed to a group of Portuguese Christians.[86] That Sancian was devoid of certain minimal traits required of a missionary and colonial outpost—sustained church and state activity, a defined Portuguese public, and established commercial networks that supplied the basics for living a Christian life—compelled his companions, in particular Xavier's trusted friend Pereira, to remove his sacred remains from this barren island, and its (un)deserving inhabitants, Portuguese and native alike. Moreover, by the fact that *in spite of* his poor treatment in life and death on the island of Sancian, Xavier still exhibits numerous signs of his incorruptness makes his sanctity appear even that much more significant.

Xavier's translation from Sancian is not only a ritualized activity; his corpse also emits additional "signs of wonder," thus sanctioning his continued travels in death. Lucena describes how Xavier's corpse was first returned to his coffin—"without removing the lime"—and then taken in procession on the shoulders of several Portuguese settlers where it was transferred to Pereira's ship, the *Santa Cruz*.[87] De Souza informs us that "after the loading," and as this ship[88] cast off from Sancian destined for Malacca, the typhoons, "so terrible and so frequent in those latitudes, seemed to have subsided, for the time at least, to allow safe passage to such a sacred cargo."[89] That Xavier's incorruptness in death fails to sanctify the territory of Sancian itself seems to echo this Jesuit's failure to enter China to start up a mission during his lifetime. However, that a small degree of Xavier's sanctity rubs off onto the waters surrounding Sancian,[90] that which safely carries his sacred corpse not only enforces the "seaborne" character of the Portuguese empire in Asia during the sixteenth century, including their unsurpassed naval superiority at this time, but suggests that Xavier did not leave this biographical site completely untouched in both life and death,[91] and that his protectors were justified in "translating" Xavier's sacred remains from Sancian, their hopes pinned on Malacca at this point.

Thus far, I have thematized Xavier's initial burial and translation from Sancian, suggesting the initial development of a discourse of sanctity on the part of his Jesuit biographers that incorporates certain corporeal traits or "signs of wonder": a pleasant smell, a wholeness, a lack of decomposition, and spurting blood, the production and distribution of relics of corpse and cloth, and new sites—the waters surrounding Sancian but not the island itself—that travel alongside his corpse. At the same time that the details of his translation promote his sainthood through the act of storytelling, they also expose the vulnerabilities of Portuguese statehood (ideological, religious, and political), and enforce his removal from this particular location.

B. Malacca (1553)

> At the end of the 16th century, Melaka was a quite different city from the one of Albuquerque's days. It was now a Portuguese stronghold in an increasingly hostile environment, a political, military, economic, and religious centre . . . it was the privileged crossroads of trade routes, and checkpoint of men and merchandise.[92]

In the following section, we continue on the path of Xavier's journey to sainthood, stopping off in Malacca (or Melaka as it is now called) to reveal another chapter in the story of Xavier's postmortem travels in the Indian Ocean. Specifically, I examine the reception of his corpse, his five-month interment here, and his ultimate translation from this now waning Portuguese colonial outpost. Once again, my approach is thematic, summarizing the defining characteristics of Xavier's corporeal experiences in Malacca as told by his Jesuit biographers. His body continues to exhibit numerous signs of sanctity, both replicating many of those witnessed in Sancian and producing and circulating additional markers in relation to his new location. Here, more so than in the former case, Xavier's saintliness does spread by way of contagion onto other (missionary and colonial) bodies precisely because it is a more developed colonial outpost, his stronger biographical attachments to this site also significant. However, in the end, Xavier's poor treatment during his interment here exposes the vulnerabilities of church, state, and public, thus prompting his subsequent removal from Malacca. His (Jesuit) companions are propelled once again, just as they had been earlier, to translate his corpse to a new setting (in this case, Goa), the discursive power of his sanctity once again expanded in the act of travel within the Indian Ocean world.

First, in the month-long journey from Sancian to Malacca—arriving on 22 March 1553[93]—Xavier saves the ship carrying his precious cargo from destruction, an act that simultaneously justifies his translation from Sancian and sanctifies the waters surrounding Malacca. Teixeira, himself an eyewitness to these momentous events, reports that the *Santa Cruz* was "saved from another ship that had been in front, because [Xavier's] body had come in that ship."[94] Moreover, Pinto notes the arrival of his corpse in Malacca as marking his return "nine months and twenty-two days" since he had first set off for his (failed) mission in China,[95] thus reinforcing his biographical ties to this site. Specifically, it was Xavier who had initiated the Jesuit order in Malacca in 1548 and had been bequeathed a church by its acting Portuguese governor to promote the city's religiosity.[96] Xavier's corpse thus travels, in reverse, the circuit of his life story.

Second, Xavier's incorrupt corpse is honorably received in Malacca, his reception transformed into a ritual that serves to inscribe him with meaning in this new context—a trait typical of European saint's relics. Teixeira informs us that "by the great devotion that everyone had in him and with great happiness, they were determined to receive him with the most solemnity they could," especially Diogo Pereira, for it was he, Xavier's "special devotee and friend" now-turned "ambassador," whose ship had transported him in both life and death to Malacca. It was also this same loyal friend who ordered a "great quantity of wax" (candles) to be made and the city to be decorated in preparation for his reception.[97] Valignano adds that it was also Pereira who "paid the necessary expenses," and that it was "in such a manner that all the principals of Malacca went to receive him in a procession with many candles and tapers burning, all the city converging with much devotion and reverence to see that sacred corpse."[98] Lucena informs us that this same public also "kissed" and "touch[ed] beads [of rosaries] to his corpse"[99] both intimate acts of religious devotion. Teixeira reports that this "large multitude of people" converged on Xavier "for the opinion that everyone had of that sacred father, and because of his fame that had already run throughout the city, of when he came whole and incorrupt."[100] Thus, not only was it his biographical ties to this site but also the news of the miraculous state of his corpse that led Malacca's public to ritually honor Xavier in death through the special lighting of the city with candles, and the seeing, touching, and kissing of his corpse.

Third, Xavier's corpse exhibits certain "signs of wonder"(both old and new) during his procession through the streets of Malacca, sanctifying both place and public in the process. Teixeira informs us that Xavier's procession is led by the Vicar of Malacca, who first confirms the continuing "whole-ness and freshness" of his corpse before giving "thanks to our Master" and initiating the solemnities.[101] This procession also includes "various clergy," Xavier's loyal friend Pereira, and finally, the "people of the city."[102] It is during his movement through the streets of Malacca that Xavier performs his first miracle of healing through the power of touch. Our eyewitness Teixeira describes how "a man [came] who was very sick in the chest, and that after having touched the body of the Father and entrusting himself to him, he remained healthy," a detail echoed in Lucena's account.[103]

Xavier also miraculously rids Malacca of an ongoing plague, his sanc-tity rubbing off onto this colonial outpost in a way reminiscent of Euro-pean relics which often acted to protect and secure its new community.[104] Teixeira reports that "since the time that he arrived there, the sacred body had stopped the plague, that had been going on in that city, which had killed many people," a point echoed by various other Jesuit biographers.[105] That Xavier maintains his corporeal exceptionalism, miraculously heals a member of Malacca's public, and stops a preexisting plague not only affirms his expanding powers in death, but also sanctifies his location in this colonial outpost.

Fourth, Xavier's corpse arrives at a designated church in Malacca, wherein he is interred for a second time in a simple grave. According to our same Jesuit eyewitness, the procession first stops, appropriately enough, at "Our Lady of the Mount, the church of the Jesuits," which had been granted to this religious order during Xavier's earlier residence in Malacca.[106] Pinto informs us that it was this same chapel where Xavier "had always made his home in Malacca,"[107] reinforcing once again his biographical ties such that his journey in death is largely determined by his journey in life. Moreover, it is "with deep pain and grief on the part of all,"[108] that Xavier is buried here. Gonçalves points out that it was a "Portuguese" who delivered the body,[109] a detail suggestive of the respect accorded Xavier in death and the remorse of Malacca's people, more so than in the case of Sancian's limited public wherein it had been a Chinese "native" who interred him. Valignano reports that they "took him out of the coffin, conforming to the custom of the Portuguese [by] putting only a pillow under his head and covering the face with a cloth."[110] It was then placed inside a grave located "at the entrance to the sacristy" according to de Souza[111]; afterwards, the "appropriate funeral rites" were performed, writes Gonçalves.[112] Lucena informs us that this same pillow was made of "silk"—a detail that indexes the larger Indian Ocean trade in commodities from Malacca—while de Souza reveals that Xavier's corpse was "simply wrapped in a shroud,"[113] before he was put into the ground.

Fifth, Xavier's corpse exhibits additional and now familiar "signs of wonder" upon the opening of his grave by several newly arrived Jesuits, five months after his interment at Our Lady of the Mount.[114] These signs incite additional acts of religious devotion and relic production, reinforce his continued sanctity in death, and finally, reveal the increased involvement of the Jesuits in mapping his journey to sainthood. Teixeira tells us that it was Juan de Beira, a Portuguese Jesuit who alongside several brothers, and on his way to the Moluccas—yet another colonial outpost that Xavier himself had visited in life (1546)—stopped off in Malacca desirous to see what had been described to him as the incorrupt corpse of his "special friend" to whom he was much devoted.[115] These historical details suggest not only the constant movement of Jesuits and ecclesiastical information between Portuguese sites, but also, Xavier's many biographical ties to both places and individual persons caught up in the religious, commercial, and political networks of the Indian Ocean world.

Lucena informs us that this group of Jesuits "secretly opened the hole at night"—again, amidst circumstances reminiscent of European relic translations—upon which they saw the "towel which covered his face" and the "pillow upon which was the head," both of which had "passed red blood,"[116] signs of his continuing sanctity. In addition, his corpse was found to be "as entire, fresh and fragrant as it was before being interred there," and his vestments were found to be "perfectly intact" according to de Souza.[117] Valignano tells us that his incorruption was complete despite the "fresh lime with its fire" and the "earth with its humidity," a detail that suggests that lime had been employed once again in an effort to decompose Xavier's flesh more quickly.[118] Gonçalves informs us that his preservation immediately incited acts of religious devotion, Beira and his Jesuit companions "kiss[ing] his sacred hand and feet [and] showering them with tears of devotion."[119] He also describes how Xavier's outer vestment—its preservation also a sign of its achieved relic status—was then removed by Father Melchior Nunes and eventually carried to Japan.[120] That these additional translations of Xavier's relics were about to take place serves to map his biographical ties in life onto those in death—Xavier having visited Japan as part of his larger Asian mission in the year 1549—at the same time that they spread by contagion his saintliness to additional sites located in the Indian Ocean world.

But this same group of Jesuit devotees also determines that Xavier is not fully appreciated in Malacca, due to damages evident to his corpse upon his second disinterment. Specifically, these damages expose the vulnerabilities of church, state, and public, and ultimately compel Xavier's translation from Malacca. De Souza informs us of Xavier's improper treatment during his interment by those "Portuguese" initially put in charge of his corpse. Not only was the grave that was dug "too short" to fit his body, but he was forced down into it; a "recoiling" of the neck, "deep cuts" in the neck and on the face, and a "slight bruising" of the top of the nose were all corporeal traits evidenced by Beira and his companions upon opening his grave.[121] Moreover, Xavier's simple burial—devoid of a coffin—is now viewed more critically in light of his physical damages, de Souza affirming that this was in fact a "custom [existing] among the poorer classes," while Valignano goes so far as to consider it "an act of disgrace,"[122] yet another sign confirming a lack of respect accorded to this would-be saint in death at this location.

I suggest that Xavier's poor treatment in death has everything to do with the vulnerabilities of church, state, and public in Malacca present at this time.[123] That there was no sizeable contingency of Jesuits located here to preside over his previous interment is a point affirmed by Xavier's many Jesuit biographers.[124] This, in turn, suggests not only that Xavier's burial in Malacca lacked religiosity, but that members of his own order were neither there to sanction the interment of their religious brother nor to ensure his proper burial. Moreover, Gonçalves alludes to the reason behind the fact that there were no Jesuits residing in Malacca, despite their ownership of "Our Lady of the Mount," suggesting that earlier tensions with Malacca's Portuguese acting governor, Dom Alvaro de Athaide, had led to his disapproval of the Jesuits such that they had consequently left the city as a result.[125] In addition, the governor's marked absence during the burial of Xavier's corpse—he remained at a window observing the procession through the streets according to Gonçalves—[126]suggests that Xavier's burial had occurred without a proper "balance" of church and state actors.[127]

Moreover, that Malacca had been in the midst of a plague at the time of the arrival of Xavier's corpse suggests both its lack of hygiene and the weaknesses of colonial officials to prevent its spread onto other (Portuguese Catholic and native) bodies; Xavier was forced instead to stand in for the role of the state as protectorate. Finally, this lack of an organized Jesuit presence in Malacca during Xavier's (second) burial also points to the possible general disregard for colonial policies and practices amongst Malacca's public such that there were no Jesuits to preside over daily communions and conversions, the city's residents perhaps more busily engaged in forms of trade instead.[128] De Souza informs us that it was "at that sight, [that] the authors of the secret exhumation judged it improper to hide anew, under the earth, such a treasure so neglected and so little appreciated,"[129] a rationale also typically used in promoting European relic translations. Thus, Beira and his companions felt compelled to translate Xavier's corpse to a "more decent place"—in this case Goa, both the centre of the Portuguese empire in Asia and the Indian Ocean port city that had witnessed Xavier's momentous arrival in 1542—where he would be more fully solemnized by church, state, and members of the public.[130]

Xavier's translation from Malacca to Goa, just as had been the case for Sancian, is transformed into a ritualized event wherein he is carried in procession to an awaiting ship accompanied by two of the above Jesuits. Teixeira tells us that on 15 August 1553, it was Juan de Beira who "ordered a coffin to be made, in which the father put him, decently, and asked that it be guarded with much reverence, and leaving for the Moluccas, he left there with him[Xavier] a fellow Jesuit, one of whom had arrived with him, in order to carry the body to India, and to put it in the Jesuit College of St. Paul in Goa."[131] Our biographer affirms both that Xavier's journey was to be overseen by a Jesuit, a factor overlooked in both Sancian and Malacca, and that the new home for Xavier's corpse was to be a (famed) Jesuit institution in Goa. Also, that Beira himself was destined for the Moluccas suggests once again a larger Jesuit enterprise wherein members constantly travelled between Portuguese colonial posts located in the Indian Ocean world, contributing to their civilizing development in the process.

Valignano informs us that it is the same Pereira of earlier accounts who covered the costs of the commissioned coffin for Xavier: it was "very well made, covered with damask inside, and covered on the outside with a cloth of brocade."[132] Next, according to de Souza, "the holy body was laid [inside the coffin], pending its embarkment for India, at the next monsoon."[133] It was during this waiting period that Xavier performed a miracle, thus directly sanctioning his removal from Malacca, once again in a manner reminiscent of European relic translations.[134] De Souza writes: "the interval of waiting lasted eighteen days, and a wax taper, which was lit by the side of the coffin and which could in the ordinary course of things have lasted at most ten hours, continued to burn all those eighteen days, and the wax that flowed from it weighed much more than the taper itself."[135] Gonçalves informs us that this "truly miraculous" event was witnessed by Pereira and Beira, as well as the former's cousin, who later testified to this remarkable occurrence on oath in Lisbon as part of Xavier's canonization process.[136]

Next, Xavier's corpse is carried in procession, the month now being September (1553) and nearing the coming of the monsoon season,[137] towards the shores of Malacca, "accompanied by many noblemen [wherein] he was placed on a sloop[small boat] that was already waiting, beautifully adorned with luxurious carpeting and a silk awning, on which he was taken to a ship belonging to a certain Lopo de Noronha, who was about to depart for India, and transferred aboard," according to Pinto.[138] The emphasis on noblemen—including shipowner Noronha himself—also indexes Xavier's elevated status compared to his earlier transport from Sancian on a

Portuguese merchant's ship. Not only was the ship itself and the berth reserved for Xavier's corpse richly decorated, but during his translation he was surrounded by "many smells and perfumes," according to Teixeira,[139] a detail that suggests that Xavier's own corporeal fragrance was supplemented with artificial ones to ensure that his "odor of sanctity," endured throughout the arduous journey. Lastly, Lucena and Valignano give us additional information on the men who were selected by Beira to safeguard and sanction Xavier's journey to Goa. The first was Manuel de Tavora, a Jesuit who had accompanied Beira to Malacca, and the second was Pedro de Alcaçova, a Jesuit who had only recently arrived from Japan, where he had been overseeing the Jesuit mission initiated under Xavier (1549), and who had been requested by a Portuguese colonial state official to "do some business in India" on his behalf.[140] These details affirm once again Xavier's enduring sanctity and status, his biographical ties to persons and places, as well as the fact that members of the *Society of Jesus* were often employed as agents of the Portuguese colonial state.

Finally, Xavier exhibits numerous "signs of wonder" on the voyage to Goa, thus sanctioning the larger Portuguese "seaborne" empire, his translation from Malacca, and his continued travels in death to additional colonial outposts, including brief stopovers in Ceylon and Cochin. Through these postmortem travels a discourse of sanctity expands to include additional persons, places, and publics, at the same time mapping a larger Portuguese empire in the Indian Ocean world. Both Valignano and Teixeira attest to the fact that Xavier liberated the ship through his intercession from numerous "certain dangers and shipwrecks"[141] caused by "large storms on the journey,"[142] the ship's (Jesuit) passengers "invoking the name of Father Francis to keep them free and safe."[143] Gonçalves informs us that precisely when the ship was in danger, the candles and perfumes surrounding Xavier's corpse "blazed even brighter" and "smelled even stronger," details suggestive of this would-be saint's ability to emit efficacious signs at critical moments as well as ensure his travel companions of their safeguarded journey to Goa.[144]

In this section, I have explored a series of themes to characterize Xavier's translation to Malacca, his five-month interment here, and his continuing journey in death, relying on the same set of Jesuit biographies that earlier provided a window onto Xavier's postmortem experiences in Sancian. The discourse of sanctity recounted in these Jesuit biographies incorporates additional places, publics, and practices as it travels alongside Xavier's corpse, telling a remarkable Indian Ocean story in the process. While this missionary's corpse exhibits many of the same "signs of wonder" first evidenced in Sancian (a lack of decomposition, a fragrance, the spurting of blood, relic production and circulation), Xavier also incites new acts of devotion (the lighting of tapers, a richly decorated coffin, kissing, touching, and the shedding of tears). His residence in Malacca also reflects the availability of material goods in this center of trade—silk, tapestries, perfumes, candles, and carpeting—and the greater wealth of Malacca as a Portuguese colonial outpost compared to Sancian. That Xavier spreads by contagion his powers onto other (colonial) bodies—curing a man of his sickness and ridding the city of a plague—affirms his biographical ties to this site through such men as Pereira and Beira, and suggests once again that while Malacca was a more developed colonial outpost than Sancian, it still had its own set of political and economic instabilities to contend with.

Together, these "signs of wonder" work to sanctify Xavier's location here as well as the space of Malacca and its residents. However, Xavier's ill treatment in death such that his body is buried without a coffin and subsequently damaged during his second interment also exposes the vulnerabilities of church, state, and public in this diminishing Portuguese colonial outpost. Here, interestingly, the Jesuits stationed in Malacca take on a defining role in mapping his journey to sainthood, compelling, alongside the will of Xavier himself in death, his translation from this colonial outpost to a more suitable site directly tied to his biography in life.[145] Once again, as was the case in Sancian, that Xavier maintains his sanctity *in spite of* his location makes him that much more "saintly." Moreover, it is in the act of telling his remarkable story on the part of his Jesuit biographers that value is added to the object of their storytelling, in this case Xavier himself.[146]

SECTION IV: GOA AND THE TELLING OF INDIAN OCEAN STORIES

That Xavier's corpse arrives in Goa successfully and exhibits sufficient "signs of wonder" to guarantee his permanent residency there in death is at the center of another Indian Ocean story, one that will not be (re)told here. If, however, I were to continue on Xavier's written and physical journey to sainthood, I would detail the numerous "signs of wonder" associated with Xavier, suggesting that he both replicates many of those witnessed to publics at the different sites of his earlier translations (Sancian and Malacca), and produces and circulates additional signs, now largely familiar to his oceanic readers, but in relation to his new location. Specifically, in the case of Goa, Xavier will no longer emit signs *in spite* of his location according to his Jesuit biographers. Here, to a stronger degree than in Malacca, Xavier's saintliness will spread by way of contagion precisely *because* the port city of Goa, also known as a "a bride of the sea" by the Portuguese[147] was a more developed centre for missionary and colonial activity,[148] and precisely *because* of Xavier's even stronger biographical attachments in life to this place.[149] Unlike both Sancian and Malacca, where his corpse was intermittently valued and poorly treated, Xavier is fully appreciated in Goa. Moreover, the elaborately ritualized reception of Xavier's holy relic in *Velha Goa* will be unlike either of the events that were staged in Sancian and Malacca;

that Xavier intercedes in exposing a perfect balance of church, state, and public at this valued site also explains why his postmortem travels end here. However, in choosing to confine Xavier's fate to Portuguese India, Jesuit missionaries in the future will neither let go of Xavier's sanctity nor fail to recognize the richly deserving will of this saint-in-the-making for carving out their own missionary enterprise; rather they will continue to expand his discursive power beyond the confines of Goa to map out additional sites and signs of wonder in Portuguese Asia,[150] always in search of new pathways, networks, and circuits of faith, commerce, and colonialism.

NOTES

1. Inés Županov, "The Prophetic and the Miraculous in Portuguese Asia: A Hagiographical View of Colonial Culture," in *Sinners and Saints: The Successors of Vasco da Gama*, ed. Sanjay Subrahmanyam, 155 (Oxford, UK: Oxford University Press, 1995).
2. Devleena Ghosh and Stephen Muecke, "Indian Ocean Stories," in *The Indian Ocean, The UTS Review* VI(2; 2000): 24.
3. Kären Wigen, "Introduction: Oceans of History" forum, *American Historical Review* 111(3; August 2006): 717–721.
4. Markus Vink, "Indian Ocean Studies and the New Thalassology" *Journal of Global History* 2(2007): 45. He points to the contributions of historian Michael Pearson to Indian Ocean studies, suggesting that by including humans and the sea in the equation Pearson recognized other elements of commonality in the region's cultural landscape—port cities, ships, trade, commodities, religious communities, lingua francas, and the political military presence of the Portuguese and their string of coastal forts.
5. Ghosh and Muecke, "Indian Ocean Stories," 28.
6. Devleena Ghosh and Stephen Muecke, eds. "Editors' Introduction," in *The Indian Ocean, The UTS Review* VI(2; 2000): 5.
7. Ibid. This same cultural approach (an anthropology of things) is evidenced in the writings of anthropologists such as Arjun Appadurai, ed. See his "Introduction," in *The Social Life of Things*, 3–63 (Cambridge, UK: Cambridge University Press, 1986).
8. George Marcus referenced in Stephen Vertovec, "Conceiving and Researching Transnationalism," *Ethnic and Racial Studies* 22(2; 1999): 14.
9. Ghosh and Muecke, "Editors Introduction," 5.
10. Ghosh and Muecke, "Indian Ocean Stories," 33. The authors assert that this is a deeper level of cultural analysis.
11. Igor Kopytoff, "The Cultural Biography of Things: Commoditization as Process," in *The Social Life of Things*, ed., Arjun Appadurai, 64–91 (Cambridge, UK: Cambridge University Press, 1986).
12. Ibid. Slaves and saints' relics (whole corpses and/or parts) both fit this category of being things and persons at the same time. See also Patrick Geary, *Furta Sacra: Thefts of Relics in the Central Middle Age*, (Princeton, NJ: Princeton University Press, 1978).
13. Thomas Metcalf, *Imperial Connections: India in the Indian Ocean Area, 1860–1920* (Berkeley, CA: University of California Press, 2007), 9.
14. These more recent approaches to studying the Indian Ocean have generally been applied to the postmaritime age (post 1750), following Martin Lewis and Kären Wigen. Here I want to take these newer perspectives but apply

them to older circuits in the Indian Ocean (pre 1600) in order to conceptualize the early modern period in alternate ways. See Martin Lewis and Kären Wigen "A Maritime Response to the Crisis in Area Studies," *The Geographical Review* 89(2; April 1999): 166.

15. Sanjay Subrahmanyam, "Introduction: The Portuguese and Early Modern Asia," in *Sinners and Saints: The Successors of Vasco da Gama*, ed. Sanjay Subrahmanyam, 9 (Oxford: Oxford University Press, 1995). A biographical approach is particularly useful for exploring the early modern period, because there is such a dearth of materials. Specifically, I emphasize both the life and death of Xavier as a historical actor, in the process expanding the notion of biography to suggest that what happens in death is just as telling as what happens in life.

16. Briefly, the *Estado da Índia* was the name given to the Portuguese colonial state in Goa that was formally established (after Vasco da Gama's "discovery" in 1498) under the first Viceroy, the ineffectual Dom Francisco de Almeida (1505–1510) but which was strongly fortified during the rule of Governor Affonso de Albuquerque (1510–1515). The *Estado da Índia* became a formidable presence in the sixteenth century, its decline apparent by the middle of the seventeenth century. Goa at the time of Albuquerque's rule (1510) was in effect the second capital of Bijapur, physically a compact Muslim town of recent date. Tissuari island, or the island of Goa, prior to being incorporated into Bijapur state, had been a Hindu settlement during the early days of the Vijayanagar dynasty (fourteenth century). By 1440 the whole town had shifted to the other side of Mandovi and by 1469 Goa was ruled by the Bahmanis before incorporation into the Bijapur dynasty. Goa had largely flourished during the fifteenth through sixteenth centuries because it was the principal site for the import of horses, shipped from the Persian Gulf to the Deccan. See Boies Penrose, *Goa-Rainha do Oriente, Goa-Queen of the East* (Lisboa: Commissão Ultramarina, 1960), 39. One must take note of anthropologist Vicente Rafael's argument that applies to both the Spanish and Portuguese cases of colonialism, namely that of the intimate relation of Iberian colonial rule to missionary practice and ideology as "Catholicism imbedded the structure of colonial rule within the practice of religious conversion." Vicente L. Rafael, *Contracting Colonialism: Translation and Christian Conversion in Tagalog Society Under Early Spanish Rule* (Durham, NC: Duke University Press, 1993), 17.

17. It is important to note that throughout this chapter, I do not equate a Jesuit presence with a Catholic presence; rather, the Jesuits were one of many religious orders (alongside the Franciscans, Dominicans, and later the Augustinians) vying for souls in the Portuguese East Indies in the late sixteenth century. Nor did the Jesuits have an unproblematic relationship with the Vatican; it was one of constant negotiation. Lastly, the Jesuits under analysis here were operating in a particular temporal and spatial location; their actions cannot necessarily be used to generalize the *Society of Jesus.*

18. *Francisco de Jassu y de Xavier* was born in 1506 to Basque nobility in Navarre Spain. Xavier was ordained a priest on June 24, 1537; he then traveled to Venice and Rome (1538) where he was hurriedly chosen to replace another priest for the voyage to the Indies. The *Society of Jesus* had been confirmed on Sept 27, 1540 by the Pope's decree, its founder being Ignatius de Loyola. Xavier set sail for Lisbon in 1540 to receive his orders from King John III; he then made his solemn vow as a Jesuit in the church of St. Paul in Rome on April 22, 1541, arriving in Goa in 1542 to initiate the *Society of Jesus* in Asia. See S.J. P. Rayanna, *St. Francis Xavier and His Shrine*

(Panjim, Goa: Imprimatur, 1982), 40–47. Jesuits missionizing in the East Indies during the sixteenth century mostly came under the jurisdiction of the *Padroado* (Portuguese king). Their dependence on the *Estado da Índia* for support (political, economic, and ideological) was most acute during the mid-sixteenth century when they were still establishing themselves, whereas later on, as they achieved their own successes, they operated more independently of state structures and ideologies. For example, by 1759 in Goa, the Jesuits were viewed as such a threat to the power of the colonial state that they were expelled.

19. Ibid., 68. According to Rayanna, Xavier spent about four to six months in Goa upon his arrival in India in 1542. He visited Goa "half a dozen more times" in the ten years he spent missionizing, but always "on business and in a hurry." In total, Xavier spent approximately ten months in Goa during a ten-year period. In some ways, Xavier was less a saint of Goa then of Portuguese Asia. Overall, Xavier's "evangelical campaign" took him three times to the Fishery, Malabar, and Travancore coasts, twice to Bassein and Ceylon, five times to Malacca, and once to Amboina, the Moluccas, Japan, and finally, the outskirts of China, where he would die awaiting permission to establish a Jesuit mission. See Dauril Alden, *The Making of an Enterprise: The Society of Jesus in Portugal, its Empire and Beyond 1540–1750* (Stanford, CA: Stanford University Press), Chapter 3, p. 43. Thus, on the one hand, Xavier acted as an agent of the *Estado da Índia* by dedicating himself to setting up Jesuit missions in those places where the Portuguese had already established outposts, simultaneously strengthening the power of both church and state in the process. On the other hand, this "man of God" acted as agent of the church by dedicating his efforts to establishing an even larger Jesuit umbrella organization that operated indirectly outside the confines of the colonial state, with Goa as its center. For an extended discussion, see my unpublished dissertation: "The Relic State: St. Francis Xavier and the Politics of Ritual in Portuguese India" (Columbia University, Department of Anthropology, 2004).

20. Goa officially became a Catholic diocese in 1534. The territory assigned, comprised the whole of the East, from the Cape of Good Hope to the boundaries of China. See Carlos Merces de Melo, *The Recruitment and Formation of the Native Clergy in India, 16th–19th Century, An Historico-Canonical Study*, (Lisboa: Agencia Geral do Ultramar, 1955), 11–13.

21. Inés Županov, "The Prophetic and the Miraculous," 156. Xavier directed his attentions not only at the so-called pagans, but also towards the Portuguese living in Portuguese enclaves who had lost sight of their Christian ways, helping to make sense of the larger civilizing mission. This helps explain his popularity amongst both natives and Port colonial officials, who would take it upon themselves to initiate the many transfers of his corpse, and his subsequent canonization drive. It is estimated that he converted approximately 30,000 souls as opposed to the hagiographical number of one million attributed to him. See Georg Schurhammer, "Historical Research into the Life of Francis Xavier in the 16th C," *Revista de Historia*, Julho-Dez, No. 47–48. (Lisboa: Empresa Litteraria Fluminense, 1923): 195–196.

22. The biographies in this chapter were all originally printed in Europe, with the majority of them printed from Lisbon or Rome. The reading public for these books were largely the nobility and clergy. It was they who supported Xavier's canonization in both metropole and colony. Neither can the power of the printed word be underestimated in transforming society, conceptions of language, and communities. See Benedict Anderson, *Imagined Communities* (New York: Verso, 1983); Elizabeth Eisenstein, *The Printing Press as an*

Advent of Change: Communication and Transformations in Early Modern Europe (Cambridge, UK: Cambridge University Press, 1979).

23. While these men held a variety of positions within the Jesuit Order and were either in Europe or stationed throughout Asia in various missionary capacities, some of the earlier chroniclers knew Xavier personally and were witness to some of the actual events that took place on Xavier's remarkable journey in death from China to India. Here I can only introduce the names of these chroniclers and their publications: (Spanish) Manuel Teixeira S.J., "Vita S. Francisci," reproduced in *Monumenta Xaveriana*, Tomus Secundus (Matriti: Typis Gabrielis Lopez del Horno, 1912[1581]). Fernão Mendes Pinto, *The Travels of Mendes Pinto*, ed. and trans. Rebecca Catz (Chicago, IL: University of Chicago Press, 1989 [between 1569–1578]; (Italian) Alessandro Valignano, His original title: *Historia del Principio y Progresso de la Companhia de Jesus en las Índias Orientales (1542–1564)*. It is reproduced as Alessandro Valignano S.J., "Vita S. Francisci" in *Monumenta Xaveriana*. Tomus Primus (Matriti: Typis Augustini Avrial, 1899–1900 [1588]); João de Lucena, *Historia Da Vida do Padre S. Francisco de Xavier, e do que Fizeram na Índia Os Mais Religiosos da Companhia de Jesu* (Lisboa: Noa Oficina de Antonio Gomes, 1600). Sebastiam Gonçalves S.J., *Primeira Parte da Historia Dos Religiosos da Companhia de Jesus e do que fizeram com a divina graça na conversão dos infieis a nossa sancta fee Catholica nos reynos e provincias da Índia Oriental*, (1616). Volume I, (ed.) Joseph Wicki S.J. (Coimbra: Atlantida, 1957); Francisco de Souza S.J., *Oriente Conquistado a Jesu Christo pelos Padres da Companhia de Jesus, da Provincia de Goa*, (Lisboa: Valentim Da Costa Deslandes, 1710). For additional biographical information on these Jesuit biographers—equally fascinating characters themselves, whose lives intersected with Xavier's in both life and death in curious ways, and whose biographies are dialogic in nature—see my Chapter 1: "Incorruption" in my unpublished dissertation: "The Relic State: St. Francis Xavier and the Politics of Ritual in Portuguese India" (Columbia University, Department of Anthropology, 2004).

24. The attention to Xavier's afterlife is unusual within the genre of saints' biographies (*Vitaes*). Ironically, it is only if a corpse exhibits signs of its incorruptibility that it is thought to be that of a saint and the teleological process of writing a saint's biography begins. While biographies typically end with the death of the subject, few biographies of saints pay attention to the afterlife of the saint in question; this is what makes this set of biographies dedicated to Xavier so valuable for historical analysis. Interestingly, St. Ignatius, the founder of the Jesuit order who was canonized alongside Xavier in 1622, never exhibited in death any of the signs of incorruptibility associated with Xavier.

25. I utilize these source materials to suggest that they have been overlooked by historians of Portuguese Asia for both revealing and contributing to missionary and colonial state building processes.

26. My assertion here parallels the one made by Patrick Geary with regard to "translation" narratives found in the Middle Ages in Europe. See his *Furta Sacra*, 9.

27. State documentation of the sixteenth century would typically be concerned with maritime affairs and the administration of the *Estado da Índia*, and thus would not provide the details of Xavier's journey in death. Only more hagiographical sources such as this set of Jesuit biographies would deem these morbid details significant enough to include them, which in turn, makes the following analysis possible.

28. Inés Županov, using Sebastiam Gonçalves's biography of Xavier as her case study, argues that there are constant slippages between the spiritual and material

conquest. Certain omissions and silences are observed, those that endanger a simple "biographical truth." See her "Prophetic and Miraculous," 136.

29. Ibid., 154.

30. Ibid., 136. She describes the kind of information imbedded in these texts—a mixed genre of these histories combining ethnographic and geographic information, long citations of "primary" sources such as individual letters, papal bulls, and royal edicts, as well as chronological and biographical data concerning every single Jesuit missionary sent to Asia and eastern Africa. Here I turn to these chronicles as a source of information on the *Society of Jesus* and the *Estado da Índia*, and do not assume that the fact of Jesuit authorship reveals sociological information only on the Jesuits.

31. Ibid., 155. Županov suggests that there is a territorial dimension to Gonçalves's text, arguing that "this territorial dimension coincides perhaps with a general orientation of the *Estado da Índia* by the end of the 16th century." I apply the idea of a "territorial dimension" to all the Jesuit biographies under analysis, for evidenced in them is a story of the consolidation of sea and land under the Portuguese, a point that will be fully explored as it is tied to the travels of Xavier's corpse in the Indian Ocean. This "territorial dimension" is also important for historiographical reasons, particularly since the majority of sources for this period emphasize the maritime aspects of the *Estado da Índia*.

32. I employ "church" and "state" heuristically to refer to the activities of the *Society of Jesus* and the *Estado da Índia*, respectively; nor do I mean to suggest that they can be as easily disentangled from each other as the Portuguese colonizing project was just as much a civilizing one, operating through the ideology of Roman Catholicism.

33. See Patrick Geary, *Furta Sacra*, 9–10. The value of the saint, including his body, was typically increased in the narration of his relic translations.

34. Inés Županov, "Currents and Counter-Currents: Jesuit Geopolitics in Asia (16th Century)," 1. This (unpublished) paper was presented at the *Table Rond* conference, held in Rome, October 2002.

35. Inés Županov, "The Prophetic and the Miraculous,"149. (Emphasis mine).

36. Inés Županov, "The Prophetic and the Miraculous," 155. She writes: "Jesuit missionaries endlessly in circulation from one place to another in search of missions among Portuguese and their indigenous client groups serve to 'sanctify the land' and intersperse it with *signs of wonder*"(emphasis mine).

37. Due to the limited space and scope of this chapter, my focus is on Sancian and Malacca, with an eye towards Goa as the future and most ideal potential spot for his relic translation.

38. Patrick Geary, *Furta Sacra*, 10–12, 18. As Geary writes, "Far thinking churchmen looked beyond mortal efforts to supernatural defenders, and in importing saints hoped to find a solution to their society's ills"(18). It is outside the scope of this chapter to delve into the history of the cult of saints in Europe, which had its origins in the cult of martyrs of Christian Rome; however, Xavier's potential sainthood in the Indian Ocean must be contextualized within this larger history for it follows many of the same characteristics of the genre. Thus, providing a European backdrop (ninth to twelfth centuries) for what occurs in a colonial context helps illuminate the specificities of the temporal and spatial location under analysis here, and shows how the European cult of saints was adopted and adapted to fit the needs of a burgeoning religious order located in Asia whilst operating under the umbrella of a colonial state during the sixteenth century.

39. The sweet smell, called the "odor of sanctity" that Xavier's corpse also exhibited, was often accorded to certain bodies upon death—this was not

uncommon in Medieval Europe for it served as proof that the person died a saint and for his/her sainthood. For more details, see Paul Stoller's *The Taste of Ethnographic Things, The Senses in Anthropology* (Philadelphia, PA: University of Pennsylvania Press, 1986), 7.

40. Patrick Geary, *Furta Sacra*, 7. The story of a saint's relic translation is also a story of the people who "assimilate him into their own history" by venerating his remains. In order for an object to be venerated as a relic, a new symbolic function had to be assigned—a function that had its origin in the fabric of the society in which it was to be venerated. Thus the symbolic value of a new or rediscovered relic was only a reflection of the values assigned by the society that honored it. *Any change in the nature, force, or direction of its cult had to come entirely from the society itself* (emphasis mine).

41. Patrick Geary, "Sacred Commodities: The Circulation of Medieval Relics," in *The Social Life of Things.* ed., Arjun Appadurai, 178 (Cambridge, UK: Cambridge University Press, 1986). The idea of a public ritual was essential to the creation of a relic's value; ritual had to emphasize both the identity of the remains with those of a saint and the actual miraculous power exercised by that saint through those very remains.

42. Inés Županov, "The Prophetic and the Miraculous," 136–137. The Jesuits held a monopoly in the Asian missionary field at this time. She argues that by focusing on the "exemplarity" of Xavier, these Jesuit biographies are an excellent literary crystallization of the perceptions of a collective conscience.

43. Patrick Geary, *Furta Sacra*, 9–10, 12. This idea of moving relics (whole corpses or parts) in a process named "translations" was part of the larger practice of promoting the cult of saints in Europe. "Translatio" refers to the process by which a saint's relics are moved (legally or not) to a new context and given a new meaning by its community members through formal liturgical processions. These translations were given a particular narrative structure and were either told orally or included in more comprehensive biographies of saints (*Vitaes*). Saintly attributes were to rub off onto the new site, thus sanctifying it in the process and giving the relic a new set of meanings, a new language for understanding it. Geary suggests that relic translations typically exhibited certain qualities: the search for the relic often takes place in secret and at night, its authenticity is often an issue, is miraculous upon discovery, is often not appreciated in its original context (sometimes the saint wills its removal by exhibiting signs), is sometimes difficult to move, and is honored in a joyful reception upon arriving at its new context, qualities and narrative structures that, as will become evident in the following analysis, also emerge in the case of Xavier's relic translations.

44. Inés Županov, "The Prophetic and the Miraculous," 137. The Jesuit missions, including Xavier's efforts, were not just about converting and civilizing the so-called heathens and pagans but also about improving the "corrupt customs" amongst the Catholic faithful in Portuguese Asia. In other words, Xavier was both an apostle of the Indians and the Portuguese.

45. Ibid., 139. According to the author, the real carriers of divine signs and portents were the Jesuits themselves and for the same reason all the *supernatural commerce* in Asia was their monopoly (emphasis mine).

46. Patrick Geary, "Sacred Commodities," 186. The very act of transfer removed the relic from the cultural structure in which it had originally acquired value. It thus arrived in the new community as an unproven object. Moreover, newly acquired relics had to undergo a process of social negotiation within the new community in order to "fit in."

47. Here I emphasize the power of touch or physical contact to make a case for sainthood and statehood. Specifically, it is relevant to the present discussion

to note that touch is in its nature more mutual than sight: to see is not necessarily to be seen by, but to touch is in a sense always to be touched by; this helps explain the emphasis on physical contact with a saint's relics both by a person and a place. See David Clarke, "Invoking the Body's Presence," *The American Journal of Semiotics* 9(1; 1992): 77 [endnote no. 26].

48. Despite the conflicting testimonies of his Jesuit biographers, some who suggest that Xavier's corpse was always meant for Goa, others who seem less committed to this idea, there is evidence that supports the point that all along his body was meant to be transferred to Goa, even if he did not exhibit any signs of sanctity. Xavier himself supposedly requested in life that his body be returned to Goa after his death. The words "I shall not return to Goa, my body yes, it will remain here" is credited to Xavier. See Alexandre Barbosa, "Off to a Ritualistic Start," *Goa Today*, Volume XXIX, 5 (December 1994): 12.

49. Inés Županov, "The Prophetic and the Miraculous," 142. Here a Jesuit can turn into a Portuguese and the opposite movement can be noticed as well.

50. Ibid., 137. Županov suggests that making a Portuguese saint out of a Spanish missionary was not so simple a process; he had to be fashioned in a way that revealed and served best the progressive manifestation of Portuguese glorious destiny in Asia.

51. Patrick Geary, *Furta Sacra*, 9–10.

52. T.R. de Souza, "The Portuguese in Asia and their Church Patronage," in *Western Colonialism in Asia and Christianity*, ed. M.D. David, 14 (Bombay: Himalaya Publishing House, 1988).

53. The day (Friday, Saturday, or Sunday) and the date of his death (December 2 or December 3) are a topic of much debate. The majority of early biographers assigned December 2 as Xavier's date of death; it was later revised to December 3 by church and state officials. Xavier's saint's day is celebrated the world over on December 3. Georg Schurhammer's conclusion is that he probably died close to midnight between December 2 and December 3, between a Friday and Saturday. See Moreno de Souza's unpublished article, "When Did Francis Die?" sent to *The Examiner* (1994). These differences in opinion regarding his death date are also suggestive of the differing viewpoints of the Jesuit biographers under analysis here.

54. Most historians of Portuguese Asia call it Sancian; it was also called *Sao João* (St. John) the Portuguese name given to the island, all variations derived from the Chinese *Shan-chuan tao*. According to Schurhammer, Sancian had been untilled and uninhabited until 1523, the second year of the emperor Chia Chang, when some families began to settle there because of the overcrowding of the mainland. See Georg Schurhammer, S.J., in *Francis Xavier: His Life, His Times*, transl. M. Joseph Costello (Rome: The Jesuit Historical Institute, 1977), Volume IV, Chapter VII; 620, fn. 1. Historian Lea Williams points out that after 1523, the Chinese banned all trade with the Portuguese. That is why Portuguese merchants resorted to smuggling and piracy and why Xavier was on the island of Sancian, awaiting permission to enter China. Lea E. Williams, "Inauspicious Ambience: The Historical Setting of Early Luso-Chinese Contacts," in *Indo-Portuguese History: Old Issues, New Questions*, ed. Teotonio de Souza, 37 (New Delhi: Concept Publishing Company, 1985). Sancian is located approximately 90 miles west of Macau, also a former colonial outpost in the Portuguese East Indies.

55. According to Schurhammer, Xavier embarked for China on July 22, 1552. He spent approximately two and a half months on the island of Sancian, awaiting news. In the meantime, he had requested that a small church be built on the island. There he offered Mass, instructed the children and slaves of Portuguese in Christian doctrine, visited the sick and collected alms for the poor. By the

fact that no news came regarding his mission, it has been suggested that he died from despair, a feeling of failure. More than likely he died from a high fever, and possibly tuberculosis. For additional details, see Georg Schurhammer, S.J., *Francis Xavier: His Life, His Times*, 620, 640–643.

56. That he died for his missionary cause is one of the first revealers of sainthood; a Christian burial is a sign of the respect accorded in death to a martyr. See Pierre Delooz, "Towards a Social Study of Canonized Sainthood in the Catholic Church" in *Saints and their Cults: Studies in Religious Sociology, Folklore and History*, ed. Stephen Wilson, 202–212 (Cambridge, UK: Cambridge University Press, 1983).

57. Hereafter, anything within quotation marks is my direct translation (from the Spanish or Portuguese into English) from the Jesuit biographer named. Otherwise, it is a paraphrasing or summary of their respective testimonies. I also rely on extant English translations of some of these narratives for my analysis.

58. Fernão Mendes Pinto, Chapter 215, *The Travels of Mendes Pinto*, 497–498.

59. Alessandro Valignano S.J., Chapter 30, "Vita S. Francisci," 194–197. By converting his servant, Xavier's displays his missionizing skills. Antonio de Santa Fé was present at his death. He was ordained a priest in 1560 and wrote down his own account of Xavier's death at the request of Manuel Teixeira, probably in 1556. These biographical details concerning Antonio de Santa Fé are provided by Moreno de Souza in his unpublished article, "When Did Francis Die?» The fact that there was a ship anchored in ports suggests Sancian's use as a base for trade operations.

60. Ibid. Valignano also writes that they had "much feeling concerning his death."

61. João de Lucena, *Historia Da Vida do Padre S. Francisco de Xavier*, 399–405. The presence of these settlers suggests a Portuguese community already established in Sancian, and includes, according to Jesuit biographer Francisco de Souza, one Francisco Gonçalves, a rich merchant from China, and a Portuguese settler by the name of Jorge Alvares. See Francisco de Souza S.J., *Oriente Conquistado* translated and quoted in John Castets S.J., "The Miracle of the Body of St. Francis Xavier," *Indian Catholic Truth Society* 13(1925): 3–9.

62. Alessandro Valignano S.J., "Vita S. Francisci," 194–197.

63. Ibid. It was thought that lime would act as an agent of decomposition, a common practice adopted to rid bones of their flesh. However, historian Maurice Collins provides an alternate theory for this lack of decomposition, suggesting that the particular lime used in this instance was of such a "quality or strength" that it instead acted as a preservative. See Sebastião Manrique, *The Land of the Great Image: Being the Experiences of Friar Manrique in Arakan*, ed. Maurice Collins (New Delhi: Asian Educational Services, 1995), 38.

64. Francisco de Souza quoted in John Castets, "The Miracle of the Body of St. Francis Xavier," 3–9. This limited audience is suggestive of the lack of respect accorded to Xavier by many of the Portuguese settlers in Sancian at this time.

65. Sebastiam Gonçalves S.J., *Primeira Parte da Historia Dos Religiosos da Companhia de Jesus*, 418–422. De Souza reports that one stone was placed at his feet, another at his head. See John Castets, "The Miracle of the Body," 4.

66. Ibid., 422–425. This act works to reaffirm Xavier's Spanish roots in light of his representation as "Portuguese" by his many Portuguese Jesuit biographers.

67. Manuel Teixeira S.J., "Vita S. Francisci," 898–900. Diogo Pereira was a wealthy Portuguese merchant. Not only had he befriended Xavier in life,

donating money to the Jesuit mission as a result, but also he would take Xavier's corpse to Malacca aboard his ship. Jesuits typically would travel on Portuguese ships between missionary posts, thus it was not unusual that Xavier had traveled to Sancian on Pereira's ship.

68. Ibid.
69. Ibid. Lime typically has a strong smell.
70. Fernão Mendes Pinto, *The Travels of Mendes Pinto*, 498, 499.
71. Alessandro Valignano S.J., "Vita S. Francisci," 194–197.
72. John Castets, "The Miracle of the Body," 3–9.
73. Sebastiam Gonçalves S.J., *Primeira Parte da Historia Dos Religiosos da Companhia de Jesus*, 418–422.
74. John Castets, "The Miracle of the Body of St. Francis Xavier," 3–9.
75. Ibid.
76. Ibid. Additional relics from Sancian were reported after his canonization, no doubt because of their increased value. Reportedly Xavier's earlobe was then divided amongst the same Portuguese settlers who received pieces of his cassock. The same author also reports that the pilot of the *Santa Cruz*, Francisco de Aguiar, had retained a bucket to perpetuate his memory of two things that Xavier had said to him, one that he would never be poor, the other (thing) that he would not die in the ocean. Later, his nephew tried unsuccessfully to get back this bucket from the Jesuits of Cochin, who in 1616 were using it as part of the canonization proceedings, to give to his grandmother. See Francisco Xavier da Costa, *S. Francisco Xavier em Goa* (Nova Goa: Tip. Bragança & Co, 1922), 27.
77. Characteristic of saint's relics is that they will be moved if not placed in the appropriate surroundings.
78. If his corpse had been decomposed upon arrival, it was meant as a sign that he was destined to stay there.
79. Fernão Mendes Pinto, *The Travels of Mendes Pinto*, 498–499.
80. Alessandro Valignano S.J., "Vita S. Francisci," 194–197.
81. João de Lucena, *Historia Da Vida do Padre S. Francisco de Xavier*, 399–405.
82. John Castets S.J., "The Miracle of the Body," 3–9.
83. See also Francisco Correia Afonso, *The Spirit of Xavier* (Bangalore: Good Shepherd Convent Press, 1922), 128–132. Xavier's troubles in Sancian also had to do with Malacca's governor Dom Alvaro de Athaide. It was from Malacca that Xavier left to enter China; it was this same Governor who had thwarted Xavier's efforts to set up a Jesuit mission in China. I will return to the figure of Athaide and his role during the arrival of Xavier's corpse in Malacca in the following section.
84. Fernão Mendes Pinto, *The Travels of Mendes Pinto*, 498–499.
85. John Castets, "The Miracle of the Body," 3–9. Since de Souza's account was written after Xavier's canonization, this point reinforces his more hagiographical perspective as compared to Xavier's earlier Jesuit biographers.
86. Sebastiam Gonçalves S.J., *Primeira Parte da Historia Dos Religiosos da Companhia de Jesus*, 418–422. Despite his conversion, he was still not considered Christian enough to define Xavier's burial as "Christian."
87. João de Lucena, *Historia Da Vida do Padre S. Francisco de Xavier*, 399–405.
88. Inés Županov, "The Prophetic and the Miraculous," 148. She writes: "the destiny of Portuguese navigators in Asia was more than closely related to the destiny of their ships . . . A ship was, for its proprietor, in particular, an extension of his body on which his whole existence depended. It is no wonder that the *Santa Cruz*, which belonged to Xavier's devoted follower

Diogo Pereira and carried the former to his ultimate terrestrial harbor on the island of Sancian, saw him die there and then returned his holy relics back to Melaka, earned special celestial merits and a privileged place in the narratives of Xavier's *vitae*."

89. Francisco de Souza S.J., *Oriente Conquistado*, 680–684. While some Jesuits, such as Teixeira and Lucena, assert that he was already destined for Goa at this time, others such as Valignano and de Souza argue that at this time his corpse was only destined for Malacca.

90. Inés Županov, "The Prophetic and the Miraculous," 152. She suggests that Xavier's holy intervention was focused on the "male sphere" and one of the most important was the sea. Moreover, "calming the storm was one of the saint's specialities."

91. Sancian's links to Xavier would not be completely forgotten despite the unsuitability of saint and state at this juncture. In subsequent years, passing ships would fire artillery in view of the island to honor Xavier. See J.M.S. Daurignac, *Historia de Sam Francisco de Xavier, Da Companhia de Jesus, Apostolo das Índias e do Japão, Protector do Oriente*, 3rd ed. (Goa: No Publisher Listed, 1880), 210–211.

92. Paulo Jorge Sousa Pinto, "Purse and Sword: D. Henrique Bendahara and Portuguese Melaka in the Late 16th Century," in *Sinners and Saints: The Successors of Vasco da Gama*, ed. Sanjay Subrahmanyam, 75 (Oxford, UK: Oxford University Press, 1995). His description and characterization of Malacca as a place where a "purse and sword" come together evidences its very different history and development as comparison to Sancian under the Portuguese. Specifically, prior to its becoming a burgeoning colonial outpost after its conquest by Albuquerque and the Portuguese in 1511, it was a thriving Indonesian Hindu nodal point with links to Siam and China, and a thriving centre for piracy. Thus, by the fact that it was a center of political, economic, military, and religious power sets it up as a more suitable site for the location of Xavier's corpse. However, by the fact that it was subject to numerous attacks by the Sultan of Aceh, starting after 1537, also weakened Malacca which was coupled with a decrease in trade, the Portuguese Crown's withdrawal of its investments, and a general worsening of conditions at the time of Xavier's reception. Here I thank Shanti Moorthy for helping me to characterize Malacca more accurately for this time frame.

93. All of Xavier's Jesuit biographers record this as the date of his arrival, except for Fernão Mendes Mendes Pinto who incorrectly reports his date of arrival as March 17, 1553.

94. Manuel Teixeira S.J., "Vita S. Francisci," 898, 900. He recorded his eyewitness account very soon thereafter from Cochin in 1554.

95. Fernão Mendes Pinto, *The Travels of Mendes Pinto*, 498, 499.

96. Ibid.

97. Manuel Teixeira S.J., "Vita S. Francisci," 899–900. In this section, I largely rely on Teixeira's account, since it is by far the richest, given that he was an eyewitness to the event. It is interesting that in Sancian, Diego Pereira is viewed as a merchant whereas in Malacca he is described as an "ambassador," perhaps an ambassador bearing Xavier's corpse.

98. Alessandro Valignano S.J., "Vita S. Francisci," Chapter 30, 194–197.

99. João de Lucena, *Historia Da Vida do Padre S. Francisco de Xavier*, 399–405.

100. Manuel Teixeira S.J., "Vita S. Francisci," 899–900.

101. Ibid.

102. Ibid.

103. Ibid. cf. João de Lucena, *Historia Da Vida do Padre S. Francisco de Xavier,* 399–405.
104. Patrick Geary, "Sacred Commodities," 179. During moments of weak state control, relics were prized for their ability to substitute for public authority in order to safeguard a particular community.
105. Ibid. Teixeira indexes Xavier's canonization process, stating that this story was "later affirmed on oath." In addition, Gonçalves writes "the air that was of the last plague, which still wandered corrupt, it improved in a way, that from there in front it was heard there was a notable movement and improvement." See his *Primeira Parte da Historia Dos Religiosos da Companhia de Jesus,* 418–422. Perhaps he is more cautious, given that he is writing prior to his canonization as compared to Francisco de Souza who writes, "the plague, which till then had daily claimed numerous victims, ceased completely all of a sudden, of those that were then already attacked, no one died." See his *Oriente Conquistado,* 680–684. Reportedly, in addition to the plague he averted an imminent famine in Malacca, a sign of the increasingly hagiographical accounts of Xavier's reception in Malacca in the aftermath of his canonization. See Francisco Correia Afonso, *The Spirit of Xavier,* 128–132.
106. Manuel Teixeira S.J., "Vita S. Francisci," 899–900. Georg Schurhammer provides a brief history of this chapel that was dedicated to Our Lady of Annunciation. It was also referred to as the church of the Jesuits and it served as both a site of religious activity and a landmark for navigators. It was more than likely built around 1515, on top of a Muslim king's palace, as requested by Albuquerque in 1513 and was given to the Jesuits between 1548 and 1549. See Georg Schurhammer, "The Church of St. Paul, Malacca," in *Xaveriana* (Lisboa: Centro de Estudos Historicos Ultramarinos, 1964) 532–535. It was a commonplace practice for European empires to build Christian churches on old sites of royal power in an attempt to counter the site's preexisting (Islamic in this case) sanctity.
107. Fernão Mendes Pinto, *The Travels of Mendes Pinto,* 498–499.
108. Ibid.
109. Sebastiam Gonçalves S.J., *Primeira Parte da Historia Dos Religiosos da Companhia de Jesus,* 418–422. In pointing out that the body was delivered into the hands of a Portuguese, Gonçalves compares this to Sancian, where he was carried by his Chinese interpreter and two mulattos, without any Portuguese presence at his burial.
110. Alessandro Valignano S.J., "Vita S. Francisci," 194–197. This burial practice compares to the Chinese custom of putting Xavier in a fitted box as was done in Sancian. This indexes the "saintly fashioning" of Xavier from Spanish missionary to Portuguese saint that Županov points to. See her "The Prophetic and the Miraculous," 142.
111. Francisco de Souza S.J., *Oriente Conquistado,* 680–684.
112. Sebastiam Gonçalves S.J., *Primeira Parte da Historia Dos Religiosos da Companhia de Jesus,* 418–422.
113. Francisco de Souza S.J., *Oriente Conquistado,* 680–684.
114. According the majority of his Jesuit biographers, Xavier's corpse remained in the ground from March 23 to August 15. Pinto is the only one who suggests that he was in the ground for nine months, until December 1553.
115. Manuel Teixeira S.J., "Vita S. Francisci," 900–909. Juan de Beira was accompanied by Jesuits Pedro de Alcaçeva and Melchior Nunes, the latter arriving independently in Malacca in April of that year. They were waiting until August to leave for the Moluccas because of navigation problems and

the imminent monsoons. Nunes requested to see Xavier's corpse as he had heard of how it had arrived in an "incorrupt" state.

116. João de Lucena, *Historia Da Vida do Padre S. Francisco de Xavier*, 399–405.

117. Francisco de Souza S.J., *Oriente Conquistado*, 680–684.

118. Alessandro Valignano S.J., "Vita S. Francisci," Chapter 30, 194–197.

119. Gonçalves S.J., *Primeira Parte da Historia Dos Religiosos da Companhia de Jesus*, 422–425.

120. Ibid. Nunes had earlier accompanied Beira to Xavier's gravesite in Malacca.

121. Francisco de Souza S.J., *Oriente Conquistado*, 680–684. Despite this ill treatment, Xavier's body spurted blood, which in effect makes him ever more incorrupt *in spite of* his surroundings. Gonçalves reports that it was the shaking of the earth—a sign of the will of the saint due to his ill treatment—that caused the falling of a pillar that crushed Xavier's nose. See his *Primeira Parte da Historia Dos Religiosos da Companhia de Jesus*, 422–425.

122. Alessandro Valignano S.J., "Vita S. Francisci,"194–197.

123. Paulo Jorge Sousa Pinto, "Purse and Sword," 76–77. During the early sixteenth century, the Portuguese were only interested in the city of Malacca and is structure of trade, conquering it in 1511. At first they exercised no religious pressure over Muslims or Hindus, nor did they show an interest in acquiring any land beyond the city. The second half of sixteenth century brought changes due to the fact that Islam was rapidly spreading along the Indian Ocean rim and due to the Counter Reformation in Europe which increased the Portuguese propensity for religious intolerance. As a result, in the second half of the sixteenth century, Portuguese shipping in the Indian Ocean became less safe; the straits of Malacca were particularly risky and vulnerable.

124. See Alessandro Valignano S.J., "Vita S. Francisci," 194–197. Also see João de Lucena, *Historia Da Vida do Padre S. Francisco de Xavier*, 399–405. It is more than likely that Jesuit biographer Manuel Teixeira was present but he is inexplicably not accounted for in these Jesuit biographies.

125. Sebastiam Gonçalves S.J., *Primeira Parte da Historia Dos Religiosos da Companhia de Jesus*, 418–422. It had been at the urging of Xavier himself that these Jesuits had left Malacca.

126. Ibid. He reports that Dom Alvaro asked God to "miss the intercession of them," them being those involved in his procession. Our Jesuit biographer also alludes to tensions between Athaide and Goa's acting Viceroy at the time, Dom Affonso de Noronha, a man who knew Xavier in life and who played a significant role during Xavier's Goa celebrations. Georg Schurhammer provides additional information on Dom Alvaro Athaide. The lack of support for the Jesuits in Malacca on the part of Athaide was evidenced by a witness, Galeote Pereira, of Cochin. Moreover, Athaide may have been afflicted with leprosy at the time of his governorship (which explains why he remained at a window during the procession of Xavier's corpse) and was later removed from office and died in a prison in Lisbon. In November 1552, Xavier had given strict orders to the Superior of the Jesuit residence in Malacca to leave the city because of Athaide's attitude. See Georg Schurhammer, S.J., *Francis Xavier: His Life, His Times*, Volume IV, Chapter 7, 645. These details supplement Gonçalves's account, and support claims that there was no sizeable Jesuit contingency in Malacca during Xavier's interment.

127. That the ritualization of Xavier's corpse in Malacca became a site for these palpable tensions between the acting governor and the Jesuits points to the value of relics for expressing and conducting societal disputes in a manner reminiscent of European translations. See Patrick Geary, "Sacred Commodities," 188.

128. Inés Županov, "The Prophetic and the Miraculous," 140. She confirms this point, relying on the account of Sebastiam Gonçalves to make her case. "It was not an accident that Melaka, a prosperous port town on the Malay peninsula, were sites of Xavier's many clairvoyant feats . . . not only was it an extremely 'unwholesome countrie' (sic) and filled with 'evil ayre' (sic) the city of Melaka 'was in need of a good example and the (Christian) doctrine.'" Paulo Jorge Sousa Pinto also points to the central role that trade played for Malacca as a commercial center that linked a widespread network of Portuguese fortresses and factories dispersed throughout the Indian Ocean. See his, "Purse and Sword," 80.

129. Francisco de Souza S.J., *Oriente Conquistado*, 680–684. See Manuel Teixeira S.J., "Vita S. Francisci," 900–909. This author also confirms a lack of appreciation and suggests that it was the will of the saint (Xavier here) manifesting himself through his incorruption to show that he should be moved.

130. Francisco de Souza S.J., *Oriente Conquistado*, 680–684. He suggests that this was Beira's purpose in moving him.

131. Manuel Teixeira S.J., "Vita S. Francisci," 900–909. St. Paul's was the premier Jesuit college in Asia and the epicenter of Jesuit activity in the Indian Ocean world. It had been built in 1541 on top of the ruins of an old mosque. Xavier himself had often resided at the college when in Goa on Jesuit business.

132. Alessandro Valignano S.J., "Vita S. Francisci," 194–197.

133. Francisco de Souza S.J., *Oriente Conquistado*, 680–684. He also adds that Xavier's corpse was temporarily guarded after being placed inside a coffin in a room of a house located near the shore until the coming monsoons when they were able to leave for Goa. Here it is important to recognize the defining role of the monsoons for regulating activities and creating patterns of movement in the Indian Ocean world.

134. Patrick Geary, "Sacred Commodities," 186. Moreover, the saints were too powerful to allow themselves to be taken unwillingly. A saint unable to prevent his own removal would hardly have been a desirable acquisition.

135. Francisco de Souza S.J., *Oriente Conquistado*, 680–684.

136. Sebastiam Gonçalves S.J., *Primeira Parte da Historia Dos Religiosos da Companhia de Jesus*, 422–425.

137. Francisco de Souza S.J., *Oriente Conquistado*, 680–684.

138. Fernão Mendes Pinto, *The Travels of Mendes Pinto*, 498–499.

139. Manuel Teixeira S.J., "Vita S. Francisci," 900–909.

140. João de Lucena, *Historia Da Vida do Padre S. Francisco de Xavier*, 399–405. Manuel Tavora would play a large role in the Goa celebrations surrounding the arrival of Xavier's corpse in 1554. Mendes Pinto informs us that Tavora would later be at the College of Évora in Portugal. See his, *The Travels of Mendes Pinto*, 498–499. I point to Tavora's travels (Goa, Malacca, Portugal) as reflexive of the larger circuits that the Jesuits frequently traveled, operating under the umbrella—and sometimes even as functionaries—of the Portuguese state.

141. Alessandro Valignano S.J., "Vita S. Francisci," 194–197.

142. Manuel Teixeira S.J., "Vita S. Francisci," 900–909. Again, "calming the storm was one of the saint's specialities," according to Županov. See her, "The Prophetic and the Miraculous," 152.

143. Alessandro Valignano S.J., "Vita S. Francisci," 194–197.

144. Sebastiam Gonçalves S.J., *Primeira Parte da Historia Dos Religiosos da Companhia de Jesus*, 422–425.

145. Perhaps the residents of Malacca were not so happy by this latest development. Inés Županov suggests that by a series of Jesuit manipulations and by

"theft" the Body [of Xavier] arrived in Goa, to the dismay and anger of the inhabitants of Melaka. See her "Currents and Counter-Currents," 6.

146. Patrick Geary, *Furta Sacra*, 9–10.
147. Markus Vink, "Indian Ocean Studies," 56.
148. Michael Pearson, "The Port City of Goa: Policy and Practice in the 16th C," in his *Coastal Western India*, XCHR Studies, Series No. 2 (New Delhi: Concept Publishing Company, 1981), 74. According to Pearson, it was largely because of its location and the fact that it was easily defensible that Goa became the central focus of the Portuguese empire in Asia. Also, Goa had replaced Cochin as capital of the *Estado da Índia* in 1530.
149. Various rumors circulated in the aftermath of Xavier's death. One of them helped to make a stronger case for his remains to stay in Goa, namely that Xavier himself had stated his desire for his corpse to return to Goa in death. "I shall not return to Goa, my body yes, it will remain here"; these words are attributed to Xavier himself. See Alexandre M. Barbosa, "Off to a Ritualistic Start," 12.
150. Inés Županov, "The Prophetic and the Miraculous," 144. A strong case is to be made that "the supernatural is an absolute necessary when social objectivity is not firmly lodged in impersonal and enduringly rooted political institutions. The supernatural is a product of this situation, as it is obvious in the case of Xavier's mission among the Portuguese."

BIBLIOGRAPHY

Afonso, Francisco Correia. *The Spirit of Xavier*. Bangalore: Good Shepherd Convent Press, 1922.

Alden, Dauril. *The Making of an Enterprise, The Society of Jesus in Portugal, its Empire and Beyond 1540–1750*. Stanford, CA: Stanford University Press.

Anderson, Benedict. *Imagined Communities*. New York: Verso, 1983.

Appadurai, Arjun. "Introduction." In *The Social Life of Things*, edited by Arjun Appadurai, 3–63. Cambridge, UK: Cambridge University Press, 1986.

Barbosa, Alexandre. "Off to a Ritualistic Start" *Goa Today*, Volume XXIX, 5 (December 1994): 12–13.

Castets, John. S.J., "The Miracle of the Body of St. Francis Xavier." *Indian Catholic Truth Society* 13(1925): 3–12.

Clarke, David. "Invoking the Body's Presence." *The American Journal of Semiotics* 9(1; 1992): 49–82.

Da Costa, Francisco Xavier. *S. Francisco Xavier em Goa*. Nova Goa: Tip. Braganca & Co, 1922.

Daurignac, J.M.S. *Historia de Sam Francisco de Xavier, Da Companhia de Jesus, Apostolo das Índias e do Japão, Protector do Oriente*, 3rd ed. Goa: No Publisher Listed, 1880.

Delooz, Pierre. "Towards a Social Study of Canonized Sainthood in the Catholic Church." In *Saints and Their Cults: Studies in Religious Sociology, Folklore and History*, edited by Stephen Wilson, 202–212. Cambridge, UK: Cambridge University Press, 1983.

De Lucena, João. *Historia Da Vida do Padre S. Francisco de Xavier, e do que Fizeram na Índia Os Mais Religiosos da Companhia de Jesu*. Lisboa: Noa Oficina de Antonio Gomes, 1600.

De Melo, Carlos Merces. *The Recruitment and Formation of the Native Clergy in India, 16th–19th Century, An Historico-Canonical Study*. Lisboa: Agencia Geral do Ultramar, 1955.

De Souza, Francisco. S.J., *Oriente Conquistado a Jesu Christo pelos Padres da Companhia de Jesus, da Provincia de Goa*. Lisboa: Valentim Da Costa Deslandes, 1710.

De Souza, T.R. "The Portuguese in Asia and their Church Patronage." In *Western Colonialism in Asia and Christianity*, edited by M.D. David, 11–19. Bombay: Himalaya Publishing House, 1988.

Eisenstein, Elizabeth. *The Printing Press as an Advent of Change: Communication and Transformations in Early Modern Europe*. Cambridge, UK: Cambridge University Press, 1979.

Geary, Patrick. *Furta Sacra: Thefts of Relics in the Central Middle Ages*. Princeton, NJ: Princeton University Press, 1978.

———. "Sacred Commodities: The Circulation of Medieval Relics." In *The Social Life of Things*, edited by Arjun Appadurai, 169–191. Cambridge, UK: Cambridge University Press, 1986.

Ghosh, Devleena, and Stephen Muecke. "Indian Ocean Stories." In *The Indian Ocean, The UTS Review* VI, 2 (2000): 24–43.

Ghosh, Devleena, and Stephen Muecke, eds. "Editors' Introduction." In *The Indian Ocean, The UTS Review* VI, 2 (2000): 1–5.

Gonçalves, Sebastiam. S.J., *Primeira Parte da Historia Dos Religiosos da Companhia de Jesus e do que fizeram com a divina graça na conversão dos infieis a nossa sancta fee Catholica nos reynos e provincias da Índia Oriental*, (1616). Volume I, edited by Joseph Wicki S.J. Coimbra: Atlantida, 1957.

Gupta, Pamila. "The Relic State: St. Francis Xavier and the Politics of Ritual in Portuguese India." Unpublished PhD Dissertation, Columbia University, Department of Anthropology, 2004.

Kopytoff, Igor. "The Cultural Biography of Things: Commoditization as Process." In *The Social Life of Things*, edited by Arjun Appadurai, 64–91. Cambridge, UK: Cambridge University Press, 1986.

Lewis, Martin and Kären Wigen "A Maritime Response to the Crisis in Area Studies." *The Geographical Review* 89(2; April 1999): 161–168.

Manrique, Sebastião. *The Land of the Great Image: Being the Experiences of Friar Manrique in Arakan*, edited by Maurice Collins. New Delhi: Asian Educational Services, 1995.

Mendes Pinto, Fernão. *The Travels of Mendes Pinto*, edited and translated by Rebecca Catz. Chicago, IL: University of Chicago Press, 1989[1569–1578].

Metcalf, Thomas. *Imperial Connections: India in the Indian Ocean Area, 1860–1920*. Berkeley, CA: University of California Press, 2007.

Pearson, Michael. "The Port City of Goa: Policy and Practice in the 16th C." In *Coastal Western India*, XCHR Studies, Series No. 2. New Delhi: Concept Publishing Company, 1981, Chapter 4.

Penrose, Boies. *Goa-Rainha do Oriente, Goa-Queen of the East*. Lisboa: Commissão Ultramarina, 1960.

Pinto, Paulo Jorge Sousa. "Purse and Sword: D. Henrique Bendahara and Portuguese Melaka in the Late 16th Century." In *Sinners and Saints: The Successors of Vasco da Gama*, edited by Sanjay Subrahmanyam, 75–93. Oxford, UK: Oxford University Press, 1995.

Rafael, Vicente L. *Contracting Colonialism: Translation and Christian Conversion in Tagalog Society Under Early Spanish Rule*. Durham, NC: Duke University Press, 1993.

Rayanna, P. *St. Francis Xavier and His Shrine*. Panjim, Goa: Imprimatur, 1982.

Schurhammer, Georg. "Historical Research into the Life of Francis Xavier in the 16th C." *Revista de Historia*, Julho-Dez, No. 47–48. Lisboa: Empresa Litteraria Fluminense, (1923): 195–196.

————. *Francis Xavier: His Life, His Times.* Translated by M. Joseph Costello. Rome: The Jesuit Historical Institute, 1977.

————. "The Church of St. Paul, Malacca." In *Xaveriana,* 532–535. Lisboa: Centro de Estudos Historicos Ultramarinos, 1964.

Stoller, Paul. *The Taste of Ethnographic Things, The Senses in Anthropology.* Philadelphia, PA: University of Pennsylvania Press, 1986.

Subrahmanyam, Sanjay. "Introduction: The Portuguese and Early Modern Asia," in *Sinners and Saints: The Successors of Vasco da Gama,* edited by Sanjay Subrahmanyam, 5–12. Oxford, UK: Oxford University Press, 1995.

Teixeira, Manuel. S.J., "Vita S. Francisci," reproduced in *Monumenta Xaveriana,* Tomus Secundus. Matriti: Typis Gabrielis Lopez del Horno, 1912[1581].

Valignano, Alessandro. *Historia del Principio y Progresso de la Companhia de Jesus en las Índias Orientales (1542–1564)* [original lost, reproduced as Alessandro Valignano S.J., "Vita S. Francisci" in *Monumenta Xaveriana.* Tomus Primus. Matriti: Typis Augustini Avrial, 1899–1900[1588].

Vink, Markus. "Indian Ocean Studies and the New Thalassology." *Journal of Global History* 2(2007): 41–62.

Vertovec, Stephen. "Conceiving and Researching Transnationalism." *Ethnic and Racial Studies* 22(2; 1999): 447–462.

Wigen, Kären. "Introduction: Oceans of History" forum, *American Historical Review* 111(3; August 2006): 719.

Williams, Lea E. "Inauspicious Ambience: The Historical Setting of Early Luso-Chinese Contacts." In *Indo-Portuguese History: Old Issues, New Questions,* edited by Teotonio de Souza, 32–43. New Delhi: Concept Publishing Company, 1985.

Županov, Inés. "The Prophetic and the Miraculous in Portuguese Asia: A Hagiographical View of Colonial Culture." In *Sinners and Saints: The Successors of Vasco da Gama,* edited by Sanjay Subrahmanyam, 135–161. Oxford, UK: Oxford University Press, 1995.

————. "Currents and Counter-Currents: Jesuit Geopolitics in Asia (16th Century)." This (unpublished) paper was presented at the *Table Rond* conference, held in Rome, October 2002.

9 Kuo Pao Kun's *Descendants of the Eunuch Admiral* and the Myth of Modern Singapore[1]

Susan Philip

This chapter will study Kuo Pao Kun's play *Descendants of the Eunuch Admiral* as a reexamination of Singapore's position within the Indian Ocean world; the play critically examines what Singapore has become, and proffers an alternative, almost utopian vision to offset the dystopia of a "dour and puritanical modernity"[2] which is evinced in the form of a monocular focus on material comfort. By juxtaposing the historical figure of Admiral Zheng He with a group of modern day Singaporean yuppies, it looks at Singapore's position in the past on the great Oceanic trade route, and how that position has been translated into the present. The play takes a critical stance towards what has become of Singapore as it seeks to consolidate its prime position in the global world of trade and finance; Singapore is presented as soulless and focused almost entirely on material gain. The play then tries to present another, more spiritual and joyful view of what Singapore might have been. Interestingly, however, that vision is still grounded in an ingrained perception of Singapore as a trading centre. That identity, it would appear, has become too deeply entrenched to be easily shaken off. My reading of the play in conjunction with historical references to Zheng He and the Indian Ocean world reveals a complex and nuanced vision of contemporary Singapore as a nation wholly predicated on its relationship to the sea and its associated trade routes. While today the sea routes have to some extent been replaced by air travel and new communication technologies, Singapore remains steadfastly "outward" in its outlook. For this reason Zheng He, an early master of the Indian Ocean trade routes, has been of central significance in Singapore's imagining of itself and the global position it occupies.

The specific importance of Zheng He to Singapore is highlighted by the fact that the International Zheng He Association is based in Singapore. Geoff Wade has noted that "many of the legends still current today in Southeast Asia are centred" around Zheng He,[3] while William Peterson has argued that Zheng He is "a historically significant figure whose stature in the region's history is roughly equivalent to that of Sir Stamford Raffles."[4] This comparison between Raffles and Zheng He is telling—like the Eunuch Admiral,

Raffles is part of Singapore's originary myth, one of the founders of modern Singapore. Singaporean playwright Robert Yeo's play *The Eye of History* begins with three workers reading the words on a plaque placed on the plinth of a statue of Stamford Raffles: "On this historic site Sir Thomas Stamford Raffles first landed in Singapore on 28th January 1819 and with genius and perception changed the destiny of Singapore from an obscure fishing village to a great seaport and modern metropolis"[5]—that is, from an isolated and unimportant habitation, it became a globally linked centre of trade.

Thus, two of the men most centrally implicated in the construction of contemporary Singapore's identity are intimately linked with the Indian Ocean, with trade, and with control. Zheng He's voyages were undertaken at the behest of Ming Emperor Chu Di, who desired "to control maritime trade to the south and exploit the economic advantage of such control."[6] Raffles saw in Singapore an ideal port from which the East India Company could conduct its affairs of trade. It is quite specifically these commercial ties with the past which are highlighted in current constructions of Singapore's history. Its Malay past and ancient connections with Prince Parameswara are marginalized, surviving only in another symbol of Singapore—the Merlion, a "lion head with a fish body resting on a crest of waves," designed in 1964 as an emblem for the Singapore Tourism Board:

> Designed by Mr. Fraser Brunner, a curator of the Van Kleef Aquarium, the lion head represents the lion spotted by Prince Sang Nila Utama when he re-discovered Singapura in 11 AD, as recorded in the 'Malay Annals'. The fish tail of the Merlion symbolizes the ancient city of Temasek (meaning 'sea' in Javanese) by which Singapore was known before the Prince named it 'Singapura' (meaning 'lion' (singa) 'city' (pura) in Sanskrit), and represents Singapore's humble beginnings as a fishing village.[7]

It is pertinent that even this land-dwelling animal has been retroactively mythologized into a sea creature which only peripherally refers to the ancient past,[8] focusing instead on the relationship with the sea, and hence tangentially referencing the importance of Singapore's maritime position.

What both Zheng He and Raffles (or the East India Company) took advantage of was Singapore's strategic position along a particular Indian Ocean trade route, and the safe, convenient harbour it was able to provide. Singapore was, then, an important node along a high-density, high-impact trade route. Geographically, Singapore is bounded by the Strait of Malacca, which separates Malaysia from Sumatra, the Strait of Johor (between Malaysia's southernmost tip and Singapore) and the Singapore Strait (between Singapore's southern coast and Sumatra). Since the Strait of Malacca was the most direct route from the Indian Ocean to the Pacific Ocean, as well as providing a convenient travel route between India, Indonesia and Malaysia, and China, it occupied a hugely important position in the world of trade in Zheng He's time. The Strait of Malacca functioned as a choke point, a narrow passage through which shipping must pass, en route to another place.

Singapore today is still rooted in its position along this strategic choke point. With no natural or land resources, it has had to position itself as a centre for trade and finance, rather than, for example, agriculture. Kingsbury notes that "Singapore aspires to be a regional or even global center" in areas such as private banking and finance.[9] So successfully has this global image been marketed that foreigners are attracted to buy properties there because Singapore is (according to two foreign property buyers) "an international city," and is reminiscent "of living in Malibu."[10] There seems to be no sense that they are attracted by some essence of the Singaporean identity, whatever that may be. Small and fragile, a tiny, Chinese-dominated nation-state surrounded by much larger Malay-Muslim neighbours, Singapore has built up a kind of power base by allying itself to a global trade and finance network. But these international alliances suggest a vital point, one brought up by Cheong Koon Hean, the CEO of the Urban Redevelopment Agency of Singapore: " . . . ultimately, we need to seek out answers that best suit Singapore. To find our own soul."[11]

Descendants takes a penetrating look at this question of the Singapore soul and suggests that, in the postindependence search for economic stability (which has in modern Singapore been translated into a concerted effort to build up global networks) the Singapore soul has somehow disappeared, or perhaps been trampled in the rush to make a comfortable living.

In order to achieve its current high level of economic stability, the state has exerted considerable control over its people. The state maintains its tight control over the population at least in part by reminding them that without this control, the country might sink back into the chaos from which it arose. David Birch has suggested that the state in Singapore maintains a "discourse of crisis,"[12] in which the nation is constantly threatened by a series of crises which can only be staved off by the level of control implied in their various policies—thus justifying their often draconian approach to control of the people. Birch states that:

> the future itself is constructed as only able to happen in the terms set out by the government. These are the "necessary illusions" for social management constructed by the Singapore government in order to maintain its rhetoric of containment and control.[13]

The implication is that without the controlling measures which have been put in place, Singapore's population will cease to experience the secure and comfortable lifestyle they currently enjoy.

Singapore can thus be seen as functioning as a metaphorical choke point as it exerts control over the people, in terms of both politics and culture. A choke point[14] is a strategic location which, because of its narrowness, can be fairly easily blockaded by an armed force of some kind. One could think, for example, of the Spartan army controlling Thermopylae against the vast Persian army. It is a point at which obstruction can be strategically deployed to maintain control, as commonly occurs in Singapore. Peterson states that "Singapore's phenomenal economic success is attributed by many to its adherence to a form of state capitalism where civil liberties are curtailed for the sake of economic development."[15] Equally important has been the issue of cultural control—focused on economic stability, Singapore has come to be known as a "cultural desert,"[16] whose most prominent value is "moneytheism."[17] Wee suggests that Singapore has advanced by "forsaking not only many of the political dimensions of democratic life but also its cultural dimensions."[18] Culture has been marginalized, except in the essentialized and rigid definitions of cultural identity which tie every individual down in narrowly defined terms of race, language, and religion.

Kuo Pao Kun explores this idea of extreme control in his play, linking it with the idea of wealth and comfort, and the very high standard of living for which Singapore is known (a standard that was made possible by Singapore's strategic use of its favoured position near the Strait of Malacca). He suggests, in this play, that Singaporeans have in fact been constrained to give up their personal freedom in exchange for this high standard of living; to some extent, this freedom was willingly given up precisely because the state was able to provide such ease of living. Both the state and the people are thus implicated in the ceding of freedom for easy living.

To counter this relinquishing of civil liberties into state hands, Kuo reaches after some expression of "soul," freedom and autonomy by forging links with the past. The question, as posed by Wee and Lee in their introduction to the anthology containing the text of *Descendants*, is: "can we stitch our cultural memories together with other cultures to arrive at that which can transcend the sum total of Singapore's cultural fragments? It is a large humanistic articulation,"[19] as opposed to a mere materialist articulation.

In his search for this "humanistic articulation," Kuo examines the state's strategic positioning of itself at the metaphorical choke point where it can exert control. Thus Singapore, the maritime choke point allowing for a free and lucrative flow of trade and capital, also becomes the node at which a choke hold is put on certain individual freedoms. Kuo counters this identity with a view, stitched together from cultural memories, of a trading nation reveling in wealth, splendour, generosity, and cultural exchange. Thus, Singapore in this play is envisioned as a choke point in two contrasting ways, which are in tension with each other. Through the reminiscences of Zheng He, juxtaposed with the needs and yearnings of the yuppies, Kuo takes a critical stance towards the materialistic focus and soullessness of contemporary Singapore, while displaying longing for a less rampantly consumerist orientation—what Wee and Lee refer to as "a sort of prelapsarian capitalism, one that has not experienced the Fall."[20] Kuo's nostalgia also centres on trade and materialism, but deliberately eschews the underlying pragmatism and will to control which stifle individual freedoms. He yearns, instead, for the humanism of free and open exchange.

Both these views of Singapore are rooted in the country's position along the Indian Ocean trade routes, and both are equally rooted in the myth-making that has centred around the figure of the eunuch admiral who led an enormous fleet across the oceans. Wade refers to some of the more popular views of Zheng He and his voyages:

> These were thus friendly diplomatic activities. During the overall course of the seven voyages to the Western Ocean, Zheng He did not occupy a single piece of land, establish any fortress or seize any wealth from other countries. In the commercial and trade activities, he adopted the practice of giving more than he received, and thus he was welcomed and lauded by the people of the various countries along his routes.[21]

Another Chinese scholar claims that "Zheng He was a great maritime voyager of the Ming dynasty, and an outstanding envoy of peace and friendship."[22] Wade states that these views are common in Chinese scholarship.

If this is the originary myth, it implies a benevolent outlook, openness and freedom. Trade was the route towards peaceful exchange, which also, importantly, brought in wealth. To go back to Robert Yeo's play *The Eye of History*, William Peterson reads this play as an affirmation of the idea of Singapore as being centred on the merchant-trade culture. The play states that "Raffles had intended Singapore to be a commercial enterprise,"[23] an intention later brought to full fruition by Lee Kuan Yew, and discussed by Lee and Raffles during the course of the play. Peterson suggests that: "By demonstrating that Lee has fulfilled a sacred, national dream, Yeo upholds one of the great myths that provide a foundation of the nation of Singapore."[24] The myth suggests that it was Singapore's destiny to become a "global" nation founded on commerce and exchange, and the myth of Zheng He's voyages as being primarily about friendship and diplomacy bolsters these ideas. Françoise Vergès also notes these pacific ideas when she states that: "The Indian Ocean world brings forth images that evoke encounters not placed under the signs of trauma and violence." She sees the voyages of Zheng He as being the antithesis of the (ultimately violent and decimating) arrival of Columbus in the West Indies, and highlights the cosmopolitan nature of the Indian Ocean port cities, where the people forged "a lingua franca, a creolized language and culture." While she admits that "there were wars, conflicts, slave trade," these are subsumed under "practices and idioms of cultural translation that maintained and developed a world of trade and exchange."[25]

However, the benevolent view of the voyages can be countered by looking at the colonizing or dominating tendencies of Emperor Chu Di's fleet. Wade states that a close study of voyages made during the Ming dynasty will indicate clearly "the desire of the Ming to control maritime trade to the south and exploit the economic advantage of such control"[26]:

> These missions were [. . .] intended to create legitimacy for the usurping emperor, display the might of the Ming, bring the known polities to demonstrated submission to the Ming and thereby achieve a *pax Ming* throughout the known world and collect treasures for the Court.[27]

This *pax Ming*, far from being pacific, sometimes involved acts that bordered on the declaration of open warfare. For example, Wade notes that in 1411, there was a military invasion of Sri Lanka during which:

> Zheng He invaded the royal city, captured the king, destroyed his military and carried the king and his family members back to the court. [. . .] As happened in similar scenarios in Yun-nan, the Ming appointed a puppet ruler to replace the king, presumably to act in ways beneficial to the Ming.[28]

Achieving peace, in this context, was synonymous with exerting control, to the ultimate benefit of the Ming empire. The centrality of control (rather than the much-vaunted "diplomacy") is a particularly apposite point in the case of Singapore, although the need to exert power over others is more or less contained within its borders.

Vergès points to "the ocean as a cultural space" in which one can "observe layers on layers of maps of power and resistance, which have created and still create identities, narratives, and territories."[29] In Singapore, the ocean has been taken up as a means of mapping an identity—for example, an identity as a state: Singapore is a trading nation, anchored not in the ground, but in the water, empowered in Zheng He's time by ocean currents and flows of trade, and in the modern world by increasingly transnational flows of capital. Having virtually no land—it is, after all, a state that is effectively just one large city—Singapore is centred on global relationships which are divorced from the land.[30] As Vergès notes, "power is now less rooted in possession of land than in control of international and market flows."[31] Philippe Beaujard also notes trade has the power "to unify, create, and transform cultures."[32] Indeed, a similar vision seems to have motivated Chu Di to launch his treasure fleet. In the face of opposition from his conservative Confucian advisors, he:

> threw China's doors open to foreigners and foreign merchants, saying, "Now all within the four seas are as one family." The emperor decreed, "Let there be mutual trade at the frontier barriers in order to supply the country's needs and to encourage distant people to come."[33]

It is this point which Kuo Pao Kun centralizes when he proffers his "alternative" vision of what Singapore, as trading centre, could have become or could still become. He sees trade as an avenue leading towards "an expansive Asian globalism [. . .] which [exceeds] the confines of alienated life in the modern nation, with the potential for cultural exchange still alive."[34] These two visions of Singapore, the authoritative and the individual, remain in tension throughout this play; Kuo challenges the choke hold of the state over individual liberty, with a joyful, liberating vision of Singapore as part of the maritime choke point which revels in openness and cultural exchange.

DESCENDANTS OF THE EUNUCH ADMIRAL

Kuo's *Descendants of the Eunuch Admiral* is an abstract, lyrical piece based loosely on the voyages of Admiral Zheng He. It centres, however, on contemporary Singapore, drawing fragile connections between Zheng He and a group of modern Singaporean yuppies, between ancient Singapore and Singapore today. It was first performed in English by Singaporean group TheatreWorks, with Ong Keng Sen directing, at the Victoria Theatre, Singapore, in June 1995. It was then performed in Mandarin, at the same theatre, by The Theatre Practice in August 1995. The play won the Critic's Choice for Theatre, Singapore, in 1995, and was restaged, in English, at the Victoria Theatre in 1996. This version was taken to the 1996 Theatre Festival in Cairo, where it won the Critic's Choice for Best Acting and gained a nomination from the International Jury for Best Staging. Malaysian theatre group Five Arts Centre staged the play in Kuala Lumpur at the Experimental Theatre in November 2000, with Chee Sek Thim as director.

Descendants is a rather curious and flexible piece of theatre. It does not take a linear form, and has no plot as it is conventionally understood. The text is divided into sixteen scenes of varying length, each containing speeches which could work as monologues or dialogues. There is no indication from the playwright as to how many characters there are, or of what gender they should be, or which lines they should speak. It is, therefore, entirely up to the director to make these decisions. There are also few clues about where the play is set.

Despite the lack of clues, the play appears simple: a few speakers (or possibly just one) are recounting the exploits of Zheng He. They sometimes merely narrate the stories, while at other times they take on the role of Zheng He. The retellings are interspersed with anecdotes from the lives of the speakers. About the speakers we know virtually nothing—in Scene Three, one speaker refers to "the organizational chart of our companies or departments,"[35] which suggests that they are corporate workers of some kind. However, in Ong Keng Sen's 1995 production, they are clearly identified and contextualized as "Shentonites," employed in offices in Shenton Way, Singapore's financial district. Ong refers to them as "archetypes of the successful Singapore"[36] (1996). Through their narrations they—and we—become aware of a deep connection between them and Zheng He. Kuo explores the implications of this connection in the rest of the play. In this chapter I will read Kuo's text as well as Ong's staging,[37] as the visual and physical interpretation of Kuo's very verbal play have added a deeper level of resonance to the text.

Kuo establishes very clearly the idea of a dominating state or ruler. Although Zheng He functions as the central consciousness of this play, he cannot be seen as a dominant or dominating figure. The presence of the Ming Emperor looms over all, undermining any suggestions that Zheng He has any agency. Scene Two, for example, talks about the admiral's many voyages and the bravery he displayed in undertaking them, but this paean to Zheng He is framed by references to the Emperor:

> With divine command from the Ming Emperor in 1405
> He brought the imperial influence to distant nations
>
> Over the treacherous straits and thunderous seas
> He braved savage waters to explore the Western lands
>
> For three decades Zheng He's armada ruled the ocean
> Exploring the exotic from Tenggara, India to Arabia
>
> When he returned to the splendours of the Imperial Court
> Peace and friendship had stretched as far as Africa[38]

It is made all too clear that the whole enterprise is controlled by this distant but all-powerful ruling figure. This point is emphasized in Scene Six, when Imperial Decrees are given to the various eunuchs, empowering them to carry out their duties in relation to the voyages of the treasure fleet. The Emperor tells Zheng He to go "in power, authority and peace,"[39] but it is obvious that any power devolved to the eunuchs is given solely at the whim of the Emperor. What power they have on this voyage is in fact the Emperor's power. Their verbal responses to the Emperor are indicative of their powerlessness in comparison to him: Zheng He "*humbly* receives the Imperial Decree," and "*accepts* [. . . it] with *great honour and gratitude*."[40] The ritual words Zheng He uses emphasize his subject position in relation to the Emperor.

The Emperor's total control over Zheng He becomes even more apparent in Scene Eleven, when he decides to change Zheng He's name. According to Levathes:

> Zhu Di rewarded his loyal servant and eunuch commander Ma He by bestowing on him the name Zheng. He chose that name, it is believed, because in the early days of the rebellion his horse had been killed just outside Beiping at a place called Zhenglunba. Zheng He had particularly distinguished himself in the 1399 defense of Beiping and in the final campaign south in 1402 to capture Nanjing.[41]

Levathes constructs the incident as a reward for bravery and loyal service. Kuo's treatment of the same incident, however, is slightly more sinister. Approaching Zheng He (or Ma He, as he still was) during a celebration, the Emperor suddenly cries out "Ah, how can we have a horse running in the Imperial Court!"[42]—this was taboo because superstition stated that "when horses are let free in court, there would be war and rebellion in the land,"[43] and "Ma"means "horse" in Mandarin. By changing the eunuch's name, the Emperor also defuses a hint of potential threat; the adversarial name "Ma He" is removed, and replaced by a name which focuses instead on the eunuch's great loyalty towards the Emperor. The Emperor's power to name the subject underlines the eunuch's subordinate position and his absolute dependence on his master.

The Emperor, then, is constructed as omnipotent and controlling, an all-seeing patriarch. Kuo's vision of the Emperor is interesting because it hints at a level of power not emphasized in Singapore's constructions of Zheng He's voyages. As noted earlier, the focus in Singapore's vision of its history is on Zheng He rather than on the Emperor, with the voyages centralized as missions of trade and goodwill. In the play, the Emperor is imagined as justifying the voyages by saying that "for decades now we have not extended our imperial presence and goodwill to the Western Ocean. It is therefore now my explicit wish that the power, prestige and splendour of the Imperial Court be extended once more to the farther shores."[44] This seems to chime in with the official versions. But Kuo undermines this possibility by juxtaposing the Emperor's seeming benevolence with the bleakness of his threats to the eunuchs: "The punishment for whoever fails to expedite his duties as commanded is no less than summary execution!"[45] Zheng He's reaction when the Emperor questions him about his name is also instructive: although the Emperor laughs at his own witticism and looks at Zheng He "in amusement,"[46] Zheng He responds with fear, desperately begging the Emperor's pardon. The Emperor controls his subjects through fear, because he has absolute power over them. By constantly framing descriptions of the voyages with references to the Emperor's controlling power, Kuo revises one of Singapore's originary myths to emphasize the authoritarian nature of the contemporary state.

This point is significant for the Singaporean yuppies, who are slowly realizing the closeness of their connection to Zheng He: "the more I discover, the more I am convinced that we were related, closely related—so closely related that I had to be a descendant of the eunuch admiral."[47] Kuo uses this perceived relationship to examine the position of the Singaporeans in relation to the state. The absolute authority of the Emperor, and his control of his subjects, can be linked with the high level of control held by the Singapore state over its citizens. However, that power to control is not as brutal as the Ming Emperor's. Francis Fukuyama has called the governing style in Singapore "paternalistic authoritarianism that persuades rather than coerces."[48] Kuo examines this "soft authoritarianism"[49] through the metaphor of castration, thus providing another link between modern Singaporeans and the eunuch admiral.

Castration is, naturally, a leitmotif running through this play, as Zheng He had to be castrated in order to be accepted for service in the Imperial household. Kuo presents several viewpoints, both specifically about Zheng He's castration, and about the act of castration in more general terms. Levathes states that when the Ming army took prisoners from Zheng He's home province of Yunnan, the boy's cleverness was noticed, and he was chosen to be castrated and placed in the service of Chu Di (then still a prince).[50] Kuo approaches this event from two contrasting angles in Scene Five. The first version is narrated in the first person by Zheng He, who is thus positioned as choosing subject. He declares that: "It was my own decision to become a eunuch, because our family was very poor"[51]; he remains steadfast and unwavering even in the face of his father's tears. The father is portrayed as deeply loving, suffering immense pain over his son's decision. He is unwilling to carry out the procedure if there is the slightest hint of hesitation on his son's part; he asks several times, "Doggie, you won't regret?"[52] "Doggie," it is explained, is Zheng He's pet name. The repeated question and the use of the pet name underline the close and loving relationship between father and son. In this narration, the castration is performed on a willing, choosing subject for the good of the family.

In the context of modern Singapore, we can read this castration as the conscious handing over of power by Singaporeans to the state in exchange for a chance at material comfort: if the father here is a metaphor for the state generally, and patriarchal authority figure Lee Kuan Yew specifically,[53] then Singaporeans are constructed as making sacrifices for a caring state, which reluctantly accepts these sacrifices for the greater good of the nation. Here, there is not even any suggestion of coercion of the individual—rather the reverse, in fact, with the father having to be coerced into performing the procedure, even though it will benefit him.

However Kuo deconstructs this picture of benevolence and self-sacrifice by immediately switching from first-person to third-person narrative, in order to tell a story of brutality and imposition. As soon as the first story has been told, one of the speakers says "But of course Zheng He didn't choose like this. He was summarily cut and cleansed by his masters when he was barely a teenager."[54] In this narration, the procedure is performed not by a loving and reluctant father, but by anonymous "masters" seeking to fill the Imperial Court's "huge need for eunuchs."[55] Here, Zheng He is neither the speaking nor the choosing subject, and the narration centres on the individual's utter lack of power. One wonders how much of this harsh response to the curtailing of individual power stems from Kuo's own experience as a two-term detainee under the Internal Security Act of Singapore.[56]

Yet his view is not unremittingly harsh. He is aware that in return for this curtailment of civil liberties, Singaporeans enjoy a high, even luxurious standard of living, far outstripping their neighbours and even some

developed countries in the West. Kuo does not condemn Singaporeans for
having consented to this exchange. He himself, having come out of the
harsh environment of detention, had to confront the "peculiar softness"
that governs Singaporean life.[57] As Kuo notes, this soft way of life "somehow massages you in a way so comfortable that you tend to forget that
before [. . .] you had some ideas."[58] Kuo compares this exchange of power
for an easy life to a method of castration which avoids the violence and
disfigurement experienced by Zheng He. In this method, the nanny of the
little boy chosen will massage his testicles softly, producing a pleasurable
sensation. Over time, the massage becomes harder, eventually crushing and
destroying the testicles—but the boy, so habituated to the pressure of the
massage, never experiences it as anything but "comforting, enjoyable and
even highly desirable."[59] There is no trauma and the castrated individual
appears whole. This, Kuo suggests, is what has happened to the Singaporeans. Wee and Lee also note this point, stating that the play "draws explicit
parallels between the history of Zheng He and contemporary man, and the
cost to be paid for service to the state—in this case, an anachronistic and
allegorized Chinese nation-state."[60] Although it is not overtly stated here,
if there are parallels between Zheng He and contemporary (Singaporean)
man, then there must also be parallels between the "anachronistic [. . .]
Chinese nation-state" and contemporary Singapore.

While such parallels can be inferred, it is interesting that the director
and most critics chose to avoid the political inferences. Director Ong agrees
that the play can be seen as political "but on a larger level, it's not just about
Singapore and politics but about castration in modern life—because we no
longer allow ourselves to relate to our environment."[61] This is a vague, general comment which avoids the political by apparently referencing "larger"
issues. He is more specific when he pins this idea of castration down to
being "so concerned about success" that "the little things that make up our
life" are ignored[62] (Koh 1995 a); here, he acknowledges the overwhelmingly materialistic nature of the national identity. Critic B.P. Koh sees the
play as drawing parallels "between the power struggles of court eunuchs
and modern-day office workers, using the metaphor of castration to show
how much they have sacrificed in order to climb up the corporate ladder,"[63]
thus narrowing the play's field of reference to a very particular, nonpolitical
environment. The very reluctance of Ong and the critics to engage with the
underlying political criticism is indicative of their complicity in the system
of control.

Like the yuppies, they are the descendants of the Eunuch Admiral. In
a way, the state has actually constructed them as such—as Singaporeans,
citizens of this global city and its international networks, they have inherited his legacy of trade routes and external linkages. However, in modern
day Singapore, that adventurous, pioneering heritage has been reduced to a
highly consumerist, materialistic orientation. Kuo reconsiders the myth by
revisiting the historical figure of Zheng He. In Kuo's portrayal, Zheng He

is from the start controlled by the desire for wealth, power, and prestige, so that he becomes entirely focused on these goals. But none of the power, ultimately, resides with him. This perception is reductive of the common image of Zheng He.

Zheng He, as portrayed in history books and hagiographies, is an impressive figure indeed, vibrant and larger than life. Levathes states that, according to Zheng He's family records, he departed from the stereotype of the shrill-voiced, temperamental eunuch; he was said to be:

> seven feet tall and had a waist about five feet in circumference. His cheeks and forehead were high but his nose was small. He had glaring eyes, teeth as white and well-shaped as shells, and a voice as loud as a huge bell. He knew a great deal about warfare and was well accustomed to battle.[64]

However, as depicted by Kuo, Zheng He is far from being this vital and (ironically) potent figure. Kuo describes him as "this 600-year-old legend of a molested and incarcerated man."[65] By specifically referring to him as an ancient legend, Kuo undermines the truth-value of commonly held perceptions of Zheng He, demanding that these perceptions be questioned and revisited. For Kuo, despite his power, Zheng He was "molested" (painting him as a victim) and "incarcerated" (despite being on the open seas, he is constrained and imprisoned by the Emperor's control). In Kuo's reconstructed myth, Zheng He is not the powerful figure of history. Rather, he is lost and alone.

In Scene Four, the yuppies discuss whether, upon his death, Zheng He was buried with or without his severed penis. This discussion leads them to a realization about the nature of power:

> Suddenly suspicion arises as to how fragile all these big men and women are—and how temporary and transient the power, status and authority of these people occupying high positions really are—when we found that a supremely powerful grand eunuch like Zheng He could end up so pathetically.[66]

By remembering the myth differently, (and thus remembering Zheng He differently) Kuo reevaluates the position of Zheng He's descendants in Singapore, underscoring their lack of control and individual freedom.

But, as noted earlier, he acknowledges the complicity of ordinary Singaporeans in agreeing to abdicate individual civil liberties in exchange for a better life. Like Zheng He in Scene Five's first-person narration of his castration, they have decided to become "eunuchs," stripped of personal power, "because our family was very poor. No money, no status, no education—we were fated to be poor and downtrodden forever. So, I decided that going into the imperial court to serve as a eunuch was the only way to

get us out of our condemned poverty."⁶⁷ By serving at the "Imperial Court"
of modern Singapore, Singaporeans have in fact managed to fight their way
out of poverty. Even the late David Marshall, long a critic of Lee Kuan Yew
and his domestic policies (he called Lee "at base a fascist"), was "in awe,
genuine awe, of what they [the PAP] have achieved pragmatically . . . There
is no unemployment, there is no homelessness, there is an overflowing
rice bowl."⁶⁸ Chua Beng Huat posits that the state has effectively bartered
increased material comfort for greater political control.⁶⁹ Jacqueline Lo
takes the argument a step further, stating that: "Anxiety and/or dissatisfaction with the heavy-handedness of the government has been ameliorated by
discernible material rewards as Singapore's economy developed rapidly."⁷⁰
The suggestion is that material comfort placates the people, removing the
desire to challenge state hegemony or even to express "dissatisfaction." The
choke hold is applied softly, though firmly.

Kuo's yuppies acknowledge their complicity in relinquishing agency in
return for comfort, experiencing it as a kind of spiritual emptiness from
which they wish to escape. In Scene One, the yuppies dream of entering
a "vast space [. . .]. Endless. Haunting. Unknown. But promising. And
seemingly reachable." They are ambivalent about this "unknown" space,
fearing it and yet yearning for it at the same time, because it will lead them
away from their current existence, which they describe as "a terrible insan-
ity." In this scene, distinct parallels are drawn between the yuppies and
the admiral, suggesting that the yuppies, too, are "molested and incarcerated."⁷¹ These parallels are made even more explicit in Scene Three; the
yuppies talk about a room in the Imperial Palace where the penis boxes of
the eunuchs are hung from the ceiling, rising closer to the ceiling as their
own position in the Court rises. They compare this arrangement to the
organizational charts in the companies they work in and ask, deflatingly,
"don't we look like a network of pricks?"⁷²

Kuo's text constantly compares the current position of the yuppies with
Zheng He's position as one who has literally given up his (male) power
in order to enjoy a more secure and comfortable life, at the expense of
his personal and civil liberties. In the text, their yearnings are verbalized
but not realized. Ong's staging brings them closer to their dreams. He
physically positions the yuppies in a strange limbo somewhere between
the financial markets which dominate their lives, and the potent, haunting
unknown into which they wish to escape. In the 1996 TheatreWorks production,⁷³ the stage is virtually bare, containing nothing but four chairs
upstage, and a few glass bowls downstage. At the back of the stage there
is a large screen; throughout the performance, images of balance sheets,
stock market figures, and so on are projected onto this screen, thus visually grounding the play in the world of financial markets and networks—
the modern equivalent of Zheng He's trading voyages. Four Shentonites,
dressed in black and white corporate clothes, stumble into this stark, bare
space, which is inhabited by a mysterious figure dressed in a white robe

which vaguely suggests a traditional Chinese costume, but is not a detailed replica of ancient Chinese court robes. This silent figure glides slowly and gracefully around the stage, a calm counterpoint to the frenzy and tension of the Shentonites. As the Shentonites speak, the robed figure ceremoniously divests them of their shoes and trousers or skirts, and washes their feet, ritually cleansing them of their associations with the financial world. At one point, they strip down to a costume reminiscent of bondage gear— black leather straps crisscrossing their torsos. This costume provides a rather startling contrast to the conservative black and white clothes they were wearing earlier. Taken together with the constant, dominating presence of the flickering screen in the back, it suggests that the yuppies are still in thrall to their consumerist ideologies.

Indeed, the play implies that the yuppies never manage to break their bonds with the world of finance and trade. Even when they have completely shed their constricting corporate uniform and are dressed in loose white robes, the back of the stage is dominated by the screen and its endless display of numbers. In the text, the last line is "The Market is calling me!"[74] This seems to function as a kind of motto or rallying cry for both Zheng He and the yuppies. Zheng He, entirely dependent on the Emperor, must serve the call of the Market in the form of the trade routes he sailed with the treasure fleet. The Shentonites, equally dependent on the comfortable life created for them by the state, are unable to quite escape the world of the financial markets which help satisfy their material needs—even though they are aware of spiritual emptiness.

Kuo appears, then, to be aware of the difficulty of completely escaping from the call of the markets. It is too deeply ingrained in the Singapore psyche—the island state's identity is too intricately bound up to these international financial networks. However, Kuo has an alternative vision of what the markets could be. Currently, they are a symbol of spiritual and cultural poverty, offset by economic prosperity. In Scene Thirteen, however, Kuo describes a trading mission which is replete with the splendour, sharing, and friendship which were the (ostensible) original motivation for the voyages of the treasure fleets. Zheng He and his emissaries bring goods ashore to trade. They are eagerly awaited by the people on shore, and there is celebration, feasting, and cultural exchange. In this scene, he manages to create some of the air of solemn but colourful ceremony and the sense of wonder which must have, fundamentally, been a part of the whole event.

The trading day begins with Zheng He's emissaries "getting ready to bring their goods ashore for the great trading festival"; by using the word "festival," Kuo manages to turn the event into a time of enjoyment and celebration, rather than a business transaction. It is a "joyous journey" which "brought together all sorts of people" in a "gentlemanly exchange," "a meeting of friends" which ends, when they part, "in passionate sorrow." The entire focus is on joy, friendship, and sharing among friends. Kuo also describes the items traded—"silk, brocade, china of many varieties," "fabrics made of jute, of cotton, of silk; [. . .] metalwork made of gold, of silver of bronze [. . .]; [. . .] coral, pearls, fish bones, turtle shells." He emphasizes the abundance and the exotic beauty of the goods, but subordinates the important matter of their monetary worth, simply saying that they were all "priced beforehand"—such mundane matters as haggling over price do not intrude on this festival of splendour and friendship.[75] Zheng He is buoyed by the sense that through these trading fairs, these "markets," he is leaving "a path of amazing splendour that would seep into the lives of so many people in so many places, through so many ways over so long a time."[76] After the market, he and his sailors stay awake, energized by what has happened, talking and singing through the night, unwilling for the air of celebration to end.

By focusing almost exclusively on human interaction, beauty, and celebration, while subtly sidelining matters such as prices and bartering, Kuo successfully shifts the emphasis from the financial to the humanistic. This, he suggests, is a more fulfilling way of life—although power still lies in the hands of others, living by focusing on cultural exchange and friendship will offset the emptiness that haunts the yuppies. But this scene is just one interlude, and is undermined almost immediately by the next scene which describes Zheng He as: "An outcast almost for life, exiled on the vast, open sea, he—apart from serving the emperor's imperial interest— also must have been looking deep in his heart, for his own paradise."[77] The underlying implication is that he never finds this paradise. He remains circumscribed by the Emperor's wishes.

Ong's staging also carries some of this ambivalent sense of joy tempered by the awareness of being bound to the will of a dominating power. B. P. Koh describes how the scene was staged in the 1995 English production:

> There is a sensational sequence in *Descendants of the Eunuch Admiral* in which undergraduate Janice Koh spins on the spot 300 times while delivering a 7 ½-minute speech. The scene, played out against Gabriel Faure's requiem, expresses such uplifting exhilaration that the audience breaks out in applause afterwards.[78]

Ong's use of physical movement to embody the excitement of the trading scene is interesting—it focuses not on the splendour and wealth displayed, but on the sheer joy and exhilaration experienced by those taking part. The audience was clearly caught up in that emotion. At the same time, however, it is telling that the actress spins around *on the spot*, signifying that she is constrained, seemingly unable to break free from the bonds placed on her by her willingness to cede her personal authority to the state. Yes, she can experience great joy—but always within limits.

Although the imperative to voyage and trade constrains Zheng He, the sea also offers some liberty. The yuppies ponder whether Zheng He saw these voyages as a kind of escape:

I have often wondered what Zheng He was thinking when he was alone on deck in the South Seas, in the Indian Ocean, sailing away to the distant lands, in the middle of nowhere . . . In his loneliest moments, which probably were also his freest moments . . . Was he more than the eunuch that we have generally imagined him to be, or less than the hero which the historians and legends have portrayed him to be?

Maybe he was feeling what we would be thinking when we travel out of the country. In a state of limbo, but free from constraints and controls . . . There is no doubt that if there was really a chamber in the Forbidden City storing the eunuch's treasures, Zheng He's box would be very high up near the ceiling. But the climb must have involved plenty of hard work—and often going against his own good conscience—which had to be pleasing to the Emperor.[79]

It is only when he is adrift on the ocean, in some ways beyond the control of the Emperor, that he feels some kind of autonomy in this "potent" loneliness.[80] The Shentonites overtly compare this to their own feelings when they leave the city—uncertain, but free. The state is no longer able to function as a choke point monopolizing and controlling their freedom, or at least not to the same extent.

The play ends on an ambivalent note, with the yuppies poised between accepting the inescapability of state control, and their individual dreams of liberty:

It looks as if, however well-meaning one is, however hard one tries, the fate of the cut and dried, cleansed and uprooted eunuch is all but decided . . .

But the eunuch admiral seemed never to have given up the hope of finding an alternate life. On board his drifting vessels, in the loneliness of the vast ocean, in the limbo between departing and arriving, between being a man and a non-man, he kept on dreaming, hoping, searching, struggling.[81]

It is interesting that Kuo differentiates here between the eunuch, for whom everything "is all but decided," and the eunuch *admiral*, who might still be able to find some other life. A mere eunuch is spiritually bound, unable to escape the dominant ruler. The potential for freedom and individual agency exists only for the admiral, who can travel beyond his circumscribed borders. Zheng He's "moments of transcendence [. . .] come about *only* during the voyage,"[82] that is, away from the controlling power of the state. Is this another way of looking at the idea of Singaporeans as being descendants of the eunuch admiral? Should we, in our reading, focus on the agency contained within the term "admiral," rather than overemphasizing the lack of privilege and power all too physically embodied by the figure of the eunuch?

Cheong Koon Hean (quoted earlier), stresses the need to find a Singaporean soul[83]; but this implies some level of spiritual or emotional investment by the Singaporeans in their country. Yet this entire play focuses on the finding of joy and individual potency on the Indian Ocean—which, in effect, means "away from home." Where is home for Zheng He and the Singaporeans? Where do they feel that they are "rooted"? Perhaps, given the tenor of Singapore's originary myths, there is nowhere for them to put down roots. These myths persistently focus on trade, exchange, and the building of outside links. They are myths built on water and (in the modern era of air travel and satellite communications) in the air. Steeped in an environment that privileges outside linkages and economic exchange, they have no home but the "Markets" which call to them and to Zheng He. Like Zheng He, perhaps they finally conclude that "Departing is my arriving/ Wandering is my residence."[84]

NOTES

1. Some minor parts of this chapter have been taken from my unpublished PhD Thesis entitled "Re-Scripting Identities: Performativity in the English-Language Theatres of Singapore and Malaysia" (Australian National University, 2005).
2. C.J. W.-L. Wee, "Creating High Culture in the Globalized 'Cultural Desert' of Singapore," *The Drama Review* 47(4; 2003): 85.
3. Geoff Wade, "The Zheng He Voyages: A Reassessment," ARI Working Paper, No. 31 (October 2004): www.ari.nus.edu.sg/pub/wps.htm: 10.
4. William Peterson, *Theater and the Politics of Culture in Contemporary Singapore* (Middletown, CT: Wesleyan University Press, 2001), 96.
5. Ibid., 67.
6. Geoff Wade, "The Zheng He Voyages: A Reassessment," ARI Working Paper, No. 31 (October 2004): www.ari.nus.edu.sg/pub/wps.htm: 9.
7. Singapore Tourism Board. "Uniquely Singapore." http://www.visitsingapore.com/publish/stbportal/en/home/what_to_see/landmarks_and_memorials/merlion_park.html.
8. In a rather angry article about the position of Malays within Singapore society, writer Alfian Sa'at refers to this symbol, and the mythology that has consciously been created around it: "At the Sentosa Merlion there are signs that say that Sang Nila himself saw the Merlion rising from the waters, a fact that the *Sejarah Melayu*, the Malay Annals, failed to mention. Evidently there is someone called 'Sang Nila' somewhere in the executive committee of the Singapore Tourism Board" (Alfian, 2003, 386). It would be interesting (though beyond the scope of this chapter) to look at the centrality of Zheng He and Raffles from an ethnic or racial point of view—they seem to symbolise Singapore's Chinese dominance and (economically) Western outlook. The Malay founders of Singapore have largely been written out of Singapore's history.
9. Kathleen Kingsbury, "Singapore Soars," *Time*, June 4, 2007, 20.
10. Ibid., 19.
11. Quoted in Ibid., 21.
12. David Birch, "Staging Crises: Media and Citizenship," in *Singapore Changes Guard: Social, Political and Economic Directions in the 1990s*, ed. Garry Rodan (New York: Longman Cheshire, 1993), 75.

13. Ibid., 73.
14. I would like to thank my colleague Ashraf Jamal for suggesting this idea to me.
15. William Peterson, *Theater and the Politics of Culture in Contemporary Singapore* (Middletown, CT: Wesleyan University Press, 2001), 9.
16. C. J. W.-L. Wee and Lee Chee Keng, "Breaking Through Walls and Visioning Beyond—Kuo Pao Kun Beyond the Margins," in *Two Plays by Kuo Pao Kun: "Descendants of the Eunuch Admiral" and "The Spirits Play"* (Singapore: SNP, 2003), 25.
17. S. Rajaratnam, quoted in R. S. Milne and Diane K. Mauzy, *Singapore: The Legacy of Lee Kuan Yew*, (San Francisco: Westview, 1990), 24.
18. C.J. W.-L. Wee, "Creating High Culture in the Globalized 'Cultural Desert' of Singapore," *The Drama Review*, 47(4; 2003): 84.
19. C. J. W.-L. Wee and Lee Chee Keng, "Breaking Through Walls and Visioning Beyond—Kuo Pao Kun Beyond the Margins," in *Two Plays by Kuo Pao Kun: "Descendants of the Eunuch Admiral" and "The Spirits Play"* (Singapore: SNP, 2003), 25.
20. Ibid., 27.
21. Xu Zu-Yuan, PRC Vice Minister of Communications, quoted in Geoff Wade, "The Zheng He Voyages: A Reassessment," ARI Working Paper, No. 31 (October 2004): www.ari.nus.edu.sg/pub/wps.htm: 1.
22. Kong Yuan-zhi, quoted in Geoff Wade, "The Zheng He Voyages: A Reassessment," ARI Working Paper, No. 31 (October 2004): www.ari.nus.edu.sg/pub/wps.htm: 2.
23. Robert Yeo, quoted in William Peterson, *Theater and the Politics of Culture in Contemporary Singapore* (Middletown, CT: Wesleyan University Press, 2001), 69.
24. William Peterson, *Theater and the Politics of Culture in Contemporary Singapore* (Middletown, CT: Wesleyan University Press, 2001), 69.
25. Françoise Vergès, "Writing on Water: Peripheries, Flows, Capital, and Struggles in the Indian Ocean," *Positions: East Asia Cultures Critique* 11(1; 2003): 246.
26. Geoff Wade, "The Zheng He Voyages: A Reassessment," ARI Working Paper, No. 31 (October 2004): www.ari.nus.edu.sg/pub/wps.htm, 9.
27. Ibid., 11.
28. Ibid., 16.
29. Françoise Vergès, "Writing on Water: Peripheries, Flows, Capital, and Struggles in the Indian Ocean," *Positions: East Asia Cultures Critique* 11(1; 2003): 250.
30. Contrast this, for example, with policy in Malaysia, where identity is very literally tied to the land: the Malays are referred to as *Bumiputra*, which translates as "sons of the earth or soil."
31. Françoise Vergès, "Writing on Water: Peripheries, Flows, Capital, and Struggles in the Indian Ocean," *Positions: East Asia Cultures Critique* 11(1; 2003): 247.
32. Philippe Beaujard, 2005. "The Indian Ocean in Eurasian and African World-Systems before the Sixteenth Century," *Journal of World History* 16(4; 2005): 412.
33. Louise Levathes, *When China Ruled the Seas: The Treasure Fleet of the Dragon Throne; 1405–1433* (New York: Oxford University Press, 1996), 88.
34. C. J. W.-L. Wee and Lee Chee Keng, "Breaking Through Walls and Visioning Beyond—Kuo Pao Kun Beyond the Margins," in *Two Plays by Kuo Pao Kun: "Descendants of the Eunuch Admiral" and "The Spirits Play"* (Singapore: SNP, 2003), 27.

35. Kuo Pao Kun, *Descendants of the Eunuch Admiral*, in *Two Plays by Kuo Pao Kun: "Descendants of the Eunuch Admiral" and "The Spirits Play"* (Singapore: SNP, 2003), 41.
36. Ong Keng Sen, "An Interview with Ong Keng Sen," by Mok Wai Yin, in *Descendants of the Eunuch Admiral* Program (Singapore 1996).
37. Ong Keng Sen is himself an interesting figure to consider in the context of global networks and global citizenship. He is the artistic director of TheatreWorks, Singapore's best-known and most successful professional theatre company. Although he began his career directing such homegrown, locally referential pieces as *Beauty World* and *Army Daze*, he is now very much an international figure, collaborating with other theatre practitioners from Europe, America, and Asia, creating works with a far wider scope of reference than just Singapore. One newspaper article suggests that: "After several years exploring the idea of what it meant to be Singaporean, it was inevitable that Ong turned his attention to the wider issue of Asian identity" (Cairns, 1999). This "inevitability" is, I think, part of this larger process of positioning the self and the state within an international rather than a national context.
38. Kuo Pao Kun, *Descendants of the Eunuch Admiral*, in *Two Plays by Kuo Pao Kun: "Descendants of the Eunuch Admiral" and "The Spirits Play"* (Singapore: SNP, 2003), 39.
39. Ibid., 46.
40. Ibid., 46 (emphasis added).
41. Louise Levathes, *When China Ruled the Seas: The Treasure Fleet of the Dragon Throne; 1405–1433* (New York: Oxford University Press, 1996), 72–73.
42. Kuo Pao Kun, *Descendants of the Eunuch Admiral*, in *Two Plays by Kuo Pao Kun: "Descendants of the Eunuch Admiral" and "The Spirits Play"* (Singapore: SNP, 2003), 55.
43. Ibid., 55–56.
44. Ibid., 46.
45. Ibid., 47.
46. Ibid., 55.
47. Ibid., 38.
48. Francis Fukuyama, quoted in William Peterson, *Theater and the Politics of Culture in Contemporary Singapore*, (Middletown, CT: Wesleyan University Press, 2001), 9.
49. Gordon P. Means, "Soft Authoritarianism in Malaysia and Singapore," *Journal of Democracy* 7(4; 1996): 103.
50. Louise Levathes, *When China Ruled the Seas: The Treasure Fleet of the Dragon Throne, 1405–1433* (New York: Oxford University Press, 1996), 58.
51. Kuo Pao Kun, *Descendants of the Eunuch Admiral*, in *Two Plays by Kuo Pao Kun: "Descendants of the Eunuch Admiral" and "The Spirits Play"* (Singapore: SNP, 2003), 44.
52. Ibid., 44.
53. For more on Lee Kuan Yew as Singapore's founding father and patriarch, see Haskell (2003).
54. Kuo Pao Kun, *Descendants of the Eunuch Admiral*, in *Two Plays by Kuo Pao Kun: "Descendants of the Eunuch Admiral" and "The Spirits Play"* (Singapore: SNP, 2003), 45.
55. Ibid., 45.
56. The Internal Security Act is a holdover from colonial days that allows for the detention without trial of individuals deemed to be a threat to internal

security. In Singapore, one term of detention is two years. Kuo was detained from 1976 to 1980, for allegedly spreading Marxist teaching. His citizenship was automatically revoked upon detention. Upon his release, he began working in theatre again, and in 1989 was awarded the Cultural Medallion for outstanding contributions to Singaporean theatre. His citizenship was reinstated in 1992, only after a formal application from Kuo.

57. Kwok Kian Woon, "Remembering Kuo Pao Kun (1939–2002)," *Inter-Asia Cultural Studies* 4(2; 2003): 198.
58. The Necessary Stage. "Playwright's Voice: A Forum on Singapore Theatre," in *9 Lives: Ten Years of Singapore Theatre. Essays Commissioned by The Necessary Stage* (Singapore: n.p., n.d.) 71.
59. Kuo Pao Kun, *Descendants of the Eunuch Admiral*, in *Two Plays by Kuo Pao Kun: "Descendants of the Eunuch Admiral" and "The Spirits Play"* (Singapore: SNP, 2003), 65.
60. C. J. W.-L. Wee and Lee Chee Keng, "Breaking Through Walls and Visioning Beyond—Kuo Pao Kun Beyond the Margins," in *Two Plays by Kuo Pao Kun: "Descendants of the Eunuch Admiral" and "The Spirits Play"* (Singapore: SNP, 2003), 26.
61. Susan Tsang, Castration and Modern Life, *Business Times* [Singapore] June 1, 1995. .
62. Koh Boon Pin, "A Play About Being Castrated From Life," *Straits Times* [Singapore], May 30, 1995.
63. Koh Boon Pin, "Castration and Corporate Ladder," *Straits Times* [Singapore], June 6, 1995.
64. Louise Levathes, *When China Ruled the Seas: The Treasure Fleet of the Dragon Throne, 1405–1433* (New York: Oxford University Press, 1996), 64.
65. Kuo Pao Kun, *Descendants of the Eunuch Admiral*, in *Two Plays by Kuo Pao Kun: "Descendants of the Eunuch Admiral" and "The Spirits Play"* (Singapore: SNP, 2003), 38.
66. Ibid., 43.
67. Ibid., 44.
68. David Marshall, quoted in William Peterson, *Theater and the Politics of Culture in Contemporary Singapore* (Middletown, CT: Wesleyan University Press, 2001), 12.
69. Chua Beng Huat, *Communitarian Ideology and Democracy in Singapore* (London: Routledge, 1995), 19.
70. Jacqueline Lo, *Staging Nation: Postcolonial English Language Theatre in Malaysia and Singapore* (Hong Kong: Hong Kong University Press, 2004), 138–139.
71. Kuo Pao Kun, *Descendants of the Eunuch Admiral*, in *Two Plays by Kuo Pao Kun: "Descendants of the Eunuch Admiral" and "The Spirits Play"* (Singapore: SNP, 2003), 38.
72. Ibid., 41.
73. For this analysis, I am relying on the published script, as well as the video recording of the 1996 performance at the Victoria Theatre.
74. Kuo Pao Kun, *Descendants of the Eunuch Admiral*, in *Two Plays by Kuo Pao Kun: "Descendants of the Eunuch Admiral" and "The Spirits Play"* (Singapore: SNP, 2003), 67.
75. Ibid., 59.
76. Ibid., 60.
77. Ibid., 61.
78. Koh Boon Pin, "She Spins 300 Times and Delivers 7 1/2–min Speech," *Straits Times* [Singapore], June 7, 1995.

79. Kuo Pao Kun, *Descendants of the Eunuch Admiral*, in *Two Plays by Kuo Pao Kun: "Descendants of the Eunuch Admiral" and "The Spirits Play"* (Singapore: SNP, 2003), 52.
80. Ibid., 38.
81. Ibid., 66.
82. C. J. W.-L. Wee and Lee Chee Keng, "Breaking Through Walls and Visioning Beyond—Kuo Pao Kun Beyond the Margins," in *Two Plays by Kuo Pao Kun: "Descendants of the Eunuch Admiral" and "The Spirits Play"* (Singapore: SNP, 2003), 27.
83. Quoted in Kathleen Kingsbury, "Singapore Soars," *Time*, June 4, 2007, 21.
84. Kuo Pao Kun, *Descendants of the Eunuch Admiral*, in *Two Plays by Kuo Pao Kun: "Descendants of the Eunuch Admiral" and "The Spirits Play"* (Singapore: SNP, 2003), 66.

BIBLIOGRAPHY

Alfian bin Sa'at. "The Racist's Apology." *FOCAS: Focus on Contemporary Art and Society* 4 (2003): 385–392.
Beaujard, Philippe. "The Indian Ocean in Eurasian and African World-Systems before the Sixteenth Century." *Journal of World History* 16(4; 2005): 411–465.
Birch, David. "Staging Crises: Media and Citizenship." In *Singapore Changes Guard: Social, Political and Economic Directions in the 1990s*, edited by Garry Rodan, 72–83. New York: Longman Cheshire, 1993.
Cairns, Alice. "Daring King of the New Asian Vision." *Sunday Morning Post* [Adelaide] January 17, 1999, *AgendaMetro*.
Chua Beng Huat. *Communitarian Ideology and Democracy in Singapore*. London: Routledge, 1995.
Descendants of the Eunuch Admiral. Videocassette. By Kuo Pao Kun. Dir. Ong Keng Sen, 1996.
Haskell, Dennis. "Whose Singapore?" In *Resistance and Reconciliation: Writing in the Commonwealth. Proceedings of the 12th Triennial Conference of ACLALS, July 2001, Canberra, Australia*, edited by Bruce Bennett, Susan Cowan, Jacqueline Lo, Satendra Nandan and Jennifer Webb, 236–247. Canberra: Association for Commonwealth Literature and Language Studies (ACLALS), 2003.
Kingsbury, Kathleen. "Singapore Soars." *Time*, June 4, 2007, 16–21.
Koh Boon Pin. "A Play About Being Castrated From Life." *Straits Times* [Singapore], May 30, 1995.
———. "Castration and Corporate Ladder." *Straits Times* [Singapore], June 6, 1995.
———. "She Spins 300 Times and Delivers 7 1/2-min Speech." *Straits Times* [Singapore], June 7, 1995.
Kuo Pao Kun. *Descendants of the Eunuch Admiral*. In *Two Plays by Kuo Pao Kun: "Descendants of the Eunuch Admiral" and "The Spirits Play,"* 37–67. Singapore: SNP, 2003.
Kwok Kian Woon. "Remembering Kuo Pao Kun (1939–2002)." *Inter-Asia Cultural Studies* 4(2; 2003): 193–201.
Levathes, Louise. *When China Ruled the Seas: The Treasure Fleet of the Dragon Throne, 1405–1433*. New York: Oxford University Press, 1996.
Lo, Jacqueline. *Staging Nation: Postcolonial English Language Theatre in Malaysia and Singapore*. Hong Kong: Hong Kong University Press, 2004.
Means, Gordon P. "Soft Authoritarianism in Malaysia and Singapore." *Journal of Democracy* 7(4; 1996): 103–117.

Milne, R. S. and Diane K. Mauzy. *Singapore: The Legacy of Lee Kuan Yew.* San Francisco, CA: Westview, 1990.

The Necessary Stage. "Playwright's Voice: A Forum on Singapore Theatre." In *9 Lives: Ten Years of Singapore Theatre. Essays Commissioned by The Necessary Stage*, 54–71. Singapore: n.p.

Ong Keng Sen. "An Interview with Ong Keng Sen." By Mok Wai Yin. *Descendants of the Eunuch Admiral* Program. Singapore, 1996.

Peterson, William. *Theater and the Politics of Culture in Contemporary Singapore.* Middletown, CT: Wesleyan University Press, 2001.

Singapore Tourism Board. "Uniquely Singapore." http://www.visitsingapore.com/publish/stbportal/en/home/what_to_see/landmarks_and_memorials/merlion_park.html. Accessed 2 July 2007.

Tsang, Susan. 1995. "Castration and Modern Life." *Business Times* [Singapore] June 1, 1995.

Vergès, Françoise. "Writing on Water: Peripheries, Flows, Capital, and Struggles in the Indian Ocean." *Positions: East Asia Cultures Critique*, 11(1; 2003): 241–257.

Wade, Geoff. 2004. *The Zheng He Voyages: A Reassessment.* ARI Working Paper, No. 31, October 2004, www.ari.nus.edu.sg/pub/wps.htm.

Wee, C. J. W.-L. . "Creating High Culture in the Globalized "Cultural Desert" of Singapore." *The Drama Review* 47(4; 2003): 84–97.

Wee, C. J. W.-L. and Lee Chee Keng. "Breaking Through Walls and Visioning Beyond—Kuo Pao Kun Beyond the Margins." In *Two Plays by Kuo Pao Kun: "Descendants of the Eunuch Admiral" and "The Spirits Play,"* 13–34. Singapore: SNP, 2003.

10 "That Great Ocean of Idealism"
Calcutta, the Tagore Circle, and the Idea of Asia, 1900–1920

Mark Ravinder Frost

If any one political drama dominates the intellectual history of Calcutta during the nineteenth and early-twentieth centuries then surely it must be the Swadeshi movement of 1905 to 1908. These three hectic years of boycotts, protest marches, and revived domestic industry have been seen by several historians as epoch-defining. Swadeshi (literally meaning "of one's own country") appears as that crucial moment when a nineteenth-century Bengal Renaissance discovers its radical voice and thrusts the "second city" of the British Empire to the forefront of the anticolonial struggle.[1] Recently, Swadeshi has been presented almost as an apotheosis for the very concept of Bengali "culture" itself: the point at which "culturalism," having migrated to India from northern Europe, transforms into the organising trope in a popular celebration of local and communal distinctiveness.[2]

However, from a Bengali-nationalist perspective, the years that followed the Swadeshi campaign must have appeared something of an anticlimax. In 1911, the capital of the Indian Empire moved back to Delhi; by which time the promise of a collective Swadeshi agitation that would unite Hindus and Muslims had dissipated in communal riots; by which time, also, Calcutta's intellectual scene had become saturated by the "culture of revolution" and the "philosophy of the bomb" found in the city's proliferating secret societies and seditious coffee clubs.[3] At the conclusion of World War I, leadership of the Indian nationalist movement passed to a Gujerati by the name of Mohandas Gandhi, who appropriated Swadeshi to become the nation's most famous political icon. In the 1920s, in the same decade that Gandhi presented passive resistance to the Indian nation, Calcutta experienced a major outbreak of the Hindu–Muslim violence that would periodically blight the city through the remainder of the century. In terms of a unifying Indian nationalism, by 1920 Calcutta appeared to have lost its intellectual primacy.[4]

But as much new scholarship illustrates, a landlocked, nation-state perspective provides just one prism through which to appreciate India's past.[5] Indeed, in terms of Indian intellectual history the territorial strictures imposed by a narrowly domestic investigation might not always prove the most enlightening. For if we approach the city of Calcutta not from the *mofussil* but from the sea, then a rather different tale can be told of its metropolitan rise as a centre for ideas.

In this story, Calcutta appears as a highly internationalized, globally connected, colonial port city, part of a network of other port cities across the Indian Ocean world that were linked to each other by improved maritime communications and, in particular, by a steadily faster and more reliable imperial post.[6] Through the latter nineteenth century, and especially after 1900, Calcutta literati utilised the accelerated circulation of books, periodicals, and correspondence that the imperial post facilitated to establish their cultural presence not just throughout India but across the wider Indian Ocean world. With the advent of more rapid and frequent steamship passages, they began to make voyages to other port cities that reinforced their taste for supranational intellectual sociability. In turn, a regional traffic in news, views, and ideologies flowed back into the "second city" of the Empire; in growing numbers, literati, holy men, and political activists headed to Calcutta to preen themselves in its metropolitan limelight and draw global attention to their diverse projects. In an era of heightened maritime interconnection, not only does Calcutta become a key reference point for Indian nationalist thinking, it also establishes itself as one of the most cosmopolitan centres of knowledge in the Indian Ocean world.

This is the accompanying story of Calcutta's intellectual history that the remainder of this chapter will explore. In particular, the following discussion suggests that simultaneous to the rise of Swadeshi, and surviving well after its decline, Calcutta became home and inspiration to some of the more definitive expressions of pan-Asianism and an influential discourse of Asian civilisation.[7] In such discussions, the presence of the Indian Ocean was never far away. Not only did it sustain the practical communications through which Calcutta literati (and those who joined their discussions from overseas) read, travelled and discovered the wider world beyond their city's shores, it also generated the cosmopolitan arena through which their ideas about Asia were disseminated. Not least, the Indian Ocean provided the historical authority and the metaphorical language through which a new universalism was increasingly expressed. In the writings of prominent Calcutta-based literati, Asian civilisation became an "ocean of idealism" through which, in the distant past as well as in their more immediate present, "waves," "currents," and "ripples" of Indian thought repeatedly washed up on distant "shores" and "beaches" to unite the region as one unified whole.

But before we examine these "waves," "ripples," and "currents" in detail, let us first begin at their point of origin with some of those important developments that marked Calcutta's emergence as a global intellectual centre.

THE ENLIGHTENED CITY

In 1908, the *Imperial Gazetteer* remarked of the Bengal press that "a great change has generally taken place in its character, tone and literary style." It went on to elaborate:

The principal characteristics of such papers at the present time are the increasing prominence given to political and administrative questions, a reckless, exaggerated and occasionally disloyal tone, and a colloquial, ungrammatical, and anglicized style. *With the spread of English education, the papers published in English by Bengalis are rapidly growing in importance.*[8]

This latter point is of some significance. Late-nineteenth-century Calcutta, like other colonial port cities across British Asia, had experienced a major expansion in Western-style, English-language education. By 1908, the city was home to four daily English-language papers edited by Europeans, and five edited by Indians (the *Bengalee, Amrita Bazar Patrika, Indian Mirror, Hindoo Patriot,* and *Bande Mataram*). The city's total of nine English-language periodicals compared with the twenty-three vernacular journals that circulated in the same year, the most influential of which were the following weeklies: *Hitabadi, Basumati,* and *Bangabasi.* Of these, the *Bangabasi* magazine was especially popular, at one time achieving an unprecedented subscription list of 50,000, partly through its repeated assertions that the discoveries of Western science had been anticipated by the ancient Aryans.[9]

Inevitably, the readership for Calcutta's English-language periodicals paled by comparison. In 1908, the *Imperial Gazeetteer* estimated that although one in five males in the city was literate, the English-speaking population numbered just 29,000, compared with 435,000 Bengali-speakers and 319,000 Hindi-speakers.[10] Nonetheless, the "rapidly growing" importance of the Indian English-language press can be gauged by examining its broader national and regional circulation. For instance, Calcutta's monthly *Modern Review*, which first appeared in 1907, quickly became something of a *New Yorker* for the Indian Ocean world. The journal's articles were frequently summarized or lifted wholesale by other periodicals across the region (this was an age before copyright) and the *Modern Review* as a whole became the model for similar *Reviews* in other Indian cities and in Ceylon. In Calcutta, the *Modern Review* also appeared in Bengali as *Prabasi.* Sumit Sarkar's claim that the "Indian colonial intelligentsia of the nineteenth century chose Indian languages, and not English, as their primary, indeed overwhelmingly predominant, media for imaginative expression" overlooks an obvious point: Indian literati who wrote in English periodicals (or whose works appeared, as Tagore's initially did, in English translation in such periodicals) knew that what they published might be picked up and read across the Empire. As we will see, well before the advent of what Sarkar terms the "Indo-Anglian" writing of "postcolonial times" (a genre that he argues emerged under "conditions of intensified globalisation"), Bengalis writing in English had discovered a wider national and even global public.[11]

Increasingly, the enhanced transport links that Calcutta experienced with other parts of India, and across the Bay of Bengal with Ceylon, Burma, and the Straits Settlements, brought this wider public closer to home. In the 1880s and 1890s, European Theosophists journeyed north from their international headquarters in Madras, established Theosophical branches in Calcutta, and thereby connected the city with a regional community of text which preached the superiority of Aryan civilisation from Bombay to Batavia. Meanwhile, from 1892, the Colombo-born Buddhist reformer and onetime Theosophist protégé, Anagarika Dharmapala, selected Calcutta as the ecumenical centre for his global Buddhist mission—the base from which he lobbied for the preservation of Bodh Gaya (the ancient site of the Buddha's enlightenment), received Buddhist pilgrims from across the region, and coordinated fund-raising efforts with his coreligionists in Burma, Ceylon, and Siam.[12]

Moreover, as Calcutta's contacts with other parts of the Indian Ocean world intensified, the city's local intelligentsia made increasing assumptions as to the broader region's cultural unity. Especially towards the end of the nineteenth century, in the writings of Keshub Chunder Sen, Swami Vivekananda, and Bhudev Mukhopady, three connected ideas about Asian civilisation coalesced and became paramount: (1) that India and Asia were essentially one, (2) that Asian civilisation had eschewed European materialism and was the wellspring of a superior spirituality, and (3) that, in consequence, the civilisations of Asia and Europe were bonded together in a relationship that was complementary.[13] Capturing all of these ideas, Bhudev asserted that the global role of Hinduism was to:

> absorb *all other Indian cultures* and spread to Europe and the entire world the light of true knowledge and virtue. The way of knowledge has been cleared by Bacon, Descartes, Kant and others. The Hindus have given China, Japan and the rest of Asia the light of faith, they will bring to Europe an even purer, brighter light of ineffable charm.[14]

What is equally evident by the turn of the century is that the unified Asia that Bhudev and other Calcutta literati imagined, and which they believed Indian civilisation had largely created, was one that they could, if they so chose, increasingly experience at first hand. Two celebrated Calcutta luminaries who capitalized on a burgeoning Indian Ocean lecture circuit were Vivekananda and Rabindranath Tagore. In 1893, on his way to the Chicago Parliament of Religions, Vivekananda travelled through Japan, and on his return from America in 1897 he visited Ceylon. Here, he lectured in Colombo, and a Vedantic society was shortly after established in his honour. Two decades later, Tagore visited Japan via the Straits Settlements and Hong Kong (as we will see), and on three later occasions lectured in Ceylon (in 1922, 1934, and 1943). Tagore was following in the footsteps of his elder brother Satyendranath (the renowned composer and author) who had in 1859 journeyed to Ceylon in the company of Keshub Chunder Sen. Such tours enhanced the regional celebrity of Bengal's leading literary lights—in the case of Tagore's visits to Colombo, his lectures and the performances of this theatrical troupe had the effect of inspiring several Ceylonese writers and artists to follow him back to his ashram at Santiniketan. At the same time, such tours also ensured that intellectual currents that emanated from Calcutta reached an Indian Ocean public whose participants might never actually step foot in the city.

Thus, a nineteenth-century revolution in maritime communications ensured that ideas about Asian unity became grounded in greater first-hand acquaintance with the region and in regular pan-Asian intellectual sociability. Arguably the most important site for this new sociability was the Tagore family's residence in the northern Calcutta suburb of Jorasanko (incidentally, a site also revered by many people today as the heart of the "Bengal Renaissance"). Here, the artists Abanindranath and Gaganen-dranath Tagore and the poet Rabindranath and his nephew Surendranath, entertained learned guests from Europe fascinated by the "East." But per-haps more importantly, here the Tagores also played host to those Asian literati and artists who claimed to *represent* that "East." From 1900 to 1920, the Tagore salon transformed itself from being the hub of Bengali and then Indian nationalist aesthetics into a key centre for pan-Asian ideal-ism, and it is to three of the most important thinkers who participated in this transformation that we now turn.

THE VISITOR FROM JAPAN

Born in the port city of Yokohama in 1862, the Japanese art critic, Okakura Tenshin (Kakuzo), would be remembered as one of the Tagore's most influ-ential Asian visitors. The child of a samurai family that had set up as silk merchants, in 1875 Okakura entered what would later be known as Tokyo University, where he became closely associated with William A. Hough-ton, a teacher of English literature, and Ernest. F. Fenellosa, a Harvard-educated political philosopher with a keen interest in Japanese art. After graduating, Okakura entered government service with the Ministry of Edu-cation and began to assist Fenellosa in the preservation of Japan's artistic heritage, accompanying his American associate in 1886 on a two-year tour of Europe and the United States to study the most advanced methods of art research. On his return to Japan, Okakura became involved in a range of activities and institutions dedicated to Japanese arts, crafts, and architec-ture, and in 1893 he made his first journey to China to study and collect Chinese artworks. But it was his journey to India in late 1901 that was to prove the defining experience in his rise to international prominence.

Surendranath Tagore, who made Okakura's acquaintance at a Calcutta reception organised in his honour by Sister Nivedita (the Irish devotee of Vivekenanda), has left us with an evocative depiction of his Japanese friend's Indian sojourn. At Jorasanko, Okakura worked on his "next book on the Awakening of Asia" while the rest of the Tagore family spent "wildly exhilarating evenings, sitting around his table, listening to his glowing passages deploring the White Disaster spreading over the East, in its intellectual and spiritual surrender to the western cult of Mammon." Then, in the spring of 1902, Surendranath accompanied Okakura on a tour of architectural monuments across North and Western India. During this trip, writes Surendranath, Okakura's "samurai heart went out at once to the Sikhs of the Golden Temple, and of the *kripan*-cult." On "entering any temple," he goes on, "Okakura went barefoot, wearing a *dhoti* in Indian fashion, – for him all shrines were to be approached with reverence."[15]

By the close of Okakura's eleven-month stay in India, he had produced his first major book, *The Ideals of the East*. Following its publication in London in 1903, the work circulated back in India where it "created a sensation among the English-speaking intelligentsia."[16] Okakura begins *The Ideals* with his now famous exclamation: "Asia is one. The Himalayas divide, only to accentuate, two mighty civilisations, the Chinese with its communism of Confucius, and the Indian with its individualism of the Vedas." He then continues:

> But not even the snowy barriers can interrupt for one moment that broad expanse of love for the Ultimate and Universal, which is the common thought-inheritance of every Asiatic race, enabling them to produce all the great religions of the world, and distinguishing them from those maritime peoples of the Mediterranean and the Baltic, who love to dwell on the Particular, and to search out the means, not the end, of life.[17]

The structure of *The Ideals* indicates that it was probably redrafted in response to the suggestions of Sister Nivedita who also worked with Okakura on his subsequent *Awakening of Asia* and was a habitué of the Tagore salon.[18] Both the work's opening and its final chapter on Asian ideals in society and art are manifestos calling for a revival of traditional practices and values (especially those of Indian religion and Chinese ethics) and for a pan-Asian unity in the face of encroaching Westernisation. The intervening chapters, drawn from lectures Okakura had earlier given in Japan to European disciples of Vivekananda, provide the justification for his introductory claim that it has been "the great privilege of Japan to realise [Asia's] unity-in-complexity with a special clearness. The Indo-Tartaric blood of [the Japanese] race was in itself a heritage which qualified it to imbibe from the two sources [India and China] and so mirror the whole of Asiatic consciousness." As an "unconquered race" Japan was the true repository for Asiatic thought and culture:

> Thus Japan is a museum of Asiatic civilisation; and yet more than a museum, because the singular genius of the race leads it to dwell on all phases of the ideals of the past, in that spirit of living Advaitsim which

welcomes the new without losing the old . . . The history of Japanese
art becomes thus the history of Asiatic ideals – the beach where each
successive wave of Eastern thought has left its sand ripple as it beat
against the national consciousness.[19]

Although *The Ideals* clearly reveal Okakura's powerful nationalist sentiments, much effort is spent in describing Asia's civilisational unity. Moreover, the language Okakura employs to do so is significant, indicative of
a scholar who sees the past through the lens of the present. In Okakura's
writing, India no longer stands as the primary centre of Asian civilisation
(Japan, by remaining politically independent has usurped this crown).
Rather, India along with China form the two cultural poles of an ecumene
bound together by historical maritime communication. "Down to the days
of the Mohammedan conquest," Okakura explained:

> went, by the ancient highways of the sea, the intrepid mariners of the
> Bengal coast, founding their colonies in Ceylon, Java and Sumatra, leav-
> ing Aryan blood to mingle with that of the sea-board races of Burma
> and Siam, and binding Cathay and India fast in mutual intercourse.

"Long systolic centuries" may have followed in which China and India
shrank back on themselves. However, the "old energy of communication
lived yet in the great moving sea of the Tartar hordes." Moreover, Buddhism served as "that great ocean of idealism, in which merge all the river
systems of Eastern Asiatic thought."

Throughout *The Ideals* Okakura repeats this use of maritime metaphors
to capture the intellectual exchange that he believed once generated Asian
unity. As we have seen, Japan, in Okakura's eyes, was "the beach where
each successive wave of Eastern thought has left its sand ripple as it beat
against the national consciousness."[20] Elsewhere, the author seems influenced by his own recent voyage across the Indian Ocean:

> For if Asia be one it is also true that the Asiatic races form a single
> mighty web. We forget, in an age of classification, that types are after
> all but shining points of distinctness in an ocean of approximations.[21]

In the final chapter of *The Ideals*, entitled "The Vista," Okakura underlines
further his argument that Asia was once a unified entity bound together
by religion and by centuries of maritime communication. In this respect,
pilgrimage, the "travel-culture" of the time as Okakura referred to it, was
and remained fundamentally important:

> Asia knows, it is true, nothing of the fierce joys of a time-devouring lo-
> comotion, but she has still the far deeper travel-culture of the pilgrim-
> age and the wandering monk. . . .

The "human intercourse" of the wandering "Indian ascetic" and the "Japanese peasant-traveller," whose cultural contributions were born out of harmonious interaction with nature and their fellow man, was what made Asia distinct. Such habits of journeying Okakura describes as unique "modes of experience" or "interchange." The "task of Asia today," he then argues, "becomes that of protecting and restoring Asiatic modes":

> We know instinctively that in our history lies the secret of our future, and we grope with a blind intensity to find the clue . . . But it must be from Asia herself, along the ancient roadways of the race, that the great voice shall be heard.[22]

In her "Introduction" to *The Ideals*, Sister Nivedita was at pains to balance Okakura's claim that Japan represented the perfection of Asian aesthetics with the argument more familiar to Calcutta literati that India was the origin of all Asian civilisation. In so doing she pointed to the Buddhism which she claimed Okakura saw "pouring into China across the passes of the Himalayas and by the sea-route through the straits" as in reality "the name given to the vast synthesis known as Hinduism . . ." Nivedita likewise drew on Okakura's notion of a "great ocean of idealism" uniting Asia: *The Ideals* was, in her view, about how "waves of Indian spirituality have worked to inspire nations" across this expanse. Moreover, with modern maritime communications in mind, she went on to predict:

> The process that took a thousand years at the beginning of our era may now, with the aid of steam and electricity, repeat itself in a few decades and the world may again witness the Indianising of the East.[23]

Such a reading was most probably the preferred one amongst Okakura's Indian audience, which included many of Bengal's leading intellectual lights, for whom *The Ideals* was said to have come as a "revelation."[24] Leaving aside the jostling for national and religious pride-of-place contained within the work, its core thesis—that Asia had once been united during a golden age of cultural exchange and civilisation—would have been immediately attractive to Indian readers. In today's age of so-called "Asian values" such an argument might hardly seem novel, but, as Nivedita's introduction underlined, it represented in its day a major intellectual turning point. Okakura had shown Asia "not as the congeries of geographical fragments that we imagined, but as a united living organism, each part dependent on all the others, the whole breathing a single complex life."[25]

THE HOUSEGUEST FROM CEYLON

In between Okakura's visits to Calcutta, the Tagores received another houseguest from overseas who proved to be just as influential a proponent of the region's civilisational unity. Though the Ceylonese Eurasian Ananda Kentish Coomaraswamy never met Okakura in person, both men knew of each other's work and before Okakura's death they both corresponded. In addition, both men shared mutual friends and associates through their participation in the Tagores' international circle. Like Okakura, Coomaraswamy eventually joined the Boston Museum of Fine Arts, having brought to the United States a significant collection of artworks amassed during his own travels across Asia. From Boston, after 1917, when he took up his curatorship, Coomaraswamy would produce his most important scholarly works on Asian aesthetics and on what he termed the "Asiatic philosophy of Art" that underlay its essential "diversity in unity."[26] However, it appears that fundamental to his later writings on this subject were the years previous to his move to Boston, during which he paid frequent visits (in "the pilgrim spirit" as he himself put it) to India, Calcutta, and the Tagore's residence at Jorasanko.

Educated in England as a youth, Coomaraswamy emerged from University College, London, in 1900 with a B.Sc. in Geology and Botany. Returning to Ceylon in 1902, he became director of the Mineralogical Survey of Ceylon, a body set up by the British partly in response to his research findings. However, in his spare time Coomaraswamy dedicated himself to the study of Ceylonese arts and architecture and grew increasingly distressed at what he saw as the unimpeded inroads made by Western civilisation into traditional Ceylonese life. In 1905, simultaneous to the emergence of the Swadeshi across the Bay of Bengal, he launched his own agitation for the rejection of Westernisation and the revival of local manufactures, arts and crafts. The letters, lectures, and pamphlets he circulated for this cause led the following year to the creation of the Ceylon Social Reform Society, of which he became the founding President.

The following year, Coomaraswamy made the first of what would be several visits to India in the coming decade, his second series of visits between 1909 and 1913 including a two-year sojourn. In Calcutta, he befriended Abanindranath Tagore and like Okakura settled effortlessly into the Tagore salon. (A drawing made by Nandalal Bose of Abindranath's studio circa 1910 shows Coomaraswamy, surrounded by books and a hookah, reclining on a sofa in earnest discussion with Sister Nivedita, while in the background other Tagores lie on chaise lounges, sleeping or reading.) In fact, just as they had done with Okakura, the Tagores played a major role in supporting Coomarsawamy's career. The Indian Society of Oriental Art, established in Calcutta by the Tagores and their European associates, offered the Eurasian from Ceylon a platform from which to express many of his formative ideas. The Society also entrusted him with the task of organising an exhibition of past and contemporary Indian art for the All-India Exhibition in Allahabad at the end of 1910.

By the time Coomaraswamy set off across North India to collect works for this exhibition, his intellectual star was on the rise. According to one contemporary, his essays on national aesthetics in English-language journals, especially the *Modern Review,* already brought him a "kind of hero worship" that his public lectures (which "made an impression on young minds and left crowds of them to ruminate on his central ideas") further enhanced.[27] Back in Calcutta, Coomaraswamy scored a hit with *Myths of the Hindus and Buddhists,* a best seller he had coauthored with Sister Nivedita (completing two-thirds of the text after her death in 1911) that featured lavish illustrations by Nandalal Bose, Abanindranath Tagore, and their school.[28]

In both Ceylon and India, Coomaraswamy's writings on the need for "national" aesthetics made essentially the same point. The inhabitants of these two countries had forgotten how to express their distinctive cultural selves and instead were colluding in an unthinking adoption of Western habits and mores that deprived them of their respective national identities. In a seven-page essay entitled *Borrowed Plumes,* the pamphlet which launched the "Ceylon Social Reform" campaign in 1905, Coomaraswamy tells us how he was led to question the value of advancing Westernisation by the incongruous appearance outside his home in the Kandyan highlands of a Sinhalese mother and child dressed in the "borrowed plumes" of European fashion. However, what is striking in this short work is how quickly the author's reflections on Ceylon's battle with Westernisation led him to imagine a struggle not of national but of civilisational proportions:

> I thought how different it might be if we Ceylonese were bolder and more independent, not afraid to stand on our own legs and not ashamed of our own nationalities. Why do we not meet the wave of civilisation on equal terms, reject the evil and choose the good? Our eastern civilisation was here 2,000 years ago; shall its spirit be broken utterly before the new commercialism of the West; or shall we be strong enough to hold our national ideals intact, to worship beauty in the midst of ugliness, to remember old wisdom and yet not despise the new.[29]

Coomaraswamy's broader civilisational concerns were apparent again a few years later when he wrote directly on Swadeshi in India. In an essay entitled "The Deeper Meaning of the Struggle" he warned of the dangers of an Indian nationalism that surrendered itself to materialism and particularism:

> Five hundred years hence it will matter little to humanity whether a few Indians, more or less, have held official posts in, or a few million bales of cloth been manufactured in Bombay or Lancashire factories; but it will matter much whether the great ideals of Indian culture have been carried forward or allowed to die. It is with these that Indian Nationalism is essentially concerned, and upon these that the fate of India as a nation depends.[30]

As these writings suggest, Coomaraswamy was never really a political nationalist, despite being fêted by his Madras publishers, Ganesh and

Co., during his lifetime as a "nation builder" of modern India. Rather, Coomaraswamy viewed the importance of Swadeshi-style action in terms of the cultural autonomy it granted its participants and the cosmopolitan possibilities it offered. Poets and artists, he claimed, did more to build up nations than did politicians and it was in the cultural sphere that nationalist energies ought to most be applied. He judged that "in meeting the wave of civilisation on equal terms" the various nationalities of Asia would come to a greater appreciation of those cultural ties that bound them together. That he had by 1914 distanced himself from the anticolonial political struggle in Asia was due, in no small part, to his belief that the most significant battle with European colonialism was one that required Asians to seek out their common cultural idealism.[31]

Such an attitude comes across particularly strongly in Coomaraswamy's 1907 address to the Ceylon Social Reform Society, delivered on the eve of his departure for India and entitled "India and Ceylon." In this lecture he expatiated on the "mental and spiritual relation" between the two countries and asked his audience to consider whether "Ceylon is in the future to belong in these respects to India or to Europe? Is India to be our motherland still or shall we prosper more as orphans?" To revive Ceylon's "social institutions, wealth, power, arts, industries and sciences" the country's leaders had to realise "that India in the past has been the chief factor in the growth of civilisation and culture, and that in that work even Ceylon has played no insignificant part." India represented an "open book" for the Ceylonese to study, in that it shared so many of the latter's "difficulties and doubts."

As his lecture continued, it became clear that the kind of nationalism Coomaraswamy advocated, far from accentuating the "differences between men" and hindering "a realisation of the brotherhood and unity of humanity," in fact implied "internationalism." "Nationalism," he argued, was "essentially altruistic": it was a "people's recognition of its own special function and place in the civilized world." "Internationalism" was "the recognition of the rights of others to *their* self-development, and of the incompleteness of the civilized world if *their* special culture-contribution is missing."

Arguing further in this vein, Coomaraswamy insisted that "India without Ceylon is incomplete . . . The nobler of the two great Indian epics unites India with Ceylon in the mind of every Indian." As a "mirror" to India, Ceylon provided "a more perfect window through which to gaze on India's past than can be found in India itself." His parting advice for his fellow Society members was that they should travel to India "in the pilgrim spirit," direct young men to study at Indian universities, read Indian papers and magazines and send "at least one representative to the [Indian National] Congress."[32]

After Coomaraswamy arrived in India, his concept of a pan-Indian civilisation that incorporated Ceylon broadened significantly. His writings from 1907, once he had been exposed to the cosmopolitan milieu at Jorasanko, reiterated the idea that India was the wellspring of *all* Asian civilisation. When he wrote about India and Asia in the following decade, he effortlessly (and without hesitation) slipped from discussing one entity to considering the other; and this without the supporting evidence that he would later have to hand in Boston to back his implicit claim that the two were identical. In his series of Indian essays entitled *The Dance of Shiva* (first published in 1918) "India" and "Asia" seamlessly merge. India's present condition as a "co-operative society in a state of decline" becomes within a few paragraphs "the decay of Asia" and its "rapid degradation," a degradation caused by Europe's reduction of all "Asiatic" society "from the basis of *dharma* to the basis of contract." Elsewhere, the movement of "Young India" towards "national education and social reconstruction" is quickly recast as the "development of Asia," a process in which the Western world must play a more positive role lest Asia's "degradation" lead to a replica of a Western "Industrialism or Imperialism" that might menace "European social idealism."[33]

When Coomaraswamy arrived in America in 1917 to take up his appointment with the Boston Museum of Fine Arts, his sense of pan-Asian purpose travelled with him. In one of his earliest reports for the institution that he was to be associated with until his death in 1947, he wrote:

> The Museum now possesses the materials for a logical presentation of Asiatic art as a consistent whole—a unity in that sense which Mr Okakura so often insisted upon. It is precisely the art of India, linked as it is on the one hand with that of Persia, and on the other hand with that of China—the whole foundation of Chinese Buddhist art being formally Indian—which needs to be represented in any museum pretending to deal fundamentally with the art of the Far East: and it is only due to various accidents that the art of India, which is to so great extent an art of *sources*, has been so long neglected.[34]

Such an outlook shaped Coomaraswamy's major contribution to art history, his 1927 study *Indian and Indonesian Art*, which in fact covered most parts of modern South, Southeast, and East Asia, and which argued that Indian influence had extended to China, Korea, and Japan through both overland and sea routes.[35] The following decade, he reaffirmed his Okakura-like position that "Asia, in all her diversity, is nevertheless a living spiritual unity" by drawing out common philosophical approaches to art as revealed by learned men in India, Japan, and China.[36]

But there was another key shift in Coomaraswamy's thinking evident by the time he left India and likewise at least partly attributable to his Calcutta sojourn with the Tagores. In his remarkable 1916 essay "Intellectual Fraternity," he took the occasion of the war in Europe to argue that not just Indian thinkers, but Lao Tze and Jesus, as well as "Plato and Kapt, Tauler, Behman and Ruysbroeck, Whitman, Nietzsche and Blake," all, if one looked deeply enough, shared streams of thought in common. Moreover, he wrote, "it is not only in Philosophy and Religion—Truth and Love—but also in Art that Europe and Asia are united . . ." Where the two civilisations differed was in their accumulated wisdom over the ages: "the fullness of the Asiatic experience . . . still contrasts so markedly with European youth." Nonetheless, the two sides remained compatible "and we must demand of a coming race that men should act with European energy, and think with Asiatic calm . . ." The problem of the current age was that "European progress has long remained in doubt, because of its lack of orientation." But in this "present hour of decision" there was hope, since Europe had discovered Asia, whose task it was now to reorient the West toward the creation of "a social order founded on Union."[37]

Such hopes for what Coomaraswamy at the outset of this essay termed "a common civilisation of the world" were certainly influenced by his visits to London in the early 1900s and his discovery there of Blake, Nietzsche, and of the other European writers whom he listed. Nonetheless, his new universalism retained a direct connection with Calcutta as part of a discussion almost simultaneously shared by the Tagores. For, in the very same year that "Intellectual Fraternity" appeared in print, Bengal's favourite literary son (as he later recalled) was standing with an international friend looking out over the sea near the Japanese port of Yokohama, when his thoughts also turned to the horrors of the European war. And just as Coomaraswamy had done, so Rabindranath Tagore came to the conclusion that what mankind needed was the nurture of a common, universal civilisation.

TAGORE'S EASTERN ODYSSEY

Tagore's personal journey through Swadeshi to pan-Asianism, and eventually to universal humanism, has been charted by several studies and biographies.[38] Unsurprisingly, it was a journey that both Coomaraswamy and Okakura were closely associated with. Coomaraswamy supported Tagore's work through his Indian essays, translated Tagore's poems into English, and became a regular guest at Tagore's ashram at Santiniketan. As for Okakura, Tagore described the Japanese art critic as his "intimate friend" and following their meeting in 1902 became (at least until 1916) a confirmed Japanophile. Following Okakura's first visit to India, the Tagore family welcomed a number of Japanese artists whom Okakura had recommended. Indeed, at a time when Tagore's patriotic Bengali songs were being sung down Calcutta streets by Swadeshis on the march, the Tagore salon was revealing its increasing eclecticism. At Jorasanko, Rathindranath and Surendranath Tagore established the "Vichitra" (multi-coloured) club, which hosted, among other events, Chinese- and Japanese-themed banquets, pageants, and literary soirees.[39]

Tagore's own literary adventures east of Calcutta began in earnest around the time he first made Okakura's acquaintance. In 1901, the Cambridge don G. Lowes Dickinson published his *Letters from John Chinaman*, an indictment of the activities of Western powers within China and a defence of China's civilisational superiority over Europe.[40] Tagore, under what was a widespread impression that the then anonymous author of the *Letters* was a genuine Chinese official, reviewed the work for *Bangadarshan* (The Vision of Bengal), the Bengali periodical he was then editing. Typical of his generation, Tagore surmised from the *Letters* that "there is a deep and vast unity among the various peoples of Asia" and that "Indian civilisation is one with Asian civilisation." But what Tagore added to the discussion was the notion that the progress other countries had subsequently made with this civilisation might be for Indians a source of national pride:

> If we can see that our ancient civilisation has spread to China and Japan then we can understand that it has a great place as an expression of human nature, that it is not merely the words of manuscripts. If we can see that China and Japan have experienced success within this civilisation, then our own inglorious and impoverished condition disappears, and we can see where our real treasure lies.

Tagore also rehearsed the charge that trade and politics dominated European civilisation whereas the key aspects that defined Asian civilisation were its spirituality and effective social organisation. He believed, along with Okakura and Coomaraswamy, that Asia was locked in a civilisational struggle in which its spiritual life was threatened by an invasion of Western materialism. The struggle now demanded, and would further consolidate, pan-Asian solidarity. "Asia is growing ever more eager to defend this life," the poet wrote. "In this we [of India] are not alone; we remain linked to the whole of Asia." [41]

When the Swadeshi movement began, Tagore invested it with a wider pan-Asian significance from the outset. During the antipartition agitation of 1904–1905, reports of Japan's victories over Russia in the Korean peninsula simultaneously filtered through to Calcutta and inspired Tagore to take up a Japanese theme in his writings. One of his three *haiku* poems from this period links a past when monks journeyed from India to Japan with the teachings of the Buddha, to a present in which Indians now came to Japan's door "as disciples, to learn the teachings of action." In mid-1904, Tagore took the opportunity of a public lecture on "Swadeshi Samaj" to further elaborate his pan-Asian sentiments. In Bengali he told his audience of a time when:

> China, Japan and Tibet, who are so careful to bar their windows against the advances of Europe, welcomed India with open arms as their *guru*, for she had never sent out armies for plunder and pillage, but only her messages of peace and good will. This glory, which India had earned as the fruit of her self-discipline, was greater than that of the widest of Empires.[42]

Swadeshi, at least when Tagore and Coomaraswamy spoke, was not merely an expression of local and communal difference but a celebration of the civilisation that India had given to the rest of Asia—and to be understood in these broader international terms.

Following the end of the Swadeshi campaign (until he was drawn out again in 1917 by the internment of the Theosophist and Home Ruler Annie Besant), Tagore turned his back on nationalist politics in protest against the violence advocated by Bengali revolutionaries. As a consequence, he found that he was to a degree ostracized by Calcutta's literary circles. Yet this respite from the public eye also allowed him to explore firsthand the cultural unity that he presupposed Indian civilisation had gifted the rest of the region. In February 1913, Tagore visited Okakura in Boston and during their meeting (so the poet recalled) his Japanese friend brought to life once more the splendours of an Asian civilisation and spirituality awaiting "another opportunity to have the fullness of illumination." Okakura requested that Tagore accompany him to China so that the poet might know her truly.[43] Though their joint pilgrimage never eventuated (Okakura died a few months after their reunion in Boston), such a journey continued to lure Tagore in the next two years, becoming a reality in 1916 when he undertook to lecture in Japan.

Unlike Tagore's subsequent journeys across the Indian Ocean, which inspired him to pen some of his most evocative songs and poems, his first voyage east from Calcutta came as a rude shock.[44] The ugliness and sameness of the ports of Rangoon, Penang, Singapore and Hong Kong offended his aesthetic sensibilities, leading him to rail against the capitalism and industrialisation that had (in a practical sense) brought Asia closer together.[45] Yet, however much he might himself be discomforted, these same industrial connections had brought the fame of the Indian Nobel prize winner to many parts of the region in advance of him.

This fact was no more evident than when Tagore first set foot on Japanese soil. Extensive national press coverage of his arrival in Kobe meant that when he emerged from Tokyo station he was greeted by a crowd estimated in the region of 20,000 to 50,000. Following his address to the Nihon Bijutsuin (The Japan Art Academy) on the unity of Asian art (a fitting subject considering that Okakura had been the founder of this institution), he was invited to lecture at Tokyo Imperial University. Dressed all in white and wearing a Daoist cap that had been a gift from Okakura, Tagore addressed a packed auditorium of around 2,000 people that included over one hundred Indians and a similar number of European and Americans. Speaking in English, Tagore's subject was "The Message of India to Japan."[46]

Though Okakura's *The Awakening of Japan* was not then available in Japanese translation, anyone who had read the original 1904 English edition ought to have immediately recognized a familiar literary presence. Perhaps Tagore even felt that his lecture fulfilled some remaining mission of Okakura to Japan that the latter's death had conspired to cut short.

Just as Okakura had in *The Awakening* (as we will shortly see), Tagore began his argument with the assertion that all Asia had till recently been placed under the "bondage of dejection" and had been subject (in language that directly recalls Okakura's own) to the "darkness of night." But then, suddenly, "Japan rose from her dreams and in giant strides left centuries of inaction behind, overtaking the present time in its foremost achievement." Again echoing Okakura's earlier work, Tagore insisted that he did not believe that Japan had attained its current position by "imitating the West" but rather because she was a "child of the Ancient East." Finally, in a passage reminiscent of *The Ideals*, Tagore described to his audience a united Asia that had once existed before the "darkness" fell:

> I cannot but bring to your mind those days when the whole of Eastern Asia from Burma to Japan was united with India in the closest ties of friendship, the only natural tie which can exist between nations. There was a living communication of hearts, a nervous system evolved through which messages ran between us about the deepest needs of humanity . . . ideas and ideals were exchanged, gifts of the highest love were offered and taken; no difference of languages and customs hindered us in approaching each other heart to heart; no pride of race or insolent consciousness of superiority, physical or mental, marred our relation; our arts and literatures put forth new leaves and flowers under the influence of this sunlight of united hearts; and races belonging to the different lands and languages and histories acknowledged the highest unity of man and the deepest bond of love.

The Japan of the present day, Tagore argued, had before it the "mission of the East to fulfill." Western civilisation had "presented before the world grave questions": the conflict between the "individual and the state," "labour and capital," "the man and the woman," and "the greed of material gain and the spiritual life of man," to name but a few. Tagore therefore exhorted the Japanese nation to apply its "Eastern mind," its "spiritual strength," "love of simplicity" and "recognition of social obligation," so as "to cut out a new path for this great unwieldy car of progress, shrieking out its loud discords as it runs." "Of all countries in Asia," he asserted, "here in Japan you have the freedom to use the materials you have gathered from the West according to your genius and your need. Therefore your responsibility is all the greater, for in your voice Asia shall answer the questions that Europe has submitted to the conference of Man."[47]

ISLAM AND THE IDEA OF ASIA

Between 1900 and 1920, members of the Tagore circle used ideas and expressions to convey Asia's cultural unity that so overlapped we might easily imagine them regularly borrowing one another's scripts. It is true that their individual writings on Asia never cohered into a systematic ideology; nevertheless, in fundamental respects they articulated a shared intellectual sensibility. All of these writers agreed that Asia had been united in the past by centuries of interaction and exchange. All thought the present age demanded that Asians once again become conscious of the deep, underlying unities that shaped their common experience—whether it was to save Asia from the West, or, indeed, to save European civilisation from itself.

But the way these writers imagined that Asia had actually become "one" brings to light a major omission. Tagore, Okakura, Coomaraswamy, and Nivedita all presumed Asian civilisation was derived from the key elements of Hinduism, Buddhism, and, to a lesser extent, Confucianism. Buddhism took pride of place and was crowned as "that great ocean of idealism"—the primary means by which past cultural exchange and common ideals had generated a regional unity. Other faiths such as Daoism or Zoroastrianism rarely received a mention. In the Tagore circle's discussions of Asian civilization, Islam was particularly conspicuous by its absence. The great world religion that through text, trade, and pilgrimage had over the centuries renewed and intensified global interconnection from Batavia to the Bosphorus was largely overlooked.

Not only that, when Okakura took up his pen those historical figures who professed Islam's tenets were increasingly depicted as the great disrupters of Asia's golden age of cultural intercourse. In *The Ideals* (perhaps under the influence of Sister Nivedita) Okakura described Islam as "Confucianism on horseback, sword in hand" and implied the existence of a "Western" Asia, which in the case of Baghdad and her "great Saracenic culture" demonstrated "Chinese, as well as, Persian, civilisation and art."[48] However, a year later in *The Awakening of Japan*, a book that was equally well-received by Calcutta elite, Okakura painted a starkly contrary picture. Revisiting the notion of the golden age of "Buddhaland," he revised his earlier narrative of Asian civilisation by pointing out the source of its decline:

> The decadence of Asia began long ago with the Mongol conquest in the thirteenth century. The classic civilisations of China and India shine brighter by contrast with the night that has overtaken them since that disastrous irruption. The children of the Huang-ho and the Ganges had from early days evolved a culture comparable with that of the era of highest enlightenment in Greece and Rome, one which even foreshadowed the trend of advanced thought in modern Europe. Buddhism, introduced into China and the farther East during the early centuries of the Christian era, bound together the Vedic and Confucian ideals in a single web, and brought about the unification of Asia. A vast stream of intercourse flowed throughout the extent of the whole Buddhaland. Tidings of any fresh philosophical achievement in the University of Nalanda, or in the monasteries of Kashmir, were brought by pilgrims and

wandering monks to the thought centers of China, Korea and Japan. Kingdoms often exchanged courtesies, while peace married art to art. From this synthesis of the whole Asiatic life a fresh impetus was given to each nation . . . Thus, while Christendom was struggling with mediaevalism, the Buddhaland was a great garden of culture where each flower of thought bloomed in individual beauty.

"But alas!" Okakura continued, "the Mongol horseman under Jenghis Khan were to lay waste these areas of civilisation, and make of them a desert like that out of which they themselves came." The Mogul emperors of Delhi who "had embraced the Arabian faith as they sped on their conquest through southern Asia" not only "exterminated Buddhism, but also persecuted Hinduism." It was:

a terrible blow to Buddhaland when Islam interposed a barrier between China and India greater than the Himalayas themselves. The flow of intercourse, so essential to human progress, was suddenly stopped . . . By the Mongol conquest of Asia, Buddhaland was rent asunder, never again to be reunited . . . We have not only permitted the Mongol to destroy the unity of Asia, but have allowed him to crush the life of Indian and Chinese culture. From both the thrones of Peking and Delhi, the descendants of Jenghis Kahn perpetuated a system of despotism contrary to the traditional policies of the lands they had subjugated. Entire lack of sympathy between the conquerors and the conquered, the introduction of an alien official language, the refusal to the native of any vital participation in administration, together with dreadful clash of race-ideals and religious beliefs, all combined to produce a mental shock and anguish of spirit from which the Indians and Chinese have never recovered . . . So in India the reactionary uprising of the Marathas and the Sikhs against the Mohammedan tyrants, though partially successful, did not crystallize into a universal expression of patriotism. This lack of unity enabled a Western power to shape her destinies.[49]

In their concept of Asia's geographical and cultural boundaries, other members of the Tagore circle were less hard-line. Sister Nivedita, Coomaraswamy, and Tagore all imagined India to lie at the heart of Asia, with "Eastern Asia" stretching out from Burma to Japan and "Western Asia" comprising Persia, Arabia, and perhaps long ago (at least in Nivedita's eyes) the Nile delta and ancient Greece. However, the primary focus throughout their writings was on a cultural zone that linked India with the civilisations of China, Japan, and the countries in between. Nivedita's first chapter in the *Myths of the Hindus and Buddhists* claimed that ancient Egypt and Arabia were destined "from their geographical positions, to be overrun and suffer destruction of their culture." Remarking in passing that "civilisation" in "Western Asia" would in future again "accumulate," she turned to discussing the historical intercourse between India, China, "and half a dozen minor nations" during the "Gupta empire," intercourse which "only the rise of Islam was effective in ending."[50]

Coomaraswamy's writings before 1920 similarly focused on an Asia that spread out east from India. On occasion they even presented the influence of Islamic culture as a disruption and a divergence. Writing on Ceylon, Coomaraswamy argued that the island's history gave a better insight into India's past civilisation because its art and literature were "free from Mohammedan influence." In a later discussion of Rajput painting he depicted the compositions of the Mughal court as some worldly deviation from the long Indian tradition of spiritual painting. Though he agreed that "Western Asia" (especially Persia) had cultural achievements of its own, as late as 1932 his theorizing about the philosophical unity that underlay "Asiatic art" had still not engaged directly with this oeuvre. One of his studies, in his own words, excluded "the art of Western Asia, more specifically Muhammedan art, though it would be interesting and well worth while to show to what extent Muhammedan art is truly Asiatic."[51]

By comparison, Tagore would appear to have been least dismissive of the Islamic world's contribution to a unified Asian civilisation. In his youth, the poet dreamt of being a Bedouin and devoured *The Arabian Nights*. After 1920 he visited Iraq and Persia (whose contribution to Bengali culture he acknowledged) as well as Java, where he lamented the sight of a once great Muslim society now under European subjugation.[52] Nonetheless, before 1920, Tagore seems to have had little contact with Muslim intellectuals in India. As his "Message of India to Japan" indicates, he was then primarily concerned with the "Eastern Asia" that Okakura had promised to show him.[53] In effect, though the explicitness of Okakura's rejection was exceptional, the Tagore circle shared in the exclusion of Islam's contribution both to Asian civilisation and to the historical intercourse on which they believed that Asian unity had rested. Their discovery of Asia invariably led these thinkers to look from Calcutta further east, along the ancient highways where, in their eyes, the "great ocean of idealism" was most immediate and apparent.

IDEAS OF ASIA IN CIRCULATION

What, then, was the impact of these ideas? Did they remain confined to the rarefied atmosphere of the Tagore salon, amounting to little more than an elite sideshow set against the grander narrative of popular Asian nationalism? Or, did they have an influence beyond Jorasanko, and become embedded in the wider consciousness of early-twentieth-century Asian literati?

Certainly, Tagore's "Message of India to Japan" in 1916 was a failure. His lectures in Tokyo stimulated considerable debate for a time within Japanese intellectual circles, with various "writers, religious leaders, philosophers and pan-Asianists," so historian Stephen Hay has written, using the poet's arrival to set forth "their own views on the issues he raised in their respective spheres."[54] Nevertheless, outright support for his message—that Japan should develop a modernity which held true to Asian social and spiritual ideals and so inspire the rest of the region—was minimal. Tokyo's two main daily newspapers were notably muted in their response and once Tagore had left Japan's shores his idea that all Asians shared a common civilisation passed (for a time) out of mind with him.[55] Tagore himself was stung by the way, as he recalled, some Japanese newspapers had praised his utterances for their "poetical qualities, while adding with a leer that it was the poetry of a defeated people."[56] His reception in Japan pushed him to an even stronger rejection of the Western-inspired nation-state as the be-all and end-all of Asian liberation.

However, across a colonized Indian Ocean arena, one that had received from the British Empire its regional *lingua franca*, the taste for such pan-Asianism was more evident. Even a brief survey of the Anglophone press across three port cities of the Bay of Bengal reveals periodicals that reprinted, paraphrased, imitated, emulated, and even preempted many of the core ideas about Asian unity articulated at Jorasanko.

Buddhist periodicals in Colombo and Calcutta seized on the idea that India was the original wellspring of an Asian civilisation that had spread out through Okakura's ancient "Buddhaland." Repeatedly these journals featured articles, lectures, or portions of books that highlighted, as one author saw it, a past golden age when "the high culture of ancient India was seen by the Greek and Chinese who came to India centuries before the invasion of India by Arabs and Europeans."[57] The Colombo *Buddhist* in 1895 (lifting a leader published originally in the Calcutta *Indian Mirror*) advocated the "sea-voyage moment" and called on Indians "to visit Asiatic countries, chiefly the Buddhistic ones," which "their ancestors in the far past helped to educate and civilise after the fashion of the then existing Hindu religious and philosophic ideals." A decade later, the *Maha Bodhi Journal* featured on one occasion the lecture of the Reverend Farquar, a Calcutta clergyman, and, on another, an article by Coomaraswamy on the migration of Indian art, so as to emphasize that India under Buddhist rule had spread civilisation to both China and Japan. The same journal sometimes presented India's civilizing role across Asia in squarely racial terms. "What Buddhism has done for non-Aryan peoples to civilize them," an article on "Ancient India" posited, "may be learnt by the historical works treating of Burma, Siam, China, Japan, Mongolia and Tibet."[58]

These same periodicals likewise reveal the deep impression made by the claim that "Asia is one." Interestingly, when this notion was contested, as occurred in 1916, it elicited a response from no less a figure than the former Bengali revolutionary Lala Lajput Rai. Lajput Rai was prompted to defend Asia's perceived unity publicly by the appearance in India of another work by G. Lowes Dickinson (the same author responsible for the *Letters From John Chinaman* that had partly inspired Tagore's early expression of pan-Asianism). In his *Essay on the Civilisations of India, China and Japan*, Dickinson argued that "the East is not a unity, as implied in the familiar antithesis of East and West. Between India, on the one hand, and China or Japan, on the other, there is as great a difference as between India and any western country." Lajput Rai's response was published in the Calcutta *Modern Review*, then summarized and given further circulation by Annie Besant's *New India* paper in Madras. According to the Madras organ, Lajput Rai successfully demonstrated that there was at the present time a "fundamental unity" between India, China, and Japan, partly because Western influences were "producing more or less the same results and threatening to make the East a bad and imperfect copy of the West." The West threatened each nation's "individual" ethos as well as its shared "continental" character. But despite such a threat, Asian countries manifested a greater "unity" than ever before because they were bound together by the "sameness of their religions, intellectual and social outlook, and in a manner also the sameness of their economic life."[59]

Undoubtedly, the dominant Asian story during this period (at least in terms of column inches) was the present and historical relationship between India and Japan. Preempting the Tagore circle's discovery of Japan by a few years, journals in Calcutta and Colombo drew attention to the heightened presence of Japanese scholars and monks in South Asia who travelled to the region to study, to teach, or to undertake Orientalist research. The *Indian Mirror* recorded in 1895: "Japanese visitors have been coming among us for the last few years, and we have looked upon them in much wonder, and some disdain, for the Japanese do the grossest injustice to themselves in their externals." Nonetheless, the same leader recommended that Indians visit "the first independent country in Asia" so as to understand the "spiritual power behind the Japanese race," a power the paper believed to be Buddhist. The "revival of veneration and love for India among the Japanese" was a cause for joy: "The Buddhists have many more things in common with the Hindus than the Europeans can possibly have, and are our brothers in spirit, though not in blood." The contemporary exchange that the *Indian Mirror* advocated was to consist of Japanese teaching the Hindus "manly virtues," while the Hindus in turn would reinitiate the Japanese into the "great spiritual religion which was preached to all nations in the time of Asoka."[60] On another occasion, the same paper aired the views of Japanese monks themselves. The Reverend Daito Shimaji asserted:

Japanese were spiritually united with the Indians 1350 years ago . . . It is, therefore, our sincere wish that the two nations would soon come to a better understanding of each other and entertain a closer relation materially as well as spiritually.[61]

Formal bilateral discussions with Japanese aristocrats, merchants, and students also received press coverage. In 1910, the *Maha Bodhi Journal* noted that a certain Count Otani had arrived in Calcutta to persuade Dharmapala of the need for further Buddhist propaganda efforts in Japan because, as he put it, many Japanese Buddhists still believed India was "in heaven" (Dharmapala had earlier visited Japan with the Theosophist Henry Steele Olcott). Later that year, the same journal reported on activities of the Indo-Japanese Association (established in 1904), whose purpose was to enhance trade relations between both countries. At around the same time, Indian students studying in Japan became prime movers in the establishment of another pan-Asian association, the Asian Solidarity Society, which in its brief eighteen-month existence brought together not just Indians and Japanese but also some Chinese.[62]

In addition, several books and articles featured in these periodicals reinforced the claim that Japan represented an alternative model for Asian modernity. In the same year that Tagore presented his "Message of India to Japan," his friend Pramatha Nath Bose published his *The Illusions of New India*. In this work Bose argued that the British in India had created a class of educated Indian "who can hardly be said to have a mind of his own—It is more or less a shadow, a reflection of the Western mind." What Indians needed instead was a Japanese-style education in economics, hygiene, aesthetics, culture, morals, and science. Japan had learnt its science—"science which was new to Europe as well"—from the West, but the ethics of the State she had derived from "the system of Confucius" and the "ethics of religion, morality and hygiene from Buddhist India."[63]

The closer attention that editors and contributors paid to Japan, no doubt largely through the writings of Okakura, meant that Confucianism also emerged to take its place alongside Buddhism as the philosophical inspiration behind Japanese advances. The Allahabad *Hindustan Review*, for instance, featured an article by the American P. S. Reinsch, entitled "Energism in the Orient," which claimed that Japan had the "virility of a giant" and had taken "the two foremost sages [Buddha and Confucius] for her spiritual and ethical guidance."[64] Whereas in 1895 Japan's defeat of China had been portrayed by at least one Buddhist paper in Colombo as the victory of a "modified Buddhistic metaphysic" over the "unspirituality, narrowness and selfishness of the old Agnostic's philosophy," by 1910 Confucian teachings and commentaries were being featured in the *Maha Bodhi Journal*, the flagship pan-Buddhist magazine organ across India, Burma, and Ceylon.[65]

Finally, the Tagore circles' own ideas about Asian unity made a significant impact beyond the Indian Ocean. As we have begun to appreciate, Okakura and Coomaraswamy, as respected scholars who took up appointments in the United States, fed their thoughts about Asian aesthetics directly into Western academe, helping to sustain an Orientalism that some critics might accuse of being essentialist and reductionist.

Likewise, Tagore himself, although he did not take up an academic appointment, became a prime mover in Orientalist scholarship back in India. A few months after his revelatory moment at Yokohama, he wrote to his son Rathindrinath (then in charge of his ashram at Santiniketan) outlining his plan for the creation of a world university.[66] In pursuit of this project, Tagore relied heavily on the support of Sylvain Levi, the French Orientalist then building his career around establishing the migration of Indian civilisation into central and eastern Asia. In late-1921, Levi arrived at Santiniketan for the launch of Tagore's Visva-Bharati University and to set up its Department of Chinese and Tibetan Studies. Such a grand educational edifice to Asia's civilisational unity continues to thrive over eighty years later.

In a sense, the founding constitution of the Visva-Bharati University represents the Tagore circle's closing manifesto on Asian unity—the point at which two decades of discussion finally become institutionalized. By today's standards the university's overall raison d'être might sound rather postmodern: to study the mind of man "in its realisation of different aspects of truth from diverse points of view." Nonetheless, its more immediate goals recall those "exhilarating" evenings spent in debate at Jorasanko:

[1] To bring together . . . the various scattered cultures of the East, the fittest place for such endeavour being India, the heart of Asia, into which have flowed the Vedic, Buddhist, Semitic, Zoroastrian, and other cultural currents originating in different part[s] of the Orient from Judea to Japan; to bring to a realisation the fundamental unity of the tendencies of different civilisations of Asia, thereby enabling the East to gain a full consciousness of its own spiritual purpose, the obscuration of which has been the chief obstacle in the way of [2] a true co-operation of East and West, the great achievements of these being mutually complementary and alike necessary for Universal Culture in its completeness.[67]

Only, the discourse of Asian civilisation had by now transformed into an academic discipline with a clearly defined set of desired outcomes. And it was at this point—as the first students filed into their lecture halls and took their places to listen to renowned authorities such as Sylvain Levi— that the idea of Asia entered a new stage in its Indian Ocean history, becoming a concept that would henceforth be as much "passed down" as it was "passed around."

ANOTHER ORIENTALISM?

The dynamic nature of the idea of Asia that the Tagore circle and other Asian literati explored raises an immediate question: How can we argue that such an idea was simply, at its heart, a European Orientalist construction?

Obviously, the broader context in which this discourse of Asian civilisation was generated and circulated was colonial: "Asia is one" was especially well received amongst multilingual literati accustomed to life in colonial entrepôts, the maritime nodal points through which European imperialism worked most visibly to knit the region closer together. But if we went further and argued that the idea of Asia as a cultural unity was largely a European Orientalist fantasy—one swallowed wholesale by colonized minds across the Indian Ocean world—then we would be on less stable ground.

European Orientalist scholarship, especially European archeological excavations of Buddhist sites in India, certainly inspired the literati we have studied in their imagining of a golden Asian past. Nonetheless, the impact of European Orientalism should not be overstated nor asserted without some sense of chronology. For one thing, as the careers of Okakura and Coomaraswamy indicate, certain Orientalist scholarship was informed by Asian thinkers from the outset. But more than that, the concept of a unified Asia appears to have become embedded across the Indian Ocean world (at least in the port city journals of India and Ceylon) before European scholars were drawn on to systematically substantiate it. By the time these scholars did make an impact, the idea that Asia was one (with India at its heart) had gone global, thanks largely to the writings of Asian literati who derived their arguments from their experience of the region and who already presupposed its cultural unity.[68].

For Asia was by now an entity that the region's inhabitants, utilising modern methods of social communication and engaging in transoceanic debates, had begun to explore, to imagine, and to define for themselves. So much so that in key respects the discourse of Asian civilisation emanating from within the Indian Ocean world stands clearly apart from representations of the "East" or the "Orient" that Edward Said and his followers have seen as embedded in Western literature and the Euro-American academy.[69] In looking back at the "Night of Asia," as Okakura called it, certain Asian writers did reiterate the belief that in comparison with the West their societies had become atrophied, bereft of internal stimuli, even effeminate and lacking in "manly virtues." However, such a condition was seen to be historically contingent and not an inherent or defining characteristic of the region. The Asian past the literati we have studied preferred to invoke was one in which the region was united by maritime intercourse and the ecumenical strands woven by wandering pilgrims—a golden age of peaceful coexistence and dynamic cultural exchange that only passed with the arrival of foreign invaders. In this respect, Islam was the main historical culprit, but the foe in more recent time was clearly European colonialism.

Moreover, in the early-1900s Asia's golden age appeared on the verge of a rebirth. Once more we return to the point that many Asian literati seemed as much inspired by the "great ocean of idealism" of the present they lived in as by an ancient one that had come centuries before. The modern Indian

Ocean might have relied on steam and electricity for its "energism," it might have been punctuated by ugly, industrial port cities; nonetheless, it was an equal source of visionary aspiration and cosmopolitan hope—the grand universal filter through which even a provincial expression of difference such as the Swadeshi Movement took on a far greater pan-Asian, even global, significance.

NOTES

1. For an important discussion of the way Swadeshi has been represented as the culmination of a "Bengal Renaissance" (with "Calcutta lying at the heart of both") see Sumit Sarkar, *Writing social history* (Oxford, UK: Oxford University Press, 1997), 159–185. Earlier, Sarkar traced the ideological origins of Swadeshi back through Bengal's nineteenth century "renaissance," in *The Swadeshi movement in Bengal, 1903–1908* (New Delhi: People's Publishing House, 1973), 24, 34–35.
2. Andrew Sartori, *Bengal in Global Concept History: Culturalism in the Age of Capital* (Chicago, IL: University of Chicago Press, 2008).
3. To borrow the description of Haridas and Uma Mukherjee, quoted by Roger Lipsey, *Coomaraswamy: Vol. 3—His Life and Work* (Princeton, NJ: Princeton University Press, 1977), 78.
4. At least, that is to say, in the minds of subsequent generations of Bengali literati. See Sarkar, *Writing Social History*, 184–85.
5. One of the most important additions to this literature is Sugata Bose's *A Hundred Horizons: The Indian Ocean in the Age of Global Empire* (Cambridge, MA: Harvard University Press, 2006). Other works with a similar oceanic scope are discussed throughout this chapter.
6. See Mark Ravinder Frost, "Asia's Maritime Networks and the Colonial Public Sphere, 1840–1920," *New Zealand Journal of Asian Studies* 6(2; December 2004): 63–94.
7. For an alternative discussion of this theme, see Prasenjit Duara, "The discourse of civilisation and pan-Asianism," *Journal of World History* 12(1; 2001): 99–132.
8. *Imperial Gazzetteer: Vol. VII*, (Oxford: Clarendon Press, 1908), 337. My emphasis.
9. Tapan Raychaudhuri, *Europe Reconsidered: Perceptions of the West in Nineteenth Century Bengal* (New Delhi: Oxford University Press, 1988), 11.
10. *The Imperial Gazetteer of India, Vol. IX*, 261, 267–269, 283. The statistical breakdown for literacy from the 1901 Census for Calcutta is 20.9 percent amongst males and 3.8 percent amongst females. Among Christians, 75.9 percent were literate, among Hindus 26.5 percent and among Muslims 12.2 percent.
11. Sarkar, *Writing Social History*, 173–74. Sarkar is clearly thinking of fiction, but even here his argument neglects the rise of English-language periodicals run for and by Indians, and their publication of Indian-authored verse and short stories. The *Modern Review* featured English translations of Tagore's short stories and poems from December 1909.
12. Mark Ravinder Frost, "'Wider Opportunities'": Religious Revival, Nationalist Awakening and the Global Dimension in Colombo, 1870–1920," *Modern Asian Studies* 36(4; October 2002): 936–67; also *Enlightened Empires: New Literati in the Indian Ocean World, 1870–1920* (Singapore: Singapore University Press, *forthcoming*).

13. This is to paraphrase (and modify slightly) the conclusion of Stephen Hay in *Asian Ideas of East and West: Tagore and His Critics in Japan, China and India* (Cambridge, MA: Harvard University Press, 1970). For Hay's fuller discussion see ibid., 21–26.

14. Quoted by Raychaudhuri, *Europe Reconsidered*, 86. My emphasis.

15. "Kakuzo Okakura by S. Tagore," *Okakura Kakuzo: Collected English Writings, vol. 3*, ed. Sunao Nakamura (Tokyo: Heibonsha, 1984), 233–42.

16. Hay, *Asian Ideas*, 39.

17. "The Ideals of the East," *Okakura: Collected Writings, vol. 1*, ed. Sunao, 6–129, 13.

18. "A bibliographical introduction," ibid., 433–436; see also Rustom Barucha, *Another Asia: Rabindranath Tagore and Okakura Tenshin* (New Delhi: Oxford University Press, 2006).

19. "Ideals of the East," *Okakura: Collected Writings, vol. 1*, ed. Sunao, 14–16.

20. Ibid., 14–16.

21. Ibid., 13–14.

22. Ibid., 129–32.

23. Ibid., 7–11.

24. On the impact of this work on Bengali nationalists see Rathindranath Tagore, *On the Edges of Time*, 2nd ed. (Calcutta: Visva-Bharati, 1981), 68.

25. "Ideals of the East," *Okakura: Collected Writings, vol. 1*, 11.

26. "Introduction to the Art of Eastern Asia," *Coomaraswamy: Vol. 1—Selected Essays, Traditional Art and Symbolism*, ed. Roger Lipsey (New Jersey: Princeton University Press, 1977), 101–127.

27. These are the words of Muhammed Hafiz Syed, a prolific writer, scholar, and translator, quoted by Lipsey, *Coomaraswamy: Vol. 3—Life and Times*, 88.

28. Sister Nivedita and Ananda K. Coomaraswamy, *Myths of the Hindus and Buddhists*, 5th ed. (London: George G. Harrap and co, 1920), first published in 1913.

29. Ananda K. Coomaraswamy, *Borrowed Plumes* (Kandy: Industrial School, 1905).

30. Ananda K. Coomaraswamy, *Essays in National Idealism* (New Delhi: Munshiram Manoharlal, 1981), 1–2.

31. On Coomaraswamy's attitude to political nationalism and the role of poets and artists in nationalist struggles see Lipsey, *Coomaraswamy: Vol. 3—Life and Times*, 83–4, 90.

32. *Ceylon National Review* 2(4; July 1907): 15–22.

33. *The Dance of Shiva*, revised ed. (New York: Noonday Press, 1969), 19–20, 166.

34. *Annual Report of the Boston Museum of Fine Arts*, 1917, quoted by Walter Whitehill, *Museum of Fine Arts, Boston—A Centennial History* (Cambridge, MA: Harvard University Press, 1977), vol. 1, p. 365.

35. A. K. Coomaraswamy, *History of Indian and Indonesian Art* (New Delhi: Munshiram Manoharlal, 1972), 150–55.

36. Coomaraswamy, "Introduction to the art of Eastern Asia."

37. "Intellectual Fraternity," *Dance of Shiva*, 135–139.

38. See especially Krishna Dutta and Andrew Robinson, *Rabindranath Tagore: The Myriad-Minded Man* (London: Bloomsbury, 1995); Hay, *Asian Ideas*; Bose, *A Hundred Horizons*.

39. Dutta and Robinson, *Tagore*, 209.

40. G. Lowes Dickinson, *Letters From John Chinaman and Other Essays* (London: Allen & Unwin, 1946), 7–44.

41. Tagore's review is quoted at length by Hay, *Asian ideas*, 34–5.

42. Quoted in ibid., 43–44. This lecture was also later published in English. See Rabindranath Tagore, *Greater India* (Madras: S. Ganesan, 1921).
43. Tagore quoted by Hay, *Asian Ideas*, 48–49.
44. On these subsequent voyages see Bose, *A Hundred Horizons*, 233–271.
45. Dutta and Robinson, *Tagore*, 200–201.
46. On Tagore's arrival in Japan see Hay, *Asian Ideas*, 57–63.
47. The "Message of Indian to Japan" was later published as "Nationalism in Japan" in R. Tagore, *Nationalism* (Delhi: Macmillan, 1976); see especially 29–42. See also Okakura's "The Awakening of Japan," *Okakura: Collected Writings—vol. 1*, ed. Sunao, 169–264.
48. "Ideals of the East," 13–14. The same views are evident in Okakura's *The Awakening of the East*. See *Okakura: Collected Writings—vol. 1*, ed. Sunao, 146–47.
49. Ibid., 178–82.
50. Nivedita and Coomaraswamy, *Myths of the Hindus*, 1–3.
51. Coomaraswamy, "India and Ceylon" and his "Introduction to the Art of East Asia." Coomaraswamy eventually engaged with "Western Asia" in 1933 when he became the Boston Museum of Fine Art's Fellow for Research in Indian, Persian, and Mohammedan Art. On Coomaraswamy's attitude to Mogul and Persian painting see Lipsey, *Coomaraswamy: Vol. 1—Life and Times*, 94–104, 260–65.
52. Dutta and Robinson, *Tagore*, 144–45, 277–80, 315–22; Bose, *A Hundred Horizons*, 233–71.
53. Tagore, *Nationalism*, 40–41. Tagore's engagement with Bengal's Muslim literati appears to have begun in the 1920s through his friendship with the young poet Kazi Nazrul Islam. In 1926 Tagore agreed to speak at the University of Dhaka, the same institution whose creation he had opposed the previous decade.
54. Hay, *Asian Ideas*, 118; see also 82–123.
55. Of course, the idea that "Asia is one" would from the late 1930s become the rallying call for Japan's military conquests across Asia.
56. Tagore, *Nationalism*, 23.
57. The quote is from Pramatha Nath Bose, *The Illusions of New India* (Calcutta: W. Newman & Co., 1916), reviewed and summarized by the *Maha Bodhi Journal (MBJ)* 24(6; June 1916): 146–51.
58. "The Hindus and the Japanese," *Buddhist* 24 May 1895; "India and Japan," *MBJ* 25(8; August 1907): 109–12; A. K. Coomaraswamy, "Indiana—on Indian Art in China," ibid., 20(7; July 1912): 216–18; "Ancient India," ibid. 20(4; April 1912): 117–20; see also "India's influence on Japan in the past," ibid., 16(6; June 1908): 85–87; and "Japan and India," ibid., 18(8; August 1910): 585–86.
59. Dickinson, *John Chinaman and Other Essays*, 45–87; "The Unity of the East," *New India* 6 December 1916.
60. Reprinted as "The Hindus and the Japanese," *Buddhist*, 24 May 1895.
61. Rev. Daito Shimaji, "India and Japan in Ancient Times," *Indian Mirror*, 8 December 1909; reprinted in *MBJ* 18(2; February 1910): 372–4.
62. "News and Notes," ibid., 18(2; February 1910): 378–84; "Japan and India"; Rebecca E. Karl, *Staging the World: Chinese Nationalism at the Turn of the Twentieth Century* (Durham, NC: Duke University Press, 2002), 169–176.
63. "Review of 'Illusions of News India' by Mr Pramatha Nath Bose," *MBJ*, 24(6; June 1916): 146–51. See also "What Lessons India Should Learn from Japan at the Present Moment," ibid. 16(9; September 1908): 137–40, reprinted from the *Indian Mirror*. Pramatha Nath Bose was the well-known author of *Epochs of Civilisation* and *A History of Hindu Civilisation under British Rule*.

64. The global journey of this article is revealing in itself. Reinsch's piece first appeared in the Chicago *International Journal of Ethics* in July 1911, before being picked up by Allahabad's *Hindustan Review*, and then reprinted again from this latter periodical in the *Maha Bodhi Journal* early the following year. See "News and Notes," *MBJ* 20 (1; January 1912: 30–32.
65. "Buddhism v. Confucianism," *Buddhist*, 8 Mar. 1895; "Confucius and Some of His Sayings and Apothegrams," *MBJ* 17(9; September 1909): 309–11; and 18(12; December 1910): 685–688.
66. Hay, *Asian ideas,* 126–127.
67. Quoted in Hay, *Asian ideas,* 133–134.
68. For a fuller discussion of the contribution of European Orientalists to the "Greater India" idea of Asia after 1920, see Susan Bayly, "Imagining "Greater India": Indian visions of colonialism in the Indic mode," *Modern Asian Studies* 38(3; 2004): 703–744.
69. Edward W. Said, *Orientalism* (New York: Vintage, 1994).

BIBLIOGRAPHY

Barucha, Rustom. *Another Asia: Rabindranath Tagore and Okakura Tenshin.* New Delhi: Oxford University Press, 2006.
Bayly, Susan. "Imagining 'Greater India': Indian Visions of Colonialism in the Indic Mode." *Modern Asian Studies* 38(3; 2004): 703–744.
Bose, Pramatha Nath. *The Illusions of New India.* Calcutta: W. Newman & Co., 1916.
Bose, Sugata. *A Hundred Horizons: The Indian Ocean in the Age of Global Empire.* Cambridge, MA: Harvard University Press, 2006.
Buddhist. "Buddhism v. Confucianism," 8 Mar. 1895. "The Hindus and the Japanese," 24 May 1895.
Coomaraswamy, A. K. *Borrowed Plumes.* Kandy: Industrial School, 1905.
———. "India and Ceylon." *Ceylon National Review* 2(4; July 1907): 15–22.
———. "Indiana—on Indian Art in China." *Maha Bodhi Journal* 20(7; July 1912): 216–18
———. *The Dance of Shiva, revised ed.* New York: Noonday Press, 1969. First published in 1918.
———. *The History of Indian and Indonesian Art.* New Delhi: Munshiram Manoharlal, 1972. First published in 1927.
———. *Coomaraswamy: Vol. 1—Selected Essays, Traditional Art and Symbolism,* edited by Roger Lipsey. Princeton, NJ: Princeton University Press, 1977.
———. *Essays in National Idealism.* New Delhi: Munshiram Manoharlal, 1981. First published in 1909.
Daito Shimaji, Rev. "India and Japan in Ancient Times." *Indian Mirror,* 8 December 1909.
Duara, Prasenjit. "The Discourse of Civilisation and Pan-Asianism." *Journal of World History* 12(1; 2001): 99–132.
Dutta, Krishna, and Andrew Robinson. *Rabindranath Tagore: The Myriad-Minded Man.* London: Bloomsbury, 1995.
Frost, Mark Ravinder. "Asia's Maritime Networks and the Colonial Public Sphere, 1840–1920." *New Zealand Journal of Asian Studies* 6 (2; December 2004): 63–94.
———. "'Wider Opportunities': Religious revival, nationalist awakening and the global dimension in Colombo, 1870–1920." *Modern Asian Studies* 36 (4; October 2002): 936–67.

————. *Enlightened Empires: New Literati in the Indian Ocean World, 1870–1920.* Singapore: Singapore University Press, *forthcoming.*

Hay, Stephen. *Asian Ideas of East and West: Tagore and His Critics in Japan, China and India.* Cambridge, MA: Harvard University Press, 1970.

Imperial Gazzetteer. Vol. VII–IX. Oxford: Clarendon Press, 1908.

Karl, Rebecca E. *Staging the World: Chinese Nationalism at the Turn of the Twentieth Century.* Durham, NC: Duke University Press, 2002.

Lipsey, Roger. *Coomaraswamy: Volume 3—His Life and Work.* Princeton, NJ: Princeton University Press, 1977.

Lowes Dickinson, G. *Letters From John Chinaman and Other Essays.* London: Allen & Unwin, 1946.

Maha Bodhi Journal. "India's Influence on Japan in the Past," 16(6; Jun. 1908): 85–87; "What Lessons India should learn from Japan at the Present Moment," 16(9; September 1908): 137–40; "Confucius and some of His Sayings and Apothegrams," 17(9; September 1909): 309–311; "News and Notes," 18(2; Feb. 1910): 378–84; "Japan and India," 18(8; August 1910): 585–86; "News and Notes," 20(1; January 1912): 30–32; "Ancient India," 20(4; April 1912): 117–20; "Review of 'Illusions of News India' by Mr Pramatha Nath Bose," 24(6; June 1916): 146–51.

New India. "The Unity of the East," 6 December 1916.

Nivedita, Sister, and Ananda K. Coomaraswamy. *Myths of the Hindus and Buddhists,* 5th ed. London: George G. Harrap and Co., 1920. First published in 1913.

Okakura Kakuzo: *Collected English Writings,* Three Volumes. Edited by Sunao Nakamura. Tokyo: Heibonsha, 1984.

Raychaudhuri, Tapan. *Europe Reconsidered: Perceptions of the West in Nineteenth Century Bengal.* New Delhi: Oxford University Press, 1988.

Said, Edward W. *Orientalism.* New York: Vintage, 1994.

Sarkar, Sumit. *The Swadeshi Movement in Bengal, 1903–1908.* New Delhi: People's Publishing House, 1973.

————. *Writing Social History.* Oxford, UK: Oxford University Press, 1997.

Sartori, Andrew. *Bengal in Global Concept History: Culturalism in the Age of Capital.* Chicago, IL: University of Chicago Press, 2008.

Tagore, Rabindranath. *Greater India.* Madras: S. Ganesan, 1921.

————. *Nationalism.* Delhi: Macmillan, 1976. First published in 1917.

Tagore, Rathindranath. *On the edges of time,* 2nd ed. Calcutta: Visva-Bharati, 1981.

Whitehill, Walter. Museum of Fine Arts, Boston—A Centennial History, Vol. 1. Cambridge, MA: Harvard University Press, 1977.

11 "Is It the Same Sea As Back Home?"

Transformative Complicities As Travelling Tropes in Fictions from Sri Lanka, Mauritius, and South Africa

Miki Flockemann

> "The sea in our loins. A tear-drop for an island. A spinning blue glob-
> ule for a planet. Salt. A wound."
>
> (Romesh Gunesekera, *Reef*) [1]

Romesh Gunesekera's *Reef* presents a delicate balance between differently conceived worlds—coexisting, separating, colliding, intersecting, or swimming apart. The novel explicates flows between the "small world" of the tear-drop island of Sri Lanka, and the wider worlds of travelling ideas, peoples, goods, as well as peoples as goods. The ripples of events seem to run inward and outward, both synchronic and diachronic, apparently expanding and contracting seamlessly. This is achieved through a narrative offering a species of "history from below" in which Sri Lanka's spiral into civil war between the 1960s and 1980s coexists with the material realities of life in the kitchen, seen from the inside, through the eyes of a servant. At the same time, this perspective encompasses the prehistoric deep-sea mountains at "the bottom of the world" just off the fort town of Galle, and beyond the coral reef where one can apparently drift effortlessly to Indonesia and back.[2] All this against the insight gained that, "human history is always a story of someone's diaspora."[3] Arguably, *Reef* can be read as exemplary for exploring the connectedness that is the subject of much recent scholarship on the Indian Ocean world as contact zone.[4] This connectedness, however, is also at the heart of the complicities and ruptures that are tracked in the text.

The complicit subjectivities fictionalized in *Reef* offer scope for analyzing the confluence of debates on complicity within forms of acquiescence or resistance. I argue that Gunesekera's representation of the simultaneous temporality of different worlds (historical, geographic, mythical, experiential, material, and imagined) enables encounters with others and strangers.

This, as Anthony Appiah claims, is crucial for a revised and "partial" cosmopolitanism, "where to be a citizen of the world means to enter into an imaginary conversation with strangers."[5] In order to offer a wider context for this discussion, I draw connections with two texts situated within or abutting on the Indian Ocean, namely, *Boy* (2004) by Lindsey Collen, set in Mauritius,[6] and *Thirteen Cents* (2000) by K. Sello Duiker, located in Cape Town.[7] These three diversely located coming-of-age narratives are touched by the same sea, and this entails intertwined but distinct colonial legacies. In turn, this illustrates the network of connections characterizing the Indian Ocean world; after all, the Portuguese explorers, the Dutch East India Company traders, followed by the British colonists, all left similar imprints that can be tracked from Cape Town to Sri Lanka.[8]

It has been noted that the representation of migrancy in imaginative literature is the most effective vehicle for exploring what has become a worldwide "determining influence," especially as migrants live in multiple worlds which require negotiation and constant self-re-fashioning.[9] Connecting the texts is the representation of an ever-widening spiral of different "worlds" encountered by the protagonist-narrators. These range from the circumscribed world of Duiker's *Thirteen Cents* where the Cape Town street child is a migrant in his own home city, to the unfamiliar worlds glimpsed and imagined within and beyond the Mauritian coastline in Collen's *Boy*. In *Reef*, however, worlds are encountered physically, through the imagination, through narration and books, and of course through migration and exile.[10] The ocean itself features strongly throughout, both as threshold to new and connected worlds, and as horizon marking the limits of the familiar, or known world.[11]

Like *Reef*, Collen and Duiker's texts use the narrative lens of boyhood to track a coming to consciousness.[12] In drawing comparisons between these narratives of boyhood my aim is to uncover the potentially transformative creativity released through the complicitous relationships described in *Reef*, as well as through the narrator's often transgressive situation within the domestic sphere. As diasporic text speaking through the flows of the Indian Ocean world, *Reef* offers a useful counterpoint to the more limiting complicities explored in Collen's *Boy* and Duiker's *Thirteen Cents*. This chapter also hopes to illustrate why, as Isabel Hofmeyr points out, it is productive to address South African writing through a wider lens—specifically that of the Indian Ocean world.[13] Hofmeyr notes the paucity of literature which attempts to think of the Indian Ocean islands in relation to South Africa, and identifies Mauritius for its "critical sets of interactions with South Africa," noting that that such work could "open up new vistas of narrative possibilities for South African literary history."[14] I suggest that Sri Lanka is another island that yields fruitful vistas for comparison, not only for writing from South Africa, but from Sri Lanka as well. Relevant here is the broad claim by some diaspora scholars that representations of the Asian diaspora differ from those commonly associated with the Black

Atlantic in terms of offering a more diffuse, ambiguously layered, and less dichotomized experience.[15] This has implications for the possible futures posited in *Reef*.

Before outlining the comparative framework employed, it is necessary to explain how the concept of complicity will be applied here. The significance of the simultaneous temporality of diverse "worlds" will also need to be addressed when analyzing how complicity can be seen to operate as destabilizing, even productive, rather than primarily collusive or entropic. In general terms, complicity is associated with implicit culpability, coercion, connivance, or collusion. For South Africans the notion of complicity is of course extremely pertinent given our recent history. Of interest is how these local discussions on complicity can extend perspectives on a text like *Reef* which deals with a similarly traumatic recent history. A useful framework for this discussion is Mark Sanders' *Complicities: The Intellectual and Apartheid*,[16] which explores how intellectuals grapple with complicity in imaginative literature.

Sanders outlines various modalities of complicity: for instance, "acting in complicity" entails active collaboration in "acts subject to a system of accountability," while "responsibility in complicity" refers to an acknowledgement of complicity by virtue of a shared "foldedness of human-being."[17] Responsibility thus "requires motivated acknowledgment of one's complicity in injustice."[18] However, it is also this recognition of the "foldedness of human-being" that forms the basis of complicity *and* for opposition.[19] Sanders proposes "to consider resistance and collaboration as interrelated and to explore the problem of complicity without either simply excusing or accusing the parties involved."[20] He claims that, "without relinquishing the pejorative force of the word *complicity*" (his emphasis), his project is to "mount a conceptual generalization of complicity as the very basis for responsibly entering into, maintaining, or breaking off a given affiliation or attachment." He notes that, "in order to resist, victims needed to be aware of and overcome an intimacy of psychic colonization that led them to collaborate with the oppressor." Sanders points out repeatedly how the literary is an ideal vehicle for "representing the complexity of complicity."[21]

Reef certainly lends itself well to an exploration of complicities, since the dual perspective offered by Triton as an older man reflecting on the experiences of his youth shifts between the "then" and the "now," and offers scope for tracking the evolution of the relationship between Triton, the houseboy, and Salgado his employer. Also typical of the *bildungsroman* genre is the account of a series of "new lives" for Triton: first, when at the age of eleven he is brought from his rural village to the Colombo home of Salgado, a gentrified intellectual and marine biologist; another new life begins when he is put in charge of the household following the dismissal of the disgraced head servant. This leads to the discovery of his extraordinary talent for preparing creatively conceived dishes. When the delectable Miss Nili enters their monkish home she ushers in another "new era" for Salgado and Triton. Finally, after Nili and Salgado's relationship disintegrates against the backdrop of Sri Lanka's escalating civil war, Triton begins another new life in exile with Salgado in the United Kingdom. The subtle forms of complicity to be explored here are introduced early in the novel and are intertwined with each new life.

When the eleven-year-old Triton is offered the position of head servant after the expulsion of his arch enemy, Joseph, Triton decides that he does not need to go back to school. Instead, he claims that he will "watch" and "learn" from his dreamy and well-meaning young employer who is described as a leftover of a feudal system of Sinhala privilege. When Salgado halfheartedly suggests that Triton, who is clearly "a smart *kolla* [boy]," should go to school after all, Triton answers:

> "No, Sir." I was sure, at that time, that there was nothing a crowded, bewildering school could offer me that I could not find in his gracious house. "All I have to do is watch you, Sir. Watch what you do. That way I can really learn."
> He sighed, slowly releasing us into the future. "Let's see."
> So I watched him, I watched him unendingly, all the time, and learned to became who I am.[22]

At face value, what is described here is Salgado's awareness, as suggested by his involuntary sigh, of complicity in colluding with the boy's decision, thereby denying Triton his opportunity to complete formal schooling. At the same time, it also reveals the boy's unwitting complicity in maintaining a feudal system of patronage, where the convenience of the master overrides the obligation to the servant. However, the last sentence complicates these easy judgments, since the emphasis on Triton's "watching" suggests agency and evaluation, and the tension between "then" and now, in "becoming" who he "is" later, reveals an awareness of the contingencies of identity, such as outlined by Stuart Hall. According to Hall, diaspora identities involve "'becoming' as well as 'being.'" He claims that these identities "belong to the future as much as to the past" since they "come from somewhere, have histories. But like everything else that is historical, they undergo constant transformation."[23] Clearly, in *Reef* we are not dealing with a "mimic man" or "nervous native" who aspires to replicate his neocolonial master, but something altogether different. This is where Sanders' explication of complicity is helpful.

As noted earlier, in his discussion of an inevitable "responsibility in complicity" which is necessary for opposition, Sanders stresses the recognition of a "folded togetherness of human-being."[24] In other words, "complicity arises at the point of foldedness with the other."[25] He argues that the literary stands for, and offers the "possibility for staging complicity in responsibility not possible in actual life."[26] This is demonstrated by another aspect of the dual perspective offered by Triton's situation as simultaneously cultural (Sinhala) insider, and class-inflected outsider to Salgado's world. Given that Triton, as cook-housekeeper, is "everything" to Salgado, he is privy to the most intimate aspects of the household, including Salgado's personal habits, his books, circle of friends, passion for preserving the coral reef, and apparent innocence about the political realities pressing onto their carefully managed small world. At the same time Triton, as a young man of eighteen, is allowed glimpses into Salgado's relationship with Nili since he is positioned as a kind of vicarious third party: this is demonstrated when, in preparation for Nili moving in, he unpacks her undergarments and marvels at the strangeness of lacy bits of cloth; this intimacy with the couple is piquant and transgressive, for he handles her underwear, yet is a servant, expected to fulfill every whim. At the same time, it is because he is "only a cook" that he is privy to the growing politicization of Salgado's research assistant, Wijetunga—something that his mentor Salgado appears oblivious to.

The liminal stage of fictionalized childhood and dual perspectives offer an intermediate space in which to rehearse "the entering into, maintaining, or breaking off a given affiliation or attachment" referred to by Sanders.[27] For instance, Triton is at first delighted at Nili's addition to "my small world." However, her arrival also results in the expansion of this deliberately contained arena of genteel domestic intimacy which has up til then safely included Salgado's obsession with the coral reef which surrounds Sri Lanka, protecting the island in a living, self-renewing layer from being swamped by the ocean. Salgado's perhaps prophetic fear that " as the coral disappears, there will be nothing but sea and we will all return to it"[28] does posit other, imagined, future "worlds," but these are perceived as metaphysical, somehow less threatening than the immediate encroachment of Sri Lanka's growing political instability as the country slides into civil war. Triton's attempt to maintain the small world of Salgado's gracious home suggests, as Meg Samuelson (quoting Martin and Mohanty) points out, "an illusion of safety and coherence based on the exclusion of specific histories of oppression and resistance, the repression of differences even within oneself." Samuelson's discussion of the continuing exclusions haunting South Africa's so-called rainbow nation has a strong bearing on this interplay between different worlds in *Reef*. Noting Njabulo Ndebele's claim that "an uncanny doubling—or 'split personality'—may be the site from which new forms of creativity, appropriate to our new context, will arise,"[29] Samuelson, like Sanders, argues persuasively that the literary is an ideal form in which to explore the encounter with the stranger outside and within.[30]

The simultaneous temporality of different worlds evoked in *Reef* is one of its most suggestive narrative strategies. In a discussion of Ernst Bloch's essay on nonsynchronism, Keya Ganguly refers to how "coming into the present"—"that is to be synchronous with it" has implications for "the *still possible future* from the *past*" (Bloch's emphasis).[31] At the risk of oversimplifying a complex argument, one could say that this has a bearing on the way different temporal "worlds" are represented in the novel, particularly as Triton experiences them as simultaneously "coming into present." A good example of this is the pivotal Xmas dinner which marks Triton's triumph as master chef, and exposes him to a cosmopolitan cross-section of Sri Lankan society and foreign guests. During the dinner, which is prepared with military precision by Triton, he comes into close contact with Nili's intoxicating body as he serves her ("she didn't notice"[32]) while at the same time listening to an equally intoxicating pageant of Sri Lankan history recounted by the unusually loquacious Salgado:

> I was spellbound. I could see the whole of our world come to life as he spoke: the great tanks, the sea, the forests, the stars. The past resurrected in a pageant of long-haired princes clutching ebony rods . . . His words conjured up adventurers from India north and south, the Portuguese, the Dutch and the British, each with their flotillas of disturbed hope and manic wanderlust.[33]

Salgado's voice brings the past into the present for Triton, and it seems to him as if these different realities are all contingent on one another; he is spellbound both by Nili's perfume and the romanticized Sinhala past. This is yet another new life opening up before Triton. However, when he goes to the kitchen, his domain, to clean up, there is a shift in mood, as he becomes aware of the world of grinding labor that still awaits him: "It tired me just to look at the pile of dishes and plates and the half-eaten carcass."[34] At this point Nili suddenly appears to give him a book of recipes from around the world. As her hand touches his to give him the gift, he is filled with expectation. However, when he sees that she has included "a hundred-rupee note. A piece of paper with drawings etched somewhere in Surrey: a picture, names that meant nothing to me; swirls of coloured ink,"[35] he is devastated. In that gesture he reads that to her he is just a servant: "*Missy*, I wanted to call out and bridge the gulf between us. I was only a servant but I wanted there to be more than money between us in our small world."[36] This dispels Triton's hope that he can maintain the utopian world he has created: instead, he is inevitably confronted with both the presence of the past (albeit a highly selective version of it), and his own status in the present world of circulating global economies etched in swirls of coloured ink. These realities do not negate each other, cannot be kept separate, but are all in the present, synchronous with it. This is what makes the apparent "gulf" all the more painful for him. At the same time, as I will argue, this recognition of worlds in balance is a significant facet of potential for transformation.

While Nili and Salgado enjoy a life of hedonistic pleasure against the backdrop of growing political discontent and the formation of revolutionary groups inspired by events in Cuba, Wijetunga, Salgado's research assistant, attempts to enlist Triton as a comrade in the call for revolutionary change. Witjetunga introduces Triton to the slogan, *"we have to destroy in order to create,*"[37] but Triton rejects Wijetunga's attempt to invoke him as "brother" with the excuse, "But I am only a cook."[38] This is ironic since his most pressing desire is to be seen as more than just a cook by Salgado and Nili. Nevertheless, growing awareness of his own complicity crystallizes into consciousness during an ill-fated poker party that results in the final rupture of Salgado and Nili's relationship. Triton's disillusionment with Salgado's lifestyle and that of his drunken poker cronies is brought to a head when, as of old, he is summoned by the call, "*kolla.*" In stark contrast to his characteristic ever-solicitous conduct, Triton for the first time refuses to be hailed by others as "boy" (just as he had rejected Wijtunga's appellation of "brother"). This scene represents another example of Sanders' consideration of "resistance and collaboration as interrelated."[39] Just at the moment where Triton resists his class-inflected naming, he acknowledges his own complicity in it.

This recognition of compliance is signaled when Triton, in a frenzy of self-recrimination, calls himself "stupid *kolla*" for allowing himself to be trapped in this world of his own making. Suddenly he understands Witjetunga's call for brotherhood; yet even that is complicit with Triton's own caste-based Buddhist/Sinhala prejudice against the spite-filled Joseph. Triton as a boy had seen Joseph as "not one of us" (effectively repressing the other within), claiming that the unsavory and mendacious Joseph belongs "stuck up some palm tree, high on *toddy*, keeping the demons happy like the rest of his people."[40] (It is suggested, but never directly stated, that Joseph is associated with the aboriginal and looked down upon Veddahs.) In this moment, Triton's awareness of his complicity overturns the sense of triumph he had felt at Joseph's expulsion. On his departure, Joseph had spat at his feet and cursed: "you bastards, you are going to eat shit one day, shit."[41] This comes back to Triton now, as he half-recognizes, belatedly, his own complicity in the impotent rage of Joseph and others like him, who have turned into the "stupid monsters"[42] who carry out the carnage that is to come. However, in keeping with the way the fictional account lends itself to the "complexity of complicity," this moment of awareness does not result in any sudden neat reversal of attitude and political consciousness; instead, the novel explores the evolving relationship between Triton and Salgado, and invites reflection on the significance of the simultaneous temporality of different worlds, the layered modernities within the household, and the different universalities outside.[43]

The perspective of boyhood becomes integral to tracking and comparing an emerging awareness, or refusal, of complicities. For instance, like *Reef*, Lindsey Collen's *Boy*—originally published in Creole as *Misyon Garcon*—uses the narrative of the developing self as a meditation on the culturally heterogeneous developing world that is Mauritius. On the other hand, Sello Duiker's *Thirteen Cents* presents a searing indictment of failed expectations which mock the newly democratic era in South Africa. As witness accounts, all three texts create an interplay between marginality and centrality to the events being described. From exile in the United Kingdom, Triton asks: "Is it the same sea here as back home?"[44] and one could argue that the ocean itself is metonymic of this connectedness between the three narratives, since its presence is like an undertow suggestive of other potentialities, other worlds, as well as shared colonial legacies. Of course it is not literally the "same sea" he encounters in the United Kingdom, but the novel suggests that at another level it is and—as Salgado cautions—"we will all return to it" eventually.

The famous claim by Heraclites, "you don't step twice into the same river," is echoed in Collen's *Boy* when the seventeen-year-old Krish undertakes an impromptu journey across the island partly to avoid dealing with the disappointment of failing his final exams, and partly in response to suppressed emotions following the death of his older brother, a passing he has not properly mourned. As he watches the Belil River flowing into the sea he notes: "Towards the sea it drifts. Grand for so small a river. It passes but is here, passes but is here,"[45] and this refrain signals his new consciousness of being in the present, but also always in flux, "becoming," as Hall puts it. Although he finally conquers his fear of the sea when he goes on an impromptu fishing trip, this fear nevertheless appears justified when they encounter a drowned girl in shallow waters, with a rock tied to her chest. Krish both desires and fears the sea: sitting on the beach he contemplates how far he can see—"Is it Madagascar"?[46]—or "If I look down to my left, would I, if I went straight, get to the South Pole"?[47] The boy's sense of convergence and flux can be read in terms of the social dynamic of self and identity associated with metonymies of islands and oceans.[48] For instance, the glimmering of other worlds on the horizon opens Krish to an awareness of the lives of strangers as he encounters individuals from across the social class spectrum on his trek across the island. However, it also makes him suddenly recognize, for the first time, his own unconscious complicity in their economic hardships. After being offered hospitality by a group of striking unionists, he recognizes that he has been blissfully unaware of what was happening on his own doorstep: "Me sleeping away. I, a colonizer of my own land. I am giddy at my own ignorance, my own internal emptiness."[49]

The more starkly dichotomized world of the thirteen-year-old Azure in *Thirteen Cents* presents a contrast to the expansive sense of other worlds and realities in *Boy*, but more especially in *Reef*. It might be tempting to suggest that this is in keeping with the fact that Cape Town is associated (mistakenly) with the meeting point between the warm Indian Ocean and cold Atlantic Ocean worlds. The problem with this is that it invites a symptomatic reading and generalizes what is a particular aesthetic response to the post-apartheid experience. Admittedly this is an extremely bleak, and, some might say, pathological aesthetic that describes the legacy of apartheid as a lingering psychosis. Duiker claims in an interview that in *Thirteen Cents* he wanted to show "how violence is not only a way of dominating people," but also how "violence is used by people to communicate with each other to convey a message." He goes on to claim that, "we are part of a violent culture, and we never knew a day of rest, nor did we receive help to enter into a process of healing after apartheid. That is our fate, and the cause of our psychosis that we carry around with us."[50] While the reference to fate suggests a paralyzing complicity which enables repression to continue, what we have here is also an attempt to tell the "other side" of the story of postapartheid South Africa.

Duiker aims to shock: in his account the most vulnerable members of society replicate the "games" of the "grown-ups" with apparently willful cruelty. This should be read in the light of warnings about "a pervasive rhetoric of amnesia" in which "the 'morbid' aspects of South Africa's bloody road to democracy" are being prematurely forgotten in the interests of discourses of nation-building.[51] At the same time it draws attention to the staggeringly high levels of violence involving minors as victims and as perpetrators—with the Cape having the highest levels of juvenile crime.[52] In *Thirteen Cents* the process of learning is by means of negatives, of un-learning to hope. Azure learns the same lesson again and again. This involves a series of betrayals and boils down to the realization that in his world only money counts and no one is to be trusted. Even his father said once: "I made you. I can take you out of this life."[53] The conclusion Azure comes to shows how the apparently endemic pathology of violence which is a legacy of apartheid expresses itself through the language of sexuality in a perversion of nurturing relations between parents and children: "Grown-ups have children so that they can say, Oh God I'm going to come. I'm going to shoot all over you."[54] For Azure there are no alternative worlds on the horizon, no choices worthy of making. Except, that is, in dreams and visions associated with altered states of consciousness as he moves away from the city and climbs to a cave on Table Mountain where he communes with shamanic figures from the past. Here he has a vision of the sea rising up over Cape Town swallowing the city and rolling up along the sides of mountain to where he has taken refuge. This purging vision resonates with Witjetunga's call in *Reef*, "we have to destroy in order to create."

Unlike the benign process of learning that is described in Collen's *Boy*, where even Krish's recognition of complicity is a privileged insight (akin to waking from sleep), learning for Azure follows a different path. The postapartheid child, in apparent complicity, follows wealthy white men for sex so that he can be paid for performing "tricks" with them simply to survive on the streets. After the death of his parents, Azure, like many others, becomes a migrant (or more accurately, vagrant) in his own city. However, Azure also embodies a much older legacy, linking the three texts: that of the human cargo traded via the Dutch East India Company. Ancestors of people like Azure were brought to the Cape, disinherited and unnamed, and then renamed in the master's voice. These slave legacies are repeated when, in the ritual ceremonial enslavement to the gang who now own him,

Azure is renamed, has his shoes taken away, and is beaten, imprisoned, and sodomized as part of a typical practice of social alienation engineered by the gang boss. He seems to be caught in a spiral that goes back even further than apartheid, though his father's words seem to be a chilling parody of that system. In this way, Duiker's narrative inserts the slave legacy back into the present postapartheid city, waking us from the willed amnesia. It is telling that in *Thirteen Cents*, when the boy's parents named him Azure, they drew attention to his multivalent identity by signaling the apparent anomaly of the startling sea-blue eyes set in a dark-skinned face. When the gang boss renames him simply "Blue," he indirectly both affirms Azure's connection to the colonial past, and denies his individuality and potential agency in the present and future. This is in stark contrast to *Reef*, where naming is imbricated in Triton's process of "becoming." For instance, when Salgado for the first time uses his given name rather than the generic "*kolla*," he implicitly validates Triton's performative "enactment" of his future identity as culinary artist. Triton's ecstatic, even spiritual response to this recognition indicates both the potential for change and the recognition of what Hall (1996) refers to as his "rootedness" in a personal history. Triton experiences the moment of naming, "*Triton made it*," as "clean, pure and unstinting."[55] He describes Salgado's voice as seeming "like a channel cut from heaven to earth right through the petrified morass of all our lives, releasing a blessing like water springing from a river-head, from a god's head. It was bliss. My coming of age."[56]

In *Thirteen Cents*, however, the experiences of a street child in postelection Cape Town expose the layers of psychic and physical violence that seem to have seeped into the cracks of the streets—a veritable archive of violence. The novel has been heralded as offering something new in mapping the city from below, highlighting the defining structure of our globalized modernity.[57] Even now, remains of the older slave past are being excavated, literally accidentally unearthed, as bulldozers shift the ground for another multinational business venture in the mother city.[58] The fictional staging of complicity, when Azure follows or seeks out the very men who are to prostitute or enslave him in gangster culture, leads Azure to a radical but cyclical and destructive urge to return to beginnings. By way of contrast, in *Boy* the sheltered and self-absorbed Krish does expand his horizons of experience, yet there is something too easy about this, and at times the narrative flags on account of the occasionally overzealous emphasis on Krish's newfound awareness of the "foldedness of human-being." *Reef*, however, most effectively of the three texts, demonstrates and grapples with, "the complexity of complicity." Gunesekera achieves this through employing a transformative aesthetic; this entails intersections between the mythic and creative realms associated with childhood and the material contingencies of the adult entering history, and attempting to address the future.

As suggested earlier, there are several factors that contribute to the productive, rather than simply resistant complicity in *Reef*. Firstly, there is the evolution of the (complexly complicitous) relationship between Triton and Salgado. Secondly, there is Triton's propensity for imaginative and creative responses—something he demonstrates from childhood; and thirdly, we have the travelling trope of connectedness outlined in the introduction to this chapter. Finally, the simultaneous temporality of diverse worlds also plays a crucial role in Triton's ability to imagine a future. For example, the first time that Triton encounters Salgado is when he hears his voice from another part of the house. Triton is captivated immediately: "I had never heard language so gently spoken."[59] His response is not only triggered by a sensation, but the appeal for him is its "newness" or strangeness in terms of its unaccustomed gentleness. It is both an aesthetic and cognitive response, but also indicates an ability to recognize, in keeping with Appiah's claims for a revisioned cosmopolitanism, a potential self in a stranger, as well as a potential for transformation in the present. His genius in the kitchen seems a logical extension: he can take ingredients and imagine how unusual combinations will work to create new dishes, or familiar ones with new tastes. Cooking is a form of creative expression and agency as Triton identifies himself in terms of what he can "make," again emphasizing the potential for "becoming" rather than the more static class- and caste-bound "being" one usually associates with someone in his position.

Given Triton's gradual disillusionment with Salgado's ineffectualness and collapse after the Nili affair, one could ask, why does he remain loyal to Salgado? Is this a complicit loyalty, since Triton is now fully aware of the spoiled paradise they inhabit, with more than just the ocean pressing around them? Why does he not join Wijetunga who had, after all "worked it all out"? Instead, Triton takes it upon himself to nudge the apparently emotionally paralyzed Salgado back to health. Ironically, it is from the new small world of their cramped apartment in London that they witness, via the flickering television images, the horrors of the 1971 riots in Colombo, the news of "ghastly beheadings on the beach"[60] foreshadowing the brutality to come. Having at last indirectly witnessed what is happening in Sri Lanka from the vantage point of exile, Salgado decides to return to look after Nili; Triton, however, remains behind in an attempt to "make" a future. Triton is fully aware, however, that he has to learn to "perform" like one who has "found his vocation at last."[61] This indicates the hard-won self-reflexivity of Triton's enactment of agency. According to Judith Butler, the identity that is "assigned" is reiterated in performance,[62] but one hardly ever carries out these assignments to expectation. However, as Culler explains, in the "gap" that is created by the different ways of carrying out the assignment, "lie possibilities for resistance and change."[63] It seems that in his awareness of the performative "enactment" of his vocation, Triton also acknowledges the responsibility (and the cost) of resistance and change. This is, he says "the only way I could succeed: without a past, without a name, without Ranjan Salgado standing by my side."[64] Needless to say, this is an impossibly ambivalent situation. The past must be kept at bay in order to live in the present, but this entails loss, and the precariousness of keeping the past at bay renders one as vulnerable as the easily breached coral reef that once held Sri Lanka in a protective embrace.

It has been claimed that the illusion of return to origins is a key feature of the diasporic imaginary: according to Avtar Brah "home is a mythic space of desire in the diasporic imagination [. . .] It is a place of no-return even if it is possible to visit the geographic territory that is seen as the place of origin."[65] Triton seems to grasp this in justifying his decision to stay on in the United Kingdom without Salgado—he will at last have "a place to call his own."[66] However, as suggested earlier, this is a performative act rather than a claim to belonging, evident in the use of the third person to refer to himself. Even at the end of the novel, it seems Triton is still in the same liminal space, both insider and outsider, characteristic of the "doubleness" of diaspora experience.[67] At the same time, it could be said that the novel counters critique leveled at the "inbetween" position associated with the diasporic condition, where "its feted mobility becomes a form of detachment from the very circumstances in which political resistance is possible."[68] Instead, as I have explained, the way the novel balances the temporality of worlds militates against that detachment.

This balance is captured in the opening sequence, appropriately called "The Breach" when Triton, now in his forties, sees a familiar stranger in a cubicle of a London parking lot and sees in the young Tamil refugee's face "almost a reflection of my own."[69] The act of "allowing the stranger in," when Triton steps into the cubicle with the young refugee, triggers a flood of memory that flows through the breach opened by this encounter. This recollection becomes the narrative, *Reef*, and should be read as a transformative aesthetic, rather than an attempt to "return" to Sri Lanka (as undertaken by Salgado).

While *Reef* posits simultaneous worlds, in *Thirteen Cents* the mind-altered vision of an alternative world is one which does not coexist, but destroys the corrupted "present" world. The apocalyptic ending of *Thirteen Cents* envisions a tsunami of water, wind, and fire as the sea rolls in over Table Mountain as if to reclaim the afflicted land. In *Reef*, on the other hand, it is the tide of memory as narrative. The future posited in *Reef* is bounded by the past it still floats upon. All his young life Triton had tried to maintain his world, hold it intact, and keep out strangers. However, the connectedness that was Salgado's pet theory presents itself to him as a lived reality at last, when he realizes that history is always the story of someone else's diaspora. This connectedness cannot be escaped, even if it holds one in an uneasy, indeed complicitous, balance with the present.

Reef received critical acclaim as a debut novel and was short-listed for the Booker and Guardian fiction prizes in 1994; nevertheless, it was criticized in some quarters for not doing "justice" to the political realities of Sri Lanka's civil war, or for "diluting" or "straining" the personal narrative with references to the political context.[70] However, as I have argued,

these inclusions and interruptions are integral to Gunesekera's transformative aesthetic. This is also demonstrated in the choice of epigraph, "of his
bones are coral made," as frame for the narrative. Indeed, *Reef* has been
seen as another Asian *Tempest*, reenvisioning the master–servant, island–
mainstream, self–other, centre–periphery relationships associated with
this.[71] It is telling that the epigraph comes from a speech which stresses
transformation, and is in keeping with the focus on "becoming" that has
informed my reading:

> Full fathom five thy father lies;
> Of his bones are coral made;
> Those are pearls that were his eyes;
> Nothing of him that doth fade,
> But doth suffer a sea change
> Into something rich and strange.[72]

It would be a mistake to see this emphasis on transformation as negating
the uncompromising call by Wijetunga for revolutionary change ("we have
to destroy in order to create"), which is also embedded in Duiker's equally
uncompromising indictment of the lingering malady of apartheid's older
violence. In fact, both *Reef* and *Thirteen Cents* can be seen as foreground-
ing a spiral rather than the linear teleology tracked in Collen's *Boy*: Duiker's
representation of postapartheid violence loops back via present and future
to the slave and colonial history, while in *Reef* this circularity suggests not
a reiteration, but the potential for renewal, for resisting the trap of replicating past histories. This happens, not through negation or deliberate erasure
in forgetting, but rather as transformed into "something rich and strange,"
the narrative itself. The South African experiences represented in Duiker's
deliberately polemical fiction can, by comparison with *Reef* (and *Boy*), be
read as existing along a continuum of coexisting potential worlds, rather
than simply contradicting these. For Triton, the possibility of "making"
a future within the present can still be sighted on the imagined horizon,
even though it is, as Triton acknowledges, like "painting a dream." This
admittedly tentative and qualified move towards a future in Gunesekera's
Reef opens up possibilities for further conversations between writings from
across the same, but not the same, sea.[73]

NOTES

1. Romesh Gunesekera, *Reef* (London: Granta Books, 1994), 172.
2. Gunesekera, *Reef*, 169. Gunesekera lives in the United Kingdom, but grew
   up in Sri Lanka and the Philippines. He has also published a collection of
   short stories, *Monkfish Moon* (1992); other novels are *The Sandglass* (1998),
   Heaven's Edge (2002), and *The Match* (2006).
3. Gunesekera, *Reef*, 174.

4. Isabel Hofmeyr, has written extensively on the Indian Ocean world and its connection to South Africa. Referring to the antiquity of this economic and cultural network, she draws on Sugata Bose's *A Hundred Horizons: The Indian Ocean in an Age of Global Imperialism* (2005), which characterizes this "interregional area" as a "set of articulating trade systems that have interlinked Malays, Chinese, Indians, Arabs and Africans. It is an arena in which Britain, Denmark, France, Germany, Holland, Italy, Portugal, Spain and the USA came into contact with Africa, the Middle East and the Orient." Isabel Hofmeyr, "The Black Atlantic Meets the Indian Ocean: Forging New Paradigms of Transnationalism for the Global South Literary and Cultural Perspectives," *Social Dynamics* 33(2; 2007): 3–32, 6.

5. Appiah argues that in such an imaginary conversation, the connection is "not through identity but despite difference" Anthony Appiah, *Cosmopolitanism: Ethics in a World of Strangers* (London: Penguin, 2006), 135.

6. Lindsey Collen, *Boy* (London: Bloomsbury, 2004). Collen was born in South Africa but lives in Mauritius, where she is a well-known trade union activist and writer. In my view, *Boy* is not in the same class as her excellent earlier novels which present densely tessellated narratives of engendered oppressions and strategies for survival: *The Rape of Sita* won the Commonwealth Prize, but was banned in Mauritius in a storm of controversy around Collen for daring to fictionalize taboo subjects such as rape. Other works are *There is a Tide, Getting Rid of It*, and *Mutiny*.

7. Sello K. Duiker, *Thirteen Cents* (Cape Town: David Philips, 2000). In a compilation celebrating the work of Duiker (who committed suicide in 2005), and another young writer, Phaswane Mpe (who died in the same year), Mbulelo Mzamane notes how they have been described as "chroniclers of the 'new' SA," Mzamane, *Words Gone to Soon: A Tribute to Phaswane Mpe and K. Sello Duiker.* (Pretoria: Skotaville Media and Communications Ltd, 2005), xi. *Thirteen Cents* was Duiker's his first novel, for which he won the Commonwealth Writer's Prize for Best First Book in 2001. His second novel, *The Quiet Violence of Dreams* won the local Herman Charles Bosman Prize in 2002. His latest book, published posthumously is aimed at a young audience.

8. For instance, this legacy is marked by the quasi-identical and massive seventeenth century five-sided castle forts built by the Dutch East India Company on the cliffs in Galle, Sri Lanka, and Cape Town, mirroring one another across the ocean.

9. Paul White, "Geography, Literature and Migration," in *Writing Across Worlds*, ed Russell King, John Connell and Paul White (New York: Routledge, 1995), 6.

10. Perhaps, as has been suggested, these "worlds" could also be seen as different or contesting universalisms; as Hofmeyr puts it, the Indian Ocean is "the site par excellence of 'alternative modernities,' those formations of modernity that have taken shape in an archive of deep and layered existing social and intellectual traditions" ("Forging New Paradigms," 13). She notes: "these intellectual circuits produced in a world of crosscutting and contesting universalisms [produced] a view of colonialism less as an encounter of the local and the global than as a contestation of different universalisms" ("Forging New Paradigms," 7–8).

11. This has been seen as metonymic of the dynamics of self and identity; drawing on Certaux's "Writing the Sea," Daniel Yon notes that "the ideas of indeterminacy and endless fluidity that are inscribed onto the ocean . . . are themselves engineered meanings . . . a discourse that helps to make intelligible this otherwise vast and unknown space." Daniel Yon, "Race-Making/

Race-Mixing: St Helena and the South Atlantic World, *Social Dynamics: Oceanic Worlds/Bordered Worlds.* 33(2; 2007):144–145.

12. A common trend in explorations of the developing self in the developing country has been to focus on the experiences of the girl child, since her marginal and necessarily multivalent position is productive for analyzing the interface between private and public domains (see Helena Maria Lima, "Revolutionary Developments: Michelle Cliff's *No Telephone to Heaven* and Merle Collins' *Angel, Ariel* 24(1; 1993): 35–56.

13. This wider lens is thus a corrective to the more common North-South Black Atlantic and African axis. Hofmeyr (drawing on Campbell) identifies some of the differences between the Atlantic model and that of the Indian Ocean; for instance, the trade was largely female, and "involved predominantly household slaves rather than plantation workers." Consequently, "boundaries between slave and free were much more blurred than in the Atlantic; and, furthermore, the association of race and slavery did not exist in any marked form" ("Forging New Paradigms," 11).

14. Hofmeyr, "Forging New Paradigms," 22. See also Meg Samuelson, "Re-imagining South Africa via a Passage to India: M.K. Jeffreys's Archive of the Indian Ocean World," *Social Dynamics: Oceanic Worlds/Bordered Worlds* 33(2; 2007): 61–87.

15. Monika Fludernik draws on Vijay Mishra's "The Diasporic Imaginary" to categorize diaspora models that have been identified by Khachig Toloyan, William Safran, James Clifford, and Robin Cohen, including "Old and New Diaspora of victimhood and mobility." Monika Fludernik, "The Diasporic Imaginary: Postcolonial Reconfigurations in the Context of Multiculturalism," in *Diaspora and Multiculturalism: Common Trends and New Developments,* ed. Monica Fludernik, (Amsterdam: Rodopi, 2003) xi–xxxviii.

16. Mark Sanders, *Complicities: The Intellectual and Apartheid* (Durham, NC: Duke University Press, 2002).Sanders, *Complicities,* 9.

17. Ibid., 9.

18. Ibid., 8.

19. My emphasis, ibid., 9.

20. Ibid., x.

21. Ibid., 113.

22. Gunesekera, *Reef,* 43.

23. Hall is referring to Caribbean identity following a history of transportation, slavery, and migration. Stuart Hall, "Cultural Identity and Diaspora," in *Contemporary Postcolonial Theory,* ed. Mongia, Padmini (New York: Arnold, 1995), 112.

24. Sanders, *Complicities,* 11.

25. Ibid., 21.

26. Ibid., 92.

27. Ibid., x.

28. Gunesekera, *Reef,* 172.

29. Meg Samuelson, *Remembering the Nation, Dismembering Women? Stories of the South African Transition* (Durban: University of KwaZulu-Natal Press, 2007), 223.

30. Ibid, 223. Sanders relates complicity to the concept of hospitality: of "allowing the stranger in" (125), and quotes Fanon: "One's human-being depends on a relation to an other and this involves an affectual and an ethical dimension" (*Complicities,* 183). In view of the recent waves of xenophobia which have exposed the contradictions underlying South Africa's postulated rainbow nationhood, this will no doubt be a significant arena for future analysis as writers grapple with the aftermath of these events.

31. In Keya Ganguly, "Temporality and Postcolonial Critique," in *The Cambridge Companion to Postcolonial Literary Studies*, ed. Neil Lazarus (Cambridge, UK: Cambridge University Press, 2004), 174.
32. Gunesekera, *Reef*, 79.
33. Ibid., 85.
34. Ibid., 94.
35. Ibid., 98–99.
36. Ibid., 99.
37. Ibid., 110.
38. Ibid., 111.
39. Sanders, *Complicities*, x.
40. Gunesekera, *Reef*, 29.
41. Ibid., 42.
42. Ibid., 42.
43. See Hofmeyr, "Forging New Perspectives," 8.
44. Gunesekera, *Reef*, 172.
45. Collen, *Boy*, 85.
46. Ibid., 71.
47. Ibid., 71.
48. See Yon, "Race-Making," 144.
49. Collen, *Boy*, 154.
50. In Fred De Vries, "Interview with K Sello Duiker," *Cape Librarian* 48(2; 2004): 22–24.
51. Gugu Hlongwana, "The Junction Avenue Theatre Company's Sophiatown and the Limits of National Oneness," *Postcolonial Text* 2(2; 2006): 1.
52. Karyn Maughn, "Shock Report on Youth Crime in Province," *Cape Times*, March 27th, 2008, p 1.
53. Duiker, *Cents*, 144.
54. Ibid., 144.
55. Gunesekera, *Reef*, 64.
56. Ibid., 64–65.
57. Lizzy Attree, "Already Falling Apart," *Wasafiri* 46(2005): 30–36.
58. Holiday, "living dead return," 9.
59. Gunesekera, *Reef*, 7.
60. Ibid., 173.
61. Ibid., 180.
62. Judith Butler, "Gender as Performance: An Interview with Judith Butler." *Radical Philosophy* 67(1994): 33.
63. Referring to Butler's discussion of how identity is gendered, Jonathan Culler offers a useful clarification which can be applied to the "assignment" Triton performs here. Jonathan Culler, *Literary Theory* (Oxford, UK: Oxford University Press, 1997), 105.
64. Gunesekera, *Reef*, 180.
65. In Minoli Salgado, "Nonlinear Dynamics and the Diasporic Imagination," in *Diaspora and Multiculturalism: Common Trends and New Developments*, ed. Monica Fludernik (Amsterdam: Rodopi, 2003)188–189.
66. Gunesekera, *Reef*, 180.
67. Uma Parameswaran, Uma, "Dispelling the spells of Memory," in *Diaspora and Multiculturalism: Common Trends and New Developments*, ed. Monika Fludernik (Amsterdam: Rodopi, 2003), ix.
68. Andrew Smith, "Migrancy, Hybridity, and Postcolonial Literary Studies," in *The Cambridge Companion to Postcolonial Literary Studies*, ed. Neil Lazarus (Cambridge, UK: Cambridge University Press, 2004), 257.
69. Gunesekera, *Reef*, 1.

70. See Neil Gordon's review in *Boston Review*, April/May 1995 issue: http://64.233.183/seach?q=cache:0130ArVOylwJ:bostonreview.net/BR20.2/ Gordo. Accessed November 2, 2008.
71. Iyer Pico, "The Empire Strikes Back" *The New York Review of Books*, June 22, 1995, p 30-1.
72. Shakespeare, *The Tempest*, 1.ii.
73. Gunesekera, Reef, 2.

BIBLIOGRAPHY

Appiah, Kwame. *Cosmopolitanism: Ethics in a World of Strangers*. London: Penguin Classics, 2006.
Attree, Lizzy. "Already Falling Apart." *Wasafiri*. 46(2005): 30–36.
Butler, Judith. "Gender as Performance: An Interview with Judith Butler." *Radical Philosophy*. 67(1994): 32–39.
Collen, Lindsey. *Boy*. London: Bloomsbury, 2004.
Culler, Jonathan. *Literary Theory*. Oxford, UK: Oxford University Press, 1997.
De Vries, Fred. "Interview with K Sello Duiker." *Cape Librarian*. 48(2; 2004):22–24.
Doubt, Jenny. "A Sensitive Linguistic Journey." *African Review of Books*. http://72.14.205.104/search?q=cache:QIHTWGAUpuIJ:www.africanreview ofbooks.c. (Accessed November 6, 2007)
Duiker, K. Sello. *Thirteen Cents*. Cape Town: David Philips, 2000.
Fludernik, Monika. "The Diasporic Imaginary: Postcolonial Reconfigurations in the Context of Multiculturalism." In *Diaspora and Multiculturalism: Common Trends and New Developments*, edited by Monika Fludernik. Amsterdam: Rodopi, 2003. xi–xxxviii.
Ganguly, Keya. "Temporality and postcolonial critique." In *The Cambridge Companion to Postcolonial Literary Studies*, edited by Neil Lazarus, 162–182. Cambridge, UK: Cambridge University Press, 2004.
Gordon, Neil. Review of *Reef*, *Boston Review*: April/May 1995 http://64.233.183.104/ search?q=cache:0130ArVOylwJ:bostonreview.net/BR20.2/Gordo.   .(Accessed February 11, 2008).
Gunesekera, Romesh. *Reef*. London: Granta Books, 1994.
Hall, Stuart. "Cultural Identity and Diaspora." In *Contemporary Postcolonial Theory*, edited by Mongia, Padmini. New York: Arnold, 1996, pp 110–121.
Hlongwana, Gugu. "The Junction Avenue Theatre Company's Sophiatown and the Limits of National Oneness" *Postcolonial Text*, 2(2; 2006). http://postcolonial. org/index.php/pct/rt/printerFriendly/425/191
Hofmeyr, Isabel. 2007. "The Black Atlantic Meets the Indian Ocean: Forging New Paradigms of Transnationalism for the Global South Literary and Cultural Perspectives." *Social Dynamics: Oceanic Worlds/Bordered Worlds*, edited by Meg Samuelson and Shaun Viljoen, 33(2; 2007): 3–32.
Holiday, Anthony. "The 'Living Dead' Return to Haunt the 'New' South Africa," *Cape Times*, 30 July, 2003, 9
Iyer, Pico. "The Empire Strikes Back," *The New York Review of Books*, June 22, 1995, p30-1.
Lima, Helena Maria. "Revolutionary Developments: Michelle Cliff's *No Telephone to Heaven* and Merle Collins' *Angel*." *Ariel* 24(1; 1993): 35–56.
Maughan, Karyn. "Shock report on youth crime in province," *Cape Times*, March 27, 2008, p 1.

Mzamane, Mbulelo. *Words Gone to Soon: A Tribute to Phaswane Mpe and K. Sello Duiker.* Pretoria: Skotaville Media and Communications Ltd, 2005.

Parameswaran, Uma. "Dispelling the spells of Memory." In *Diaspora and Multiculturalism: Common Trends and New Developments,* edited by Monica Fludernik. Amsterdam:Rodopi, 2003. xxxviiii–1xv

Salgado, Minoli. "Nonlinear Dynamics and the Diasporic Imagination." In *Diaspora and Multiculturalism: Common Trends and New Developments,* edited by Monica Fludernik, 183–198. Amsterdam: Rodopi, 2003.

Samuelson, Meg. *Remembering the Nation, Dismembering Women? Stories of the South African Transition.* Durban: University of KwaZulu-Natal Press, 2007.

Samuelson, Meg. "Re-imagining South Africa via a Passage to India: M.K. Jeffreys's archive of the Indian Ocean World." *Social Dynamics: Oceanic Worlds/Bordered Worlds,* edited by Meg Samuelson and Shaun Viljoen, 33(2; 2007): 61–87

Sanders, Mark. *Complicities: The intellectual and Apartheid.* Durham, NC: Duke University Press, 2002.

Smith, Andrew. "Migrancy, hybridity, and postcolonial literary studies." In *The Cambridge Companion to Postcolonial Literary Studies,* edited by Neil Lazarus, 241–261. Cambridge, UK: Cambridge University Press, 2004.

White, Paul. "Geography, Literature and Migration." In *Writing Across Worlds,* edited by Russell King, John Connell, and Paul White, 1–19. New York: Routledge, 1995.

Yon, Daniel A. "Race-Making/Race-Mixing: St Helena and the South Atlantic World." *Social Dynamics: Oceanic Worlds/Bordered Worlds,* edited by Meg Samuelson, Meg and Shaun Viljoen, 33(2; 2007): 144–163.

12 Making Home on the Indian Ocean Rim

Relocations in South African Literatures

Meg Samuelson

> *In my veins courses the blood of the Malay slaves who came from the East. Their proud dignity informs my bearing, their culture a part of my essence. The stripes they bore on their bodies from the lash of the slave master are a reminder embossed on my consciousness of what should not be done.*
> *[. . .]*
> *I come from those who were transported from India and China, whose being resided in the fact, solely, that they were able to provide physical labour, who taught me that we could both be at home and be foreign, who taught me that human existence itself demanded that freedom was a necessary condition for that human existence.*
> *[. . .]*
> *I am an African.*
>
> Thabo Mbeki, 1996

On the occasion of the adoption of the new constitution, then-Deputy President Thabo Mbeki presented an image of Africa—and South Africa in particular—as cut across and comprised by oceanic passages. This chapter begins to sketch the ways in which such movements, and the literary texts that retrace their passages, introduce into South African cultural studies the Indian Ocean paradigm (previously occluded in favour of autochthonous or Atlantic paradigms) and deflect attention away from the agonistic relationship with the North or West (depending on one's location) that marks much cultural production in the so-called postcolonial world.[1] Docking on the exclusionary shores of erstwhile white South Africa, such passages— oceanic and literary—hone analytic tools with which to meet a xenophobia, articulated first in apartheid racism (which cast Africans as "strangers" in their own land, and Asians as foreigners to be repatriated) and now transmuted into hostility towards continental Africans and Asians, rearing its ugly head in the postapartheid present. In this present, casting one's

gaze back across the ocean raises pertinent questions around home, belonging, and Africanness that help to move us beyond the bankrupt politics of
autochthony[2] and gesture towards ways of imagining the nation anew: no
longer in terms of the "closed doors" that the metaphor of the national
home encapsulates,[3] but rather as a ship coming to port in a diverse range
of harbours bordering the fluid territory of the Indian Ocean world.

My enquiry is framed by the extract from Mbeki's speech quoted in this
chapter's epigraph, in which the deputy president celebrates the inauguration of a new constitution that sunders postapartheid South Africa from its
exclusionary predecessor and which produces, at least on paper, a nation
characterized by its tolerances and freedoms. Mbeki's attempt to capture
the constitution's spirit in his poetic tribute to the roots and routes that
comprise an "African identity" has evoked a range of different responses.
Ronit Frainman-Frenkel, for one, regrets its construction of some South
Africans as "foreign": "Why is it that South African Indians continue to be
seen as not fully South African? Why are they both foreign and at home in a
country in which they have lived for a hundred and fifty years?"[4] Such questions emerge out of a long history that has cast South Africans of Indian
descent as foreigners, that has denied their citizenship, and that for decades
engaged "the Indian question" as an issue pertaining only to repatriation.
In the wake of such a hostile history, and in a postapartheid present that
at times again threatens to abject these members of the national polity,[5]
Frainman-Frenkel's concerns are clearly valid. I, however, find in Mbeki's
phrasing and pronoun usage—"who taught *me* that *we* could both be at
home and be foreign"—an occasion for rethinking notions of "home," and
their valence in nationalist discourse, in potentially rich and provocative
ways. Who is this uncanny "we," inhabiting a home that is simultaneously
foreign? What is the source and import of this (un)homely state?[6]

Engaged more in mapping the waters than in docking on solid land, this
chapter begins to explore, rather than seeking to answer, such questions by
drawing into focus the unity and spread of the Indian Ocean world from the
perspective of the South African shore. Previous studies of South Africa's
Indian Ocean cultural heritage have illuminated the contributions to South
Africa made by indentured and "passenger" Indians, who began to arrive
in colonial Natal in 1860,[7] and have excavated from beneath apartheid's
repressive discourses and practices the Creole culture forged in the slave-
holding households of the early Cape, with their African-Asian-European
compositions.[8] This chapter sets a broader, and hence necessarily sketchier,
scene in order to draw into one frame (a) the three waves of Indian traffic:
Dutch East Indian Company (DEIC) slaves, indentured labourers imported
under British colonialism, and the traders, or "passenger" Indians, who
followed them;[9] (b) the mingling of multiple Indian Ocean cultures in the
Cape, without excluding Africa or separating South(east) Asian strands
from African ones in the weave of Cape culture; (c) the larger "interregional arena"[10] of the Indian Ocean, that takes us as far afloat as China,

rather than tacking back and forth on a narrow route from one subcontinent to another. This variegated, entangled scene is traced through a set of narratives—fictional, semifictional and (auto)biographical—produced in the postapartheid era and spanning geographical and temporal locations, seeing us travelling from the shores of China, South and Southeast Asia, and Mozambique to the port cities of Cape Town, Durban and their hinterlands, and from the beginning of DEIC rule in the mid-seventeenth century through colonial rule and the apartheid regime, to the dawn of a new era.

Established by the DEIC in 1652 as a refreshment station for ships on the spice route between Holland and Batavia, Cape Town functioned since its inception as an "oceanic crossroads."[11] Subject to the authority of Batavia, it was, as Nigel Worden puts it, "integrally a part of the Indian Ocean world,"[12] and looked, for the next century and more, "on the Indian Ocean as its dominant hinterland."[13] Officials moved back and forth between the Cape and Batavia, *transplanting* the mores of the Indian Ocean trading zone into this backwater founded precisely to perform the function of a *garden*. Their influence may have been fleeting, had they not brought with them the human cargo that embedded the Indian Ocean world more firmly on the southern tip of Africa. Slaves at the Cape were seldom imported in large consignments, and often arrived haphazardly, many being sold individually by owners returning to Holland for their retirement after long careers in Southeast Asia. The result was that "slaves at the Cape came from an exceptionally diverse and widespread range of regions in the Indian Ocean world, providing a virtual map of VOC [DEIC] trading activities."[14]

For a textured narrative account of the first fifty years of the DEIC settlement, informed by a career in the Cape Town Archives, readers can turn to Dan Sleigh's weighty novel, *Islands* (first published in Afrikaans as *Eilande*), which is remarkable, in particular, for the ways in which it binds together the early Cape and the island of Mauritius within the framework of a shared Indian Ocean world.[15] Russel Brownlee's *Garden of the Plagues* enters midway into the story *Islands* covers, and writes the ocean as the permeable boundary of early Cape Town, whose inhabitants cling to the edge of Africa, their eyes turned always to the sea.[16] Slaves populate the pages of both novels, but take centre stage in Rayda Jacob's *The Slave Book*, set in the early nineteenth century in the years leading up to abolition under the new British colonial administration.

The publication of *The Slave Book* was a significant landmark—or watermark—in that the history of slavery was long ignored and suppressed in South Africa, not least due to the non-African origin of many Cape slaves, and hence the intractability of this memory in marshalling a united antiapartheid front.[17] The largest proportion of Cape slaves hailed from Madagascar, India, and the Indonesian archipelago. In the Cape, as Jacobs shows, a new Creole culture emerged in which Islam—which in previous centuries "wove a new pattern of economic and cultural unity through [the] vast interregional arena" of the Indian Ocean[18]—provides a structuring device. *The Slave Book* shows how Islam produces a sense of unity out of discordance, and enables the recreation of home and community among a randomly produced group comprised of members who hail from Celebes, Ceylon, Java, Malabar, and Malaya. Watching such a diverse group perform *salat* together, the character Harman reflects:

> He didn't know what they were saying, didn't know them, their origins—and they were a strange mix, of all colours and manner of dress and manner—but [he] somehow understood the importance of their worshipping together in that room. No one was doing anything different. All were following the imam up front.[19]

The Islam presented in the novel reveals the routes by way of which it has been rooted in the Cape. *Riempie-sny,* or the cutting of orange leaves on the Prophet's birthday,[20] and the performance of *tariq ratiep* trances,[21] mark the particular points of departure, such as Indonesia, from which Islam was transported to South Africa, and where it has been, in turn, inflected by the experience of slavery. As Sangora, a slave and spiritual leader, explains of *ratiep*:

> It's not part of our religion [. . .] It's a display of faith, a tradition. Brought here from overseas by the slaves. It's good for people who don't have a belief system to see what you can do if you have faith. A normal man needs his God. Now what about a slave? As a slave you have to have faith or you'll give up. You don't have anything else.[22]

In large part a celebration of slave resilience, and of the infusion of Indian Ocean cultural and religious practices into the Creole matrix of the Cape, *The Slave Book* unfolds in romance mode as it attempts to construct viable homes on African soil.[23] We have to step off the land, and return to the ocean, in order to gain a more sober sense of the relations between white men and slave women that, in part, produced the Creole Cape. On land, the novel deflects the threat of rape that Somiela faces from her owner, and allows her instead to enjoy a consensual, romantic union with another "white" man. The brutality of the intimate relations between slave and slave owner is parenthetically presented only in the elliptical back story of Somiela's mother, Noria, which begins on the Malabar coast, where her mother sells her to the captain of a ship. Noria is passed from vessel to vessel, and man to man, until she finally finds herself on the auction block at the Cape. Her mother's betrayal, the rejecting "home" of origin, brackets this traumatic journey between the loss and remaking of home, and it is with the latter project that this novel is concerned.

Jacob's construction of the Cape as "home" is produced not only by its romantic gaze, but also, as Pumla Gqola has argued, by its abjection of the African; in this case, the Mozambican Prize Negro *mandoor*, Kanaga, onto whom the rapacity that might otherwise have been written into white masculinity is projected.[24] It is salient, here, to observe Jeremy Cronin's recent comments on the ways in which Cape Town's Creole past and present could productively be harnessed to trouble current fetishisations of an "authentic, pure, rooted and timeless African identity"; such a project, however, will fail to offer "an effective disruption," he points out, "if we fall into a counteractive chauvinism, imagining Cape Town rooted in the marriage of Europe and Asia to the exclusion of Africa."[25]

One of the most recent offerings in South African literature—Yvette Christiansë's *Unconfessed*—shifts the homely boundary to insert yet again the abjected "stranger" into the nation. Sila van Mozbieker—later renamed Sila van der Kaap in a treacherous move aimed to deny her freedom—hails from Southeast Africa. For her, the ocean—popularly imagined as a space of connection, encounter, and potential—is a space of separation and a persistent nightmare from which she longs to flee. Hailed as South Africa's reply to Toni Morrison's magnificent *Beloved*, *Unconfessed* unfolds as a monologue addressed by Sila to the son she killed during her long incarceration for infanticide on Robben Island.

The shift in focus—from Southeast Asia to Southeast Africa, and from the Cape destination to the oceanic passage—is salient. As Patrick Harries argues, in his study of Mozbiekers, the historiographical focus on creolisation at the Cape—itself a potent response to the separating discourses of apartheid and the autochthonous claims of new nationalism—led to a focus on the institution of slavery that partially occludes the slave trade. Historians, he argues, "underestimate, or ignore, the traumatic conditions under which individuals were captured and shipped to the Cape," while producing a paradigm unable to account for the "vestiges or survivals of cultural practices brought to the colony by African slaves."[26] While the first one hundred and fifty years of Cape slavery were dominated by South and Southeast Asian slave sources, in the late eighteenth century first the Dutch and then the Batavian and British administrations at the Cape began to import large numbers of slaves from Mozambique and its surrounds. Though still drawn from diverse geographical, linguistic and ethnic groups, African slaves "were sufficiently numerous to form a broad identity as "Mozbiekers.""[27]

The "passage to the Cape" from Mozambique, argues Harries, "was at times more traumatic than the mid-Atlantic crossing,"[28] and had exceptionally high fatalities, with chilling tales of mortality and suffering, "horror and death,"[29] emanating from slave-trading vessels. For Sila, the ocean is indeed a space of death, and marks forever her sense of separation from home, while, on Robben Island, it continues to isolate her from the mainland. Like the characters that populate *The Slave Book*, the young Sila inhabits a heterogeneous world. She shares a household with Philip from Malabar and Amerant from Batavia; "then there were those of us who are called Mozbiekers. We all came in ships and we never got that rolling world out of our ears because, on some days, one of us would stumble and the others knew the ocean was sending us a message."[30] Similarly to the *The Slave Book,* rape is rendered an oceanic experience, but, unlike the more romantic novel, in *Unconfessed* the ocean and what it encodes never recedes; of the master who drives her to infanticide, she recalls: "she thought about the ocean and heard it rush through the chambers of her ears at night as Van der Wat sweated on her"[31]; "Now she thought of that time as endless washing, scrubbing, sweeping, polishing, worrying about her children, and listening to the ocean in the chambers of her ears while Van der Wat did what he had to do."[32] Each upheaval, displacement, and further reduction of her freedom is recast through the image of the ship. When *Oumiesies,* who promised but failed to manumit her slaves, dies, Sila reports: "I wanted to ask Johannes why the world was leaning too far on one side like that day they put me in the boat."[33] Her capture itself is presented only through the elliptical memory of being pushed into the hulk of a ship floating unsteadily on water: "Then the world leaned too far to one side and we all spilled into the darkness that stank and would not be still. It has never been still."[34]

As she serves her sentence on the isolated island, Sila dreams of moving far out of the reach of the sea:

> I have had enough of water that washes me away from all those years of a childhood to which there is no return. Not that it is the childhood I desire, but the years before this place.
>
> When I leave this island—and I will leave this place—I will take up what little I may have, gather my children—and I will find all of you, even if I am an old, old woman—and I will walk into that land and not stop until there is not a scent of salt water. There will be no edge of the world. There will be no more waves, no more ships, no more surf on the rocks.[35]

Before this conclusion, in which she turns her back on oceanic worlds in favour of solid land, Sila has comforted her dying friend and lover, Lys, a Khoi woman imprisoned with her on Robben Island, with a more tentatively sketched alternative world that we may, fancifully no doubt, read as the "new" South Africa with its multicoloured, rainbow flag:

> I dreamed of a big ship that came and on it were such people as you have never seen. And they flew a flag of colors that would not be still. Do you think, Lys, that you could be at home with such a people? If I tell you about them, do you think you could be at home with them?[36]

This cuts to the quick of my enquiry: can indigenous Lys be "at home" in this new nation, multihued and cut across by oceanic passages?

The end of apartheid did indeed see renewed attention to the ships that have docked on South African shores. Freed from the exigencies of the struggle and the urgency of presenting a united front, South Africans whose ancestors had been transported across the Indian Ocean to make their home on African soil have begun to retrace these journeys and, in the process, reveal South Africa's formation and entanglement in previously occluded Indian Ocean worlds.[37]

China, in particular, is a long-ignored South African homeland from which the fogs of obscurity have only just begun to lift, not least due to two publications: an illustrated history of the Chinese in South Africa compiled by Melanie Yap and Dianne Leong Man and Darryl Accone's family (auto)biography, *All Under Heaven: The Story of a Chinese Family in South Africa*. Both emphasise the tension experienced by Chinese immigrants between the perceived need to assimilate, fit in, and adapt to their new society and the equally pressing desire to transport intact their cultural traditions across the ocean. Both also point out that most Chinese immigrants embarked for South Africa as economic migrants, intending to return to China, and yet never making this homeward-bound journey.[38]

All Under Heaven anticipates this outcome in the sense of foreboding that descends on a young Ah Kwok as he sets off for what is intended to be a temporary sojourn in Johannesburg: "It was as if in leaving the soil of Canton he had committed some irrevocable action."[39] In the closing epilogue, after the author has revealed himself as a member of the extended family that will issue on South African soil, we see Ah Kwok (now under the name he had to take in order to gain entrance to South Africa, Ah Leong) gazing back over the water:

> On holidays at the coast, Ah Leong would stand looking eastwards over the Indian Ocean, hands clasped behind his old but upright back: east towards China, towards the home he had left when not yet a teenager, certain in his youthful optimism he would return soon. He never set foot on Chinese soil again. He spent the last 73 years of his life in Namfeechow.[40]

The very act of writing, tracing the voyage out in reverse, becomes in itself a form of return, an expiation for past ancestral loss and displacement, yet one which turns east *not* in order to depart from South African shores, but rather to enrich and complicate the cultural heritage of the nation that is now home.

The impossibility of return is written into the very plot of *All Under Heaven*: one branch of Accone's family does attempt repatriation when the apartheid noose tightens around its neck. The second section, "Sea" (the book is divided into four sections: Sky, Sea, Earth, and Fire), opens not, as we might expect, on the voyage out, but on the voyage in. Its opening chapter, "On the *Diamaru*, Indian Ocean, 1923," finds Gertie and Andrew, the eldest children of Martin and his European-South African wife, Cornelia, returning "to live on the soil of what Father always called home."[41] The

Indian Ocean becomes, on the voyage, the "repository of [their] hopes"[42] as they sail toward a homely world imaginatively set in contrast to the estranging web of legislation they have to negotiate in South Africa. These hopes seem fulfilled as they near China, stopping in Singapore, where they feel "curiously at home" due to the number of Chinese in whose features they recognize their own, while seeing in the Malays uncanny images of "the Coloureds in Namfeechow"; as Gertie points out: "the Malays were taken from this part of the world by the Dutch, who ruled here, and used slaves in the new Dutch settlement at the Cape. That's why these people seem so familiar."[43] Yet, while they wait in their father's home village for their parents and siblings to join them, they find themselves often out of place in what should be "home." The impossibility of return is then finally underlined in the passage of their parents.

Following their eldest children to China, Cornelia and Martin relive their youthful romance as Cornelia once more finds her previously closeted white world "enlarged"[44] by the Indian Ocean world Martin has traversed:

> On the voyage from Durban to Mauritius, Martin [. . .] told them of the island where he had spent his youth, of its wavy trees, rugged mountains and endless plantations of sugar cane. [. . .] Cornelia listened almost as raptly, for in her husband's recounting she was transported back to the heady early days of their romance, when she would hang on every word of his as he spoke of Mauritius and, going further back, of China.[45]

Recalling the moment when "their eyes, and two worlds met,"[46] she is brought to the present with a start, realizing that she "was on board the ship, not in the safe, cosy corner of [Martin's] shop"[47]; both sites—Martin's Chinese shop in Johannesburg and the ship crossing the Indian Ocean—speak to the connections and entanglements that present alternative realities to the stratified, bounded worlds that apartheid aimed to produce.

There is, moreover, no return to the point of origin from the polygot reality of the Indian Ocean world. When they pass through a violent storm, Cornelia and Martin comfort one another with the thought that "[i]t shall be part of the story of our passage, our journey from the West."[48] In the calm that follows, however, Martin slips on the stairs leading to the deck, and dies from his injuries. The boundlessness of the ocean turns ominous: "Worries encircled Cornelia as the ocean did the ship. She was a 37-year-old widow with seven children, bound for a country that she had never seen, in which she knew no one, and whose language she could speak with only moderate fluency."[49] Without Martin by her side, and stunned by the yawning gap between his nostalgic remembrances of "home" and the reality she finds, Cornelia and her children return to South Africa. While Cornelia later moves on to Australia, Gertie remains in South Africa to become one of the author's grandparents.

The use of untimely death to fend off the return "home" in order to force the remaking of home on the other side of the Indian Ocean is also employed in Aziz Hassim's *The Lotus People*, which plots itself over three generations in order to reach from India to South Africa. "Unfold[ing] between India and South Africa," argues Isabel Hofmeyr, "it shifts the axes of our thinking":

> It moves our attention from the Atlantic to the Indian Ocean. This shift is an important one. South African literature is generally imagined as a combination of 'Europe' and 'Africa' or as a weave of Europe/Africa/ North America. Hassim's novel, however, redefines South Africa as part of the Indian Ocean. It consequently extends our thinking about the multiple inheritances that make up South African society. It is a story of how we combine various international traditions—from both the Atlantic and Indian Ocean; and of how these inheritances are refor- mulated and shaped into a 'home-made' cosmopolitanism.[50]

Presenting Durban's Casbah as "a miniature replica of a major city in India,"[51] the novel shows how the "imaginary homeland," as Sugata Bose puts it, "could in a sense travel to Africa"[52]; in the process of being "carried across" the ocean, it is translated into new structures and idioms, jostling alongside Africa and Europe in a process which is often as painful as it is provocative. Yahya's generation face the shock of arrival in an inhospitable British Natal that tries to fend off their landing:

> when I first came here I truly believed that I was coming as a free man. A pioneer. On the first day that we docked in Durban they held all the Indians on board our ship as virtual prisoners, on the pretext that the ship was in quarantine. The European passengers who had traveled so closely with us had been happily welcomed and allowed to disembark. It was only after several days of the utmost privation, and when the port authorities had run out of every excuse they could think of, did they allow us to set foot on solid land.[53]

Generations to follow will continue to feel the earth turn to water beneath their feet as white South Africa advances a series of repatriation schemes, finally recognizing those of Indian descent as a South African population group only in 1961. The result is a sense of ontological insecurity in the second generation; Yahya's son, Dara, sees the Indian caught between two groups: unyielding whites and militant blacks. The 1949 riots in which Africans attacked Indians[54] loom large in his memories, as he recalls the "brutal savagery of the Zulu hordes."[55] While he claims to have "made this country our home,"[56] he prepares, in his old age, to return to India:

> Look around you, at this continent of Africa. What has it taught you? In country after country the white man has been the exploiter and has

enriched himself. The Indian the victim now has been bludgeoned into paying the price, by the incensed indigenous inhabitants whose memories are short and their greed to emulate the now defeated rulers greater than their powers of logic. [. . .] The conclusion is inescapable. *We must leave this country. Now!* [57]

His son, Jake, however, responds emphatically: "We belong here, we are part of the struggle."[58] Keenly aware of the need to resist apartheid "divide and rule" tactics *and* to translate cultural practices into South African homes, the novel's project is in part to record and remind postapartheid South Africa of the significant role played by Indians and South Africans of Indian descent during the antiapartheid struggle; through the pages of this work—and others—walk figures such as M.K. Gandhi, Dr. Goonum, Dr. Naicker, Dr. Dadoo and Fatima Meer. Into this project is woven another: retaining cultural memories of India so that "home" becomes, as R. Radhakrishnan writes, "a mode of interpretive in-betweenness, [. . .] a form of accountability to more than one location."[59] Relocating across the Indian Ocean, then, foregrounds the south-south solidarities and transfertilisations,[60] and the blend of "nationalism and universalism,"[61] out of which anticolonial positions were crafted and from which new national homes were made, and open up new directions that bypass the North and West in order to plot alternative configurations.

But the weave of India and Africa that *The Lotus People* produces threatens to fray around the 1949 riots. The idiom employed to represent this crisis moment seems to have been drawn from the colonial repertoire: before we see the Africans, we hear "the roar, like distant thunder,"[62] of their approach; when they move into focus, the soundtrack changes to "blood-curling yells."[63] The "sheer mass" of these "hordes" is finally seen rampaging through the streets, "mercilessly clubbing their screaming victims."[64] But the tension such depictions create is quickly eased as the mystery surrounding Jake is abruptly resolved. The novel's structure, which sees it jumping back and forth between past and present, ensures that the chapter following the riots will reveal Jake to be the famed undercover *Umkhonto we Sizwe* operative and freedom fighter: *Aza Kwela*. The movement that takes place across this temporal juxtaposition is then mirrored in the larger family epic. Dara's plans to return to India—which his surviving son, Sam, resists with the insistence that "[w]e are an integral part of this country"[65]—are thwarted by his sudden death. Ending with the next generation preparing to take up the national liberation struggle, the novel concludes with an insistence that those who have traversed the Indian Ocean have now firmly put down roots in their new homeland.

A similar process is traced in Ronnie Govender's *The Song of the Atman*, a fictionalized reconstruction of the life of the author's uncle, Chin Govender. The novel begins with a letter from Chin to Devs, a son he had illegitimately conceived with a black woman, due to his insistence that he could only marry an Indian woman.[66] The import of the letter becomes evident only at the close of the narrative, which itself opens with the words: "The choppy seas shot spray into his face."[67] At first glance, the reader may expect to be transported into the passage from India. Chin, however, is not making a transoceanic crossing; rather, he is traversing the Table Bay to visit Devs, imprisoned on Robben Island for antiapartheid sabotage. Only in the following chapter do we cut back to the oceanic passage, and even here only from the perspective of a first generation South African Indian who, significantly, is not a member of the extended family traced by the novel:

> His father had come to South Africa from Bihar in India, where he and others like him had been fed stories of gold nuggets being picked up on the streets of Durban. It was a different story, of course, when they arrived, aching to get away from an India impoverished by waves of Arab and British imperialism. The word 'indenture', as he has his fellows were to discover, was a polite word for slavery.[68]

Presenting indenture as a form of slavery, Govender resists the homogenization of South Africans of Indian descent under the sign of "the greasy Indian who was only interested in making money, by fair or foul means, and who still regarded India as the motherland."[69] Following other postapartheid texts in relating the transoceanic passage to South Africa, it evidences anxiety about the implications of doing so, which is in turn resolved by transposing the passage onto that to Robben Island: the passage undertaken by the heroes of the national liberation struggle.

When we are again directed to the transoceanic passage, Govender once more employs it as an occasion to consider transplantation: routing as rooting, and oceanic travel as the making of home.

> The first indentured labourers had brought with them seeds and seedlings, which they managed to keep alive despite the long, taxing journeys on rickety sailing vessels and, later, steamships. Given the conditions, this was a minor miracle. Among the plants and seeds they brought were tamarind, peepul, mango, jackfruit, coconut, avocado, guava, china guava, different types of gourd, curry leaf, mustard, dhania, chillies and bringals. Their homes were surrounded by mango, avocado, jack fruit, banana and custard-apple trees, curry-leaf bushes, hedges of granadilla and double-bean vines, and neatly ordered front gardens of snapdragons, marigolds, carnations, dahlias, roses and pride-of-Indias. With some exceptions, regularly whitewashed exterior walls and glossy-painted interiors—often somewhat garish, in bright primary colours—reflected an abiding pride in one's home.[70]

The spectre of the 1949 riots looms once more and is again carefully managed. Cast, firstly, as a white conspiracy ("Much of the violence was clearly orchestrated by unseen forces"[71]), this painful history that sets autochthon against immigrant is finally dismissed as irrelevant to the fully transplanted subject, as the following exchange between Chin and his nephew, Guru (who is recruited to the antiapartheid movement by Devs and, after this statement, is made to pay the ultimate price for national liberation), reveals:

> 'We are living well. What more do you want? Indians are caught between. If the black people get into power you won't have a chance. Look at what happened during the 1949 riots . . . '
>
> Guru said quietly, 'I am not an Indian. I am a South African [. . .] I am a South African—like your son Devs!'[72]

The final novel to be discussed in this brief survey casts home adrift once more. Imraan Coovadia's romp across "East," "South" and "North," as the three sections of *The Wedding* are entitled, opens with Ismet Nissan, the narrator's grandfather, travelling through India by train. Reflecting bitterly on the fragmentation of the Indian polity, he glances out the window in time to catch a glimpse of "the most beautiful lady in the world."[73] Leaping out of the carriage in which he is about to come to blows with a family of Sikhs, he cuts a hilarious figure in the village, where he is finally able to secure Khateja as his wife, under the strict condition, stipulated by her, that the marriage will never be consummated. Her hard-won independence is only relinquished later in South Africa, when narrative fate (she is, after all, the narrator's grandmother) demands of her that she produce a new "race" of Indo-Africans.

Their train-bound honeymoon behind them, Ismet takes Khateja home to Bombay, where she and her mother-in-law enter into a domestic feud that nearly engulfs them in a conflagration of flames. As Khateja refuses to be domesticated into her wifely role, the mother-in-law embarks on a domestic strike; refusing to prepare another meal until Khateja pulls her weight in the kitchen. Into this stalemate, Ismet introduces his plans to travel to South Africa. His reasons for migrating are threefold: the domestic feud that is driving him to slow starvation, the desire for a "sea change,"[74] and, finally, the dream of "founding a new race"[75] that besets him when he visits a friend in search of culinary sustenance, only to be regaled by hyperbolic stories of the "brave new world" across the oceans, whose extolled wonders include its ability to tame impetuous women. The benefits of a few years in South Africa, his informant claims, can be viewed in his wife: "You should see her now, completely obedient, asking me every minute what I am wanting, what are my wishes, what she can do for me. Absolutely in love."[76]

In Ismet's fantasies of arrival:

> Khateja the ice queen would melt.
>
> As the ship pressed close on the African coast she would reach for his hand and squeeze it tightly.
>
> 'I am scared, Ismet', she would tell him [. . .]

That aboriginal forge Africa would throw them ever more tightly into each another's arms. There would be an untamed volcano, a chop-licking leopard circling around in the evening-time, the poisoned darts of the bone-nosed natives whistling through the air to make sure they would turn always to the other for reassurance. Cooing and mooning, adoring inaugural twosome.

From Khateja's womb would spill a legion of children [. . .] A hundred, a thousand, peopling the vast land.[77]

This vision is allegorical not only of a new Indo-African people; it is suggestive also of the ways in which "India" and "Indians" are themselves presented as products of this "aboriginal forge," driving previously divided groups into one another's arms, while Ismet's imagery suggests that such productions of India are based on an othering of Africa that sails very close to colonial constructions. Ismet and Khateja are, in turn, both uniquely individual in their idiosyncrasies and made to stand for a larger population. While Ismet, in religion, point of disembarkation, and profession, belongs to the "passenger" Indian class, the fact that he and Khateja make their journey out onboard the SS *Truro* (the name of the first ship to disgorge its cargo of indentured labourers onto South African soil in 1860), links them also to this second wave of Indian traffic.

One of the novel's major themes concerns the "making" of India and Indianness in South Africa. Coovadia develops the notion that Gandhi was, in South Africa, able to see India as a whole—was able, in effect, to imagine India into being:[78]

thanks to its piebald, multistriped composition, the municipality of Durban inculcated in the mind of the expatriate Mohandas Gandhi, who was currently residing there, the outrageous conviction that each disparate subcontinental belonged to the same nationality—and so, in a sense, Durban created the nation-state of India.[79]

Forged on the "black water" (*kala pani*) between India and South Africa, as numerous commentators have noted, was a new sense of Indian identity:

Within Natal, there were thus indentured workers, free Indians and passenger Indians. The indentured Indians came from a variety of villages, spoke many languages and were from different castes in India. But from the minute the journey from India began a new identity was starting to develop, one that would grow further on African soil. [. . .] The voyage across the ocean itself meant breaking the rules of caste, and confinement on the ship did not allow any finicky regulations governing whom one should eat with.[80]

The act of crossing the ocean, Bill Freund points out, sundered the social bonds that secured individuals within the Hindu caste system[81]; regrouping again on dry land, Indian migrants "allow[ed] themselves to inhabit a world somewhat different to India yet similar enough to keep the memory of India alive."[82] This translation, Freund suggests, was managed through the creation of:

> a double cultural world [. . .] On the one hand, there was a neo-Indian world [. . .] which looked very Indian indeed to outsiders. On the other hand, there was the attraction of the marketplace, the hybrid colonial cultural world outside the house which held great appeal and also had to be entered for practical reasons.[83]

Freund's observations mirror those of Partha Chatterjee, in his discussion of the ways in which nationalist ideology in colonial Bengal resolved both the "woman's question" and its own contradictory nature through a separation of spheres: the material and the spiritual, which were then mapped onto the gendered Victorian separation of private and public, or "home and the world." According to Chatterjee, the Bengali elite forayed into the world of modernity while enshrining self-identity in the home, where it remained uncontaminated by the compromises made in the public sphere. The home, then, became the "inner sanctum" of nationalist identity, guarded and embodied by women.[84]

Ismet attempts to produce such a division of spheres in Durban by having Khateja set up home while he strikes out in search of material success. As they unpack in their new abode, this seems entirely possible, as "India, multifold, many-fingered, articulated, cloth-covered India issued from their luggage."[85] But Ismet's plans snag on Khateja's intractability. Living on "bunny chow," a hybridized South African-Indian dish, Ismet grows troubled by the extent to which India is accommodating itself to its new surroundings:

> [A] man cannot live by bunny chow alone: It was time, to start shooting off roots, to set seeds in the patient earth, time to husband their pool of resources. Had they traveled so far to embrace stagnation? India is a portable country, to some extent, which moves as people do, accommodating itself freely to new environments, but if they started off forsaking her, forgetting her in this and that detail, what would happen at the end of time?[86]

The solution, as he sees it, is for Khateja to prepare authentic Indian dishes inside the "inner sanctum." Making home, as this text brings into focus, is a gendered activity that calls on women to transport, recreate and maintain "home." For Ismet, the potential gains are twofold: the domestication of his wife and the preservation of "India"; both aims unite in the production of the "home-country wife" that he tries to effect:

> This was his idea: stand the fractious Khateja before an iron pot and a paraffin stove, have her stirring with spoons one-two hours a day, washing meat, dicing vegetables, slicing up loaves of brown bread on a cutting slab, frying, ladling, marinating—at some point, indubitably, lo! a real traditional Indian-style home-country wife and gentle-fingered lady would emerge from the membranes of dissension, would cast them off, chrysalis-like (or so Ismet imagined). Ushering a new race of beings onto the world-historical stage without first pausing to refit the original mother, truly that would be madness.[87]

However, both cultural identity and domesticity are shown to be duplicitous, carrying within themselves subversive modes of resistance that Khateja is able to use to her advantage. Turning to the resources an Indian kitchen can offer, she deftly thwarts Ismet's efforts. Her elaborate culinary production is, on the first sitting, an apparent success; the second meal strikes Ismet as being a tad hot on the palate, but speaking sufficiently of India's portability to allow him to begin feeling "perfectly at home. He looked at the blacks in their blue overalls, light-bodied men sweating in the heat and moving boxes or grumbling, and he wanted to put his arms around them."[88] Into her third, and final, meal, Khateja pours: "Six bags red chili powder, twelve grated green chilies, a big glass bottle of black pepper that had a broad maroon label with a pirate ship and skulls on it, for good measure a fifth or a pint of Tabasco sauce in the prawns."[89] The pirate ship label, familiar as Robertson's line of spices, gestures back to the very start of this story, in which the spice route draws South Africa, as refreshment station, into the Indian Ocean world.

Eventually, and inevitably given the grandson-narrator, Khateja is tamed; but her spirited defense does at least ensure that the "inner sanctum" of the home is redefined as a space of potential subversion. Rather abruptly, we leave this generation, and these shores, to end up, with the narrator, in the North. Ensconced in a Sikh-driven taxi, we join him en route to a cinema where he watches a film about a family of Indians in Kampala, Uganda, which evokes the fragility of the "home" that has been constructed on the other side of the Indian Ocean:

> People are happy. Then, in 1972, Idi Amin, struggling with the thought, comes to a conclusion. He furrows his brow and announces, 'Africa is for the Africans. That means,' and he pauses for a second, scans the paper in front of him, and continues, 'that means that Asians have no place here. They should go somewhere else'.[90]

Their heartfelt appeals that "this is our home" fall on deaf ears.

Stepping out of the cinema, the narrator concludes:

> Standing there outside the theatre, underneath the awning, on the pavement in Times Square, an eternity after Ismet Nassin saw the most beautiful woman in the world, [. . .] amid the Hispanic dope dealers and the Jewish daughters and the Irish cops and the Pakistani mothers and the limousine-ferried real-estate magnets and the black rap addicts and the sweatered and suede-jacketed students—standing there, for an instant, I imagined I was at home.[91]

* * *

The "world-*in*-the-home" that the movements traced in this chapter have produced, struggled against, and ultimately celebrated, gives way to a sense of home-in-the-world.[92] It is in such uncanny states—which Mbeki's speech begins to reach towards, even as his presidency may have foreclosed their potential—that new national homes, with open rather than closed doors, can be imagined. None of the narratives discussed here—all written in the new era—are able to bring their stories up to the present, except in the odd coda or epilogue. Yet all speak eloquently of the ways in which we can reimagine a postapartheid world. In the unhomely structures through which their subjects flit, we may hear ghostly echoes of the return of the repressed, as the postapartheid nation, which imagines itself as a home for all, attempts to stem the "flood" of immigrants slipping through its borders, this time travelling over land rather than sea.

NOTES

1. See Hofmeyr (2007) for an overview of the differences that the Indian Ocean paradigm imparts.
2. See Mbembe.
3. George, 18. I have elsewhere explored the poetics of home in postapartheid writing in ways resonant with the argument presented here, but without reference to the Indian Ocean world (see Samuelson, *Remembering*, 195–230).
4. Frainman-Frenkel, 5.
5. I refer here to the controversial, yet highly popular, song, "*AmaNdiya*" ("The Indians"), by the famous playwright and musician Mbongeni Ngema, which includes lyrics such as "We struggle so much here in Durban, as we have been dispossessed by Indians [. . .] I have never seen Dlamini emigrating to Bombay, India. Yet, Indians arrive everyday in Durban—they are packing the airport full" (quoted in Nyamnjoh, 57). For further commentary, see Nyamnjoh (56–63) and Frainman-Frenkel (25).
6. On the uncanny/unhomely (i.e. *unheimlich*), see Freud.
7. See, *inter alia*, Dhupelia-Mesthrie.
8. See, *inter alia*, Shell.
9. The first wave of Indian traffic to South Africa has generally been ignored, or sundered from studies of the second and third waves. As Uma Dhupelia-

Mesthrie notes, "Indian slaves would not preserve a distinct identity as Indians [. . .] They would eventually become known as Malays, a term which ultimately referred to all Muslim slaves irrespective of their geographical origins, or they would disappear into that general category of people known as coloured"; their experiences and contributions have been elided the "general history of Indian South Africans. The main marker of that history is 16 November 1860, when the first of what by 1911 would total 384 ships, dislodged its human cargo from India on the shores of Natal. They arrived under the indentured system, which has since been described as 'a new system of slavery', since it was meant to replace slavery, which was abolished in the British colonies in 1834" (10).

10. Bose, 18.
11. Ward.
12. Worden, 42.
13. Harries, 101.
14. Worden, 30.
15. Worden's recent comparison of the port towns of Cape Town and Port Louise draws out some of the implications of such a connection.
16. For a comparative study of these two texts and their representations of a littoral world, see Jamal.
17. See Ward & Worden.
18. Bose, 18.
19. Jacobs, 156.
20. Jacobs, 31.
21. Ibid., 154–55.
22. Ibid., 157.
23. Similarly romantic, and far more disturbing in its ability to sublimate the experience of slavery, is André Brink's *Rights of Desire*, in which the ghost of a decapitated slave woman, Antjie of Bengal, returns to offer benediction to an aging white man, allowing him to feel finally at home in the new South Africa.
24. Gqola, 56.
25. Cronin, 52.
26. Harries, 92.
27. Ibid., 93.
28. Ibid.
29. Ibid., 108.
30. Christiansë, 156.
31. Ibid., 21.
32. Ibid., 28–29.
33. Ibid., 174.
34. Ibid., 283.
35. Ibid., 333.
36. Ibid., 327.
37. Noting the importance of asserting a united South African identity under apartheid, Dhupelia-Mesthrie notes: "The new South Africa allows those who rejected Indianness at the height of apartheid to explore their roots and to be what they want to be" (27).
38. See Yap and Leong Man, 31.
39. Accone, 46.
40. Ibid., 281.
41. Ibid., 49.
42. Ibid., 53.
43. Ibid., 56.
44. Ibid., 92.

45. Ibid., 109.
46. Ibid., 110.
47. Ibid., 114.
48. Ibid., 118.
49. Ibid., 122.
50. Hofmeyr, 2003.
51. Hassim, 168.
52. Bose, 150.
53. Hassim, 61.
54. See Dhupelia-Mesthrie; Freund, 57–58.
55. Hassim, 23.
56. Ibid., 25.
57. Ibid.
58. Ibid., 26.
59. Radhakrishnan, xiv.
60. See Boehmer.
61. Bose, 31.
62. Hassim, 149.
63. Ibid.
64. Ibid., 151.
65. Ibid., 285.
66. Govender, 165.
67. Ibid., 13.
68. Ibid., 19.
69. Ibid., 269.
70. Ibid., 154–55.
71. Ibid., 271.
72. Ibid., 309.
73. Coovadia, 6.
74. Ibid., 105.
75. Ibid., 119.
76. Ibid., 117.
77. Ibid., 120.
78. See, *inter alia*, Brown.
79. Coovadia, 142–42.
80. Dhupelia-Mesthrie, 13.
81. Freund, 9.
82. Ebr.-Vally, 22.
83. Freund, 9–10.
84. See Chatterjee, 238–39.
85. Ibid., 148.
86. Ibid., 157.
87. Ibid., 164–65.
88. Ibid., 176.
89. Ibid., 178.
90. Ibid., 278.
91. Ibid., 280.
92. See Bhabha, 11.

BIBLIOGRAPHY

Accone, Darryl. *All Under Heaven: The Story of a Chinese Family in South Africa.* Cape Town: David Philip, 2005.

Bhabha, Homi K. *The Location of Culture.* New York: Routledge, 1994.

Boehmer, Elleke. *Empire, the National, and the Postcolonial, 1890–1920: Resistance in Interaction.* Oxford, UK: Oxford University Press, 2002.

Bose, Sugata. *A Hundred Horizons: The Indian Ocean in the Age of Global Empire.* Cambridge, MA: Harvard University Press, 2006.

Brink, Andre. *The Rights of Desire: A Novel.* London: Secker & Warburg, 2000.

Brown, Judith M. "The Making of a Critical Outsider." In *Gandhi and South Africa: Principles and Politics,* edited by Judith M. Brown and Martin Prozesky, 21–33. Pietermaritzburg: University of Natal Press, 1996.

Brownlee, Russel. *Garden of the Plagues.* Cape Town: Human & Rousseau, 2005.

Chatterjee, Partha. "Nationalist Resolution of the Women's Question." In *Recasting Women: Essays in Indian Colonial History,* edited by Kumkum Sangari and Sudesh Vaid, 233–53. New Brunswick, NJ: Rutgers University Press, 1990 [1989].

Christiansë, Yvette. *Unconfessed: A Novel.* New York: Other Press, 2006.

Coovadia, Imraan. *The Wedding.* New York: Picador, 2001.

Cronin, Jeremy. "Creole Cape Town." In *A City Imagined,* edited by Stephen Watson, 45–54. Johannesburg: Penguin, 2006.

Dhupelia-Mesthrie, Uma. *From Cane Fields to Freedom: A Chronicle of Indian South African Life.* Cape Town: Kwela, 2000.

Ebr.-Vally, Rehana. *Kala Pani: Caste and Colour in South Africa.* Cape Town: Kwela, 2001.

Frainman-Frenkel, Ronit. "'On the Fringe of Dreamtime . . . ': South African Literature, Race and the Boundaries of Scholarship." Ph.D. thesis, University of Arizona, 2004.

Freud, Sigmund. "The 'Uncanny." 1919. In *Standard Edition of the Complete Psychological Works,* Vol 17, translated and edited by James Strachey, 217–56. London: Hogarth, 1955. .

Freund, Bill. *Insiders and Outsiders: The Indian Working Class of Durban 1910–1990.* Pietermaritzburg: University of Natal Press, 1995.

George, Rosemary Marangoly. *The Politics of Home: Postcolonial Relocations in Twentieth-Century Fiction.* Berkeley, CA: University of California Press, 1996.

Govender, Ronnie. *Song of the Atman.* Johannesburg: Jacana, 2006.

Gqola, Pumla Dineo. "'Slaves don't have opinions': Inscriptions of slave bodies and the denial of agency in Rayda Jacob's *The Slave Book*." In *Coloured by History, Shaped by Place: New Perspectives on Coloured Identities in Cape Town,* edited by Zimitri Erasmus, 45–63. Cape Town: Kwela Books, 2001.

Harries, Patrick. "Making Mozbiekers: History, Memory and the African Diaspora at the Cape." In *Slave Routes and Oral Tradition in Southeastern Africa,* edited by Beningna Zimba et al., 91–123. Maputo: Filsom, 2005.

Hassim, Aziz. *The Lotus People.* 2002. Johannesburg: STE, 2003.

Hofmeyr, Isabel. Review of *The Lotus People,* by Aziz Hassim. First published in *The Sunday Independent.* *The Lotus People* website. http:///www.lotuspeople.co.za/archives/000020.html. 2003 (accessed 22 May 2007).

Hofmeyr, Isabel. "The Black Atlantic Meets the Indian Ocean: Forging New Paradigms of Transnationalism for the Global South—Literary and Cultural Perspectives." *Social Dynamics* 33(2; 2007): 3–32.

Jacobs, Rayda. *The Slave Book: A Novel.* Cape Town: Kwela, 1998.

Jamal, Ashraf. "Africa's Appendix." Forthcoming in *Eyes Across the Water,* edited by Pamila Gupta, Isabel Hofmeyr and Michael Pearson. Pretoria: Unisa Press.

Mbeki, Thabo. "I am an African." [Statement of Deputy President T. M. Mbeki, on Behalf of the African National Congress, on the Occasion of the Adoption by the Constitutional Assembly of 'The Republic of South Africa Constitution

Bill 1996.] 8 May 1996. http://www.anc.org.za/ancdocs/history/mbeki/1996/sp960508.html (accessed 15 Jan, 2005).

Mbembe, Achille. "African Modes of Self-Writing." Translated by Steven Rendall. *Public Culture* 14(1; 2002): 239–273.

Nyamnjoh, Francis B. *Insiders and Outsiders: Citizenship and Xenophobia in Contemporary Southern Africa.* Dakar: Codesria; London: Zed Books, 2006.

Radhakrishnan, R. *Diasporic Mediations: Between Home and Location.* Minneapolis, MN: University of Minnesota Press, 1996.

Samuelson, Meg. *Remembering the Nation, Dismembering Women? Stories of the South African Transition.* Pietermaritzburg: University of KwaZulu-Natal Press, 2007.

Shell, Robert C-H. *Children of Bondage: A Social History of the Slave Society at the Cape of Good Hope, 1652–1838.* Johannesburg: University of the Witwatersrand Press, 1994.

Sleigh, Dan. 2004. *Islands.* Translated by André Brink. London: Secker & Warburg, 2004.

Ward, Kerry. "'Tavern of the Seas'? The Cape of Good Hope as an Oceanic Crossroads during the Seventeenth and Eighteenth Centuries." Conference Proceedings: Seascapes, Littoral Cultures, and Trans-Oceanic Exchanges, Library of Congress, Washington, D.C., 2003. http://www.historycooperative.org/proceedings/seascapes/ward.htm. (accessed 30 April 2007).

Ward, Kerry and Nigel Worden. "Commemorating, Suppressing, and Invoking Cape Slavery." In *Negotiating the Past: The Making of Memory in South Africa*, edited by Sarah Nuttall and Carli Coetzee, 201–227. Cape Town: Oxford University Press, 1998.

Worden, Nigel. "Cape Town and Port Louis in the Eighteenth Century." In *The Indian Ocean Rim: Southern Africa and Regional Co-operation*, edited by Gwyn Cambell, 42–53. London: Routledge, 2003.

Worden, Nigel. "Indian Ocean Slavery and its Demise in the Cape Colony." In *Abolition and its Aftermath in Indian Ocean Africa and Asia*, edited by Gwyn Campbell, 29–49. London: Routledge, 2005.

Yap, Melanie and Dianne Leong Man. *Colour, Confusion and Concessions: The History of the Chinese in South Africa.* Hong Kong: Hong Kong University Press, 1996.

13 A Travelling Science

Anthropometry and Colonialism in the Indian Ocean

Rochelle Pinto

The Medical School in colonial Goa (a Portuguese colony from 1510 to 1961, located in the western Indian Ocean) has been the focus of a number of studies that situate the institution within the matrix of nineteenth-century colonial imperatives and philosophies. Of the many significant aspects of the school that delineate its place in the exercise of colonial power, the following quote about its historiography seems apt for the purposes of this chapter.

> Accounts of the collective saga of the doctors of Goa turn on a core that combines the following two narrative strands in a form that is unique and seemingly paradoxical: on the one hand, it emphasizes the constant discrimination to which they were subjected by Portuguese authorities; on the other, it exalts the glories of their contribution towards the Portuguese colonization of Africa. The glorification of the past and of the imperial vocation is conjoined to the historiography of the twentieth century about the Medical School and reaches its peak between 1940 and 1950, when Portugal tried to sustain an archaic style of national imperialism in a world that had turned in another direction.[1]

Cristiana Bastos among others has suggested a range of ways in which to explore the effect of the Medical School as the locus for the hierarchisation of "Western" medicine over prevailing medical practices, or as a discursive filter for the appearance and disappearance of indigenous populations in medical texts, as the hosts of disease or the site for its control.[2] The emphasis in Bastos' work however, has been to demonstrate how the Medical School further filtered the ideological currents emanating from the metropole, modifiying them according to the political exigencies of the local elite in the colony of Goa. Some of her essays have traced the changes in imperial ideology through the length of the Salazarist dictatorship from 1926 to 1974; with particular attention to the elaboration of notions of racial difference which provide a grid onto which one can map similar shifts occurring in the colonies.[3]

The School therefore appears enmeshed within a layered and dynamic semantic field, the site for the articulation of racialist and colonial ideology that not only sifted whites from others, but also Catholic Goans from Hindu Goans, upper-caste Goans from lower-caste Goans, and Goan doctors from African subjects. Far from being passive and parasitic recipients of a racialised discourse that they used to bolster their position within a colonial racial grid, Bastos indicates that the Goan elite seized upon the Medical School and contemporary medical and racial discourse to fashion categories and spaces for itself that had not hitherto existed. The production of texts that reveal the nature of intellectual activity within this subordinated elite was aided by nineteenth-century legislation that officially recruited the Medical School of Goa to dispense medical services to African colonies.[4] These texts, produced by Goan doctors who were in a position to observe, record, describe, and make deductions about the nature of race, constitute a body of work that reveals much about contemporary interest in anthropology, anthropometry, race theory, and colonial improvement.[5]

This chapter is a study of a few of these anthropometric and ethnographic texts produced in the context of Portuguese colonies in the Indian Ocean by Goan doctors recruited in the service of the empire. I trace how the texts of Alberto Germano da Silva Correia and Constancio Mascarenhas, two doctors associated with the Medical School in Goa, negotiated the discourse of race. I examine the construction of race in these texts, in an attempt to add to the body of work that urges that we examine racial difference as it emerged in nondominant or atypical contexts.[6] The majority of these texts were produced from the late nineteenth century until the 1930s, a period associated with the consolidation of the Salazarist dictatorship in Portugal, and modern state practices that reaffirmed Portugal's hold over the colonies. With reference to race, the Estado Novo renewed its rationale of colonial rule based on scientistic theories of race that were supported by the setting up of institutions and societies devoted to the study and classification of racial difference. An article that elaborates the ideologies of race that were dominant during the 1930s (as opposed to the 1950s) emphasizes that the legal separation of colonial populations into "civilized" and "primitive" reinforced racial difference, while simultaneously declaring the colonies as politically one with the Portuguese nation.[7]

The texts produced by Goan doctors during this time are of interest, as they manifest the contradictions that emerged when norms for calibrating racial difference were deployed by colonial subjects who were privileged in relation to other colonies, while subordinated in relation to the metropole. They also, however, indicate that though the discourse of racial difference within the ambit of the Indian Ocean appeared to be similar to that which held sway in other parts of Europe, it had remnants and strains of different and prior ways of establishing difference that were specific to the Iberian experience of colonialism. The simplicity of the division of civilized from primitive that accompanied diversified norms of classification and scientific ordering, in itself indicates that a closer inquiry into the intellectual legacies of Portuguese colonial rule may be of interest. This chapter, however, retains a focus on the varied and sometimes unpredictable uses of anthropometry in the hands of colonial subjects who were both threatened and empowered by the discourse of race.

This study could be situated within arguments that suggest that the nineteenth-century classificatory systems which dominated European state practice may not adequately account for the workings of race within empires formed prior to the eighteenth century.[8] The Dutch, Spanish, and Portuguese colonial experience, for instance, suggests the emergence of modern structures of articulating difference much before Anglo-American dominance, as well as the persistence of consistently different modernist adaptations of a Christian (and perhaps specifically Catholic) worldview.[9] Perhaps the most visible difference between the implementation of practices of racial classification in British as opposed to Portuguese colonies was the creation and absorption of mixed-race elites into the administration of empire and, sometimes, the polity of the metropole. This fact alone prevents a study of Portuguese colonialism from assuming that the distance established between "West" and other, through the distance between the "white" race and others, was ever secure as a scientific or political category in Portugal; or that it denotes the same kind of difference that one assumes in relation to Anglo-American practices.

The fact that Portugal itself had to prove its European identity from the thirteenth century on, striving to distance itself from the intellectual and racial proximity of Arab and African traditions, signifies both its early investment in the discourse of racial segregation, as well as the many intellectual currents that were not invested in identifying difference along racial lines. At the simplest level, among the currents that combined with and/or militated against establishing difference on the basis of phenotype and purity of blood was the persistence of Catholicism as a political philosophy. Despite the numerous categories denoting purity of blood to separate Christians from Jews and Muslims, and later, blacks and mestiços from the pure Portuguese, the transition to being a Portuguese subject routed through conversion to Christianity persisted, and was used as a legal means of mobility by various colonial elites.[10]

The conflation of Catholicism with citizenship was simultaneously a political, legal, and religious category, though less dominant from the end of the eighteenth century, and virtually submerged in the Salazarist definition of the Portuguese state. A sign of its persistence as a political trope is evident, however, in the continuing and broad amorphous division between civilized and native, which allowed certain populations within the colonies to be recognized as citizens and others as natives.[11] The criteria for recognition under Salazar, however, were comportment, dress, language, and profession—markers that were cultural rather than religious, signifying the entry of markers that were nonreligious to regulate entry into the ranks of citizens.[12]

Therefore, beyond the framework of binary difference suggested by the experience of British and Northern European colonialism, the experience of creolized populations in contexts ranging from the Seychelles to Brazil has suggested the need to account for assimilation to "sameness" as a strategy of colonial power, in the construction of racial difference. If these different constructions of race were compared for their relative significance in the context of the *disciplinary* reach of racial discourse, connoting modern state practices of enumeration and individual disciplining, then one would have to concede that a binary understanding of race had an overarching influence particularly in the nineteenth century.

In the day-to-day running of the Portuguese empire, a range of racial terms were generated among Portugal's colonies, without any great degree of internal consistency between one colony and another, though segregation in various realms of life was systematically effected as much in Portugal as in the colonies.[13] The need to pinpoint what was different about race within Portuguese colonialism has less to do with asserting degrees of racial oppression or evidence of segregation that is only too similar to that practiced in other empires, than with tracing what strategies of power were enabled by the inconsistencies in racial discourses. This discussion of anthropometric studies conducted in the early twentieth century on different races in Africa and India suggests that these texts are poised on the divide between ways of defining and constituting difference within Portuguese colonialism, and the simultaneous pressure exerted by the legitimacy of knowledge production about Indians generated within British colonialism. The colonial elites of Goa, themselves created through an assimilationist model of colonial rule, adopted contemporary thinking about race with the intention of modernizing their own domain of practice, by incorporating and responding to the newest theories on race. They were positioned, however, to indicate the fissures and the inapplicability of some of these theories to their own situation and to reproduce some of its contradictions.

The enumeration of the Goan elite within the racial and religious constructs of the Portuguese empire, along with their enumeration within categories of caste and ethnicity that were defined predominantly by the anthropological surveys of the British colonial empire on the Indian subcontinent, placed them at the crossroads of two kinds of enumeration that denoted potentially differing positions on a racial and ethnic grid vis-à-vis groups within Goa, British India, and two different colonial powers. A snapshot view of this elite group may be necessary to indicate why their encounter with theories of race provoked the writing of these texts. Though the actual extent of racial mixing between Portuguese and Goans is unknown and is unlikely to have numerical magnitude, the uppermost echelon of the privileged class in Goa was constituted by rival groups of mixed-race subjects as well as colonial (as opposed to metropolitan-born)

Portuguese, and Goan subjects who were a porous and mobile class of competitive indigenous elite. The Goan and mixed-race elite pushed against discrimination within church, state, and the circuits of knowledge production to assert their place in the world.

When we consider the spectrum of elites, however, it is evident that the Portuguese (whether colonial born or metropolitan) were not the only contenders. Goan elites were also defined by caste structures of Catholic Goan society, and participated in the rivalry among the upper castes. Furthermore, they had greater access and privilege in the realm of state politics, higher education, and bureaucracy in comparison to Hindu upper castes. Outside of the tensions among upper castes, other caste groupings, with differing degrees of power, existed among both Catholics and Hindus. A reading of texts about race in the context of India and Africa produced by the Catholic elite necessarily evokes this pantheon of subject-positions, among which the elite were variously defined. The tensions that are visible in these texts were not only generated by the subordination of Goans to the Portuguese therefore, though this was the most dominant and visible impetus for their production, but was symptomatic of the wider and more complicated realm of colonial knowledge production that a location within the Indian Ocean denotes.

In the following sections I trace how the writings of Alberto Germano da Silva Correia and Constancio Mascarenhas, as doctors associated with the Medical School in Goa, negotiated the discourse of race. The intersections and divergences of discourses of race and caste may be a useful entry point for a discussion of how Indian elites may have functioned as a conduit and a constitutive force in the production of these discourses in the western Indian Ocean.

RATIONAL COLONIALISM

While the production of racial categories had begun much earlier, the mid- to late-nineteenth century in Portugal saw these categories being rerouted through institutions, laws, and texts for the organization of information about the colonies that would respond to the European demand for the scientific and rational colonialism that Portugal was said to lack.[14] At a time when colonies had been lost, and large areas of Africa had been apportioned to various European powers, the accumulation of information and its appropriate showcasing worked as a discursive defense against the decline in the number and profitability of Portugal's colonial holdings across the world.

The Sociedade Geografia de Lisboa (Geographical Society of Lisbon), set up in 1875, initiated a series of geographical and anthropological expeditions to Africa, and became one of the visible nodal Portuguese institutions that would parade the production of knowledge driven by enlightenment thought.[15] The collections of photographs, craniums, artifacts, and anthropological and historical data from the various expeditions ensured that the holdings of the Sociedade were regarded as a source of archival information, but also as a model for branches and offshoots of the organization within the colonies themselves. Such efforts were driven by demands internal to Portugal and its colonies that cited the political effectiveness of Anglo-American and European discourses on race, civilization, and colonial governance. In 1877, therefore, the permanent Commission of Geography urged the government to send expeditions into Central Equatorial Africa.[16]

In a study of the trajectories of intellectual and institutional discourses around anatomy, natural history, and evolutionary theories that constituted the domain of anthropology, Ricardo Roque makes the argument that there was a consolidation of the authority of anthropology as a university discipline in the 1930s, particularly after the public excitement generated by the display of African subjects at the Portuguese Colonial Exhibition in Porto in 1934.[17] With the state and university speaking in one voice, Roque argues, there was an attempt to command and direct the involvement of parallel institutions in the colonies to contribute to the anthropological agenda set by Portugal. The Colonial Act of 1930 and the Salazarist regime's boost for a nationalist rearticulation of colonial rule facilitated this.[18]

Despite the evident investment in of the emergent discipline of colonial anthropology, the same historians emphasize the evidence of discontinuity, incompleteness, and instability in the way these initiatives were actually manifest.[19] They point to the fact there is no simple link between the circulation of anthropological texts, their reception in the colony, and their impact on colonial governance. Others suggest how the imperatives of local colonial institutions, such as the Medical School in Goa, in fact determined the shape of structures that were set up to be the colonial handmaidens of metropolitan power.[20]

Within this context, a further impetus to the intellectual endeavours of Goan doctors was the need to combat their professional subordination to universities and medical practice in Portugal. The school in Goa would not be given the status of a university, such that doctors had to further their training in Portugal to be ranked on par with those based in the metropole. Ricardo Roque further suggests that the status of the colonial intelligentsia was not acknowledged in metropolitan circles despite the simultaneity of interests and a relatively fluid circulation of texts between colonies.[21] This was particularly evident in the case of Alberto Germano da Silva Correia, a military doctor and teacher, trained in Goa, Porto, and Lisbon, and in the Parisian school of anthropology.[22]

PRODUCING STRONG BODIES: MODIFYING THE DISCOURSE OF RACE

The focus of studies on Correia's work has tended to be his writing on the *luso-descendentes*, the mixed-race populations in the colonies, and the *descendentes,* the direct descendants of the Portuguese, and, in particular those in India. Correia's focus on mixed-race populations can be viewed in context of the fact that in the nineteenth century, climate continued to be seen as the main factor responsible for physical and cultural difference. Cristiana Bastos emphasizes that though "race had come to be seen as a stable biological entity" by the nineteenth century, the Portuguese were dogged by the fear that people who moved from one climate to another would undergo physical change. Northern Europeans pointed out that miscegenation in India, Brazil, and Africa had led the Portuguese down the path of "darkness, degeneration and caffrealization."[23] In a study on the migration of impoverished Madeirans, and therefore white Portuguese, to various colonial plantations in search of employment and fortune, Bastos indicates that the figure of the Madeiran is one among the many facets of Portuguese colonialism that disrupts the identity of a singular white colonizer. Migrant Madeiran bodies, she reveals, became the focus for late-nineteenth-century Portuguese studies on how *caffrealization* or indigenisation and acclimatization inevitably spelt the medical, physical, and cultural degeneration of the white race.[24]

In opposition to this, Correia's modification of the theory of degeneration among the Madeirans carved out a racial niche for mixed-race elites. His work on the hygiene and acclimatization of the white race in the tropics constructed an approach that he extended to the study of Angola and Portuguese India.[25] According to Correia, the ability of the Madeirans to acclimatize, and survive, was a marker of the strength and endurance of the Portuguese race. They adapted and did not succumb easily to tropical diseases, unlike their Northern European counterparts. By implication, this theory could be extended to mixed-race elites to legitimize their presence within the field of anthropometry and to suggest that it was beneficial to empire building. This insertion of *luso-descendentes* disturbed the apparently neutral and scientifically graded racial order that distinguished white races from others, to force the figure of the mixed-race colonial onto the stage of anthropometry.

Such disjunctions indicate that the continuous relocation and circulation of the Catholic Goan elite and Portuguese administrators in various parts of the Portuguese empire did not produce a consistent cumulative anthropological discourse, but a discontinuous one. For the demands of absolute scientificity required that the Portuguese, the colonial-born Portuguese, the mixed-race populations, and the Catholic Goan elite also be systematically accounted for within theories of race. As a continuum of the prevalent trends in European anthropology to focus on the ethnogeny of the nation itself, the Portuguese presence in other parts of the world seemed to demand study through methodologies that were gaining currency. *Índia Portuguesa* emerged as a distinct entity that was a comparative parallel to Africa, as well as to the metropolitan categorization of the white race.

Commentaries on Correia have therefore emphasized that the demand of universal applicability made by emergent sciences was in fact at the behest of the colonial anthropologist.[26] In the face of occasional indifference and skepticism from the metropolitan academic establishment, the envisioned cosmopolitanism and circulation of modern learning was effected by the colonial doctor as a means of having colonial identities enumerated and therefore legitimized through science. As Ricardo Roque asserts, this confounds the binary of center and periphery in plotting the flows of knowledge production.[27]

Correia's text on Portuguese India began with a harangue that echoed the exhortation that simultaneously rang around the metropolitan circles of anthropologists, urging the state to mobilize its resources for the systematic organization of information about colonial peoples.[28] He starts with an expression of intense disappointment with the state of ethnographic study in Goa. His dominant concern in the preface to his text was the paucity of work on Portuguese India, and the glaring omission that he saw in contemporary scholarship caused by the absence of work in this area. "What is known about the racial composition of the population of India Portuguesa? Nothing," he stated.[29] "What is known about the ethnic origins of the inhabitants of Goa Daman and Diu? Nothing once again," he said.[30] He went on to list the various recommendations that had been issued from the mid-nineteenth century onwards, urging the collection of data of various sorts from the colonies; none of these had apparently been seen as pressing. His comments on the flaws and absences in his own text were in fact a bitter commentary on the indifference within the Goan administration and intelligentsia to his attempts to inaugurate a new disciplinary space. He said:

> Mine is not an anthropometrical work because with the absolute lack of anthropological instruments, I had no opportunity to provide any measurements of the normal or the criminal. This cannot even be an anthropological study because in this country of doctors, lawyers and metaphysicists, nothing, absolutely nothing exists that makes an ethnological study of its inhabitants possible.[31]

Correia's theory of white adaptability, however, was tempered with warnings against cultural contamination, which he saw as debilitating. Portuguese descendants, according to him, had retained both their cultural and racial strength, by keeping marriage alliances within the community. Bastos argues that Correia's own position within the empire, as a *mestiço*, was implicated in these theories. The decline of the *descendente* in colonial politics, and the taint of racial mixing, made visible through the increasing rigidity of racial typing in Europe, were compensated for through his theory of Portuguese adaptability.

CATEGORICAL LIMITS

If all the works of an individual doctor like Correia are analyzed together with the work of Goan anthropologists collectively, it would seem that the production of racialist discourse by colonial doctors was an effort to provide an adequate template for the vast racial range and context provided by the experience of Portuguese colonialism. This not only necessitated the inclusion and explanation of *descendentes* (both Portuguese and *mestiço*), but was also a challenge to the very scientificity of racial ordering that made clear divisions between one race and another possible.[32]

The work of the second Goan anthropometrist under consideration in this chapter, Constancio Mascarenhas, reveals how this challenge was complicated by the fact that he traversed the uneven categories of caste and tribe borrowed from census reports in British India, which had different implications from the connotations of racial and caste categories in Goa. The works of anthropometrists in Goa tended to be discontinuous when they analyzed populations in terms of ethnicity and/or race. They separated the study of the white and mixed-race descendants of the Portuguese, from an ethnological study of Hindu Goans. If we were to locate what it was about Correia's text that was not entirely metropolitan, and yet not completely a creolized position, it was the distinction he drew between the need to study the white and mixed-race populations in terms of a racialised anthropology and the Hindu population of Goa in terms of caste.

Among the indigenous peoples of Africa and India, all those who could not be counted as assimilated whites or as indigenous Catholics or as assimilated citizens became the object of ethnographic and racial study. In 1909, the Sociedade Geografia de Lisboa sent a set of photographs from Goa and Africa to the International Photography Exhibition in Dresden.[33] Within this collection, it was groups of Hindus, such as temple dancers, priests, local kings, and idols, who emerged as the focus of exotic speculation and/or ethnographic study. Similarly, a wide range of people from Africa, distinguished by profession, "tribe" and place, and familial relations, were seen as objects of spectatorship.

How were the Goan elite to resolve these divisions within the domain of a science that was supposed to be universally applicable? With the proliferation of categories of caste, tribe, ethnicity, and race in neighbouring India, and with the need to categorize themselves among mixed-race or assimilated Brazilians, Timorese, Africans, and Portuguese, it was the quantificatory techniques of anthropometry that promised a uniformity of measurement across difference. This was, however, a fragile unity, and the prefaces and forewords of the writers were revelatory of their fractured anthropological vision, despite their lists of measurements and morphological traits. In particular, the work of Mascarenhas—written in the 1930s, at a moment when anthropometry was being discredited for its association with racist ideology, and when the competing discipline of sociology had achieved considerable prominence—bears the marks of a fraught position within colonial anthropology.

Anthropometric studies conducted by Correia and Mascarenhas examined temple dancers, Muslims of Portuguese India, the Marathas of

Portuguese India, *Curumbins*, an "agricultural caste" in Goa, the Ranes of Satari, and Southern Indian tribes.[34] The writings of both these doctors in French, Portuguese, and occasionally, English, were addressed to an international audience of French, American, and other European theorists who were acknowledged authorities on race theory and anthropology. The Goans justified their findings with contemporary theories that fed into the formation of international protocols for anthropometry and anthropology.[35]

Mascarenhas' choice of samples typified the groups that would be encountered within the Portuguese empire. His expertise was brought to the study of samples of 447 Portuguese craniums, 26 Hindus, 49 Africans, 4 Timorese, and 116 Angolans.[36] Rather than producing a theory of uniformity, it would appear that the perception of group after group through the lens of anthropometry pushed Mascarenhas to elaborating the limits of his own discipline. He therefore sustained his belief in the scientificity of anthropometry precisely on the grounds that it had revealed the unsustainable relation between race and anthropometry; the fact that it produced data, but not data that had anything useful to say about racial difference.

On the whole, the thrust of arguments in Mascarenhas' craniometric studies were to emphasise differences in formations that were independent of race, or rather, similarities across race that suggested that certain kinds of anthropometric features could not be seen as the attributes of a particular race. Mascarenhas in fact explicitly combated the belief that deductions about mental ability could be made on the basis of anthropometry. Within a history of changing perspectives on race and anthropology, he evidences the shift from a biological understanding of race to a socio-historical one. What could anthropometry then do for the two groups that Goan doctors represented most frequently (Africans and non-Catholic Indians)?

Mascarenhas' divergent approach when choosing a methodology for the study of Hindus of Goa and British India as opposed to Africans is revelatory of the political quandaries of the Catholic Goan elite, rather than being a systemic inconsistency, arising from the juxtaposition of two different ways of categorizing difference. Inclusion within a category of race or caste would not only position them differently in the eyes of each colonial government (a positioning that would alter depending on whether they were located in Goa, in British India, or in Portuguese or British Africa), but would also affect their hierarchisation in relation to fellow Goans.[37] Within scientific texts, however, the inability to reconcile the inadequate and asymmetrical systems of classification had to be compensated for with ethnographic explanations to account for cultural difference. Mascarenhas' own doctoral work was on the castes of India, to explain how an inequitable system persisted despite Buddhism. His student, Vassudeva Camotim (or Vasudev Kamat), combined ethnography and anthropometry and extended these methods to the study of his own privileged caste group, the Saraswat Brahmins in Goa.[38]

Such uncertainties over categories were not the preserve of these anthropometrists alone. Studies on colonial ethnography in British India have traced the shifts in theories of race from the eighteenth century on, and the shifting legitimacy of the grounds on which racial identity was proved.[39] Others have suggested that notions of caste and tribe drew on a racialised understanding of difference, and that evolutionary and linguistic theories of race helped sustain a theory of civilization in which the white race was the most advanced, and the rest were graded in degrees of proximity to white. Crispin Bates' "Race, Caste and Tribe in Central India: The Early Origins of Indian Anthropometry," for instance, suggests that the longue durée of evolutionary time allowed for the mapping of distinctions of caste and tribe, in themselves never stable or convincing as empirical categories, onto the "scientifically" proven distinctions between races.[40] Simply put, this meant that upper-caste Indians could be categorized as potentially belonging to the Aryan race, and lower castes, but most especially tribes, could be categorized as the racial "other." Such categorizations of caste that changed in accordance with differing administrative theories and theories of social difference, helped enormously in the administration of property and populations. But, Bates argues, the furthest reaches of racial primitiveness was reserved for those about whom the British knew least, and therefore feared the most.[41]

Both upper-caste Indians (under British rule) and upper-caste Goans could potentially benefit from the implication of their proximity to the white race. Yet, the studies conducted by Catholic Goans placed Hindu Goans at a distance from themselves through *caste* categories denoting occupation and political hierarchy while they themselves were identified exclusively through race. Typically, in the case of texts about the Ranes or Southern Indian tribes, ethnographic descriptions identified what was distinctive about the clothing, marriage, and occupational patterns of these various groups, and preceded anthropometric tables. There was little connection between ethnographic essays and anthropometric tables, which were juxtaposed as incremental and discrete information. While membership within an upper caste had potential benefits for a Hindu Goan, the elite Catholic's classification within racial categories would be the only appropriate category that would justify their proximity to the colonizer in both Goa and in Africa.

INFALLIBLE DOGMA: ARGUING AGAINST RACE

It was in relation to black Africans, who, unlike the Indians, could not be housed in racial proximity to the white race, that Mascarenhas was pushed to provide a lengthy account of racial difference and the failures of contemporary methodology. It was the unassimilated African who was most jeopardized by anthropometry and racial classification, a system that had lost its legitimacy for Mascarenhas. Given the fallibility of racial theory, there had to be another explanation for what was still, to Mascarenhas, visible "backwardness" of the African continent as a whole. This difference, however, he was certain, was not racial in as far as race was a scientific and therefore technical category. His defence of the African is indicative of the eclectic sweep of arguments that the Goan doctor was called upon to produce, once disabused of the conviction that anthropometry was a useful tool for ascertaining difference.

Mascarenhas insisted on historical contingency as the reason for the "backwardness" of isolated black populations against the overarching consensus with regard to their inherent resistance to civilization. His publication of 1934, *The People of Angola*, embodies the dilemma of the scientist who, on discovering the inadequate scientificity of his theory, also discovers its implication in nonscientific power structures. The text depicted the black person caught between the civilized who used him as a workhorse, and the evangelist who saw in him a brother of the same species.[42] Between these two views, he stated, "the Negro dragged himself along in his primitive and obscure existence."[43] It was the duty of rational and scientific methods of colonialism to civilize the black African, according to contemporary wisdom. However "if one cast an eye over the indigenous populations of Africa," said Mascarenhas, "one could not encounter even one that had been shifted towards western civilization." "Would it be necessary" he asked, "to then agree with the various authorities who assert that the ferocity and savagery of the African barred him from entry into the civilized world? Would one have to adopt this as an infallible dogma?"[44]

From the anatomico-physiological and the anthropological point of view, there had been attempts, he stated, to prove the distinctiveness of the African, but these in fact could not be supported scientifically. It was through the psycho-moral realm, he suggested, that one had to account for what he saw as the unquestionably primitive nature of African society. Mascarenhas' argument extended beyond those of the anatomists, to incorporate recent work by genetic sociologists, and inevitably, to philosophies of civilization. He was particularly vociferous about those who propagated that the primitive mind had certain intrinsic antirational, mystic preoccupations. He argued against Levy-Bruhl's, François Cosentini's, and Raoul Allier's contentions that the inherently passive primitive mind had to eventually give way to the Western, or that the primitive mind being completely ordered by mysticism, could not conceive of contradiction, or of the objective representation of things and concepts.

Interestingly, the persistent nature of Mascarenhas' argument against typifications of the African led him to contest the teleological assumptions of evolutionary time. He did this by citing empirical examples of the behaviour of Africans that did not match the traits that were supposed to typify primitive behavior; examples from practices of supposedly civilized peoples which in fact corresponded to contemporary beliefs about the primitive. Against the idea therefore, that unregulated sexual activity led to the dissipation of civilizations, which was said to characterize India as well as Africa, Mascarenhas argued that India was however not ranked in the category of the primitive, just as the prevalence of polygamy among Muslims, and the sexual dissoluteness of the Greeks had not led to an argument of primitiveness. He argued therefore, that civilizations went through different phases, and could not be characterized in any fixed way. Against Bergsonian philosophy, which he opposed in favour of Cartesian rationality, Mascarenhas suggested that it was through conflict and fights that civilizations developed, and it was only the absence of contact with other civilizations in sub-Saharan Africa that maintained people in their primitive state.

This rationalist argument against determinist racism not only developed into an argument for a philosophy of action as a civilizational strategy for growth and survival, but led to critical questions about the links between governance and concepts of civilization in colonial Africa—was it not perhaps the notion of a backward civilization that was used in the governance of Africa that in fact produced that state to match the idea? The anticolonial stance in these arguments is evident, but the more interesting aspect to Mascarenhas' work is the progressive steps through which what began as an argument against the applicability of anthropometry for the analysis of race developed into an argument about the categories underpinning theories of governance and civilization.

The study of blacks in America, according to Mascarenhas, indicated the great transformation that contact with heterogeneous cultures had achieved, but the significant difference between America and Africa, he stated, was that after the wars of independence, the state in America worked actively for the betterment of its people, whereas politics in the colonies were driven by different impulses. Mascarenhas not only shifted the burden of civilizational states to the nature of the state or colonial governance, but also historicized the changing notion of the civilizing mission that had shaped colonial relations. This had particular relevance to the history of Portugal, which under Salazar had refreshed the historiography of its imperial past as the earliest civilizing mission in various parts of the world, particularly Africa.

If Mascarenhas' location in time and in the line of vision of the particular racial spectrum afforded by the Portuguese empire had produced this relentless questioning of race theory, why was it only in connection with Africa that such an interrogation had emerged? Why could his own place in the multiple classificatory grids of race and caste not elicit it? The many possible answers to this question reflect the shifts in race theory in the contexts of the Atlantic world and the development of Portuguese colonialism.

Linda Martín Alcoff's "Philosophy and Racial Identity" for instance, positions itself in the impasse created by antiessentialist theories of race, on the one hand, which dissolve the category of race, and the pressing political need, on the other, to assert race as an ontological entity, such that its continuing prevalence is not undermined by theories that question the epistemological validity of its existence.[45] Alcoff discusses the possibilities of Paul Gilroy's *The Black Atlantic: Modernity and Double Consciousness* as a way to elude this bind. For Gilroy, and others who follow a similar argument, the assertion of racial identity "is a concept not organized around sameness, . . . not as sameness opposed to difference but as substance opposed to absence."[46] It is in the possibility of making an "interested positionality" visible, Alcoff suggests, that the category of identity needs to be understood.

Gilroy and Alcoff struggle with the liberal discourse of sameness and difference as well as critiques of identity, as assertions that are still enmeshed in the implications of liberal categories. This critique provides a possible entry into plotting the difference of Portuguese discourses on race. Alcoff for instance also cites David Theo Goldberg who argues "that the universal sameness that was so important for the liberal self required a careful containment and taxonomy of difference. Where rights require sameness, difference must be either trivialized or contained in the Other across a firm and visible border."[47] Against this, it is possible to suggest that the assertion of sameness was never fully secularized within Portuguese colonialism. With Portuguese citizenship and notions of nation and national subjectivity never fully articulated outside of religious Christian terms, the scientific legitimization of colonial difference was not as crucial to the colonial state's support of racial segregation (as suggested earlier, this does not imply that it was not prevalent, just that it did not require the justification required by states who had distanced the definition of the national subject from Christian categories).[48] This argument would seem to dovetail with the almost commonsensical historiographical claim in nationalist histories of Portugal, which suggest that it was a Christian rather than commercial spirit that drove politics at home and in the colonies.[49]

Against such a claim, Diogo Ramada Curto throws out a series of challenges in his essay, "Portuguese Imperial and Colonial Culture," where he cites a range of political traditions that were in practice in colonial interactions between the sixteenth and seventeenth centuries.[50] Ramado Curto provides instances of how racial difference was onceptualized and practiced within the early modern period from across the colonies, through republican ideals, monarchist paternalism, and entrepreneurial slave petitions for manumission. He also gestures to a combination of humanism, antiquarian methodology, and Christian mythmaking in the construction of the narrative of a Christianised rather than a technologised colonial tradition, to assert the impossibility of single-cause explanations as an adequate historical explanation for Portuguese history.

To return to Alcoff and Goldberg's argument, it could be asserted (following Curto) that the absence of a singular dominant discourse generated from within Portugal for the understanding and administration of colonial difference produced no singular response that urged sameness with the colonizer, but fractured and diverse arguments against oppression. As Ramado Curto discusses some of the dilemmas attendant on deciding at which level of generality to pitch one's analysis as a historian of Portuguese colonialism, he emerges with the evocative phrase "dynamism of the oceans," to depict the extensive reach of the empire and the diversity of coexisting political vocabularies.

As this chapter attempts to define the discursive position of the texts produced by Goan doctors, the challenge posed is to identify the political positioning that produced their vision. This positioning cannot be conveyed by defining their place in a racial hierarchy (which was simultaneously overwritten by multiple categories), or within a scientific moment (simultaneously inscribed by a Christian discourse of civilization and secularized scientism).

To combine both the theoretical concerns described above, of complicating the history of Portuguese colonialism, and of identifying the assertions of racial identity as substantive and positioned articulations against the demarcation of absence, this chapter suggests that the "subaltern elite" of Catholic doctors found themselves situated between the civilizational Other represented by the African and the enumerated Other of British colonialism, the caste-bearing Hindu. This position was empowering as it inserted the Catholic Goan doctor in the position of a racially superior knowledge producer vis-à-vis Africa, but it also created an epistemological space between two kinds of enumeration that enabled a critique of anthropometry and instability in the claims of classification.

The visibility of caste in India and the attempt to order it as a subset or variation on race had a significance in the context of British colonial administration that it did not have for early-twentieth-century Portuguese colonialism. In the case of Portuguese colonialism, the privileging of upper castes and the rationalization of caste into colonial structures already had a relative stability from the sixteenth and early seventeenth century. Enumeration and the elaboration of difference in the nineteenth century was not as significant a concern for routine administrative governance in the gambit of Portuguese colonialism.

This assertion may be better explained if we draw from Bethencourt's and Curto's demand for an understanding of the Portuguese empire as a discontinuous one, demanding a study of the highly variable configurations of power in the local contexts of Portugal's colonies.[51] Bethencourt also emphasizes, however, that discontinuity does not necessarily lead to the embracing of the fragment and the production of unresolvedly isolated historical moments. It would appear that the tension within Alcoff's race theory about the potential theoretical dissolving of race as a node of power following antiessentialist critiques is also mirrored in the historian's anxiety about arriving at a methodology to understand Portuguese colonialism without falling into either/or positions with regard to the macro and micro view, the mono-causal and the fragmentary view. This would seem to be the contemporary dilemma facing the historiography of Portuguese colonialism—to arrive at coherent explanations for the multiplicity of political formations across the empire and across time, without taking recourse to a centralized vision that the macro view brings, or a resolutely localized difference that the micro view tends to produce. I would contend that the position of the Catholic Goan doctor between Africa and India exactly enacts the typical movement of Portuguese colonialism, producing figures and moments that cut across intellectual, chronological, and geographical terrains that appear theoretically stable.

While the upper castes within the tribe-caste classification of the British were assured a certain position of power that could be extended to the Hindu Goan, the Catholic Goan had far more to gain from being defined by race. Yet, for a scientist invested in the claims of neutrality and even equality of the scientific method, the category of caste too did not pose a very great threat, as it was recognized by the Portuguese as the remnants of a great but declining Indian civilization. It was the African who remained the least assimilable quantity in the Portuguese empire. The privileged positioning of the elite Goan doctor could not be better displayed than in the defence of the African subject. However it was the reality of their self-definition as members of caste groups as well as their publicly acknowledged identity as racialised subjects and the fact of inhabiting these diverse, discontinuous categories which they had participated in elaborating, that may have prevented Germano Correia and Constancio Mascarenhas from using their potential access to whiteness to legitimize a theory of Portuguese racial synthesis that erased the question of power between colonizer and colonized—a stance associated famously with the Brazilian sociologist, Gilberto Freyre.[52]

The diverse discursive pressures weighing on Mascarenhas to reconcile the classificatory logic produced by the colonizing traditions of Britain and Portugal may have propelled him towards resolving their inconsistencies. But, closer home, the Salazarist reassertion of colonial relations could also have generated his vehement engagement with race and his anticolonial diatribe, applied however, to the safely distanced figure of the oppressed African.

NOTES

1. Cristiana Bastos, "O ensino da medicina na Índia colonial portuguesa: fundação e primeiras décadas da Escola Médico-cirúrgica de Nova Goa," *História, Ciências, Saúde-Manguinhos* 11(1; 2004).
2. Ibid., 11.
3. See Rosa Cabecinhas and Luís Cunha, "Colonialismo, Identidade Nacional e Representações do 'Negro,'" *Estudos do Século XX* 3 (2003), for a detailed exposition of the shift in ideologies of race leading up to and within the Estado Novo.

4. Cristiana Bastos, "Doctors for the Empire: The Medical School of Goa and its Narratives," *Identities* 8, no. 4 (2001). Bastos elaborates on decrees issued between 1844 and 1847 that sought to control the teaching and administration of medical practice in African and Asian colonies.

5. Ricardo Roque, "Equivocal Connections: Fonseca Cardoso and the Origins of Portuguese Colonial Anthropology," *Portuguese Studies* 19(1; 2003).

6. Francoise Verges, "Writing on Water: Peripheries, Flows, Capital, and Struggles in the Indian Ocean" *positions: east asia cultures critique* 11 (1; Spring 2003): 241–257.

7. Rosa Cabecinhas and Luís Cunha, "Colonialismo, Identidade Nacional E Representações Do 'Negro,'" *Estudos do Século XX*, 3 (2003).

8. Ann Laura Stoler, *Race and the Education of Desire—Foucault's History of Sexuality and the Colonial Order of Things* (Durham, NC: Duke University Press, 1995).

9. Miguel Vale de Almeida, "From Miscegenation to Creole Identity: Portuguese Colonialism, Brazil, Cape Verde," in *Creolization: History, Ethnography, Theory*, ed. C. Stewart (Walnut Creek, CA: Left Coast Press, 2007).

10. Hebe Mattos, "'Pretos' and 'Pardos' Between the Cross and the Sword : Meanings and Uses of Racial Categories in the 17th Century Portuguese Empire." Within the history of ideologies of race, however, this can also be explored as the persistence of a religious theory of monogenesis despite the dissemination of theories of polygenesis.

11. Marcelo Caetano, *Colonizing Traditions, Principles and Methods of the Portuguese* (Lisboa: Agencia Geral do Ultramar, 1951).

12. This would alter by the 1950s, when the postwar fear of anticolonial movements prompted a cynical extension of rights of citizenship to most colonial subjects, and a hasty embracing of "lusotropicalism" a celebration of racial mixing within Portuguese policies, as an official stance on the racial assimilation of nonwhite subjects.

13. Mattos, "'Pretos' and 'Pardos' Between the Cross and the Sword : Meanings and Uses of Racial Categories in the 17th Century Portuguese Empire." For a description of segregation in schools in Mozambique in the 1930s, see Mário Malheiros, "L'Enseignement," in *Colonie de Moçambique*, (Paris: Exposition Coloniale Internationale, 1931).

14. Jose Joaquim Lopes de Lima, *Ensaios sobre a Estatistica das Possessoes Portuguesas na Africa Occidental e Oriental, na Asia Occidental* (Lisboa: Imprensa Nacional, 1862). Or, the Secretary to the Governor General in Goa, J. H. da Cunha Rivara's preface to Augusto Estanislau Xavier Soares, *Descripção da Villa de Sofalla, de seus principaes edificios, população, agricultura, commercio, etc., deguida de Cathalogo de seus Governadores, e dos de Moçambique, pois que esta provincia foi separada do governo da India* (Nova Goa: Imprensa Nacional, 1857). Photographic images of African labour generated for international exhibitions between the nineteenth and twentieth centuries were intended to combat universal consensus that Portugal's colonies were preserved in a state of extreme underdevelopment. Eric Allina, "'Fallacious Mirrors': Colonial Anxiety and Images of African Labor in Mozambique, ca. 1929," *History in Africa*, 24(1997): 9–52. http://links.jstor.org/sici?sici=0361-5413%281997%2924%3C9%3AFMCAAI%3E2.0.CO%3B2-F

15. Roque, "Equivocal Connections: Fonseca Cardoso and the Origins of Portuguese Colonial Anthropology."

16. Germano Correia, *Os 'Luso-descendentes' da Índia—estudo antropo-aclimológico e histórico-demográfico* (Nova Goa: 1920).

17. Ricardo Roque, "A antropologia colonial portuguesa (c. 1911–1950)," in *Estudos de sociologia da leitura em Portugal no século XX*, ed. Diogo Ramada Curto (Lisbon: Fundação Calouste Gulbenkian).
18. Cristiana Bastos, "Race, medicine and the late Portuguese empire: the role of Goan colonial physicians," *Institute of Germanic & Romance Studies* 5(1; 2005): 24.
19. Roque, "Equivocal Connections: Fonseca Cardoso and the Origins of Portuguese Colonial Anthropology." Roque's discussion of Fonseca Cardoso emphasises that there may not be a stable connection between colonial imperatives, knowledge production and the life of the anthropological text as artifact. Bastos, "Race, Medicine and the Late Portuguese Empire: The Role of Goan Colonial Physicians," 27. Bastos mentions the Portuguese administration's "lack of interest" in exercising "colonial biopower."
20. Bastos, "Race, Medicine and the Late Portuguese Empire: The Role of Goan Colonial Physicians."
21. Roque, "A antropologia colonial portuguesa (c. 1911–1950)."
22. Bastos, "Race, Medicine and the Late Portuguese Empire: The Role of Goan Colonial Physicians," 30. Correia also served in Angola, aside from his professional involvement in European institutions.
23. Cristiana Bastos, "Migrants, settlers and colons: The biomedicine of displaced bodies" (paper presented at the Conference Diaspora and Disease, SOAS, London, March 31–April 1 2005).
24. Ibid.
25. Correia, *Os 'Luso-descendentes' da Índia—estudo antropo-aclimológico e histórico-demográfico.*
26. Roque, "A antropologia colonial portuguesa (c. 1911–1950)."
27. Ibid.
28. Correia, *Os 'Luso-descendentes' da Índia—estudo antropo-aclimológico e histórico-demográfico.*
29. Ibid.
30. Ibid.
31. Ibid.
32. This difficulty in achieving a consistent tabulation was visible elsewhere as well. At the International Congress of Orientalists, held in Lisbon in 1892 and organized by the Sociedade Geografia, a comparative account of the Orient and America, or, a comparative account of the uses and customs of the inhabitants of Portuguese India and those of Brazil, proved to be inconclusive, unable to draw any definite mark of similarity between the American Indian and the "Oriental," or between the Brazilian and the "Oriental," and suggested that Portuguese was in fact closer to Sanskrit than any indigenous American language. A. Lopes Mendes, *O Oriente e a America, apontamentos sobre os usos e costumes dos povos da India Portugueza comparados com os do Brazil, memoria apresentada a X sessão do Congresso Internacional dos Orientalistas*, Lisboa, Imprensa Nacional, 1892.
33. *Relação annotada das photographias enviadas a 'Exposição Internacional de Photographia' de Dresde*, 1909, Typographico Colonial, Sociedade de Geographia de Lisboa, Lisboa.
34. Alberto Germano da Silva Correia, *Les bayadères et les autres courtisanes de l'Inde Portugaise. Étude anthropologique et physio-pathologique.* (Bastora: Tipografia Rangel, 1940), Alberto Germano da Silva Correia, *Les ranes de satary. Étude anthropométrique* (Bastora: Tipografia Rangel, 1928), Alberto Germano da Silva Correia, *The mussulmans of Goa* (Bangalore: 1935), Alberto Germano da Silva Correia, *Os maratas da Índia Portuguesa. Estudo antropométrico* (Porto: Edições de 1 Exposição Colonial Portuguesa,

1934), Constâncio and Vassudeva Camotim Mascarenhas, *Os Curumbins de Goa*, ed. Sociedade Portuguesa de Antropologia e Etnologia (Porto: Imprensa Portuguesa, 1959).
35. Constâncio Mascarenhas, *Anthropometrical Notes on some Southern Indian Tribes* (Bastora: Tipografia Rangel, 1936).
36. Constâncio Mascarenhas, *Essais d'Anthropologie anatomique et de Zoomorphologie* (Bastorá: Tipografia Rangel, 1935).
37. In this regard, Crispin Bates' observation that categories of race and caste tell us more about the enumerator than the enumerated, or about the exercise of power and hierarchy between categories, seems apt. Crispin Bates, "Race, Caste and Tribe in Central India: The Early Origins of Indian Anthropometry," *Edinburgh Papers In South Asian Studies* Number 3 (1995).
38. Voicunta Camotim, *Os Bramanes Sarasvatas de Goa* (Nova Goa: Minerva Indiana, 1929).
39. Shruti Kapila, "Race Matters: Orientalism and Religion, India and Beyond c.1770–1880," *Modern Asian Studies* 41(3; 2007).
40. Bates, "Race, Caste and Tribe in Central India: The Early Origins of Indian Anthropometry."
41. Ibid., 14-15.
42. Constâncio Mascarenhas, *Os Povos de Angola*, Tipografia Rangel, Bastorá, 1934.
43. Ibid.
44. Ibid.
45. Linda Martín Alcoff, "Philosophy and Racial Identity," in *Philosophies of Race and Ethnicity*, ed. Stella Sandford (London: Continuum, 2002).
46. Ibid., 27.
47. Ibid., 13.
48. See, for instance, the persistence of division of people into civilized and primitive, or citizen and indigenous evidenced in Ferreira Diniz, *Populações Indígenas de Angola*, Imprensa da Universidade de Coimbra, 1918.
49. This would form one strand among arguments that defensively explain the difference of Portuguese colonialism against the Anglo-American charge of underdevelopment or cruelty, by emphasizing its humanity, its early abolition laws, its commercial failures, etc.
50. Diogo Ramada Curto, "Portuguese Imperial and Colonial Culture," in *Portuguese Oceanic Expansion, 1400–1800*, ed. Diogo Ramado Curto (USA: Cambridge University Press, 2007).
51. Francisco Bethencourt and Diogo Ramada Curto, "Introduction," in *Portuguese Oceanic Expansion, 1400–1800*, ed. Diogo Ramado Curto (USA: Cambridge University Press, 2007).
52. Gilberto Freyre, Portuguese integration in the tropics; notes concerning a possible Lusotropicology which would specialize in the systematic study of the ecological-social process of the integration in tropical environments of Portuguese, descendants of Portuguese and continuators of Portuguese (Lisbon: [Realizaðcäao Grafica da Tipografia Silvas], 1961).

BIBLIOGRAPHY

Almeida, Miguel Vale de. "From Miscegenation to Creole Identity: Portuguese Colonialism, Brazil, Cape Verde." In *Creolization: History, Ethnography, Theory*, edited by C. Stewart, 108–132. Walnut Creek, CA: Left Coast Press, 2007.

Bastos, Cristiana. "Doctors for the Empire: The Medical School of Goa and its Narratives." *Identities* 8(4; 2001): 517–548.

———. "O ensino da medicina na Índia colonial portuguesa: fundação e primeiras décadas da Escola Médico-cirúrgica de Nova Goa." *História, Ciências, Saúde-Manguinhos* 11(1; 2004): 3. Trans. Rochelle Pinto..

———. "Migrants, settlers and colons: The biomedicine of displaced bodies." Paper presented at the Conference Diaspora and Disease, SOAS, London March 31–April 1, 2005.

———. "Race, medicine and the late Portuguese empire: the role of Goan colonial physicians." *Institute of Germanic & Romance Studies* 5(1; 2005): 23–35.

Bates, Crispin. "Race, Caste and Tribe in Central India: The Early Origins of Indian Anthropometry." *Edinburgh Papers In South Asian Studies* 3(1995): 2–35.

Bethencourt, Francisco, and Diogo Ramada Curto. "Introduction." In *Portuguese Oceanic Expansion, 1400–1800*, edited by Diogo Ramado Curto. USA: Cambridge University Press, 2007.

Cabecinhas, Rosa, and Luís Cunha. "Colonialismo, identidade nacional e representações do 'negro.'" *Estudos do Século XX* 3(2003): 157–84.

Caetano, Marcelo. *Colonizing Traditions, Principles and Methods of the Portuguese*. Lisboa: Agencia Geral do Ultramar, 1951.

Camotim, Voicunta. *Os Bramanes Sarasvatas de Goa*. Nova Goa: Minerva Indiana, 1929.

Correia, Germano. *Os 'Luso-descendentes' da Índia—estudo antropo-aclimológico e histórico-demográfico*. Nova Goa, 1920.

da Silva Correia, Alberto Germano. *Les bayadères et les autres courtisanes de l'Inde Portugaise. Étude anthropologique et physio-pathologique*. Bastora: Tipografia Rangel, 1940.

———. *Les ranes de satary. Étude anthropométrique*. Bastora: Tipografia Rangel, 1928.

———. *The mussulmans of Goa*. Bangalore, 1935.

———. *Os maratas da Índia Portuguesa. Estudo antropométrico*. Porto: Edições de 1 Exposição Colonial Portuguesa, 1934.

Freyre, Gilberto. *Portuguese integration in the tropics; notes concerning a possible Lusotropicology which would specialize in the systematic study of the ecological-social process of the integration in tropical environments of Portuguese, descendants of Portuguese and continuators of Portuguese*. Lisbon: Realizaðcäao Grafica da Tipografia Silvas, 1961.

Kapila, Shruti. "Race Matters: Orientalism and Religion, India and Beyond c.1770–1880." *Modern Asian Studies* 41(3; 2007): 471–513.

Lopes de Lima, Jose Joaquim. *Ensaios sobre a Estatistica das Possessoes Portuguesas na Africa Occidental e Oriental, na Asia Occidental*. Lisboa: Imprensa Nacional, 1862.

Malheiros, Mário. "L'Enseignement." In *Colonie de Moçambique*. Paris: Exposition Coloniale Internationale, 1931.

Martín Alcoff, Linda. "Philosophy and Racial Identity." In *Philosophies of Race and Ethnicity*, edited by Stella Sandford, 13–28. London: Continuum, 2002.

Mascarenhas, Constâncio. *Anthropometrical Notes on some Southern Indian Tribes*. Bastora: Tipografia Rangel, 1936.

———. *Essais d'Anthropologie anatomique et de Zoo-morphologie*. Bastorá: Tipografia Rangel, 1935.

Mascarenhas, Constâncio, and Vassudeva Camotim. *Os Curumbins de Goa*. Edited by Sociedade Portuguesa de Antropologia e Etnologia. Porto: Imprensa Portuguesa, 1959.

Mattos, Hebe. "'Pretos' and 'Pardos' Between the Cross and the Sword : Meanings and Uses of Racial Categories in the 17th Century Portuguese Empire."

Revista Europea de Estudios Latinoamericanos y del Caribe No. 80, April (2006).

Ramada Curto, Diogo. "Portuguese Imperial and Colonial Culture." In *Portuguese Oceanic Expansion, 1400–1800*, edited by Diogo Ramado Curto, 314–57. USA: Cambridge University Press, 2007.

Roque, Ricardo. "A antropologia colonial portuguesa (c. 1911–1950)." In *Estudos de sociologia da leitura em Portugal no século XX*, edited by Diogo Ramada Curto. Lisbon: Fundação Calouste Gulbenkian.

———. "Equivocal Connections: Fonseca Cardoso and the Origins of Portuguese Colonial Anthropology." *Portuguese Studies* 19(1; 2003): 80–109 (30).

Soares, Augusto Estanislau Xavier. *Descripção da Villa de Sofalla, de seus principaes edificios, população, agricultura, commercio, etc., deguida de Cathalogo de seus Governadores, e dos de Moçambique, pois que esta provincia foi separada do governo da India.* Nova Goa: Imprensa Nacional, 1857.

Stoler, Ann Laura. *Race and the education of Desire—Foucault's History of Sexuality and the colonial order of things.* Durham, NC: Duke University Press, 1995.

14 Whiteness in Golden Goa
Linschoten on Phenotype

Arun Saldanha

The emergence of white identities during early modernity was largely the effect of the encounters between different bodies on the coasts of the Indian and Atlantic Oceans. This chapter uses the observations made by the late-sixteenth-century traveller Jan Huygen van Linschoten during his stay in Goa to think through some conceptual issues pertaining to processes of racialisation in the Indian Ocean world. "Golden" Goa, then the capital and most important economic node of the Portuguese *Estado da Índia*, exhibited both early forms of cosmopolitanism and the solidification of racial intolerance and prejudice. Following a "physiological" approach to race derived from Nietzsche and Foucault, we can infer from Linschoten's account that racialisation was an incipient material process in which the variations of human phenotype was not incidental, but central. However ambiguous in the light of miscegenations and conversions, phenotype was from the beginnings of early modernity an important if ambivalent vehicle of social difference.

THE EMERGENCE OF WHITENESS

Historical sociologists and historical geographers have recently contributed much to our understanding of how deep the racial dimension of the global present is. Howard Winant, for instance, provides ample evidence of the intertwining of racial politics with democracy itself.[1] In particular, globalization and modernity cannot be understood without understanding whiteness and its emergence within the world's diverse populations and migrations.[2] Europeans started recognizing themselves as white through a gradual hierarchical demarcation and coding of human phenotypical variation. As Foucault showed in his lectures on what he termed *biopolitics*, the fundamental investment of European states in the institutional purification of domestic populations went hand in hand with the ethnic nationalisms and racist typologies of the nineteenth century, and the holocausts of the twentieth.[3] In the wake of Foucault, Ann Laura Stoler kindled new research into the everyday and intimate nature of colonial regimes. In effect, Stoler demonstrates how an infatuation with the literary and the discursive has blinded postcolonial theory to these more mundane and fleshy matters.[4] Conjoining the interests of Stoler and Winant, then, the Foucauldian study of oceanic colonialism would do well to ask in what ways the embodied encounters between sixteenth- and seventeenth-century Europeans, on the one hand, and Africans, Asians, Australians, and Americans, on the other, prefigured later regimes of white supremacy. I want to affirm that racialisation and the concomitant "becoming white" of European bodies are not mere effects of racial discourses, but a material process that phenotypically variable bodies are themselves engaged in.

In contrast to most critical work on colonialism, the conception of race I am advocating here attempts to retrieve the Nietzschean side of Foucault. Foucault's genealogical counter-method draws much of its force from Nietzsche's attack on the historian's obsession with origins. Instead of attempting to represent the past as one continuous lineage running unproblematically from an origin to the present, genealogy is interested in what Nietzsche calls *Herkunft*, which could be translated as "descent":

> the ancient affiliation to a group, the bonds of blood, tradition or social class. The analysis of *Herkunft* often involves a consideration of race or social type. But the traits it attempts to identify are not the exclusive generic characteristics of an individual, a sentiment, or an idea, which permits us to identify them as "Greek" or "English"; rather, it seeks the subtle, singular, and subindividual marks that might possibly intersect in them in a network that is difficult to unravel.[5]

Through Nietzsche, Foucault managed to privilege the messy contingencies of what he calls "emergence." What matters is the spatial arrangement and dissipation of bodies and things, not the clear agency and causality identified in traditional historical writing.

This nonlinear sense of history is important for a complex understanding of race. The question "How did Europeans *become white* when they were elsewhere, amongst visibly different populations?" has been answered extensively, of course, in the history of ideas, as in Winthrop Jordan's classic *White Over Black*, or differently, in Edward Said's standard *Orientalism*.[6] However, Nietzsche's suggestive turning toward an "[e]ffective history, on the other hand, shortens its vision to those things nearest to it—the body, the nervous system, nutrition, digestion, and energies; it unearths the periods of decadence and if it chances upon lofty epochs, it is with the suspicion—not vindictive but joyous—of finding a barbarous and shameful confusion."[7] Nietzsche's "physiological" approach to culture demands probing further than ideas or knowledge about race, and into the concrete movements, passions, and "confusions" of bodies—bodies of flesh, genes, sinews, brain chemistry, and sexual desire, greatly overflowing what literature and thought can make of them.

Ever since his brother-in-law and sister canonised him as the most erudite apologist of German and European supremacy, Nietzsche's relationship to the critical theorisation of race has of course been an extremely contentious one. Nietzsche's more astute interlocutors, notably since Walter Kaufmann in the 1950s, have nonetheless pointed out that the profoundly creative and irreverent force of Nietzsche's philosophy is not easily assimilable to any project of biopower.[8] A recent collection called *Critical Affinities* has made an important beginning in making Nietzsche speak to some of the concerns of critical race theory.[9] I want to propose, similarly, that the historical description of what Foucault calls *emergence*—here, the emergence of new uneven and ambiguous relationships between white and brown bodies under colonialism—is yet to learn much from Nietzsche. "Emergence is thus the entry of forces; it is their eruption, the leap from the wings to the center stage, each in its youthful strength."[10] Nietzsche's worth for the study of race and colonialism can be drawn out from his critical investigations into corporeality and the circulation of energy, into the herd-like clinging to stereotypical thinking and behaviour (such as nationalism and racism), and into the ever-present potential for decay and violence behind the façade of opulence, particularly that of European civilisation.

> That will to power in which I recognize the ultimate ground and character of all change provides us with the reason why selection is not in favor of the exceptions and lucky strokes: the strongest and most fortunate are weak when opposed by organized herd instincts, by the timidity of the weak, by the vast majority. My general view of the world of values shows that it is not the lucky strokes, the select types, that have the upper hand in the supreme values that are today placed over mankind; rather it is the decadent types—perhaps there is nothing in the world more interesting than this *unwelcome* spectacle—[11]

More than usually in the social sciences this will entail understanding racialisation as an embodied and otherwise physical phenomenon, "constructed" not simply through language and mind but a whole host of ecological factors, which in fact operate underneath or beyond the human realm.[12] This means that the much-aligned *biological* dimensions of race—skin colour, body shape, genetic makeups, immunity systems, etc.—are important to how bodies are positioned in racial hierarchies.[13] This does *not* mean that racialisation (for example, the economic and cultural hegemony called "whiteness") follows automatically from phenotype (for example, relatively lighter skin). Physical differences are always over-coded, and sometimes obscured, by differences in the ways a body is dressed, comports itself, uses artefacts, speaks, worships, has sex, eats, walks—in short, by cultural difference. Moreover, the phenotypical body is itself altered by diet, exercise, medication, tanning, etc. Hence racial difference cannot be a raster of distinct "races." It is, as is generally acknowledged in race and ethnic studies, an ongoing institutional process of social interactions and cultural representations. However, I want to argue that racial difference is *also* made of genes, blood, food, bricks, drugs, and even of the divine. This heterogeneous and multilayered nature of racialisation means that it cannot be reduced to any of these components, and its social outcomes are never given.

PHENOTYPICAL ENCOUNTER

The port and merchant city of Goa was during early modernity the proud capital of the Portuguese empire around the Indian Ocean—the *Estado da Índia*. Conquered by Afonso de Albuquerque in 1510, Goa during the sixteenth century embodied a geographical concentration of cosmopolitan and economic experimentation on a par with cities like Antwerp, Venice, Alexandria, Surat, Malacca, and Canton (Guangzhou). Dubbed "Golden Goa" (*Goa dourada*) by travellers enthusiastic about its mercantile and ecclesiastical wealth, it was the most intense node of missionary activity of the Indian Ocean. In 1760 it was abandoned as imperial capital after many decades of corruption, disease, wars, and economic decline. The capital moved to Panjim (Panaji). Of the old imperial city of Goa (Goa Velha, or Old Goa) some of the large Baroque churches and cathedrals remain; the rest was left to decay. The territory of Goa was integrated into India in 1961.

As is well known, Portuguese colonialism was from the start highly ambivalent about the question of race. Officially the Lusitanian empire claimed it transcended phenotypical difference under a shared Catholic faith. In practice, as Charles Boxer argued for many decades, the Portuguese continued everyday racism both subtly and legally in all of its colonies.[14] Scholarship on the Portuguese maritime empire is well established; my contribution lies rather in providing a cue for further research and theorisation. Golden Goa is an apt place to start thinking about the historical-geographical emergence of race around the Indian Ocean world.[15] No mercantile or intervention from Europeans was free from a particular coding of human phenotype, though it needs to be concretely ascertained how and why that coding operated. I use "phenotype" quite literally here, meaning the physical characteristics of a closely related population of organisms as opposed to their genotype. Human phenotypical variation is continuous and probabilistic, of course, but *race* as a system of classification aims to group bodies together into discrete and essential identities. I would like to suggest not just that racial differences already framed early modern travel writing and Golden Goa's cosmopolitanism, but that the whiteness that resulted from it was therefore ambivalent.

The Dutchman Jan Huygen van Linschoten worked for the Archbishop in Goa from 1583 to 1587. Linschoten was a true early-modern traveller, eager to learn of the world's diversity, with an eye for detail, an ear for facts—and a hand to write and sketch them.[16] His *Itinerario, Voyage ofte Schipvaert naar Oost ofte Portingaels Indien*, published in 1596 and immediately translated into English, is a key text in the history of European geography.[17] Copiously illustrated and containing the latest maps and economic information, the *Itinerario* was a bestseller at a time Europe was becoming aware of the vast riches and curiosities lying just within reach in Asia and the Americas. I'm going to understand the book's descriptions of Goa's inhabitants not so much as ideological distortions of reality, but as witnesses of embodied encounter, of how real phenotypical differences were concretely produced and negotiated *through* practices.[18] This approach presumes a basically realist assumption that there exist physical differences between populations that are noticed, stereotyped, and elaborated through interaction. This does not mean that Linschoten was "objective," only that some striking elements of the actual situation in Goa can be inferred from his sensationalist descriptions. Within a planet entering a new phase of accelerations in cultural intermixing, Linschoten was living and writing from a vantage point.

RACIAL TAXONOMY

Let us first concentrate on Linschoten's remarks on the phenotypes he encountered. Goa harboured in excess of 60,000 residents by the early seventeenth century. The *Itinerario* constructs a detailed typology of the Goan populations, thereby demonstrating its role as node in flows of migrants and ideas across the Indian Ocean world: the Portuguese and the *mestiços*; Brahmins, and Hindus in general; Gujuratis and *Banjans* from Cambay; *Canares* and *Decanijns*, labourers and shop keepers from what is now called Karnataka; Arabs; Abyssinians; "the Black People of Mosambique" (i.e. slaves bought from the Southeast African coast); *Malabares* and *Nayros*, labourers and gentry from the Kerala coast; and Jews. Ethnic groups in Goa Linschoten does not discuss as such include Armenian, Bengali, Burmese, Chinese, Croatian, Danish, Dutch, English, Flemish, French, German, Italian, Japanese, Korean, Malay, Ottoman, Persian, and Sinhalese. Most migrants were poor soldiers and sailors, but some were successful merchants, living in constant tension with the Portuguese rulers and clergy. It is worth remembering that Linschoten's category "white" was politically and culturally far from homogeneous.

Figure 14.1   "The Mohammedans of Cananor and archenemies of the Portuguese/ Inhabitants of Malabar between Goa and Cochin and the coast where pepper grows." Courtesy of the Library of the University of Amsterdam.

Racial taxonomy is notoriously fraught by the wild phenotypic variation it attempts to contain. It should come as no surprise that Linschoten realised the *mestiços* already undermined his typology of phenotypes:

> The Portingales in India, are many of them married with the naturall borne women of the countrie, and the children procéeding of them are called Mesticos, that is, half countrimen. These Mesticos are commonlie of yelowish colour, nothwithstanding there are manie women among them, that are faire and well formed. The children of the Portingales, both boyes and gyrls, which are borne in India, are called Castisos, and are in all things like unto the Portingales, only somewhat differing in colour, for they draw towards a yealow colour: the children of those Castisos are yealow, and altogether like the Mesticos, and the children of Mesticos are of colour and fashion like the naturall borne Countrimen or Decaniins of the countrie, so that the posteritie of the Portingales, both men and women being in the third degrée, doe séeme to be naturall Indians, both in colour and fashion.[19]

Extremely few white women undertook the long and perilous journey to India, and there was much marriage, concubinage, and rape between converted Indians and white soldiers and merchants already from Albuquerque's days. Albuquerque in fact famously promoted intermarriage as biopolitical settlement strategy. For the Dutch and the English, as for racial theorists in the centuries ahead, it was clear that this genetic and cultural integration in the Portuguese colonies inevitably meant the loss of European rigour. Linschoten was already fully attuned to cataloguing differences in human phenotype, mentioning it as a matter of course about almost all the populations he encountered on his journey in the Indian Ocean. Skin colour had by his time become the prime marker of difference. Of the Goan natives, Linschoten noted "They are in a manner blacke, or of a dark browne colour."[20] Of the Jain Gujuratis living in Goa, he writes:

> They are of a yellowe colour like the Bramenes and somewhat whiter, and there are women among them which are much whiter and clearer of complection than the Portingale women. They are formed and made both in face, limmes and all other things like men of Europe, colour only excepted.[21]

The contemporary hand colouring of the bodies in certain first edition copies of the *Itinerario*'s plates has Goan skin as light brown and slaves' skin as grey. The Portuguese and the Chinese all have bright pink cheeks. This sense of bodily difference, mixing wonder with disgust, can be found in Marco Polo or Ibn Battuta, of course, but the point is that by the late sixteenth century it had become commonplace. Since geographical writing of the time was done by men travelling without their wives, it is to be expected much attention was given to local women and their alleged addiction to sex.

The incipient anthropology of Linschoten and his collaborators already showed a hierarchical taxonomy of mental characteristics along what, by the time of Comte Arthur de Gobineau, were confidently called "races."[22] The Portuguese were insolent southern Europeans and incapable of colonial rule; the North Indian and Arab merchants were deceitful; the Goan natives cowardly, effeminate, and stupid, worse even than slaves.

> These Canarijns and Corumbijns are the most contemptible, and the miserablest people of all India, and live very poorly, maintaining themselves with little meate. [. . .] They are so miserable, that for a penny they would indure to be whipped, and they eate so little, that it seemeth they live by the aire, they are likewise most of them leane and weake of limmes, of little strength and very cowardes, whereby the Portingales doe them great outrage and villanie, using them likes dogges and beasts.[23]

Figure 14.2 "'Costume and appearance of the Indian merchants, bold in their business'"; Cambayans; Brahmins. Courtesy of the University of Amsterdam

Phenotypical difference is enhanced by all sorts of material inscriptions and adornments. The *caffares* (kaffirs), the slaves from Mozambique and the East African coast, Linschoten calls "black as pitch, with curled and singed hayre both on their heads and beards, which is very little, their noses broad, flat and thicke at the end, great bigge lippes: some have holes, both above and under in their lippes, and some times besides their mouthes through their cheekes, wherin they thrust small bones, which they esteeme a bewtifying."[24] It needs to be emphasised that though I am presenting an emergent white perspective, racialisation is a mutual process. The description above continues:

> there are some among them that have their faces and all their bodies over rased and seared with irons, and al figured like rased Sattin or Damaske, wherein they take great pride, thinking there are no fairer people then they in all the world, so that when they see any white people, that weare apparell on their bodies, they laugh and mocke at them, thinking us to be monsters and ugly people: and when they will make any develish forme and picture, then they invent one after the forme of

a white man in his apparell, so that to conclude, they thinke and verily perswade themselves, that they are the right colour of men, and that we have a false and counterfait colour.

As Linschoten repeatedly states that the *caffares* live "like beastes," this momentary decentring of the European anthropological gaze is clearly written for comical effect. Yet the passage illustrates the intensity of phenotypical encounter, in which both whites and Africans, however unequal their power relation, revel in its absurdity. Note too the importance of clothing *on top of* phenotype. For Linschoten and his European readers, the first acquaintance with naked dark skin and piercings is grotesquely fascinating.

White superiority did not come straight from theology or science. It was reproduced through reiterated embodied interactions between European and non-European bodies in which the former kept noticing those things he found compellingly *different*—fascinating, enticing, or disgusting. François Pyrard de Laval, the French traveller, writes in his 1619 memoir on Goa:

You see there [at the market] very pretty and elegant girls and women from all countries of India, most of whom can play upon instruments, embroider, sew very finely, and do all kinds of work, such as the making of sweetmeats, preserves, etc. All these slaves are very cheap, the dearest not being woprth more than 20 or 30 perdos, of 32½ sols each. Girls that are virgins are sold as such, and are examined by women, so that none dare use any trickery. [. . .] Some of these girls are very pretty, fair, and comely, others are olive-colored, brown and of all colours. But those to whom they are most attracted are the Caffre girls of Mozambique and other places in Africa, who are as wondrously black, with curly hair; they call these *Negra de Guinea*. It is a remarkable fact which I have observed among all the Indian peoples, as well males as females, that their bodies and perspiration have no smell, whereas the negroes of Africa, from both sides of the Cape of Good Hope, stink in such wise that when they are heated it is impossible to approach them: their savour is as bad as that of green leeks.[25]

What few studies of Orientalism would note is that difference in the colonies was smelt, tasted, felt. This has now been cautiously proposed in Mark Smith's *How Race Is Made*, writing about the southern United States in the days of slavery. By repeatedly noting the way slaves looked, sounded, and smelt, whites not only carried around stereotypes of blacks in their heads, but learnt how to sense and react to the presence of a black body. It is obviously not the case that racism and racial typology are the *necessary* outcome of phenotypical and sensory encounter. But in hindsight, they can be analyzed by stressing the materiality of encounter.[26]

FIDALGOS

If race is an embodied practice, the artefacts that bodies utilise then become indispensable on top of phenotype to distinguish oneself. Goa's public spaces appear to have been rife with style consciousness. Linschoten's observations on the way the Portuguese in Goa underlined their whiteness through dress and comportment spurred the European imagination for centuries.

> The Portingales are commonly served with great gravitie, without any difference betwéene the Gentleman and the common Citizen, townesman of soldier, and in their going, curtesies, and conversations, common in all thinges: when they go in the stréetes they steppe very softly and slowly forwards, with a great pride and vaineglorious maiestie, with a slave that carrieth a great hat or vaile over their heads, to keepe the sunne and raine from them.[27]

White Goans quickly understood why the Nayro upper caste of Malabar chose to "wear the nayls of their hands very long": to "shew that they are Gentlemen, because the longnesse of the nayles doth let and hinder men from working or doing any labour."[28] The *fidalgo* ("son of a somebody") desire of the Portuguese to show off privilege, integral to the Portuguese aristocracy since the late Middle Ages though often more or less "bought" in the colonies, was famous across Europe. This desire overcame the contempt that was otherwise held towards the Nayros, and white men soon started growing their nails too.

For *fidalgos*, as well as for priests, sailors, and soldiers, it was important to comport oneself as a respectable subject. Greeting each other with what today would seem exaggerated courtesy was central to establish a shared sense of being white citizens of Goa. "When they méete in the stréetes a good space before they come together, they beginne with a great Besolas manos, to stoope with their bodies, and to thrust their foot to salute each other, with their hattes in their hands, almost touching the ground."[29] This visible and collective monitoring by ritual greeting consolidated the identity of these men as Portuguese and as white. If disrespect was shown, harsh retaliation was an accepted way to reinstate the importance of honour:

> when they séeke to bee revenged of any man that hath shewen them discurtesie, or for any other cause whatsoever it bee, they assemble ten or twelve of their friends, acquaintance or companions, and take him wheresoever they find him, and beat him long together, that they leave him for dead, or very neare dead, or els cause him to be stabbed by their slaves, which they hold for a great honor and point of honestie so to revenge themselves, whereof they dare boast and bragge openly in the stréetes.[30]

Racial difference is thus played out *ecologically*, over and through the built environment. One of the most comfortable and largest hospitals of the world was then located in Goa. The Royal Hospital, however, admitted "only Portingals, for no other sick person may lodge therein, I mean such as are called white men, for the other Indians have an Hospitall by themselves."[31] Segregating the entire island of Goa off from the mainland, all nonwhites needed to be physically marked with ink to be identified at the city gates.

> And the Indians, Decanijns, and other Moores and heathens, that are resident in Goa, and therein have their habitation, when they goe into the firme land to fetch their necessarie provisions, coming to those places which are called Passos, they must everye man have a marke, which is Printed on their naked armes, and so they passe over to the other side, and at their returne againe they must shew the same marke.[32]

Racialisation was achieved through an array of material and corporeal arrangements. Not just dress, parasols, jewellery, but walls, greeting style, duels, and mode of transport (the Portuguese riding a horse or being carried

Figure 14.3   In such manner the Portuguese of pedigree and wealth are carried around here. Courtesy of the Library of the University of Amsterdam.

around in a palanquin), even slaves and servants, were accessories of white bodies in the early modern Indian Ocean world. Linschoten's pictures of Portuguese colonial nobility became famous in Europe. He even speaks of the music that accompanied the festivities of the Portuguese—racial accessories need not be touchable, but they do need to be somehow sensible to everyone involved.

ON EVIL WOMEN

The intense role that sexuality played in the cohering of white masculinities in the writings of colonial regimes has been studied.[33] Women of the Indian Ocean world were to white travellers prototypes of seductive and mysterious exuberance, and Linschoten can be credited for consolidating these perceptions like no other European author of the late sixteenth century. Of Goa's white and *mestiço* women, he reported:

> When they goe to church, or to visit any friend, they put on very costly apparrell, with bracelets of gold, and rings upon their armes, all beset with costly Jewels and pearles, and at their eares hang laces full of Jewels. Their clothes are of Damaske, Velvet, and cloth of gold, for silke is the worst thing they doe weare.[34]

Within Goa's masculinist *fidalgo* culture, white women were mostly invisible, jealously guarded by their husbands and locked up in their palaquins (litters) and houses.[35] This was in telling contrast to how other women were treated. Most Portuguese *soldados* and sailors took Hindu women of lower castes as mistresses or wives, but these enjoyed little social standing. Many of the black women were used by their owners for prostitution. As Linschoten famously told Europe (with a moral indignation that would later prove hypocritical), slavery was completely entrenched in Goan society. The buying and selling of sub-Saharan Africans, though not instigated by the Portuguese, was certainly facilitated by white Christian notions of humanity and subhumanity. Rich families kept dozens, even hundreds, of slaves for household chores, production of handicrafts, and sex. In the sexual exploitation of African women slaves at Goa, therefore, we find the clearest instance of the Indian Ocean's early modern racism.

Linschoten's many misogynous statements on Indian women spurred a stubborn myth about the origins of the licentiousness of the *Estado da Índia*. All Golden Goa's vices, especially those connected to sex, were to be blamed on Indian women. Linschoten's description of the practice, allegedly invented by Indian women, of drugging their husbands with the hallucinogenic plant *datura* (jimson weed) in order to be with their lovers, was repeated by many European travellers after him.[36] Pompa Banerjee recognises Linschoten's key place in the history of European stereotypes of sati, the Hindu ritual, immediately outlawed by the Portuguese, whereby a widow throws herself into her husband's funeral pyre, which had fascinated European men since Marco Polo. Linschoten's fanciful drawing of sati sketched the irrational exuberance of the ritual firmly into the European mind.[37] Despite the obvious patriarchy of the ritual, he is convinced even here the fault lies with the Indian women:

> The first cause and occasion why the women are burnt with their husbandes, was (as the Indians themselves do say), that in time past, the women (as they are very leacherous and inconstant both by nature, and complexion) did poyson many of their husbands, when they thought good (as they are likewise very expert therein:) thereby to have the better means to fulfill their lusts.[38]

Of the Malabares, Linschoten first says reassuringly that "Of face, body, and limmes they are altogether like men of Europ, without any difference, but onely in colour." However, they were "the most leacherous and unchast nation in all the Orient, so that there are verie few women children among them of seven or eight years olde, that have their maiden-heads."[39]

All European travel writing of the colonial era strongly sexualised native women, done as it was by men experiencing long periods of heterosexual abstention within exotic landscapes.[40] But women of the Indian Ocean world—the mysterious East where spices came from—were perceived as especially immoral. "For all the care & studie that ye women and wives of India have," Linschoten posited, "is day and night to devise meanes to satisfie their pleasures, and to increase lust, by all the devises they can imagine, and to make their bodies the apter thereunto."[41] Even women-slaves "leave their mistresses in the Churches, or slip into somme shoppe or corner, which they have redie at their fingers endes, where their lovers méet them, and there in hast they have a sport, which done they leave each other: and if she chance have a Portingal or a white man to her lover, she is so proud, that she thinketh no woman comparable unto her, and among themselves doe bragge thereof."[42] Sexual intercourse did cross, but never erased racial boundaries.

In his racialising misogyny, Linschoten was simply following the general attitude towards native women amongst the white colonist class. Treating Linschoten's misogyny as prototypical of later Orientalism should not detract attention from the real desires and fears which fed it. That is, a Nietzschean physiology of "emergence" understands Linschoten's descriptions not just as stereotypical, but as skewed documents of actual physical encounter: bodies divided by class and race barriers were indeed having sex in the colonies. It is in fact sex that to some extent allowed for racism to develop. In addition, Linschoten's exaggerations reveal that elaborate stereotypes about the visibly distinguishable groups in Goa circulated amongst the white populace, while his authority on the matter would be considered impeccable by men hungry for news of such tantalising matters in Europe. By repeating these stereotypes in talk, writing, and practice, therefore, further coherence of a white identity was achieved. But already in the sixteenth century, whiteness—in this case, the cohesion of the Portuguese in the cultural and economic system of the Indian Ocean—was already felt to be a precarious structure, at mercy of the seductive lewdness of Indian and Indianised women.

THE PLEASURES OF COSMOPOLITANISM

Through entertaining certain feelings and prejudices, through architecture and a certain demeanour in public spaces, and through the use of artefacts such as expensive textiles and palanquins carried by slaves, Goa's white population was materially distinguishing itself from the rest of the city. Yet some practices did not underscore racial differentiation and thereby complicated the distinguishing efforts of the whites. Culture that was shared across phenotypes mainly concerned the pleasures of food, fashion, gambling, sex, drugs, and music. During the large *festas* in the *Estado da Índia*, chiefly organised by the church, the entire city participated. According to Boxer, writing about Macao, there were processions and games, parades with elephants and horses, music was played continuously on loud trumpets and drums, and the fidalgos were dressed up in the most exquisite clothes.[43] If Goa's festival and drug culture were studied "from below," in their physiological effects as Nietzsche might have done, racial difference therefore indeed appears messy and confused as almost everyone participated in them.

Spices, of course, were the Indian Ocean's most wanted luxury item, used by all who could afford them. In his book *Spice*, Jack Turner shows with a mass of evidence that the boundaries between spice, intoxicant, medicine, aphrodisiac, magic potion, incense, and poison have never been clear-cut; the only thing that unites these is their luxurious rarity.[44] More mundanely, colonists also seem to have enjoyed "going native" to some extent. In India, the Portuguese quickly preferred eating rice with their hands and pouring water into their mouths like Indians do.[45] But it is intoxication that made plain the decadence of the Portuguese élite. A drug commonly used to kill boredom was betel nut (*paan*).

> The Portingales women have the like custom of eating these Bettele leaves, so that if they were but one day without eating their Bettele, they perswade themselves they could not live: Yea, they set it in the night times by their Beddes heades, and when they cannot sleepe, they doe nothing els but chaw Bettele and spit it out againe. In the day time wheresoever they doe sit, goe, or stand, they are continually chawing thereof, like Oxen or Kine chawing their cud: for the whole exercise of

many Portingales women, is onely all the day long to wash themselves, and then fal to the chawing of their Bettele.[46]

The celebration of cosmopolitanism's pleasures and confusions should not blind us to the persisting economic and racial differences, however. Only the Portuguese and wealthy *mestiços* had the leisure time available for decadent living. Only they could have slaves and native women working, playing music, and dancing in their houses. In a passage worth quoting at length to elucidate Goa's social stratification, Linschoten explains that while opium and *bhang* (cannabis leaves) were used as aphrodisiacs and sedatives amongst the upper strata whites, *mestiços*, and Muslim merchants, they were used by the poor and unfree (immigrant labourers and blacks) to simply cope with existence—much like today.

> Bangue is also a common meate in India, serving to the same effect that Amfion [opium] doth. [. . .] The Indians eate this seede or the leaves thereof being stamped, saying, that it maketh a good appetite, but useth most to provoke lust; as it is commonly used and sold in the shops, it is mingled with some poulder of the leaves and the seede together: They likewise put greene Arecca unto it, therewith to make a man drunke or in a manner out of his wits: Sometimes also they mixe it with Nutmegs and Mace, which doth also make a man drunke: Others (that is to saye, the rich and welthy persons) mix it with Cloves, Camphora, Ambar, Muske, and Opium, which (as the Moores likewise affirme) maketh a man pleasant, and forgetting himselfe, performing all kind of labour and toyle without once thinking of any paine: but onely laughing, playing, and sleeping quietly. The common women or whores use it when they meane to have a mans companie, thereby to be lively and merrie, and to set all care aside. It was first invented by Captaines and souldiers, when they had layne long in the field, continually waking and with great travell, which they desiring to rememedie and againe to comfort themselves, thereby to settle their braines doe use Bangue, in such manner as is foresaid. It causeth such as eate it, to reele and looke as if they were drunke, and halfe foolish, doing nothing but laugh and bee merrie, as long as it worketh in their bodies. It is verie much used by the Indians, and likewise by some Portingales, but most by the slaves thereby to forget their labour: to conclude it is a certaine small comfort to a melancholy person.[47]

It was Linschoten's astute observations on interracial sex, however—perhaps the most blatant of cosmopolitanism's pleasures—that resounded throughout a deeply Christian Europe. As Boxer argues, there was in the Portuguese empire simultaneously an ideology of racial equality, some promotion of intermarriage, and the maintenance of the medieval Lusitanian notion of *pureza de sangue* (purity of blood), which turned from an aristocratic concept to a subtle valorisation of whiteness.[48] But for white men, purity was less of an issue when it came to concubines or prostitutes. Unlike in other colonial regimes (see Stoler's work), there was a lot of genetic exchange between phenotypically diverse populations of the Portuguese Indies. By cohabiting with white men, nonwhite women were likely to augment their status, but obviously also underlined the desirability of being white. Many natives and slaves were forcefully converted to Christianity, thereby to some extent "whitening" themselves culturally, but again, underlining the superiority of the Catholic faith.

The pleasures of cosmopolitan festival and interracial sex did little, in the end, to avert the ascendancy of modern racism. By the time the famous Orientalist Sir Richard F. Burton visited Goa, miscegenation had long fallen out of practice, and cultural boundaries between white and native were as strong as they were in British India, if somewhat less overt. "No better proof of how utterly the attempt to promote cordiality between the European and the Asiatic by a system of intermarriage and equality of rights that has failed in practice can be adduced," Burton wryly noted, "than the utter contempt in which the former holds the latter at Goa."[49] From a relatively murky situation of self-proclaimed pomp, rampant slavery, and many forms of interracial prostitution, the colonial cities of the Indian Ocean world had by the middle of the nineteenth century become entirely entrenched in the biopolitical maintenance of racist hierarchy.

CONCLUSIONS

To conclude, whiteness in Golden Goa was complicated. This is not a platitude but points to what white identities physically *consisted of* at this stage in global history. On the one hand, contemporary accounts such as Linschoten's suggest that even before organised imperialism, phenotypical difference greatly mattered in everyday interactions and social stratifications, through attraction (interracial sex, traveller's curiosity) and feelings of superiority and inferiority. Material culture, architecture, ways of moving and speaking and drinking, hospitalisation, all supported the creation of a particular kind of Lusitanian whiteness.

The Portuguese version of colonisation was derided by the northern Europeans. It was felt by the Dutch and the English—united through their Germanic languages and Protestantism, both eager to intercept the Portuguese import of spice—that the difference of climate and the passion of the tropics was irrevocably seeping into the white bodies in Goa, turning them rapidly into Indians. "There die many men within the Towne, by meanes of their disordered living, together with the hoteness of the country," as Linschoten sums it up.[50] Tropical promiscuity certainly coexisted with a profusion of venereal disease, stomach ulcers and the occasional overdose. To Linschoten and his Dutch and English readers, as to Burton centuries later, the impurities of Portuguese whiteness in *Goa dourada* were not merely moral, but pathological, hereditary, and final. Given his obsession with European degeneracy and the triumph of petty morality over independent thinking, Nietzsche would have concurred: "The values of the weak prevail because the strong have taken them over as devices of leadership."[51]

It is essential that bringing phenotype, genetics, and physiology into the analysis of racial difference not be seen as a return to biological reductionism. Practices like chewing *paan* and adultery were so widespread that they didn't neatly map onto phenotypical variation. This only confirms that racialisation is a completely contingent process, and connections between phenotype and culture cannot be predicted. In a postcolonial world still dominated by white men, it is clear that the complications of whiteness in the Asian colonies did not herald its demise. For all the miscegenation, the exoticism, and the cosmopolitan feasting, whiteness after Linschoten only became more obsessed with the purity it by definition couldn't capture.

ACKNOWLEDGEMENTS

The author thanks the Library of the University of Amsterdam for reproductions from microfiche of Linschoten's *Icones*.

NOTES

1. Howard Winant, *Racial Conditions: Politics, Theory, Comparisons* (Minneapolis, MN: University of Minnesota Press, 1994); *The World is a Ghetto: Race and Democracy Since World War II* (New York: Basic Books, 2001); *The New Politics of Race: Globalism, Difference, Justice* (Durham: Duke University Press, 2004); for the basic argument see Michael Omi and Howard Winant, *Racial Formation in the United States From the 1960s to the 1980s* (New York: Routledge, 1986).
2. Alistair Bonnett, *White Identities: Historical and International Perspectives* (Harlow: Prentice Hall, 2000).
3. Michel Foucault, *"Society Must Be Defended": Lectures at the Collège de France, 1975–1976*, eds. Mauro Bertani and Alessandro Fontana, trans. David Macey (New York: Picador, 2003).
4. Ann Laura Stoler, *Race and the Education of Desire: Foucault's History of Sexuality and the Colonial Order of Things* (Durham, NC: Duke University Press, 1995); *Carnal Knowledge and Imperial Power: Race and the Intimate in Colonial Rule* (Durham, NC: Duke University Press, 2002); Ann Laura Stoler, ed., *Haunted by Empire: Geographies of Intimacy in North American History* (Durham, NC: Duke University Press, 2006).
5. Michel Foucault, "Nietzsche, Genealogy, History,' in *Language, Counter-Memory, Practice: Selected Essays and Interviews*, eds. and trans. Donald F. Bouchard and Sherry Simon (Ithaca, NY: Cornell University Press, 1977), 145.
6. Winthrop Jordan, *White Over Black: American Attitudes Toward the Negro, 1550–1812* (Chapel Hill, NC: University of North Carolina Press, 1968); Edward W. Said, *Orientalism: Western Conceptions of the Orient* (New

York: Knopf, 1978). See also Ivan Hannahford, *Race: The History of an Idea in the West* (Baltimore, MD: Johns Hopkins University Press, 1996).

7. Foucault, "Nietzsche, Genealogy, History," 155.

8. Walter Kaufmann, *Nietzsche: Philosopher, Psychologist, Antichrist*, fourth edition (Princeton, NJ: Princeton University Press, 1974); see also Gregory Moore, *Nietzsche, Biology and Metaphor* (Cambridge, UK: Cambridge University Press, 2002).

9. Jacqueline Scott and A. Todd Franklin, eds. *Critical Affinities: Nietzsche and African American Thought* (New York: SUNY Press, 2006).

10. Foucault, "Nietzsche, Genealogy, History," 149–150.

11. Friedrich Nietzsche, *The Will to Power*, trans. and ed. Walter Kaufman (New York: Vintage, 1967), 364.

12. Arun Saldanha, "Reontologising race: the machinic geography of phenotype," *Environment and Planning D: Society and Space* 24 (1; 2006): 9–24; *Psychedelic White: Goa Trance and the Viscosity of Race* (Minneapolis, MN: University of Minnesota Press, 2007); compare Karim Murji and John Solomos, eds., *Racialization: Studies in Theory and Practice* (Oxford, UK: Oxford University Press, 2005).

13. For example, Richard Lewontin, *Human Diversity* (New York: Scientific American Library, 1982). I will expand on the biological dimensions of race in *The Political Phenotype: Antiracist Science After Man*.

14. For example, Charles R. Boxer, *Race Relations in the Portuguese Empire, 1425–1825* (Oxford, UK: Clarendon, 1963).

15. See especially Michael N. Pearson's *The Portuguese in India* (Cambridge, UK: Cambridge University Press, 1987) and *The Indian Ocean* (London: Routledge, 2003).

16. Charles McKew Parr, *Jan van Linschoten: The Dutch Marco Polo* (New York: Crowell, 1964); Roelof van Gelder, Jan Parmentier and Vibeke Roeper, eds. *Souffrir pour parvenir. De wereld van Jan Huygen van Linschoten* (Haarlem: Arcadia, 1998); Arun Saldanha, "The itineraries of geography: Jan Huygen van Linschoten's *Itinerario* and Dutch expeditions to the Indian Ocean, 1594–1602," forthcoming.

17. Jan Huygen van Linschoten, *Itinerario, Voyage ofte Schipvaert van Jan Huygen van Linschoten naer Oost ofte Portugaels Indien* . . . (Amsterdam: Cornelis Claesz, 1596). Published in English as *John Huyghen van Linschoten his Discours of Voyages into ye Easte & West Indies* . . . trans. W.P. [William Philips] (London: John Wolfe, 1598). My quotes will be from the annotated Hakluyt edition: *The Voyage of John Huyghen van Linschoten to the East Indies. The First Book, Containing his Description of the East*, 2 vols., eds. Arthur Coke Burnell and P.A. Tiele (London: Hakluyt Society, 1885).

18. Compare the iconographic analysis of Ernst van den Boogaart, *Civil and Corrupt Asia: Image and Text in the* Itinerario *and the* Icones *of Jan Huygen van Linschoten* (Chicago, IL: University of Chicago Press, 2003).

19. Linschoten, *Voyage*, vol. I, 183–184.

20. Ibid., 261.

21. Ibid., 255.

22. Arthur de Gobineau, *Essai sur l'inégalité des races humaines*, 4 vols. (Paris: Firmin-Didot, 1853–1855).

23. Linschoten, *Voyage*, vol. I, 260, 263.

24. Ibid., 271

25. François Pyrard de Laval, *The Voyage of François Pyrard de Laval to the East Indies, the Maldives, the Moluccas and Brazil*, trans. and ed. Albert Gray and H.C.P. Bell (London: Hakluyt Society, 1888), vol. 2, part I, pp. 65–66.

26. Mark M. Smith, *How Race Is Made: Slavery, Segregation, and the Senses* (Chapel Hill, NC: University of North Caroline Press, 2006).
27. Linschoten, *Voyage*, vol. I, 193.
28. Ibid., 282.
29. Ibid., 194.
30. Ibid., 194–195.
31. Ibid. 237.
32. Ibid., 180.
33. Apart from Stoler's work, see Anne McClintock, *Imperial Leather: Race, Gender and Sexuality in the Colonial Contest* (New York: Routledge, 1995).
34. Linschoten, *Voyage*, vol. I, 206.
35. More on Portuguese patriarchy in Charles R. Boxer, *Mary and Misogyny: Women in Iberian Expansion Overseas, 1415–1815* (London: Duckworth, 1975).
36. Linschoten *Voyage*, vol. I, 250–251.
37. Pompa Banerjee, *Burning Women: Widows, Witches, and Early Modern European Travelers in India* (New York: Palgrave Macmillan, 2003), 91–93.
38. Linschoten, *Voyage*, vol. I, 278.
39. Ibid., 207–208.
40. Jeniffer Morgan, "Male Travellers, Female Bodies, and the Gendering of Racial Ideology, 1500–1700," in *Bodies in Contact: Rethinking Colonial Encounters in World History*, eds. Tony Ballantyne and Antoinette Burton, 54–66 (Durham, NC: Duke University Press, 2005).
41. Linschoten, *Voyage*, vol. II, 70.
42. Linschoten, *Voyage*, vol. I, 215–216.
43. Charles R. Boxer, *Fidalgos of the Far East, 1550–1770: Fact and Fancy in the History of Macao* (The Hague: Martinus Nijhoff, 1948), 148.
44. Jack Turner, *Spice: The History of a Temptation* (New York: Vintage, 2004).
45. Linschoten, *Voyage*, vol. I, 278.
46. Linschoten, *Voyage*, vol. II, 64.
47. Ibid., 115–116.
48. Boxer, *Race Relations.*
49. Richard F. Burton, *Goa, and the Blue Mountains, or Six Months of Sick Leave* (London: Richard Bentley, 1851).
50. Linschoten, *Voyage*, vol. I, 185.
51. Nietzsche, *Will To Power*, 459.

BIBLIOGRAPHY

Banerjee, Pompa. *Burning Women: Widows, Witches, and Early Modern European Travelers in India.* New York: Palgrave Macmillan, 2003.
Bonnett, Alistair. *White Identities: Historical and International Perspectives.* Harlow, UK: Prentice Hall, 2000.
Boxer, Charles R. *Fidalgos of the Far East, 1550–1770: Fact and Fancy in the History of Macao.* The Hague: Martinus Nijhoff, 1948.
———. *Race Relations in the Portuguese Empire, 1425–1825.* Oxford, UK: Clarendon, 1963.
———. *Mary and Misogyny: Women in Iberian Expansion Overseas, 1415–1815.* London: Duckworth, 1975.

Burton, Richard F. *Goa, and the Blue Mountains, or Six Months of Sick Leave* London: Richard Bentley, 1851.

Foucault, Michel. "Nietzsche, Genealogy, History." In *Language, Counter-Memory, Practice: Selected Essays and Interviews*, edited and translated by Donald F. Bouchard and Sherry Simon. Ithaca, NY: Cornell University Press, 1977.

———. *"Society Must Be Defended": Lectures at the Collège de France, 1975–1976*, edited by Mauro Bertani and Alessandro Fontana, translated by David Macey. New York: Picador, 2003.

Gobineau, Arthur de. *Essai sur l'inégalité des races humaines*, 4 vols. Paris: Firmin-Didot, 1853–1855.

Hannahford, Ivan. *Race: The History of an Idea in the West.* Baltimore, MD: Johns Hopkins University Press, 1996.

Jordan, Winthrop. *White Over Black: American Attitudes Toward the Negro, 1550–1812.* Chapel Hill, NC: University of North Carolina Press, 1968.

Kaufmann, Walter. *Nietzsche: Philosopher, Psychologist, Antichrist*, fourth edition. Princeton, NJ: Princeton University Press, 1974.

Lewontin, Richard. *Human Diversity.* New York: Scientific American Library, 1982.

Linschoten, Jan Huygen van. *Itinerario, Voyage ofte Schipvaert van Jan Huygen van Linschoten naer Oost ofte Portugaels Indien . . .* Amsterdam: Cornelis Claesz, 1596.

———. *John Huyghen van Linschoten his Discours of Voyages into ye Easte & West Indies.* Translated by William Philips. London: John Wolfe, 1598.

———. *The Voyage of John Huyghen van Linschoten to the East Indies. The First Book, Containing his Description of the East*, 2 vols., edited by Arthur Coke Burnell and P.A. Tiele. London: Hakluyt Society, 1885.

McClintock, Anne. *Imperial Leather: Race, Gender and Sexuality in the Colonial Contest.* New York: Routledge, 1995.

McKew Parr, Charles. *Jan van Linschoten: The Dutch Marco Polo.* New York: Crowell, 1964.

Morgan, Jeniffer. "Male Travellers, Female Bodies, and the Gendering of Racial Ideology, 1500–1700." In *Bodies in Contact: Rethinking Colonial Encounters in World History*, edited by Tony Ballantyne and Antoinette Burton, 54–66. Durham, NC: Duke University Press, 2005.

Moore, Gregory. *Nietzsche, Biology and Metaphor.* Cambridge, UK: Cambridge University Press, 2002.

Murji, Karim, and John Solomos, eds. *Racialization: Studies in Theory and Practice.* Oxford, UK: Oxford University Press, 2005.

Nietzsche, Friedrich. *The Will to Power*, translated and edited by Walter Kaufman. New York: Vintage, 1967.

Omi, Michael, and Howard Winant. *Racial Formation in the United States From the 1960s to the 1980s.* New York: Routledge, 1986.

Pearson, Michael N. *The Portuguese in India.* Cambridge, UK: Cambridge University Press, 1987.

———. *The Indian Ocean.* London: Routledge, 2003.

Pyrard de Laval, François. *The Voyage of François Pyrard de Laval to the East Indies, the Maldives, the Moluccas and Brazil*, 2 vols. in 3 parts, translated and edited by Albert Gray and H.C.P. Bell. London: Hakluyt Society, 1888.

Said, Edward W. *Orientalism: Western Conceptions of the Orient.* New York: Knopf, 1978.

Saldanha, Arun, "Reontologising Race: The Machinic Geography of Phenotype." *Environment and Planning D: Society and Space* 24(1; 2006): 9–24.

———. *Psychedelic White: Goa Trance and the Viscosity of Race.* Minneapolis, MN: University of Minnesota Press, 2007.

————. "The Itineraries of Geography: Jan Huygen van Linschoten's Itinerario and Dutch Expeditions in the Indian Ocean, 1594–1602," under review.

Scott, Jacqueline, and A. Todd Franklin, eds. *Critical Affinities: Nietzsche and African American Thought.* New York: SUNY Press, 2006.

Smith, Mark M. *How Race Is Made: Slavery, Segregation, and the Senses.* Chapel Hill, NC: University of North Caroline Press, 2006.

Stoler, Ann Laura, *Race and the Education of Desire: Foucault's History of Sexuality and the Colonial Order of Things.* Durham, NC: Duke University Press, 1995.

————. *Carnal Knowledge and Imperial Power: Race and the Intimate in Colonial Rule.* Durham, NC: Duke University Press, 2002.

————. ed., *Haunted by Empire: Geographies of Intimacy in North American History.* Durham, NC: Duke University Press, 2006.

Turner, Jack. *Spice: The History of a Temptation.* New York: Vintage, 2004.

Van den Boogaart, Ernst. *Civil and Corrupt Asia: Image and Text in the Itinerario and the Icones of Jan Huygen van Linschoten.* Chicago, IL: University of Chicago Press, 2003.

Van Gelder, Roelof, Jan Parmentier, and Vibeke Roeper, eds. *Souffrir pour parvenir. De wereld van Jan Huygen van Linschoten.* Haarlem, Netherlands: Arcadia, 1998.

Winant, Howard. *Racial Conditions: Politics, Theory, Comparisons.* Minneapolis, MN: University of Minnesota Press, 1994.

————. *The World is a Ghetto: Race and Democracy Since World War II.* New York: Basic Books, 2001.

————. *The New Politics of Race: Globalism, Difference, Justice.* Durham, NC: Duke University Press, 2004.

15 Power and Beliefs in Reunion Island

Christian Ghasarian

A historical area of circulation and encounters of people and ideas, the Indian Ocean is a space where local social stratifications and colonialism have established hierarchical systems upon individuals. During the last two centuries, Europe played an important role in redefining its places and people. Yet, as always and everywhere, human life in this part of the world has been made of adjustments to situations and continuous negotiations of reality.

Away from geopolitical strategies of the Indian Ocean, a forgotten island offers a very interesting example of everyday intersections between global and local forces. From the beginning of its construction as a society, in spite of its isolation and the fact that it is structurally turned more toward the inlands than toward the sea, Reunion Island has been a place of cultural encounters and mixing. Different power relationships and different meanings related to different systems of value have been and still are constantly produced, affirmed, challenged, and contested in this small French multicultural society that constitutes a very interesting social laboratory for the study of historical and cultural dynamics. Located 9,500 km away from Paris and 200 km east of Mauritius, the island belongs to the so-called Archipelago of the Mascareignes (including Mauritius and its small isolated dependency, Rodrigues). With 800,000 inhabitants today (among whom 130,000 live in the capital, Saint-Denis) and an important demographic growth and urbanization, it perfectly expresses the human capacity to combine and reorganize models and practices originated in different places. People have developed numerous creative resources to organize their life between their ancestral system of value and the social structure they had to deal with: two dimensions subject to external influences and particularly evident in the religious domain.

To understand the dynamics of power and beliefs in Reunion, it is necessary to retrace briefly the historical constitution of the society. Since its discovery by European navigators at the end of the seventeenth century and the following progressive settlement of a population, the island has been a place of diverse exploitations, including the human kind. Until it became a French Department in the middle of the twentieth century, it was a colonial society. Yet, an unusual type of the colonial system was established there as no human settlements were found on the island when the Europeans came and it was an apparently uninhabited place. The first nation to anticipate the benefit of exploring the island, through the exploitation of expatriated people, was France.[1] This colonial society was therefore built without any fight, massacre, or subordination of native people, as the first subordinated people were extracted from their ancestral place of life on African coasts in the Indian Ocean. Displaced against their will and under very harsh authority, these people adapted to the oppressive society and, in their own way, participated in its construction.

POPULAR BELIEFS: A HISTORICAL OVERVIEW

Official history says that the first people to live on the island were a bunch of convicts abandoned there by the French government in 1663. A few years later, they were found to be in very good health and the colonisation of the promising island was decided. From that time the society was constructed through a progressive addition of people coming under different conditions from different places. All these people were carrying their own specific worldview and system of value. They experienced life on the island through their personal localization in its social stratification. For a while, these localizations were based on a simple division: dominant white colons coming from France and submitted slaves brought in from Africa and Madagascar to work in the sugarcane plantations.

In terms of beliefs, the whites were Christians and they established their religion on the island as the official one. Christianity was therefore, from the beginning, the religion of the dominants. It was also imposed on slaves who still tried to maintain a meaning in their life through hidden ancestral worships. The dominants' disapprobation of the display of non-Christian attitude was very strong until the end of the twentieth century on the island. Slaves and their descendants basically had no choice other than to adopt Christianity and to go to Church, as the Catholic institution was intimately related to the colonial power. Yet, being officially Christian did not prevent them from being involved in non-Christian cults in their private life. It is in this context of a forced acculturation conjugated with an unavoidable creolisation of ideas and practices that the music called *maloya* was born on the island.[2] Originating from Mozambique, where the term *maloya* means witchcraft, it was frightening to the general population because it also involved alcohol, fire, and uncontrolled trance states. Played and danced discreetly in the fields after the work hours, away from the disapproving eyes of the white masters (*Maîtres Blancs*), this music has for a long time represented a symbol of resistance to the oppressive power. It was first played publicly during the day of the celebration of the abolition of slavery in 1948. Then it remained underground, only played during the Malagasy cults of the ancestor (*kabar* or *sèrvis kabarè*), and was even forbidden when the local Communist Party took it as a symbol to claim independence. It is only during the last three decades that it has gained legitimacy to the point of being appropriated as a powerful symbol in the local discourse on identity. This form of resistance will be reinforced, as we will see below, by the arrival of indentured workers from India, a population who also did everything to keep their Hindu worldview and practices in spite of the local pressure to convert them.

The system of plantation and slavery lasted until its abolition in 1848 by the French government (a few decades after the French Revolution). From one day to another, 62,000 slaves suddenly became French citizens and could live freely on the island. Yet, their living and economic situations did not improve significantly, as they were still in the lowest rungs of society. A salient cultural fact of Reunion Island is related to the popular culture that has produced a complex mixture of beliefs that profoundly marked people's imaginations until today. Numerous altars (*chapèl*) are visible in various public places (roads, paths, gardens, etc.), which often show Christian deities such as the Virgin Mary or a powerful local saint called *Saint Expedit*. Although related to Christianity, this religious figure, which represents a Roman soldier, is not fully recognized by the Catholic Church outside the island, notably because of its ambivalence, as he can be evoked to protect but also to punish.[3] This apprehension of a saint is obviously influenced by the inclusive Hindu conceptions that, in the popular cults, do not trace a rigid frontier between the god that helps and the one that reprimands.

In a context of social violence inherited from the slave and colonial system, religious beliefs played a role in the human organization of meaning. If Christianity was the only and ultimate religion for the dominants and those who were in one way or another part of their world—that is practically all the population of the island—it was not really the best symbolic framework for a subaltern social counter-power to be invoked and expressed. It is therefore towards the popular cults that most of the inhabitants of Reunion in search of empowerment have turned. In these circumstances, the Malagasy ancestral worship of the dead (*sèrvis Malgache*), based on animal sacrifices, food offerings, and human possession, was practiced in the private domestic sphere. An expression of the preservation of ancestral conceptions, this cult has been maintained for a long time in a relatively hidden way until the last two decades. To involve oneself in this cult of the ancestors affirmed and expressed the connection and respect due to one's own genealogy. As a form of social solidarity, it meant being united with significant others and fellow workers in a practice based on shared conceptions. But it was also to place oneself under the protection of ancestors: those who could help in case of needs and problems, such as disease or social conflict. Revering the ancestors while going to the church was therefore a personal statement and a search for power, with the idea that the most potent help came from the peripheries and margin of the dominant system. The search for protection and help outside Christianity was also found in the cult very early rendered by a very important part of the population from the lower rungs of society, dedicated to the bandit Sitarane.[4] The grave of this man, who was the last to be decapitated on the island, is a place where numerous wishes and offerings of alcohol (*rheum*) and cigarettes were (and still are) discreetly made by people trying to empower themselves.

In the local imaginary, the wishes of people involved in what we can call the peripheral, subaltern and nonofficial cults on the island are very often thought to be malevolent. This idea is reinforced by the fact that the Church condemns these practices, which are most of the time accomplished in secrecy at night. A pervasive discourse on sorcery and its threat is widespread in popular culture. Always attributed to bad intentions towards others, sorcery is implicitly or explicitly opposed to the proper official religious attitude. This explains why most inhabitants have been doing their best to publicly display their Christianity, and thus their insertion into the mainstream life; an understandable attitude and concern if we take into account the way the local society has been constituted and has evolved.

It should be noticed that although sorcery has mostly been attributed to descendants of African slaves, most of the people of the island, including the whites who came too late to acquire land to exploit on the littoral and who took refuge in the highlands, where they started to build an economy of subsistence (*Petits blancs*), have been involved with their own logic and system of reference to activities designed as "sorcery." Coming from the countryside of France, mainly Bretagne, this very poor population of whites brought its own ancestral conceptions to Reunion, notably through a medieval French book of "sorcery recipes" called *Le petit Albert*. Through time and ethnic blending, this knowledge mixed more or less with other conceptions and practices already occurring on the island. Sorcery and popular cults with their many options thus became a space of resistance to dominant models and a practice of empowerment for the general population.

Constructed on an accumulation of violence—dislocation from the place of origin, slavery, and isolation—Reunion society has favored the creation of an imaginary of threats: those of the social world, that have a long time been important because of the simple presence of different humans, with whom one necessarily has to deal in a multicultural society, and those of the invisible world, that are probably even more dangerous. The supernatural forces that inhabit the invisible space are for the inhabitants most often negative entities (*bébèt*) ready to harm humans if they are fragile, if they do not protect themselves, if they commit a fault or, for most of the cases, if they are the object of other people's jealousy. It is in this logic that the concept of the evil eye is very widespread in the society. Coming from people who are voluntarily or not, consciously or not, jealous, the evil eye (*mové zië*) is supposed to constitute a real threat to someone's physical and/or psychic integrity.[5] Babies and children are particularly vulnerable to these dangers and this is why they are especially protected. The strong presence of the concept of the evil eye in Reunion Island perfectly illustrates the combination in this society of the cumulated dangers of the social and the invisible world.

CHRISTIANITY & HINDUISM: AN UNAVOIDABLE RIVALRY

From the second part of the nineteenth century, the social order and beliefs of Reunion society became more complex through the influx of big numbers of people from India (Hindus from Tamil Nadu from 1860 and Muslims from Gujarat a few decades later) and China (Chinese from Canton practicing the ancestor cult, mostly between 1860 and 1880). While there was already a certain amount of South Asians working in the plantation before the abolition of slavery, this event launched a new and intensive recruitment of laborers from Tamil Nadu as the white landowners tried to replace the slave workforce with an indentured migration of workers from the French colonies in South India (Pondicherry, Karikal). Coming from the lower fringes of the Indian society, these workers, principally men (the workforce was needed), replaced—voluntarily or not[6]—emancipated slaves who did not want to continue working in the plantation for the white landowners. Their living conditions were very hard, close to that of the slaves they replaced: promiscuity, harsh authority from employers at the workplace. Many Tamils tried to escape and return to India after the completion of their work contract, which was officially for five years. But very few were indeed able to do so and most of them had to stay and adapt to their new place of life.

More than Muslims and Chinese, Hindus were subject to a strong pressure to acculturation as their religion faced the strongest oppositions in the larger multicultural society. On the contract indentured workers signed in India before embarking to Reunion, it was specified that they could freely practice their Hindu religion. Their disappointment was extreme when they realized they could not do so and that they were, on the contrary, expected to convert to Christianity and to go to church. Those in power in the social stratification negatively perceived the Hindu's noncompliance to this principle. The larger society also participated in the pressure to conform to the dominant religious model. Therefore, adopting Christian attitudes was a way to express one's insertion in the society. For the indentured workers, the colonial religion was unavoidable, as they had to do with the rules they faced, and the adoption of Christianity was massive. Yet it was not really the complete conversion that the Catholic priests and political administration— two interlinked powers in the colonial society—were expecting to happen. Submitted to the same pressure to become Christian, the Chinese had to go to church—but still practice until today their inherited cult of the ancestor.

In fact, in spite of the religious pressure they faced, indentured workers did everything they could to maintain their Hindu beliefs. At first, they discreetly did their ancestral rituals in the fields under the guidance of a man familiar with the basic Hindu prayers. After many complaints were sent to the British consulate explaining that their religion was not respected in Reunion Island, South Asians were allowed to build small Hindu temples in the plantations. Some of these temples still exist today and continue to gather devotees. Being able to pray to their Hindu gods was very important for the newcomers in a society that did not see them as persons to respect. As for the African and Malagasy slaves before, it helped them to keep referring to a former worldview, and to endure their hard conditions of life. In a structured situation, in which Christian ways were forced upon the migrants and were related to the structures of power in the society, it was a way to deflect adversity with the feeling of being protected by ancestral gods.

Slowly gaining more confidence, Hindus devotees started to express more publicly their religion, as some ceremonies require carrying the gods and goddesses in processions from a river to the temple, often through villages. This visibility of an alternative religion immediately provoked a strong reaction from the larger society. Indeed, the Hindu religion displayed by the indentured workers on the island was from the beginning a popular religion; based on animal sacrifices, priest possessions, fire walking, and *cavadee*.[7] These practices deeply impressed non-Hindus who saw them as "extravagant" behaviors without understanding the religious logic behind them. The colorful gods, the ritual drumming, the emotions displayed by followers, the blood flowing during goat sacrifices, the needles in the body, the walking on fire, the priest's possession, etc., all these religious aspects, deeply meaningful for devotees, made no sense for outsiders and were therefore heavily condemned. The most virulent disapprobation came from the priests who saw—or pretended to see—in these practices the expression of evil. This very hard external judgment on Hinduism was also due to the fact that it rapidly became a concurrent religion attracting the lower rungs of the society. This has to be put in context with the important intermarriages between Hindu men and non-Hindu women.[8] Along with the unavoidable blending of Hindu migrants with already settled people of African background, Hindu ceremonies thus offered a kind of space of practice not related to the dominant and highly politically marked Christian religion. Involvement in a new and alternative religion could then constitute a form of political resistance to the colonial system.

In order to protect themselves from other people's possible threats and to express their own power in the society, Hindu migrants used the mystery associated with their religion by other people. They also did not miss opportunities to say that their Hindu gods were much more powerful than the Christian saints they also venerated at church. A study I conducted in the 1990s in Reunion Island shows that, in cases of very important matters (illness, wishes, etc.) Tamils still turn to their Hindu gods to be protected and get what they want. Such attitudes have deeply impressed others at the bottom of the economic system, who felt they could also get profit from participating in Hindu rites. Seeing fellow dark-skinned men (and in a fewer cases, women) involved in a very demanding subaltern and somewhat mysterious religion (with fasts, corporeal austerities, and various privations of pleasures), and apparently getting their wishes granted as they kept repeating their rituals, helped them develop a feeling of possible empowerment for themselves too. The ambivalence of some Hindu gods and goddesses, who can protect and punish, also played a role in the attraction caused by this religion.

Understandably, Christian priests have for a long time developed a very depreciative discourse on Hindu practices. I remember hearing, in the early 1980s, a priest saying publicly in Church that "the religion of fire walking, the religion of needles planted in the skin, is the religion of Satan!" This kind of intolerant and authoritarian judgment of an alternative belief system expresses the priest's feeling to be on the side of the power structure of the society. It is based on the assurance of representing the first, main, and dominant religion on the island. A depreciative shortcut for defining Hinduism was thus to assimilate its practices to another form of "sorcery." Analyzing the dichotomist discourse opposing religion to sorcery, anthropologists have pointed out that it comes from the dominant localization in society. In other words, accusing others of practicing "sorcery" is to place oneself in the normative realm, defined as the establishment's "religion." Clearly at the margin of the dominant structure in the society, popular Hinduism has thus been assimilated by many co-insulars to dangerous practices conducted by bad intentioned persons; an attitude neglecting the fact that the "sorcery" of some is the religion of other. The problem of Hinduism in Reunion Island was from the beginning that it was a religion of the lower spheres of society, as with African and Malagasy cults, also previously associated with sorcery. The "sorcery accusation" was thus a ready-made slot to fulfill an imaginary function. Yet, from the perspective of the people involved, these beliefs and practices are all about empowerment. Trying to gain some control on events in their life through religion, notably an alternative one, was just a normal thing to do when the social system did not leave too much room for emancipation.

In a political and religious context of acculturation and discrimination of other people's differences, being Christian, as discussed previously, was a strategic move to fit to the main models of the mainstream society. That did not, of course, prevent people from sincerely engaging in the imposed religion. Yet, the involvement had a necessary public character, while Hinduism was on the other hand practiced in the domestic temple at home, in the community temple in the village or, later, in town. A religious double system of reference slowly developed for people from South India who learned to distinguish their Christian public involvement from their Hindu private one. This cognitive mindset, which is not limited to the religious domain, has allowed a lot of cultural continuities and persistence in the multicultural context of Reunion Island. It helped people to act differently according to the institutions and situations they had to be involved in without feeling out of place. Unavoidably being Reunion people (*réunionnais*), therefore Christians, they could also remain people of Tamil descent, i.e. Hindus (or *malabars*), and express their Indianness where possible.

Two examples of the managing of a double system of reference can be found in the name given to children when they are born. First: almost systematically, and for a long time, the first name given in families of South Indian descent was "Jean" for a boy and "Marie" for a girl; a clear demonstration of the Christian adherence. Yet, the second name, used at home by relatives and therefore the most significant for a person, although it was also a Christian name, was chosen by the parents after consultation with a Hindu priest; the first letter of this second name being in accordance with the Hindu astrology, in order for the child to be protected during his/her life. Second: when going to the church, a Tamil mother will expose publicly her Christianity with a very visible cross on her blouse while wearing, unseen under the same blouse, a Hindu protective talisman that was blessed by a Hindu priest during a ceremony at the temple.

RELIGIOUS PARTICULARISM: A SOCIAL DYNAMIC

An important proportion of the population of the island was for a long time composed of poor white colons and people from African backgrounds, while the number of mixed people was continuously growing as intermarriage increased. The so-called "indigenous heritage" of the island has thus been very soon a mixture of ethnic origins: French, African, Malagasy, Indian, Chinese, and, of course, Métis. After almost three hundred years of colonial system, the island became the ninety-seventh French Department in 1946, a change of status that was followed by the importing of all the French Institutions into the society. Yet, this transformation did not erase the established social inequalities, with white masters, French administration, and the Church on one side, and the popular culture on the other side. Although it was no longer official, dark skin color persisted as an object of stereotypes, expressing the social structure of society. The sudden massive influx of educated public workers from France (mostly teachers) participated, through ethnic blending, to end the sharp separation between the white insulars' higher status and the non-whites' lower one.[9] Yet, from the colonial society to the Department, a structured system of privileges and poverty persisted. Wealth and material transfers are still not equally distributed in society. More than before, the island is dependant on France and, through this, involved in a huge consumption of goods (new cars, clothes, etc.). Desired and acquired because of their valued symbolic status, these goods are, in a capitalist logic, exported by the larger French institutions without any concern about their local cultural reception.[10]

In the religious domain, the weight and power of Christianity upon people's consciousness has been maintained until very recently through many events and institutions. Until today, most people of Tamil descent are baptized and married at church. At their death, their funeral also takes place in church. Beyond the religious symbolism, these participations in Christian ceremonies still display to the larger society their Christian involvement and, therefore, their social conformity. Classes in catechism for children of non-European backgrounds help to integrate the general population to the main social and religious models. It is striking that the fear to not express a Christian conformity was still prevalent a few decades ago for the children in catechism. Indeed, a woman of South Asian descent told me of being severely punished as a child in one of those classes for having drawn only three apostles on a paper at the request of the teacher who had asked the pupils to draw "all Jesus' apostles." She was heavily beaten with a metallic ruler on the bottom of her joint fingers a number of times corresponding to the missing apostles on her drawing.

The progressive penetration of modern and global models into the society slowly changed its internal *rapport de force*. From the opening of the island to tourism in the 1970s to the current project to create a natural park that will cover 42 percent of the island, Reunion society has been the focus of a growing interest from outside for its cultural specificities. It is in this context that 20 December, the date of the abolition of slavery, has been declared a holiday (*fèt Kaf*); runaway slaves who escaped to the hills (*marrons*) became the new emblematic figures of resistance to oppression and the real historical heroes of the colonial society; *maloya*, the music and dances born in the slave camps, long forbidden and hidden, gained a positive interest as a cultural specificity; and the project of creating the Maison des Civilisations et de l'Unité Réunionnaise (MCUR; with a 61.3 million Euros cost) in 2010. Since the 1980s, this ideological context of tolerance and cultural awareness gave more space for the expression of religious particularism and allowed non-Christian cults to be more accepted in the society at large. This was true for the Malagasy ancestor cult (*sèrvis malgache*), Hinduism as well as Islam, with the daily calls for prayer at the Mosque built in 1905 in the Capital Saint-Denis.

Today, religious ostracism is no longer taken for granted in Reunion. Yet, the acculturation process to the French models is still going on, while the island obtained in 2002 the institutional status of "Region" (*Région Réunion*) in France. Power relationships through religious beliefs and practices are still pervasive, although they may take an unexpected form. As an example, a new kind of criticism of the popular Hinduism nowadays comes not anymore from outsiders but from insiders themselves. At a time when the larger society finally became accustomed to the processions and other public demonstrations, an attitude favored by the development of tourism on the island, popular Hinduism, which was maintained under difficult circumstances by Tamils in colonial society, is now discredited by a new generation of people of Tamil descent itself. Reunited in cultural associations to preserve and express the pride of their religious differences, these persons, educated for the most part, are willing to dissociate themselves from the practices of animal sacrifices, priest possessions, and other spectacular aspects related to popular Hinduism. They wish to operate what they call a "return to the sources." In this logic, they hire Brahmin priests from Mauritius and Tamil Nadu to take charge in the ceremonies in the urban temples. Doing so, people involved in this revival movement (locally called the *renouveau tamoul*) import a new kind of Brahmanic Hinduism, based on so-called "benevolent deities" only accepting vegetal offerings. In the well known dynamic of sankritisation, they depreciate popular Hindu beliefs and practices, even if those are, in a religious continuum, intimately linked to the Brahmanic Hinduism they want to refer to. They also import celebrations from India such as *Dipavalee* (the Hindu festival of the lights) to Reunion Island: a new public event (full of color, Indian food, music, and dance) on the island that older devotees (*Malabars*) do not see as expressing the deep religion of their ancestors.

By a strange irony of history, actors of this Tamil revival are currently in the process of putting an end from inside to practices that have been maintained by their own ancestors in spite of the heavy acculturation pressures they endured. Power and status is again at stake in this situation. On one side, in accordance with the positive representation of Hinduism by European outsiders, involvement in what is considered to be the "real" form of Hinduism is supposed to express a higher position in the society. On the other side, those, mostly elders and families of lower status living in the countryside, who still want to give animal offerings to "carnivore deities," as their ancestors always did, consider that the power they need and are searching for through their popular rituals cannot be put aside for a more aesthetic—but less intense—"new" form of Hinduism. If the former generally want to call themselves *Tamouls* (a rather new identity term on the island), the latter still call themselves *Malabars*, even if this appellation is a historical colonial mistake,[11] as their ancestors adopted this term to define themselves on the island.

From colonialism (with the pressure to be Christian) to modernity (redefining what Hinduism should advantageously present of itself) and the new insider's representations of "tradition," devotees of popular Hinduism have been facing many difficulties to express their beliefs and through them, to keep alive what they considered to be a superior conception of the order of the world than the colonial system's. In the last few months, the criticism of popular Hinduism, as well as the resistance operated by its followers, has taken another form. Endorsing the Church's historical condemning of the local Hindu practices, a condemnation itself expressed by the members of the *renouveau tamoul*, the French State, through its local Prefecture, is currently engaging a legal battle against the popular Hinduism through its core practice: the animal sacrifice to the gods. Two systems of understanding of this religious act are at stake: on one side, the hygienic policies decided in the European Parliament (for the French State) and the replacement of animals with vegetables offerings (for the Tamil revival), and, on the other side, the devotees' offering of a sacrifice to the gods who need them to help humans. It should be remembered that the person who sacrifices an animal (most often a goat) considers it to be the best possible sacrifice to the gods. In the Hindu conceptions, the animal is therefore not killed but "offered" to the gods. Animal sacrifices being at the core of popular Hindu beliefs and practices, devotees cannot imagine putting an end to them without weakening their faith. This is why a huge mobilization started among devotees of popular Hinduism to prevent the French State to interfere with their cult. Without judging here the good or bad in relation to offering a sacrifice to the gods, one can notice that a state, here the French one, can still, in 2007, interfere with religious practices, as it did—and renounced—more than one century ago on the same island. Neocolonialism may thus be an insidious form of postcolonialism, as the assimilationist logic is still in process in the now French Department. That example clearly shows that some cultural differences are still not considered as such by the French State in its former colony.

From slavery to indenturism and structural dependency to France, a political power is expressing its authority: dominant models are imported upon others. That explains why many natives of Reunion Island feel their status is marginalised in the French Republic. The status of the Creole language, and the call from local intellectuals to get an official acknowledgement of the existence of bilingualism in Reunion, offers another example of the current identity issues taking place. It is important to keep in mind that the logic of acculturation in Reunion Island took place on different levels: the religious, object of our focus here, but also the linguistic and cultural. South Indians had to learn and speak Creole, the local language, and some elements of French, the official language of the island, while the second generation of migrants rapidly lost the usage of the Tamil language. They also had to dress the local way, to comply with the local administration, etc. However, cultures have resources and in spite of the forces of acculturation they are subject to, many South Indian patterns have persisted in an adapted manner as in the cooking (in the public sphere) and the system of value (in the private sphere).

It is necessary to take into account the circumstances, voluntary or non-voluntary, of the migration, when analyzing the beliefs and practices displayed by people in Reunion Island. When the immigration was voluntary, as for the white colons, Catholicism was the normal way. When it was forced, as for slaves and indentured workers from India, there was a good chance that people involved themselves in subaltern beliefs, supposedly to allow them to express a form of resistance to political and ideological power. Made of resistances, negotiations, and dialogic processes, the local cultural life still continuously adjusts itself to a social order decided and established from an outside place—France—through its Republican institutions. The social stratification of Reunion society thus gave space to cultural and personal adjustments. Through time and through diverse cultural references, people could find spaces of resistance to the dominant structure through music, beliefs, and everyday life. In spite of—or maybe because of—its long oppressive character, the multicultural society, also permitted creativity.[12] Although ancestral genealogies are lost and the interlinkedness of cultures on the island is significant, most people can today refer to two or more ancestries. The numerous ethnic blending in Reunion Island have created a diverse population with people expressing daily their multiethnic descent, and where the definition of roots can be optional (from Reunion? France? India? Africa? etc). This combination of cultures in one person expresses the complexity of the society.

Religious power is related to priority in residency and political insertion on the island. At stake is a competition for the application—and sometimes imposition—of a model upon others, even if all these models have their origin outside the island. The 1980s saw, for example, the emergence of a diverse Islamic community with the arrival of people from Comores. These lower status Muslims occupy a relatively subaltern position in the already well-established Gujarat Muslim community who, although it is a religious minority, gained a rather good (and for some families a very good) economic status in society. Economic stratifications added to antecedence in the migration thus draw a power line among the fellow believers.

To summarize my point, in Reunion, it is in the religious sphere, the private one from the point of view of French citizenship, that the most complex and strong expressions of human diversities and search for answers and power are expressed. Catholicism was, from the beginning, the religion of social integration. It was the official space for the expression of a political power but coexisted with non-Christian beliefs which, although underground for a long time, unavoidably became alternative responses to the dominant social order. The acceptance these beliefs obtained occurred when the only and unique space for social integration occupied by Catholicism left room to new imported institutions to the island since the 1950s, bringing economic development, formal secular education, etc., with Departmentalization. The empowerment these former subaltern beliefs have experienced in the last three decades is related to (and explicable by) the cultural and social changes that have taken place in the society on the island and beyond.

NOTES

1. It is striking that the meanings "explore" and "exploit" are expressed with the same term *explorar* in the Portuguese language.
2. *Maloya* is based on drumming, songs with words related to oppression, and suggestive moves of one or more dancers.

3. For a study of the way this figure became a saint on the island, see Regnier (1995).
4. Sitarane has deeply impressed the collective memory as being a very cruel bandit fighting against the political administration of the islands in the eighteenth century.
5. According to Hindu conceptions, the danger of the evil eye is related to a cosmic mechanism: in the invisible world full of positive and negative entities, anything, be it a person, a possession, an object, etc., can be hurt to various degrees by a force or spirit who has been attracted by the object of the desire of a human eye or thought.
6. Many indentured workers from India were taken away against their will from their villages.
7. *Cavadee* is a Tamil ceremony during which devotees participate in public processions, with the body pierced with long needles.
8. Hindu men came to the island in much bigger proportion than Hindu women, as the migrant ratio was one woman for ten men.
9. Among the diverse reasons behind this new attitude on the island was the humanist change and evolving value system in France since the time of colonialism, combined with European men's attraction towards the exotic beautiful island girls: a problematic smoothing of the existing social stratification.
10. The different capacities to buy and consume were the cause of riots a few years ago on the island.
11. At the time of the colony, the term *Malabar* was generally attributed by the colons to all indentured workers, although these did not come from the Goa area but from Tamil Nadu.
12. It should be remembered that it was a slave of the Island, Edmond Albius, who invented the artificial fecundation of vanilla in 1848.

BIBLIOGRAPHY

Barat, Christian. *Nargoulan. Culture et rites malbar à la Réunion*. Saint Denis: Editions du Tramail, 1989.
Barat, Christian, Michel Carayol, and Robert Chaudenson. *Magie et sorcellerie à La Réunion*, Saint Denis: Livres Réunion, 1981.
Benoist, Jean. *Hindouismes créoles*. Paris: Éditions du Comité des Travaux historiques et scientifiques, 1998.
Cambefort, Jean-Pierre. *Enfances et familles à La Réunion*. Paris: L'Harmattan, 2001.
Chaudenson, Robert. (sous la direction), *Encyclopédie de la Réunion*. Saint-Denis: Livres Réunion éditions, 1980.
Eve, Prosper. *Île à peur. La peur redoutée ou récupérée à La Réunion des origines à nos jours*. Saint André, Réunion: Océan Editions, 1992.
Fuma, Sudel. *L'esclavagisme à la Réunion 1794–1848*. Paris: L'Harmattan/ Université de la Réunion, 1992.
———. *Histoire d'un peuple. La Réunion, 1848–1900*. Saint-Denis: Editions CNH/Université de La Réunion, 1994.
Ghasarian, Christian. *Honneur, chance & destin. La culture indienne à La Réunion*. Paris: L'Harmattan, 1991.
———. "Dieu arrive! Possession rituelle et hindouisme populaire à La Réunion," *Ethnologie française*. "Mélanges," n° 4, tome 24, Paris, 1994.
———. "Interpreting a Hindu rite: a critique of a psychoanalytic reading," *Berkeley Journal of Asian Studies*, Vol. VII, University of California Berkeley, 1996.

————. "We have the Best Gods! The Encounter Between Hinduism and Christianity in La Réunion," *Journal of Asian and African Studies*, Vol. XXXII, n°3-4, December, Leiden, Netherlands, 1997.

————. "Language Strategies in La Réunion." *Cahiers*, University of Hull, n° 4.3, Autumn, England, 1998.

————. "Patrimoine culturel et ethnicité à La Réunion: dynamiques et dialogismes." *Ethnologie française*, n° 99/3, Paris, 1999

————. "Reunion." In Melvil Ember and Carol Ember, eds. *Countries and their cultures*. New York: Macmillan, 2001.

————. "La Réunion: acculturation, créolisation et reformulations identitaires," *Ethnologie française*, "Outre-mer: statuts, cultures, devenirs," n° 4, Paris, 2002.

Govindin, Sully-Santa. *Les engagés indiens, Ile de La Réunion—XIXe siècle*. La Réunion: Azalées Editions, 1994.

Nicaise, Stéphane. *Le continuum religieux créole: une matrice du catholicisme à l'île de la Réunion*. Villeneuve d'Ascq: Presses Universitaires du Septentrion, 2001.

Nicole, Reine May. *Noirs, cafres et créoles; études de la représentation du no-blanc réunionnais*. Paris: L'Harmattan, 1996.

Ottino, Paul. "La Réunion: L'organisation familiale des blancs des hauts." In Bernard Chérubini, ed. *Le monde rural à La Réunion*, L'Harmattan: Université de La Réunion, 1996.

Paillat-Jarousseau, Hélène. *Une terre pour cultiver et habiter. Anthropologie d'une localité de l'Ile de La Réunio.*, (Préface de Maurice Godelier). Paris: L'Harmattan, 2001.

Pourchez, Laurence. *Grossesse, naissance et petite enfance en société créole*, livre et CD.Rom. Paris: Karthala, 2002.

Prudhomme, Claude. *Histoire religieuse de La Réunion*. Paris: Karthala, 1984.

Reigner, Philippe. "La fabrication des Saints," *Terrains*, 24, Paris, 1995.

Verges, Françoise. *La Mémoire enchaînée. Questions sur l'esclavage*, 2007. Paris: Albin Michel, 2006.

16 Through Magical Flowers
Tourism and Creole Self-fashioning in La Reunion

David Picard

Orom makes us halt in front of a camellia tree. He starts telling a story about a lady who couldn't stand the odour of flowers. She would not use perfume either. The only flowers she had in her garden were camellias. Because camellias are odourless. And they are also beautiful. This is why the lady was called the *Dame aux Camellias*. He will tell us about a properly Creole way of utilising camellias. It was used in processions; people would throw camellias on the path before processions passed. Yet, maybe the most interesting way of using the flowers, especially the white ones, was simply as soap. He picks a large white camellia flower from the tree and rubs it between his hands. After a certain time, a white soapy mousse appears between his fingers. Ah! The group of tourists watching him is astonished. He smiles and seems happy about the success of his experiment. He continues explaining. Before, everything was used. Today we constantly by pass flowers and plants that previously had multiple utilities. Some people still know about these flowers and plants, but they are no longer in use. To make the children, his children, use them—no, that's not what he wants to do. However he thinks it is important for the children to know about these flowers and plants and how to use them. So, the white camellias for washing cloth. Efficient! He has finished his explanation. We are ready to continue the tour.

Orom is around 40. He grew up in Hell-Bourg, a village deep inside the valley of Salazie. His parents did not own land and had to work for local farmers. These had mainly small farms, with narrow patches of land and small herds of cattle. The surplus of local produce was usually sold to the markets and the large domains outside the valley. Since the 1960s, most of these small-scale agricultural concerns were facing competition from imported goods. La Reunion had become a *department d'outre-mer* (DOM) in 1946. In 1963, Michel Debré, French prime minister under de Gaulle and fervent defender of France's overseas colonial interests, was elected a member of the French parliament, representing the first circumscription of La Reunion. During his mandate, he engaged in an eager struggle against the Communist

Party of La Reunion, a movement led by Paul Verges claiming the island's autonomy.[1] To counter the political influence of the communist party, Debré often violently reestablished the colonial rhetoric of France as a motherly *Mère-Patrie*.[2] He distributed free milk to the newly created school canteens and initiated a wide-ranging economic and social development programme for the island. A new college was founded in the south of the island. The island's economy was opened to imports from the French mainland. The French welfare state was introduced, giving the population, especially the women, previously unknown access to consumption. At the same time, the translation of the republican *Mère-Patrie* rhetoric in the context of social welfare redistributions systematised a postcolonial form of dependency which left the island's population incapable to reciprocate,[3] quasi-powerless to construct and emancipate an autonomous island mythology.

Debré organised the migration of young Reunions to the French mainland (along with the forced migration of more than a thousand children taken away from their parents in La Reunion to repopulate deserted areas in France). The optimism of the dominant development doctrine of the 1960s reached Salazie and other rural areas of the island at that time. To make the agricultural sector more productive, hamlets were regrouped into villages, new access routes were built and a land reform was initiated to improve agricultural exploitations. People without land, like Orom's parents, remained with little to do and often had to leave for the urban centres at the island's coast or, via one of Debré's emigration programmes, to the French mainland. In this context of rural decline, Orom left Salazie and moved to Saint-Denis, the largest town on the island's coast. In the years that followed, he worked as a musician for private parties and as a waiter in different restaurants.

During the 1990s, with the end of the Cold War, the political and ideological tensions between republican and autonomist movements slowly vanished or metamorphosed into new ideological battlegrounds. Through capital transfers from France in the form of public sector wages, social allocations and investments in transport, health and education systems, and through the integration of La Reunion to the European Union's structured funding schemes, the island achieved by far the highest gross domestic product (GDP) per capita in the Indian Ocean region. At the same time, despite higher incomes and high educational levels for females, the population continued its rapid growth. The artificially created economy was unable to absorb the ever-increasing numbers of job seekers, leaving almost 40 percent of the active population unemployed during the 1990s. Unlike other islands of the Southwestern Indian Ocean (e.g. Mauritius, Seychelles, Zanzibar) which developed agriculture, textile, tourism, IT and financial service industries, La Reunion was not successful in diversifying its economy and creating export-driven sectors. Tourism in particular remained for long a highly contested development option.

During the 1970s and 1980s, a powerful local lobby penetrating different sociopolitical classes asked not to "sell the best beaches of the island to foreigners."[4] During the 1980s and 1990s, the emergence of environmental movements and governmental agencies for the protection of the environment further reinforced this antitourism discourse. Tourism started to become seen as "destroying" or "polluting" "local culture," landscapes, and environments. Antitourism discourses thus paradoxically inverted the symbolic system underlying the postcolonial narrative of the republican rhetoric. The Creole, hitherto visualized as impure with regard to an idealised centre (France the *Mère-Patrie*[5]), was elevated as a new ideal now threatened by the influence of mass tourism emanating precisely from this *Mère-Patrie* (now renamed the *metropole*). The emergence of an aesthetics of diversity in the political centres of the Western world (emanating in a context of fear of "cultural homogenisation" during the 1980s and 1990s) thus created conditions in La Reunion that allowed a spectacular revolution of self-representations. Tourism (and the imagined threat of tourism) seemed to turn the rhetoric employed during the postcolonial context of the Cold War on its head. The Creole became a global ideal-type, a newly fashionable model to think a world in continuous contact, exchange, and transformation. Tourism to places like La Reunion made this idea tangible. At the same time, it implied the transformation of La Reunion into a new form of social theatre.

Most of the ambitious tourism development plans of the early 1960s were never implemented. Many hotels built by local promoters consequently had no planning permission and often occupied public land. The development of residential areas around former fishing villages of the west coast were not integrated into a wider planning scheme. The absence of such a scheme resulted in often chaotic urbanisation marked by inadequate road, water treatment, and housing infrastructures. During the 1990s, at a rhetoric level, if tourism was to be developed at all, it had to be "integrated" to the island's social and natural environment. While the vast majority of tourist and commercial activities were situated along the island's beaches, a largely common public discourse located La Reunion's tourism resources and potentials mainly in its mountainous interior. It is here "that the island's heart beats," indicated the 1995 Regional Development Scheme (Région Réunion 1995). The "integrated development" of this space became a policy priority. While the largest part of the population by then lived on the coast, the new vision for La Reunion seemed to advocate that its future lay in its steep valleys and high plains, in the "traditions" and "heritage" of its vanished or vanishing rural populations. "Valorising cultural heritage and diversity" became a new master narrative, transcending regional development policies, newly organised village festivals, newly created museum interpretation sites and the marketing campaigns by local supermarkets for almost anything.

Within this wider dynamic, the *Commissariat à l'Aménagement des Hauts* (CAH), a government agency created during the early 1970s to coordinate the reorganisation of the rural economies of the islands' valleys, launched the first training programme for local tourist guides (*Guides de Pays*). This programme led to a recognised professional diploma, the BAPAAT.[6] According to an internal strategy paper, the initiative was based on the assumption that a "youthful human resource in the rural areas with often limited professional qualifications had an intimate knowledge of the environment and was willing to communicate this to (tourist) visitors."[7] The official aim of the programme therefore was to structure small-scale tourism products within a new type of tourism market based on "the discovery of a territory through its cultural, natural and economic heritage" (ibid.). This aim was part of a wider strategic development objective to increase the number of tourist nights spent in the rural areas of the island.

Between 1996 and 1997, twenty-eight people participated in the training programme. During their studies, they received bursaries from the government agency CAH. Orom, approached by agents of the CAH, decided to take part in the 1996 course. During 710 hours of teaching and learning, he passed modules in enterprise management, heritage communication, and project development. He also had to do a professional internship. As part of this course, he was asked to develop a professional project, a tourism product that he could run independently after accomplishing the course. Orom did his internship with a mountain hiking company then new to Salazie. He also collaborated with the ecomuseum of Salazie, a new museum initiated by university researchers that was then preparing its very first exhibition. Tutored by the director of this new museum, a French anthropologist, Orom developed an ethnobotanical guided walk. It is the walk on which I have been accompanying him over the past weeks, a walk that follows almost step by step a standard programme of explanations, jokes, and performances. We are on this walk right now. It will follow the usual agenda.

Having left the camellia tree behind, Orom leads us on a small path into the forest. He makes us stop besides a tree. It is a *filaos* (casuarina), he explains. Why "*filaos*"? he asks. Because when it rains, water drops form little chains: *fils à eau* (threads of water). It is a word game and the tourists don't get it immediately. Ah, *fils à eau!* they say after a moment. They get it. Orom tells the group that his parents were too poor to buy furniture wood, so they used the *filaos* for the construction of their houses. The wood needed to be cut during the winter months, three days before or after full moon. Ah! The tourists seem to understand. Usually one or two would then say that it's like that in their country. Another would normally contest it as new age humbug. Today, they just seem to acknowledge. Orom picks a little red flower and says it is called a *capucine* (nasturtium). He opens it and explains that it can be used in cooking. Put into a flour paste and deep-fry it to make *beignets de capucines*. Very nice. You can also use it as hair

shampoo, especially the ladies. It is efficient against pellicules (dandruff).
It's also good against colds. If you have a cold, you simply suck the sweet
juice. He asks if anyone wants to try. No one wants to try. He points to a
bush with red leaves. As a man, he explains, you should never plant this
in your garden. According to Creole beliefs, you would never get married.
Wow. The tourists look at the leaves and comment. They are all married.
So there is no problem. They laugh and we move on.

Orom stops to point out what he calls the *choca* (aloes). It is not the
"sugar dance," he says (he says it in English), but the *choca*. The tourists
look at him and start understanding his humour. They usually like him.
The *choca* was used as building material, but also to produce cords and
strings. The ladies in the past used it as sewing thread. We can try to stretch
it and will see: it's "hyper-resistant." The tourists give it a try and it proves
to be, well, "hyper-resistant." Another way of using the *choca* is to cut its
resin to wash cloth with. It helps to bring out the colours, to make the cloth
shine. The only problem was that, when it started raining, the cloths got
very itchy. That's it. Questions? No questions. We move on.

At the next stop, Orom points towards a bush. What would "we" (the
tourists) do with this in our world, he asks. We would of course use it
to create hedges. It is the privet (*troène*). In La Reunion, he says, people
wanted to do like people in Europe and planted the privet to build hedges.
Yet, they didn't manage to keep trimming these hedges because they grew
too fast. The privet developed into a biopest. That's why the Creoles call
it the "Invading Beauty" (*Belle Envahissante*). It grows very, very fast and
wherever it sets foot, nothing else is able to grow, he explains. Even worse,
it produces flowers that make the honey bitter. There is not much to do
against it. Some people tried to develop a mushroom to destroy the plant.
But this needs another ten years of experimentation, he says, to be sure that
the mushrooms will not parasite other plants. He turns to another plant,
another biopest threatening the forests of the island. It's called the "maroon
vine" (*vigne marronne*). It's full of thorns. We can touch it to see. We don't
touch it. It produces a little hairy berry. In Creole, he says, people call
this . . . he hesitates a second then says that today people call it the *tabac*.
What does *tabac* mean in Creole? The tourists guess wrong. It's the female
sexual genitals. He couldn't say why, he says with a smile (to say that of
course he knows: it's the visual analogy between the berry and a vagina).
Hahaha. The plant comes from Asia and was introduced here by sailors. It
was used to create protective hedges so slaves couldn't run away. Because
it's not so easy to flee with thorns in your foot and the dogs behind, he adds,
with a smile. Also, the slaves who fled within the island planted the *vigne
marronne* to protect themselves against the slave hunters. *Marronner* (to
maroon) means running away, he explains.

The group leaves the forest and follows the road for a couple hundred
meters. Then they go back into the forest. Orom talks about asparagus.
There is asparagus in La Reunion. An old man has shown him. He spreads

the branches of a small bush and takes a plant in one of his hands. It's the local asparagus. He has tried it and tells us he can confirm that it tastes good. Especially in omelettes. It gets very big because it is warm and water is abundant. We pass by so many things without seeing them, he tells us. But the old man has told him about this one, the wild asparagus, and he has tried it. It is excellent. And we can see it now. Orom turns towards another bush and points out a green fruit. It is called the "friend of the tree," he says, because it is an epiphyte. It is not a parasite, he explains, so it is an epiphyte. In La Reunion, they call it "delicious fruit." Why? Because when it is ripe it tastes and smells like pineapple, passion fruit, and banana. When ripe it tastes very, very good, he adds. He smiles again when he says "very, very good," announcing a double-sense. In Creole, he says, the fruit is called the "miss's pleasure" (*plaisir mam'selle*). He leaves it to us to guess why.

At the next stop, Orom fetches leaves from a bush and distributes one to each of the tourists. It's the leaves of the *brinjelier*, he says, a variation of the aubergine. It does not produce fruit, only small yellow seeds when it is ripe. But the flower looks like the one from an aubergine plant. Nowadays, many people just walk by and it has no signification for them. But he, Orom (he uses his name in the third person), could never just pass by a *brinjelier* without talking about it. Why? Because this plant was part of his parents' quotidian life. After eating, the leaves were used to clean greasy cooking pots. It is the "Creole sponge," also used to polish wooden floors. Nowadays, he continues, people use chemical products to accelerate the ripening of bananas. And it works. But how did they do so before they had chemical products? They used the leaves of the *brinjelier* and put alternate layers of bananas and leaves in a bag. Three or four days later, the bananas were ripened. It works, it's bio and you don't need any chemical products, he concludes. Easy. Another way of using it: when you see someone coming out of a bush scratching his bum, then he has used the wrong side of the leaf. He smiles again. The tourists understand the joke and examine both sides of the leaf he has handed them. Which side do they think is the good one? he asks. The tourists make their choice. Orom points at two of them and starts laughing. They got it wrong, he tells them. They are the persons coming out of the bush scratching their bums. Because they chose the side they shouldn't use. When he was a child he got it wrong only once, he says. The tourists are laughing and the tour moves on. We leave the forest and follow the road. After about 200 meters we will arrive at Laslo's garden plot.

Laslo is Orom's maternal uncle. I am living in the house of his sister who treats me like a member of her extended family. Lalso, when I meet him, therefore kisses me on the cheeks, a sign of social intimacy (as opposed to the more common handshake). Laslo is about sixty-five-years-old, a former forest labourer and dockworker in the harbour of La Reunion. Since his retirement, he spends most of his days in his garden plot, maintaining the courtyard, the kitchen, and a small wooden house, looking after the fruit trees and vegetables, and receiving friends for a talk and a coffee. He has also started selling fruit and vegetables that he puts on a table by the road. The garden plot belonged to his parents and he was brought up here. Some members of his immediate family still live in small houses next to the plot. Laslo has recently moved to a purpose-built house in a nearby village called Mare-à-Poule-d'Eau and only comes back here during the day. Through his local guide training in 1996 and 1997, Orom became conscious about the value newly attached to "popular culture," "Creole traditions," and "heritage." Following this training, he was temporarily employed by the ecomuseum of Salazie to help with a new exhibition with the theme of "The nature of know-how" (*La nature des savoir-faire*) inaugurated in 1998. Along with ethnographers from the University of La Reunion, he participated in the collection of objects and in the erecting of exhibition displays. Laslo, who by then had just moved out of his old house, wanted to demolish the old wooden buildings in order to expand the gardening. Orom convinced him to keep these and to transform the plot into a "heritage site." To ease the access to this garden, Orom and Laslo built a ramp between the road and the pathway leading to the old wooden house. With the financial and technical help of the ecomuseum of Salazie and the ethnologists of the University of La Reunion, Orom and Laslo added a straw hut to the existing structures, using traditional building materials and techniques. The building of this straw hut was visually documented by a team of university ethnologists.[8] From 1997, Laslo became a privileged informant for the ethnologists working for the Salazie Ecomuseum. Repeatedly interviewed, observed, photographed, and filmed, Laslo was progressively transformed into an enigmatic figure representing and embodying the essence of an immediate past, of a popular culture that has just been "lost." Various fragments of his life, especially those related to "traditional life," were widely represented at the 1998 ecomuseum exhibition. He also appeared in academic articles published in the Journal of the National Museum for Popular Arts and Traditions[9] and in numerous journalistic photo-reportages about Salazie and its "popular traditions" in international and local media. Since 1998, local tour operators programmed the visit of Laslo's garden as a tourist destination. International travel journalists invited by La Reunion's tourist board were taken to Salazie to visit Laslo's garden.

While Laslo was transformed into a kind of popular heritage celebrity at the local level, he seemed little concerned about this new public persona. In private, in the presence of his friends and family, he usually avoided talking about it. Only once he showed me a collection of French and American travel magazines in which he appeared. These he had put out of sight, in a toolbox in his kitchen. Otherwise, he seemed to have continued life as usual. In the morning, he usually started his day by sweeping the courtyard of his garden plot and the floor of the wooden house. As with most people in La Reunion, he wanted to have his courtyard and house "clean," free of dust. He then built a fire in the kitchen to boil water and make cof-fee. The doors of the kitchen were usually wide open and a radio turned on. He fed his cats and then spent the rest of the morning looking after his plants. At lunchtime, he usually ate a meal that he had brought with him to the garden and then slept for a while in the kitchen and, later, in the newly built straw hut.

This daily routine was slightly altered when tourist groups were expected for a visit. It was in most cases Orom who would bring these groups here, sometimes also other guides working for tour operators based on the coast. The relationship with these guides was always personal; Laslo knew them personally and the guides knew they had to call him before a site visit. As a sort of entrance fee (Laslo would not call it this), Laslo received 5 French francs per visitor (approximately 1 Euro). Sometimes tourists also left tips. Tourist groups usually arrived between 10 and 11 a.m. and the site visit took about one hour. When tourist groups were expected, Laslo, after sweeping and cleaning the courtyard and the house, and after lighting the fire and making coffee, usually went into his garden to pick a selection of fruits and vegetables according to the season: bananas, passion fruits, tree tomatoes, lychees, mangoes, pineapple, etc. These he placed on a table in the wooden house. He also placed a christophene (*chouchou*) on a rock in the courtyard between the house and the kitchen. He rearranged the fire so it wouldn't produce too much smoke. Orom had told him to do so he once explained me. And he turned off the radio and hid it under a pillow. When the time of the visit approached, he usually got nervous—like an actor before going on stage. He repeatedly went back and forth between the kitchen and the house for a last check, picking up leaves fallen in the courtyard, stroking the cat. During this time, he would hide behind bushes and trees, not to be seen, watching out for signs that would announce the arrival of the tour-ist group. Once he spotted the tourists through the woods, he would jump into his kitchen and hide behind the half-closed kitchen door. Sometimes, I was hiding with him and, especially in the beginning of my fieldwork, he explained to me what would happen next. The tourist guide, usually Orom, or one of the tourists would ask, in a loud voice, if someone is home (*"Il y a quelqu'un?"*). Once this sentence had been uttered, Laslo would open the kitchen door, slowly step down into the courtyard and walk down the path towards the street, to welcome the visitors.

Today, as usual, after leaving the forest Orom guides the group towards the entrance of Laslo's garden plot. In the Creole garden, he explains, there is no entry gate. However, there is an invisible boundary that visitors should not trespass without being invited by the owner of the plot. A specific type of plant marks this boundary. The group halts and Orom explains that there are three questions one can ask to be granted the licence to enter a house. The group chooses among these options and, all shouting together, loudly enquires if someone is home (*"Il y a quelqu'un?"*). After a short while, an elderly man appears on the path under the trees, smiling and inviting them to come in. Orom presents the man as Laslo, his uncle. Laslo and the tourists shake hands and then enter the garden plot. Orom takes the group to the courtyard between the kitchen and the wooden house. What will follow is a relatively sophisticated performance acted out in the interplay between Orom, Laslo, and the tourists. Orom and Laslo direct and dominate this performance, while the tourists assume the role of passively participating audience. Orom usually starts by announcing that he has his own way of seeing things, but that he also respects the way his parents understood and still understand the world. He picks up different plants in the garden and explains the way they have been used by his parents. Laslo intervenes at specific moments, when Orom—seemingly spontaneously—asks him to develop or confirm one of his stories or explanations. Orom speaks in French, with a slight Creole accent, whereas Laslo speaks in Creole. When Orom addresses Laslo, he talks to him in Creole and then explains to the tourists in French what he has asked him or what Laslo has answered. In most cases, this "translation" would not be strictly necessary as Laslo's Creole is pretty much understandable for French-language speakers. Orom and Laslo follow an unwritten script, which seems to have emerged from the frequent repetition of the visit. They play different roles, Orom the mediator between "tradition and modernity" and Laslo the living representative of a lost past. Orom talks about contemporary issues, about scientific proofs for the naturalist knowledge of his parents, about economic, social, and environmental problems. Laslo talks about his parents, about how life was before, about how to use certain objects, about the medical use of plants. Laslo confirms Orom's explanations by adding stories of his childhood, his own past. The same set of stories is consequently told within a framework of a standard itinerary. These stories are always based on objects, plants, fruits, or buildings "found" along this itinerary. Many of these are props whose presence appears accidental, but which have purposefully been placed in specific locations.

After his introduction to the front yard, Orom asks the group to enter the wooden house. Laslo no longer lives here, he explains. He lives in the village down the road. However, he is here everyday, whether there be cyclones, volcanic eruptions, earthquakes, or landslides, because, he explains, Laslo loves this kind of life. It is fantastic that he has kept this kind of traditional life while everything around him has changed. And, he adds with a smile (announcing a joke), sometimes Laslo's mobile phone rings. Besides that however, everything has been kept as it was before. This is why, Orom says, two years ago he had the idea to show this place to visitors. He explains the architecture of the house and Laslo points out where exactly he, his brothers and sisters, and his parents had slept. Orom explains the building technique of the house, the wood used, the "intelligent" aeration system, the beliefs related to the position of the door and the windows. Laslo adds short anecdotes. The visit to the house is concluded with the invitation of the tourists to try some of the fruits put on the table. The group then leaves the house and enters the kitchen, a wooden construction around an open fireplace, covered by a straw roof. The kitchen used to be the place for people to meet, a social space, Orom explains. It is here that people received visitors, where the family came together to eat, where important decisions were made. The house, on the contrary, was only used for sleeping. It was always kept clean and nicely decorated, so people who passed by could look inside. His parents rarely received visitors in the house; it was far more convivial to receive people in the kitchen. This, he concludes, is proper Creole hospitality.

The tourists sit down on wooden benches around the fire. Orom talks about different objects in the kitchen, how these were used in former times. Laslo talks about how the family came together here, how they were not allowed to talk while taking their meals, how his father used to punish him and his brothers, how his mother was compassionate with them when they were punished. Orom's stories about "how the world has changed so quickly in recent years," very commonly trigger more generic conversations, typically[10] about "how globalisation has left the world empty of values," "how young people can't connect to the world and become violent," "how hard it is for people to find jobs," "how the Americans have imposed their values to the world." Orom usually takes a specific "position" within these conversations. He would explain that his motivation to guide tourists is so that he can bring people together that come from different horizons, he can bring alive a commonly lived Creole moment. He would often explain that his past, the traditions he grew up with, are disappearing as well. He would then suggest singing a song, *Mon Ile*, a popular song about La Reunion. Although this suggestion may appear spontaneous, it is part of the standard visit programme. The song's lyrics are about the singular beauty of the island, a declaration of love by the singer for the place where he grew up. Through the emotion transported by Orom's voice, the ambience of the fireplace in the dark and smoky kitchen and the mood created by the previous conversations on some lost condition, the performance of this song generally generates an emotionally very moving moment. Some of the tourists start crying, hiding their faces with their hands. Even I, who have many times participated in this almost ceremonially choreographed moment, have the shivers.

When the song is finished, Orom stands up and invites the tourists to go back into the garden. He leads them to the old style straw hut he and Laslo have built close to the kitchen. The tourists enter and it is mainly Laslo's part now to explain that people really lived in this kind of house before. Orom watches through the window. The bed doesn't "run," he says, smiling. It is fixed to the wall so it can't "run." And before, as it was often raining and people like Laslo's parents had no TV, it was important that the bed didn't "run." It explains, he says, the large number of children in the Creole families. The tourists smile. They understand Orom's underlying suggestion that the bed that didn't run, the bed solidly fixed to the wall, allowed making love very frequently. Laslo adds, seriously, that even during a cyclone, the bed didn't "run." Orom with a complicit smile, makes a wry face, continues building on his double meaning, "even during a cyclone" meaning "even during making love with a lot of passion." The juxtaposition of Laslo's serious and Orom's metaphorical understanding of "during a cyclone" amplifies the comic nature of this situation. So, the bed doesn't run, hmm, Orom concludes, again with a smile. For the rest of the day, sentences about things that "don't run" would become running jokes among the tourists.

I have been accompanying Orom for many weeks now with the initial objective to study the constitution and construction of local selves in the intersubjective space of tourism and its "contact zones"[11] or "borderlands."[12] I wanted to know how the cultural flows are governed in the tourism contact zone, how much agency local actors have with regard to the creation of self-formulations and their mobilisation as values produced for tourism; how the tourism contact zone constitutes or transforms transnational social and cultural spaces. Like many other tourist guides, Orom has learnt to interact with tourists. He has observed their reactions, has understood how to anticipate expectations, how to throw rhetoric hooks, build tensions and then nullify it through comedy or tragedy. Orom constantly flirts with gender, phenotype, time, space, and moral boundaries. He projects tourists into a kaleidoscope of possible roles and existences, of selves in which tourists recognise their own histories and desires of being and belonging. Through the quick juxtaposition of such possible roles and existences, through the editing of images of poverty against images of progress, of cruelty against happiness, of order against chaos, he takes tourists on an emotional rollercoaster ride. In one moment, they can identify with Orom's implicit critique of modernity, of the disarticulation of social life and the loss of the beauty and social solidarity of an idealised past. Orom repeatedly talks about the rich naturalist knowledge of the generation of his parents; a knowledge that he explains is now being forgotten. People don't know anymore how to use plants. In the next moment, Orom "edits" this nostalgic narrative against an optimist's narrative of social progress. He talks about his children who now can go to school for free, who have access to modern medicine, to the mass media, to travel. He talks about himself who, of black phenotype, born into a family with no land ownership, is now able to look after his children, who himself has accessed a realm of modernity. The striking poverty of the past, the cruel times of slavery and social injustice, of severe punishment, are over. In the subsequent moment, he juxtaposes this narrative of social progress against a narrative of social complexity, of social fragmentation—where people belong to a variety of different, usually nonarticulated contexts. On the one hand, he makes himself part of a world of the past, a world that does not exist anymore, a world that was cruel and miserable, that was also happy somehow in its poverty and solidarity. On the other hand, he identifies with an equally contradictory present, where knowledge, traditions, and values, the essence of former lives, struggle to survive. Where life is accelerated through a disenchanting modernity, a potentially dangerous modernity that threatens the solidarity and integrity of life. A modernity that at the same time is a necessary ontological condition to "be in the world," to have access to technology, medicine, transport, and knowledge; to participate in a social and symbolic realm of a global modernity at the local level.

Some of his rhetoric and nonverbal performances appear as part of all guided tours. They form a kind of core register of structural possibilities, of scripts that are acted out through the guide's performance. These are usually based on the opposition between a here and now, and an alien world: the past, Western modernity, female gender, wilderness, etc. The tourists are habitually made to identify with roles related to these alien worlds. In many ways, they "become" strangers, representatives of a global modernity, or of the former coloniser (France). These roles are generally embedded in moral frameworks. Orom projects himself into the role of the castaway, the runaway slave who escaped the cruelty of a society dominated by the French coloniser. He thus creates a situation usually uncomfortable for the mainly French tourists who, at least implicitly, are identified with the role of the former coloniser. In some cases, by addressing the tourists through terms like "your ancestors did that . . ." Orom makes this role attribution quite explicit.

Orom has a particular talent to dissolve these uncomfortable situations through forms of comedy or tragedy. He jokes, for instance, about the difficulty those marooned had to run with thorns in their feet. The violent story of slavery and hardship is dissolved; it becomes a comedy Orom and the tourists can laugh about. They "can" laugh about the past because Orom (whose ancestors are supposed to have been slaves) laughs about the past. The rhetorically built ontological difference between the self-victim and the other colonial exploiter (implicitly projected onto the local–tourist relationship) is nullified. In the end, everyone is at a same level, a member of a common contemporary humanity. Orom dissolves his story about social progress in a similar way, by using a form of tragedy. He talks about a commonly experienced loss of authenticity and disenchantment brought about by the modernisation of the world. Here again, he merges the initially ontologically separate entities of tourists and La Reunion into a collective condition. Everyone is caught up in the same types of contradictions. On the one hand, social progress is professed as a moral imperative leading to better chances and equality. On the other hand, the consequences of social progress, the breaking up of forms of order and traditional metanarratives, the disarticulation of traditional forms of solidarity, bring about a deep nostalgia and a feeling of "lost values" and "happiness." Through his experience as a tourist guide, Orom can anticipate how tourists will react to these narratives, how they often project their own contradictions of life into the stories he tells basically

about himself. He can fairly well anticipate that tourists perceive the rhetorically constructed tragedy of his life as an allegory for their own tragedy of life. Orom is a brilliant performer able to spontaneously rearrange
scripts and interpret them in ways that take tourists on an emotional
journey. His performance is marked by changing rhythms and the stac-
cato of dramaturgic turning points, by a juxtaposition of moments that
create deep aesthetic emotions, heartbreaking feelings of sadness, thrills
of erotic temptation, soaring vibrations of happiness, and profound sensa-
tions of existential human connectivity.

Particular situational contexts generate further possibilities to refine the
role-play. Sometimes, it suddenly started raining and Orom spontaneously
improvised his rhetoric in this specific context. He would use the rain to
talk about modernity and the progress brought about by "good roofs"; to
evoke nostalgic images of the past, of being a child walking through the
warm summer rain. Or he would simply develop a juicy, sexualised metaphor about the effect of rain on flowers, the effect of men on women, the
effect of La Reunion on organic matter imported to the island. Sometimes,
the tourist group comprised particularly pretty or funny girls that play-
fully engaged in Orom's sexualised metaphors. They often threw images
back to him and the dialogue that developed from there sometimes reached
hilarious climaxes. In such contexts, Orom variably mobilised explanations, grimaces, or jokes, out of a preexistent personal register, which he
configured with regard to the situational context. Sometimes, new jokes
or stories emerged through the contact with tourists. Sometimes, tourists
made spirited or funny jokes or connections that Orom would later readapt
and, if these proved successful, integrate into his register. "Register" here
means of course not a written list of things to do or to say, not a set of pro-
cedures literally followed, but an ensemble of scripts and possible ways of
acting them out in specific situations.

The most "rigid" set of role attributions mobilised in the interplay
between Orom and the tourists concerns attributes of origin and territorial
belonging. In the discourse underlying his guide performances, Orom persistently relates his existence to a form of belonging to La Reunion whereas
the tourists remain related to a world outside, usually the European French
mainland. The separation between these worlds is discursively marked by
the respective ascription of attributes and qualities. In Orom's discourse, La
Reunion is depicted as a place full of juices, colours, and flavours, luscious
odours, monstrously magnified vegetables and plants, flowers that look like
sexual organs. Furthermore, it appears imbued with quasi-magical qualities
capable of transforming imported things, of awakening the vitality of ordinary European garden flowers, of sexualising people, plants, and objects,
of making things bigger, more tasteful, and juicier. Orom constructs the
island as a magical garden able to liquefy categorical boundaries between
people and things, to dissolve ontological difference, to reinstate the reign
of an idealised essential nature of all things.

By relating his own belonging to the island, these magical qualities implicitly inflect on his own persona. Through his tourism performance, he constitutes himself as part of the island's nature; as a man with an intimate connection to this nature; a man imbued with the spiritual and sexual power of this nature. At the same time, through other references (e.g., his narratives about social progress and nostalgia), he draws himself as a self-conscious and cultivated person, as a man who speaks the language of humanistic culture, who defends humanistic values.

The ideological backdrop to Orom's self-constructions cannot be seen as entirely due to his own creativity. The different facets of the persona constructed through his tourism performance are conspicuously similar to tropes developed by nineteenth- and twentieth-century Western philosophy, art, and literature. Ideas related to the figure of the noble savage in particular and its relationships to an untamed, quasi-magical nature have formed here one of the leitmotifs. The emergence of this figure as part of the Western worldview can be seen as a nostalgic reaction by Western elites to the disenchantments brought about by modernist thinking and social progress.[13] It can also be seen as a reactualisation of a more generic figure of utopian existence, the idea of an ideal place that human societies have commonly projected into some form of more or less fantasized geographical realm. Islands seem particularly apt to attract such poetic and often quasi-religious ascriptions—possibly because of their geographically marginal situation and the clearly identifiable spatial separation with their immediate environment.[14] Paradoxically, island populations very commonly seem to adopt this trope projected upon them and adapt it as a narrative to formulate their own being and participating in the world.[15] To "adopt" does not mean here a process of acculturation, of cultural assimilation to a presumably "dominant culture," of "cultural involution" or "ethnocide." It rather means a process of appropriating and translating alien elements into local narratives and patterns of signification. It means the "auto-ethnographic"[16] use of images and terms used by alien authors and artists; it means the recycling and resignification of alien matter picked up in the metaphorical gardens of contact at the local scale.

Orom does not adopt the a priori alien trope of the noble savage directly from nineteenth-century literature. He has never read nineteenth-century literature. During the nineteenth century, the feudal elites in La Reunion and (their) bourgeois artists, many of them first or second generation European immigrants to the island, adopted European leisure, literature, and artistic fashions and applied these to their immediate social and natural environments. They developed secondary residences along the sandy west coast and around the newly established bath stations in the mountainous inside of the island. A whole new corps of romantic literature, poetry, and painting enchanted the island's "rough" and "wild" nature and the beauty and heroism of its "savages" (most notably metamorphosed into the maroons, historical figures of slaves who fled the sugarcane plantations and found a more or less fragile freedom in the island's mountainous wilderness). These artworks circulated mainly within the social networks of the island's bourgeois families in La Reunion, the Indian Ocean, and the urban centres of the French mainland, namely Paris. While reimagining the island's geography and initiating the development of what would later become its tourism industry, these new practices and writings seemed to have had little contact with, or impact on, the island's large proletariat.

Since the 1960s, La Reunion's autonomy movements appropriated some of these romanticised hero stories and the related symbolism of the island's mountainous wilderness, created by the island's nineteenth century European elites, to formulate a rhetoric supporting the island's cultural and historical independence.[17] The story of maroons opposing the violent condition of slavery and oppression imposed by the European coloniser and finding freedom in an almost motherly nature seemed to provide a pertinent allegory to make sense of feelings of neocolonial oppression through the French state during the 1960s and the longing for independence and autodetermination that was at the heart of the island's independence movement. Today, ideas about La Reunion's wild nature, both in a fantastical geographical and in a metaphorical sense remain fundamental in debates about the island's "identity." They often form the ideological and symbolic core of debates on La Reunion's cultural identity and belonging, on its specific form of creolisation and modernity, on its ontological nature. They consistently reappear in political controversies and provocations, in spatial planning documents, heritage development, tourism policies, and various public and private cultural productions including music, poetry, local festivals, contemporary art, and museum displays. They provide the script for performances and texts incessantly repeated and reconfirmed by the local media,[18] by public discourses, by educational programmes, by locally produced fashion, supermarket advertisements, and festive events. As a form of both global and local discourse, these scripts are permanently reappropriated and transformed, contested and reinterpreted according to specific contexts and interests enabling people to adopt and communicate new identities. It is most likely that Orom has learnt about the romantic interpretations of the island through his contact with this diffuse and multipolar media context and that he has consequently adapted these interpretations for his own purposes.

Almost anything can become a metaphor for anything else. The actual matter used to communicate is maybe less important than what it is made to "say."[19] In the intersubjective contact between Orom and the tourists, the metaphorically signified seems at least as important as the metaphorical matter used. Had Orom been an electronics technician, he would probably translate his personal drama by talking about video-recorder technology or remote controlled toilet heaters. But he is not an electronics technician and the aesthetic needs of tourists require that flowers, landscapes, artworks, and stories of the past create events leading to what Stephanie Hom calls "the tourist moment." From this point, it is a historical accident that Orom was given the opportunity to become a tourist guide. It was determined by historical events in Western Europe that have led to the development of a particular type of tourism, also of a particular form of French colonialism leading a former French prime minister to move to La Reunion and struggle against local independence movements. While there is no positive logic in historical events and their consequences, they still do happen and configure specific contexts and conditions of social life. They set frames of references within which or along which individual lives emerge and develop. In La Reunion, these frames of references have been shifting rather radically within the past century. The political economy of colonial society, based on the production and export of sugar and the exploitation of cheap labour introduced as slaves and contract workers, has progressively been inverted. The origin of wealth is no longer associated with the fertility of cash crop land or cheap labour, but with French and European Union cash flows arriving in the island in form of subsidies, public sector wages, and public infrastructure investments. The formerly agricultural populations have, to a large part, been resettled in urban coastal areas. Many of them are jobless and receive social welfare allocations. Others have managed to integrate public sector jobs or work in the quickly emerging building and service sector industries, nourished by the population's newly acquired purchasing power.

Through the metaphorical language of his "guide discourse," Orom talks about this historical rupture at a personally lived level. He talks about the end of an era, the end of the plantation society that has left his parents and himself without a clear idea of the future; that has dissolved the moral order of social life and projected him into the uncertainties of a new era. The sense of tragedy he develops by talking through the flower is his own tragedy. It translates his ambiguous feelings about his newly found social freedom and the simultaneous loss of a life he has grown up with. One could say that he simply has become an adult; that he lives the tragedy of life that all people go through when realising that, never again, will they be the people they were when they were children, that something fundamental has been irrevocably lost. One could also say that the experience of becoming an adult and the narratives that emerge from this personal experience are mobilised to make sense of a wider context of social rupture. In this sense, Orom could be understood to mobilise a personal coming-of-age narrative to make sense of a historical moment of change. In the intersubjective context of the tourism contact zone, the effect of this rhetorically performed projection is to make tourists become aware of the changes that occur in their own lives through the same coming-of-age narratives. In this sense, Orom creates a situation where tourists are made to feel that they have lost something very precious, that the changes brought about by "globalisation" imply a loss of childhood and innocence.

At the same time, for a moment, Orom gives the tourists this metaphorical childhood back. Through his humour, through his tragedy, through his singing, he creates a moment of existentially perceived authenticity, of "genuine" human connectivity and being. At the end of a visit, tourists frequently talk about the emotional journey they went through. Some take it lightly and say it was "good entertainment." But then again, one of the defining elements of "good" entertainment in Western culture is to take the audience on an emotional journey. The Western entertainment industry is classically based on the creation of heroes the audience is made to identify with. Orom wants to live a Creole moment, he says. He talks about virility, about the sexual nature and power of the island to transform things, about the beauty of its people, about the tragedy of struggling against time, about wanting to preserve the magic of the island. He paints the island as a garden in which heterogeneous parts have come together and now form a whole. He draws an aesthetics of diversity based on the complicity of different constituting parts. To define this world, Orom constantly returns to the term "Creole." Through his words, this term is made to signify a form of solidarity between flowers in Laslo's garden, populations in La Reunion, humans and nature, male and female gender, of La Reunion and the world outside. "Creole" becomes a way of being in the world, a romanticised ethno-method to living contradictory relationships. It becomes a way to package the accidents and complexity of social history in models and stories, a magic remedy to make sense of oppositions and boundaries other than through racial or class categories. It is a narrative that suggests an alternative cosmos based on forms of solidarity and interfluidity, an idealised world of harmony, a utopia come real within a here and now. Tourists can make sense of this narrative; they can identify with this Creole world, with La Reunion as an island of peace and intercultural understanding, with Orom as a Creole hero. Orom knows that Orom-the-Creole-hero is a successful plot. It is his job and it is this job that legitimates his participation in the social life of the village. It is the performance of "being Creole" for tourists that constitutes him as a social persona within the context of his immediate social environment.

Half an hour later, the tourists have left and Orom asks me if I want to join him for a drink in his house. We walk up the street from the central square of the village and talk about one of the girls that was part of the group. Talking about girls is one of the themes of interest we share. It is an easy start for a conversation. Then we talk about things that have happened in the village, the preparations for the village festivities that will take place in two months. The reality of the visit guided during the morning quickly disappears. When we arrive at his house and meet his wife and kids, the emotional theatre of the morning, the songs, the stories and the tears, seem to have vanished. They seem only significant in terms of a job Orom has done, as his profession. It is not talked about any further than that. Orom's son brings each of us a bottle of beer and we drink together. Over the past months, a certain complicity has developed between us. I have met his family, been invited to some of his Sunday family picnics. We had some private parties in my house. We have a couple of times gone to Laslo's garden plot to fix things or just for a coffee. To justify my presence during his guided walks, he has started introducing me as his "assistant" and even integrated me into some of his jokes and explanations. Paradoxically, I am attributed the role of the ethnographer from the University of La Reunion who is interested in documenting "traditional culture." The performance of ethnography has become part of the realm consumed by tourists.

A couple of weeks after my arrival in the village, after finishing a guided tour, Orom started a conversation about his job. He asked me not to think badly of him, but that he would "normally not work everyday." I didn't understand what he wanted to tell me. He said that other people in the village guided tourists every day. That they often even had several groups a day. In these cases, the contact with tourists becomes very industrial, he said. It is like slavery, he added. You do the same thing over and over, and you lose its essence. When I had met him on one of the early days in the village, he had told me about how important it was to him to "preserve" and "valorise" Creole traditions, a discourse not much different from the one he usually performs for tourists, local development agents, or the ethnologists of the Salazie Ecomuseum. He had invited me to accompany him during his tours. It was only later that he realised that I would eventually stay in the village for quite a few months. He told me that his wife had asked him to go work while I was around, to "give a good image" both of his family and the village. During my fieldwork in other contexts in La Reunion, I had repeatedly come across the term of "giving a good image." It seems to indicate a communicative dimension to individual acts embedded within a collective normative framework. The finality of doing things often seems to lie less in the immediate transformation of a reality or the reestablishment of a kind of order, than in the public display of the very act of doing things. In this sense, acts like gardening or going shopping frequently seem to be associated with social significations that go far beyond the presumable immediate utility of these acts. They seem social performances of "giving a good image," meaning projecting a certain image of the self into a local social realm.[20] In this sense, going shopping or gardening become scenes of a social theatre; scenes for a local audience that allow assumption of certain roles and images associated with these roles. People would often take a shower, dress up, and clean the car before going shopping, as a preparation for the dramaturgic act of shopping in the realm of an inter-subjective space created between the social performer and the eye of the neighbourhood or other audiences watching (or imagined to be watching) the act of shopping.

Similarly, within the village context, the publicly performed act of guiding tourists seems to legitimate a social role for Orom. This role is almost ritually reaffirmed during village festivals and public ceremonies. During these events, Orom would dress up in his tourist guide uniform and perform "Creole traditions." Wearing khaki shorts, a white T-shirt with "Tour Guide" for a logo, hiking boots, and a straw hat on his head, he would sing Creole songs before a local audience. In the eyes of this local audience, he would look precisely like a tourist guide. People do not dress like this in La Reunion. Hiking boots are for tourists. Straw hats are for elderly men living in rural areas. "Modern men" in La Reunion don't wear hiking boots or hats. The songs Orom performs during these local events are pretty much the same he performs for tourists. Through this kind of performance, Orom dramatises himself as a professional performer for tourists, as a tourist guide. Like local farmers would festively perform their attachment to the earth and the fruits they gain from it, Orom performs his attachment to "Creole traditions" as core values of his tourism activity. This is at least how many people in the village see it. Performing "Creole traditions" thus becomes a means of local participation. Until recently, most people here did not really care about Orom's narratives *per se*. The act of performing seemed to be primary, over whatever content these performances contained. It was only during the late 1990s, when tourism became economically more important in the village, that La Reunion's politicians declared its development to be a strategic objective in the struggle against the high unemployment rate on the island, that a process of objectifying "Creole traditions" took place within a wider public realm. During this epoch, with the help of public subsidies, the active involvement of neo-rural villagers and the technical advice of public sector "experts," Orom's village was entirely transformed. Houses were repainted (according to colour schemes developed by the governmental agency for architecture and heritage, *Service départmental d'architecture et du patrimoine* (SDAP), reflecting an "authentic system" of "Creole aesthetics"—it's probably total nonsense, as shown by Niollet's[21] ethno-historic work on local architecture), wooden facades repaired, a central square built, heritage highlights made visible through signposts. In La Reunion's Regional Development Plan (SAR), the village was projected to become an "authentic Creole village" (Région Réunion 1995), the embodiment of a Creole self. The Salazie Ecomuseum, then newly created, suggested the development of different "living" interpretation sites. The idea was that these sites would not "alter" the populations, but help to valorise their "knowledge" and "traditional" activities. A slow "grande transformation"[22] took place. The value of labour and agricultural activities, and the ways in which these were socially and symbolically articulated, shifted fundamentally. The production system of tourism was less interested in agricultural production processes and products *per se*, than in their aesthetic value, in the performance of working the earth and in the result of this work: "cultural landscapes," "hand made products," "bucolic life," etc. La Reunion started shifting from an initially agricultural to a more horticultural logic of gardening.[23] Performing "Creole traditions" or a "Creole lifestyle" became means of participating in a wider social realm, means for La Reunion to participate in the symbolic realm of a global modernity, a means for Orom's village to participate in the realm of a regional modernity in La Reunion, a means for Orom to participate in the realm of a local modernity in his village.

One of the problems, one among many problems leading to the failure of the Salazie Ecomuseum, was that performing "Creole traditions" may well constitute a role within a local realm, but it does not provide economically sustainable jobs. The philosophy of social participation underlying projects like the Salazie Ecomuseum, and local development in La Reunion in general, often appeared more anchored in forms of social utopia than in developmental pragmatism. Social participation became part of the product, part of the enacted performance, part of the role played by local guides. Yet, Orom's activity is not sustainable because it is not what he wants to do eight hours a day, every day. After "admitting" to me that he doesn't normally work every day, he worked much less, maybe once a week. However, he would be present when local TV crews would shoot reportages about the village, when travel journalists or agents would visit the valley, or when local or national politicians would be shown the "successes" of local development programmes in Salazie. Often, I was not sure whether his job had a commercial economic end to it at all, whether the remuneration he gained from it was more than a symbolic sanction reaffirming that he was actually doing a job. Orom seems to work within the realm of a specific cultural economy where the symbolic capital gained by upholding a specific public image is possibly more important than the precise content of this image or the commercial revenues generated by the activities it relates to. This produces an inversion of liberal market logic where production is aimed at generating products, income, and profit. Orom's, and possibly also his village's and the island's, self-fashioning based on the performance of a specific idea of Creole life for outsider and tourist audiences paradoxically seem not to target primarily the generation of cash incomes, but to achieve a form of recognition and social participation within the wider realm of a local modernity.

The ambivalence of this new economy lies in that the performance of social life and social environments become symbolic and economic resources mobilised within the intersubjective field of tourism production. Within this context, specific frames regarding the form and configuration of this performance are imposed by the tourists' eye and its taste for romantic and magical themes.[24] These themes do not suddenly appear in the situational context of the tourist journey, but seem related to the historicity of modernist thinking, especially the often discussed idea of disenchantment and the related quest for authentic experience through tourism in distanced places.[25] Within this context, tourism can be seen as a powerful social institution re-enchanting spaces like La Reunion through ideas of innocence, beauty, and authenticity.[26] At the same time, by means of developing transport and accommodation facilities and negotiating tourism-related international policy frameworks, it makes such spaces securely accessible. In the case of La Reunion, these processes emerge at least as soon as in the mid-nineteenth century when travel to the European colonies becomes more frequent and better regulated. Within this context, travelling and local artists and writers, usually belonging to the bourgeois and aristocratic European elites, introduce romanticist fashions and project them onto the island's population and environment. The dialectics of the romanticising tourist gaze hence seems long in place when European tourist arrivals significantly grow during the 1990s and transform tourism into an industry. People in places like La Reunion are therefore not suddenly exposed to romanticising images of themselves when mass tourism emerges. On the contrary, the nineteenth-century romantic formulations of the island, especially the figure of the maroon, were used in an autoethnographic fashion by the local autonomy movements of the 1960s and 1970s. The stories of the maroons and the natural environment in which they found freedom: the island's interior here became powerful allegories and spatial embodiments for the anticolonisation struggle. With the emergence of tourism, these stories and the places in which they evolve are resignified. In this new context, people like Orom readapt the tropes of freedom and slavery, of heroism and alienation, into new stories which in turns are capable of becoming wider social narratives for his village's and La Reunion's being in the world. As an effect of time, the performance of these narratives becomes more solid. Through organised political institutionalisation, public media flows, public events, school teaching, and local tourism, they progressively become collectively sanctioned public culture narratives. Through the naturalisation of such subjectivities and self-enchantments, the very system of tourism production and the contexts of relationships it is framed by become symbolically integrated. While using the semantics and structural oppositions of former stories and symbols, and thus giving an impression of continuity, tourism constitutes a new form of being in the world.

NOTES

1. Gauvin, 1996.
2. Verges, 1999.
3. Ibid.
4. Serviable, 1983.
5. Verges, 1999.
6. Brevet d'Aptitude Professionnelle d'assistant Animateur Technicien de la Jeunesse et des Sports.
7. DATAR, 1996, 1–4, translation by the author.
8. Pandolfi & Quezin, 1998.
9. MNATP, 1999.
10. The vast majority of the tourists Orom interacts with could be categorised as French urban middle class. The quasi-systematic repetition of conversational themes in a given moment of the guided tour hence could be related to a more generic "French middle class culture of communication," a cultural epistemology historically formed within a specific frame of the French nation-state and its strongly centralised social institutions (e.g., education, media, army, public service, governance corps). A discussion of this hypothesis would go beyond the focus of this study.
11. Pratt, 1992.
12. Bruner, 2004.

13. MacCannell, 1976.
14. Delumeau, 2000.
15. Doumenge, 1984.
16. Pratt, 1994.
17. Lilette , 999.
18. Idelson, 1999.
19. Barthes, 1957.
20. Picard, 2008a, 2008c.
21. Niollet, 1999.
22. Polanyi, 1983.
23. Picard, 2008b.
24. Picard, 2008d.
25. MacCannell, 1976.
26. Picard, 2009a, 2009b.

BIBLIOGRAPHY

Barthes, Roland. *Mythologies*. Paris: Seuil, 1957.
Bruner, Edward. M. *Culture on Tour: Ethnographies of Travel*. Chicago, IL: University of Chicago Press, 2004.
DATAR. *Note sur la filière Guides de Pays*. Saint-Denis: CAH, 1996.
Délumeau, Jean. *History of Paradise. The Garden of Eden in Myth and Tradition*. Champaign, IL: University of Illinois Press, 2000.
Doumenge, Jean-Pierre. "Enjeu géopolitique et intérêt scientifique des espaces insulaires." In *Nature et Hommes dans les îles tropicales*, 1–6. Talence: CEGET-CRET, 1984.
Gauvin, Gilles. *Michel Debré et l'île de la Réunion*. Paris: L'Harmattan, 1996.
Hom Cary, Stephanie 'The Tourist Moment,' *Annals of Tourism Research* 31 (1): 6177, 2004.
Idelson, Bernard. La presse quotidienne régionale (P.Q.R.) acteur social local. Analyse d'un discours de presse: le cas du "Quotidien de La Réunion" (1976–1997). Saint-Denis de La Réunion: Université de La Réunion, 1999.
Lilette, Valérie. *Le mythe du marronnage. Symbole de « résistance » à l'île de La Réunion*. Saint-Denis de La Réunion: Université de La Réunion, 1999. .
MacCannell, Dean. *The Tourist*. New York: Schocken, 1976.
MNATP. *Tropiques métis*. Paris: Ministère de la Culture, 1999.
Niollet, Laurent. *L'habitation en bois-sous-tôle*. Hell-Bourg: Ecomuséé Salazie, 1999.
Pandolphi, Paul, and Eric Quezin. *De hier à aujourd'hui. La case en paille, un patrimoine à préserver*, 17 min. Saint-Denis: Université de La Réunion, 1998.
Picard, David. "La relation à l'étranger à La Réunion." In *Anthropologies de La Réunion*, edited by Christian Ghasarian, 77–93. Paris: Editions des Archives Contemporaines, 2008a.
Picard, David. Coral Garden Economics: International Tourism and the Magic of Tropical Nature. *Études Caribéennes* 3(9/10): 99–121, 2008b.
Picard, David. "Giardinaggio Creolo: Turismo e resilienza culturale nell'Isola della Riunione. Transl. Valerio Simoni." In *Scenari turistici. Sguardi antropologici sulle località turistiche*, edited by Chiara Cipollari, 45–58. Roma: CISU 2009.
Picard, David. "Cultivating Human Gardens: Tropical Island Tourism in the South Western Indian Ocean"." In *Eyes Across the Ocean. Navigating the Indian Ocean*, edited by P. Gupta, I. Hofmeyr, and M. Pearson. Pretoria: University of South Africa Press, 2009d forthcoming.

Picard, David. "Tropical Gardens and Formations of Modernity." In *Thinking Through Tourism*, edited by J. Scott and T. Selwyn. Oxford: Berg, 2009a forthcoming.

Picard, David. *Tourism, Magic and Modernity: Cultivating the Human Garden.* Oxford: Berghahn, 2009b forthcoming.

Polanyi, Karl. *La Grande Transformation. Aux origines politiques et économiques de notre temps.* Paris: Gallimard, 1983.

Pratt, Mary-Louise. *Imperial Eyes: Travel Writing and Transculturation.* New York: Routledge, 1992.

Région Réunion. *Schéma d'Aménagement Régional.* Saint-Denis: AGORAH, 1995.

Vergès, Francoise. *Monsters and Revolutionaries: Colonial Family Romance and Métissage.* Durham, NC: Duke University Press, 1999.

Serviable, Mario. *Le tourisme aux Mascareignes-Seychelles.* Saint-Denis: Université de la Réunion, collection des Travaux du Centre Universitaire, 1983.

17 Black Bag

Ashraf Jamal

When he clears his office he puts the videotapes in a black bag. The letters on the bag read CDG, a clothing company. He'd bought her a dress at the CDG branch in Antwerp when he'd stopped to see his mother and sisters en route back from a conference in Arles. Two years later he still has the bag. She's cut the dress, destroyed everything he's given her, which of course means that everything must be replaced. Which it can't be. Nothing can be replaced. Certainly not the moment when he sees the dress and knows it is hers. Green silk for her black skin. *La Negresse Verte.*

She jeers at his love for her. You European men, she says, always collecting. Nothing stops her from perceiving herself as a collectable. A curio. He has grown tired of her jeering. She does not believe in his love. Why should she, when the moment he elects to marry her is the moment he stops the relay of black women who visit his bed. Always his bed, not theirs. What does he know of their beds, their lives? This is the question she asks of him. What do you know of me, where I come from, who I am? The question does not stop the marriage. The reception occurs at the Hohenort in Constantia. The wedding photos too have been destroyed. She holds nothing sacred. A barbarian, he says one night, the boys asleep, the two of them screaming at each other over the badminton net.

He continues packing. She, he knows, is affecting his work. The book on Nerval has stalled indefinitely. He used to be able to work at home, but she has taken to invading his study. She does not read French. What is the good of books that no one can read? If she understands nothing, no one else will. An implacable and brutal logic. A barbarian's logic. He does not admit then, as he does now, that the goad harbours a degree of truth. The monographs he writes are by no means bestsellers. Her word, her measure in the value of words. Not that she reads—she doesn't. She knows nothing of books. She doesn't even read the newspaper. When she pages through a magazine, it is the pictures that draw her. What women wear. She does not care for the agony column. She does not bother with features on couples therapy, adoption, venereal disease. She pauses when she finds information on beauty products that pertain to her skin colour, the texture of her hair.

She slips the dresses off the images of white women. The flesh of a white women is a rack that divides her from what she wants.

He thought then that is was he she wanted. He knows now that he wanted to think this. Had he too grown tired of the pliability of the women who visited his bed? Did he think that in her he'd found his equal? The word is absurd. As absurd as the sentiment he affixes to it. He thinks of the two of them screaming on either side of the badminton net. The neighbours complained the next morning. Who could blame them? The indignity of it all still galls him. No peace at home, precious little at work. At least the term is coming to a close, his headship of the department too. Not a particularly good administrator, he thinks. If he were to believe her, he is not good at anything at all. Her claim does not convince him. And yet her jeering and scorn has taken its toll. He thinks he has had enough. He knows of course that such a state is impossible. One never has enough. But now the notion consoles him. It lends congruence to this process he undertakes, this closing shop.

While arranging his books and packing them into boxes he alights on a posthumous collection, Chatwin's *Photographs and Notebooks,* a rare volume in English in a library devoted to French literature. He is interested in Chatwin's travels through Africa, the link with Rimbaud. He opens the section devoted to Chatwin's travels in Mauritania, lingers.

> They are black here
> Mica black
> Obsidian black
> And their mouths are stone hard
> When you pay for their mouths
> Stone hard and pink at the edges.
> But the African back
> Expanse of volcanic dunes
> Black and rippling
> And the rump
> And the walk
> Both sexes are irresistible.

He does not share Chatwin's taste for boys. But this is immaterial. He lingers on the words, *obsidian, mica.* He knows the stone hard mouths. They are mouths he has paid for. Her mouth. Can he blame her resentment now? He knows he cannot. When he first sees her in a dry-cleaning shop he is smitten. He discovers her name, where she lives, that she is a single mother. One day he suggests taking her and the boy to the Boswell Wilkie Circus. Neutral ground. They go early. Six a.m. He is an insomniac. The decision has little to do with the fact that he does not sleep. He wants the boy to see the tent erected, the performers as ordinary folk, the animals being fed. It is the same, she will discover, with everything he approaches. Always at dawn when the moments hidden from view reveal human toil, the rigours concealed in art. This, she has learnt all too well, is how he approaches the hearts and minds of the artists he has made his province. Nerval, Mallarmé, Proust. This, he thought then, is how he would approach her.

He drives from his house in Rhondebosch to the flat in Lavender Hill she shares with her mother, two sisters, her son. She too has sisters. Driving towards her he discovers no lavender, no hill, but a flattened expanse of dune and scrub. Sea air has corroded the window frames, eaten through the untreated concrete blocks. A labour camp, he thinks, no worse than the tenement blocks on the outskirts of Paris. A breeding ground for resentment. *La Haine.* He wills the scent of lavender, it will not come. He imagines her in a taxi heading for work in Wynberg, a white enclave. He thinks of her, incorrectly, as a victim of history. In time he will learn that she is no one's victim. Her ignorance redeems her. Her mockery too. But then, on that morning driving to the circus in Green Point, she is quiet, pliant. The boy sleeps. He is ten years old. She, how old was she when he was born? Barely sixteen he imagines. The boy is pale. A white man's boy. She reveals nothing of the father. This occurs later. Then, in the Volvo, the roof opened, he glances, imagines her as the mother of their child. He does not think, then, of divorce. He does not imagine her stripping him of everything, even his pension. Then he sees only her beauty, her mouth with its pink edges. Mica, obsidian.

He shuts the book in the cardboard box. A fool, he thinks. He. Chatwin. Fools both. To think that he and she could become equals. What was he thinking of? How could he have invited her into his life? What does she know of Mallarmé and Nerval? Nothing, clearly. Ten years later nothing at all. Then again, what does she truly know of his life? Everything, he realises now. He looks at the black bag, the contents as thick as three volumes of an encyclopaedia. Twelve videotapes. She found them hidden behind his books in his study at home. She had the key made when he'd said he'd had enough of her barging in, disturbing him. She'd thrown the videotapes in the bin. He'd rescued them. They'd screamed at each other across the badminton net. She'd had enough of his perversity. Her word. A word he dwells upon now. *Perversity. Perversion. Pervert.* Is this what he is? Perverse? She cannot imagine a man with a serial affection for black women. It's degrading, she says. Beneath me. It is not he she thinks of but herself. What is she? Who is she? A white man's whore? The words sail through night. The neighbours listen. Do they smirk? Do they say fool, stupid fool? And why does he care for what they think? The girls get younger and younger, she says. The men stay the same. Always a white man, a black woman. Never a black man, a black woman. A black man, a white woman. She's watched each and every video. Is that what you do when you do it to me? Is that what I am? He feels her pain acutely, he cannot absolve himself. Why, she asks, why not a white woman? He can find no answer. What is wrong with you? Here he dwells. Confronted with her pain, he believes there must be something wrong. How explain the obsession? Her word. It is true that white women do not move him. Why? She is not alone in asking the question. There is his mother, his sisters in Antwerp. When he takes her there with the two boys—they have had a son—the mother, the sisters, look and look. Unlike her first son the second is dark, as dark as her. His son's hair, like hers, is intemperate; it will not yield to a white man's comb. This is what the mother and the sisters see. They look at her, at him. They want to know why he has brought them here to the cobbled streets of Antwerp. She, he knows, wonders too. They are married, it does not matter. She is the white man's whore, the white man's concubine. He doesn't prepare her for his mother's and his sisters' disgust. He leaves her stranded, naked. She, he knows, sees through their mocking affection. She screams to be back home. She wants nothing of his life. A mistake, he well knows, dragging the family to Antwerp. Why mix obsession with marriage, why procreate?

He is outcast. At forty-nine this is not what he would have wished. A bad administrator. She placed the divorce papers on the laptop in his study. He knows he'll give her what she wants. He does not care enough to withhold anything. Silence is better. The secretary appears at the door. Flaxen. Old. She has never given him the respect that is his due. Does she know of the black bag? Is the secrecy of his longing all too evident? She too regards him as a bad administrator, of this he is certain. Does she wonder what he is doing in Africa? Does she use the word he hates so much? Decadent. A state of moral and cultural deterioration. He replaces the *a* with an *e*. Decedent. A deceased person. Is that what she sees? Someone dead?

The secretary hands him three supplementary exam papers. He'll evaluate them tonight. He knows the grades before he has even marked them. He knows the examinees. He feels their judgement too. Out of touch, he's heard them say. Insensitive. They think he is homosexual because he does not care for them. Women and their instinct! Women and their overweening regard for themselves! They do not care for his disregard. Especially when they are pretty, which they are, which even he has acknowledged. What kind of a French man is he? Why won't he soften the procedure of learning? Why is he such a stickler? They forget he is Belgian, not French. They know nothing of his love for mica, obsidian. The flaxen haired secretary does. She has made it her business to know things. He persists: Has she opened the black bag? Has she read the titles of the films? Did she instinctively know what the contents were? Better *Recherche du temps perdu, Fleurs du mal!*

He slips the exam papers in his briefcase. He tells the secretary he'll be home for the remainder of the week. He does not tell her that someday soon it will not be his home. His only concern is his son. There, at least, eternal love has lodged. The boy's French is coming along well. He has a zest for the world the mother renounces. He imagines the son with him in Reunion. He has a job offer, if he wants it. He has tried each and every university in France. No one will have him. The fact that he has published with Gallimard means little, next to nothing. Do they know he has abandoned

Europe? Is he the second son—in truth if not in fact—divested of all claim
to rightful ownership, compelled to seek his fortune in the colonies? What
fortune, then, has he found? A profession he has grown to detest. A wife
who will not have him. A son, young as he is, who dreams of the *École
Supérieure*. At least, he thinks, at least something of him will survive if
she'll allow it. Much as he wills this dream he doubts its fruition. Here, at
least, he must make his stand. He has evaluated the rights a husband and a
father have. Absurd though this country is, it has acknowledged that right,
a father's right. The boy has an EU passport. The mother too. But what
good is the European Union when no university will have him? If not him,
then the boy. Surely she will allow the boy his freedom? He is not certain.
Nothing about her is certain. Aggressive, yes. Resentful, yes. But certain?
What can she know of certainty? Her family votes for the National Party.
And she? Does she vote? He doubts this. While she is made of history she
does not invest her faith there. The ANC are fools, she says. They understand nothing. And she? What does she understand? Enough to know that
she doesn't have to work for a dry-cleaning company. Enough to know she
can take him to the cleaners!

He thinks he'll take the job in Reunion. The prospect of island life
appeals to him. The irony of the name—*Reunion*—does not escape him.
He knows he is done with the mainland. Done with Europe. Done with
Africa. The boy will come with him. It will be his one proviso. Will he succeed? Here, for the first time, he prays. He is not a man given to prayer. He
is a man of little faith. He believes he has known love. It is mica, obsidian.
He knows he'll love his son always. But what of the other boy? Has he not
learnt to love him too? And what of the mother, the one who will not have
him? What of her? Is he such a thing of scorn? Inadmissible. Admissible
no longer. Surely no mere black bag could divide them? Then what? Has
he been asleep all these years? Ten. A decade. Decadent. Decedent. He has
always been drawn to the resonances of words. A book is a teacup. Words
are leaves. When he looks at the book of his life, what does he see? The
question stalls, will not go away, will not be answered. She recommends a
therapist before she gives up the ghost. He surprises himself by taking up
the suggestion. He thinks she is surprised too. She says nothing. She does
not want him to regale her with confession. She is not his altar. Better the
white man's whore than his black Madonna. He respects her decision to
cede all love, all faith in her. It is not in her that the answer lies. She knows
this. How, he does not know. But she does. Her stone mouth tells him so.
How could he think he could vault the contract between them? How could
he have ever believed he could soften her mouth? *Reunion* . . . the word will
not go away. Not only ironic, he thinks now, but obscene. Her deeds, her
words, possess no irony. They are not obscene. Is this why he will not fight
her? But what of the boy? What will he do to keep the boy? He realises now
that there is nothing he will do. In the art of war he is a novice. And she?
He can find no word to match her skill. So much for equals.

He shuts the door to the office. The number on the door will remain the same, the nameplate will change. A good thing too. During his headship he has displayed little skill in generating a student body. In South Africa, French is not the language of trade. Better if he were a specialist in Chinese! He well knows France's investment in South African culture, in cultural exchange. But culture, as she well knows, means little if not nothing. And exchange? What exchange could possibly exist when distrust and faithlessness divide the world? Trade, that's what counts. He knows this well. He has been a devoted consumer. Did he care for the hard mouths? No. Was it his own gratification alone that mattered? Again no. Then what, what has he been doing here? He passes the secretary. A chain dangles from her overlarge spectacles. She, he thinks, is asking the same question. What is he doing here? It does not escape him that this was also Chatwin's question. He hands her the keys to the office. Someone else will move the boxes. In his hand he holds the briefcase, the black bag he presses to his chest. He does not care that the CDG bag is reinforced, the seal zip-locked. He knows the treachery of plastic. The secretary gazes at the bag he holds to his chest. Her suspicion, he realises, is mixed with concern. She actually cares! In turn he smiles broadly. He wishes her well over the Christmas season. He even asks after her heart. She happily informs him of her travails. He makes a mental note to ask questions of this nature in the future. Questions that gratify, that bind. *Union. Reunion.* Clutching the black bag to his chest he thinks of an island. A piece of land surrounded by water. A detached and isolated thing.

18 Telling and Selling on the Indian Ocean Rim

Ashraf Jamal

In the heart of this 250-year-old fort we will trade anecdotes and faint memories, trying to swell them with the order of dates and asides, interlocking them all as if assembling the hull of a ship.

Running in the Family, Michael Ondaatje

The fort is in Jaffna, Sri Lanka. Built by the Portuguese in 1560, rebuilt by the Dutch in 1686, surrendered to the British in 1705, half demolished in 1994 during the war between the Tamils and Sinhalese, at the time when Ondaatje publishes *Running in the Family* in 1983 the fort is still intact and serves as the temporary residence of his politician uncle assigned to dealing with race riots. It is in this secluded if beleaguered fort that Ondaatje assembles his story—part fact, part rumour, the two interlocking like the hull of a ship. The metaphor is apt. In its terrestrial echo, the fort, whose very existence assumes the ship, Ondaatje sets the stage for the trading of anecdotes and blurred memories. Like the ebb and flow of the ocean that wash this arrested world, Ondaatje seeks to "swell" anecdote and memory with chronology and interlineary gloss; interlocking them "as if assembling the hull of a ship."[1]

What Ondaatje reminds us of here is how history works; how truth is served by imagination; how, without the trade in anecdote there would be no trade at all, for story is integral to commerce, a thing bartered and exchanged, integrally bound up with the currency of fiction and the narrative of self: one's deeds, encounters, recollections. Moreover, the history which Ondaatje pieces together is one defined first and foremost by maritime culture, for without the movement of people across the oceans, and their merger with those on its shores, we would not have had the racial and cultural mix which came to define the Ondaatje's as it did all those situated on the littoral that separates sea from umland, umland from hinterland. In the case of Ondaatje's lineage this world produces a scenario in which "everyone was vaguely related and had Sinhalese, Tamil, Dutch, British and Burgher blood."[2]

In a sense, Sri Lanka, because it is an island, is in fundamental ways informed by the ocean. However, such a generalization erases the distances which inform and shape those who live in the interior and those whose lives are informed by the border country between shore and sea. For the purposes of this exploration, therefore, what is most significant is the connection between land and sea, storytelling and seagoing trade, the commodification of memory in the process of making a sale. This is the age-old and tried and tested practice of the merchants who trafficked across the Indian Ocean, for the telling of a story was none other than a suspension (of disbelief), a means to soften the sting, and a way of connecting remote places. A kind of seafaring song line, a marker for cosmopolitanism, the trading in stories stitched the world together. As geography, stories gave shape to abstraction; they allowed for strange worlds by making them familiar (albeit with an ample dose of fiction, the better to disguise the origins of a trade). Rather than simply fixing the deal—rigging it as it were—stories dramatized the flow of lives, goods, beliefs, and conjectures.

Joseph Conrad understood the merit of storytelling as an alloy all too well, for it is the act of telling stories, of situating and dramatizing the context in which listener meets teller, and these in turn reach beyond time and place to another world—a world elsewhere—that has formed the deep structure of his writing. There was nothing unique in the mode which Conrad adopted. Like Ondaatje, he is a trader in anecdote; a purveyor of rumour; a master of the resonant detail, the psychic twist, and the inevitable mystery which clings to fact. "No story is ever told just once,"[3] Ondaatje adds, having begun to assemble his ship. And it is not surprising, therefore, that when one listens to a Conrad story for the first time one immediately senses the residue or trace of its retelling. It is as though the author's very layering, his adjectival insistence (to quote F.R. Leavis who couldn't stomach Conrad's vagueness), his Promethean yet frustrated will to unlock an enigma, come to shape the very telling; for it is only when something is told then told again that one realizes that repetition—a kind of dullness—is also a clue to mystery.

More prosaically, Ondaatje adds, "whether a memory or funny hideous scandal, we will return to it later and retell the story with additions and this time a few judgements thrown in. In this way history is organized."[4] This embroidery, this spinning of yarns in which "each memory [forms] a wild thread in a sarong,"[5] reaffirms not only the conceit—the thread of story—it also reaffirms the connection of this conceit to the history of trade. For, as Michael Pearson reminds us in *Port Cities and Intruders*, it was precisely cloth, namely from Coromandel and Gujarat, which was often bartered and exchanged in the meetings between littoral peoples and those who crossed the ocean. These fabrics varied from lay cotton to the finest of silks, and with the trading thereof arose the means to reproduce their designs.

What I'm getting at is that exchanges were not solely economic and utilitarian; they were also imaginary and creative. My supposition, therefore, is not the prevailing one, that the currency of trade was the fulcrum of the Indian Ocean world; a view which, now in the process of being reevaluated, has allowed Sugata Bose in *A Hundred Horizons* to note that "the overemphasis on trade has tended to obscure much else that went along with it, especially the flow of ideas and culture."[6] With this qualification Bose then adds: "The exploration of the Indian Ocean as a cultural milieu is quite as important as its role as a trading zone."[7] My own qualification is by no means as cautious. Rather, mine is a view which stresses that it is precisely trade which is informed by the flow of ideas and culture. Stephen Muecke and Devleena Ghosh, in *Cultures of Trade: Indian Ocean Exchanges*, concur, for "as much as the East was plundered for profit, the return cargo was a strangely powerful complex of cultural forces, as heady as the perfumes, as fabulous as the imagined and real treasures, as reproductive as the libidinal fantasies of the exotic."[8]

Whether addressing the matter of interregional and relatively localized trade, or the long and exacting arm of empire, one nevertheless returns to the prevalence of a less tangible freight which Muecke and Ghosh I think correctly interpret as always already an imaginary and libidinal investment. Engseng Ho's distinction, that "non-Europeans entered into relations with locals that were more intimate, sticky, and prolonged than the Europeans could countenance"[9] is therefore one I do not wish to emphasise here. Sticking rather with Muecke and Ghosh's more loosely encompassing reading, my intent in this chapter is to reflect on the contingent and generative power of stories in the midst of other modes of exchange. From this perspective, then, the connections between telling and selling, or of storytelling as seam, are never quite a matter of exchanging one thing for another—or of exchanging silver, gold, or cowrie shells, say, for a bolt of Coromandel cloth—for factored into the exchange, at its enigmatic heart as it were, lay desire, the imagination, the need for dreams, for the other as the deepening of one's unconscious world. Of course, one could cynically add that trade, particularly on the East African rim, was shaped by something for nothing, or something more for something less (say ivory for cloth), but this still begs the questions: Whose something? Whose nothing? Michael Pearson addresses this matter compellingly in *Port Cities and Intruders*.

Holding onto the notion of telling and selling as an act of trade, I'd wager that the stories which came with an enigma had the greatest life span. After all, is it not commonly recognized that once you know the end few care? This certainly explains why Joseph Conrad's enigmatic novella, *Heart of Darkness* remains the most heatedly debated and most written about modern fiction. Or why *The Seven Voyages of Sinbad the Sailor* remains a legendary narrative. That Salman Rushdie revisits this age-old narrative in *Haroun and The Sea of Stories*, affirms its durability. In *Haroun*, Rushdie speaks of the Indian Ocean as a treasure trove of notions, thereby locating conjecture and fantasy as its core. Sugata Bose, in *A Hundred Horizons*, reaffirms this view: "there is no question that the history of the Indian Ocean world is enmeshed with its poetry and in some ways propelled by it."[10] Fernand Braudel, in *A History of Civilizations*, further captures the integrality of stories and trade:

> Narrow as it was, the street in any Muslim country was always very lively – a permanent meeting place for people who enjoyed open-air display. It was the essential artery, the rendezvous for story tellers, signers, snake-charmers, mountebacks, healers, charlatans, barbers and all those professionals who are so suspect in the eyes of Islam's moralists and canon lawyers.[11]

Note the counterpoint of the professional and amateur, a distinction also central to Edward Said's *Reith Lectures*. While the professional constrains and overdetermines a given field of engagement – maintains his parochial "bit of turf" – the amateur, given to exploration, allows for openness and speculation – elements key to the nexus of story telling and trade. Therefore, is this not precisely why the traffic in commodities needed stories? And is this not perhaps why the products which first inspired the circumnavigation of the earth were none other than luxuries; so that it became their seeming extraneousness to the fundamentals for living that, all the more, enabled the very reason for living? And are stories then not precisely the spice of life; a way through the world; a way of travelling without physically having to thumb a ride, grab a cheap flight, or get on a boat? And is this not what traders were doing all the while: making life easier for those unable, unwilling, or afraid to move? There are numerous examples in legal documents, court laws, and other forms of written and unwritten legislation, which sanctify the trader or merchant who physically moved between contact zones, particularly war zones, so much so that they became sultans in their own right (well, certainly in their imaginations and the imaginations of those who encountered them). Or, if not sultans, then certainly these traders assumed increasingly magisterial identities. As Philip D. Curtin reminds us in *Cross-Cultural Trade in World History*, "long-distance trade required *someone* to go abroad and become a foreigner."[12] Then again, if we consider the case of Ben Yigu in Amitav Ghosh's *In an Antique Land*, then the merchant would not have become entirely foreign; rather, under the sign of the littoral, he would have fused difference and fashioned an itinerant identity.

It is certainly this habit of spinning a yarn which has made the Indian Ocean trader a figure of notoriety in the moral Western imagination, and yet, is it not precisely this manipulation of trust, this seductive *entre* into the big sale, which is in fact not typical of the Asian trader, but the very condition of trade itself? By shifting the blame and the notoriety of this practice to the East—by Orientalizing it—the West found the means whereby it could rationalize its more direct and bloody approach to the divestment and diversion of an age-old custom of exchange; a custom which, in truth, defines the cultural logic of global capital today. For aren't we buying into the spin when we purchase any item? And if we feel empowered in the act of doing so, is this not because of a constitutive disempowerment which allows us to yield, to give over our cash in the name of desire rather than sense?

Ondaatje thoroughly understands the interlocking of sense and nonsense in the traffic of ideas. Like Mandeville, he raids the world's scriptorium of

ordinary madness and does so in ways blithely unsettling yet deeply pro-
voking. The epigraphs to *Running in the Family*, culled from the fourteenth
and twentieth centuries, read:

> I saw in this island fowls as big as our country geese having two heads
> . . . and other miraculous things which I will not here write of. (Oderic,
> Franciscan friar)

> The Americans were able to put a man on the moon because they knew
> English.
>   The Sinhalese and Tamils whose knowledge of English was poor,
> thought the earth was flat (Douglas Amarasekera, Ceylon Sunday
> Times 29.1.78)

What counts for Ondaatje is not the matter of truth versus falsity, but truth
as dare. Spinning fiction is a hazardous but also an intrepid enterprise, for
it requires just enough plausibility—a highly relative ingredient—in order
to compel the listener or reader. Because there was always a vested interest in keeping the sources of trade a secret, distortion became a matter of
economic necessity. This necessary distortion persists today. So that just as
one could say that seafarers blundered upon knowledge, worked through
a disorienting (sometimes deranging) process of trial and error, similarly,
one could say that error was constitutive to the imagining, discovery, and
trafficking in the world.

If Raymond Williams in the *Country and the City* describes the provincial context of the nineteenth-century English novel as a "knowable community"[13] informed by the interdependence of the individual and his or
her society, then the unknowable and ceaselessly morphing world produces
selves that are untethered (literally, after Conrad, at the end of their tether),
unmoored, disorientated, forced to make things up as they go along, and,
piece by piece, put together a sense of something that is integrally unknowable and nontotalizable. This fractured sensibility is conveyed by Ondaatje
when, noting that the Nuwara Eliya Tennis Championships had ended and
there were monsoons in Colombo, he casts a pointed glance at archival
headlines at the same time and notes the following:

> 'Lindberg's Baby Found—A corpse!' Fred Astaire's sister, Adele, got
> married and the 13th President of the French Republic was shot to death
> by a Russian. The lepers of Colombo went on a hunger strike, a bottle
> of beer cost one rupee, and there were upsetting rumours that ladies
> were going to play at Wimbledon in shorts.[14]

What this curious list of coterminous events reveals is the Western orientation of a particular Sri Lankan newspaper at a particular time. This is not
an instance of that much touted aura of globalization, as enigmatic today
as it ever was, but, rather, the privileging of another set of coordinates

which, in a Brechtian sense, suspends the contiguity of events and high-lights not only their disconnectedness but their remoteness, so that they begin to form a constellation with no map. Hearsay rather than evidence, story rather than fact, these events manifest an emergent consciousness, dominant today, in which the world resembles a kind of rummage sale; a place where stories appear in an arbitrary and nondirected fashion, where purposiveness and currency is lost, and it matters not a jot what occurs right here or elsewhere.

Brecht's genius, Walter Benjamin well recognized, was to try and freeze this chaos, to foreground its disjointed workings, and effect a dialectic at a standstill. If through his epic theatrical stratagems Brecht attempted to stop the world so he could get off, the traders-as-artists of yore were moving the world along so that the listener to their travels could get *on*. The reason why Brecht worked through demystification—the precise inverse of our trader-traveller—was because the world as he saw it had lost not only its reason, but its reason for mystery. Ondaatje, on the other hand, recognizes both brute fact and brute fantasy. For in both inclinations he sees first and foremost the matter and act of will. The fantastic for Ondaatje is an equally conscious gesture, no more absurd than the most reasoned point of view. If Ondaatje sees this it is because, unlike Brecht, he sees the humour and hence the life inherent in a world defined by farce.

Adam Smith's bald proclamation in the *Wealth of Nations* (1776) that the greatest moments in world history were the discovery of America and the rounding of the Cape of Good Hope is an instance of farce. To readdress Columbus's blunder and Diaz's provenance, overshadowed in Portuguese history by the ventures of Vasco da Gama, one needs both Brecht's ability to demystify received truth and Ondaatje's ability to see the whimsy within it, for if histories are made up they can be made anew, notwithstanding the will to power and its undertow which underwrites any given ideology.

Stories are a kind of cargo culture, freighted, with enough heft to get beyond its point towards something less obviously consequential and yet utterly significant. Stories transact as a supplement—an addition, but also, more deftly, a substitution—for once the deal is made, the monies exchanged hands, the object purchased, there remains what Luis Bunuel pithily termed that obscure object of desire. It is this obscurity—the inverse, upside-down role of stories as acts of exchange—which stays long after that which has been traded has been consumed or collected. If this is so it is because stories cannot be consumed or collected for the simple reason that they are only ever absorbed in part, and if, say in book form, they are collected, their existence unread is meaningless. As memory and as thing, stories are corruptible, and not only because they shift in language and context, but because, as translations, as metaphors, and acts of transfer, stories are organisms defined by loss and accretion.

Makeshift, moved by context stories, whether motivated by belief or anecdote, effectively end up reflecting the culture of the listener more than the teller. But then this is a chicken-and-egg notion because the listener in turn becomes the teller. This is no mere rotation, however, because the story endlessly shifts by virtue of perception, time, and place. If it reveals anything, then, it is this shift, this disorientation and reorientation. As an archeological trace or record, therefore, stories are compelling indexes of littoral cultures, for it is these cultures—less integrated, more heterogeneous— which best adopt and adapt stories in passing. They reach their most intense resonance in a given society when told by traders who are also consummate actors. I would suggest that the same effect occurs when stories that are told not as anecdote but as belief lay hold upon the imagination of the listener. The diasporic impact of Islam in the Indian Ocean world is a case in point. It is argued that Islam appealed to littoral societies in East Africa, India, and Southeast Asia because of its monotheistic force. This, however, did not mean that the animistic forces at play in these littoral worlds were automatically expunged. Rather, the argument goes that Islam was effectively adapted and transmogrified. This is all well and good, but at bottom this argument still supposes a prior integrity to Islam. But what if adaptation and transmogrification is the name of the game of religion? What if monotheism remains, at base, a paradoxical will to generate and counter mystery? If so, then any providential answer always marks an a priori stress.

Now it is this stress, which affects one's imagination as much as it affects one's reason, which lies at the root of storytelling. The desire for an end to a story, whether as anecdote or as article of faith, just as much as the desire for a good beginning and a suspenseful and dramatic middle, does not mark its psychic effectiveness but its customer-friendly utility. Stories, in other words, are not, as I understand it, about beginnings, middles, and ends: these are mere detours. What I think counts more is their unfinishedness, their indeterminacy within the *longue duree*. Such a notion of storytelling, such a culture of listening inbetween—suggestive here of the Javanese dance-drama, the Wayang Kulit, which one can enter or leave at any point, a structure also central to Brecht's Eastern-influenced epic theatre—is, I would venture, the mainstay of Eastern business practice. One also thinks here of Sheherazad's unending story designed to stave off death, which from a non-thanaturgical perspective also invites the notion of incompletion as a gesture of survival. Labyrinthine stories, then, or Ondaatje's insistence throughout his work of the collectivity of stories, their creation from multiple perspectives, suggest an idea of storytelling which, while it flirts with conclusion, pays lip service to consolidated subject positions and drives, nevertheless promotes a logic of movement that multiplies, disperses, and calls forth a hydra-headed and oceanic sensibility.

I am aware that this proposition has barely been proven. And yet, if one were to consider the peripatetic movements of Ibn Battuta—while acknowledging his Arabic-centrist disregard for the perspicacity of local knowledge and desire, a disposition central to Islam's hegemonic dominance on the Indian Ocean littoral—or if one considers the relative failure of Islam as a discourse to take hold of the Hindu-influenced Indian subcontinent—a religion relatively akin to Islam in its fixation on absolute determinants—one nevertheless is drawn to why Islamic practice necessarily morphed. My view on this matter is directly influenced by Michael Pearson's perception that littoral societies—whether in East Africa, the Indian Subcontinent, or the Indian Ocean's most porous "border," Southeast Asia—are principally moved by a cultural logic of inbetweeness, or, as Pearson illustrates by drawing from the ocean itself, by an amphibious habitat best illustrated by the mudskipper, a strange creature that survives equally on land and on sea.

This amphibious sensibility is crucial to Pearson's understanding of the ambivalence and openness of coastal communities. It is worth noting here that Martin Luther used that very word to deride Erasmus, author of *In Praise of Folly*, when he described him as the king of the amphibians: the king of *but*. Questions are central to such a position, which of course is why Erasmus was summarily damned. Erasmus's position was notoriously a *non*-position. So is Ondaatje's, so is Conrad's, and so too is the position of the mobile skeptic and opportunist: the Indian Ocean merchantman. For each custom is a genuflection, truth an aside, story an invocation and an incantation. Dissimulating prayer, their reiterations, however, allow for difference. For littoral societies—precisely those located at the mouth of an oceanic transaction—this sensitivity to difference could not but have appeared appealing. Remember here that prior to the autocratic force of the Portuguese, the first to claim themselves lords of the sea—having barely traversed the distance to the Cape of Good Hope, their ticket to the East and all its riches—says much about all prior maritime transactions in the Indian Ocean. The Chinese called for tribute and not dominance; the Arab and Indian worlds, largely defined by land-based systems of dominance, sought a relatively passing if constant transaction of goods. For them, stories, as an integral aspect of a continuous and relatively marginal currency, were central to exchange. If Islam in this regard could be perceived as a dimension of mutual opportunism, the Christianity transported from the West—and I'm not speaking here of the Christianity that stems from Africa and Syria and predates it—conceived of tribute as subjection.

With the Portuguese insistent, though partial, dominance in the Indian Ocean, story became secondary to adherence to the utility of an absolutist law. Islam, by contrast, was opportunistic but not punitive, willing to make allowances for difference as long as trade continued and religion deferred to. As Pearson argues, the littoral societies in East Africa, West India, and Southeast Asia were not converted but, through pragmatic understanding, embraced. In littoral societies, therefore, one does not find the born-again syndrome but the deft leverage of intellectual, spiritual, and economic possibilities. Which is why, regarding the trading of stories, Islam works in a fabulist manner natural to all stories defined by aporia (the unsayable), mystery (the unbreachable), and anecdote (the right and rites of the secular).

When, like Adam Smith, one proclaims the discovery of America and the rounding of the Cape of Good Hope to be the most significant events in history, one effectively pronounces the death knell on organized, deferential, though relatively free trade in the Indian Ocean, and announces the effective sovereignty of Portuguese, then Dutch and British dominance in an economy in relation to which, barring profit, they are effectively alienated. This alienation is a deliberate one for the precise reason that these Western powers could find no logic for their position there other than for the sake of profit. Consequently, stories—understood as open-ended, shaped by the *longue durèe*—effectively wither or become repressed and, ultimately, justifiably resentful; for it is the West which, within the Indian Ocean economy, institutes the culture of non or privative reciprocity. Thereby stories become one-sided; the listener-subject is abstracted, dialogue grinds to a halt, and that invigorating desire defined by the qualifier—*but*—ceases.

Indigenous and intercultural oceanic knowledge effectively dies—or better, becomes encrypted—at the precise point at which the West's scripting of the East reaches its apex; for lest we forget the West has for millennia prior to the rounding of the Cape sought the riches of the East. Taking it with a grasping impunity required that those who stood in its way be diminished. There lies the massive industry of Orientalism in which military force is supplemented and, more significantly, shaped by discourse. Here, once again, we witness the end of story at the precise moment when story, as printed text, thanks to Gutenberg, gains dominance. That the East would come to believe in its defamation and essentialization, says reams about the diminishing power of the scripted word. Henceforth oral knowledge is putatively contained. What was once a custom-based yet libertarian sphere—that of telling stories to make or not make a sale—becomes the belated fascination of anthropologists and ethnographers. An aqueous historical time and space becomes a stripling in a grand or master narrative.

This is not, of course, to dismiss the fact that authoritarian systems were not in place prior to the Portuguese invasion of the East. Undoubtedly they were, most notably the Persian Safavid and Mughal systems, as well as the domineering though benevolent Chinese system under the Ming Dynasty. However, what is notable in all of these systems of governance is their land-based orientation, so much so that the Mughal Empire decreed the sea as belonging to the Portuguese, thereby reinforcing Portuguese opportunism. Imperial economies of dominance aside, however, what interests me are those littoral societies for whom landed power defined by state has always proved secondary to their watery transactions. For while these littoral societies doubtless fed the dominance of these land-based empires, they nevertheless remained outside their systems of servile deference. Free agents of a sort, these communities scattered across diverse points along the Indian Ocean rim seemed finally to have more in common with sea-based communities elsewhere than with an inland community on their doorstep. Belonging to a floating world, these communities—like the desert caravanserais and all nomadic societies—have effectively defined themselves as much by a passing faith as they have by a defining element. In our case that element is not desert or outback—metaphors for seas—but water, and with water its effluent and traffic; its dilatory, pulsating, and planetary rhythms. Indeed, pushing the point, one could argue that it is these littoral communities in the most ancient ocean which best represent what Paul Gilroy described as a "planetary humanism"[15] and Fernand Braudel a "human ocean."[16]

I am, of course, in no way promoting the Indian Ocean as the only body of water significant in this regard, though the pithy description of it as the "cradle of globalization" has a tempting veracity. My view, rather, after Andre Gunder Frank, is to assert that no body of water—given the density of its coves, the intimate proximities of its connections, the beneficence of its monsoon winds, and the fact, prior to 1500, that it was the most easily navigable and consistently traversed water—gestures more self-assuredly to its provenance as a watery cradle and substantive axis for the exchange of goods, cultures, beliefs.

One can, however, rely on V.S. Naipaul not to sentimentalize or eulogize the historical significance of the Indian Ocean. Departing from Southampton, via the Suez Canal, along the coast of East Africa towards Mozambique, the protagonist of Naipaul's *Half a Life* communicates a studied indifference to the import of that particular littoral. Willie, Naipaul's protagonist, tries to deal "with the knowledge that had come to him on the ship that his home language had almost gone, that his English was going, that he had no proper language left, no gift of expression."[17] This atrophy, a striking aspect of Naipaul's worldview, is nevertheless instructive. His protagonist, Willie—whose middle name he inherits from another disaffected wayfarer, Somerset Maugham—"would have liked to commit the landscape to memory, but his worry about the loss of language kept him from concentrating. It was in the same unsatisfactory way that he saw the coast of Africa: Port Sudan, on the edge of an immense desolation; Djibouti; and then, past the Horn of Africa, Mombasa, Dar-es-Salaam, and finally the port of Ana's country [now Maputo]."[18]

If Naipaul's view is instructive, it is because it provocatively records the diminution of Africa's east coast as a key player in the world's global imaginary and economy. Naipaul's position is not, I think, a merely gratuitous one. Rather, it attests to the divestment of power now linked with Africa's east coast, a divestment which is precisely mirrored in Willie's psyche, for as an errant Indian of mixed caste, both Brahmin and "backwards," misplaced in England, all the more disoriented on the journey southward, Willie embodies the dystopian condition of an alienated being. The impoverishment of language, the eroding of memory, and the loss of connectedness become the mental figuration of a disaffected world far removed from the triangulated economy of West Africa, Europe, and the Americas, which was to supercede and control the imaginations of those who lived, and live, on the Indian Ocean rim; for travelling along the east coast of Africa, then withdrawing into the hinterland of Mozambique's estates, Willie realizes that "the slow further journey in a small coasting ship to the northern province where the estate was: going back a small part of the way he had just come, but now closer to the land, closer to the frightening mouths and wetlands of very wide rivers, quiet and empty, mud and water mixing in great slow swirls of green and brown. These were the rivers that barred any road or land route to the north."[19]

The north here is also all-importantly Europe, a place to which, irrespective of longing, he does not belong, as he no longer belongs to India. The consummate itinerant, Willie concludes, while in Mozambique—though the same realization hits him anywhere in the world—that "I don't know where I am. I don't think I can pick my way back. I don't even want this view to become familiar. I must not unpack. I must never behave as though I'm staying."[20] It would be too simplistic to summarize Naipaul's position merely as that of the disaffected tourist, as the one who belongs nowhere. Rather, I feel it would be more productive to read in this morbid position a truth about the littoral condition; the condition of those who, belonging nowhere, are forced to inhabit an aporia; a condition, after Benjamin, of the actor who exists in passing.

Anthems have been sung to this condition; one need only turn to the hit lists of postmodernism and postcolonialism. But what Naipaul forcefully reminds us is that the world of stories—the trading in stories, the "gift of expression" as he puts it—has ground to a standstill. If there is no longer an effective cultural exchange it is because there is no change, only arrest, suspension, exploitation. This, I think, is directly linked to the death of mystery, the absence of ozone as Michael Pearson would put it; a mercantile extortion; the death of the other and concomitant nullification of the self. It is not, moreover, that Naipaul privileges the West over and above all other realities; rather, it is because he realizes that the evisceration of selves and the death of stories is directly linked to the failure of memory and the poverty of language: its increased inutility and withering mystery. If nobody speaks each to each it is because there is nothing to say; if nobody listens it is because there is no mystique, no aura, no desire. People, things, places, are ground down to a sameness, which, in effect, becomes a kind of nothingness. For when Willie flees Mozambique for Germany he discovers the same generic vacuity where immigrants pretend to speak on public telephones just to keep warm.

This last observation possesses a grim weight. Here speech is a decoy, a lie, which conceals that fact that unaccommodation is the new order. We are very far indeed from the beginnings of this chapter which celebrated the linkage of stories and trade. However, if this is so it is because the death of stories or the impulse for stories precisely mirrors the demystification of trade, and the adventure, risk, and mystery at its source which gave it its prior significance. Perhaps this is also because the world has shrunk, become generically familiar, void of translation. Now nothing lives behind anything else. Now depth gives way to surface. On the other hand, one could also argue that this very nothingness is the marker for a new mysticism; for people live, die, make do, and continue to create a terminus of faith to counter drift. Openness, which undoubtedly continues to exist, is no longer openness to the other, though the desperation for this need for understanding, parity, an ethics founded on compassion, remains perversely and tellingly rife.

In salvaging a consciousness of the Indian Ocean rim, its littoral worlds, one needs to ask oneself whether this emergent fascination can in fact survive the present. For if we are to give Naipaul his due, instead of damning him, one would need to recognize that no cultural terrain, or in this case no body of water, can be perceived as sacrosanct. Naipaul's disaffected vision in *Half a Life*, whether of England, India, Germany, or Mozambique, simply adds a nonutopian dimension which I feel is crucial if we are to unpick the fetish of place, origin, self, and, as seafarers of the imagination, understand how we have become shipwrecked, stranded, at a loss as intellects to find a way back or forward.

In "The Storyteller" Walter Benjamin anticipates Naipaul's vision, for if Naipaul, confronted with East Africa's coastline, finds himself void of a gift for expression it is because he intimately recognizes that the telling of stories is, after Benjamin, "something inalienable to us, the securest among our possessions . . . [but] taken from us: the ability to exchange experiences."[21] The loss of this inalienable right, which Benjamin associates with "two archaic types," the "resident tiller of the soil, and the . . . trading seaman," is connected to the death of conversation and the death of travel, for today both speech and movement have lost the aura that comes from the combination of "the lore of faraway places, such as a much-travelled man brings home, with the lore of the past, as it best reveals itself to natives of a place."[22]

Noting the important difference between telling stories and writing them down, Benjamin also notes the difference between epic and narrative forms:

> What differentiates the novel from all other forms of prose literature—the fairytale, the legend, even the novella—is that it neither comes from oral tradition nor goes into it. This distinguishes it from storytelling in particular. The storyteller takes what he tells from experience—his own or that reported by others. And he in turn makes if the experience of those who are listening to his tale.[23]

This is precisely what Conrad achieves and Naipaul fails to achieve. If Conrad effectively speaks his story for a listener, Naipaul writes astride an annulus. If Conrad's stories, after Marcel Mauss, are totemic gifts, then Naipaul's words stem from a *ressentiment* of someone who has little if nothing to say. But before we then dismiss the register of Naipaul's writing we should recognize its timeliness in the era of mechanical reproduction, and, so doing, recognize in its seeming emptiness the emergence of quite another aura. For as Benjamin cannily reminds us, it is not enough to lament the "decay" of storytelling as a "'modern' symptom," for "[i]t is, rather, only a concomitant symptom of the secular productive forces of history, a concomitant that has quite gradually removed narrative from the realm of living speech and at the same time is making it possible to see a new beauty in what is vanishing."[24]

In other words, the announcement of a loss does not make that said to be lost irretrievable. In attempting to think the asymptotic or vanishing point of storytelling one can also recover its auratic power. This, particularly, was Conrad's gift, for his stories, in their very incompleteness, recognize not only a vanishing world, but, on that cusp, also the totemic and animistic force of that world. For it is the very yearning yet in-utility of Conrad's stories, their appeal to a life beyond the moral, proverb, or maxim, which makes one understand their power in the liminal moment of exchange. If, here, I am attempting to recover the force of Benjamin's notion of the auratic it should be said that I am also alluding directly to Marcel Mauss's conception of the gift, which, as Mauss notes, is always an act of exchange, of trade. For, as Mauss reminds us:

> Souls are mixed with things; things with souls. Lives are mingled together, and this is how, among persons and things so intermingled, each emerges from their own sphere and mixes together. This is precisely what contract and exchange are.[25]

If Naipaul's protagonist possesses no "gift of expression" it is because he has no language, no impulse to wield a language which could potentially intersect with or embrace another; hence the title of his work, *Half a Life*. In this bitter phrase we are very far indeed from any commingling or transfer. Rather like the tourist who passes from one known world to the next— the globalized and hyper-real extension of Raymond Williams's "knowable community"—Naipaul's protagonist never engages with the world around or within him. The difference, of course, is that Naipaul's protagonist is constructed as a peevish invalid. But then, is this not precisely what the air-conditioned tourist has become: someone here, yet not; a mimic adventurer; voyeur; outside the circuitry it putatively engages with; for whom, a la Benjamin, story has been reduced to fragment and snapshot, and the host country and its people to sometime friend, one-night stand, or curio?

If history hurts, criminalizes, and burdens us, it also renders us weightless. If, as Derek Walcott, speaking from another ruined and ruinous shore, recognizes the sea as the source of history, then we, whoever we are, and from whatever shore—for there is no hinterland without a shore—must begin to address the changing ethics involved in the telling of the story. If Ondaatje rescues us through poetry and memory it does not follow that Naipaul damns us through the absence of both. If we are truly amphibious it is because we exist in stagnation as much as we do in the wondrous dementia that comes with satiation. And if this conclusion appears as nothing more than an idle paradox it is because, for all our knowledge, we remain thankfully stupefied and stupid. Caught on the cusp of land and sea, between worlds sedentary and nomadic, we remain the human cor-relatives of Ondaatjie's harbour in Colombo, which is "unwise"; caught between the flotsam of dailiness and the always commingling distant cur-rents. Or, recovering Naipaul's grim metaphor: bereft of words yet speak-ing all the while, we have become mimics in public telephone booths (or chat rooms, to update the metaphor); littoral zones and makeshift hearths for the exiled and dispossessed.

NOTES

1. Ondaatje, 26.
2. Ibid., 41.
3. Ibid., 73.
4. Ibid., 26.
5. Ibid., 110.
6. Bose, 11.
7. Ibid.
8. Ghosh and Muecke, 3.
9. Engseng Ho, xxi.
10. Bose, 5.
11. Braudel, 66.
12. Curtin, 6.
13. Raymond Williams, 166.
14. Ondaatje, 37.
15. Paul Gilroy, 76-84.
16. Braudel, 256-7.
17. Naipaul, 124.
18. Ibid., 124-125.
19. Ibid., 125.
20. Ibid., 126.
21. Walter Benjamin, 83.
22. Ibid., 85.
23. Ibid., 87.
24. Ibid.
25. Mauss, 20.

BIBLIOGRAPHY

Benjamin, Walter. *Illuminations.* Translated by Harry Zohn, edited by Hannah Arendt. London: Jonathan Cape, 1970.
Bose, Sugata. *A Hundred Horizons: The Indian Ocean In The Age Of Global Empire.* Cambridge Massachusetts and London: Harvard University Press, 2006.
Braudel, Fernand. *A History of Civilizations,* Translated by Richard Mayne. New York: Penguin Books, 1995.
Curtin, Philip D. *Cross-Cultural Trade In World History.* New York: Cambridge University Press, 1984.
Frank, Andre Gunder. *ReOrient: Global Economy in the Asian Age.* Los Angeles and London: University of California Press, 1998.
Gilroy, Paul. *After Empire: Melancholia or Convivial Culture?* London: Rout-ledge, 2004.

Mauss, Marcel. *The Gift: The Form and Reason for Exchange in Archaic Societies*. New York and London: Norton, 1990.

Ghosh, Devleena and Stephen Muecke, eds. *Cultures of Trade: Indian Ocean Exchanges*. Newcastle: Cambridge Scholars Publishing, 2007.

Ho, Engseng. *The Graves of Tarim: Genealogy and Mobility across the Indian Ocean*. LA: University of California Press, 2006

Naipaul, V.S. *Half a Life*. New York: Vintage Books, 2002.

Ondaatje, Michael. *Running In The Family*. London: Picador 1983.

Pearson, Michael N. *Port Cities and Intruders: The Swahili Coast, India, and Portugal in the Early Modern Era*. Baltimore and London: Johns Hopkins University Press, 1998.

Williams, Raymond. *The Country and the City*. New York: Oxford Univ. Press, 1973.

19 Post-Orientalism

Stephen Muecke

Baudelaire never made it to India,
sent there in '41 by his mother and stepfather
to cure his dissolute ways, his flânerie,
his ratbaggery and incurable genius.

Couldn't they see that a trip *là-bas* could only feed the fever?
So of course he agreed, embarking on a steamer at Le Havre,
with enough opium and books to keep him company;
the ship's chambermaid, also, mesmerised no doubt
by his melancholy and his outlandish style.

The captain spoke of his percentage in the Compagnie des Indes,
and the propagation of vanilla in Réunion and Madagascar
while prising the wine carafe gently from young Charles' grip.

At Saint-Denis he descended, under instructions,
the sea so rough that landing from the launch required climbing a
    rope ladder
hanging at the end of a jetty, two cannon balls attached to the bot-
    tom end.
"Grab the rungs at the crest of the wave, no sooner," they yelled.
But Baudelaire, the formalist, the agent of urbanity, insisted on
    climbing the ladder with books under his arm,
and slowly, pursued by the next rising wave,
reaching and engulfing him and tearing him from the ladder.
Then fished out (with some difficulty) but, amazingly, the books
    unrelinquished.
So finally he consented (*Voyons, Monsieur! Enfin!*) to leave them in
    the boat.
And on his way up again, rinsed gently by another wave.
Kept hold, arrived on top and set off for the town, calm and cool,
his hat turning and drifting in the Indian Ocean depths.

The immersion transforms the oeuvre, or is it
Emmelina de Bragard, a creole woman *aux charmes ignorés*
whom he knew

> *in a perfumed country caressed by the sun*
> *under a canopy of trees ablaze with purple.*

Baudelaire, our urban dandy, is suddenly provincialised.
Standing wet and dripping on a jetty in the Indian Ocean,
the aesthetic hemispheres turn: now he will invent
from *là-bas*

> a modernism metropolises never knew.

Oceanic feeling now flows, unstoppable, from the "exploited" places
(whose spices and perfumes literally funded the literatures of the
    modern,
giving the bourgeoisie time, money, dissolution).

The war of economic domination is won as soon as declared.
But now the postcolonial subjects set up shop
in the tourist-infested tropics, with an inexhaustible resource:
the forever incomplete desires for *luxe, calme* and *volupté*.
And sure, they spin a subtle, but substantial, economic revenge.

Like a strange and beautiful Trojan horse, our Indian Ocean poet
released an army of weird desires into the metropolis;
such an infection is never, ever misrepresentation.
You cannot argue with a virus or a verse, it takes hold, or not.

Contributors

Miki Flockemann's primary research interest is the aesthetics of transformation. Other areas she has published in include comparative studies of diasporic writings, especially by women from South Africa, the Caribbean, and the Americas. More recently her focus has extended to looking at interconnectedness between local cultural production and the Indian Ocean world. She has also published on South African theatre and performance with a focus on reading shifts in cultural trends. She has an interest in the performativity of knowledge and foregrounds this in her teaching and research. She is currently co-convenor of an interdisciplinary humanities course, and conducts a topics in theatre elective in the Department of English at the University of the Western Cape near Cape Town, where she is Extraordinary Professor.

Mark Ravinder Frost is Research Assistant Professor at the University of Hong Kong, as well as an occasional screenwriter and documentary film producer. He studied modern history at the universities of Oxford and Cambridge and has published articles on South and Southeast Asian history in journals such as *Modern Asian Studies* and the *Journal of Southeast Asian Studies*. He is the author of *Singapore: A Biography*, a popular history of the city and its people, and the forthcoming *Dreams of Other Empires: The Cosmopolitan Moment in the Indian Ocean World, 1870–1920*, a study of cosmopolitan Asian intellectuals during the emergence of anticolonial nationalism. Between 2005 and 2007, Dr. Frost worked as chief historical consultant, researcher, and script writer for the National Museum of Singapore's award-winning Singapore History Gallery.

Christian Ghasarian is Professor of Anthropology at the University of Neuchâtel, Switzerland. He has been studying the social complexity of Reunion Island since 1985. Among his publications on Reunion: Honour, Chance & Destin. La culture Indienne à La Réunion (1991); "We Have the Best Gods! The Encounter Between Hinduism and Christianity in La Réunion," *Journal of Asian and African Studies* (1997); "Reunion," in

Countries and their cultures (2001); and Anthropologies de La Réunion (for which he served as editor; 2008).

Heather Goodall is Professor of History at the University of Technology Sydney. Her publications include her monograph *Invasion to Embassy: Land in Aboriginal Politics in NSW* (1996); her coauthored biography: *Isabel Flick: Many Lives* (2004); and the coedited *Echoes from the Poisoned Well: Global Memories of Environmental Injustice* (2006). Her current research is in two areas. One project is an investigation of multicultural interactions in the environmental history of Sydney's Georges River, undertaken with indigenous, Anglo, Arabic-speaking, and Vietnamese Australians. The other is a major project investigating intercolonial relationships between colonized people in the eastern Indian Ocean, particularly in relation to decolonization and focuses on Indians, Indonesians, and Australians.

Pamila Gupta is currently a Researcher at Wits Institute for Social and Economic Research (WISER) at the University of the Witwatersrand in Johannesburg, South Africa. She received her PhD in Socio-Cultural Anthropology from Columbia University in 2004. Her dissertation, entitled "The Relic State: St. Francis Xavier and the Politics of Ritual in Portuguese India" is a historical ethnography of a series of public expositions surrounding the corpse of a Catholic missionary turned saint in Goa, India; it is currently under final revisions to be published with Columbia University Press. Forthcoming publications include: "*Goa Dourada*, the Internal 'Exotic' in South Asia: Discourses of Colonialism and Tourism" in *Reading the Exotic, South Asia and its Others* (Cambridge Scholars Press) and "The Disquieting of History: Portuguese (De)Colonization and Goan Migration in the Indian Ocean" in a special issue of *Journal of Asian and African Studies*.

Ashraf Jamal is Senior Lecturer in Art History and Visual Culture at Rhodes University, South Africa. He has published numerous essays and monographs, namely *Predicaments of Culture in South Africa* and the coauthored *Art in South Africa: The Future Present*. With Shanti Moorthy, he has edited an anthology of Southeast Asian fiction. He is also a director-playwright and fiction writer.

Christian Kull is Associate Professor in Geography and Environmental Science at Monash University, Melbourne, Australia. His research focuses on the politics of natural resource management and the environmental history of agrarian landscapes. His 2004 book *Isle of Fire* (Chicago University Press) investigates vegetation fires in the history, ecology, and environmental management debates on the island of Madagascar. His current focus, together with Haripriya Rangan, is on the movements of thorn trees and wattles around the Indian Ocean and the implications for ideas of indigeneity and for pragmatic land management decisions.

Shanti Moorthy holds a medical degree from Melbourne University and is a Fellow of the Royal College of Surgeons, Edinburgh. Formerly a dancer and *nattuvanar* with the Melbourne-based Bharatam Dance Company and freelance scriptwriter for the Bombay-based Antah UTV in Malaysia, Shanti is now a consultant otolaryngologist and Senior Lecturer in Anatomy at Monash University. She coedited the final volume of *Silverfish New Writing 7* in 2007 with Ashraf Jamal and has completed an MA in English Literature at University Malaya, situating the works of Abdulrazak Gurnah in the Indian Ocean world. She is working on a PhD in continental philosophy.

Stephen Muecke is Professor of Writing at the University of New South Wales, and a Fellow of the Australian Academy of the Humanities. Recent related publications include "The Interdisciplinary Cultural Studies Paradigm in The Indian Ocean," in *Indian Ocean Currents, Transforming Cultures*; *Joe in the Andamans and Other Fictocritical Stories* (Local Consumption Publications, 2008); and, as editor (with Devleena Ghosh), *Cultures of Trade: Indian Ocean Exchanges* (Cambridge Scholars Press, 2007).

Michael Pearson is Emeritus Professor of History at the University of New South Wales, Sydney, Australia, and Adjunct Professor of Humanities at the University of Technology, Sydney. Among his recent publications are *Port Cities and Intruders: The Swahili Coast, India, and Portugal in the Early Modern Era* (1998); *Spices in the Indian Ocean World* (which he edited; Aldershot, 1996); *The Indian Ocean* (2003); *The World of the Indian Ocean, 1500–1800: Studies in Economic, Social and Cultural History* (Aldershot, 2005); and *Metahistory: History Questioning History* (which he coedited; Nova Vega, 2007). He has also published about seventy articles and book chapters.

Susan Philip is Associate Professor in the English Department of the Faculty of Arts and Social Sciences, University of Malaya. Her area of research is the English-language theatres of Malaysia and Singapore, and she has had articles on this subject published in *Asian Theatre Journal, Australasian Drama Studies, World Literatures in English, Asiatic,* and *Southeast Asian Review of English.* Her book on the subject of identities in Malaysian and Singaporean theatre in English is currently under review with the National University of Singapore Press.

David Picard is a Researcher at CRIA (Centro em Rede de Investigacão em Anthropologìa), at the University Nova of Lisbon, Portugal and a Senior

Research Fellow at the Centre for Tourism and Cultural Change at Leeds Metropolitan University, United Kingdom. With a PhD in anthropology from the University of La Reunion, he has been a Visiting Scholar at the Institute for Development Research, Madagascar, and also at the University of California, Berkeley, United States. Publications include *Festivals, Tourism and Social Change* (for which he served as a coeditor; Channel View, 2006); *Tourism, Culture and Sustainable Development* (which he coauthored; UNESCO, 2006); *The Framed World: Tourism, Tourists and Photography* (for which he served as a coeditor; Ashgate, 2009); and *Tourism, Magic and Modernity: Cultivating the Human Garden* (Berghahn, forthcoming 2009).

Rochelle Pinto is Fellow at the Centre for the Study of Culture and Society, Bangalore. She completed her PhD at School of Oriental and African Studies, University of London, and her master's work was done at Jawaharlal Nehru University, Delhi. Her book, *Between Empires: Print and Politics in Goa* (Oxford University Press, 2007), was based on her PhD thesis. She has published in journals in South Africa and India. She is interested in forms of land ownership and concepts of natural law as they impinged on Portuguese colonial practices in general, with a specific focus on Goa. Her other interest is in public access to state archives in South Asia.

Haripriya Rangan is Senior Lecturer in Geography and Environmental Science at Monash University, Melbourne, Australia. Her research focuses on issues that address regional sustainability and resilience from the perspectives of economic geography, postcolonial development, and political ecology. She has published on regional development and forest protection in India (*Of Myths and Movements: Rewriting Chipko into Himalayan History* [Oxford University Press, 2000]), on development theory, on geographic scale, and on tribal authorities and the traditional medicine trade in South Africa. Her current focus, together with Christian Kull, is on plant exchanges around the Indian Ocean and their implications for understanding regional history and environmental sustainability.

Fernando Rosa Ribeiro is Lecturer in African Studies, University of Campinas, Brazil, and is also attached to Macau Inter-University Institute, China. He has published on ethnicity and processes of creolisation in the Caribbean, Indonesia, and South Africa. His current interests include creolisation, ethnicity, and issues of multilingualism in areas of the Indian Ocean. He has just finished the manuscript of a book on languages and writing in English and local languages in South Africa and India.

Arun Saldanha has a PhD from the Open University, UK, and is Assistant Professor at the University of Minnesota. Author of *Psychedelic*

White: Goa Trance and the Viscosity of Race (University of Minnesota Press, 2007), Arun has held Fellowships at the Institutes of Advanced Study at the University of Minnesota and Durham University, United Kingdom. His interests include critical race theory, feminist theory, and philosophy of biology, and he has published in *Environment and Planning*, *Cultural Studies*, *The Massachusetts Review*, *Social and Cultural Geography*, and *Theory and Event*. Ongoing research focuses on Dutch explorations of the Indian Ocean world, in particular the influence of Jan Huygen van Linschoten's *Itinerario* (1596). A second monograph is in the making, provisionally entitled *The Political Phenotype: Antiracist Science After Man.*

Meg Samuelson is an Associate Professor in the English Department, Stellenbosch University, South Africa. She has published articles on Southern African literatures and culture in various sources, along with the study *Remembering the Nation, Dismembering Women?: Stories of the South African Transition* (University of KwaZulu-Natal Press, 2007), and the coedited collection *Nobody Ever Said AIDS: Poems and Stories from Southern Africa* (Kwela Books, 2004). She is currently coauthoring with Dorothy Driver a study titled *South African Literatures in English: Land, Sea, City* for Oxford University Press's Postcolonial Literature series.

Lakshmi Subramanian is Professor of History, Jamia Millia Islamia, Delhi. She specialises in the economic history of early modern India and the cultural history of modern India and has several books and papers to her credit. Her most recent publications include *From the Tanjore Court to the Madras Music Academy: A social history of music in South India* (Oxford University Press, 2006) and *New Mansions for Music Performance, Pedagogy and Criticism* (Social Science Press, 2008).

Index